TADATOSHI FUJIMAKI

I hated writing back in elementary school. After writing just a few lines, I'd find myself with total writer's block. Recently, my editor said, "By the way, you just passed 1,000 pages." It's not that amazing compared to others in my field, but I was weirdly shocked by it.

People are mysterious creatures.

—2010

Tadatoshi Fujimaki was born on June 9, 1982, in Tokyo. He made his debut in 2007 in *Akamaru Jump* with *Kuroko's Basketball*, which was later serialized in *Weekly Shonen Jump*. *Kuroko's Basketball* quickly gained popularity and became an anime in Japan in 2012.

Kuroko's BASKETBALL

7 & 8

SHONEN JUMP Manga Edition
BY TADATOSHI FUJIMAKI

Translation/Caleb Cook
Touch-Up Art & Lettering/Snir Aharon
Design/Shawn Carrico
Editor/John Bae

Printed in the U.S.A.

Published by VIZ Media, LLC
P.O. Box 77010
San Francisco, CA 94107

10 9 8 7 6 5 4 3 2 1
First printing, February 2017

SHONEN JUMP MANGA

LET'S GET STARTED

7

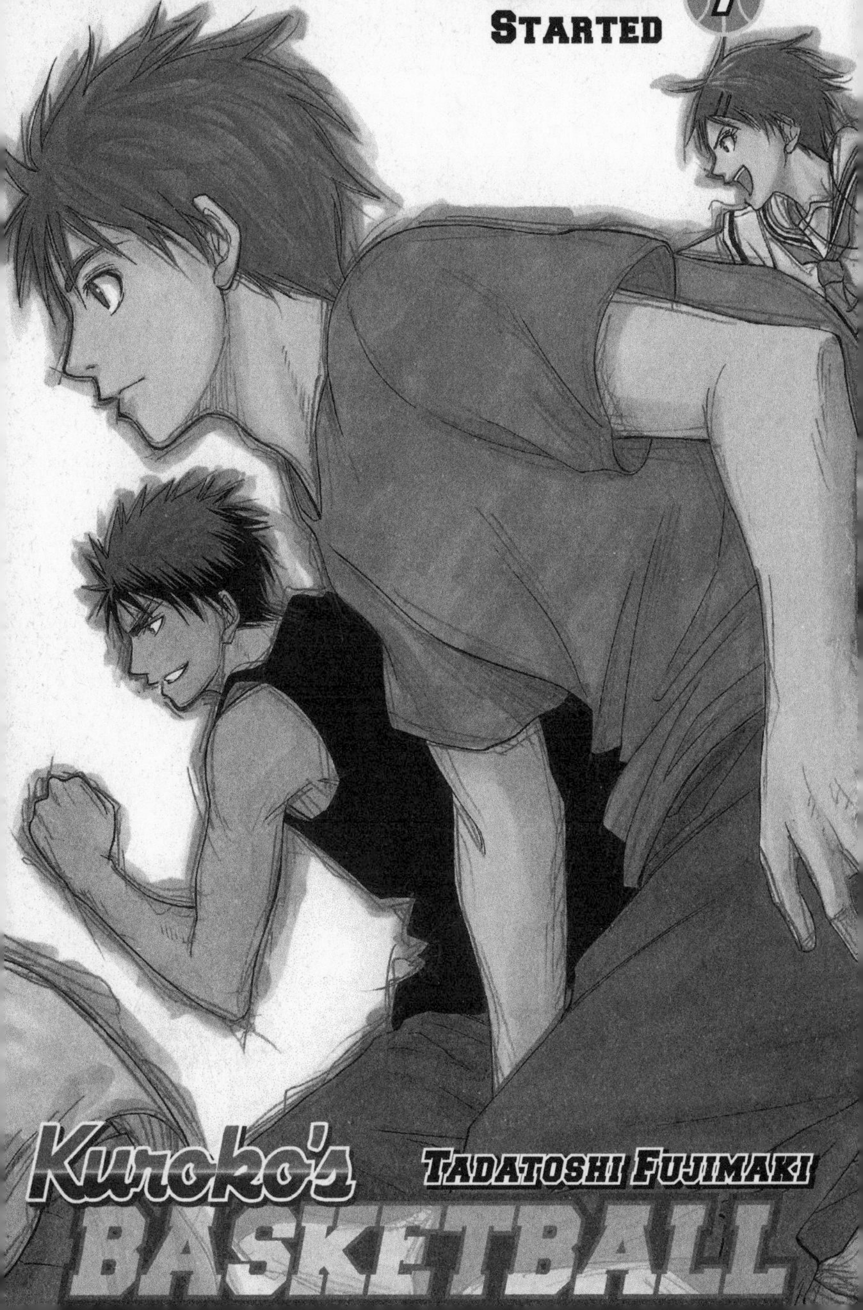

Kuroko's BASKETBALL

TADATOSHI FUJIMAKI

Characters

Tetsuya Kuroko

A first-year on Seirin High's basketball team. Gifted with a natural lack of presence, he utilizes misdirection on the court to make nearly invisible passes.

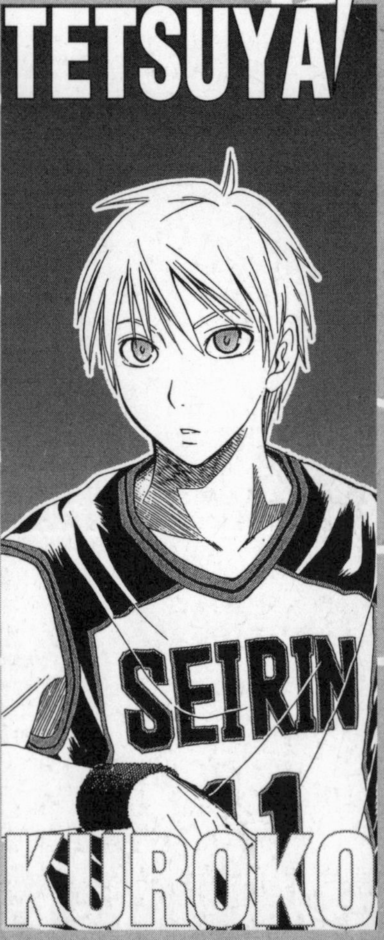

TETSUYA
SEIRIN
KUROKO

Taiga Kagami

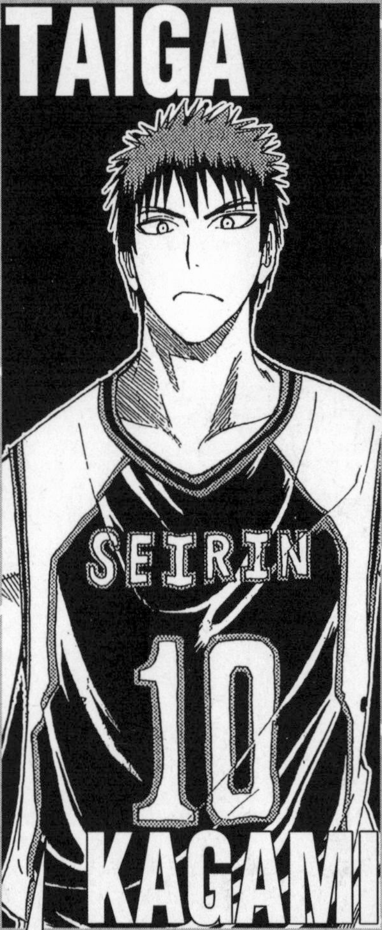

TAIGA
SEIRIN
10
KAGAMI

A first-year on Seirin High's basketball team. Though he's rough around the edges, he's a gifted player with a lot of potential. His goal is to beat the Miracle Generation.

RYOTA

KISE

One of the Miracle Generation. Any basketball move he sees, he can mimic in an instant.

SHINTARO

MIDORIMA

A first-year at Shutoku High, he's the top shooter of the Miracle Generation.

DAIKI

AOMINE

The ace of the Miracle Generation and Kuroko's former friend, he's now a first-year at To-oh Academy.

SATSUKI

MOMOI

A first-year member of To-oh Academy's basketball club, she was the team manager for the Miracle Generation during middle school.

RIKO

AIDA

A second-year and coach of the Seirin High basketball team.

JUNPEI

HYUGA

A second-year on Seirin High's basketball team. As captain, he led his team to the Finals League last year despite only playing first-year players.

Teiko Middle School is an elite championship school whose basketball team once fielded five prodigies collectively known as "the Miracle Generation." But supporting those five was a phantom sixth man—Tetsuya Kuroko. Kuroko's a first-year high school student with zero presence who joins Seirin High's basketball club. Though his physical abilities and stats are well below average, Kuroko thrives on the court by making passes his opponents can't detect!

Seirin takes their first step to making Inter-High by qualifying for the Finals League, but their first match pits them against To-oh Academy and Aomine, the ace of the Miracle Generation. Though Seirin puts up a good fight, they still suffer a lopsided loss. A dispirited Seirin then follows up that game with more losses, ending their quest for Inter-High...

STORY THUS FAR

TABLE OF CONTENTS

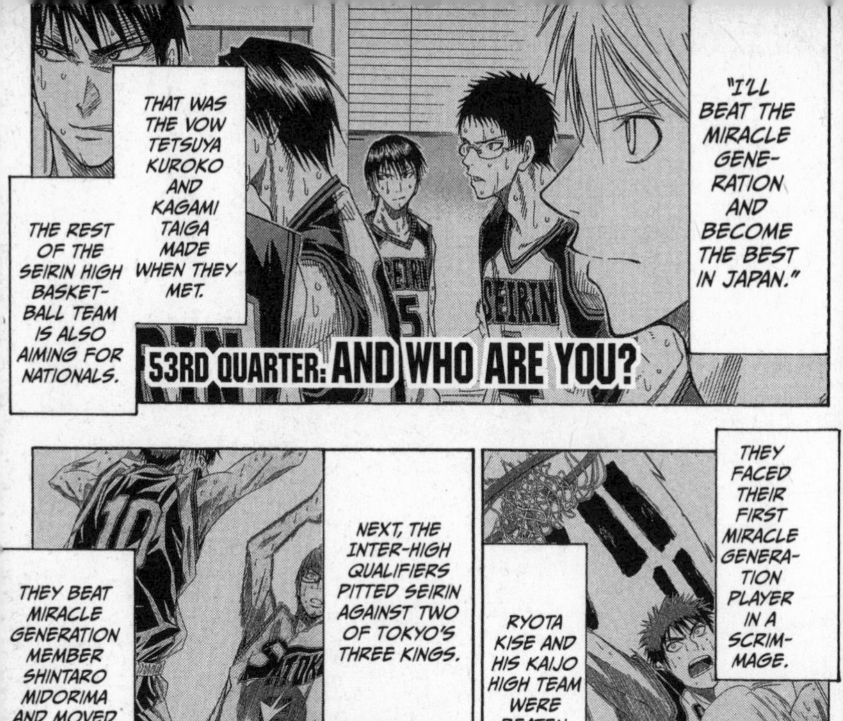
"I'LL BEAT THE MIRACLE GENERATION AND BECOME THE BEST IN JAPAN."
THAT WAS THE VOW TETSUYA KUROKO AND KAGAMI TAIGA MADE WHEN THEY MET.
THE REST OF THE SEIRIN HIGH BASKETBALL TEAM IS ALSO AIMING FOR NATIONALS.
53RD QUARTER: AND WHO ARE YOU?
THEY FACED THEIR FIRST MIRACLE GENERATION PLAYER IN A SCRIMMAGE.
RYOTA KISE AND HIS KAIJO HIGH TEAM WERE BEATEN.
NEXT, THE INTER-HIGH QUALIFIERS PITTED SEIRIN AGAINST TWO OF TOKYO'S THREE KINGS.
THEY BEAT MIRACLE GENERATION MEMBER SHINTARO MIDORIMA AND MOVED ON TO THE FINALS LEAGUE.
BUT THE ACE OF THE MIRACLE GENERATION, DAIKI AOMINE, PROVED TOO MUCH FOR THEM.
AFTER THAT OVERWHELMING LOSS, SEIRIN COULDN'T RECOVER IN TIME AND LOST THE REMAINING MATCHES.
TO-OH
SEIRIN
55

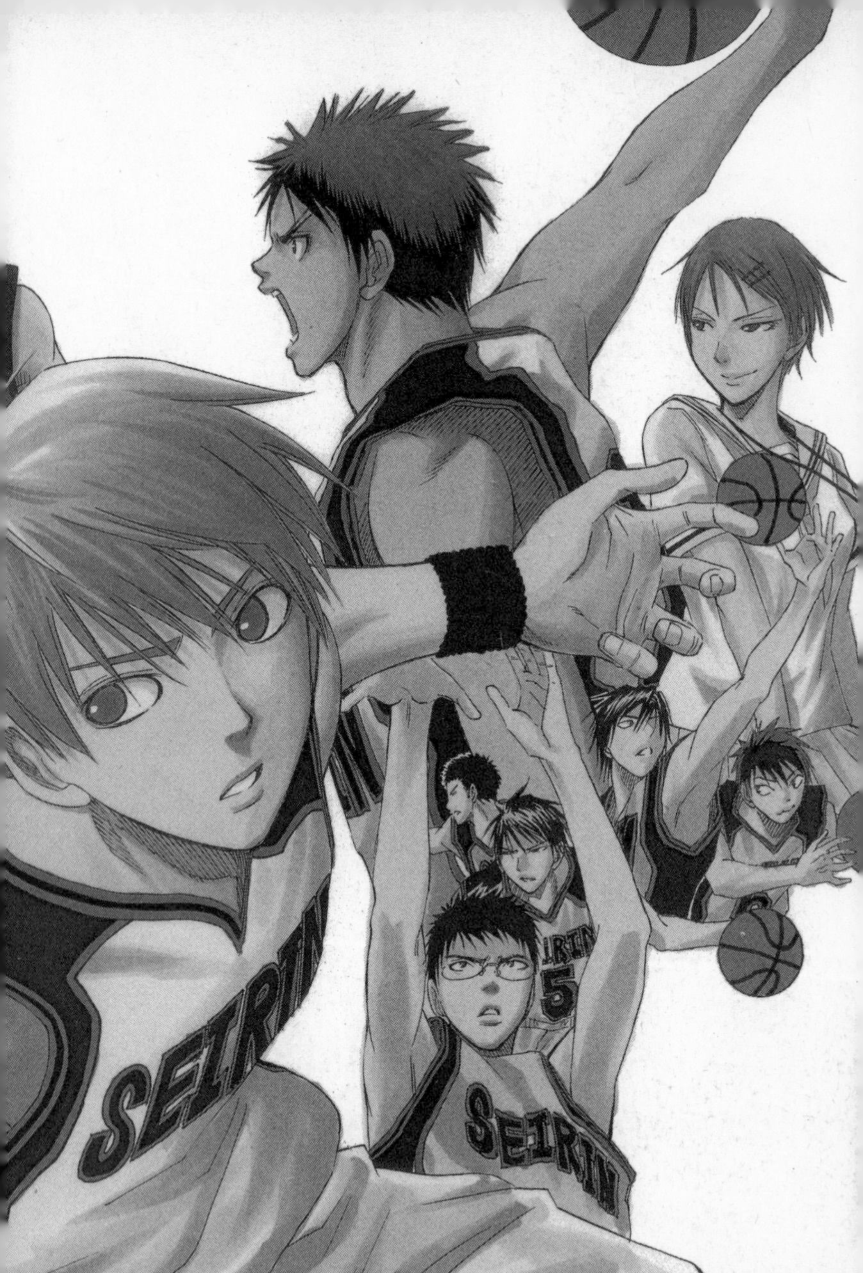
SEIRIN
SEIRIN

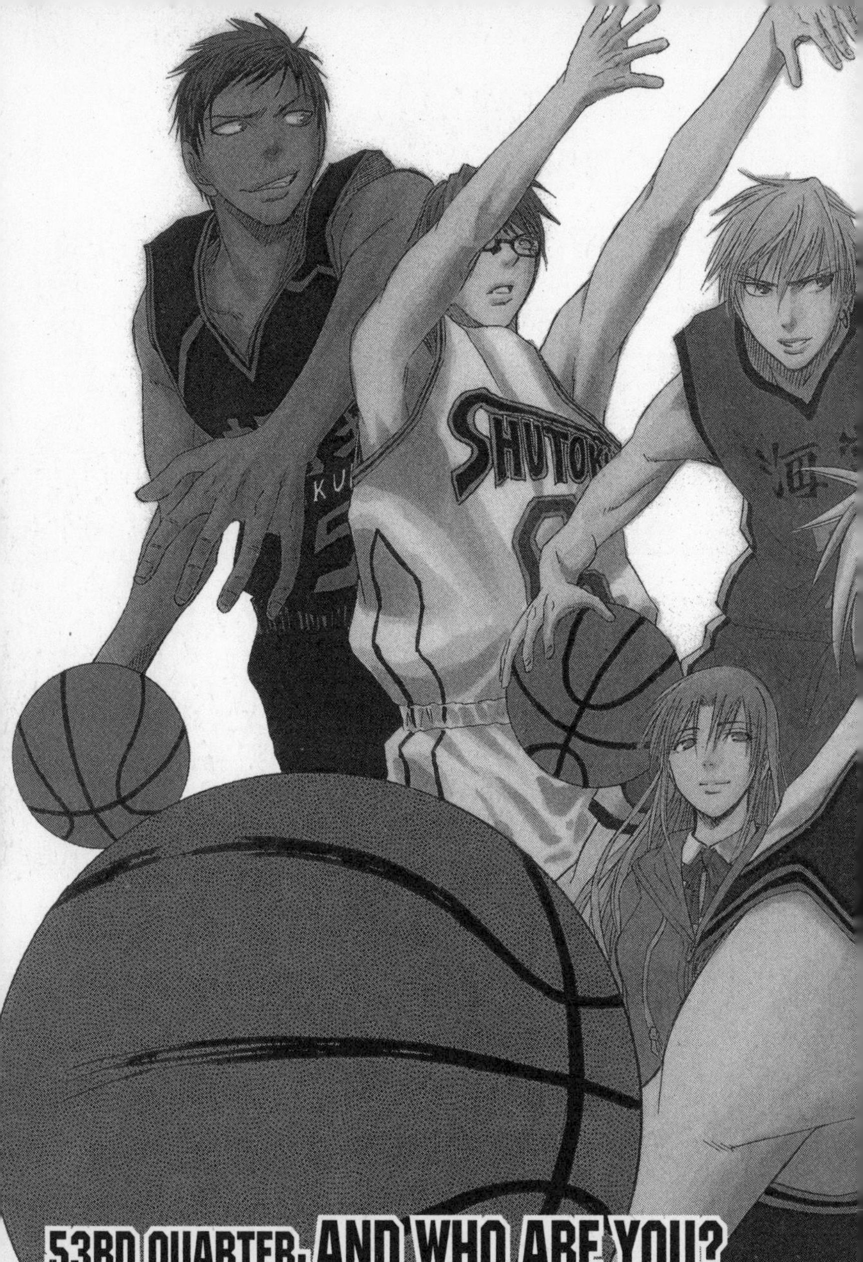

53RD QUARTER: AND WHO ARE YOU?

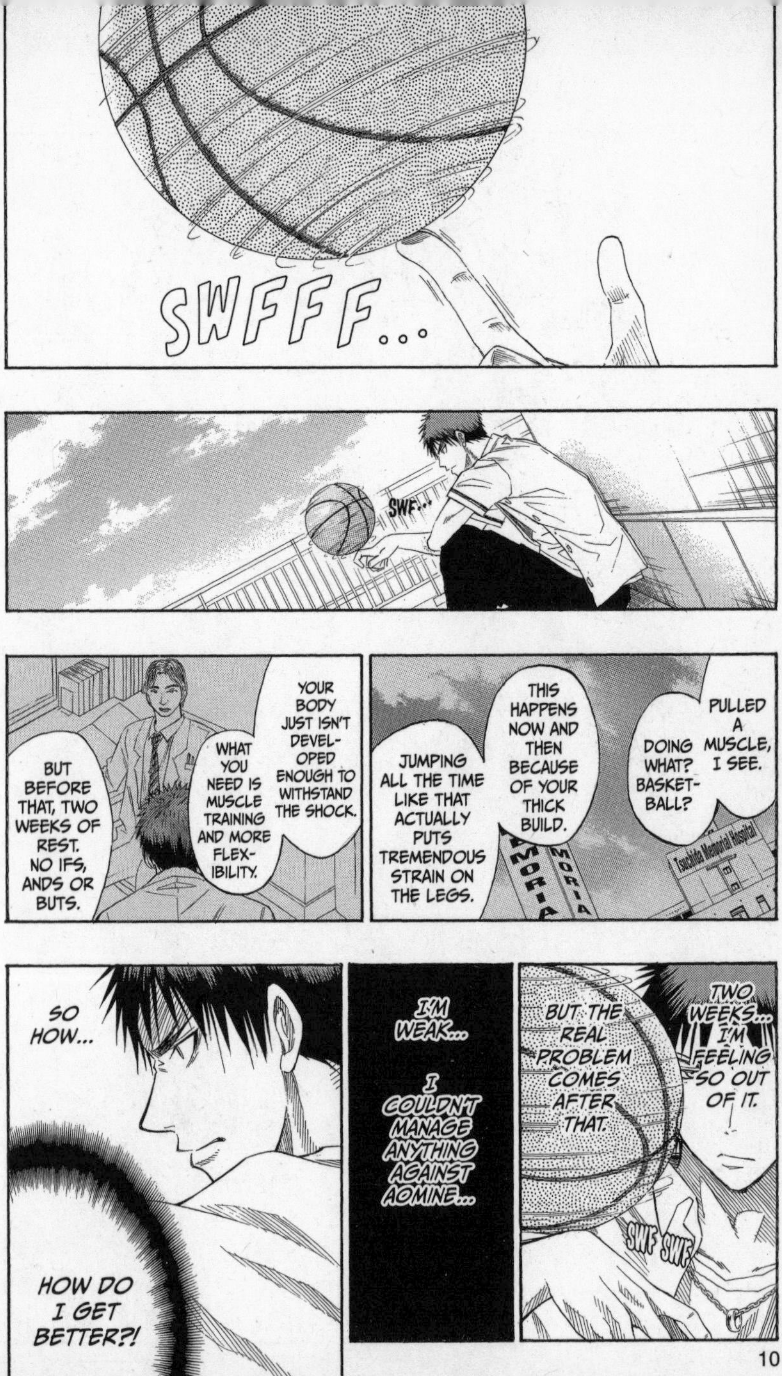

SWFFF...
SWF...
PULLED A MUSCLE, I SEE.
DOING WHAT? BASKETBALL?
Tsuchida Memorial Hospital
THIS HAPPENS NOW AND THEN BECAUSE OF YOUR THICK BUILD.
JUMPING ALL THE TIME LIKE THAT ACTUALLY PUTS TREMENDOUS STRAIN ON THE LEGS.
YOUR BODY JUST ISN'T DEVELOPED ENOUGH TO WITHSTAND THE SHOCK.
WHAT YOU NEED IS MUSCLE TRAINING AND MORE FLEXIBILITY.
BUT BEFORE THAT, TWO WEEKS OF REST. NO IFS, ANDS OR BUTS.
TWO WEEKS... I'M FEELING SO OUT OF IT.
BUT THE REAL PROBLEM COMES AFTER THAT.
SWF SWF
I'M WEAK...
I COULDN'T MANAGE ANYTHING AGAINST AOMINE...
SO HOW...
HOW DO I GET BETTER?!

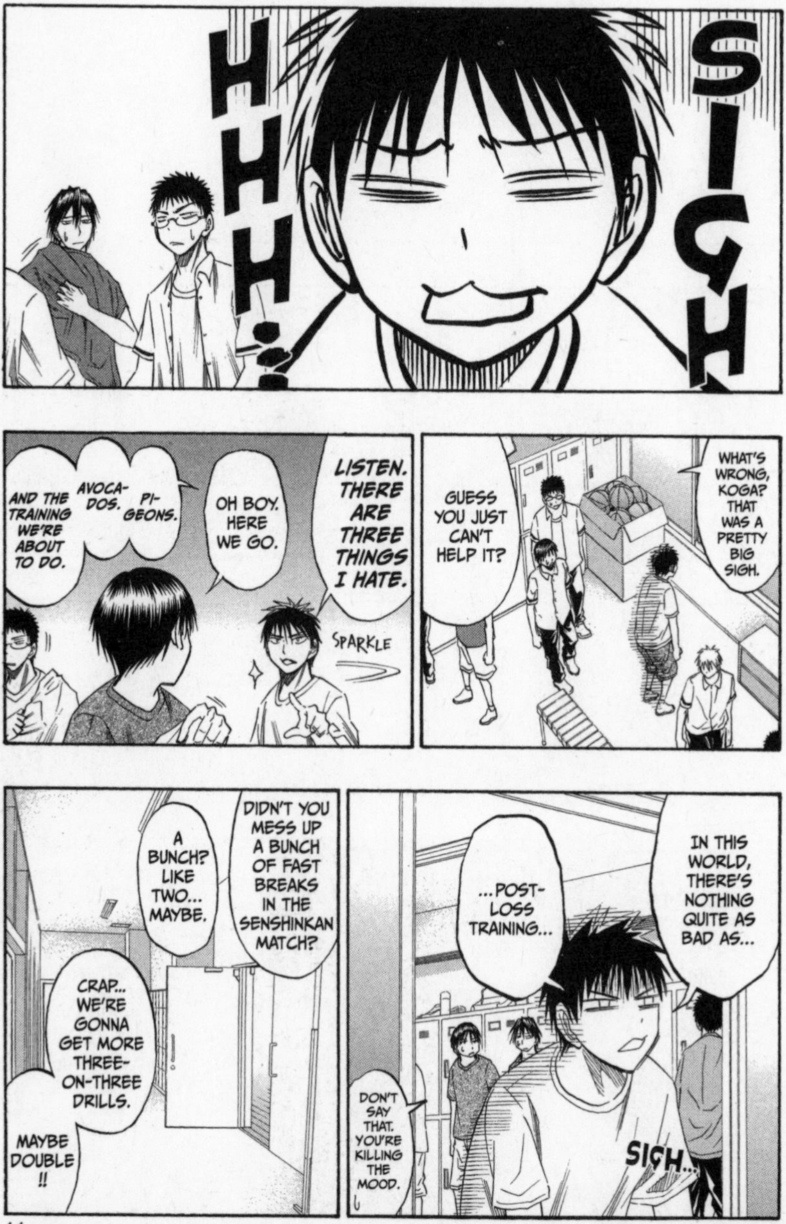
SIGH
HHHH...!!
WHAT'S WRONG, KOGA? THAT WAS A PRETTY BIG SIGH.
GUESS YOU JUST CAN'T HELP IT?
LISTEN. THERE ARE THREE THINGS I HATE.
OH BOY. HERE WE GO.
SPARKLE
AVOCADOS. PIGEONS.
AND THE TRAINING WE'RE ABOUT TO DO.
IN THIS WORLD, THERE'S NOTHING QUITE AS BAD AS...
...POST-LOSS TRAINING...
DON'T SAY THAT. YOU'RE KILLING THE MOOD.
SIGH...
DIDN'T YOU MESS UP A BUNCH OF FAST BREAKS IN THE SENSHINKAN MATCH?
A BUNCH? LIKE TWO... MAYBE.
CRAP... WE'RE GONNA GET MORE THREE-ON-THREE DRILLS.
MAYBE DOUBLE!!

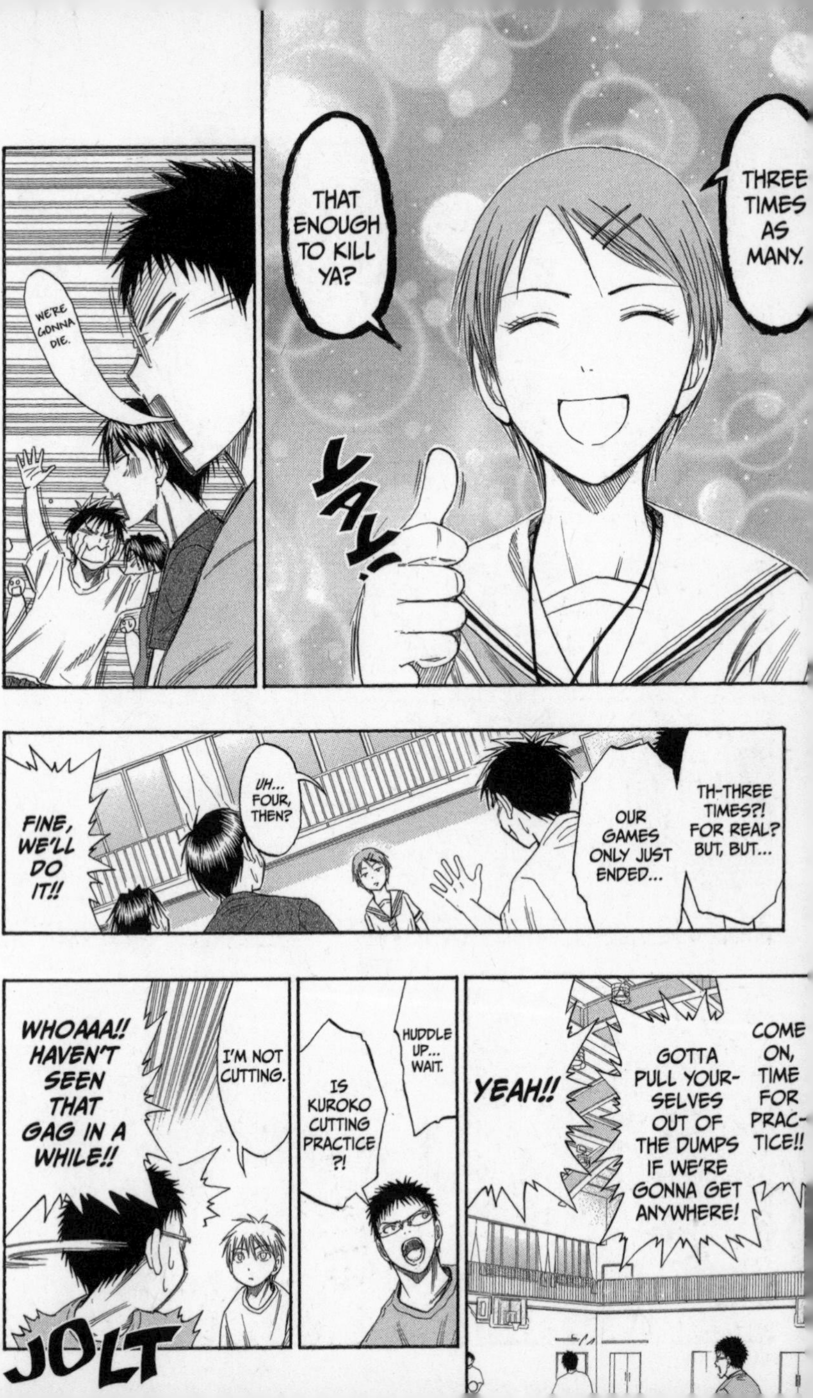
THREE TIMES AS MANY.
YAY!
THAT ENOUGH TO KILL YA?
WE'RE GONNA DIE.
TH-THREE TIMES?! FOR REAL? BUT, BUT...
OUR GAMES ONLY JUST ENDED...
UH... FOUR, THEN?
FINE, WE'LL DO IT!!
COME ON, TIME FOR PRACTICE!!
GOTTA PULL YOURSELVES OUT OF THE DUMPS IF WE'RE GONNA GET ANYWHERE!
YEAH!!
HUDDLE UP... WAIT.
IS KUROKO CUTTING PRACTICE?!
I'M NOT CUTTING.
WHOAAA!! HAVEN'T SEEN THAT GAG IN A WHILE!!
JOLT

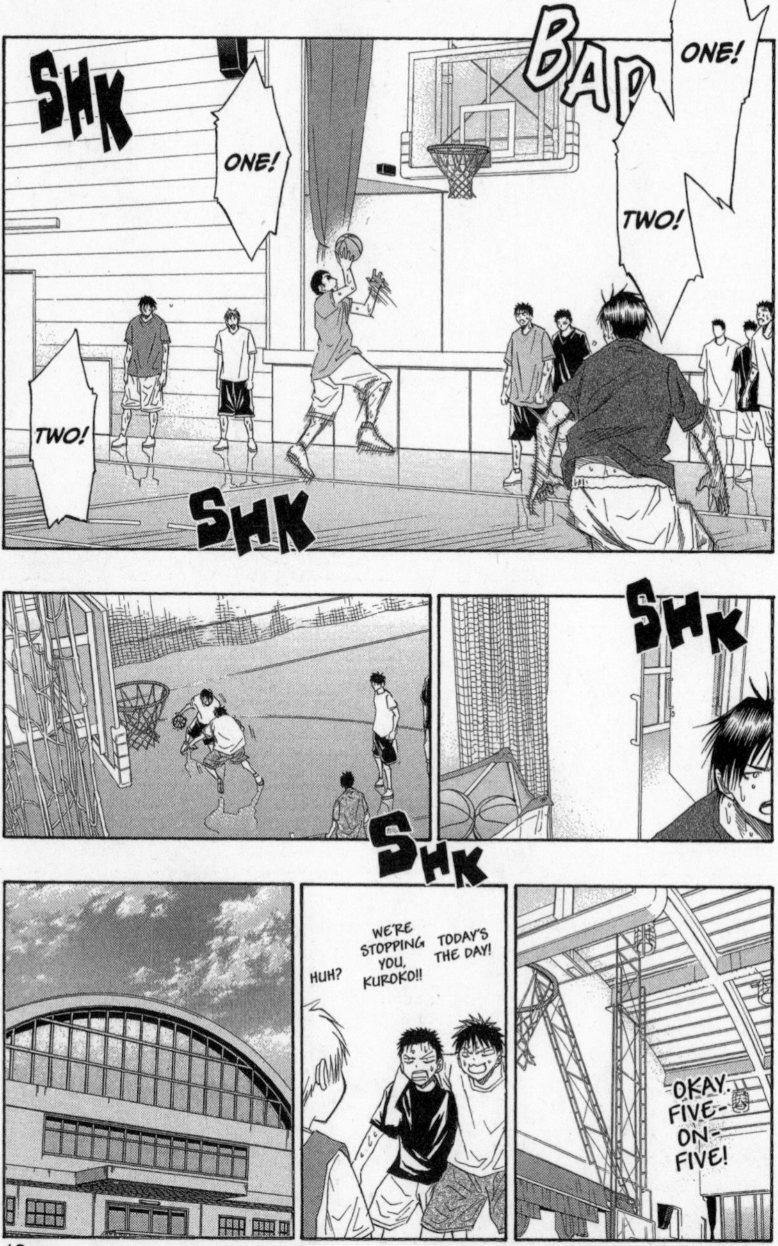
ONE!
BAP
TWO!
SHK
ONE!
TWO!
SHK
SHK
SHK
OKAY. FIVE-ON-FIVE!
TODAY'S THE DAY!
WE'RE STOPPING YOU, KUROKO!!
HUH?

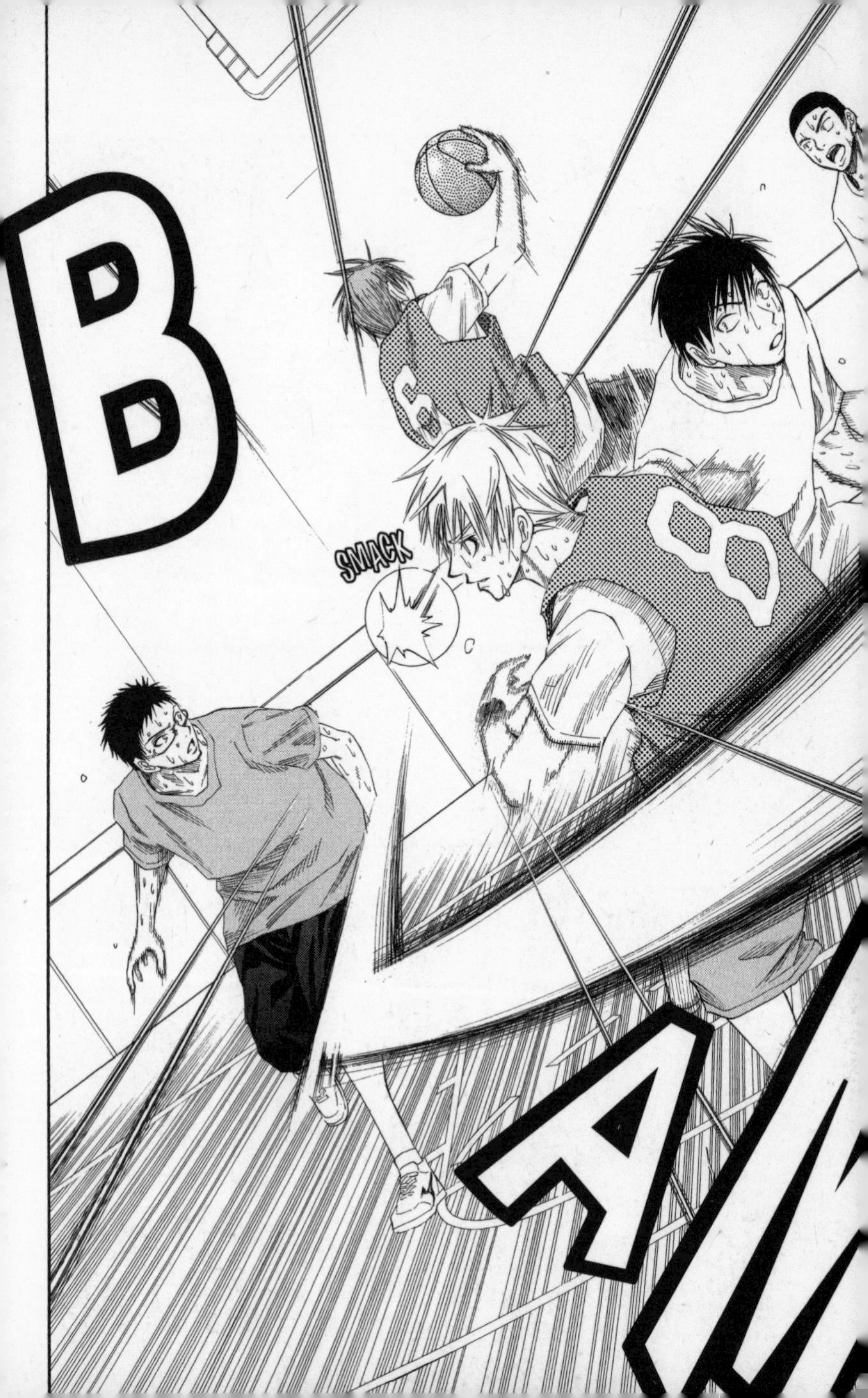
SMACK
BA

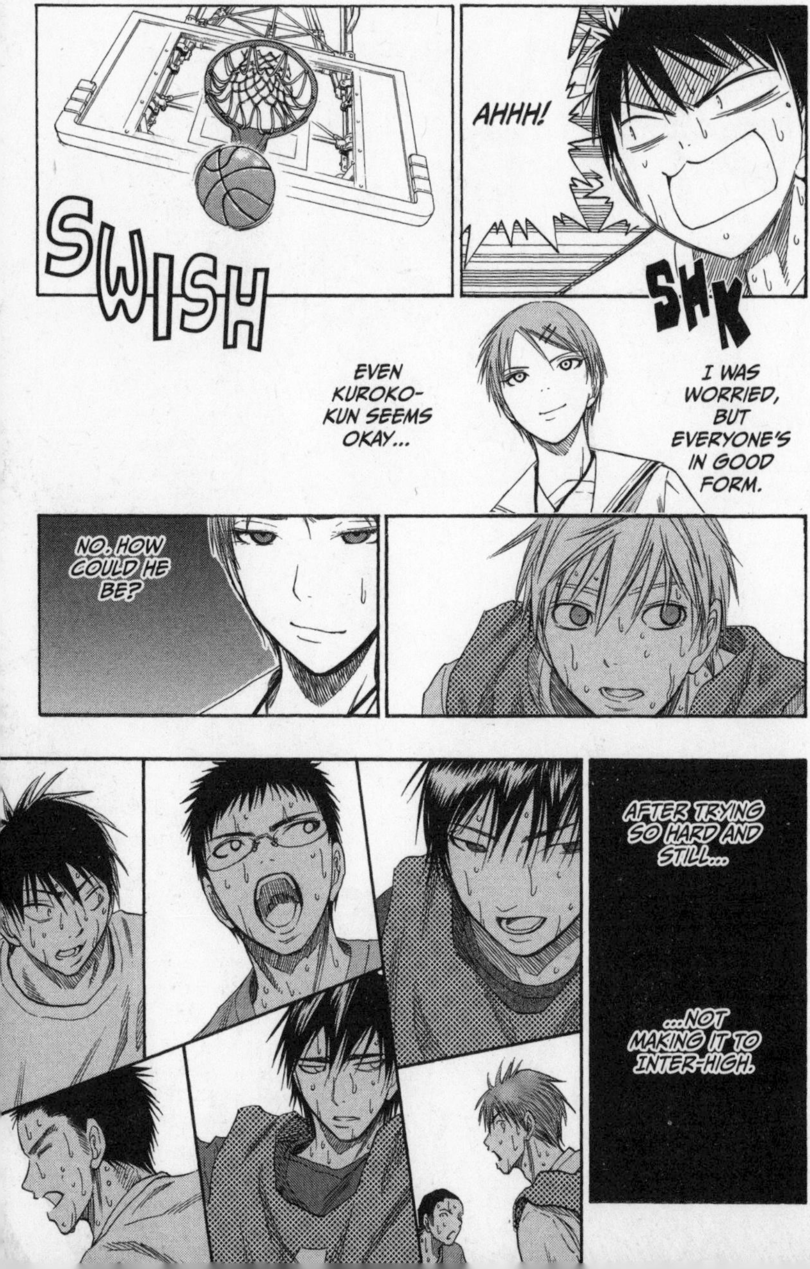
AHHH!
SHK
SWISH
I WAS WORRIED, BUT EVERYONE'S IN GOOD FORM.
EVEN KUROKO-KUN SEEMS OKAY...
NO. HOW COULD HE BE?
AFTER TRYING SO HARD AND STILL...
...NOT MAKING IT TO INTER-HIGH.

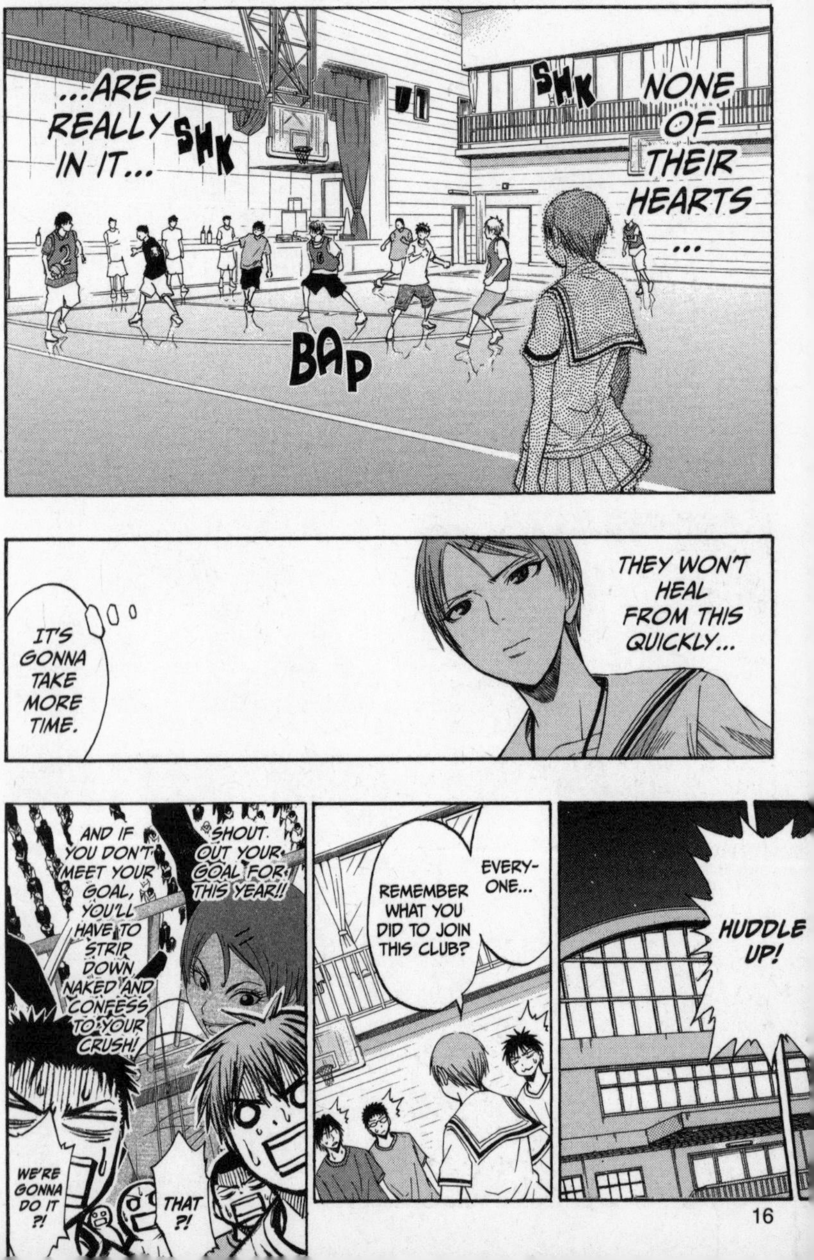
NONE OF THEIR HEARTS ...
SHK
...ARE REALLY IN IT...
SHK
BAP
THEY WON'T HEAL FROM THIS QUICKLY...
IT'S GONNA TAKE MORE TIME.
HUDDLE UP!
EVERY-ONE...
REMEMBER WHAT YOU DID TO JOIN THIS CLUB?
SHOUT OUT YOUR GOAL FOR THIS YEAR!!
AND IF YOU DON'T MEET YOUR GOAL, YOU'LL HAVE TO STRIP DOWN NAKED AND CONFESS TO YOUR CRUSH!
THAT ?!
WE'RE GONNA DO IT ?!

UH...

YOU CAN'T AFFORD TO KEEP UP THIS LOSING STREAK.

GOT IT?

BECAUSE IT GETS COLD... IN WINTER.

ESPECIALLY WHEN YOU'RE NAKED.

WINTER...?!

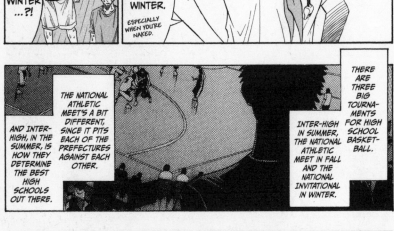

THERE ARE THREE BIG TOURNAMENTS FOR HIGH SCHOOL BASKETBALL.

INTER-HIGH IN SUMMER, THE NATIONAL ATHLETIC MEET IN FALL AND THE NATIONAL INVITATIONAL IN WINTER.

THE NATIONAL ATHLETIC MEET'S A BIT DIFFERENT, SINCE IT PITS EACH OF THE PREFECTURES AGAINST EACH OTHER.

AND INTER-HIGH, IN THE SUMMER, IS HOW THEY DETERMINE THE BEST HIGH SCHOOLS OUT THERE.

THEN THERE'S THE WINTER NATIONAL INVITATIONAL.

IT'S HELD IN DECEMBER IN TOKYO. THE FINAL BIG TITLE FIGHT OF THE YEAR TO DECIDE THE YEAR'S BEST TEAM...

THE JAPANESE HIGH SCHOOL BASKETBALL NATIONAL INVITATIONAL TOURNAMENT.

ALSO KNOWN AS...

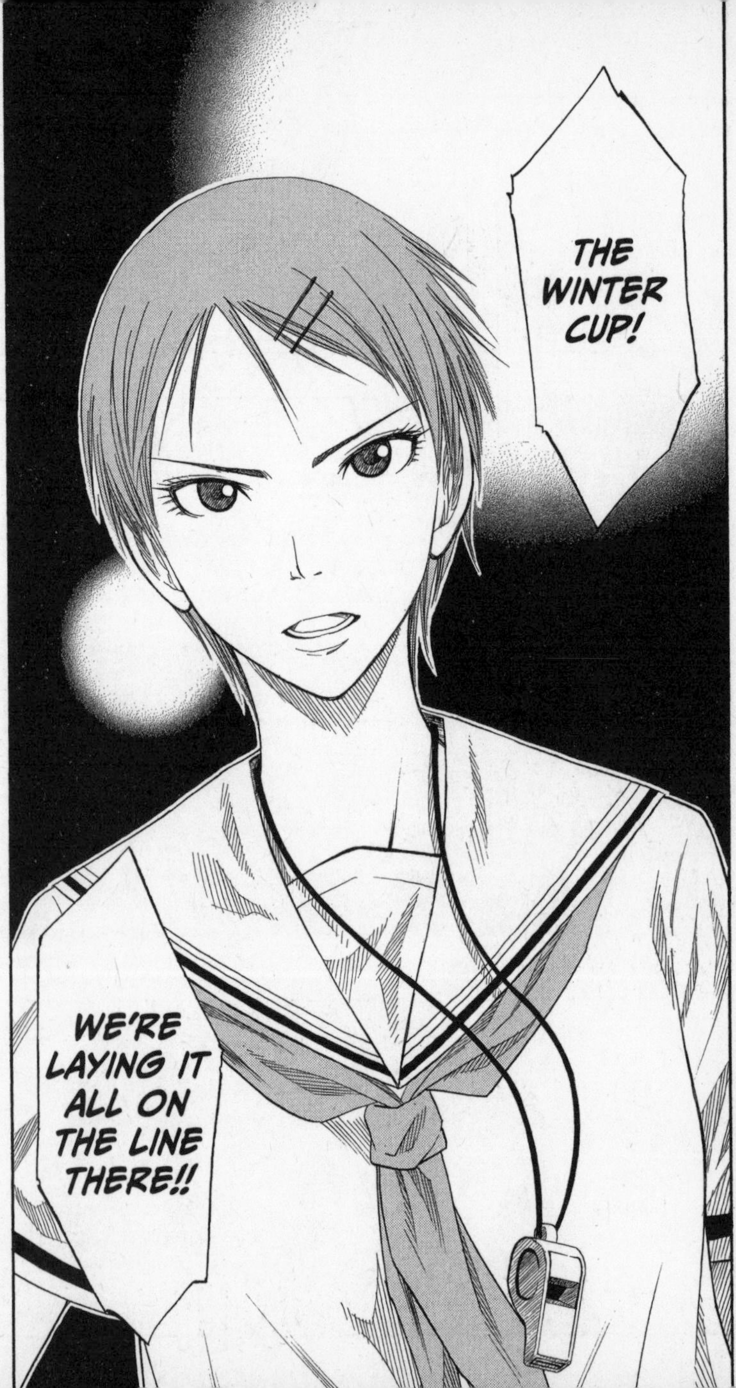
THE WINTER CUP!
WE'RE LAYING IT ALL ON THE LINE THERE!!

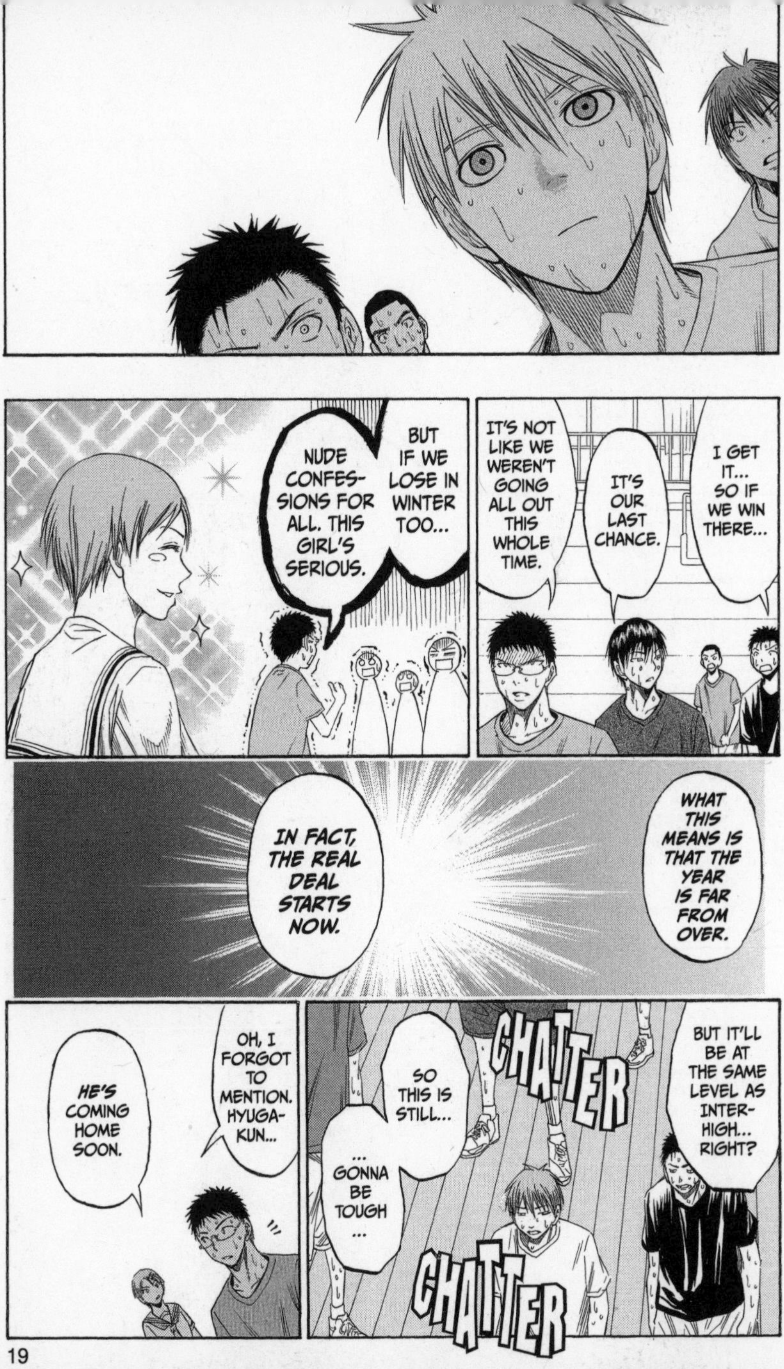
I GET IT... SO IF WE WIN THERE...
IT'S OUR LAST CHANCE.
IT'S NOT LIKE WE WEREN'T GOING ALL OUT THIS WHOLE TIME.
BUT IF WE LOSE IN WINTER TOO...
NUDE CONFESSIONS FOR ALL. THIS GIRL'S SERIOUS.
WHAT THIS MEANS IS THAT THE YEAR IS FAR FROM OVER.
IN FACT, THE REAL DEAL STARTS NOW.
BUT IT'LL BE AT THE SAME LEVEL AS INTER-HIGH... RIGHT?
CHATTER
SO THIS IS STILL...
... GONNA BE TOUGH ...
CHATTER
OH, I FORGOT TO MENTION. HYUGA-KUN...
HE'S COMING HOME SOON.

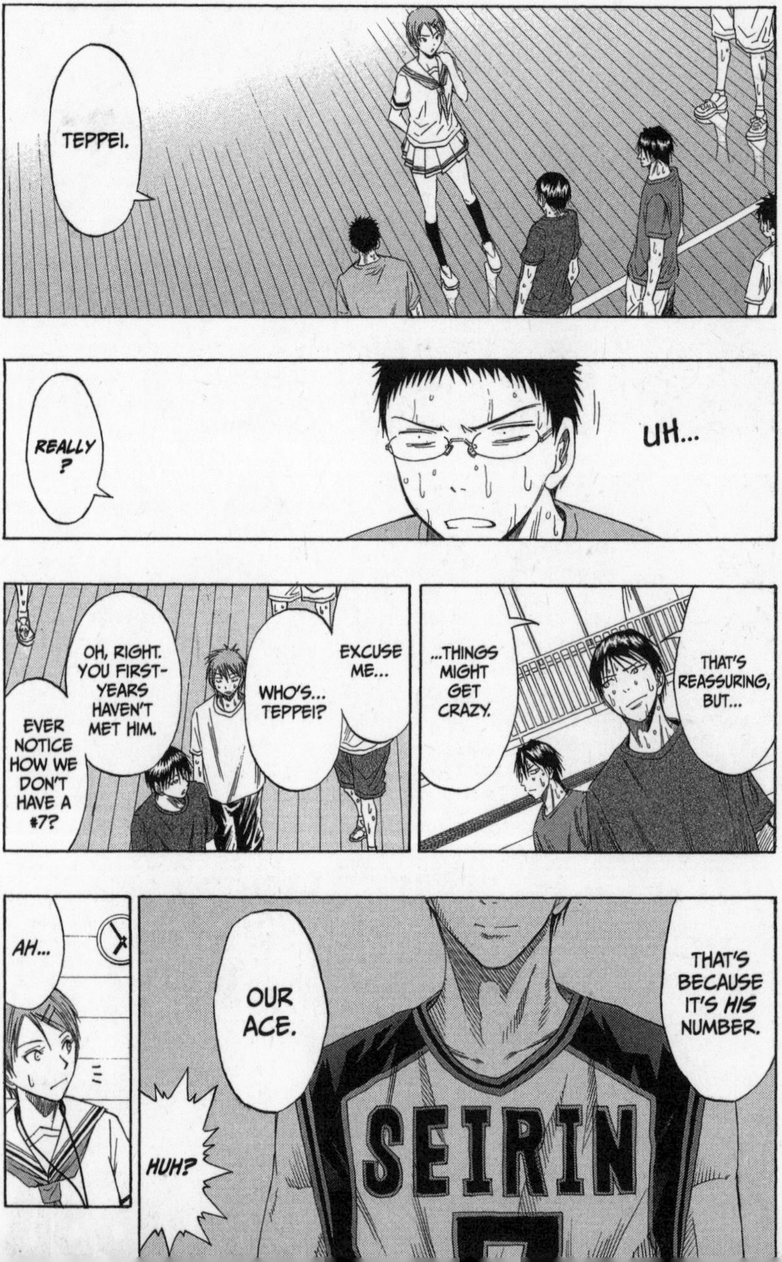

TEPPEI.
UH...
REALLY?
THAT'S REASSURING, BUT...
...THINGS MIGHT GET CRAZY.
EXCUSE ME...
WHO'S... TEPPEI?
OH, RIGHT. YOU FIRST-YEARS HAVEN'T MET HIM.
EVER NOTICE HOW WE DON'T HAVE A #7?
THAT'S BECAUSE IT'S *HIS* NUMBER.
OUR ACE.
SEIRIN
HUH?
AH...

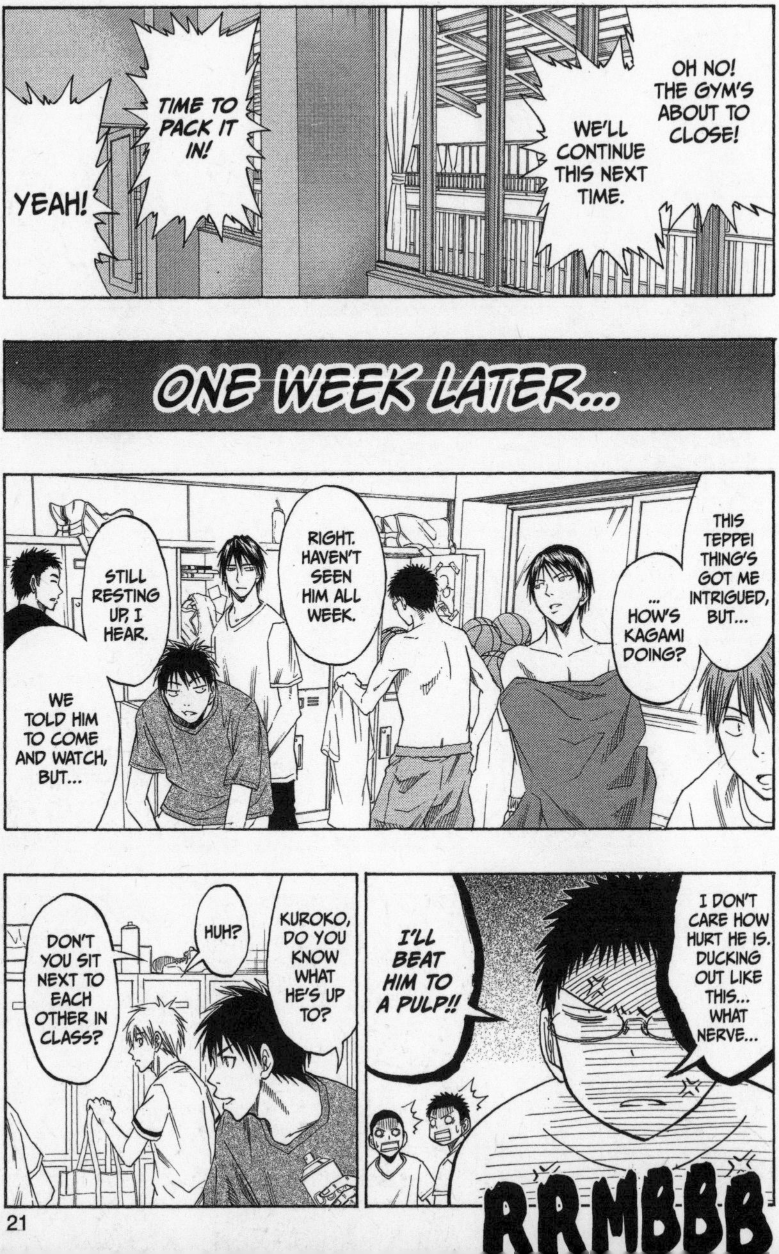
OH NO! THE GYM'S ABOUT TO CLOSE!
WE'LL CONTINUE THIS NEXT TIME.
TIME TO PACK IT IN!
YEAH!
ONE WEEK LATER...
THIS TEPPEI THING'S GOT ME INTRIGUED, BUT...
... HOW'S KAGAMI DOING?
RIGHT. HAVEN'T SEEN HIM ALL WEEK.
STILL RESTING UP, I HEAR.
WE TOLD HIM TO COME AND WATCH, BUT...
I DON'T CARE HOW HURT HE IS. DUCKING OUT LIKE THIS... WHAT NERVE...
I'LL BEAT HIM TO A PULP!!
RRMBBB
KUROKO, DO YOU KNOW WHAT HE'S UP TO?
HUH?
DON'T YOU SIT NEXT TO EACH OTHER IN CLASS?

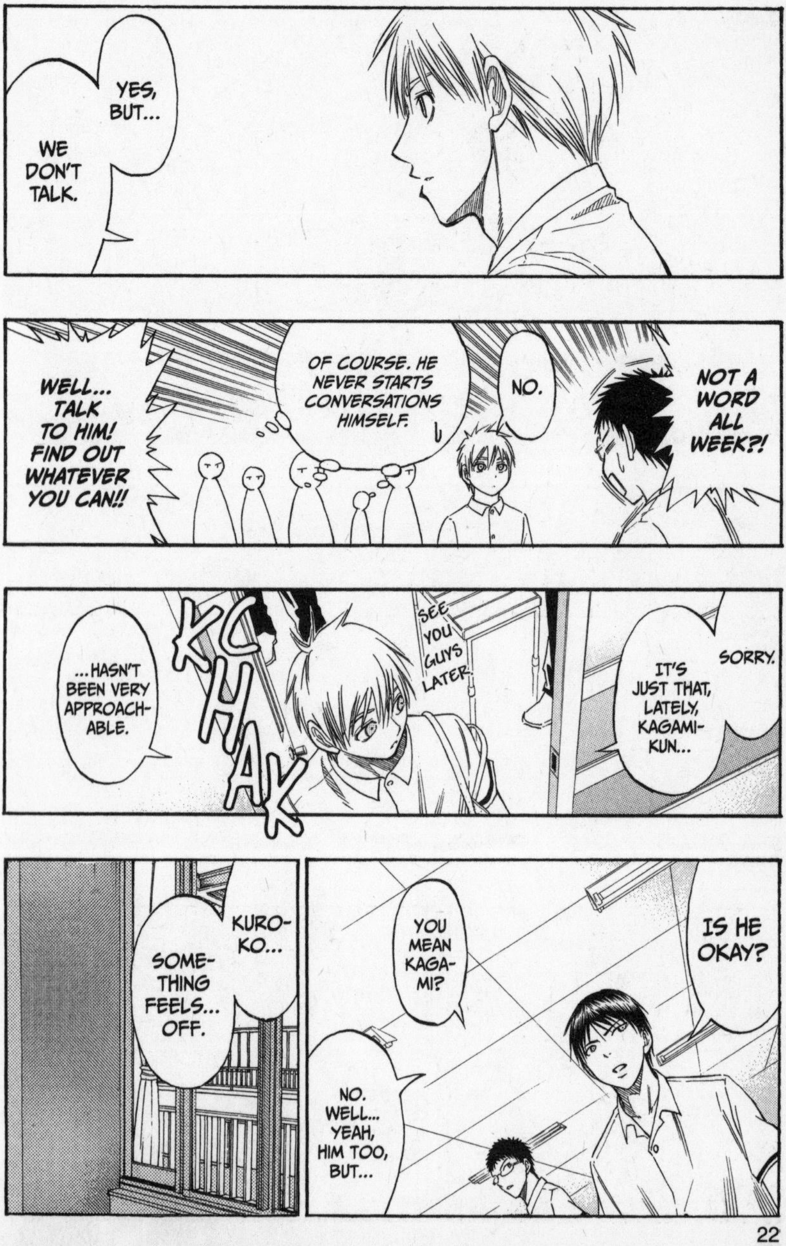
YES, BUT...
WE DON'T TALK.
NOT A WORD ALL WEEK?!
NO.
OF COURSE. HE NEVER STARTS CONVERSATIONS HIMSELF.
WELL... TALK TO HIM! FIND OUT WHATEVER YOU CAN!!
SORRY.
IT'S JUST THAT, LATELY, KAGAMI-KUN...
SEE YOU GUYS LATER.
KCHAK
...HASN'T BEEN VERY APPROACH-ABLE.
IS HE OKAY?
YOU MEAN KAGA-MI?
NO. WELL... YEAH, HIM TOO, BUT...
KURO-KO...
SOME-THING FEELS... OFF.

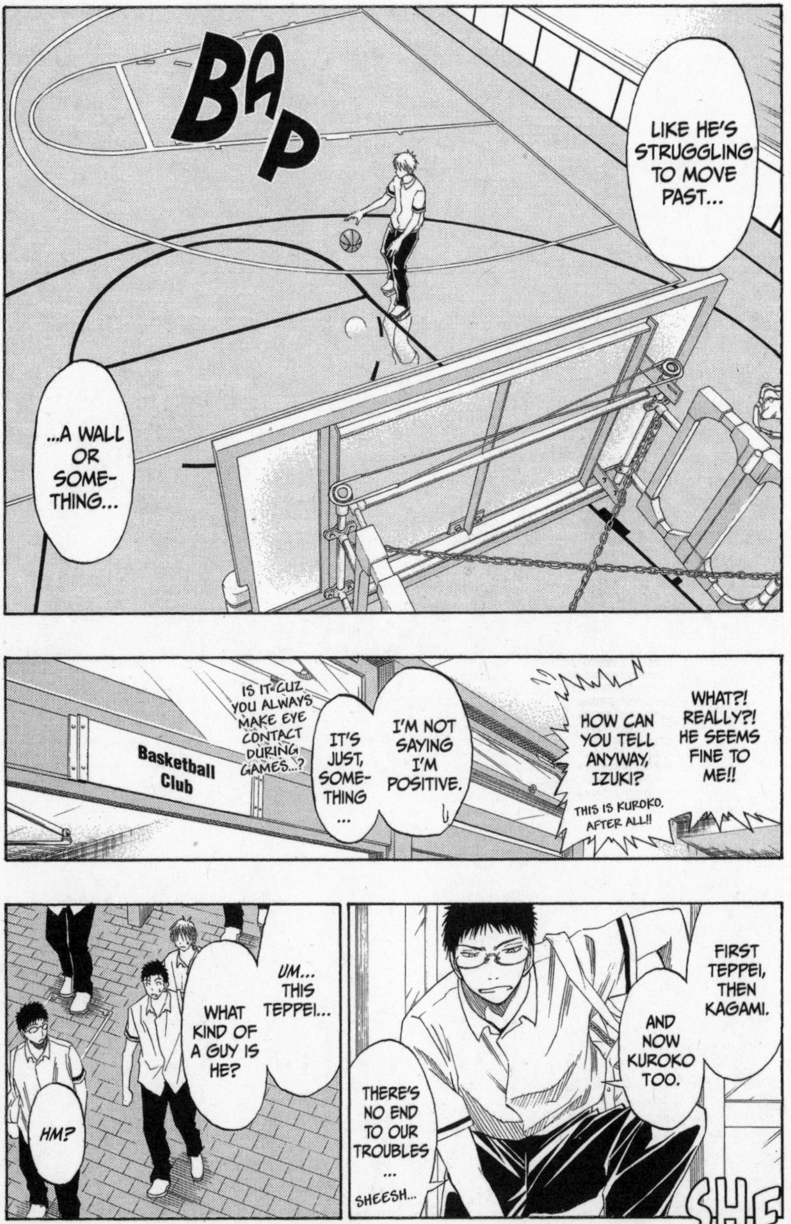
LIKE HE'S STRUGGLING TO MOVE PAST...
BAP
...A WALL OR SOME-THING...
WHAT?! REALLY?! HE SEEMS FINE TO ME!!
HOW CAN YOU TELL ANYWAY, IZUKI?
THIS IS KUROKO, AFTER ALL!!
I'M NOT SAYING I'M POSITIVE.
IT'S JUST, SOME-THING...
IS IT CUZ YOU ALWAYS MAKE EYE CONTACT DURING GAMES...?
Basketball Club
FIRST TEPPEI, THEN KAGAMI.
AND NOW KUROKO TOO.
THERE'S NO END TO OUR TROUBLES...
SHEESH...
SHF
UM... THIS TEPPEI...
WHAT KIND OF A GUY IS HE?
HM?

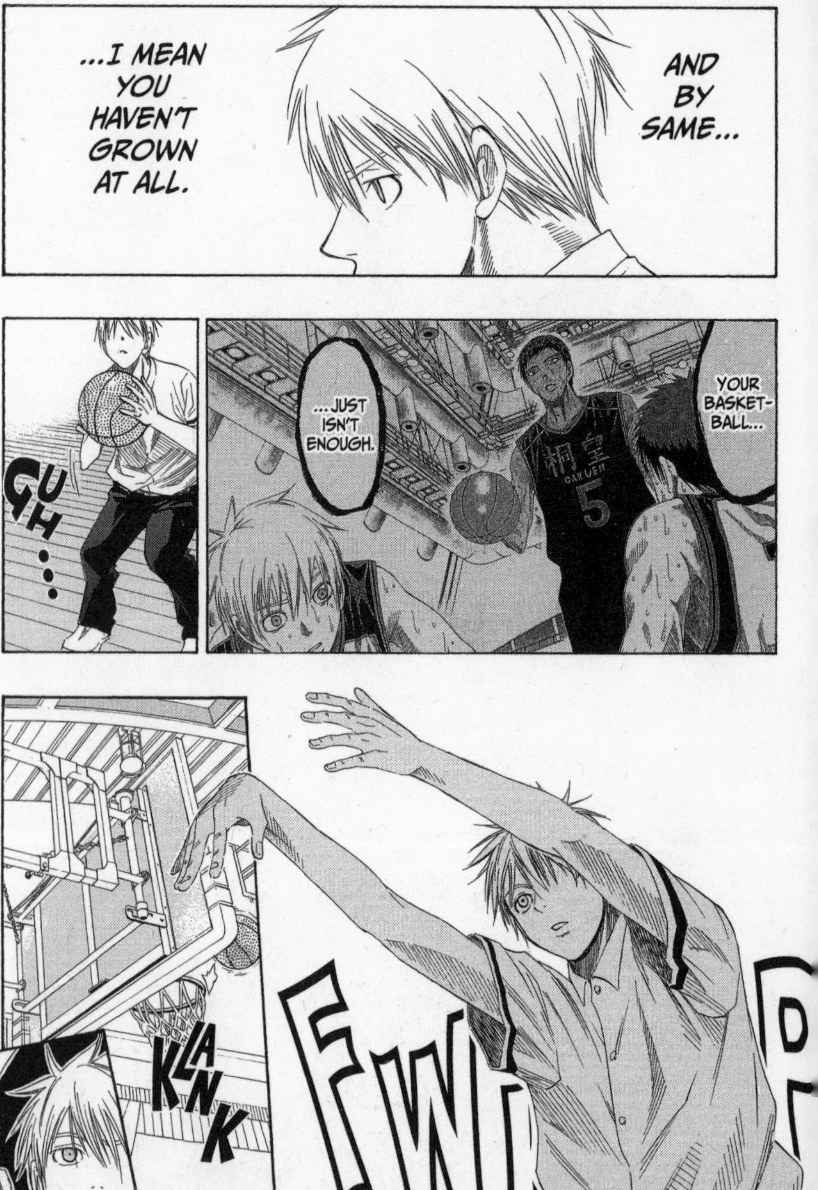
AND BY SAME...
...I MEAN YOU HAVEN'T GROWN AT ALL.
YOUR BASKET-BALL...
...JUST ISN'T ENOUGH.
桐皇
GAKUEN
5
GUH...
FWIP
KLANK

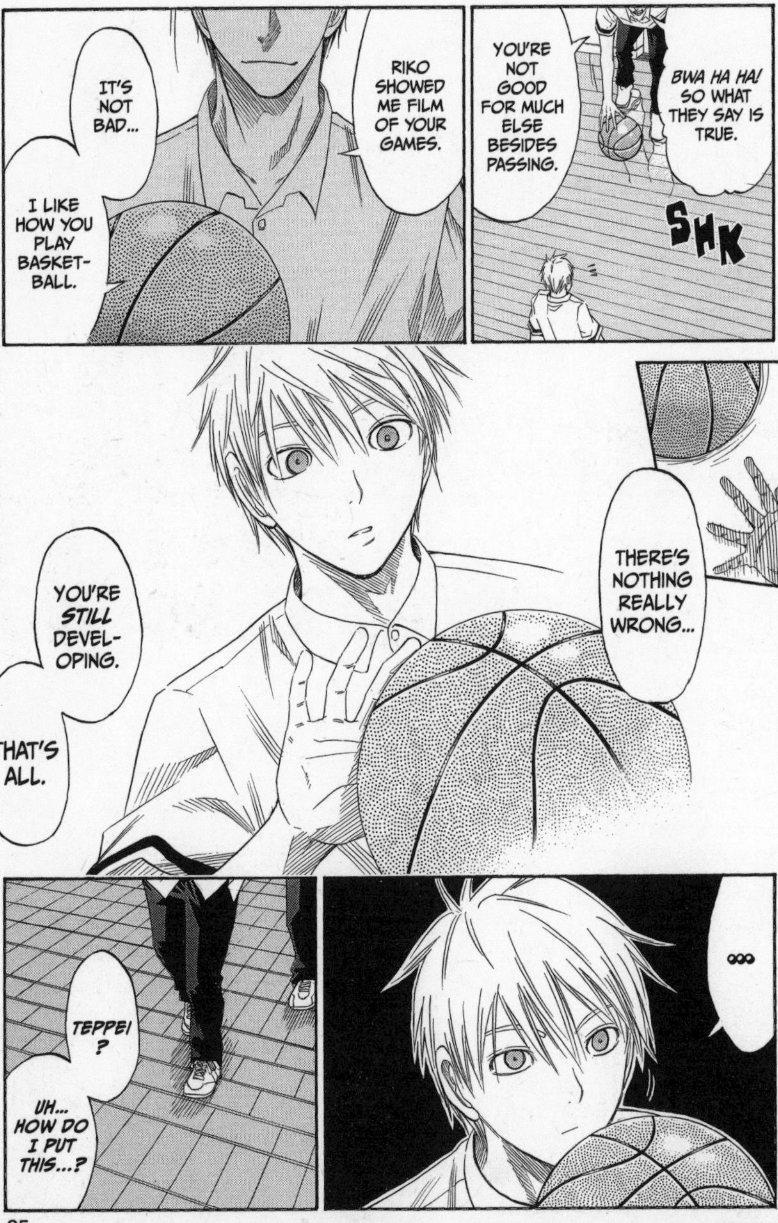
BWA HA HA! SO WHAT THEY SAY IS TRUE.
YOU'RE NOT GOOD FOR MUCH ELSE BESIDES PASSING.
SHK
RIKO SHOWED ME FILM OF YOUR GAMES.
IT'S NOT BAD...
I LIKE HOW YOU PLAY BASKET-BALL.
THERE'S NOTHING REALLY WRONG...
YOU'RE STILL DEVEL-OPING.
THAT'S ALL.
...
TEPPEI?
UH... HOW DO I PUT THIS...?

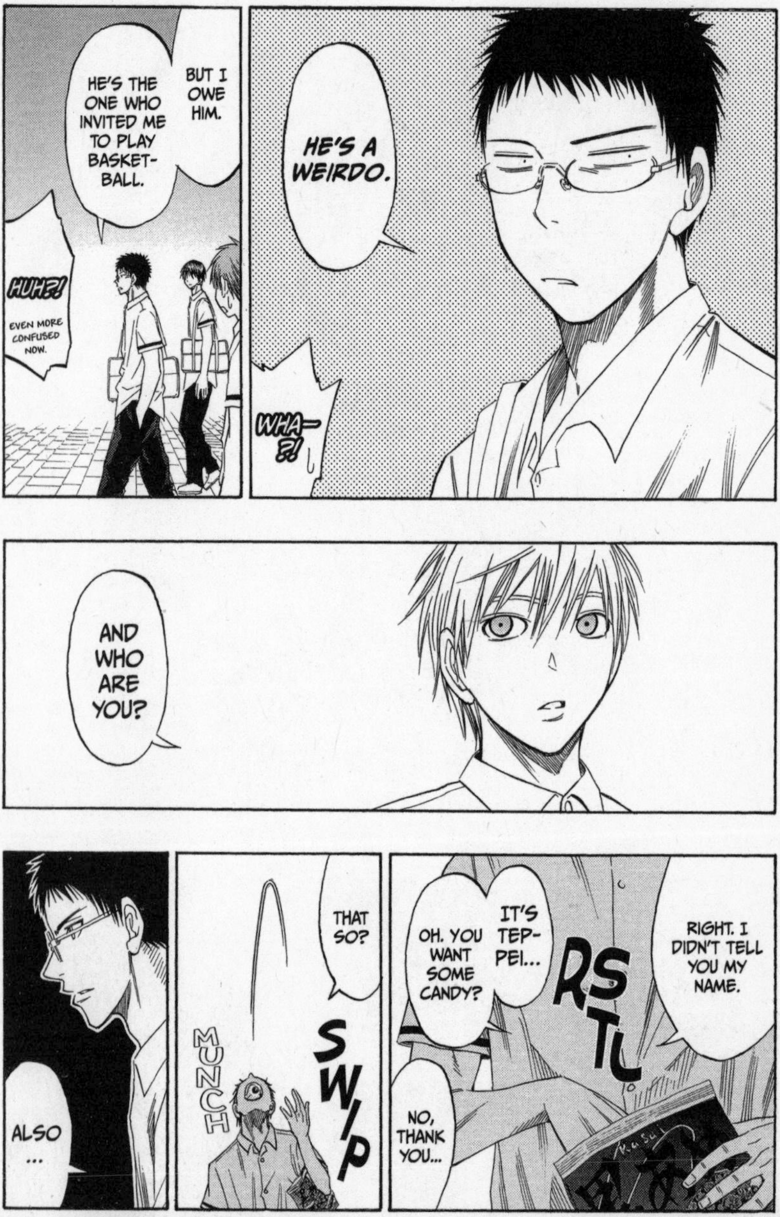
HE'S A WEIRDO.
WHA—?!
BUT I OWE HIM.
HE'S THE ONE WHO INVITED ME TO PLAY BASKET-BALL.
HUH?!
EVEN MORE CONFUSED NOW.
AND WHO ARE YOU?
RIGHT. I DIDN'T TELL YOU MY NAME.
RSTL
IT'S TEP-PEI...
OH. YOU WANT SOME CANDY?
NO, THANK YOU...
THAT SO?
SWIP
MUNCH
ALSO...

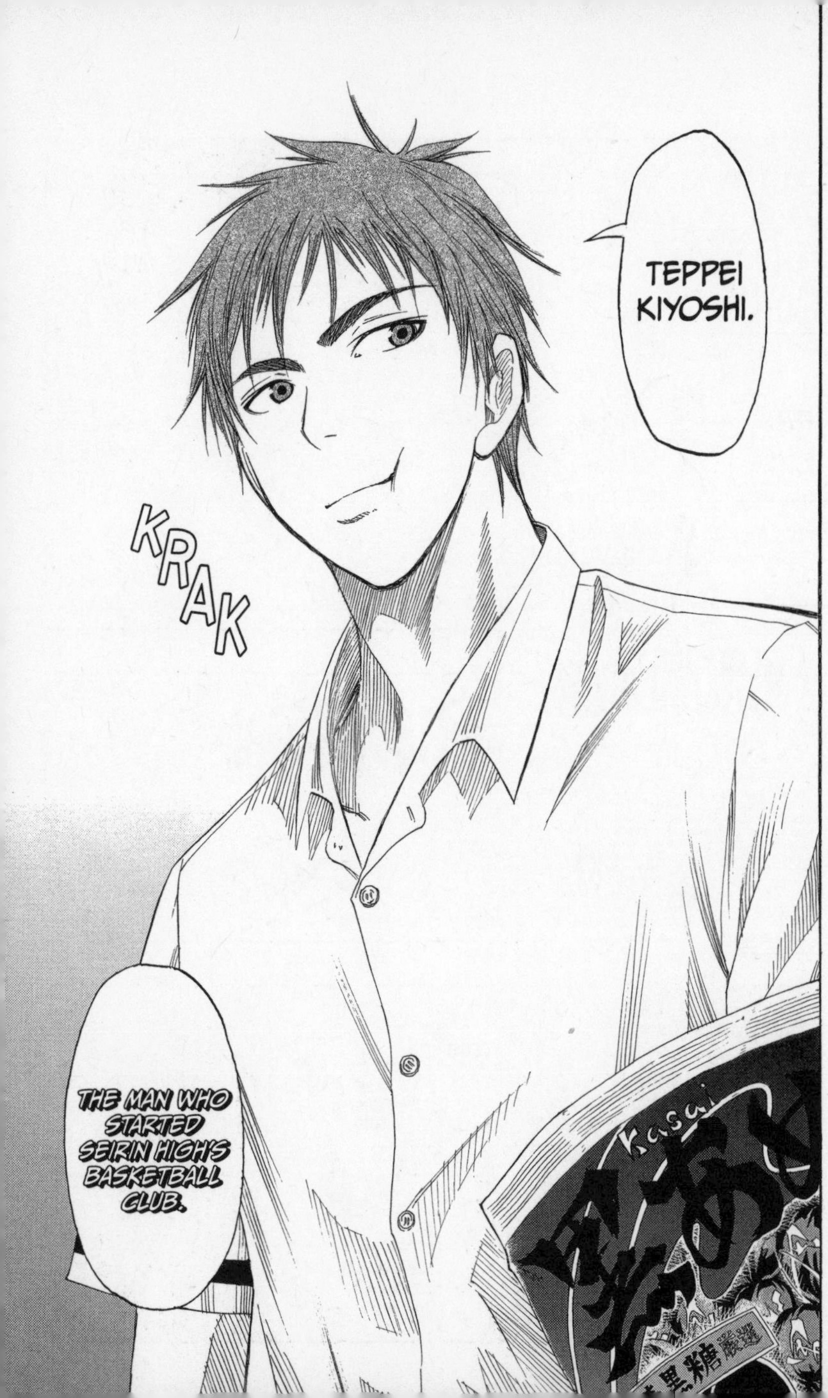
TEPPEI KIYOSHI.
KRAK
THE MAN WHO STARTED SEIRIN HIGH'S BASKETBALL CLUB.

KUROKO'S BASKETBALL BLOOPERS

TAKE 15

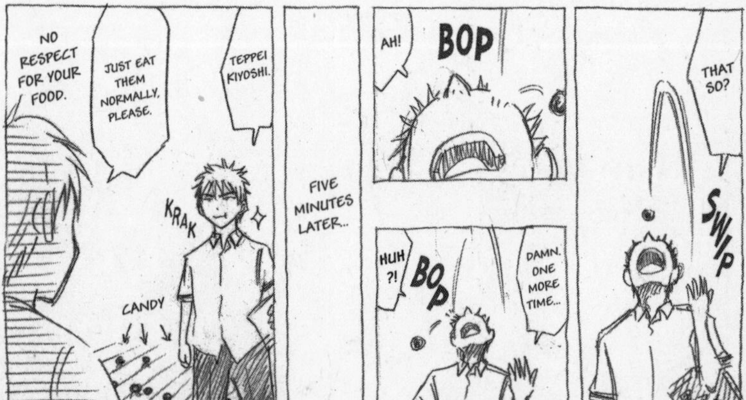

THAT SO?
SWIP
AH!
BOP
DAMN. ONE MORE TIME...
BOP
HUH ?!
FIVE MINUTES LATER...
TEPPEI KIYOSHI.
JUST EAT THEM NORMALLY, PLEASE.
NO RESPECT FOR YOUR FOOD.
KRAK
CANDY

54TH QUARTER: WHY I DON'T LIKE HIM

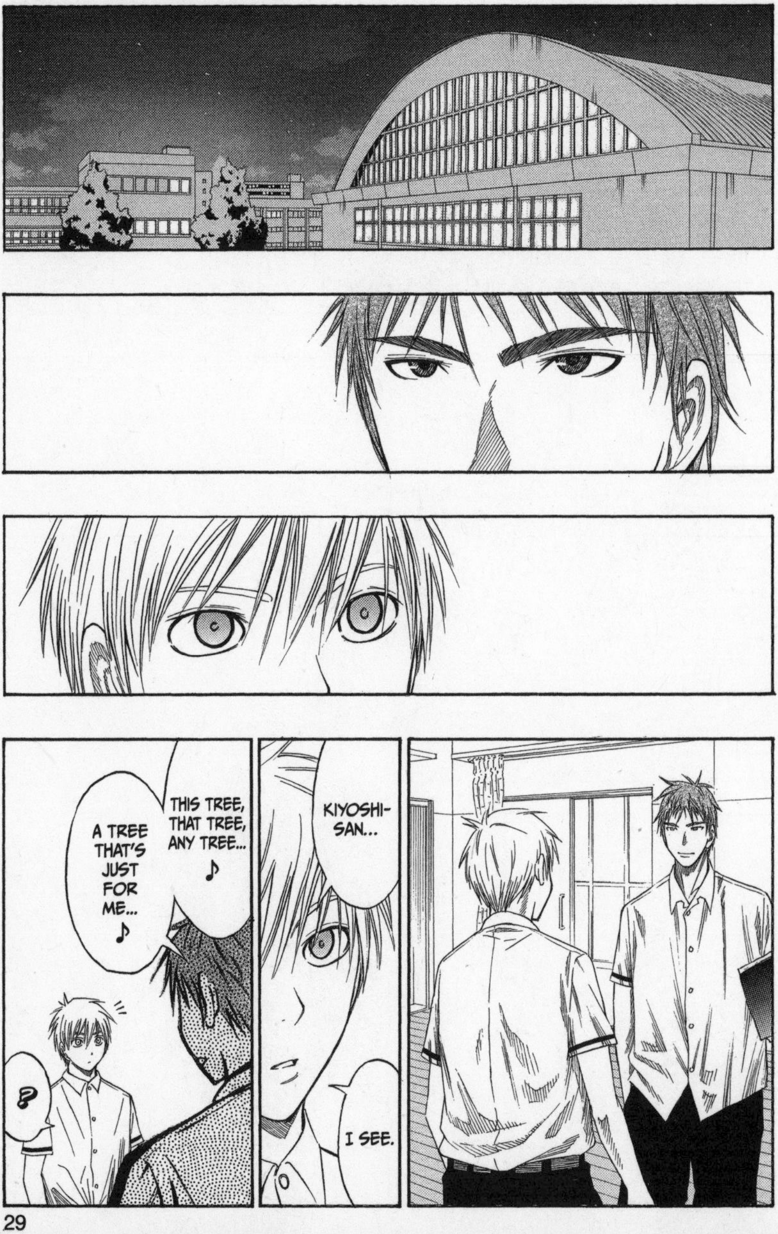
KIYOSHI-SAN...
I SEE.
THIS TREE, THAT TREE, ANY TREE... ♪
A TREE THAT'S JUST FOR ME... ♪
?

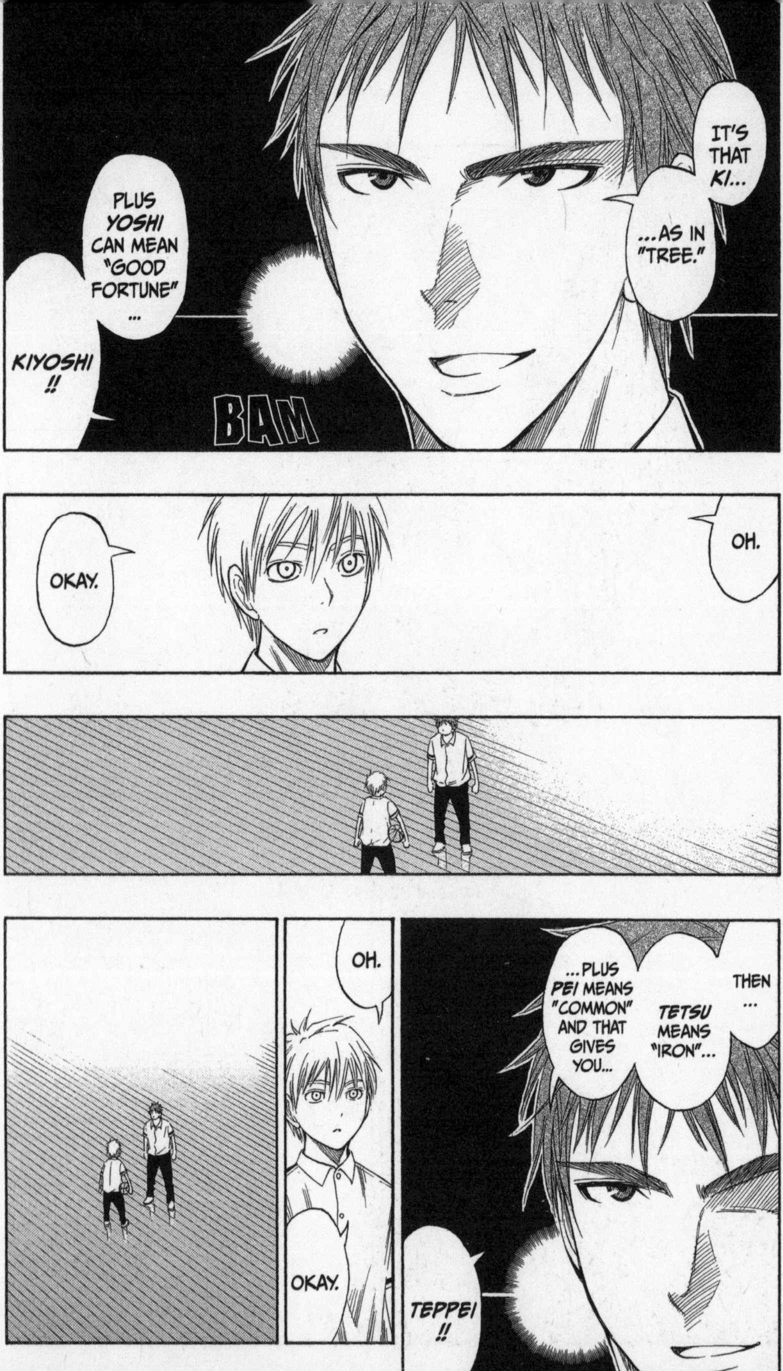
IT'S THAT KI...
...AS IN "TREE."
PLUS YOSHI CAN MEAN "GOOD FORTUNE" ...
KIYOSHI!!
BAM
OH.
OKAY.
THEN...
TETSU MEANS "IRON"...
...PLUS PEI MEANS "COMMON" AND THAT GIVES YOU...
TEPPEI!!
OH.
OKAY.

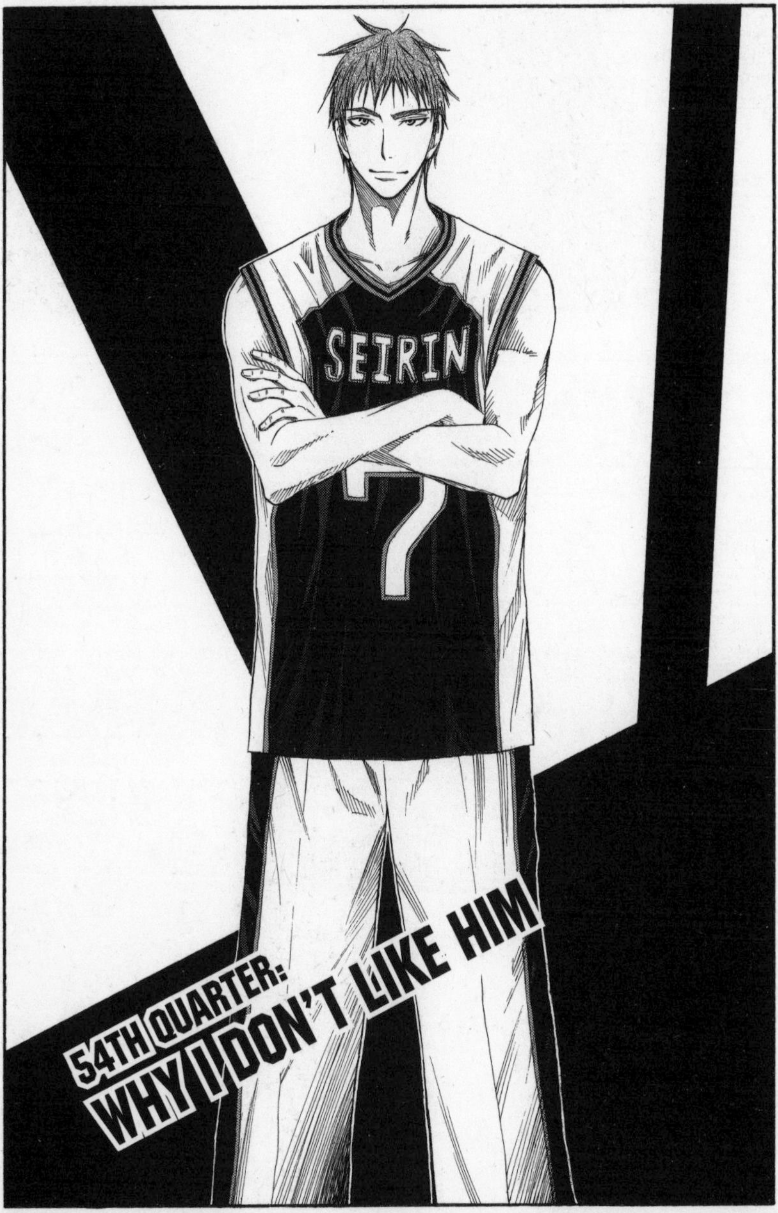
SEIRIN
7
54TH QUARTER:
WHY I DON'T LIKE HIM

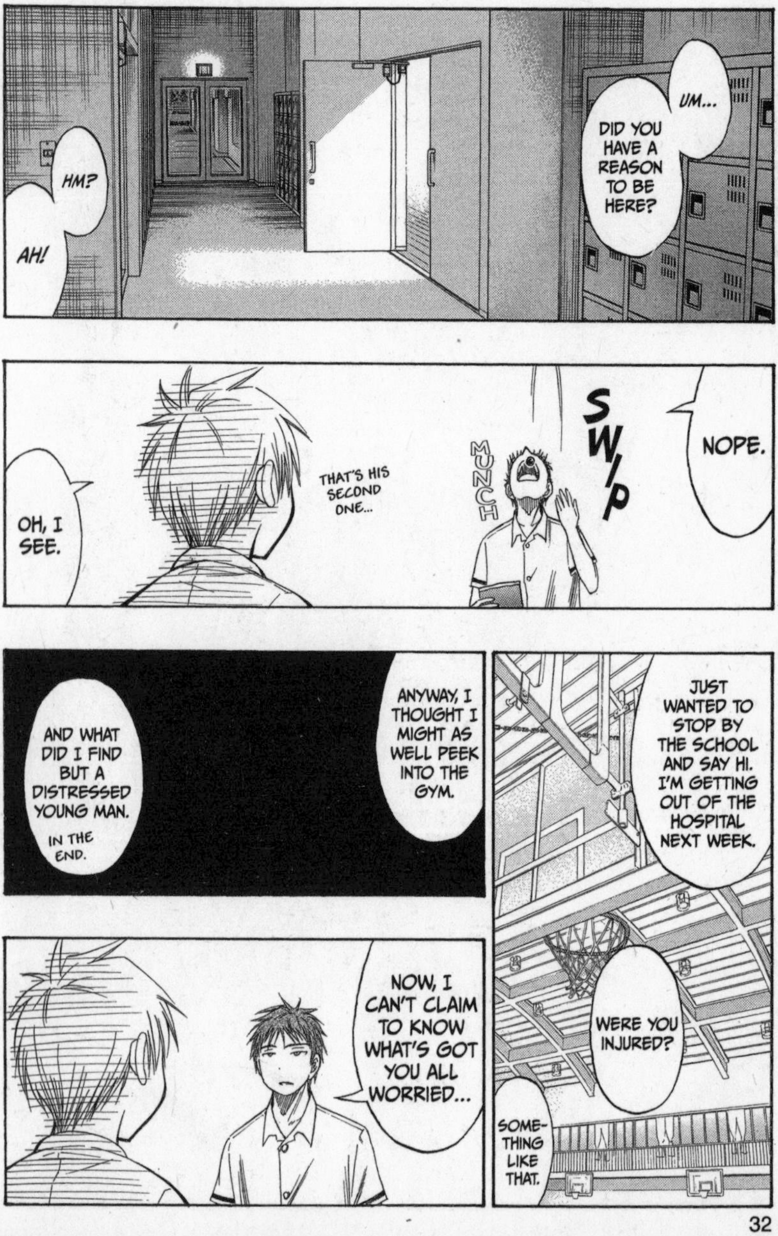
UM...
DID YOU HAVE A REASON TO BE HERE?
HM?
AH!
NOPE.
SWIP
MUNCH
THAT'S HIS SECOND ONE...
OH, I SEE.
JUST WANTED TO STOP BY THE SCHOOL AND SAY HI. I'M GETTING OUT OF THE HOSPITAL NEXT WEEK.
WERE YOU INJURED?
SOME-THING LIKE THAT.
ANYWAY, I THOUGHT I MIGHT AS WELL PEEK INTO THE GYM.
AND WHAT DID I FIND BUT A DISTRESSED YOUNG MAN.
IN THE END.
NOW, I CAN'T CLAIM TO KNOW WHAT'S GOT YOU ALL WORRIED...

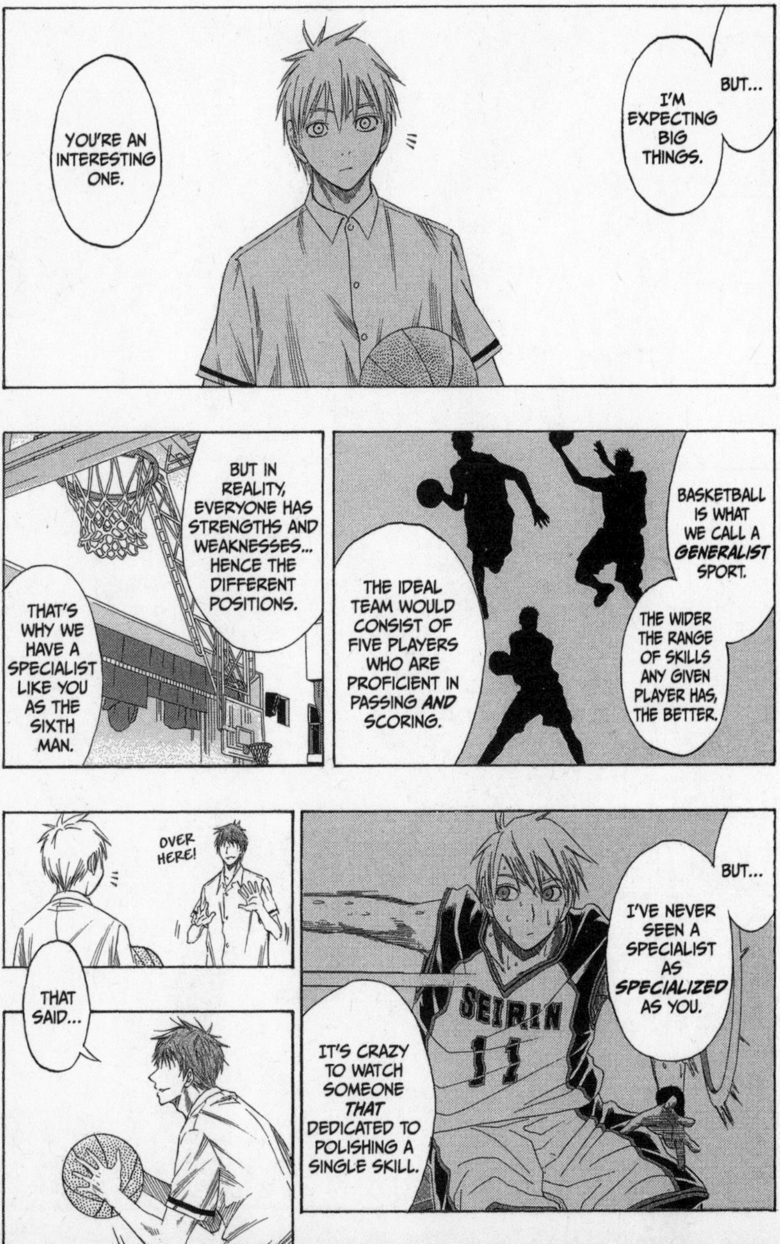
BUT... I'M EXPECTING BIG THINGS.
YOU'RE AN INTERESTING ONE.
BASKETBALL IS WHAT WE CALL A *GENERALIST* SPORT.
THE WIDER THE RANGE OF SKILLS ANY GIVEN PLAYER HAS, THE BETTER.
THE IDEAL TEAM WOULD CONSIST OF FIVE PLAYERS WHO ARE PROFICIENT IN PASSING *AND* SCORING.
BUT IN REALITY, EVERYONE HAS STRENGTHS AND WEAKNESSES... HENCE THE DIFFERENT POSITIONS.
THAT'S WHY WE HAVE A SPECIALIST LIKE YOU AS THE SIXTH MAN.
BUT...
I'VE NEVER SEEN A SPECIALIST AS *SPECIALIZED* AS YOU.
IT'S CRAZY TO WATCH SOMEONE *THAT* DEDICATED TO POLISHING A SINGLE SKILL.
OVER HERE!
THAT SAID...

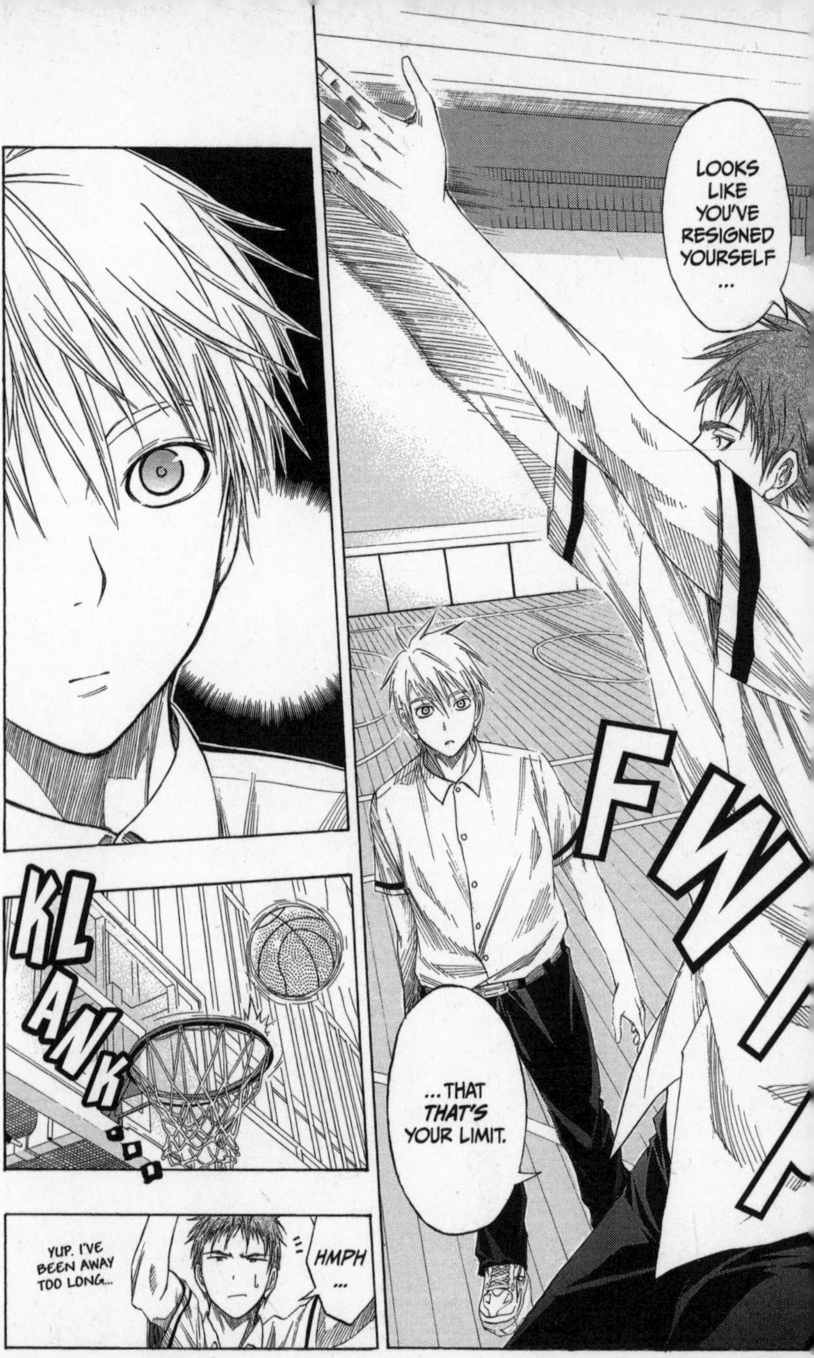
LOOKS LIKE YOU'VE RESIGNED YOURSELF ...
FWI
...THAT THAT'S YOUR LIMIT.
KLANK...
HMPH ...
YUP. I'VE BEEN AWAY TOO LONG...

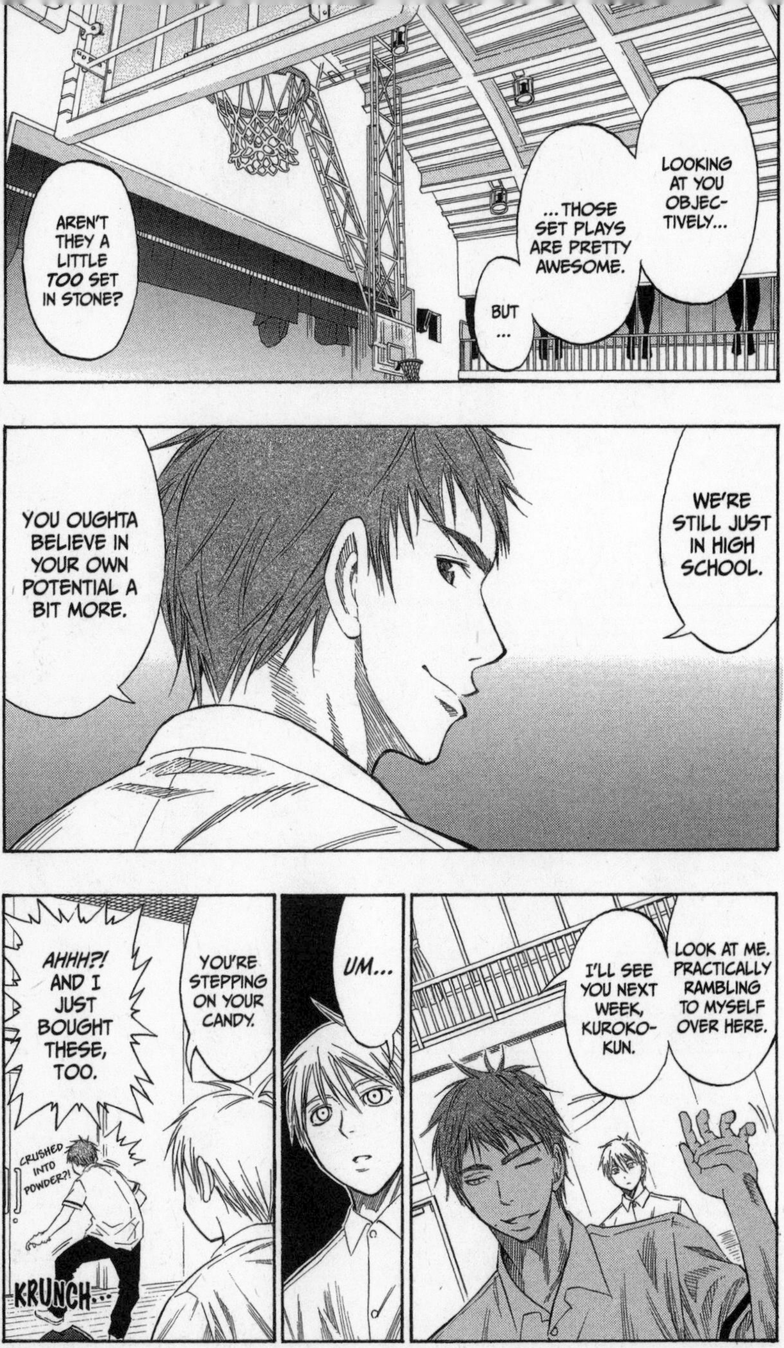
LOOKING AT YOU OBJECTIVELY...
...THOSE SET PLAYS ARE PRETTY AWESOME.
BUT ...
AREN'T THEY A LITTLE *TOO* SET IN STONE?
WE'RE STILL JUST IN HIGH SCHOOL.
YOU OUGHTA BELIEVE IN YOUR OWN POTENTIAL A BIT MORE.
LOOK AT ME. PRACTICALLY RAMBLING TO MYSELF OVER HERE.
I'LL SEE YOU NEXT WEEK, KUROKO-KUN.
UM...
YOU'RE STEPPING ON YOUR CANDY.
AHHH?! AND I JUST BOUGHT THESE, TOO.
CRUSHED INTO POWDER?!
KRUNCH...

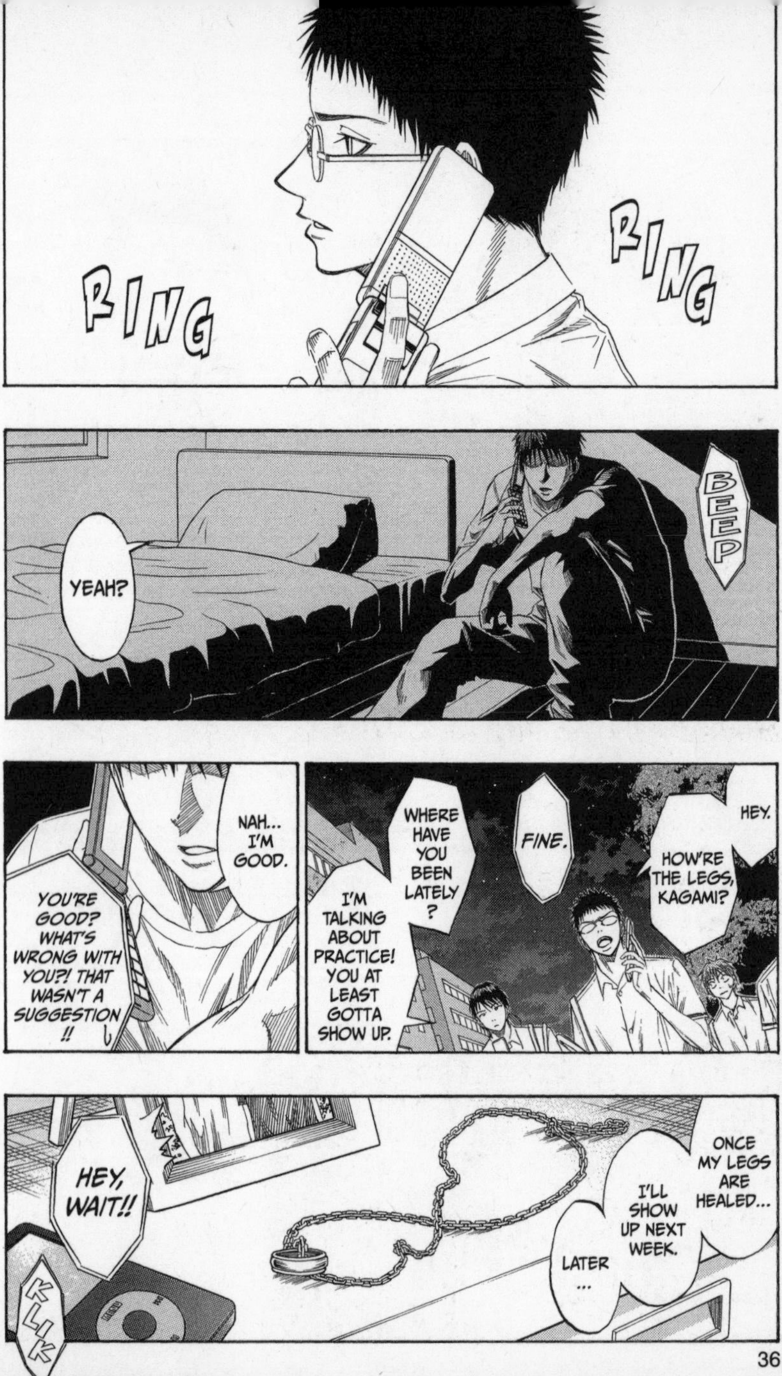
RING
RING
BEEP
YEAH?
HEY.
HOW'RE THE LEGS, KAGAMI?
FINE.
WHERE HAVE YOU BEEN LATELY?
I'M TALKING ABOUT PRACTICE! YOU AT LEAST GOTTA SHOW UP.
NAH... I'M GOOD.
YOU'RE GOOD? WHAT'S WRONG WITH YOU?! THAT WASN'T A SUGGESTION!!
ONCE MY LEGS ARE HEALED...
I'LL SHOW UP NEXT WEEK.
LATER...
HEY, WAIT!!
KLIK

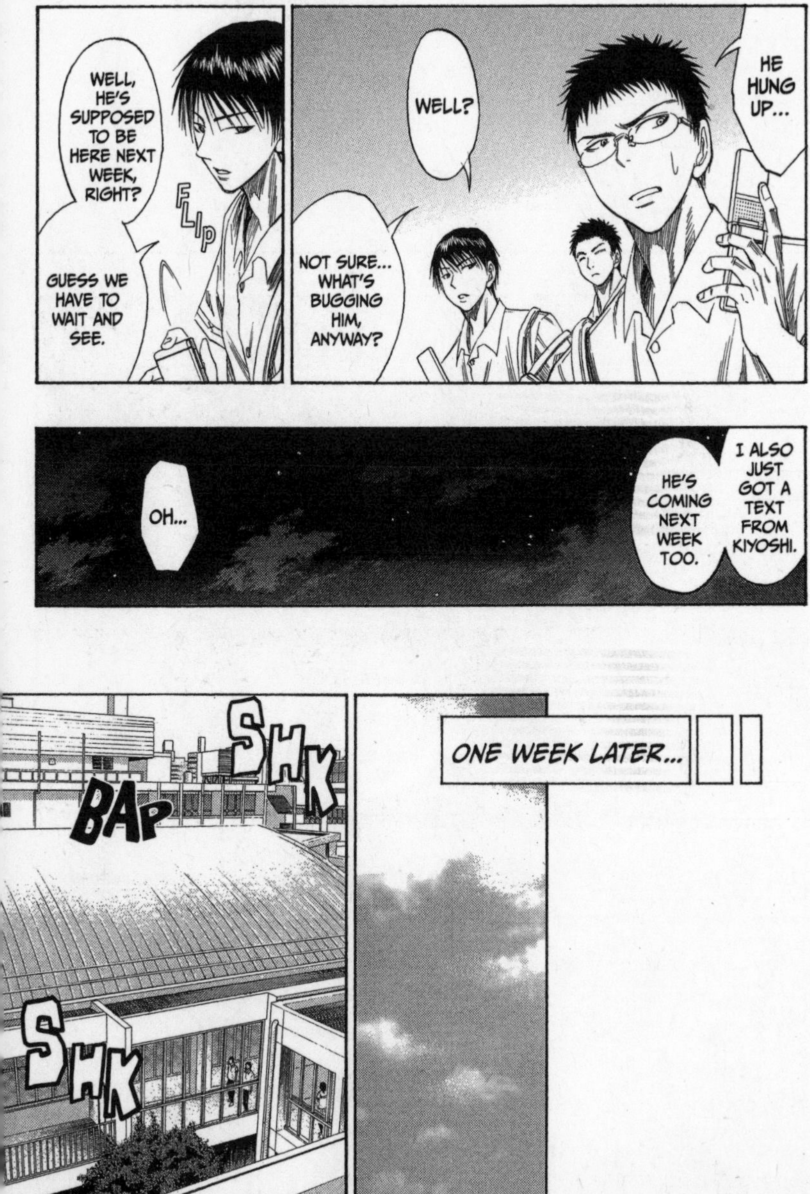
HE HUNG UP...
WELL?
NOT SURE... WHAT'S BUGGING HIM, ANYWAY?
WELL, HE'S SUPPOSED TO BE HERE NEXT WEEK, RIGHT?
FLIP
GUESS WE HAVE TO WAIT AND SEE.
I ALSO JUST GOT A TEXT FROM KIYOSHI.
HE'S COMING NEXT WEEK TOO.
OH...
ONE WEEK LATER...
SHK
BAP
SHK

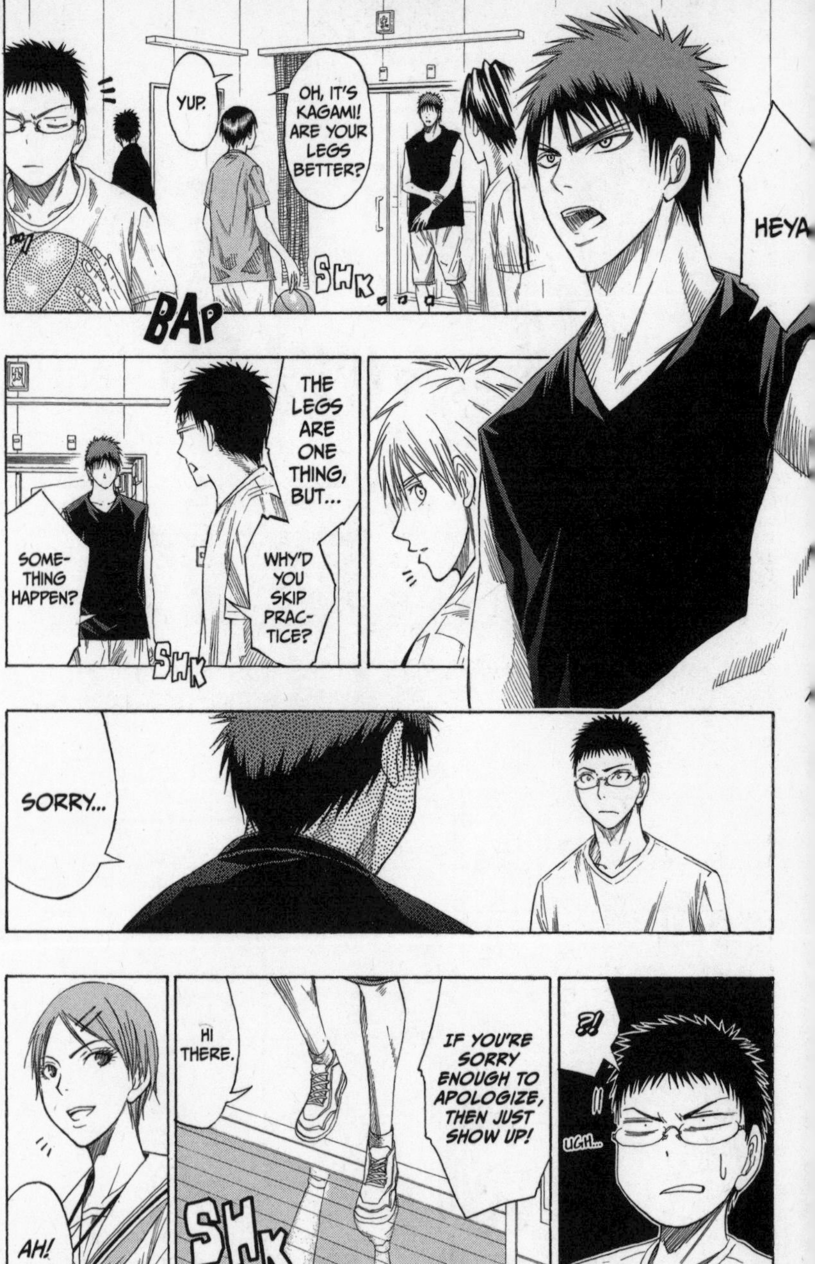
HEYA
OH, IT'S KAGAMI! ARE YOUR LEGS BETTER?
YUP.
SHK
BAP
THE LEGS ARE ONE THING, BUT...
WHY'D YOU SKIP PRACTICE?
SOMETHING HAPPEN?
SHK
SORRY...
?!
UGH...
IF YOU'RE SORRY ENOUGH TO APOLOGIZE, THEN JUST SHOW UP!
HI THERE.
SHK
AH!

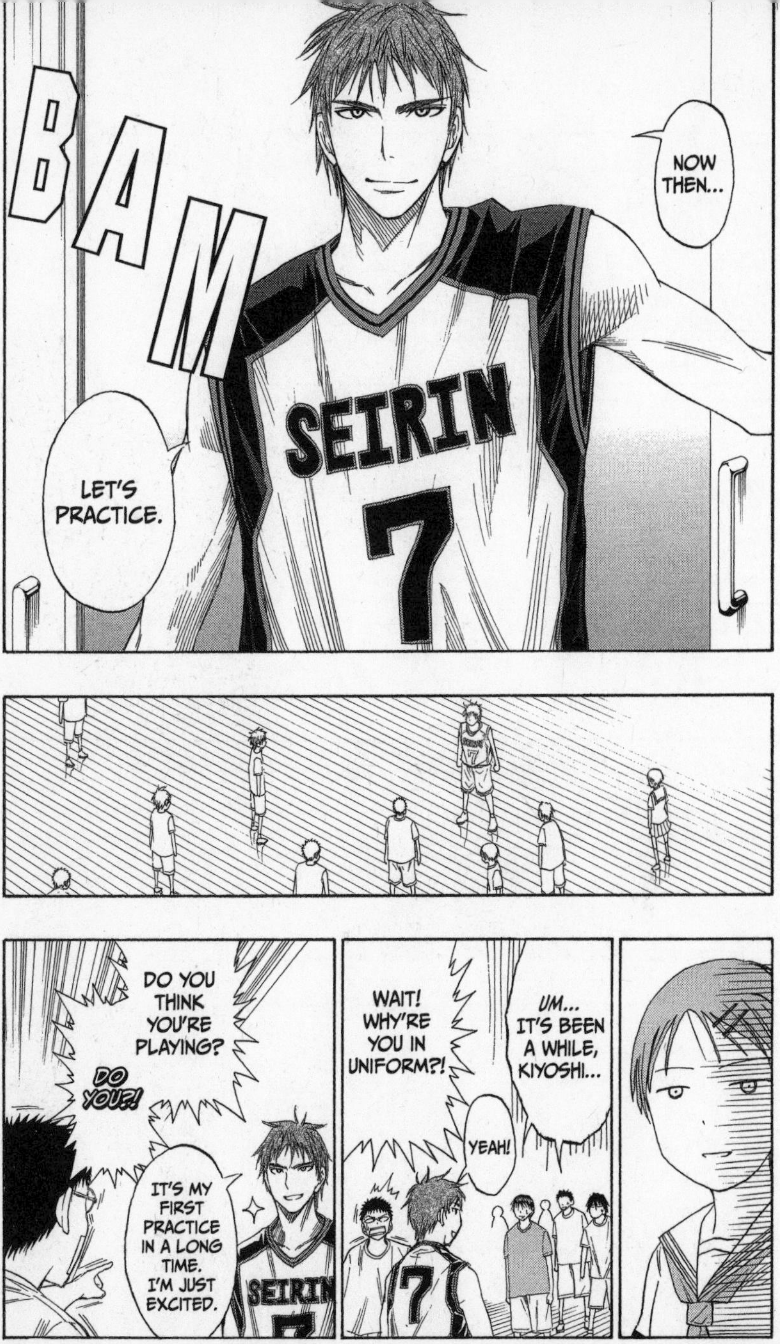
NOW THEN...
BAM
LET'S PRACTICE.
UM... IT'S BEEN A WHILE, KIYOSHI...
YEAH!
WAIT! WHY'RE YOU IN UNIFORM?!
DO YOU THINK YOU'RE PLAYING?
DO YOU?!
IT'S MY FIRST PRACTICE IN A LONG TIME. I'M JUST EXCITED.

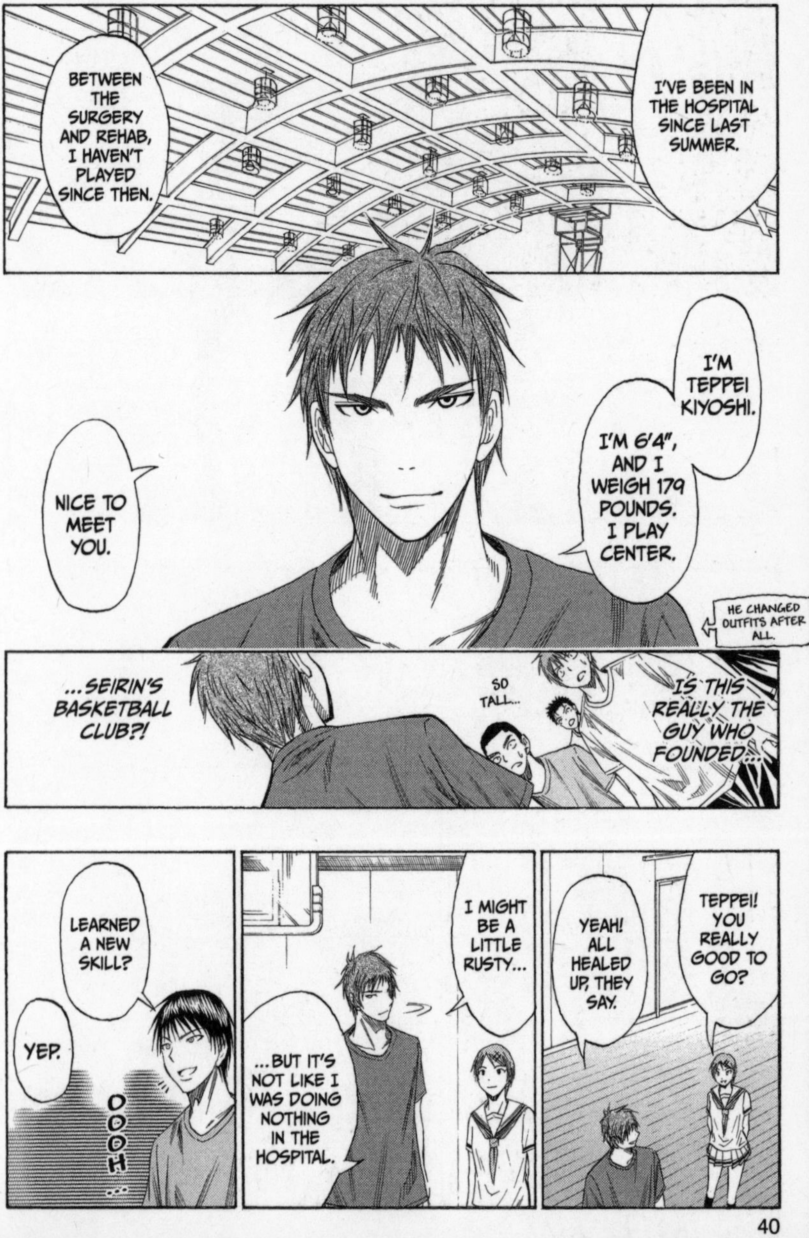
I'VE BEEN IN THE HOSPITAL SINCE LAST SUMMER.
BETWEEN THE SURGERY AND REHAB, I HAVEN'T PLAYED SINCE THEN.
I'M TEPPEI KIYOSHI.
I'M 6'4", AND I WEIGH 179 POUNDS. I PLAY CENTER.
NICE TO MEET YOU.
HE CHANGED OUTFITS AFTER ALL.
IS THIS REALLY THE GUY WHO FOUNDED...
SO TALL...
...SEIRIN'S BASKETBALL CLUB?!
TEPPEI! YOU REALLY GOOD TO GO?
YEAH! ALL HEALED UP, THEY SAY.
I MIGHT BE A LITTLE RUSTY...
...BUT IT'S NOT LIKE I WAS DOING NOTHING IN THE HOSPITAL.
LEARNED A NEW SKILL?
YEP.
OOOH...

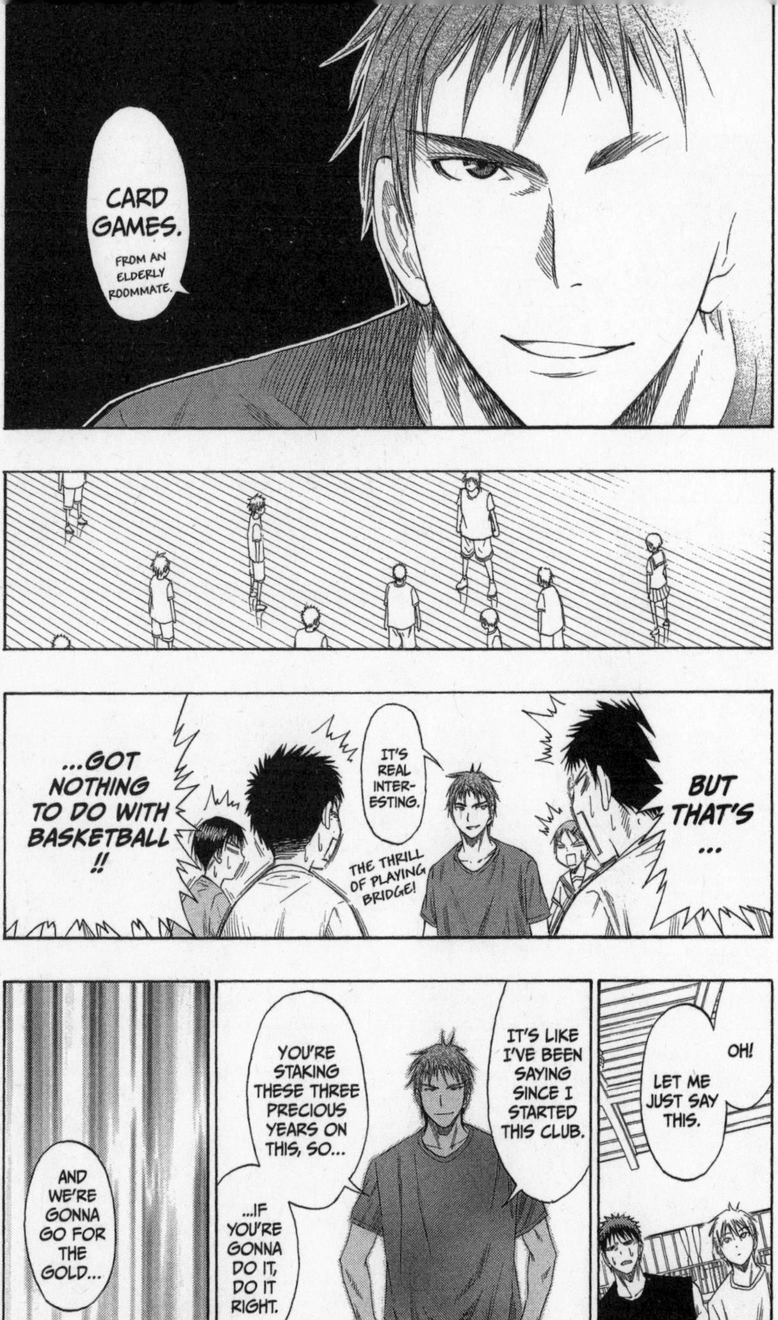
CARD GAMES.
FROM AN ELDERLY ROOMMATE.
BUT THAT'S ...
IT'S REAL INTERESTING.
THE THRILL OF PLAYING BRIDGE!
...GOT NOTHING TO DO WITH BASKETBALL !!
OH!
LET ME JUST SAY THIS.
IT'S LIKE I'VE BEEN SAYING SINCE I STARTED THIS CLUB.
YOU'RE STAKING THESE THREE PRECIOUS YEARS ON THIS, SO...
...IF YOU'RE GONNA DO IT, DO IT RIGHT.
AND WE'RE GONNA GO FOR THE GOLD...

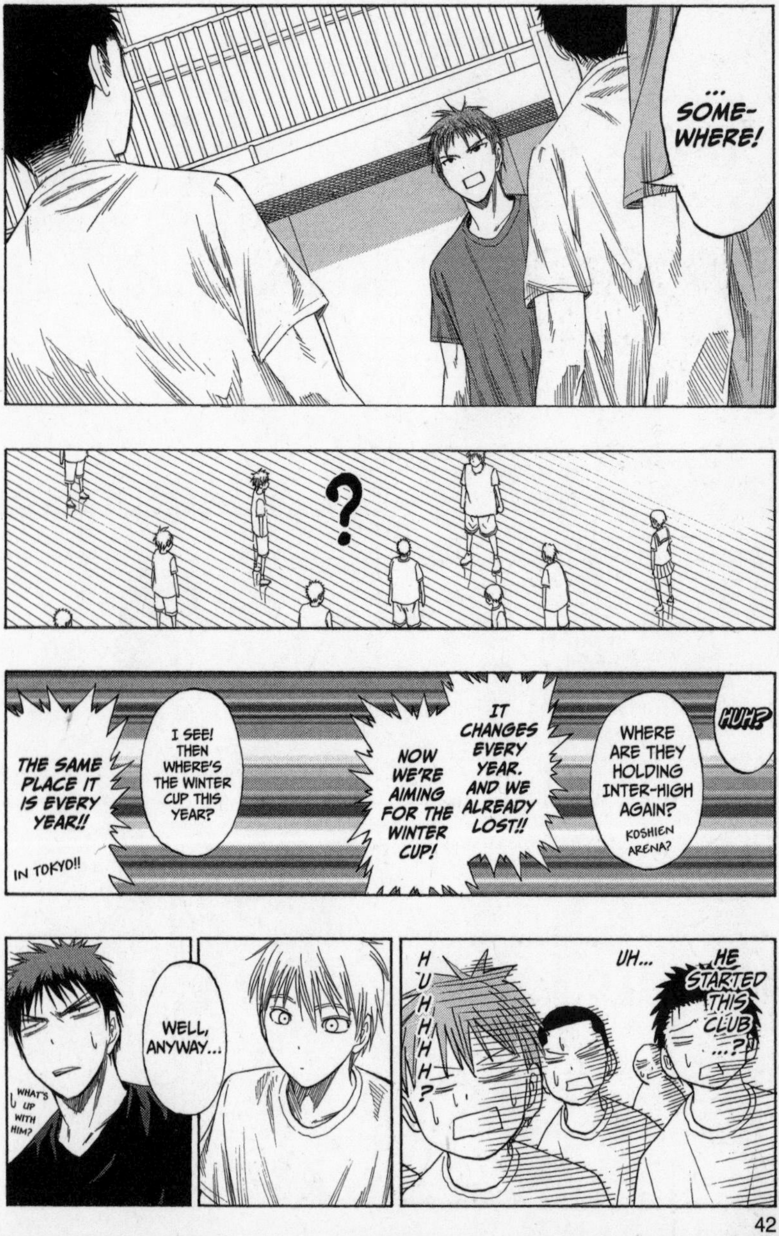
...SOME-WHERE!
?
HUH?
WHERE ARE THEY HOLDING INTER-HIGH AGAIN?
KOSHIEN ARENA?
IT CHANGES EVERY YEAR. AND WE ALREADY LOST!!
NOW WE'RE AIMING FOR THE WINTER CUP!
I SEE! THEN WHERE'S THE WINTER CUP THIS YEAR?
THE SAME PLACE IT IS EVERY YEAR!!
IN TOKYO!!
HE STARTED THIS CLUB ...?
UH...
HUHHHHH?
WELL, ANYWAY...
WHAT'S UP WITH HIM?

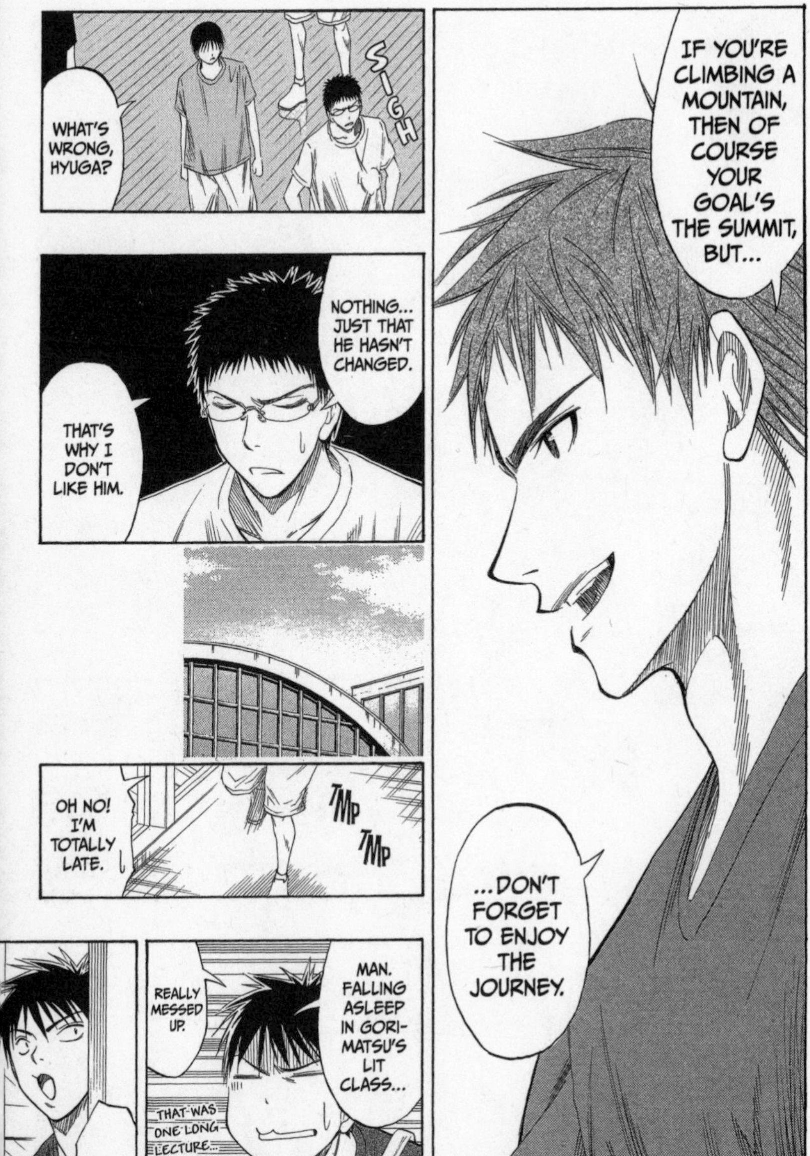
IF YOU'RE CLIMBING A MOUNTAIN, THEN OF COURSE YOUR GOAL'S THE SUMMIT, BUT...
...DON'T FORGET TO ENJOY THE JOURNEY.
SIGH
WHAT'S WRONG, HYUGA?
NOTHING... JUST THAT HE HASN'T CHANGED.
THAT'S WHY I DON'T LIKE HIM.
TMP TMP
OH NO! I'M TOTALLY LATE.
MAN. FALLING ASLEEP IN GORI-MATSU'S LIT CLASS...
REALLY MESSED UP.
THAT WAS ONE LONG LECTURE...
YO!

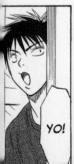

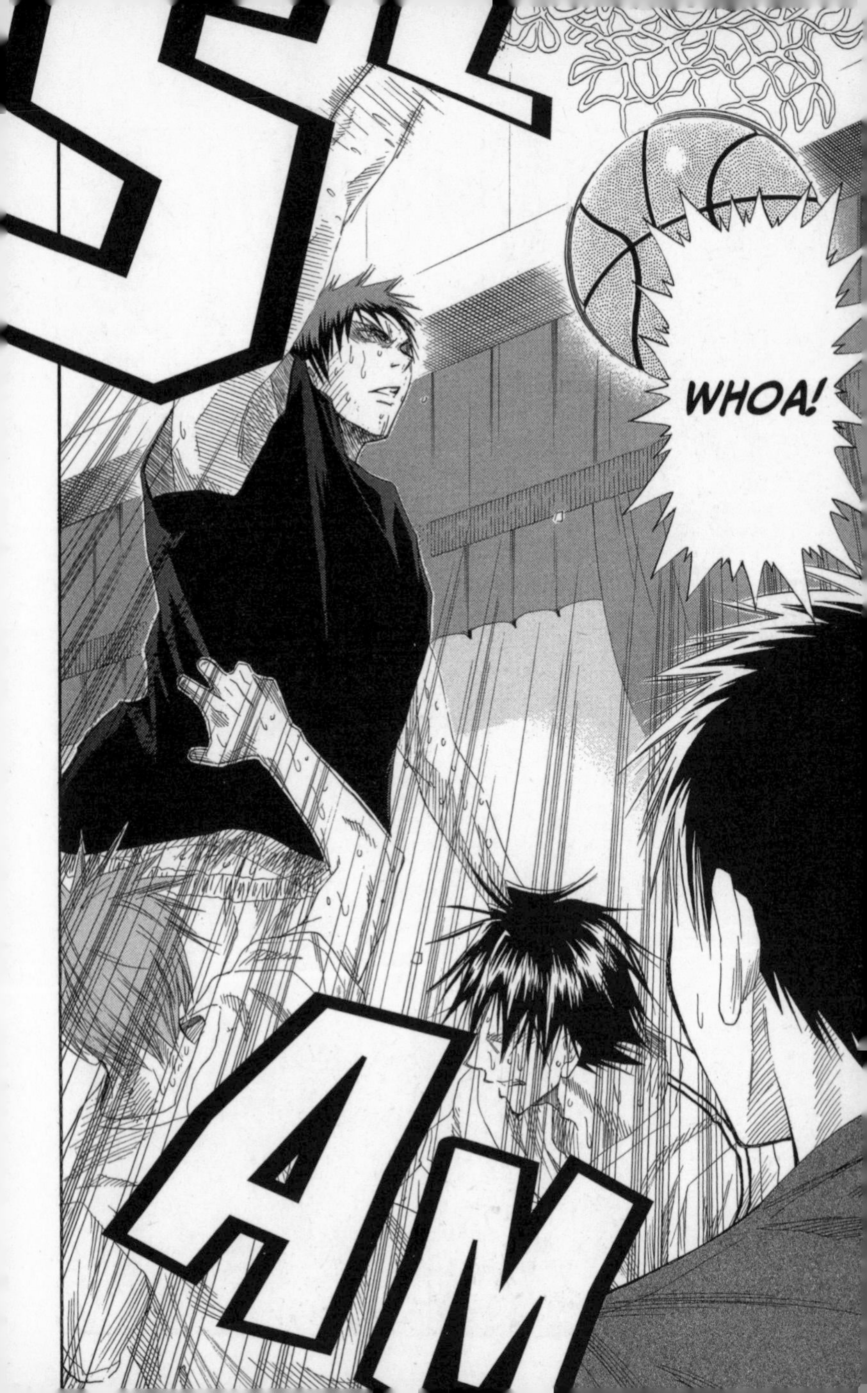
WHOA!
SL
AM

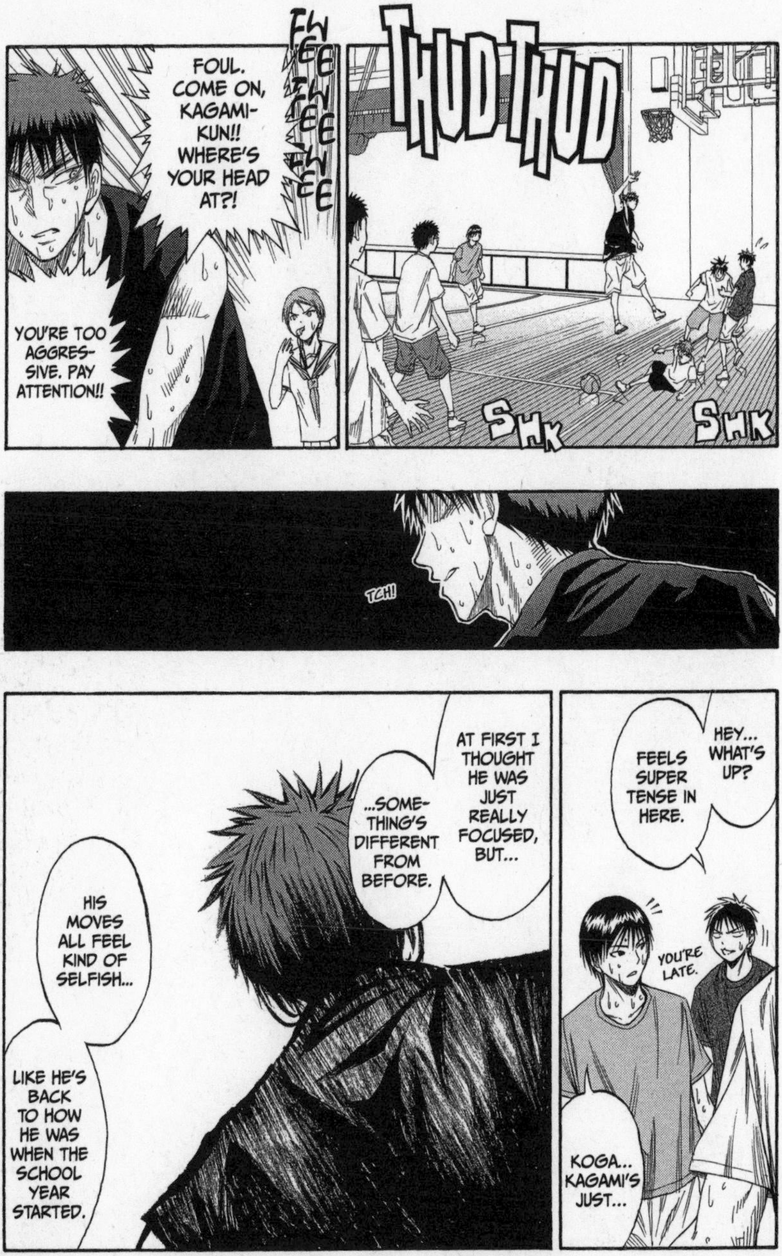

THUD THUD
SHK
SHK
FWEE FWEE FWEE
FOUL. COME ON, KAGAMI-KUN!! WHERE'S YOUR HEAD AT?!
YOU'RE TOO AGGRESSIVE. PAY ATTENTION!!
TCH!
HEY... WHAT'S UP?
FEELS SUPER TENSE IN HERE.
YOU'RE LATE.
KOGA... KAGAMI'S JUST...
AT FIRST I THOUGHT HE WAS JUST REALLY FOCUSED, BUT...
...SOMETHING'S DIFFERENT FROM BEFORE.
HIS MOVES ALL FEEL KIND OF SELFISH...
LIKE HE'S BACK TO HOW HE WAS WHEN THE SCHOOL YEAR STARTED.

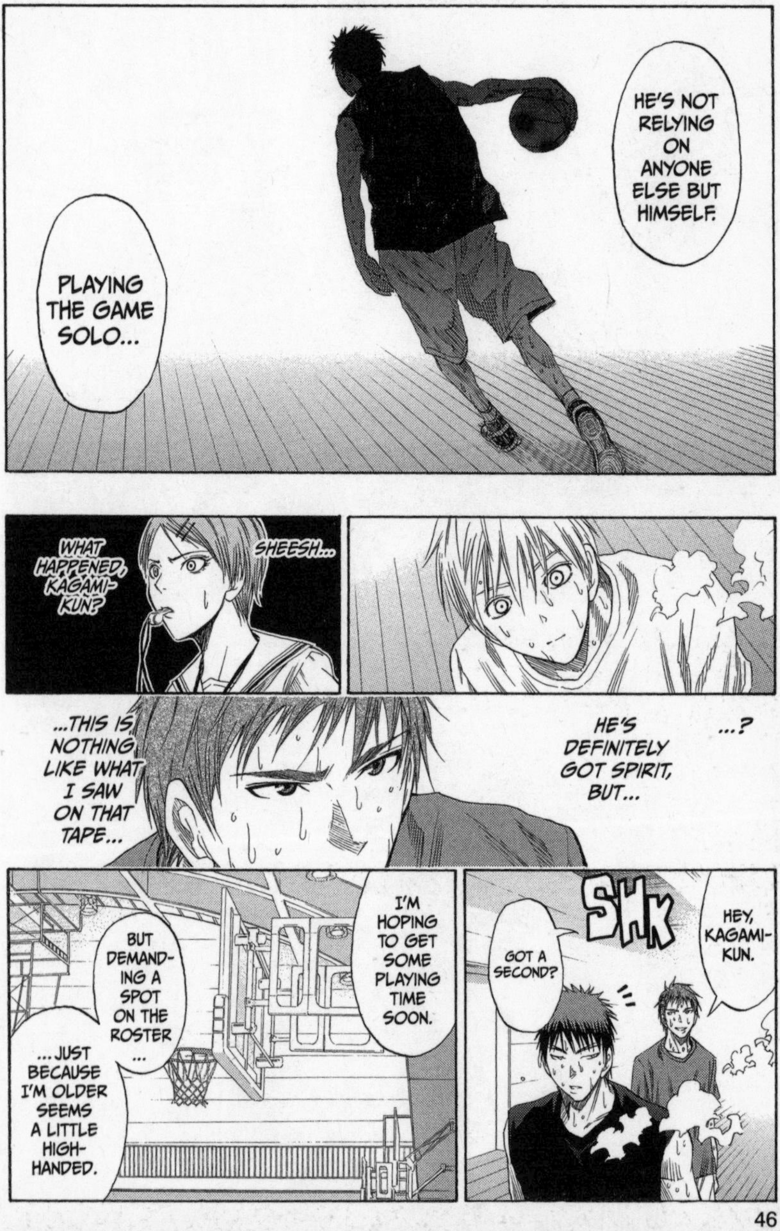
HE'S NOT RELYING ON ANYONE ELSE BUT HIMSELF.
PLAYING THE GAME SOLO...
SHEESH...
WHAT HAPPENED, KAGAMI-KUN?
...?
HE'S DEFINITELY GOT SPIRIT, BUT...
...THIS IS NOTHING LIKE WHAT I SAW ON THAT TAPE...
HEY, KAGAMI-KUN.
SHK
GOT A SECOND?
I'M HOPING TO GET SOME PLAYING TIME SOON.
BUT DEMANDING A SPOT ON THE ROSTER ...
... JUST BECAUSE I'M OLDER SEEMS A LITTLE HIGH-HANDED.

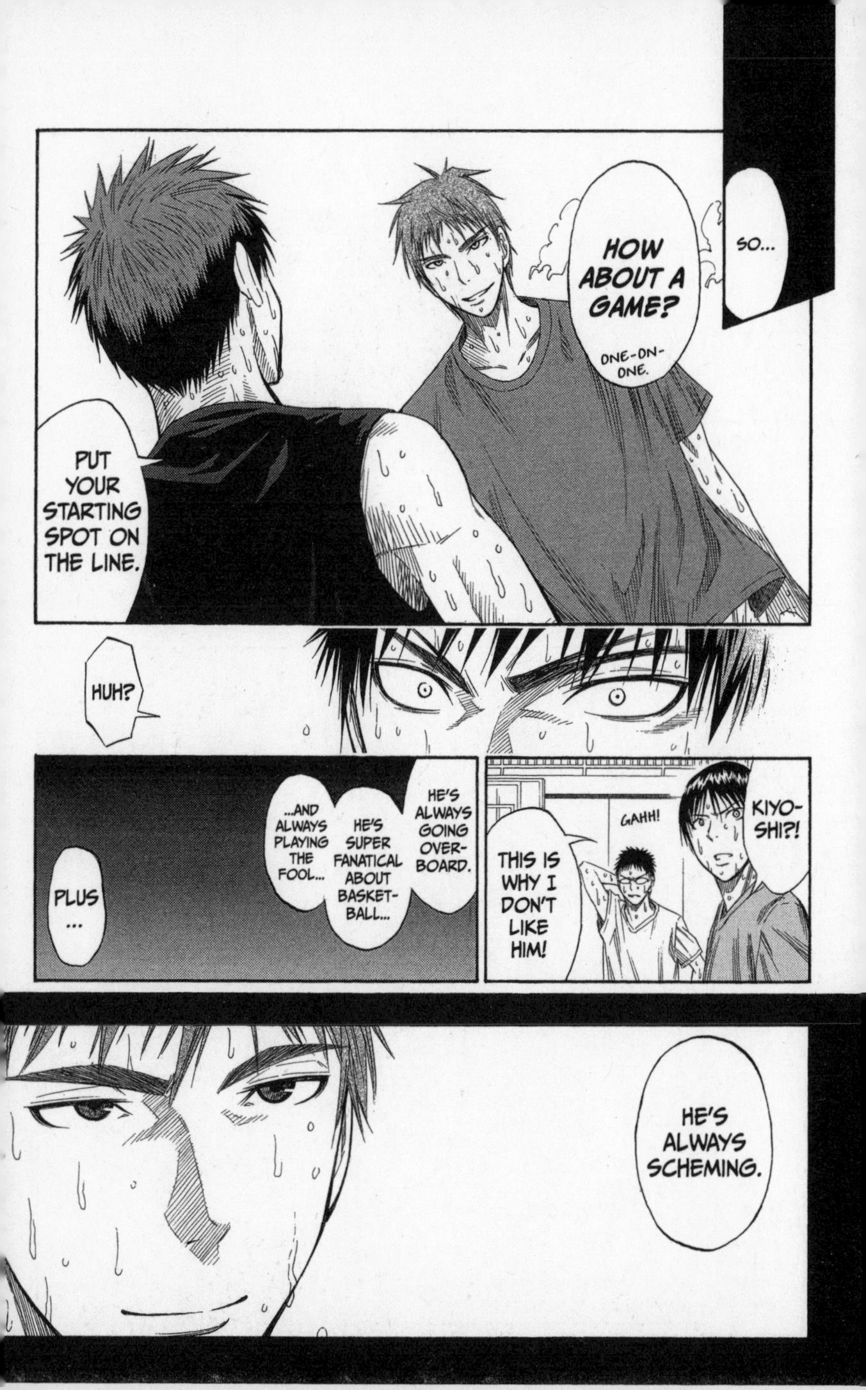
SO...
HOW ABOUT A GAME?
ONE-ON-ONE.
PUT YOUR STARTING SPOT ON THE LINE.
HUH?
KIYO-SHI?!
GAHH!
THIS IS WHY I DON'T LIKE HIM!
HE'S ALWAYS GOING OVER-BOARD.
HE'S SUPER FANATICAL ABOUT BASKET-BALL...
...AND ALWAYS PLAYING THE FOOL...
PLUS...
HE'S ALWAYS SCHEMING.

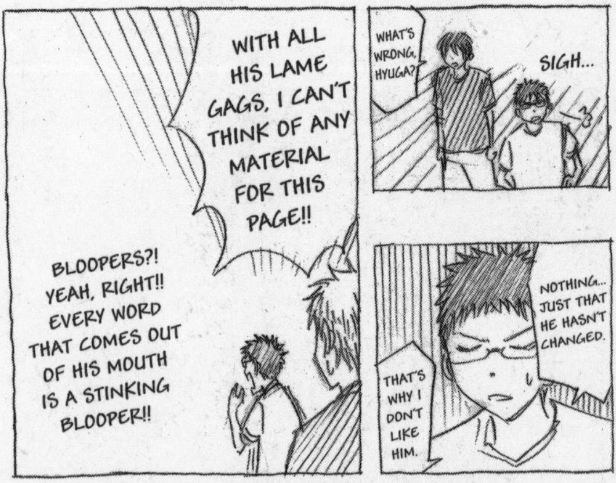
WHAT'S WRONG, HYUGA?
SIGH...
NOTHING... JUST THAT HE HASN'T CHANGED.
THAT'S WHY I DON'T LIKE HIM.
WITH ALL HIS LAME GAGS, I CAN'T THINK OF ANY MATERIAL FOR THIS PAGE!!
BLOOPERS?! YEAH, RIGHT!! EVERY WORD THAT COMES OUT OF HIS MOUTH IS A STINKING BLOOPER!!

55TH QUARTER: MY TRUE STRENGTH

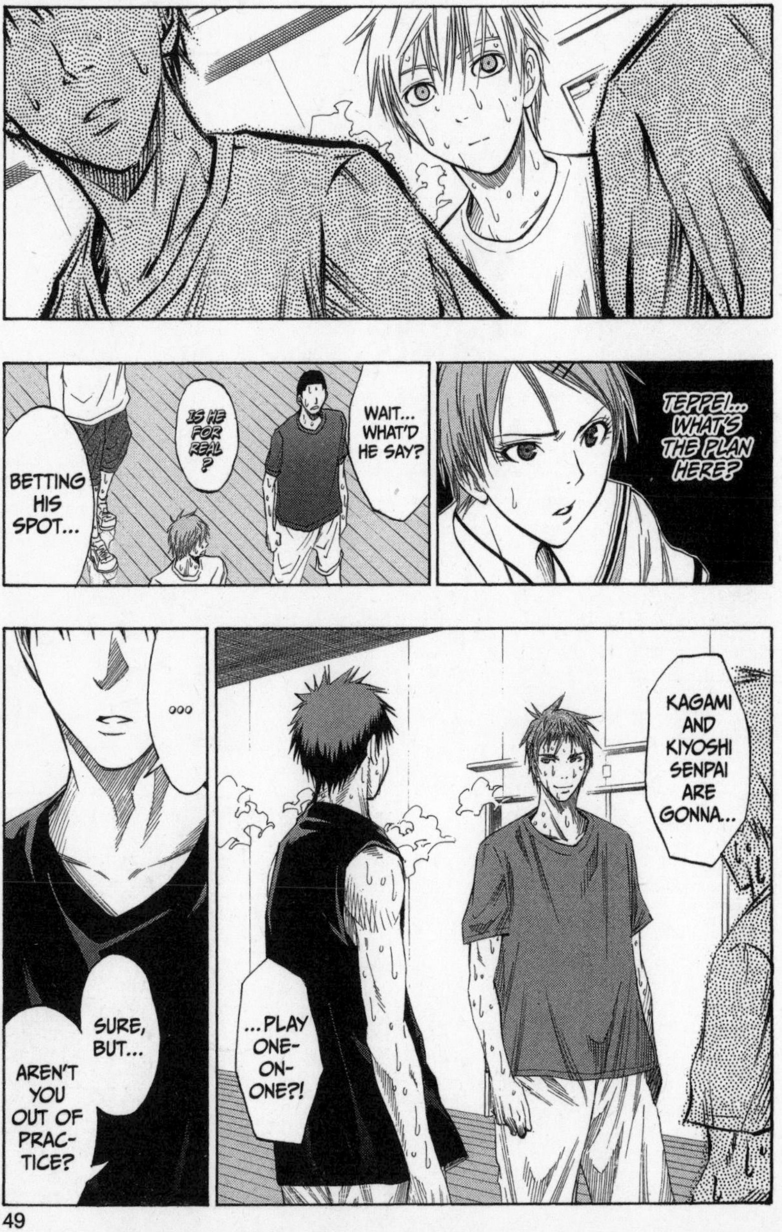
TEPPEI... WHAT'S THE PLAN HERE?
WAIT... WHAT'D HE SAY?
IS HE FOR REAL?
BETTING HIS SPOT...
KAGAMI AND KIYOSHI SENPAI ARE GONNA...
...PLAY ONE-ON-ONE?!
...
SURE, BUT...
AREN'T YOU OUT OF PRAC-TICE?

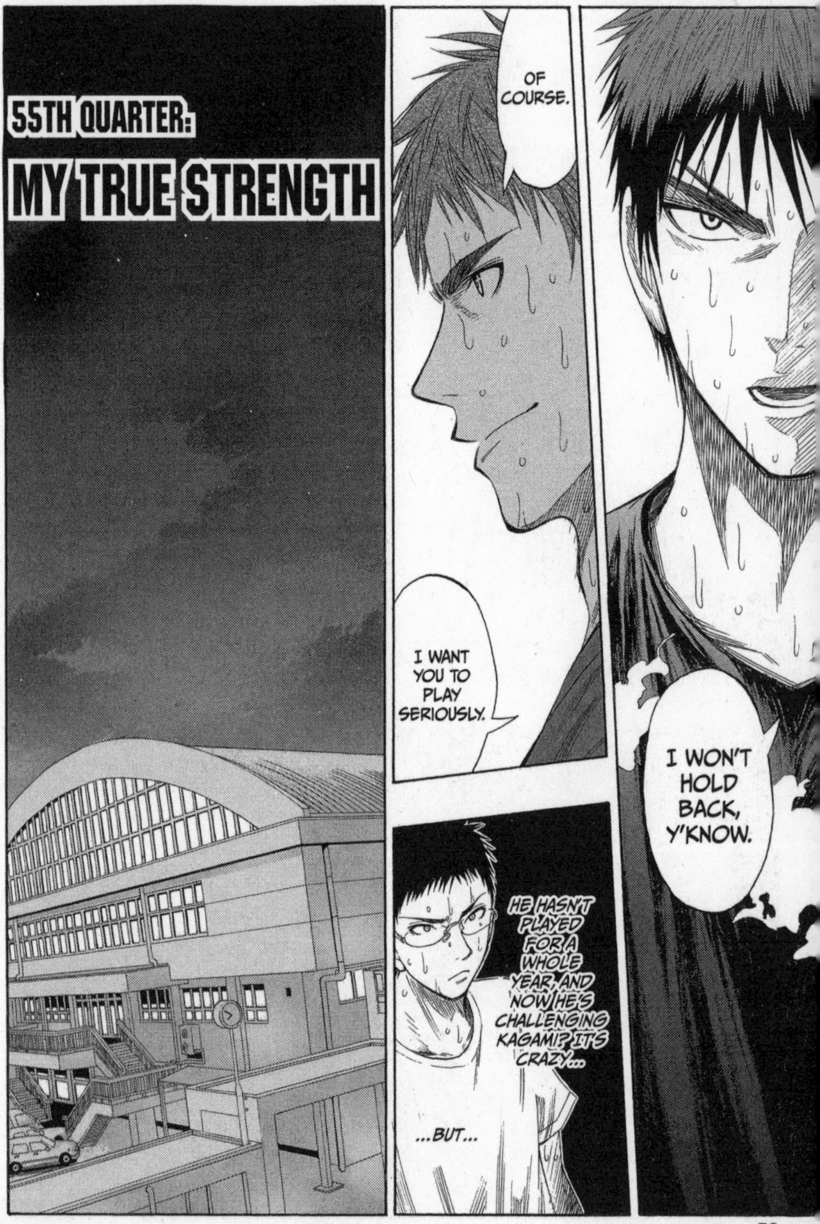
I WON'T HOLD BACK, Y'KNOW.
OF COURSE.
I WANT YOU TO PLAY SERIOUSLY.
HE HASN'T PLAYED FOR A WHOLE YEAR, AND NOW HE'S CHALLENGING KAGAMI? IT'S CRAZY...
...BUT...
55TH QUARTER:
MY TRUE STRENGTH

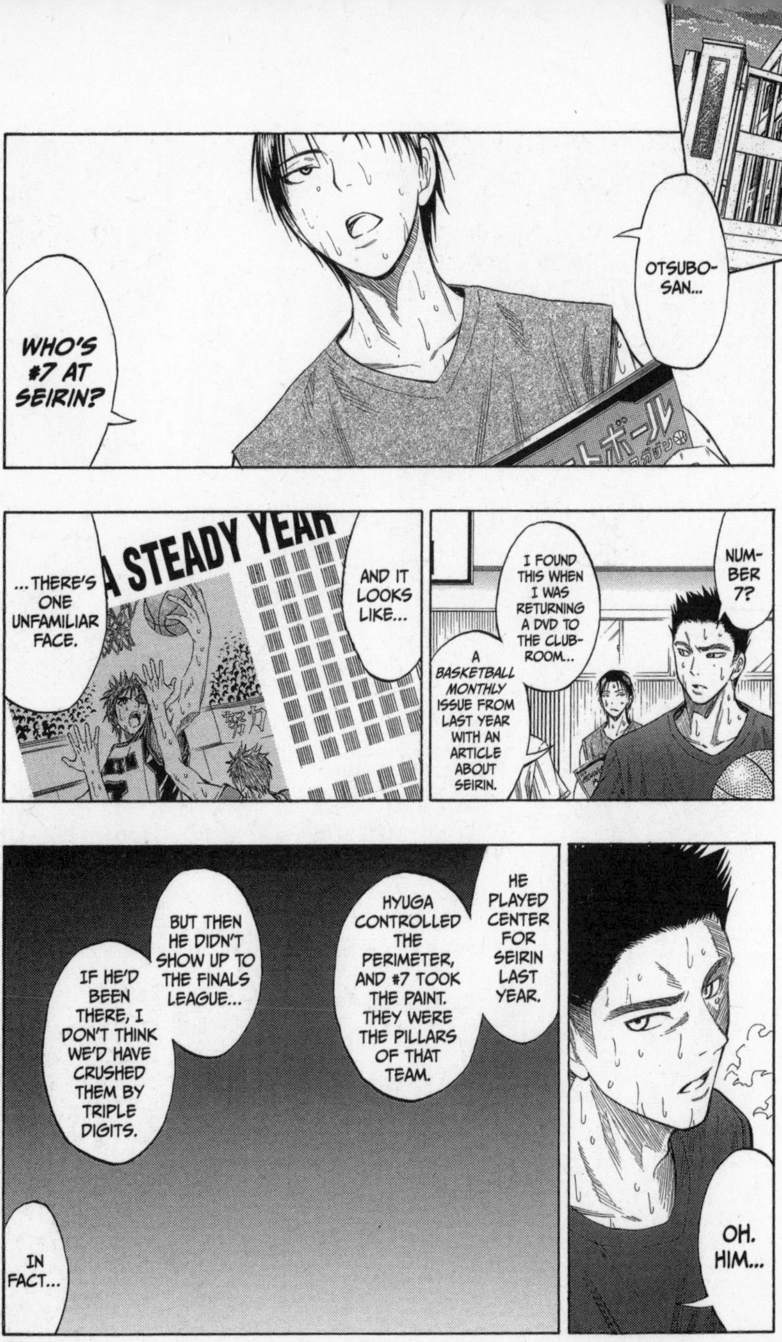

OTSUBO-SAN...
WHO'S #7 AT SEIRIN?
NUMBER 7?
I FOUND THIS WHEN I WAS RETURNING A DVD TO THE CLUBROOM...
A *BASKETBALL MONTHLY* ISSUE FROM LAST YEAR WITH AN ARTICLE ABOUT SEIRIN.
AND IT LOOKS LIKE...
A STEADY YEAR
...THERE'S ONE UNFAMILIAR FACE.
OH. HIM...
HE PLAYED CENTER FOR SEIRIN LAST YEAR.
HYUGA CONTROLLED THE PERIMETER, AND #7 TOOK THE PAINT. THEY WERE THE PILLARS OF THAT TEAM.
BUT THEN HE DIDN'T SHOW UP TO THE FINALS LEAGUE...
IF HE'D BEEN THERE, I DON'T THINK WE'D HAVE CRUSHED THEM BY TRIPLE DIGITS.
IN FACT...

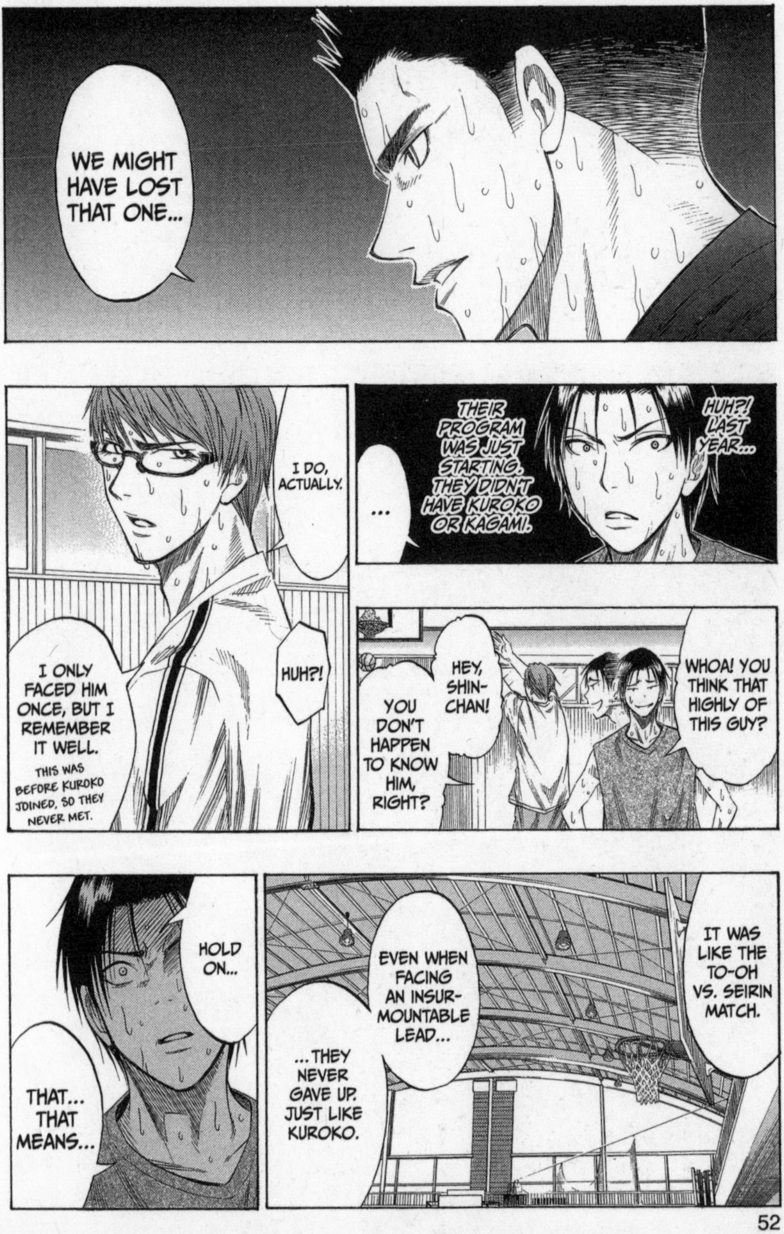
WE MIGHT HAVE LOST THAT ONE...
HUH?! LAST YEAR...
THEIR PROGRAM WAS JUST STARTING. THEY DIDN'T HAVE KUROKO OR KAGAMI.
...
WHOA! YOU THINK THAT HIGHLY OF THIS GUY?
HEY, SHIN-CHAN!
YOU DON'T HAPPEN TO KNOW HIM, RIGHT?
I DO, ACTUALLY.
HUH?!
I ONLY FACED HIM ONCE, BUT I REMEMBER IT WELL.
THIS WAS BEFORE KUROKO JOINED, SO THEY NEVER MET.
IT WAS LIKE THE TO-OH VS. SEIRIN MATCH.
EVEN WHEN FACING AN INSUR-MOUNTABLE LEAD...
...THEY NEVER GAVE UP. JUST LIKE KUROKO.
HOLD ON...
THAT... THAT MEANS...

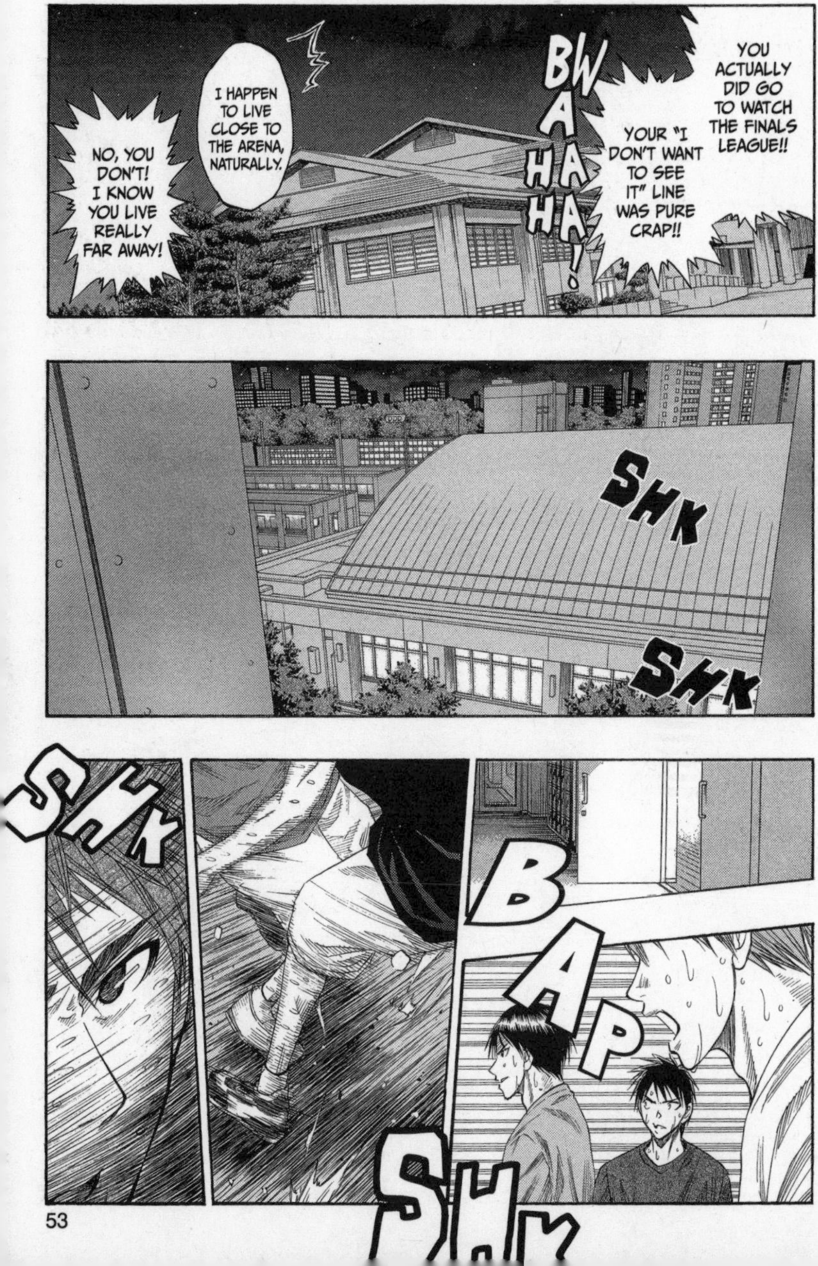
YOU ACTUALLY DID GO TO WATCH THE FINALS LEAGUE!!
YOUR "I DON'T WANT TO SEE IT" LINE WAS PURE CRAP!!
BWAHAHAHA!
I HAPPEN TO LIVE CLOSE TO THE ARENA, NATURALLY.
NO, YOU DON'T! I KNOW YOU LIVE REALLY FAR AWAY!
SHK
SHK
BAP
SHK
SHK

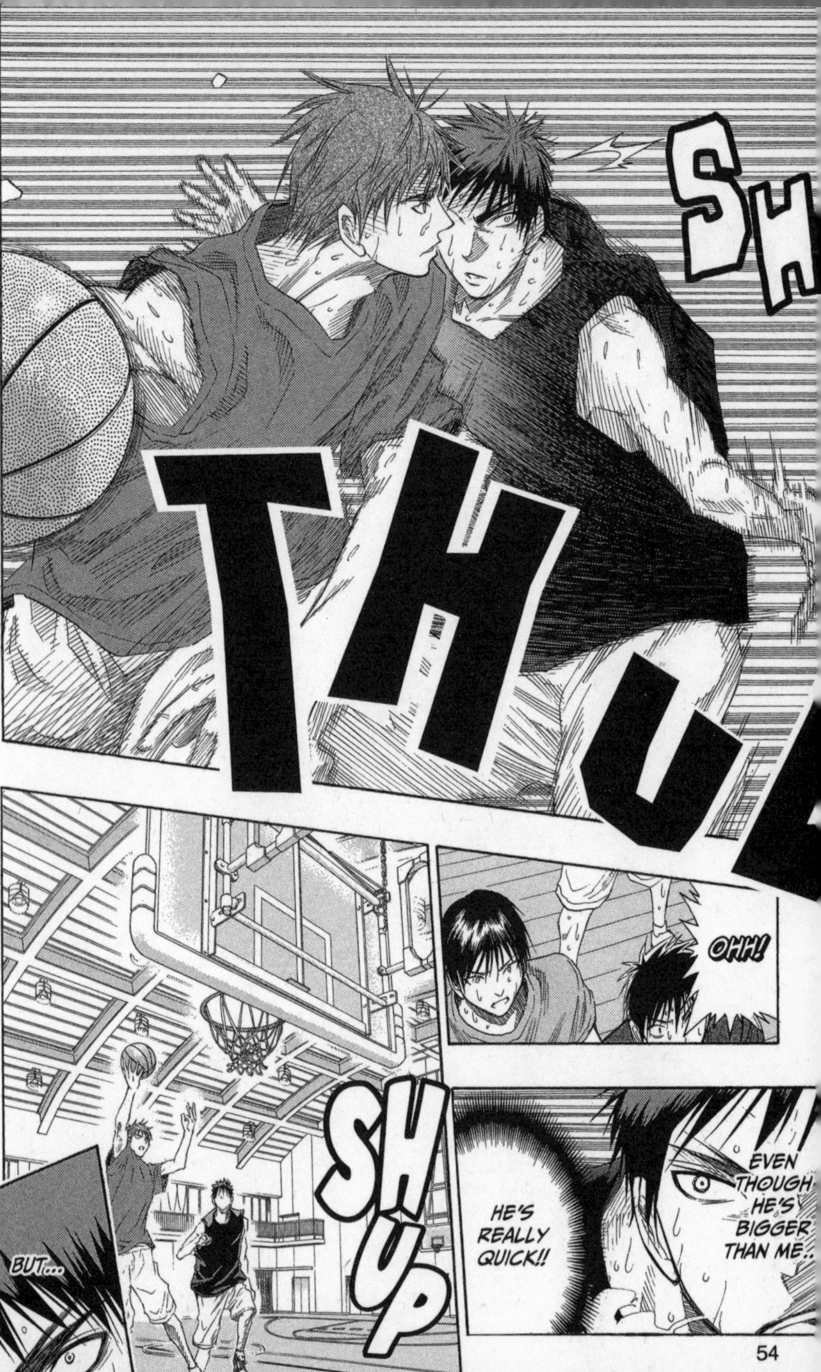
SH
THU
OHH!
EVEN THOUGH HE'S BIGGER THAN ME...
HE'S REALLY QUICK!!
SHUP
BUT...

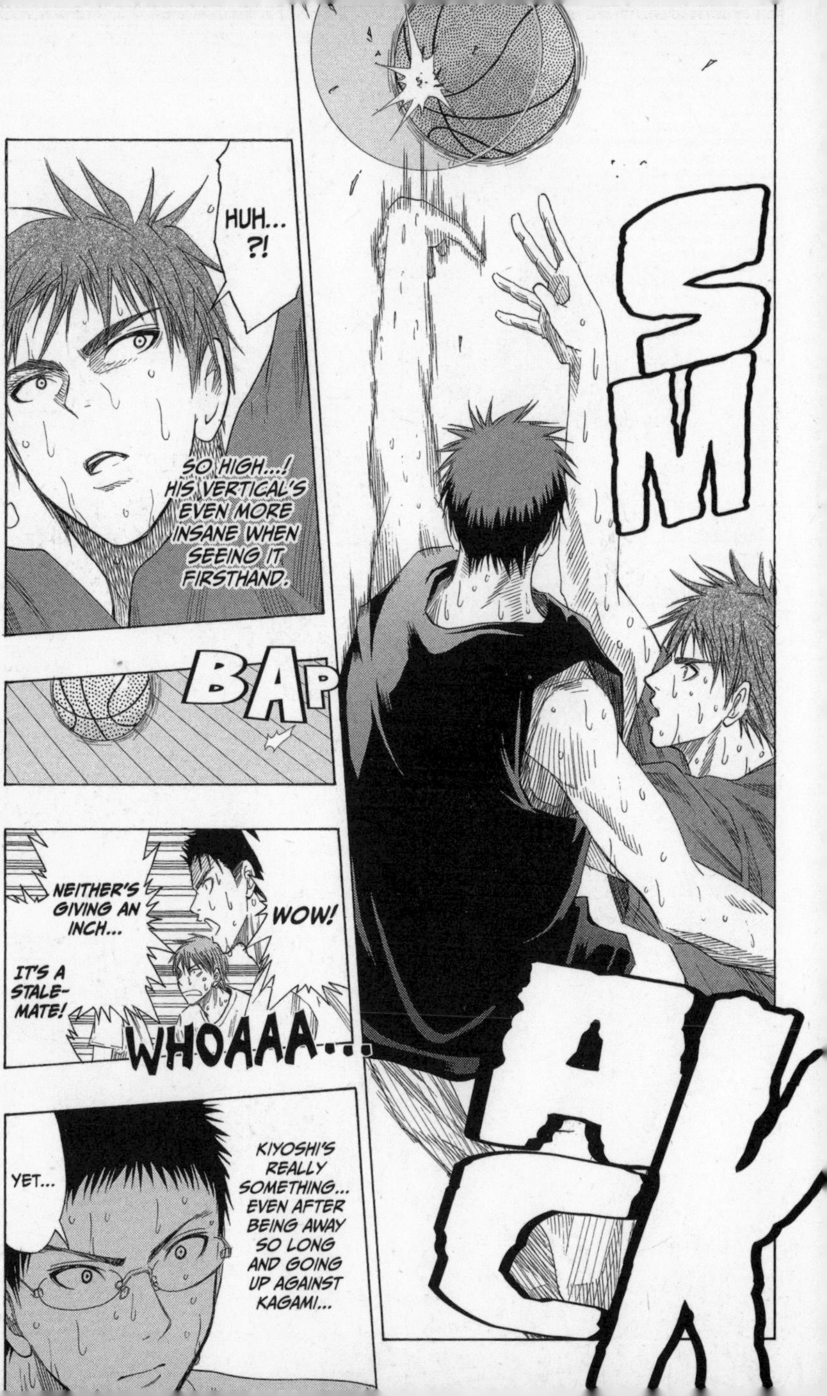
SMACK
HUH... ?!
SO HIGH...! HIS VERTICAL'S EVEN MORE INSANE WHEN SEEING IT FIRSTHAND.
BAP
WOW!
NEITHER'S GIVING AN INCH...
IT'S A STALE-MATE!
WHOAAA...
KIYOSHI'S REALLY SOMETHING... EVEN AFTER BEING AWAY SO LONG AND GOING UP AGAINST KAGAMI...
YET...

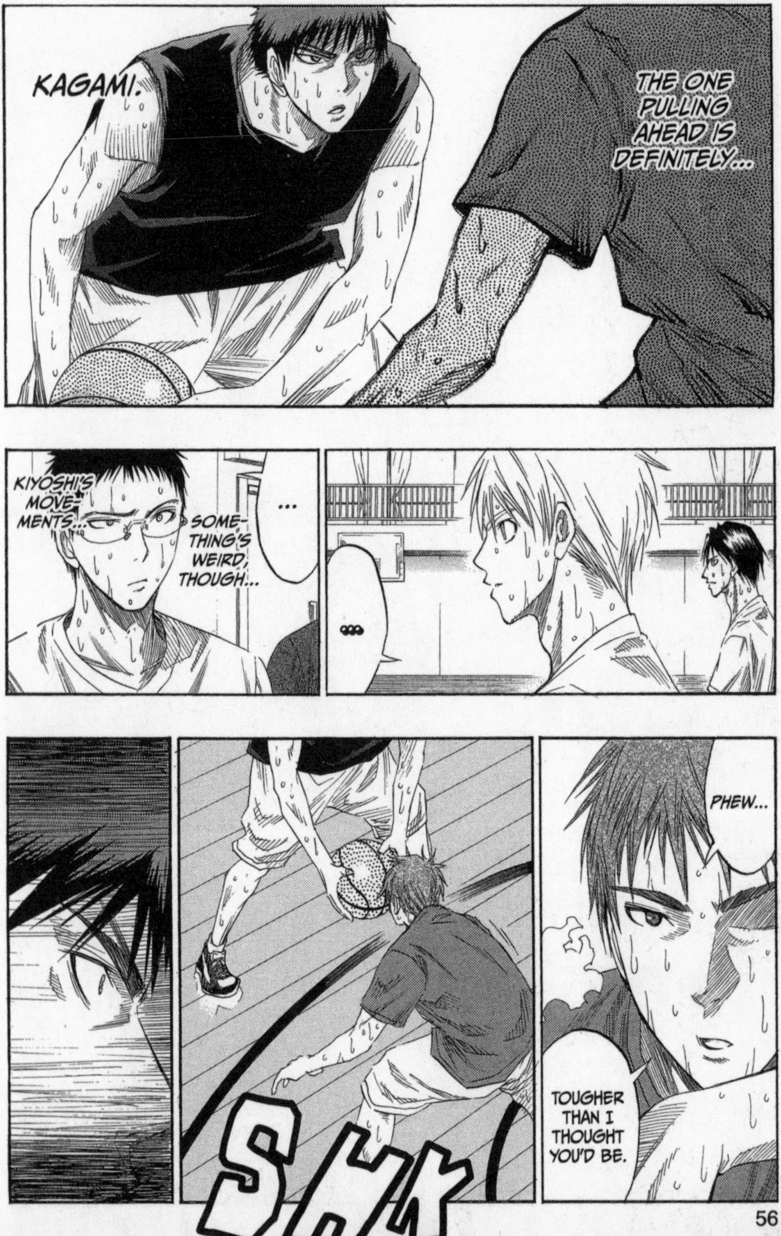
THE ONE PULLING AHEAD IS DEFINITELY...
KAGAMI.
...
...
KIYOSHI'S MOVEMENTS...
SOMETHING'S WEIRD, THOUGH...
PHEW...
TOUGHER THAN I THOUGHT YOU'D BE.
SHK

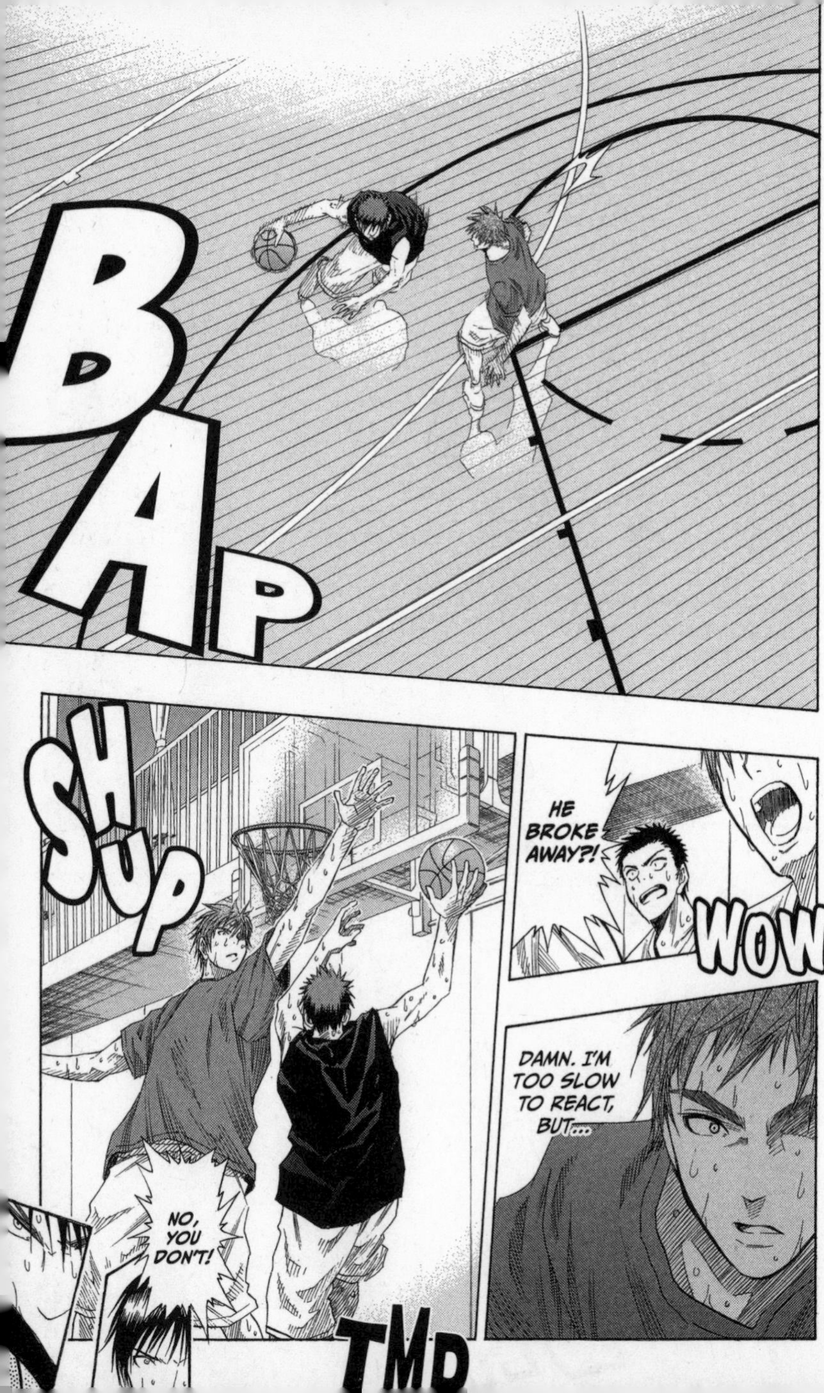
BAP
HE BROKE AWAY?!
WOW
DAMN. I'M TOO SLOW TO REACT, BUT...
SHUP
NO, YOU DON'T!
TMD

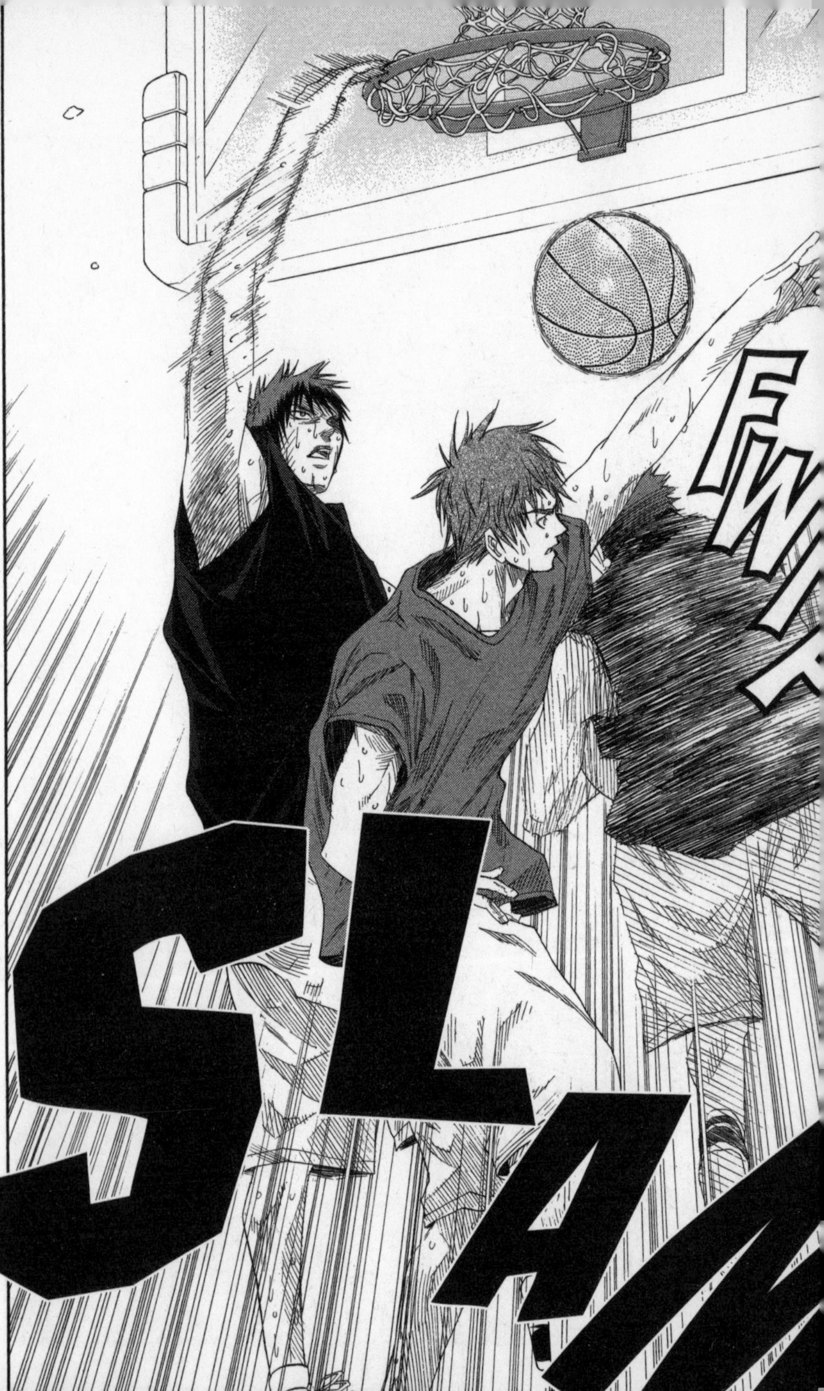
FWIP
SLAM

WHAT?!

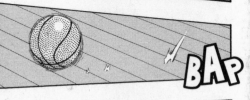

BAP

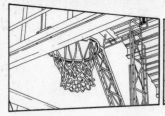

KAGAMI... WON!!

SHK

AMAZING!! PULLING OFF A REVERSE DUNK LIKE THAT!

PHEW...

...

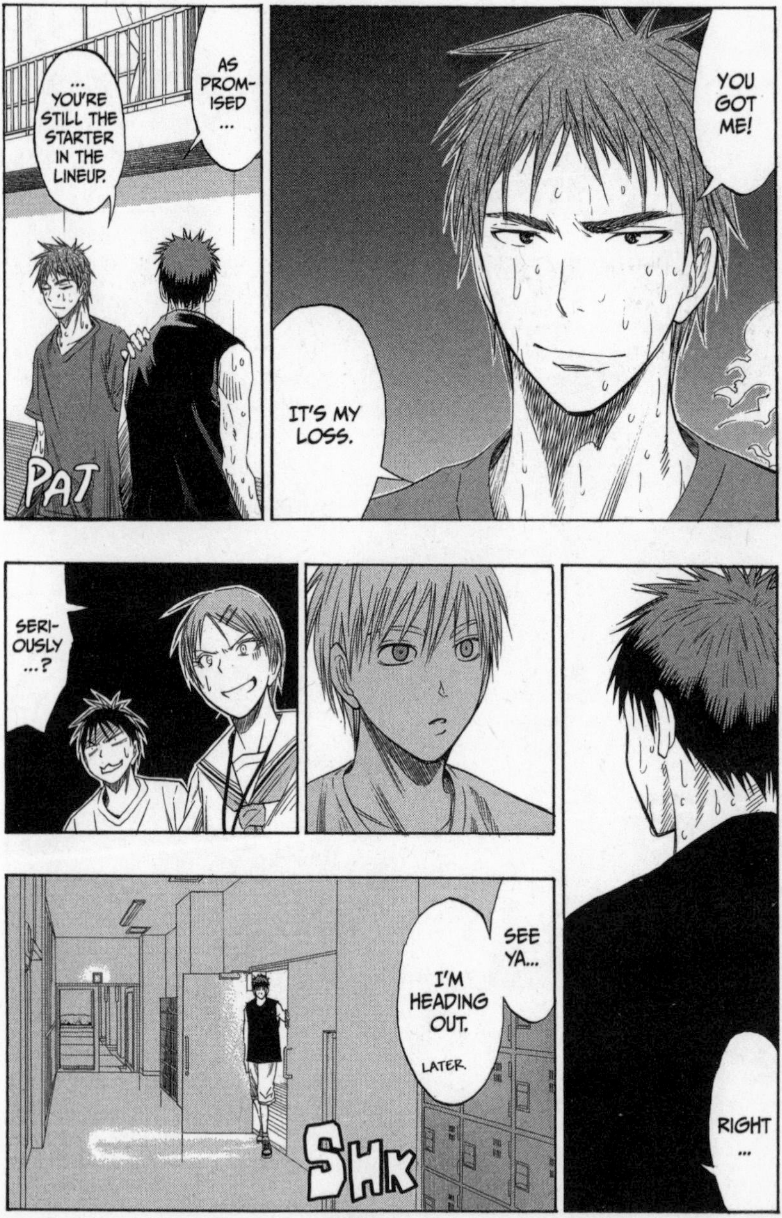
YOU GOT ME!
IT'S MY LOSS.
AS PROM-ISED ...
... YOU'RE STILL THE STARTER IN THE LINEUP.
PAT
RIGHT ...
SERI-OUSLY ...?
SEE YA...
I'M HEADING OUT.
LATER.
SHK

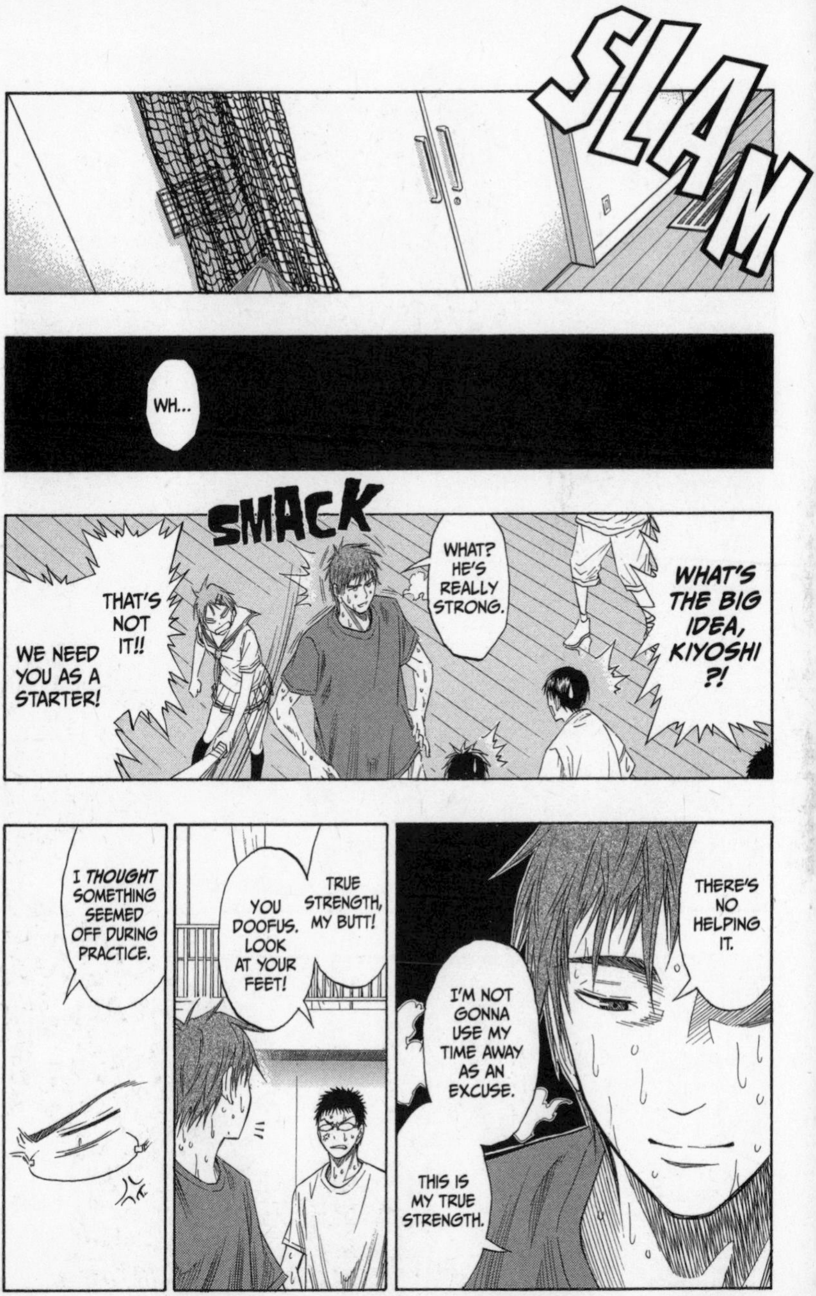
SLAM
WH...
WHAT'S THE BIG IDEA, KIYOSHI?!
SMACK
WHAT? HE'S REALLY STRONG.
THAT'S NOT IT!!
WE NEED YOU AS A STARTER!
THERE'S NO HELPING IT.
I'M NOT GONNA USE MY TIME AWAY AS AN EXCUSE.
THIS IS MY TRUE STRENGTH.
TRUE STRENGTH, MY BUTT!
YOU DOOFUS. LOOK AT YOUR FEET!
I *THOUGHT* SOMETHING SEEMED OFF DURING PRACTICE.

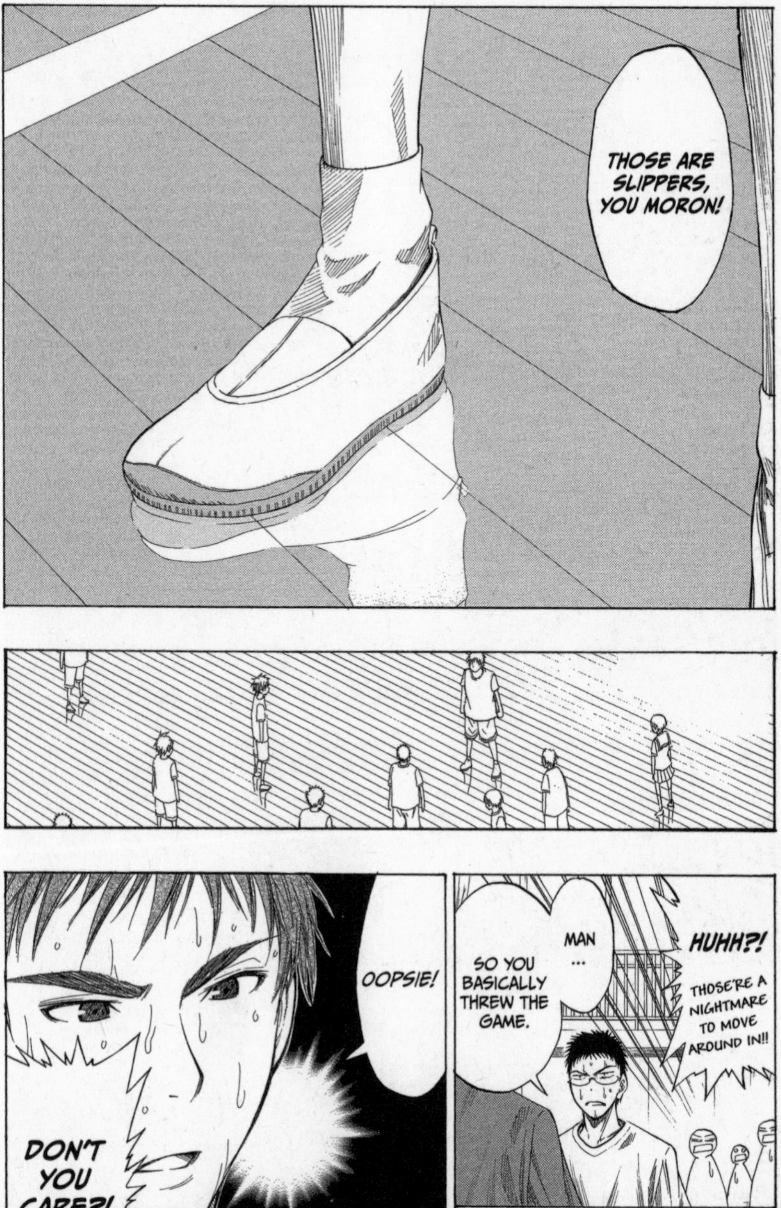
THOSE ARE SLIPPERS, YOU MORON!
HUHH?!
THOSE'RE A NIGHTMARE TO MOVE AROUND IN!!
MAN ...
SO YOU BASICALLY THREW THE GAME.
OOPSIE!
DON'T YOU CARE?!

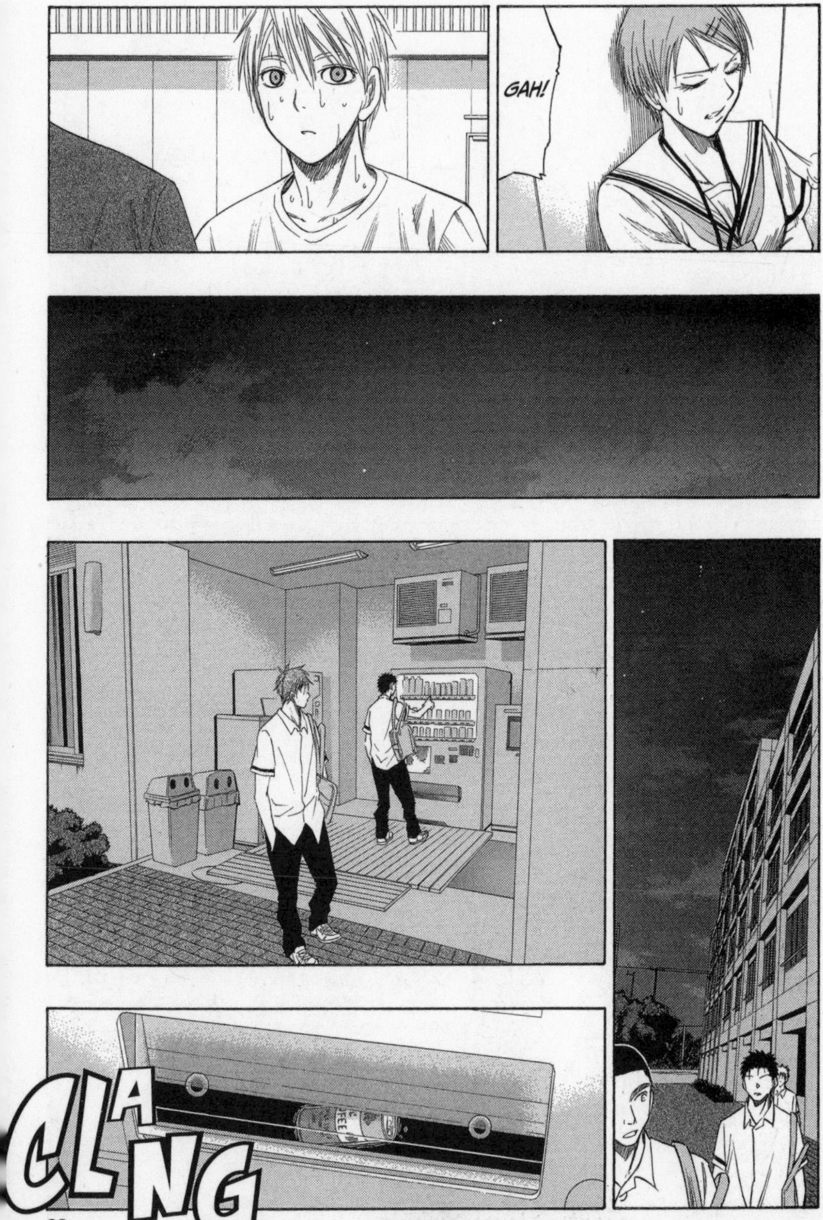
GAH!
CLANG

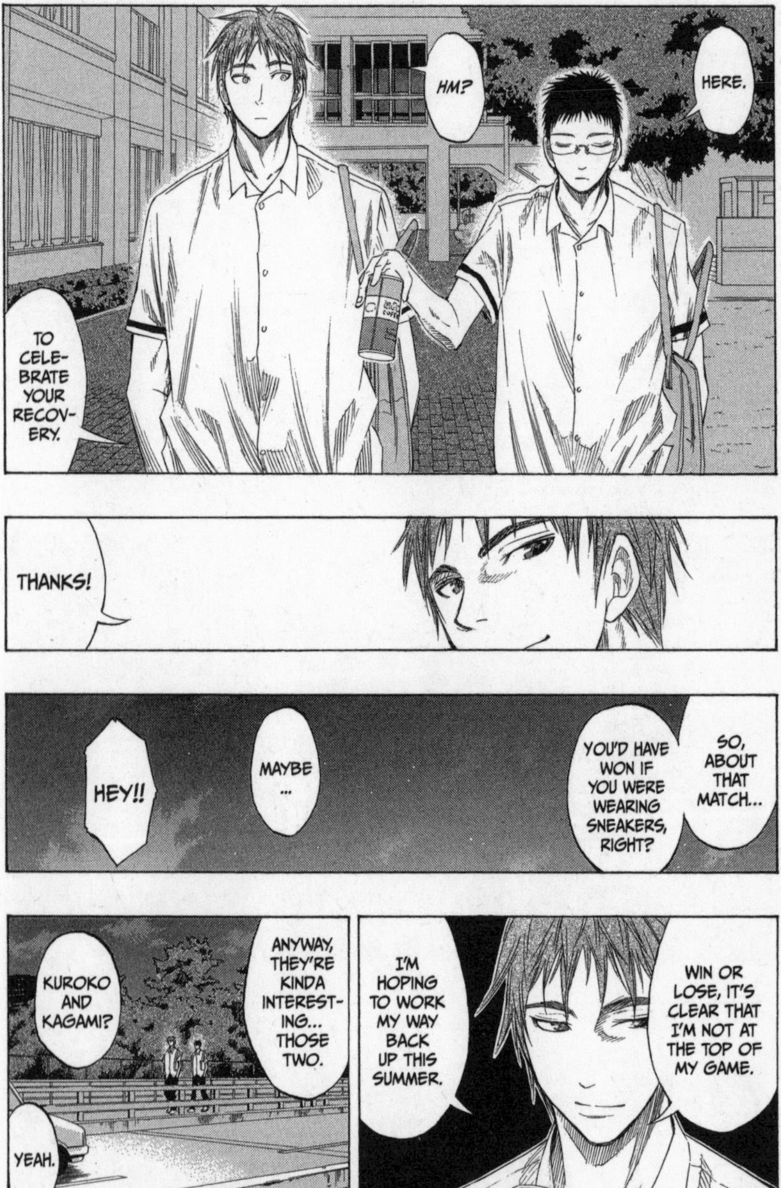
HERE.
HM?
TO CELEBRATE YOUR RECOVERY.
THANKS!
SO, ABOUT THAT MATCH...
YOU'D HAVE WON IF YOU WERE WEARING SNEAKERS, RIGHT?
MAYBE ...
HEY!!
WIN OR LOSE, IT'S CLEAR THAT I'M NOT AT THE TOP OF MY GAME.
I'M HOPING TO WORK MY WAY BACK UP THIS SUMMER.
ANYWAY, THEY'RE KINDA INTERESTING... THOSE TWO.
KUROKO AND KAGAMI?
YEAH.

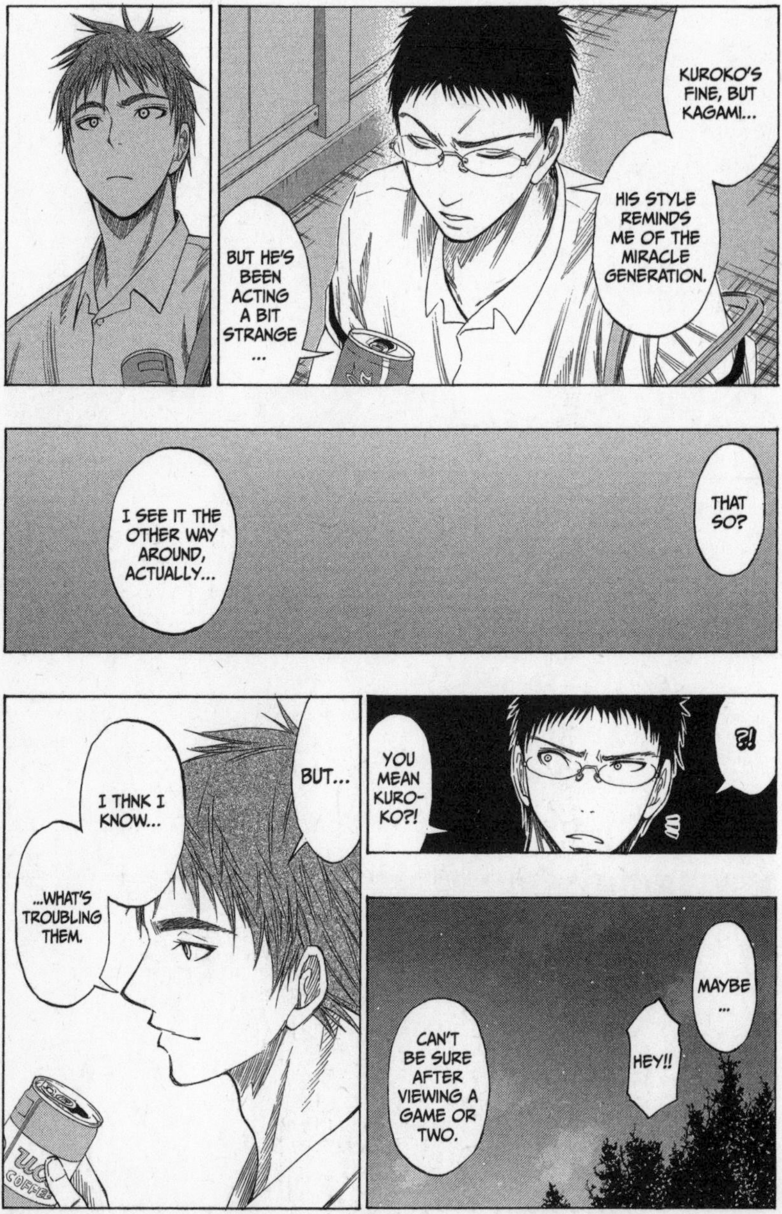
KUROKO'S FINE, BUT KAGAMI...
HIS STYLE REMINDS ME OF THE MIRACLE GENERATION.
BUT HE'S BEEN ACTING A BIT STRANGE ...
THAT SO?
I SEE IT THE OTHER WAY AROUND, ACTUALLY...
?!
YOU MEAN KURO-KO?!
MAYBE ...
HEY!!
CAN'T BE SURE AFTER VIEWING A GAME OR TWO.
BUT...
I THNK I KNOW...
...WHAT'S TROUBLING THEM.

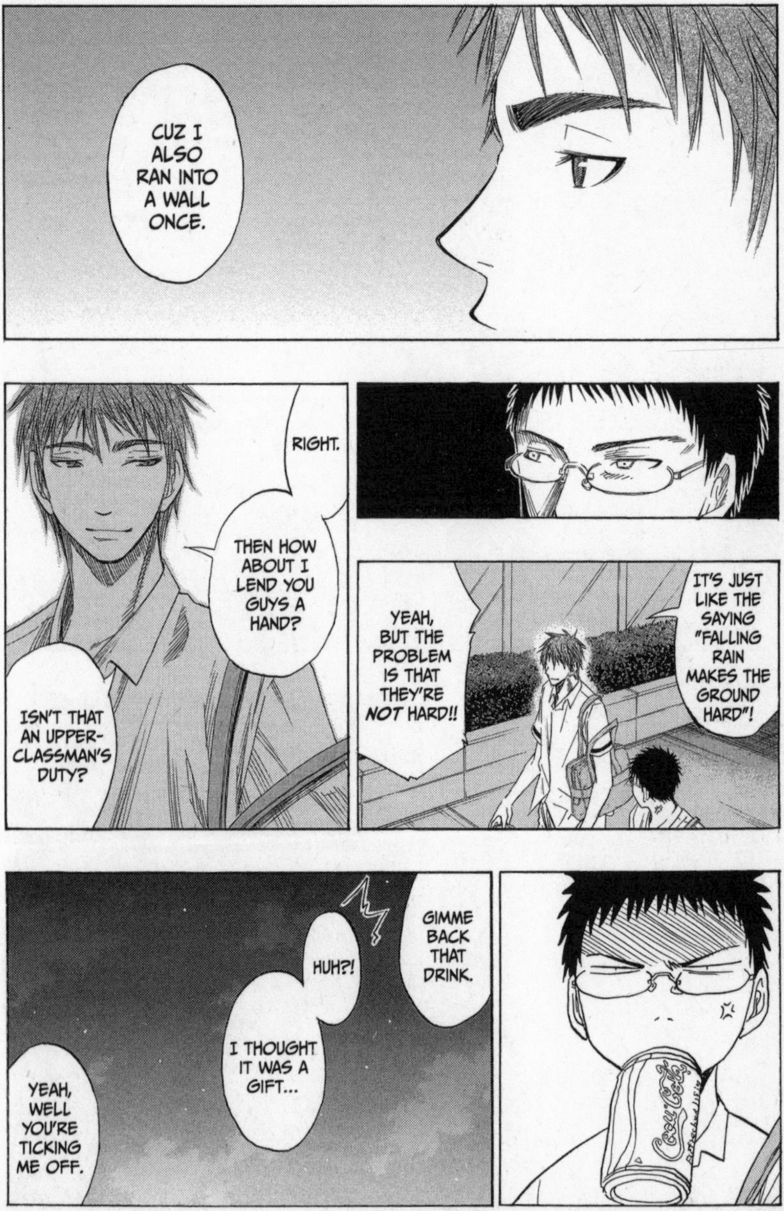
CUZ I ALSO RAN INTO A WALL ONCE.
IT'S JUST LIKE THE SAYING "FALLING RAIN MAKES THE GROUND HARD"!
YEAH, BUT THE PROBLEM IS THAT THEY'RE *NOT* HARD!!
RIGHT.
THEN HOW ABOUT I LEND YOU GUYS A HAND?
ISN'T THAT AN UPPER-CLASSMAN'S DUTY?
GIMME BACK THAT DRINK.
HUH?!
I THOUGHT IT WAS A GIFT...
YEAH, WELL YOU'RE TICKING ME OFF.

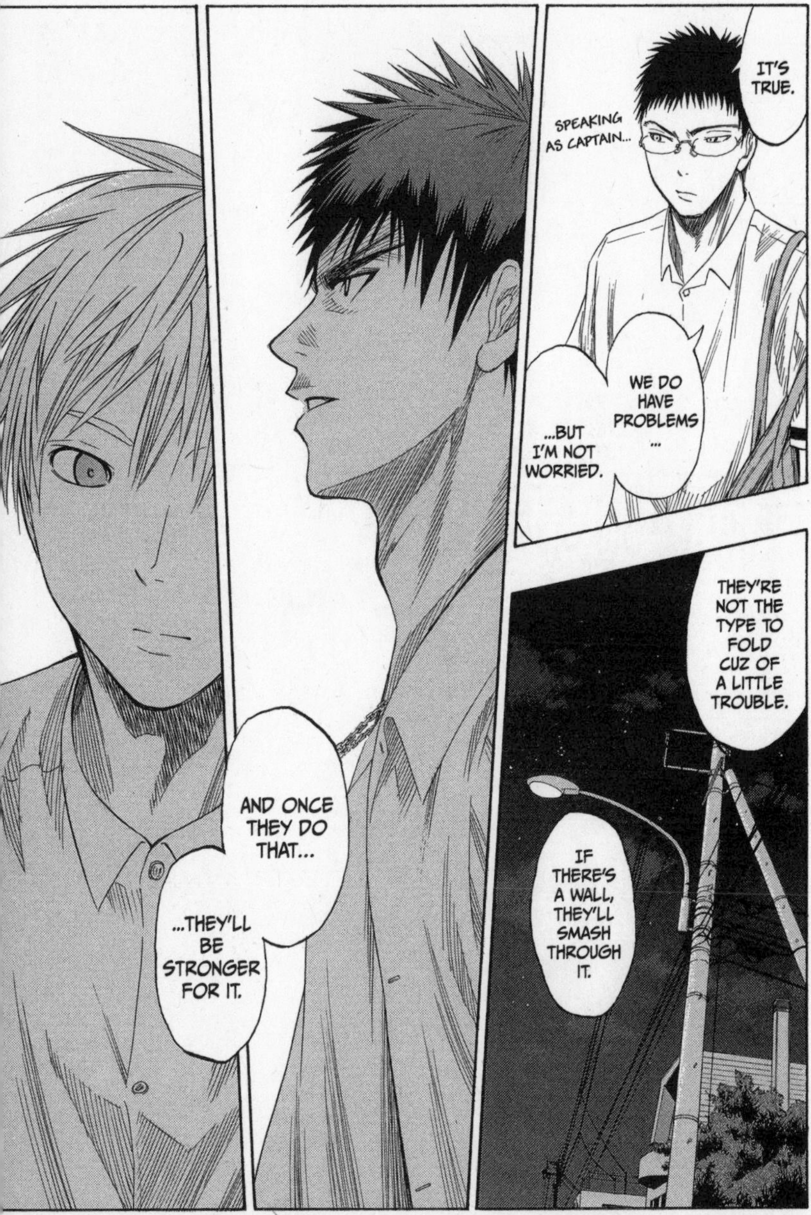
IT'S TRUE.
SPEAKING AS CAPTAIN...
WE DO HAVE PROBLEMS ...
...BUT I'M NOT WORRIED.
THEY'RE NOT THE TYPE TO FOLD CUZ OF A LITTLE TROUBLE.
IF THERE'S A WALL, THEY'LL SMASH THROUGH IT.
AND ONCE THEY DO THAT...
...THEY'LL BE STRONGER FOR IT.

KUROKO'S BASKETBALL BLOOPERS TAKE 2

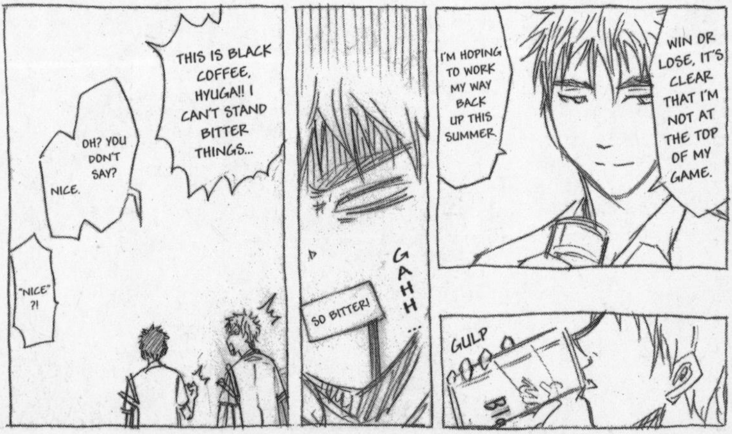
WIN OR LOSE, IT'S CLEAR THAT I'M NOT AT THE TOP OF MY GAME.
I'M HOPING TO WORK MY WAY BACK UP THIS SUMMER.
GULP
GAHH...
SO BITTER!
THIS IS BLACK COFFEE, HYUGA!! I CAN'T STAND BITTER THINGS...
OH? YOU DON'T SAY?
NICE.
"NICE" ?!

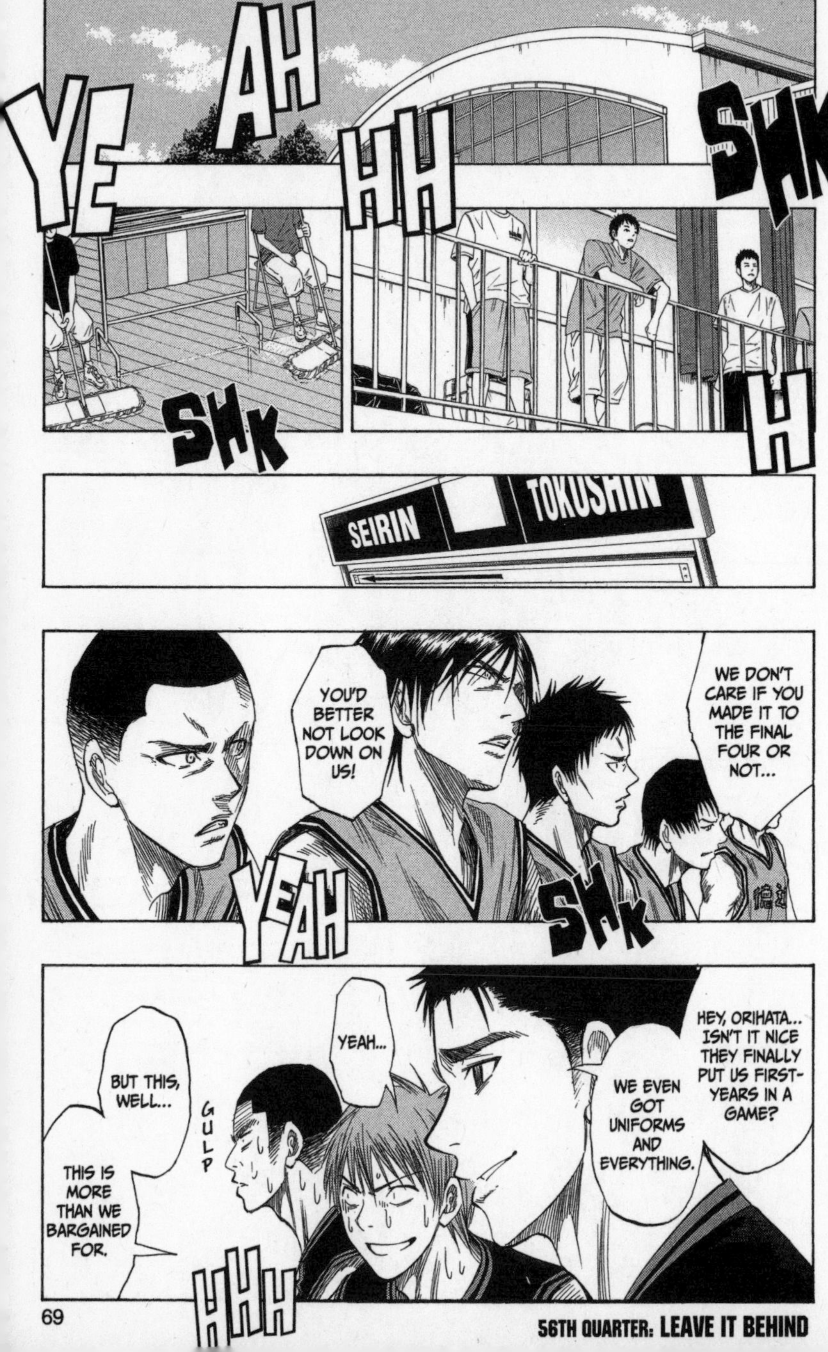
YEAHHH
SHK
H
SHK
TOKUSHIN
SEIRIN
WE DON'T CARE IF YOU MADE IT TO THE FINAL FOUR OR NOT...
YOU'D BETTER NOT LOOK DOWN ON US!
SHK
YEAH
HEY, ORIHATA... ISN'T IT NICE THEY FINALLY PUT US FIRST-YEARS IN A GAME?
WE EVEN GOT UNIFORMS AND EVERYTHING.
YEAH...
BUT THIS, WELL...
GULP
THIS IS MORE THAN WE BARGAINED FOR.
HHH

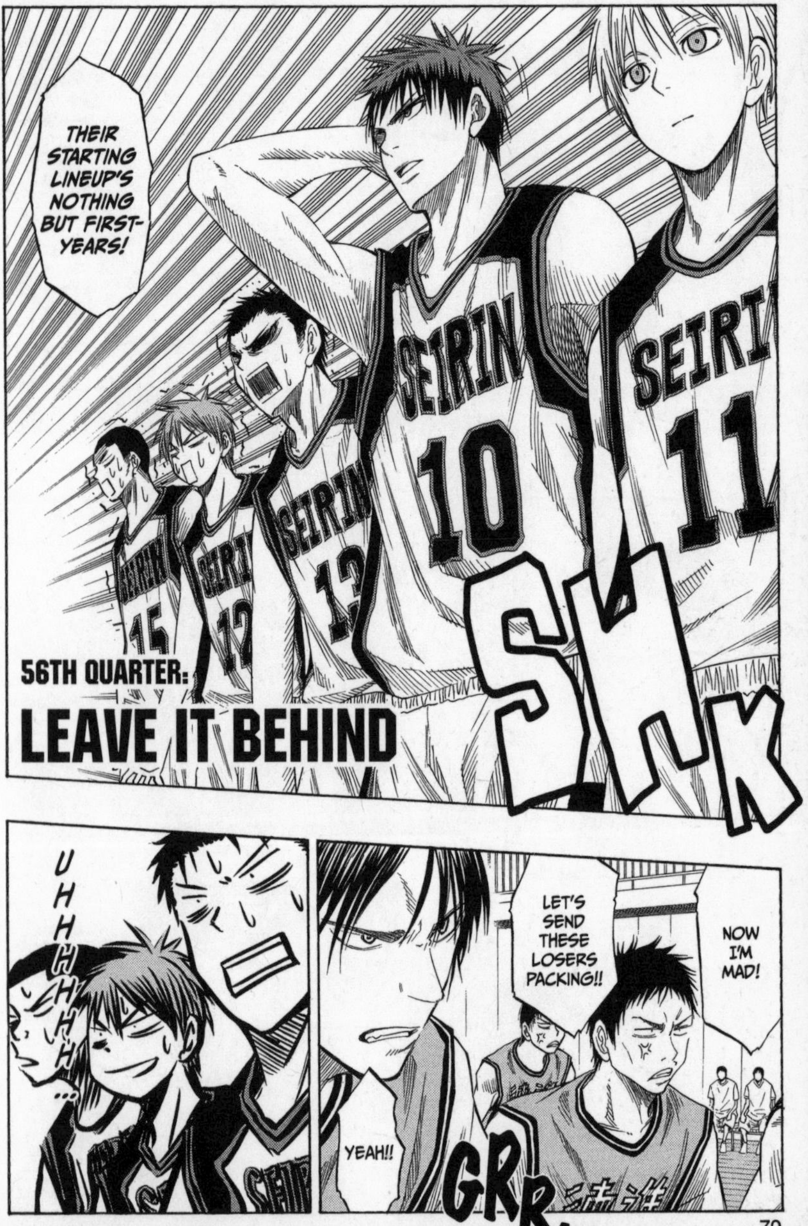
THEIR STARTING LINEUP'S NOTHING BUT FIRST-YEARS!
56TH QUARTER:
LEAVE IT BEHIND
SHK
NOW I'M MAD!
LET'S SEND THESE LOSERS PACKING!!
YEAH!!
GRR...
UHHHHHHHH...

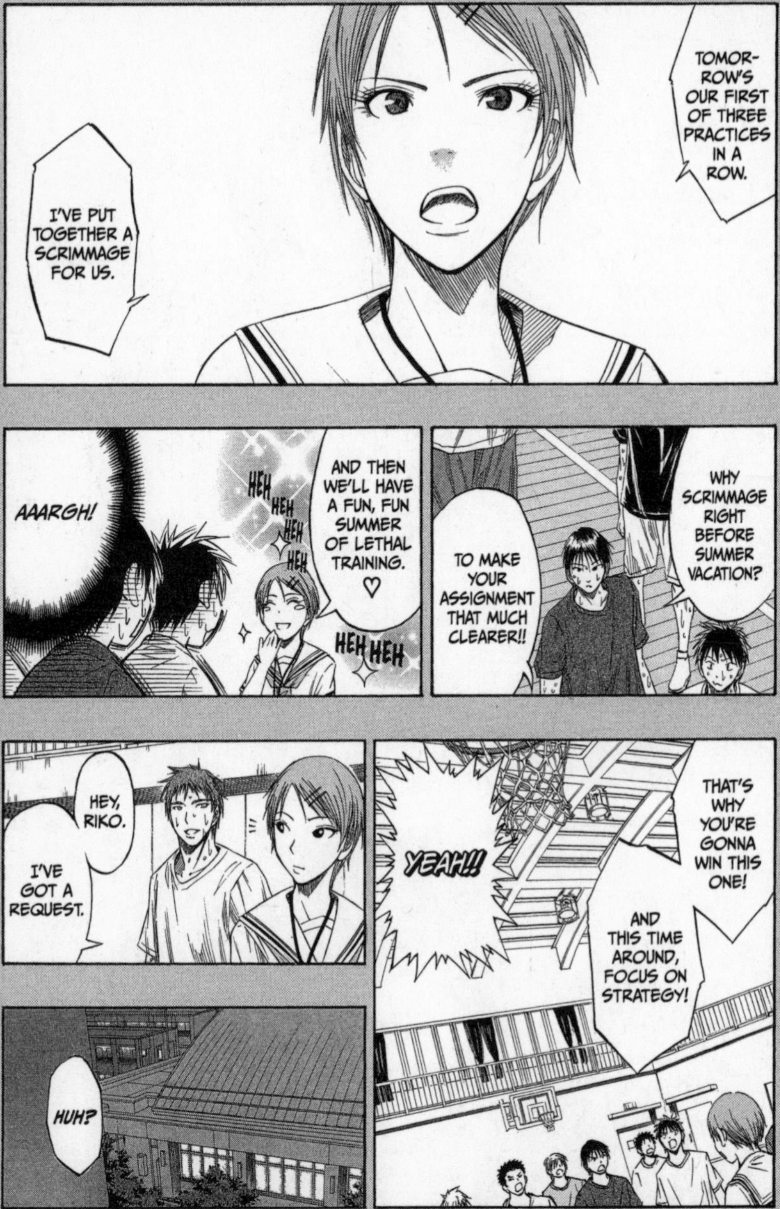

TOMORROW'S OUR FIRST OF THREE PRACTICES IN A ROW.
I'VE PUT TOGETHER A SCRIMMAGE FOR US.
WHY SCRIMMAGE RIGHT BEFORE SUMMER VACATION?
TO MAKE YOUR ASSIGNMENT THAT MUCH CLEARER!!
AND THEN WE'LL HAVE A FUN, FUN SUMMER OF LETHAL TRAINING. ♡
HEH HEH HEH HEH
HEH HEH
AAARGH!
THAT'S WHY YOU'RE GONNA WIN THIS ONE!
AND THIS TIME AROUND, FOCUS ON STRATEGY!
YEAH!!
HEY, RIKO.
I'VE GOT A REQUEST.
HUH?

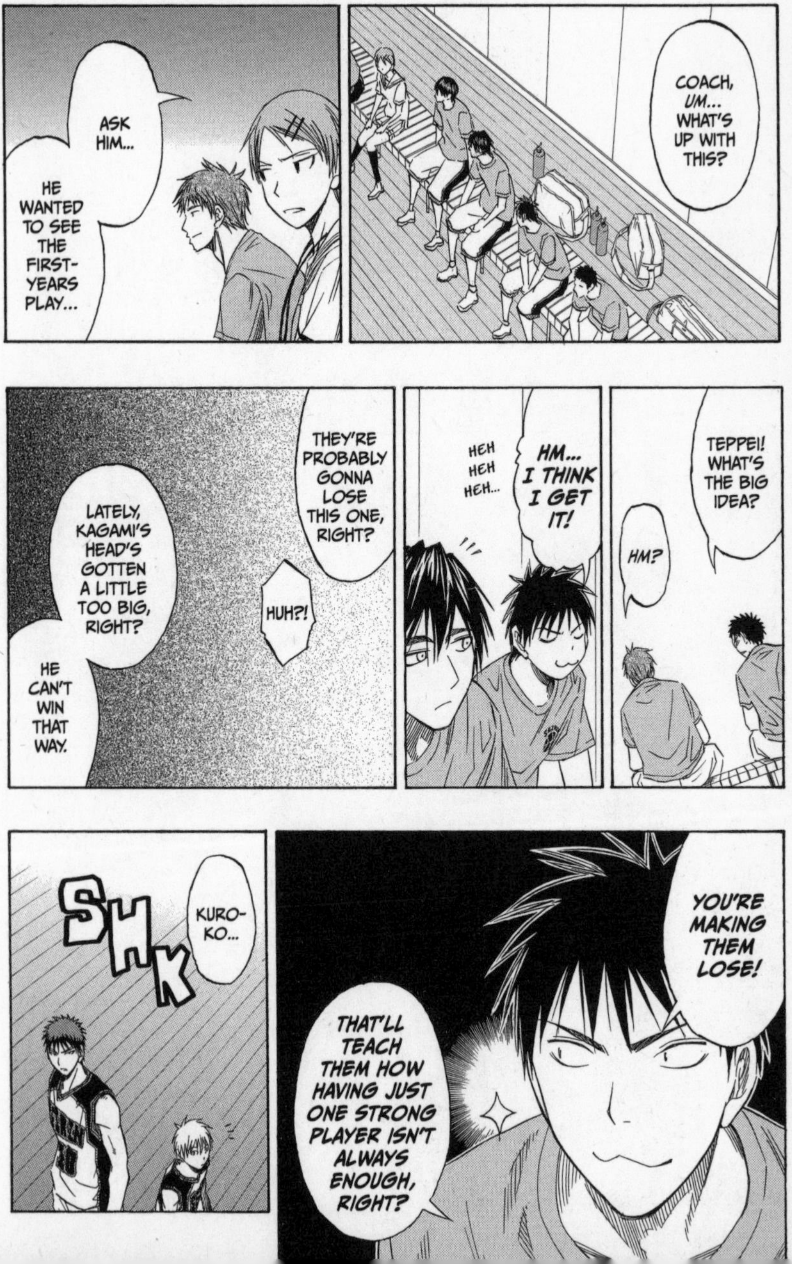
COACH, UM... WHAT'S UP WITH THIS?
ASK HIM...
HE WANTED TO SEE THE FIRST-YEARS PLAY...
TEPPEI! WHAT'S THE BIG IDEA?
HM?
HM... I THINK I GET IT!
HEH HEH HEH...
THEY'RE PROBABLY GONNA LOSE THIS ONE, RIGHT?
HUH?!
LATELY, KAGAMI'S HEAD'S GOTTEN A LITTLE TOO BIG, RIGHT?
HE CAN'T WIN THAT WAY.
YOU'RE MAKING THEM LOSE!
THAT'LL TEACH THEM HOW HAVING JUST ONE STRONG PLAYER ISN'T ALWAYS ENOUGH, RIGHT?
KURO-KO...
SHK

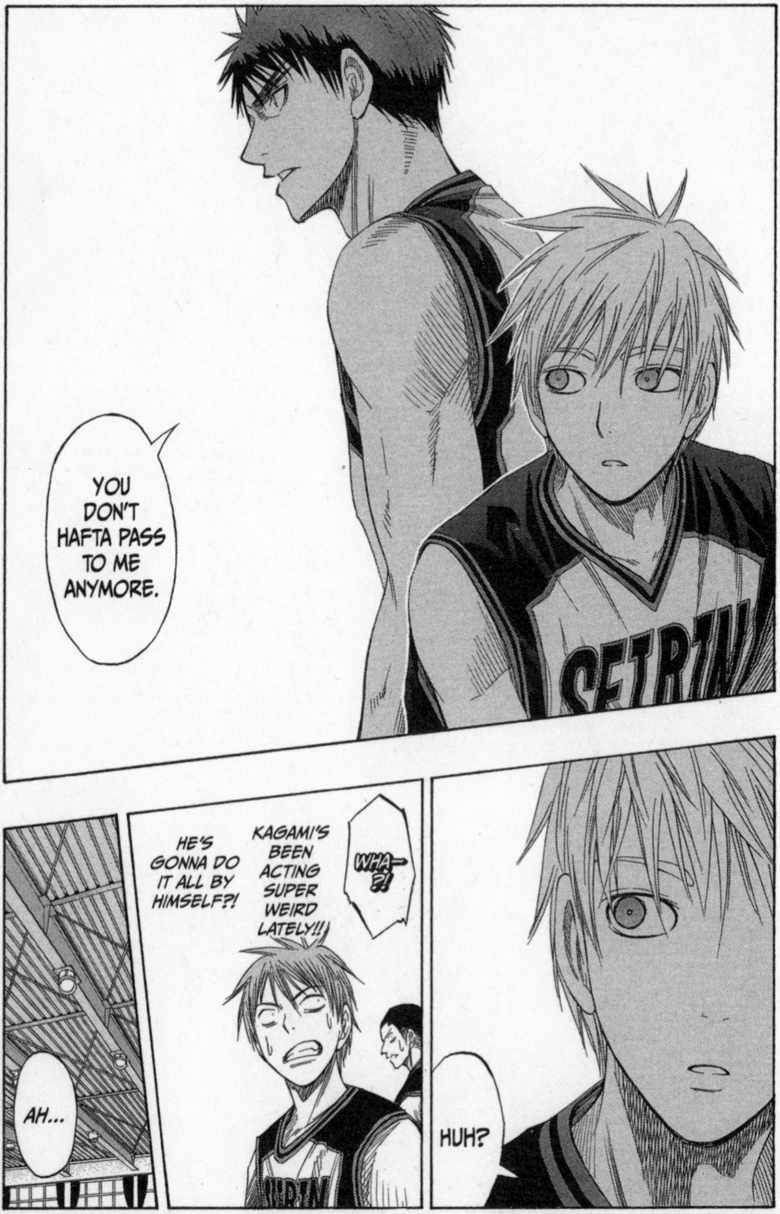
YOU DON'T HAFTA PASS TO ME ANYMORE.
HUH?
WHA-?!
KAGAMI'S BEEN ACTING SUPER WEIRD LATELY!!
HE'S GONNA DO IT ALL BY HIMSELF?!
AH...

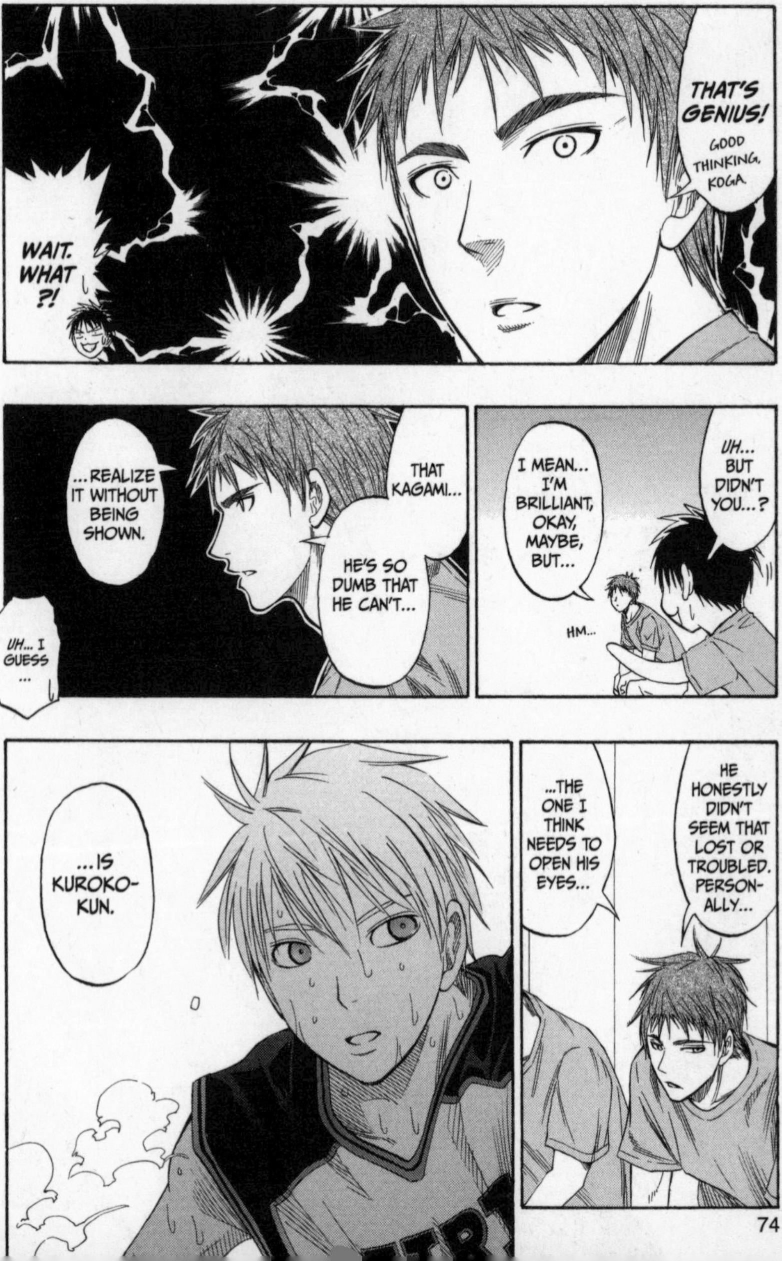
THAT'S GENIUS!
GOOD THINKING, KOGA.
WAIT. WHAT?!
UH... BUT DIDN'T YOU...?
I MEAN... I'M BRILLIANT, OKAY, MAYBE, BUT...
HM...
THAT KAGAMI...
HE'S SO DUMB THAT HE CAN'T...
...REALIZE IT WITHOUT BEING SHOWN.
UH... I GUESS...
HE HONESTLY DIDN'T SEEM THAT LOST OR TROUBLED. PERSON-ALLY...
...THE ONE I THINK NEEDS TO OPEN HIS EYES...
...IS KUROKO-KUN.

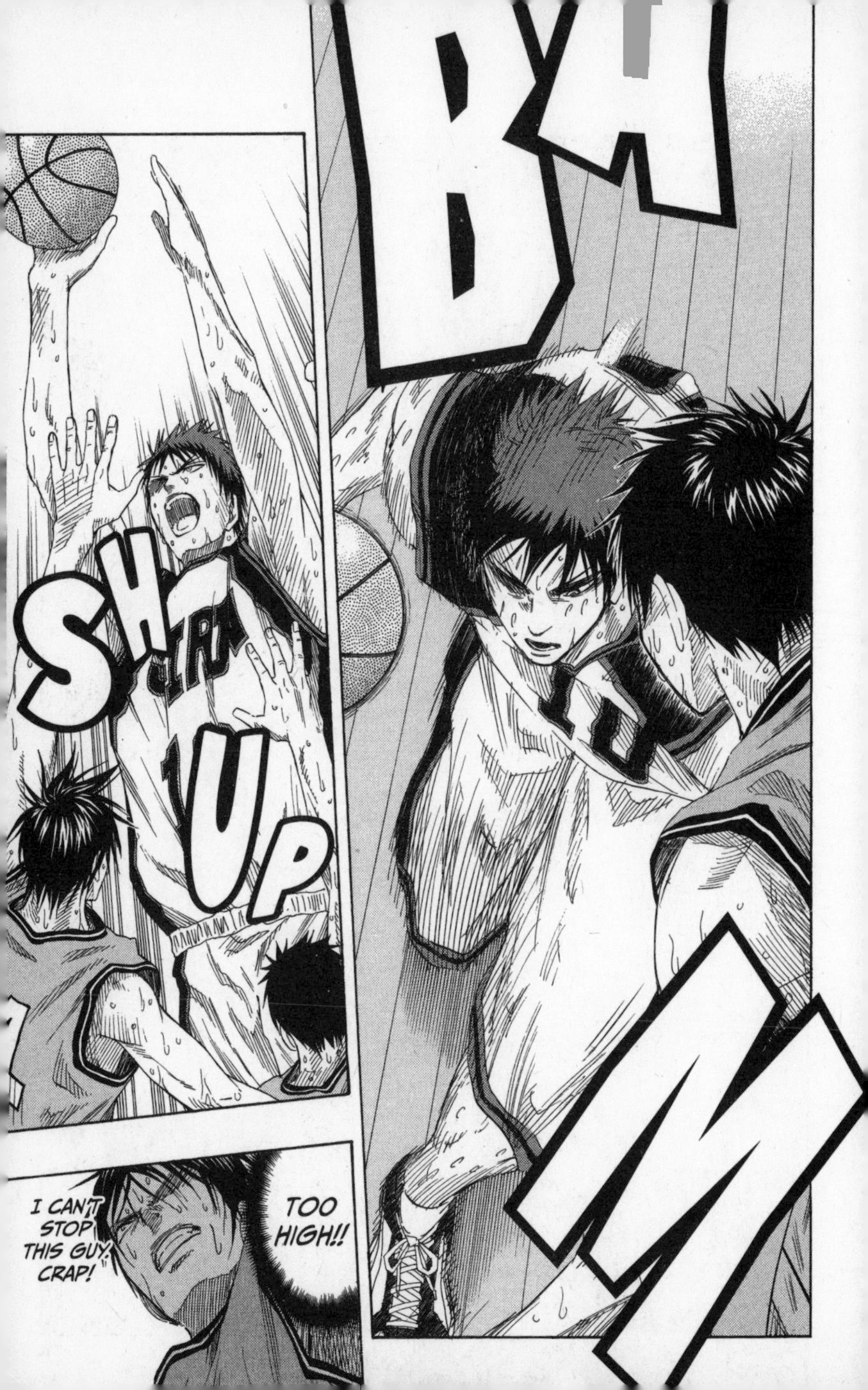
BAM
SHUP
TOO HIGH!!
I CAN'T STOP THIS GUY. CRAP!

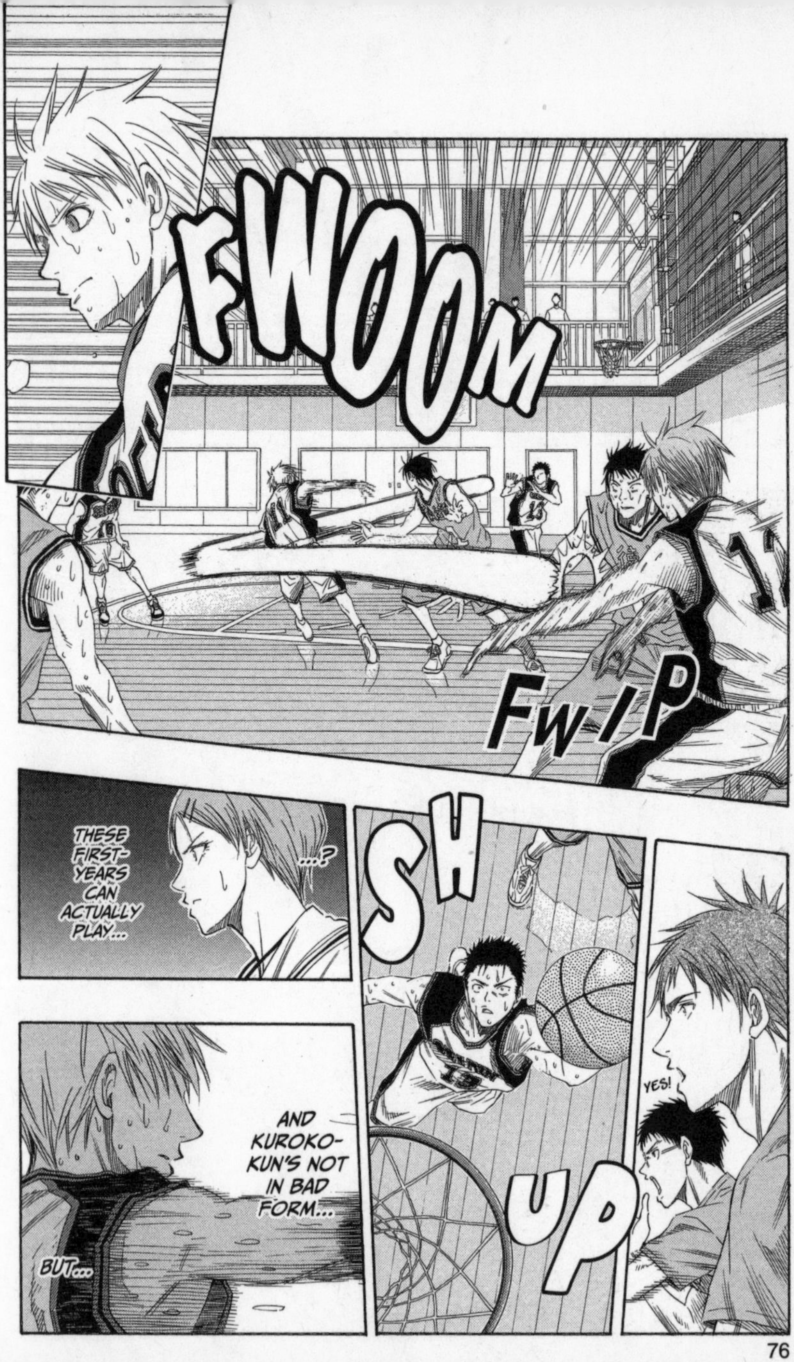
FWOOM
FWIP
YES!
SH
UP
...?
THESE FIRST-YEARS CAN ACTUALLY PLAY...
AND KUROKO-KUN'S NOT IN BAD FORM...
BUT...

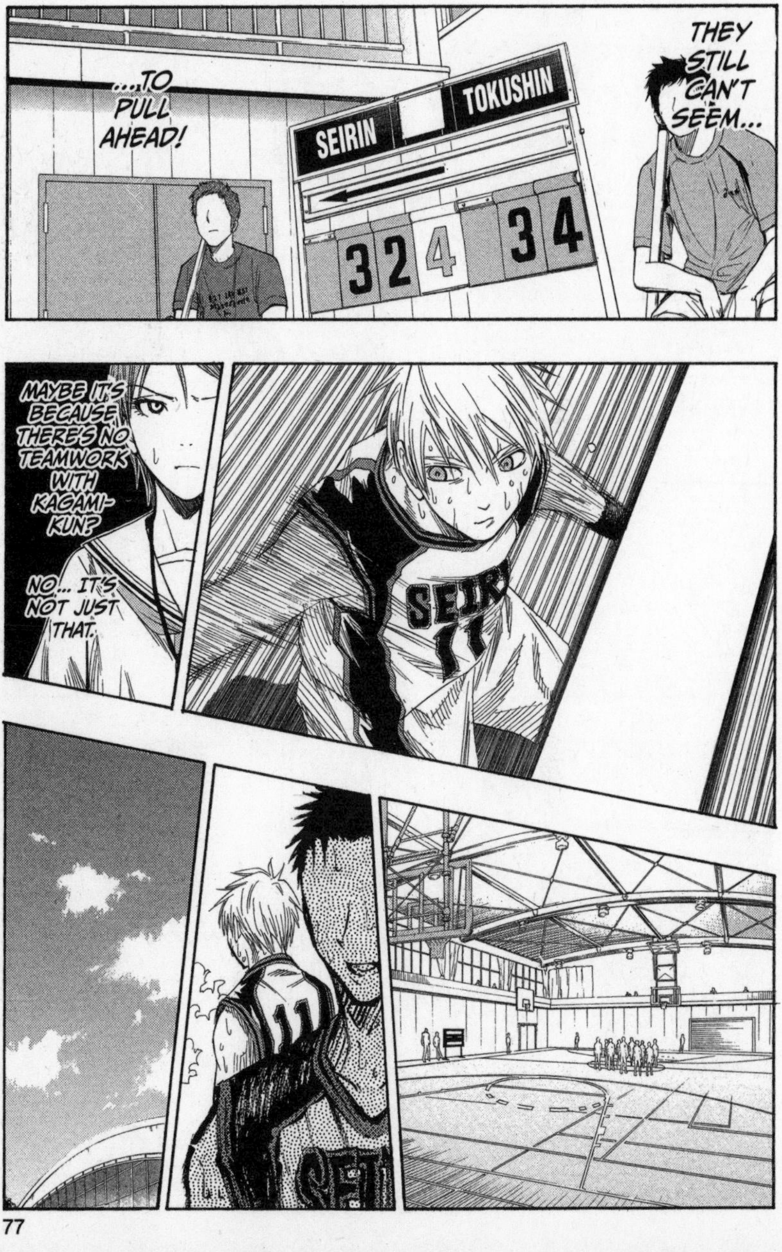
THEY STILL CAN'T SEEM...
TOKUSHIN
SEIRIN
3 2 4
3 4
...TO PULL AHEAD!
MAYBE IT'S BECAUSE THERE'S NO TEAMWORK WITH KAGAMI-KUN?
NO... IT'S NOT JUST THAT.

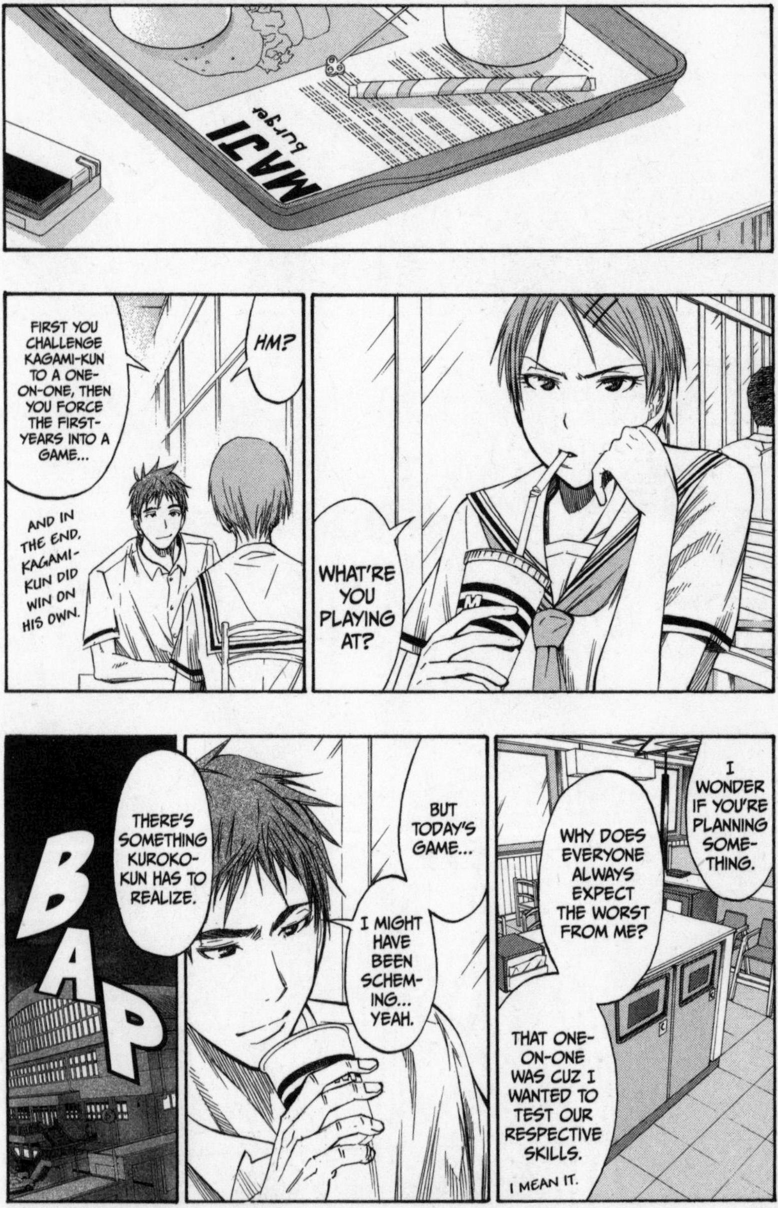
MAJI
burger
WHAT'RE YOU PLAYING AT?
HM?
FIRST YOU CHALLENGE KAGAMI-KUN TO A ONE-ON-ONE, THEN YOU FORCE THE FIRST-YEARS INTO A GAME...
AND IN THE END, KAGAMI-KUN DID WIN ON HIS OWN.
I WONDER IF YOU'RE PLANNING SOME-THING.
WHY DOES EVERYONE ALWAYS EXPECT THE WORST FROM ME?
THAT ONE-ON-ONE WAS CUZ I WANTED TO TEST OUR RESPECTIVE SKILLS.
I MEAN IT.
BUT TODAY'S GAME...
I MIGHT HAVE BEEN SCHEM-ING... YEAH.
THERE'S SOMETHING KUROKO-KUN HAS TO REALIZE.
BAP

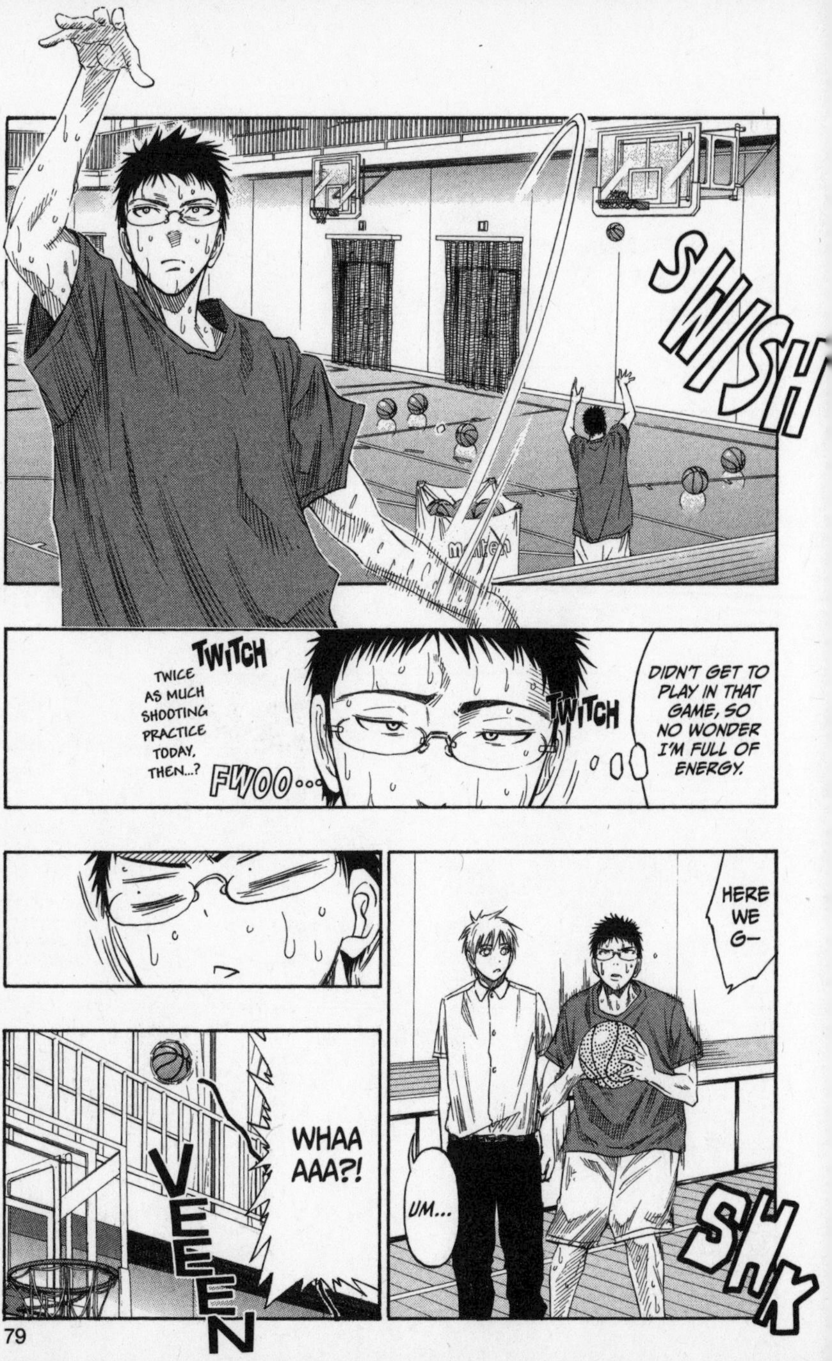
SWISH
DIDN'T GET TO PLAY IN THAT GAME, SO NO WONDER I'M FULL OF ENERGY.
TWITCH
TWITCH
TWICE AS MUCH SHOOTING PRACTICE TODAY, THEN...?
FWOO...
HERE WE G—
UM...
SHK
WHAA AAA?!
VEEEEN

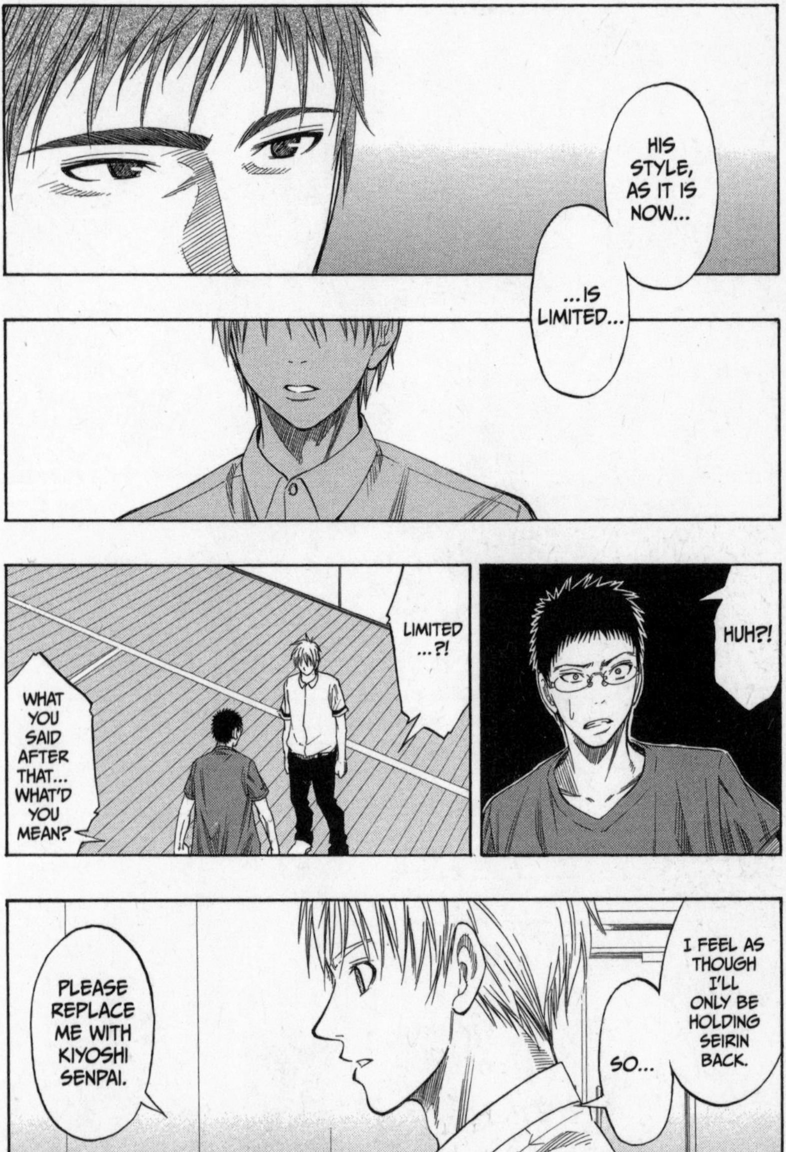
HIS STYLE, AS IT IS NOW...
...IS LIMITED...
HUH?!
LIMITED ...?!
WHAT YOU SAID AFTER THAT... WHAT'D YOU MEAN?
I FEEL AS THOUGH I'LL ONLY BE HOLDING SEIRIN BACK.
SO...
PLEASE REPLACE ME WITH KIYOSHI SENPAI.

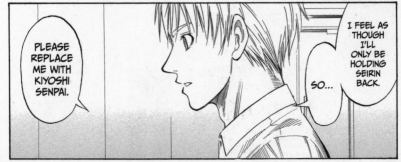

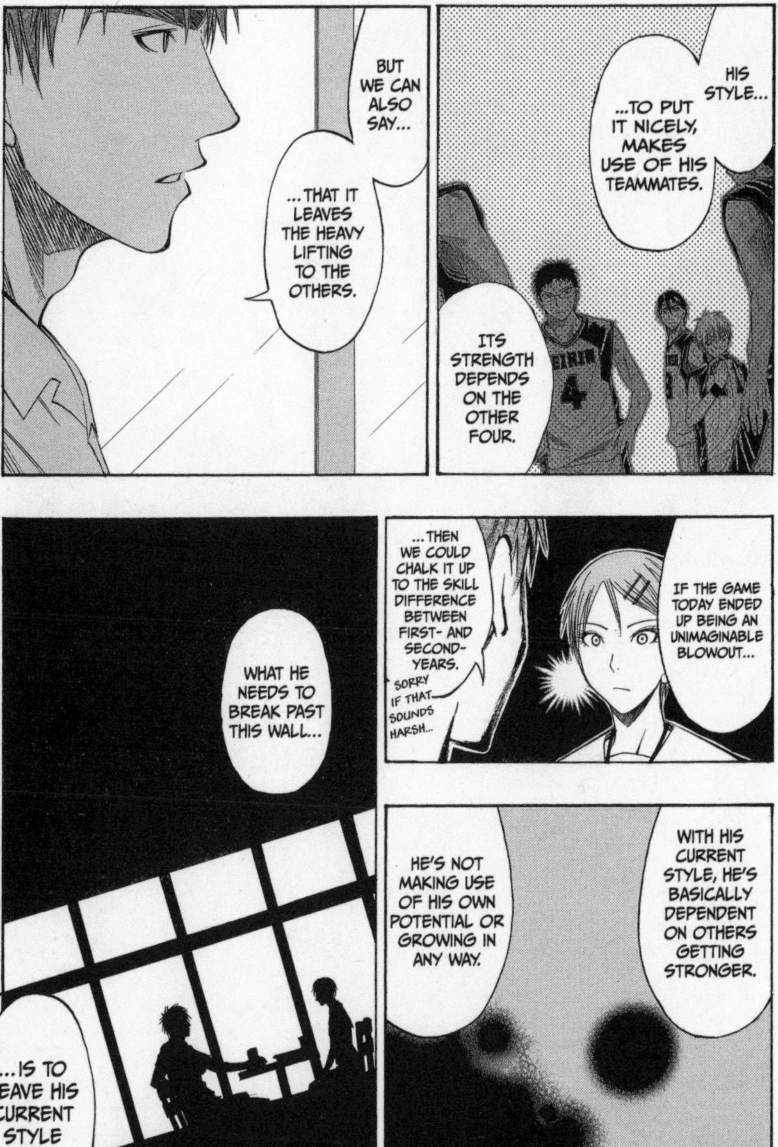
HIS STYLE...
...TO PUT IT NICELY, MAKES USE OF HIS TEAMMATES.
ITS STRENGTH DEPENDS ON THE OTHER FOUR.
BUT WE CAN ALSO SAY...
...THAT IT LEAVES THE HEAVY LIFTING TO THE OTHERS.
IF THE GAME TODAY ENDED UP BEING AN UNIMAGINABLE BLOWOUT...
...THEN WE COULD CHALK IT UP TO THE SKILL DIFFERENCE BETWEEN FIRST- AND SECOND-YEARS.
SORRY IF THAT SOUNDS HARSH...
WITH HIS CURRENT STYLE, HE'S BASICALLY DEPENDENT ON OTHERS GETTING STRONGER.
HE'S NOT MAKING USE OF HIS OWN POTENTIAL OR GROWING IN ANY WAY.
WHAT HE NEEDS TO BREAK PAST THIS WALL...
...IS TO LEAVE HIS CURRENT STYLE BEHIND.

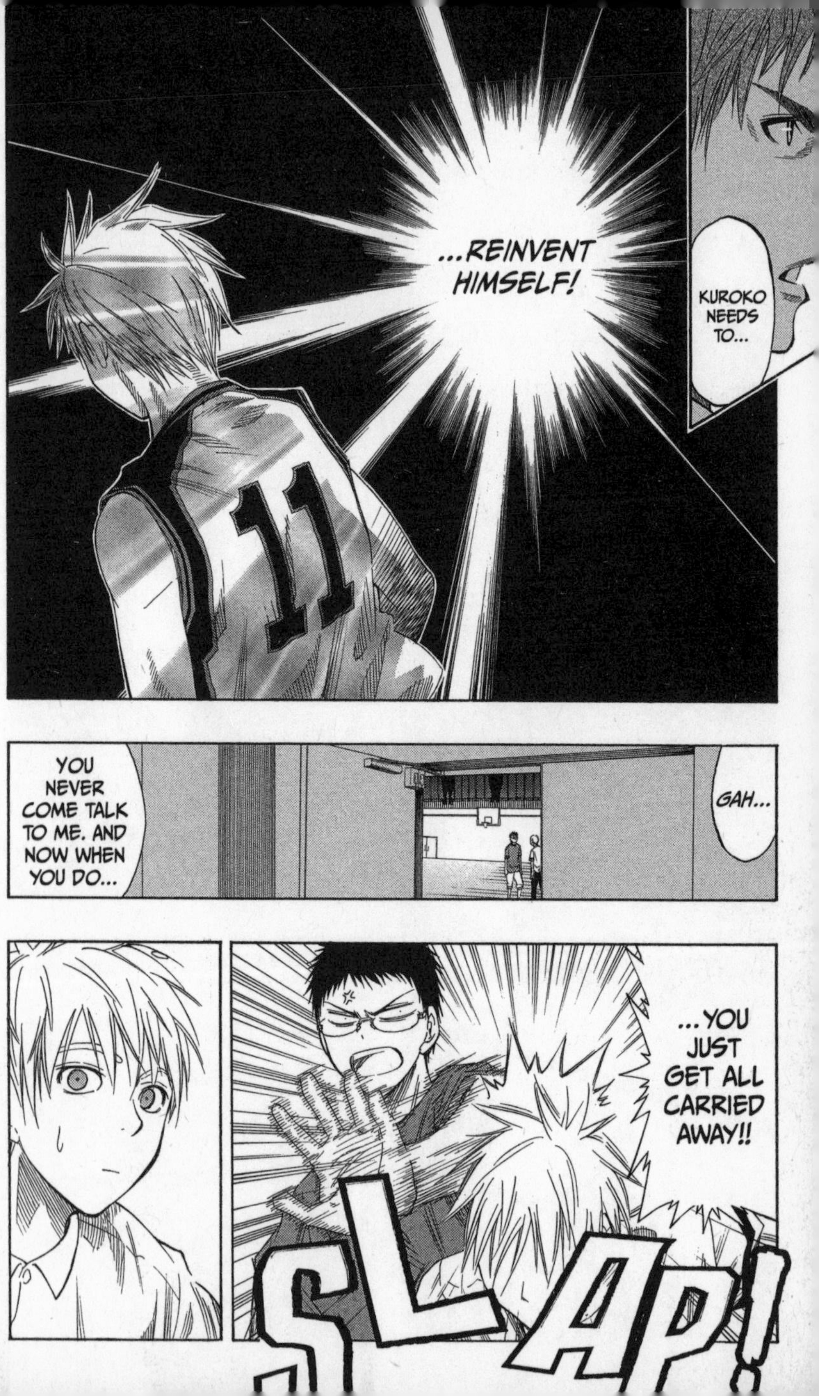
KUROKO NEEDS TO...
...REINVENT HIMSELF!
GAH...
YOU NEVER COME TALK TO ME. AND NOW WHEN YOU DO...
...YOU JUST GET ALL CARRIED AWAY!!
SLAP!

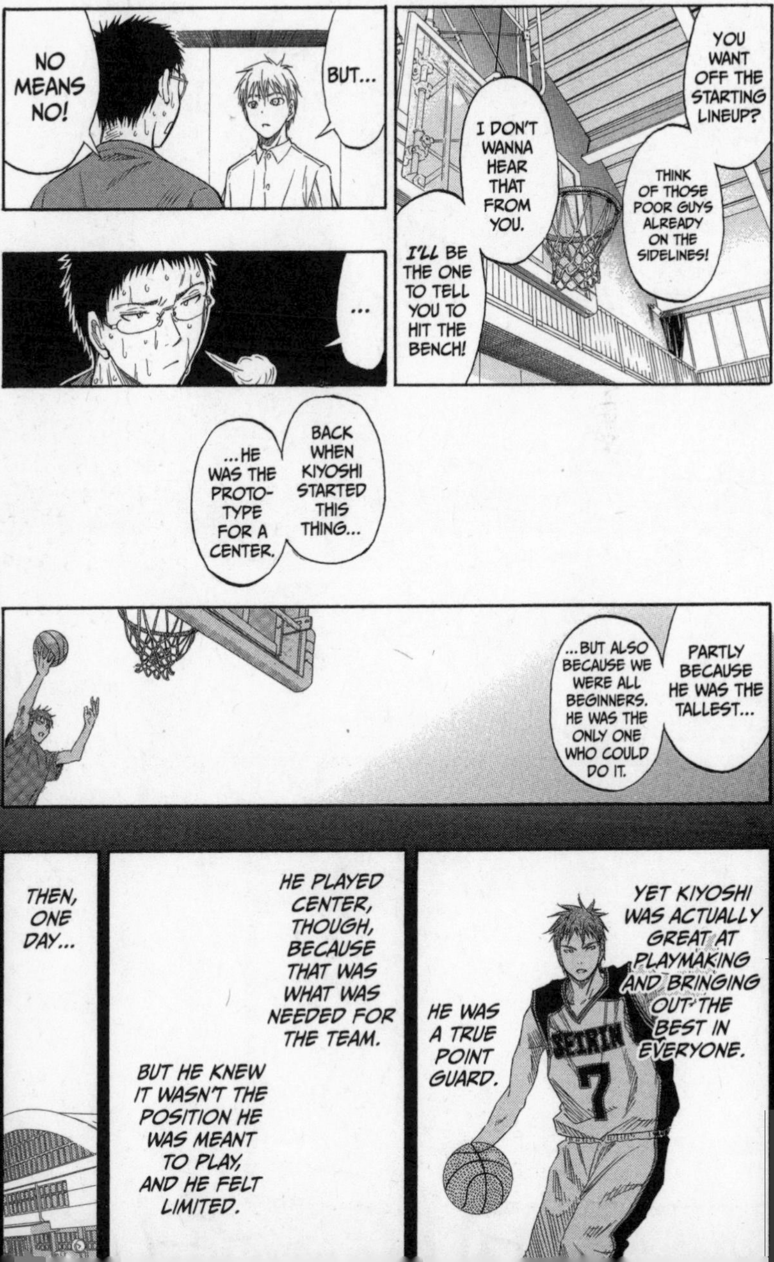

YOU WANT OFF THE STARTING LINEUP?
THINK OF THOSE POOR GUYS ALREADY ON THE SIDELINES!
I DON'T WANNA HEAR THAT FROM YOU.
I'LL BE THE ONE TO TELL YOU TO HIT THE BENCH!
BUT...
NO MEANS NO!
...
BACK WHEN KIYOSHI STARTED THIS THING...
...HE WAS THE PROTO-TYPE FOR A CENTER.
PARTLY BECAUSE HE WAS THE TALLEST...
...BUT ALSO BECAUSE WE WERE ALL BEGINNERS. HE WAS THE ONLY ONE WHO COULD DO IT.
YET KIYOSHI WAS ACTUALLY GREAT AT PLAYMAKING AND BRINGING OUT THE BEST IN EVERYONE.
SEIRIN
7
HE WAS A TRUE POINT GUARD.
HE PLAYED CENTER, THOUGH, BECAUSE THAT WAS WHAT WAS NEEDED FOR THE TEAM.
BUT HE KNEW IT WASN'T THE POSITION HE WAS MEANT TO PLAY, AND HE FELT LIMITED.
THEN, ONE DAY...

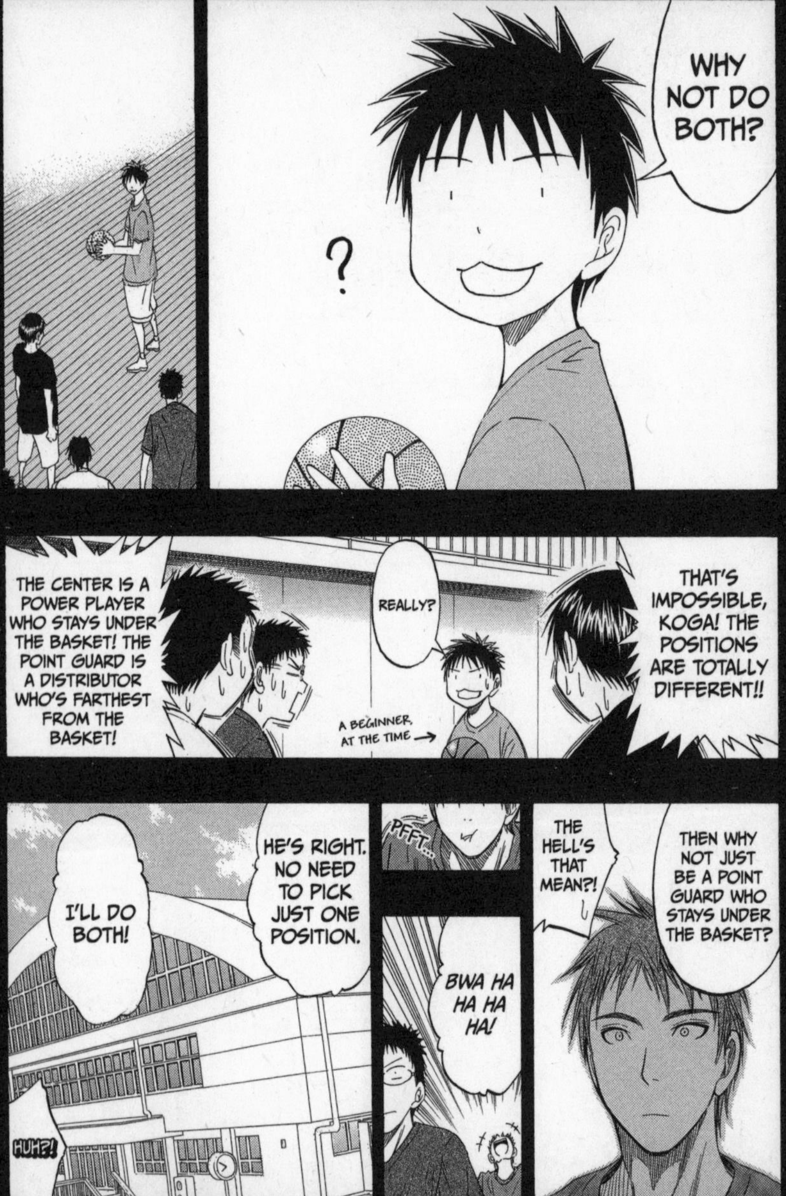
WHY NOT DO BOTH?
?
THAT'S IMPOSSIBLE, KOGA! THE POSITIONS ARE TOTALLY DIFFERENT!!
REALLY?
A BEGINNER, AT THE TIME
THE CENTER IS A POWER PLAYER WHO STAYS UNDER THE BASKET! THE POINT GUARD IS A DISTRIBUTOR WHO'S FARTHEST FROM THE BASKET!
THEN WHY NOT JUST BE A POINT GUARD WHO STAYS UNDER THE BASKET?
THE HELL'S THAT MEAN?!
PFFT...
BWA HA HA HA HA!
HE'S RIGHT. NO NEED TO PICK JUST ONE POSITION.
I'LL DO BOTH!
HUH?!

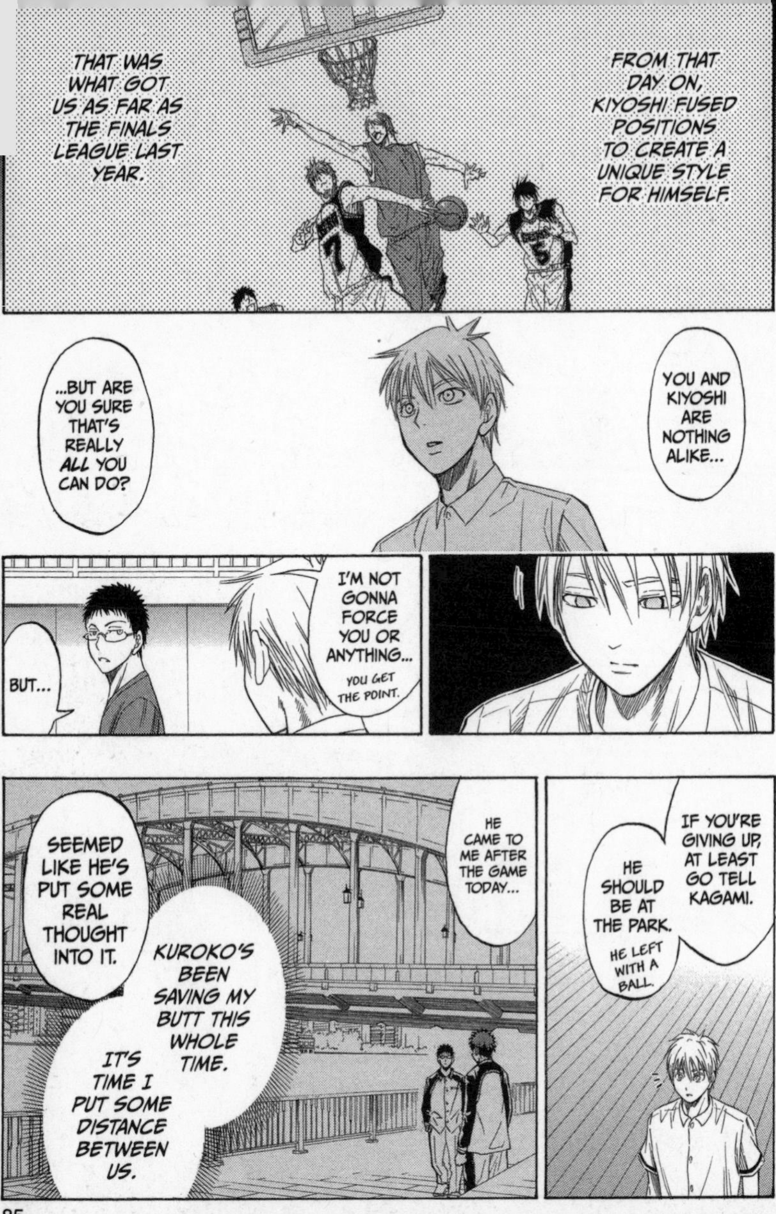
FROM THAT DAY ON, KIYOSHI FUSED POSITIONS TO CREATE A UNIQUE STYLE FOR HIMSELF.
THAT WAS WHAT GOT US AS FAR AS THE FINALS LEAGUE LAST YEAR.
YOU AND KIYOSHI ARE NOTHING ALIKE...
...BUT ARE YOU SURE THAT'S REALLY *ALL* YOU CAN DO?
I'M NOT GONNA FORCE YOU OR ANYTHING...
YOU GET THE POINT.
BUT...
IF YOU'RE GIVING UP, AT LEAST GO TELL KAGAMI.
HE SHOULD BE AT THE PARK.
HE LEFT WITH A BALL.
HE CAME TO ME AFTER THE GAME TODAY...
SEEMED LIKE HE'S PUT SOME REAL THOUGHT INTO IT.
KUROKO'S BEEN SAVING MY BUTT THIS WHOLE TIME.
IT'S TIME I PUT SOME DISTANCE BETWEEN US.

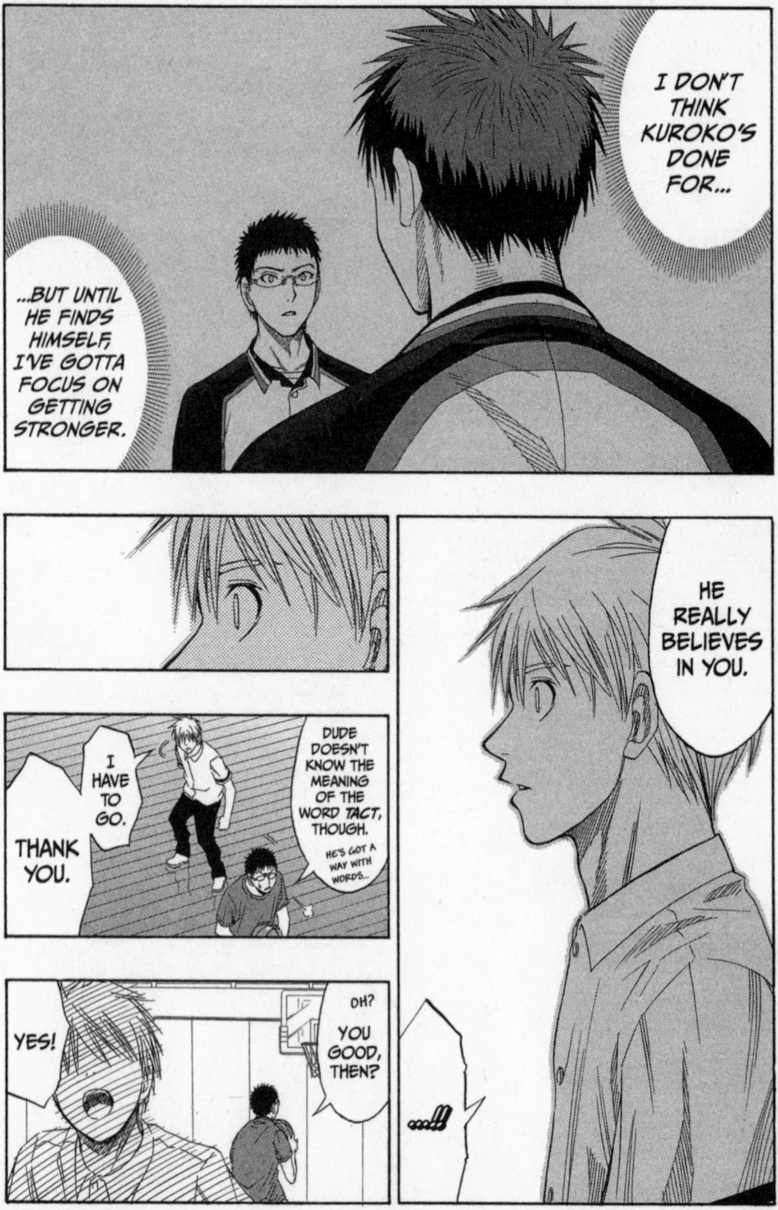
I DON'T THINK KUROKO'S DONE FOR...
...BUT UNTIL HE FINDS HIMSELF, I'VE GOTTA FOCUS ON GETTING STRONGER.
HE REALLY BELIEVES IN YOU.
...!!
DUDE DOESN'T KNOW THE MEANING OF THE WORD *TACT*, THOUGH.
HE'S GOT A WAY WITH WORDS...
I HAVE TO GO.
THANK YOU.
OH?
YOU GOOD, THEN?
YES!

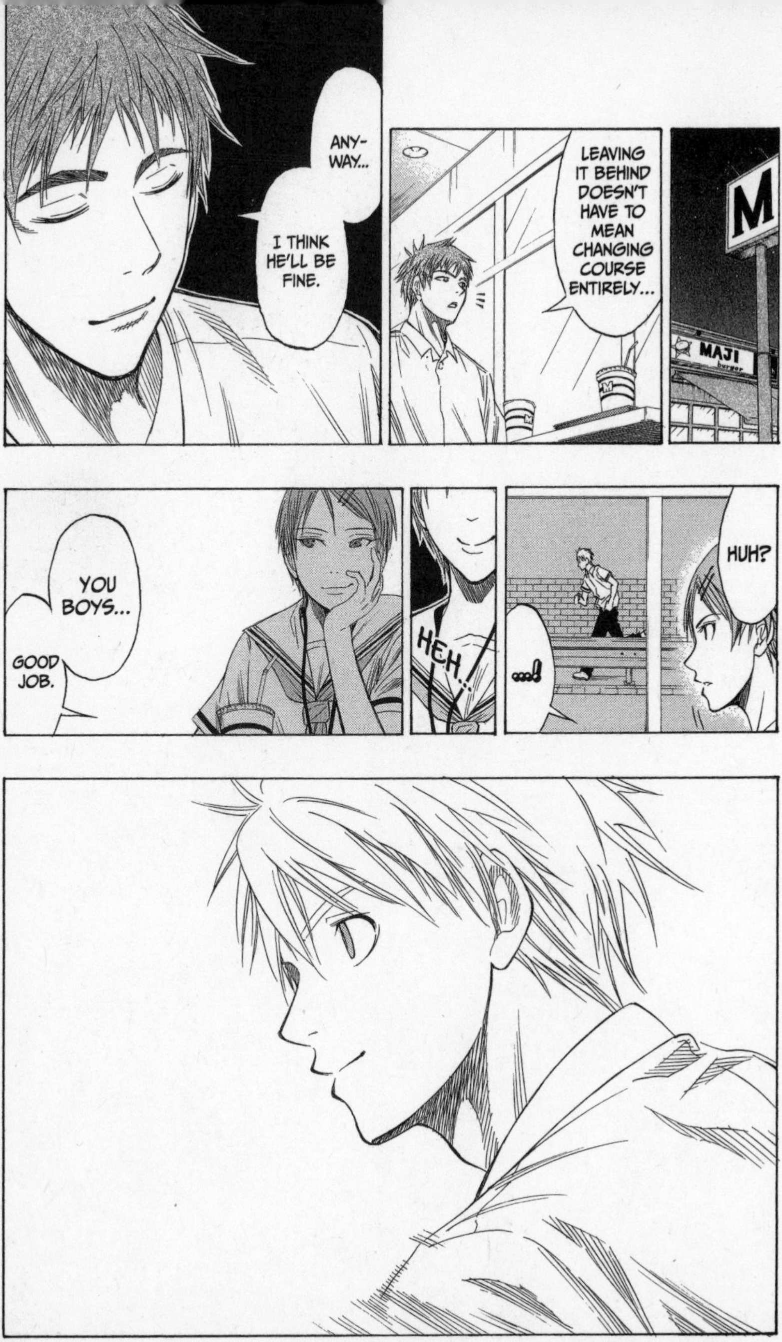
M
MAJI
burger
LEAVING IT BEHIND DOESN'T HAVE TO MEAN CHANGING COURSE ENTIRELY...
ANY-WAY...
I THINK HE'LL BE FINE.
HUH?
...!
HEH...
YOU BOYS...
GOOD JOB.

KUROKO'S BASKETBALL BLOOPERS

TAKE 3

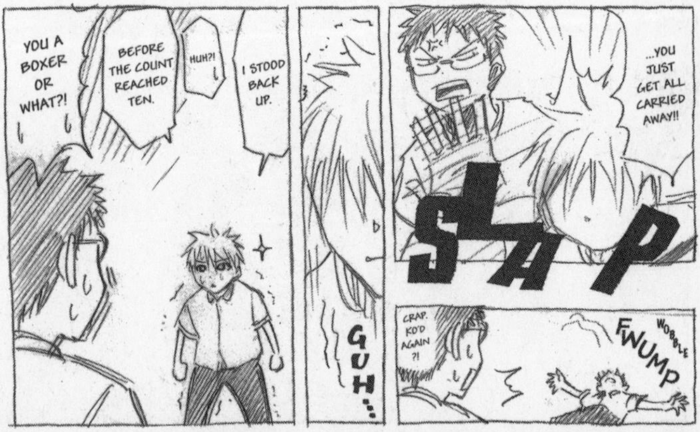
...YOU JUST GET ALL CARRIED AWAY!!
SLAP
CRAP. KO'D AGAIN?!
FWUMP
WOBBLE
GUH...
I STOOD BACK UP.
HUH?!
BEFORE THE COUNT REACHED TEN.
YOU A BOXER OR WHAT?!

BAP

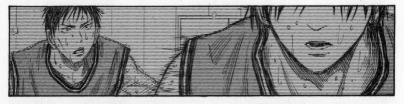

I KNOW HELP'S COMING.

THROUGH THE LEGS. DRIVE TO THE RIGHT. PASS THAT ONE GUY...

BAP

BUT I JUST COULDN'T.

I SHOULD PASS TO HIM. I KNOW.

I CAN SEE FURIHATA UNDER THE BASKET.

57TH QUARTER: NOT GONNA TRY

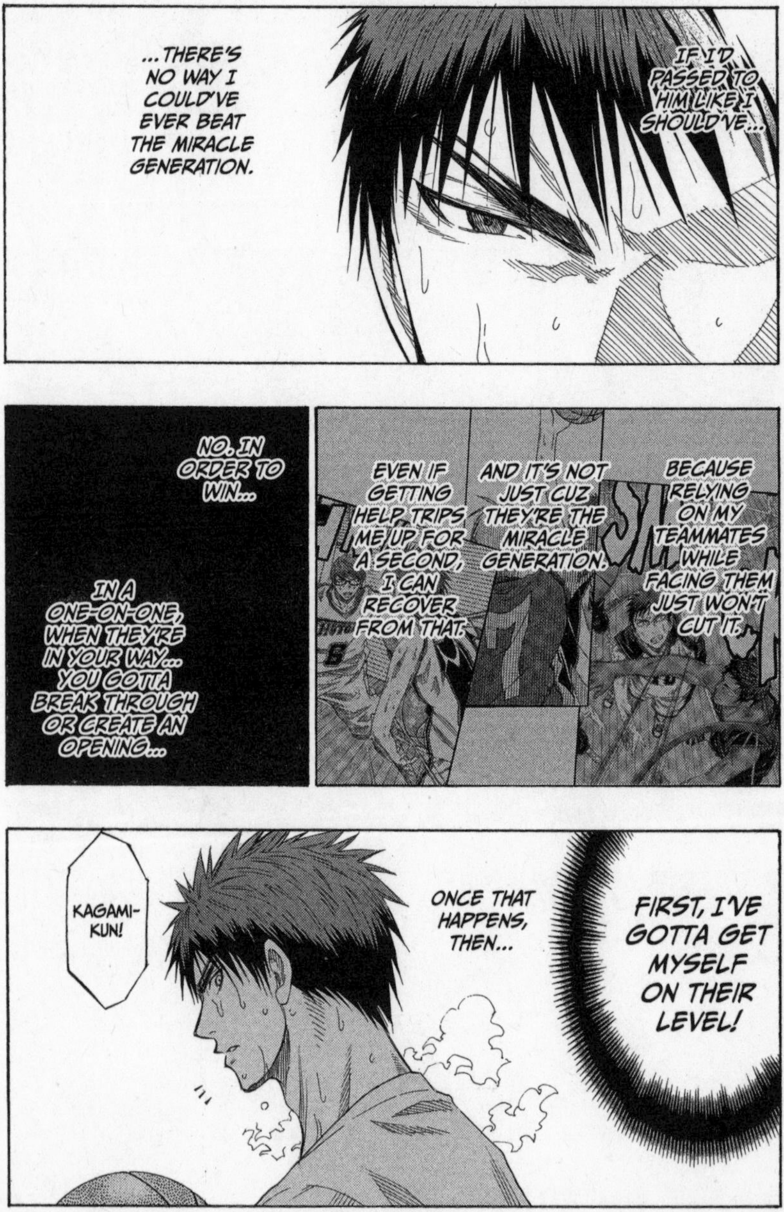
IF I'D PASSED TO HIM LIKE I SHOULD'VE...
...THERE'S NO WAY I COULD'VE EVER BEAT THE MIRACLE GENERATION.
BECAUSE RELYING ON MY TEAMMATES WHILE FACING THEM JUST WON'T CUT IT.
AND IT'S NOT JUST CUZ THEY'RE THE MIRACLE GENERATION.
EVEN IF GETTING HELP TRIPS ME UP FOR A SECOND, I CAN RECOVER FROM THAT.
NO. IN ORDER TO WIN...
IN A ONE-ON-ONE, WHEN THEY'RE IN YOUR WAY... YOU GOTTA BREAK THROUGH OR CREATE AN OPENING...
FIRST, I'VE GOTTA GET MYSELF ON THEIR LEVEL!
ONCE THAT HAPPENS, THEN...
KAGAMI-KUN!

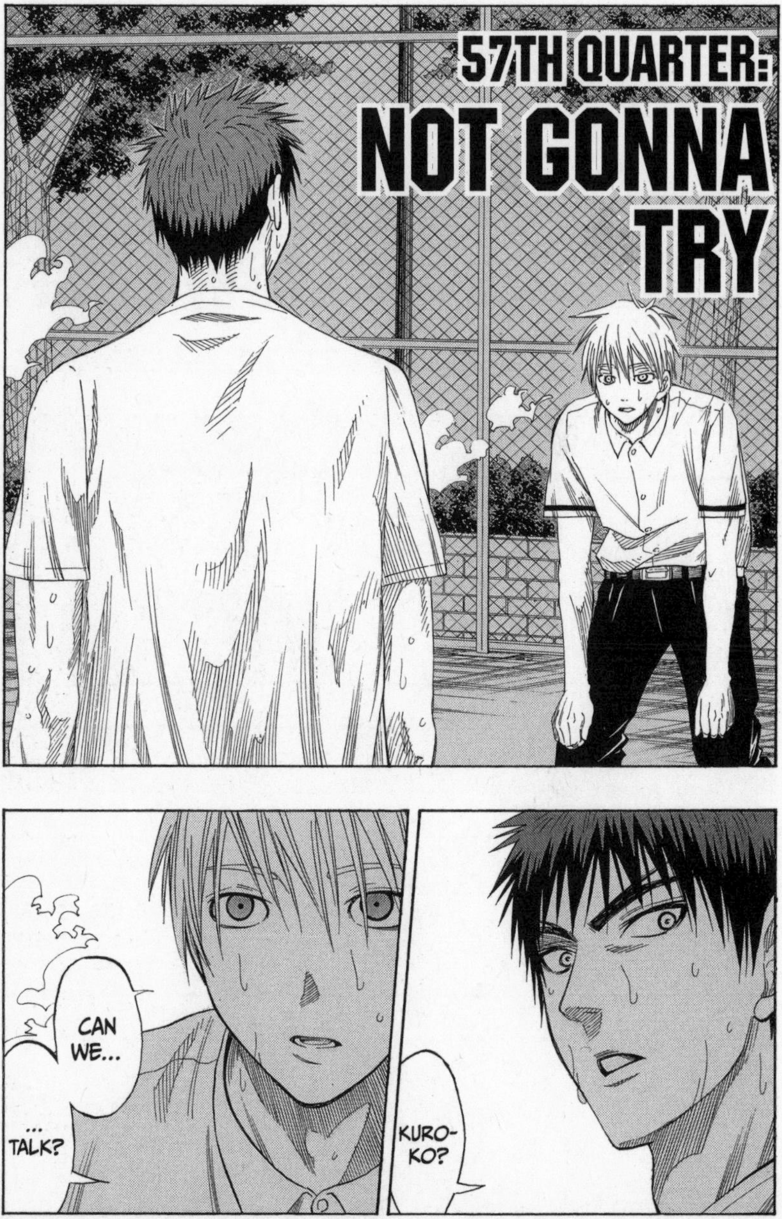
57TH QUARTER:
NOT GONNA TRY
KURO-KO?
CAN WE...
...TALK?

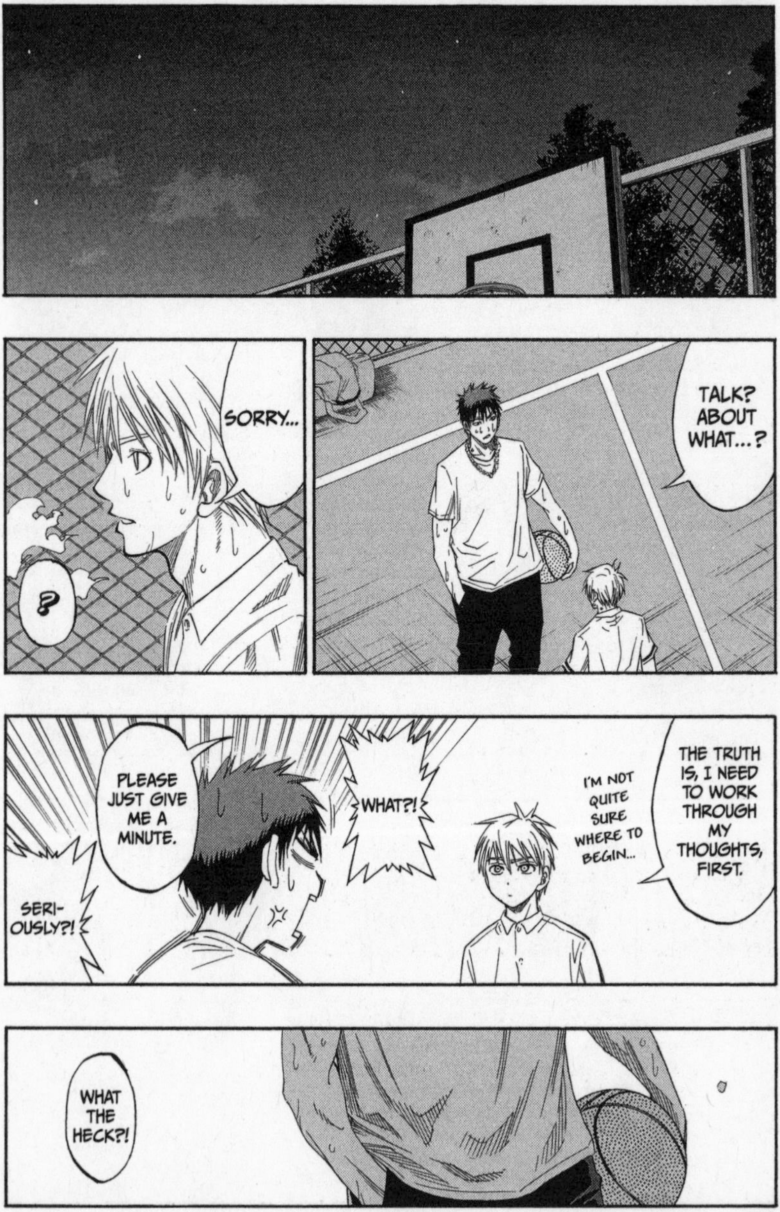
TALK? ABOUT WHAT...?
SORRY...
?
THE TRUTH IS, I NEED TO WORK THROUGH MY THOUGHTS, FIRST.
I'M NOT QUITE SURE WHERE TO BEGIN...
WHAT?!
PLEASE JUST GIVE ME A MINUTE.
SERI-OUSLY?!
WHAT THE HECK?!

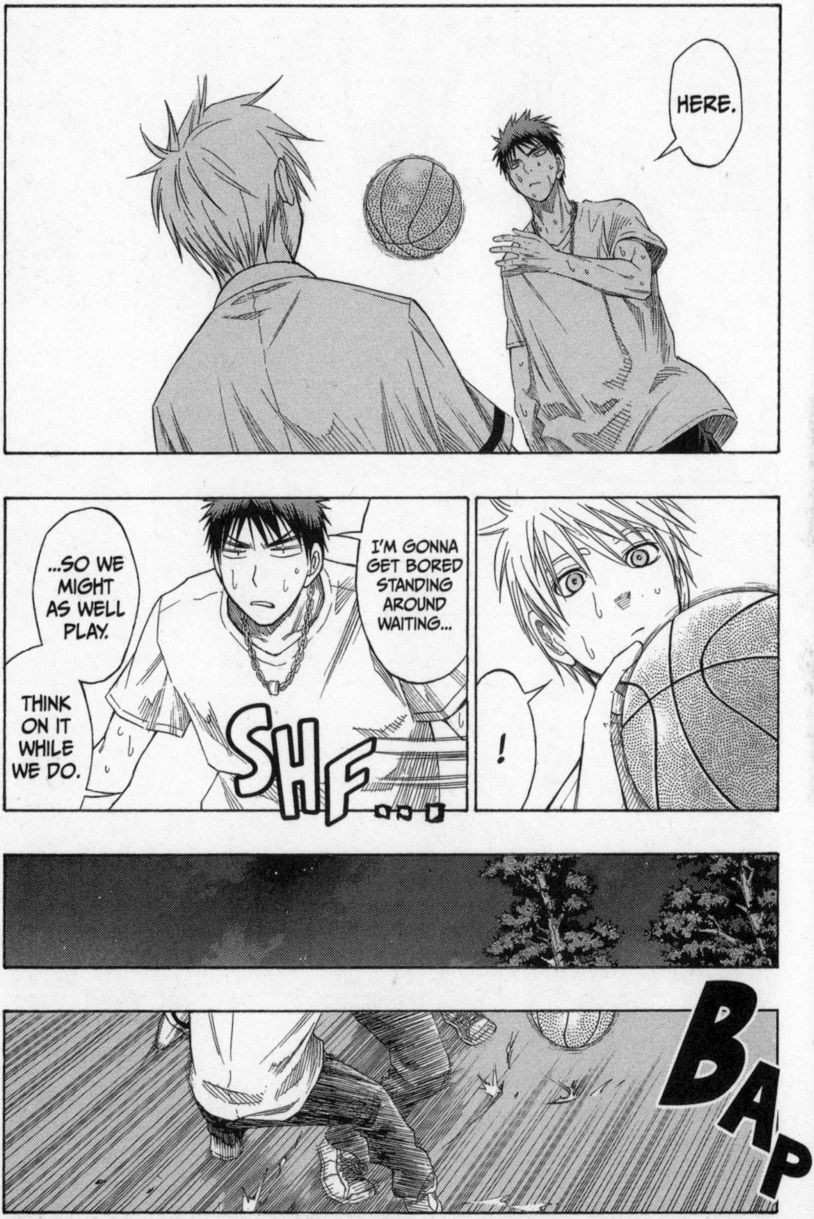
HERE.
!
I'M GONNA GET BORED STANDING AROUND WAITING...
...SO WE MIGHT AS WELL PLAY.
THINK ON IT WHILE WE DO.
SHF...
BAP

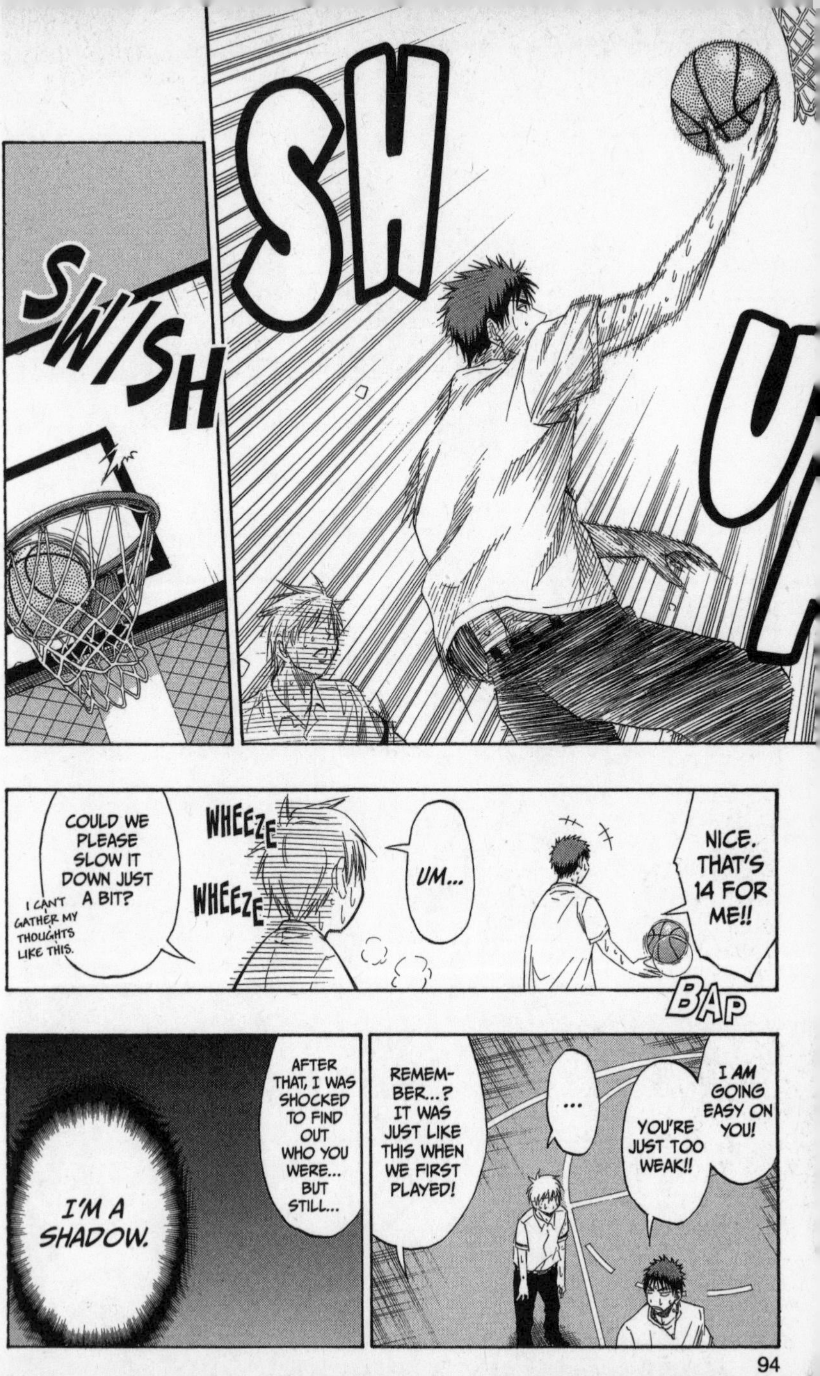
SH
SWISH
NICE. THAT'S 14 FOR ME!!
BAP
UM...
WHEEZE
WHEEZE
COULD WE PLEASE SLOW IT DOWN JUST A BIT?
I CAN'T GATHER MY THOUGHTS LIKE THIS.
I *AM* GOING EASY ON YOU!
YOU'RE JUST TOO WEAK!!
...
REMEMBER...? IT WAS JUST LIKE THIS WHEN WE FIRST PLAYED!
AFTER THAT, I WAS SHOCKED TO FIND OUT WHO YOU WERE... BUT STILL...
I'M A SHADOW.

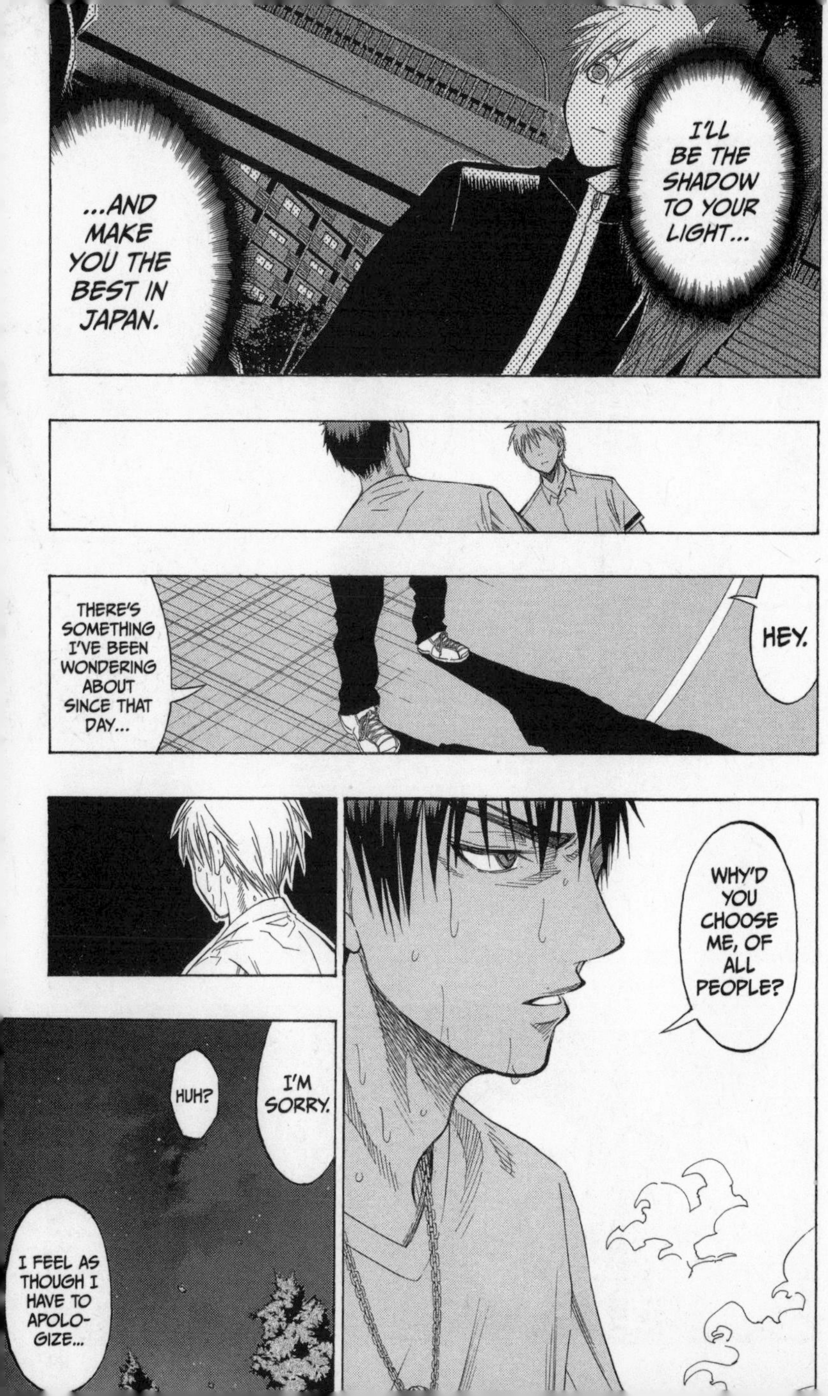
I'LL BE THE SHADOW TO YOUR LIGHT...
...AND MAKE YOU THE BEST IN JAPAN.
HEY.
THERE'S SOMETHING I'VE BEEN WONDERING ABOUT SINCE THAT DAY...
WHY'D YOU CHOOSE ME, OF ALL PEOPLE?
I'M SORRY.
HUH?
I FEEL AS THOUGH I HAVE TO APOLOGIZE...

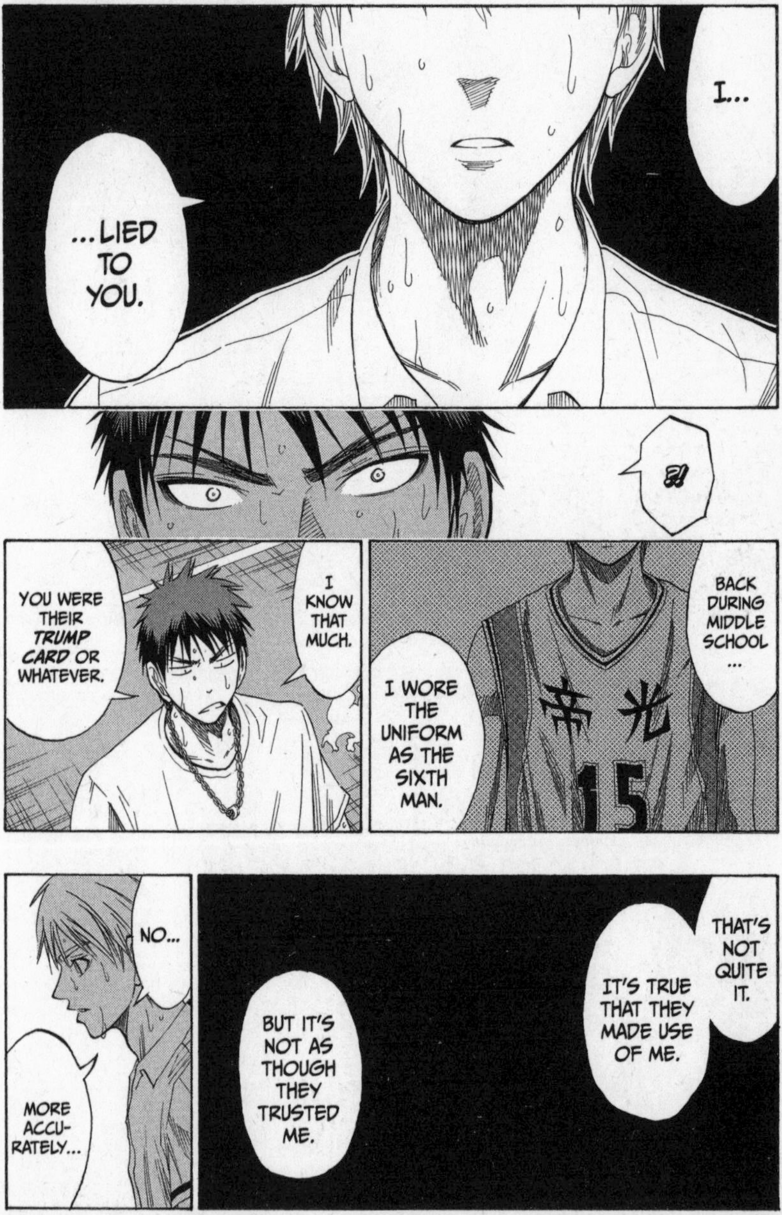
I...
...LIED TO YOU.
?!
BACK DURING MIDDLE SCHOOL...
I WORE THE UNIFORM AS THE SIXTH MAN.
I KNOW THAT MUCH.
YOU WERE THEIR TRUMP CARD OR WHATEVER.
THAT'S NOT QUITE IT.
IT'S TRUE THAT THEY MADE USE OF ME.
BUT IT'S NOT AS THOUGH THEY TRUSTED ME.
NO...
MORE ACCU-RATELY...

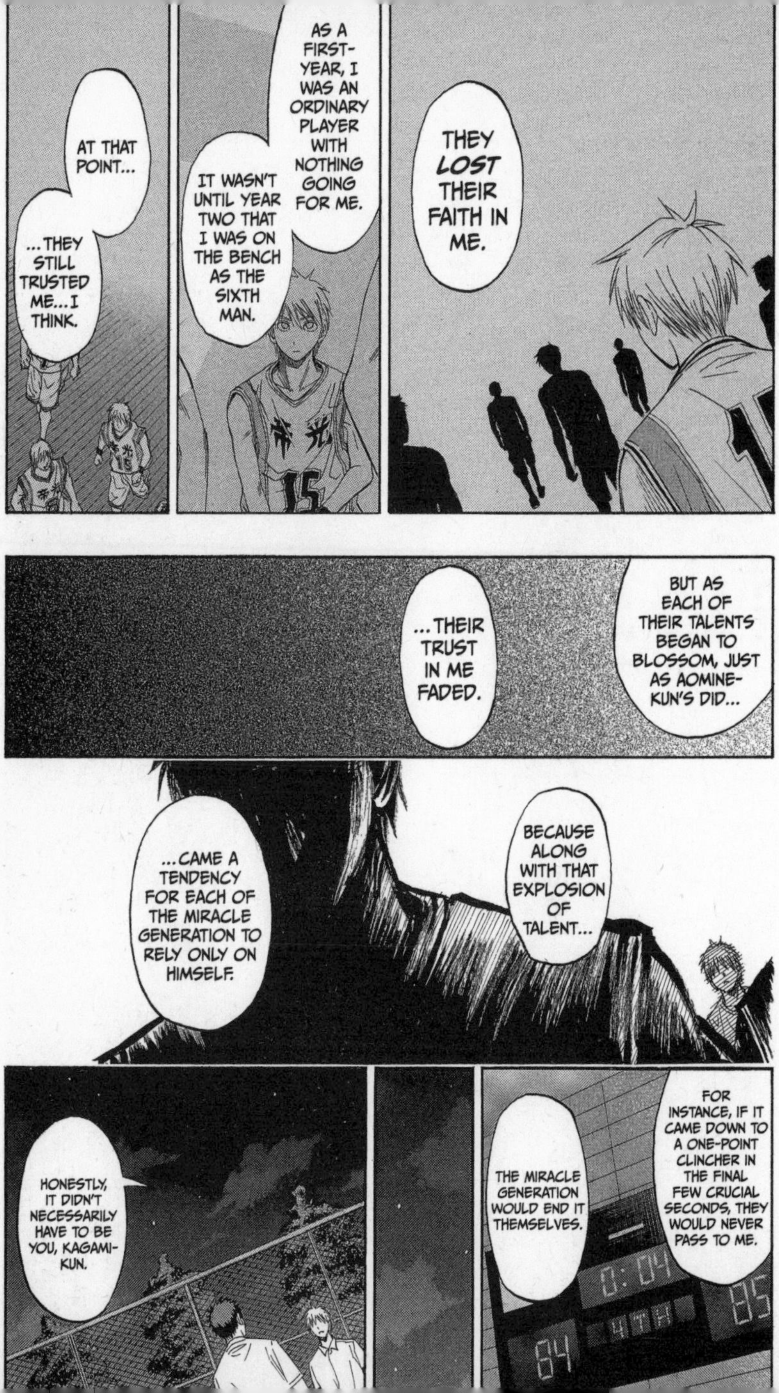
THEY LOST THEIR FAITH IN ME.
AS A FIRST-YEAR, I WAS AN ORDINARY PLAYER WITH NOTHING GOING FOR ME.
IT WASN'T UNTIL YEAR TWO THAT I WAS ON THE BENCH AS THE SIXTH MAN.
AT THAT POINT...
...THEY STILL TRUSTED ME...I THINK.
BUT AS EACH OF THEIR TALENTS BEGAN TO BLOSSOM, JUST AS AOMINE-KUN'S DID...
...THEIR TRUST IN ME FADED.
BECAUSE ALONG WITH THAT EXPLOSION OF TALENT...
...CAME A TENDENCY FOR EACH OF THE MIRACLE GENERATION TO RELY ONLY ON HIMSELF.
FOR INSTANCE, IF IT CAME DOWN TO A ONE-POINT CLINCHER IN THE FINAL FEW CRUCIAL SECONDS, THEY WOULD NEVER PASS TO ME.
THE MIRACLE GENERATION WOULD END IT THEMSELVES.
0:04
85
4TH
64
HONESTLY, IT DIDN'T NECESSARILY HAVE TO BE YOU, KAGAMI-KUN.

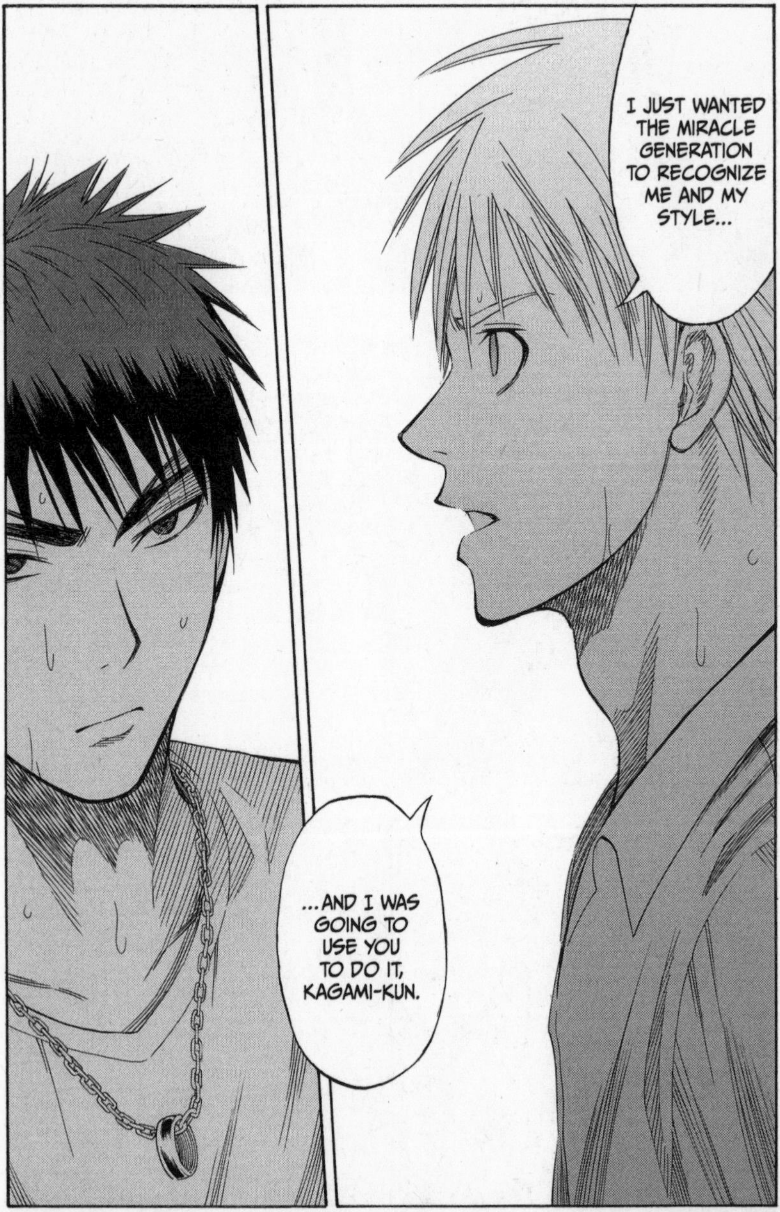
I JUST WANTED THE MIRACLE GENERATION TO RECOGNIZE ME AND MY STYLE...
...AND I WAS GOING TO USE YOU TO DO IT, KAGAMI-KUN.

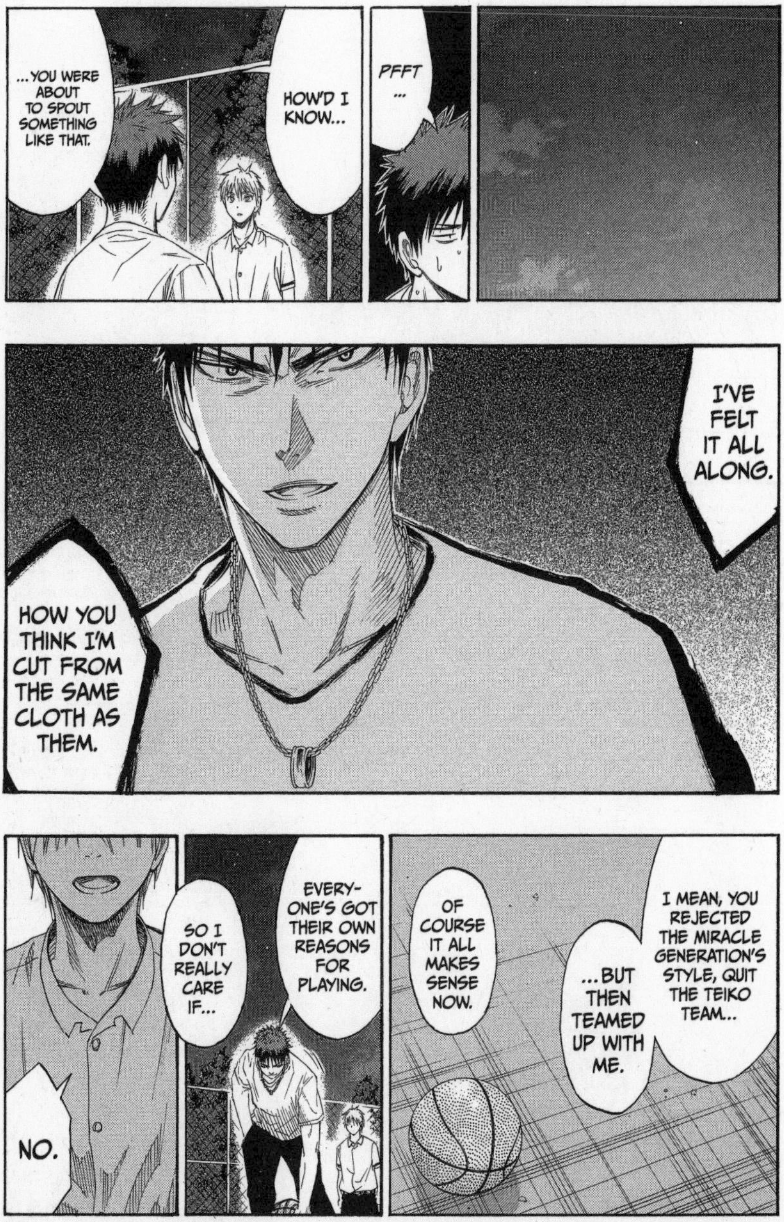
PFFT ...
HOW'D I KNOW...
...YOU WERE ABOUT TO SPOUT SOMETHING LIKE THAT.
I'VE FELT IT ALL ALONG.
HOW YOU THINK I'M CUT FROM THE SAME CLOTH AS THEM.
I MEAN, YOU REJECTED THE MIRACLE GENERATION'S STYLE, QUIT THE TEIKO TEAM...
...BUT THEN TEAMED UP WITH ME.
OF COURSE IT ALL MAKES SENSE NOW.
EVERYONE'S GOT THEIR OWN REASONS FOR PLAYING.
SO I DON'T REALLY CARE IF...
NO.

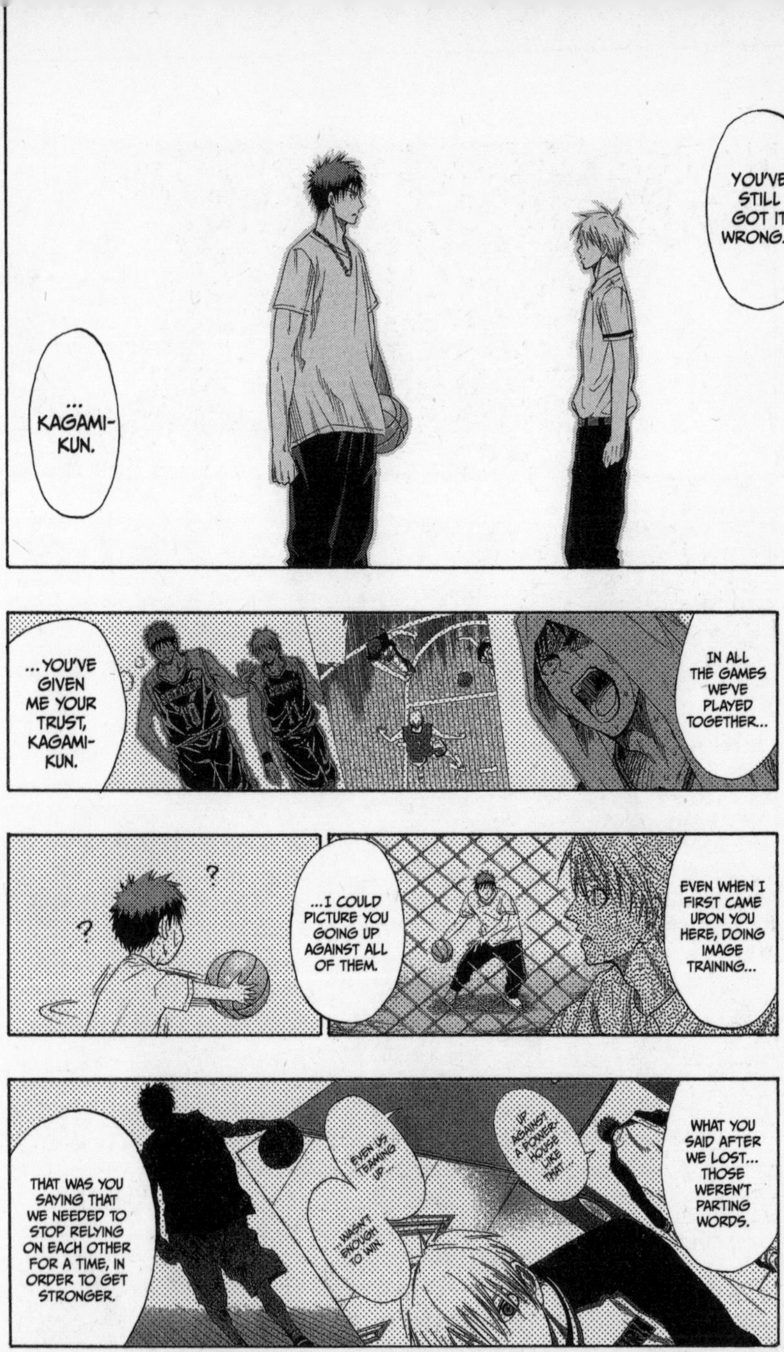
YOU'VE STILL GOT IT WRONG...
...KAGAMI-KUN.
IN ALL THE GAMES WE'VE PLAYED TOGETHER...
...YOU'VE GIVEN ME YOUR TRUST, KAGAMI-KUN.
EVEN WHEN I FIRST CAME UPON YOU HERE, DOING IMAGE TRAINING...
...I COULD PICTURE YOU GOING UP AGAINST ALL OF THEM.
WHAT YOU SAID AFTER WE LOST... THOSE WEREN'T PARTING WORDS.
UP AGAINST A POWERHOUSE LIKE THAT...
EVEN US TEAMING UP...
WASN'T ENOUGH TO WIN.
THAT WAS YOU SAYING THAT WE NEEDED TO STOP RELYING ON EACH OTHER FOR A TIME, IN ORDER TO GET STRONGER.

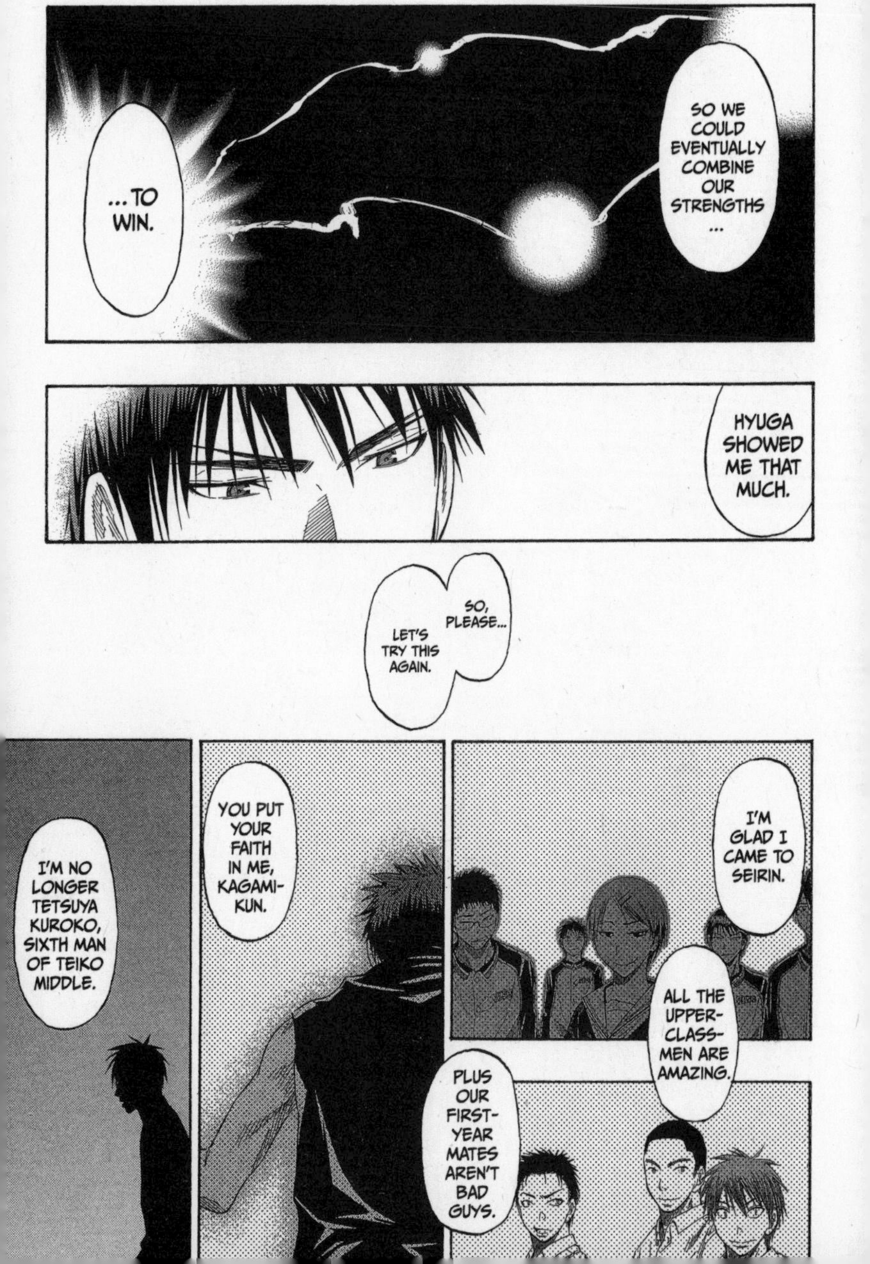
SO WE COULD EVENTUALLY COMBINE OUR STRENGTHS ...
...TO WIN.
HYUGA SHOWED ME THAT MUCH.
SO, PLEASE...
LET'S TRY THIS AGAIN.
I'M GLAD I CAME TO SEIRIN.
ALL THE UPPER-CLASS-MEN ARE AMAZING.
PLUS OUR FIRST-YEAR MATES AREN'T BAD GUYS.
YOU PUT YOUR FAITH IN ME, KAGAMI-KUN.
I'M NO LONGER TETSUYA KUROKO, SIXTH MAN OF TEIKO MIDDLE.

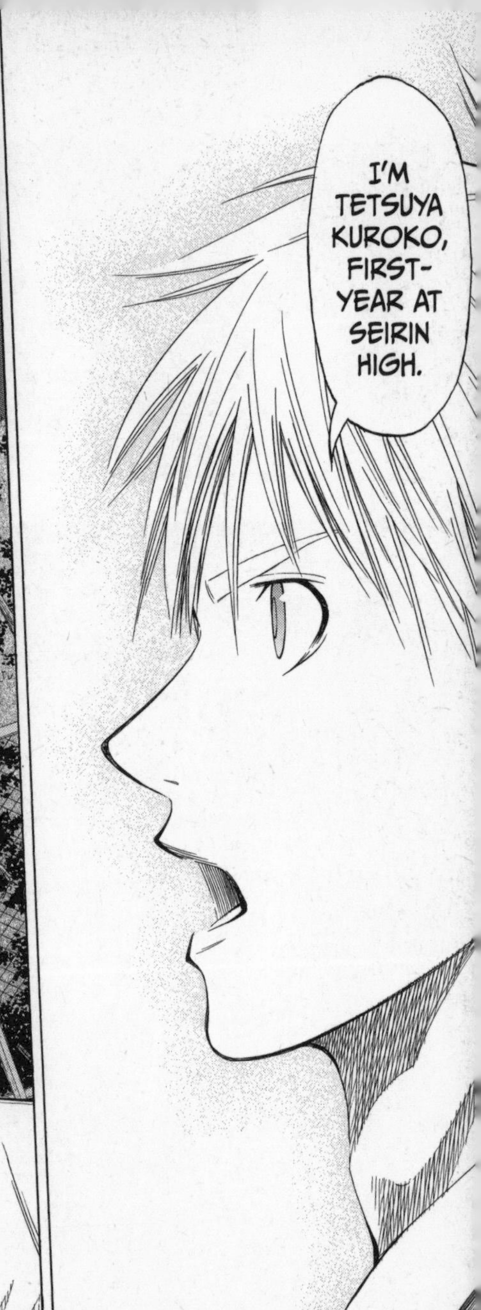
I'M TETSUYA KUROKO, FIRST-YEAR AT SEIRIN HIGH.

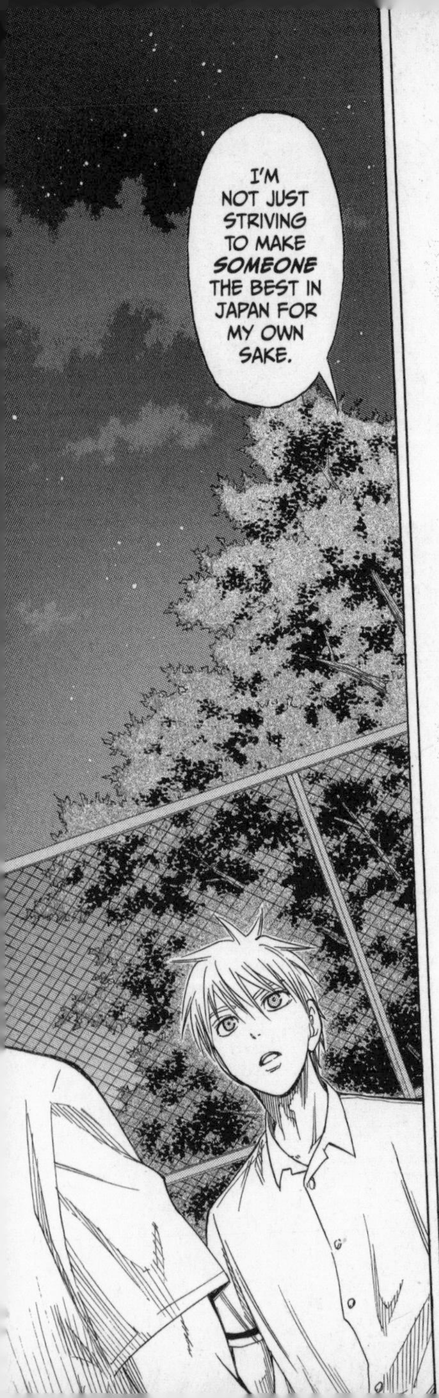
I'M NOT JUST STRIVING TO MAKE *SOMEONE* THE BEST IN JAPAN FOR MY OWN SAKE.

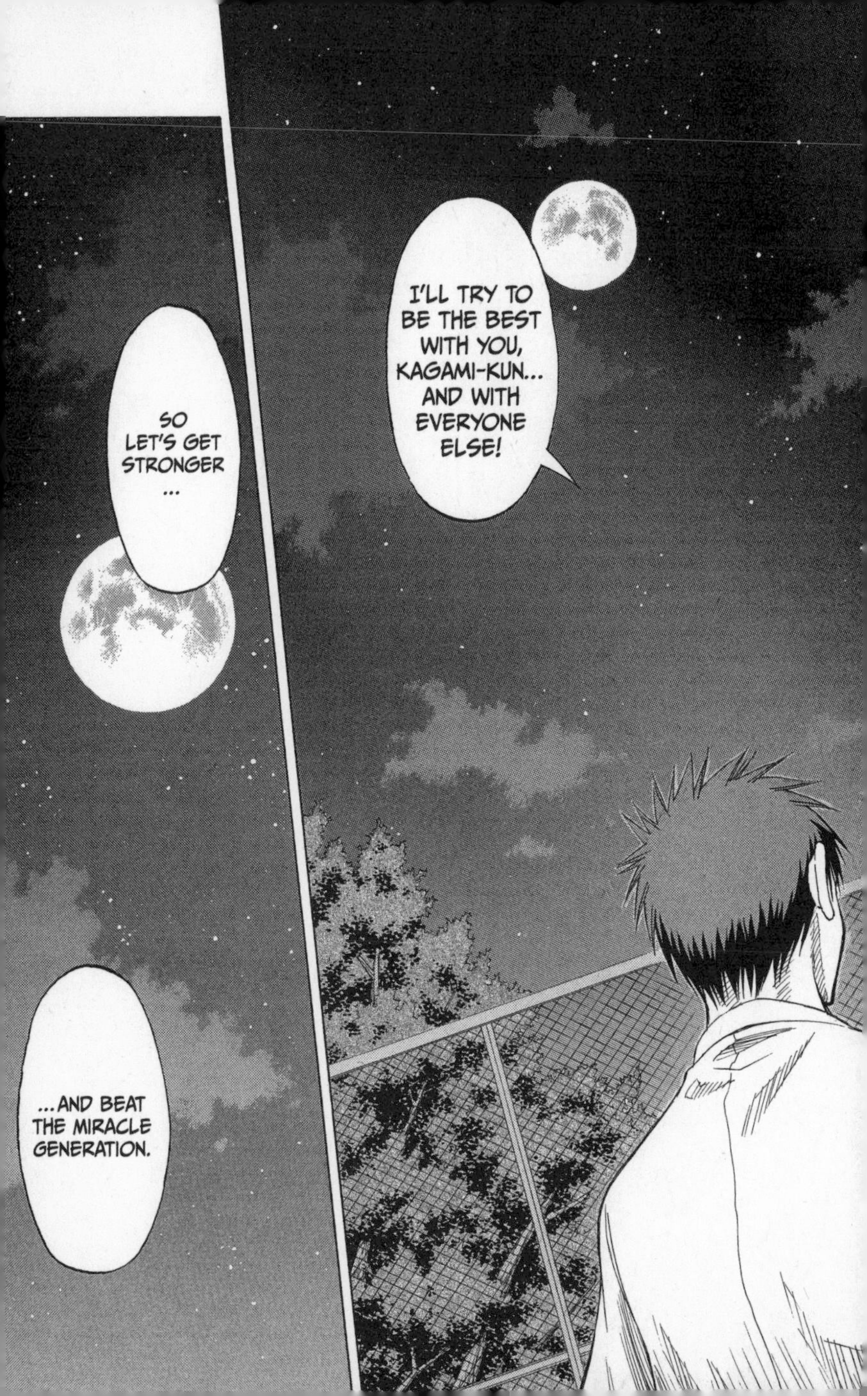
I'LL TRY TO BE THE BEST WITH YOU, KAGAMI-KUN... AND WITH EVERYONE ELSE!
SO LET'S GET STRONGER ...
...AND BEAT THE MIRACLE GENERATION.

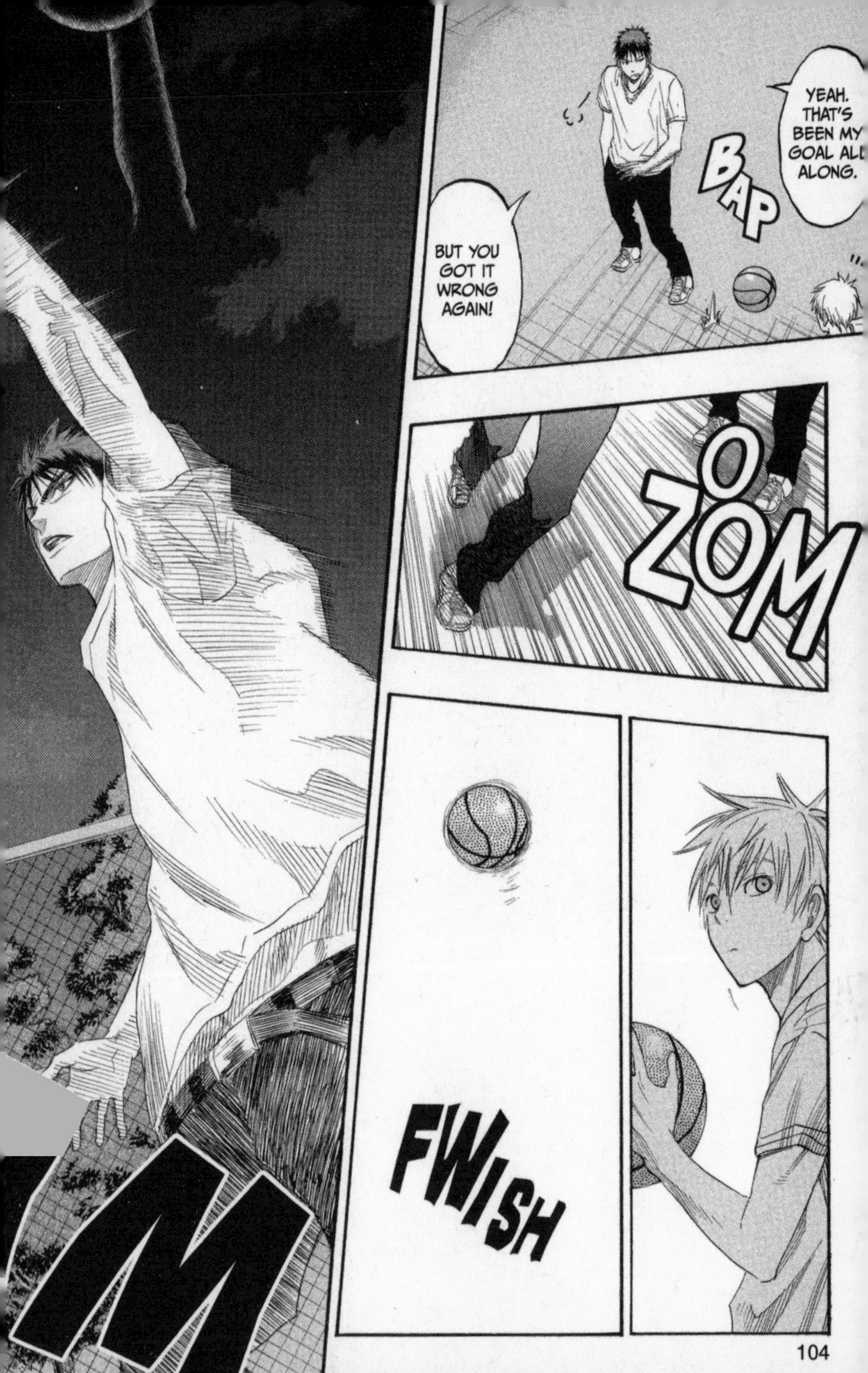
YEAH. THAT'S BEEN MY GOAL ALL ALONG.
BAP
BUT YOU GOT IT WRONG AGAIN!
ZOM
FWISH
M

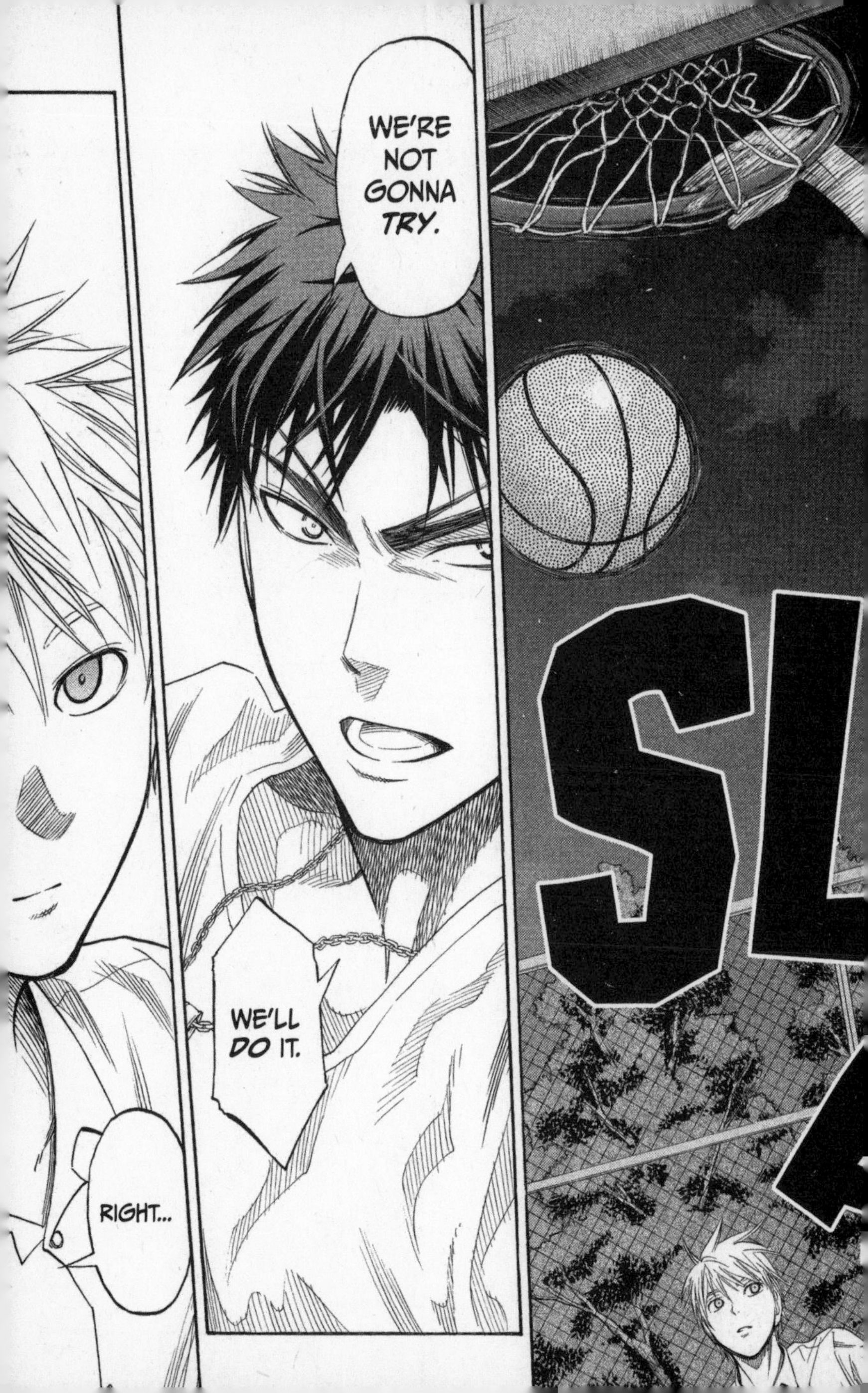
SL
WE'RE NOT GONNA TRY.
WE'LL DO IT.
RIGHT...

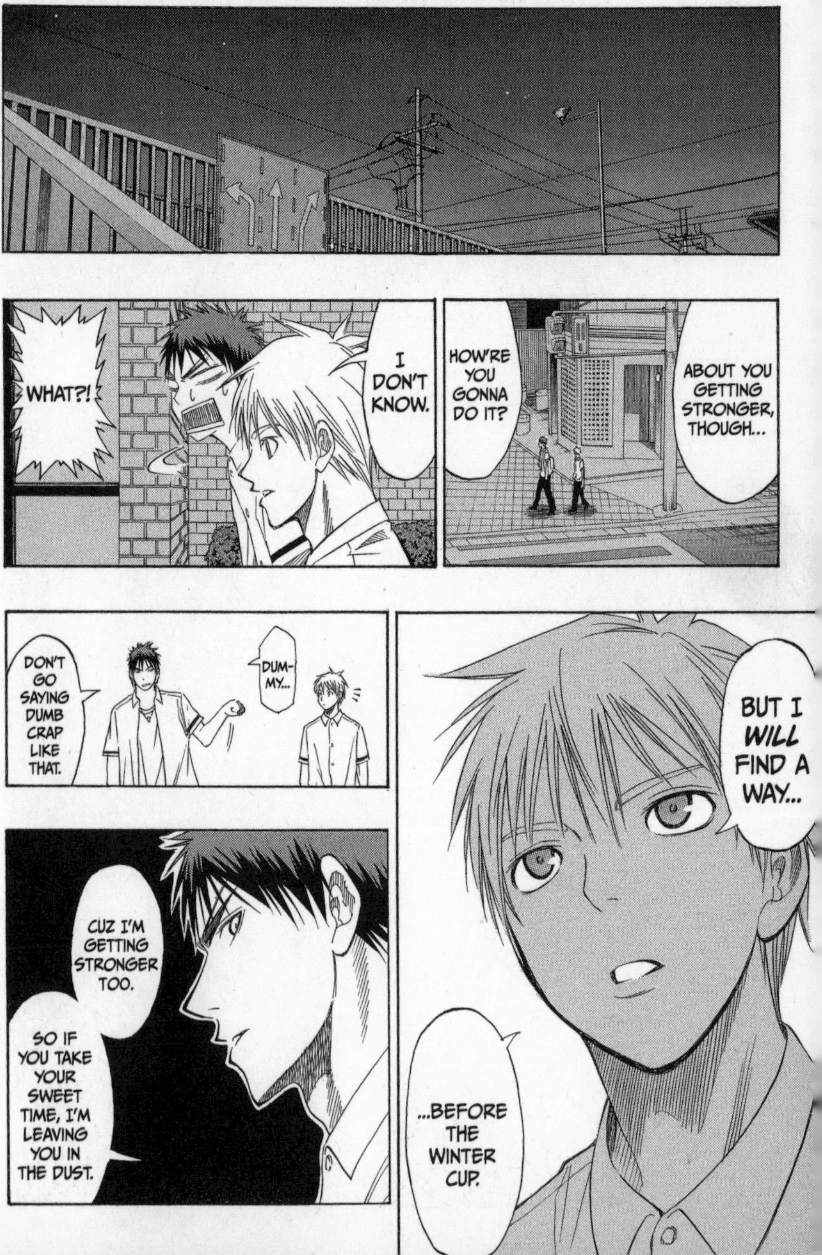
ABOUT YOU GETTING STRONGER, THOUGH...
HOW'RE YOU GONNA DO IT?
I DON'T KNOW.
WHAT?!
BUT I *WILL* FIND A WAY...
...BEFORE THE WINTER CUP.
DUM-MY...
DON'T GO SAYING DUMB CRAP LIKE THAT.
CUZ I'M GETTING STRONGER TOO.
SO IF YOU TAKE YOUR SWEET TIME, I'M LEAVING YOU IN THE DUST.

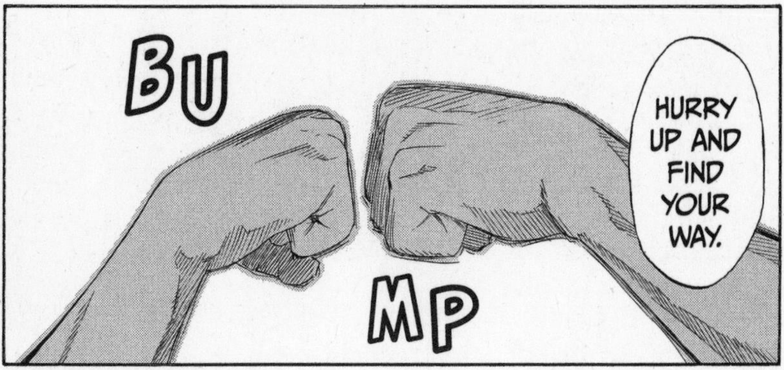
HURRY UP AND FIND YOUR WAY.
BUMP

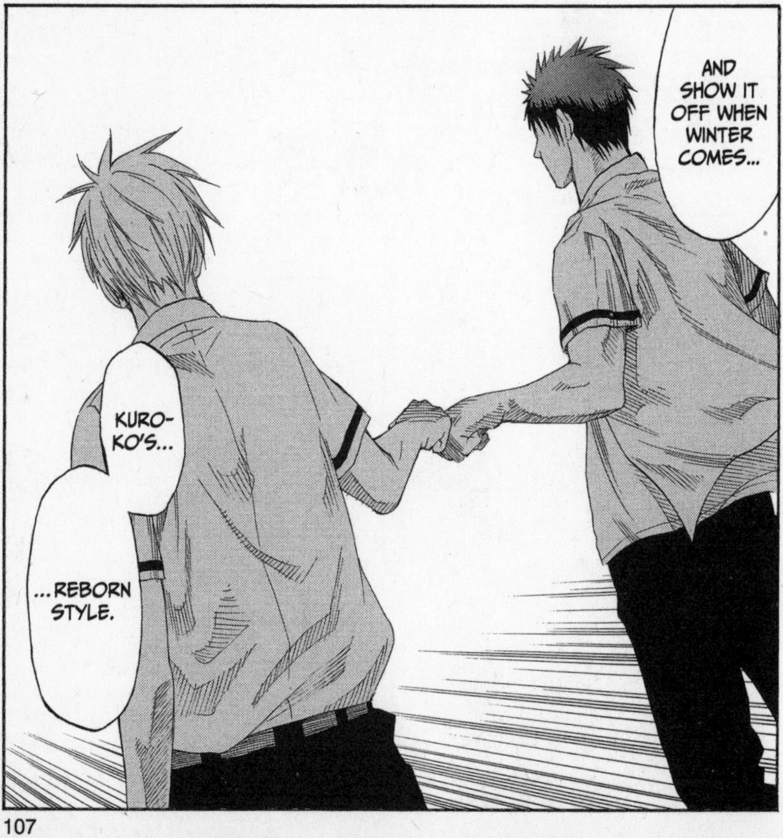
AND SHOW IT OFF WHEN WINTER COMES...
KURO-KO'S...
...REBORN STYLE.

KUROKO'S BASKETBALL BLOOPERS

TAKE 1

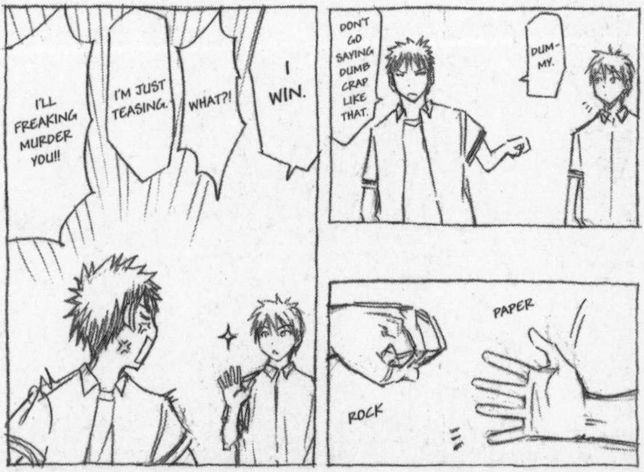
DUM-MY.
DON'T GO SAYING DUMB CRAP LIKE THAT.
PAPER
ROCK
I WIN.
WHAT?!
I'M JUST TEASING.
I'LL FREAKING MURDER YOU!!

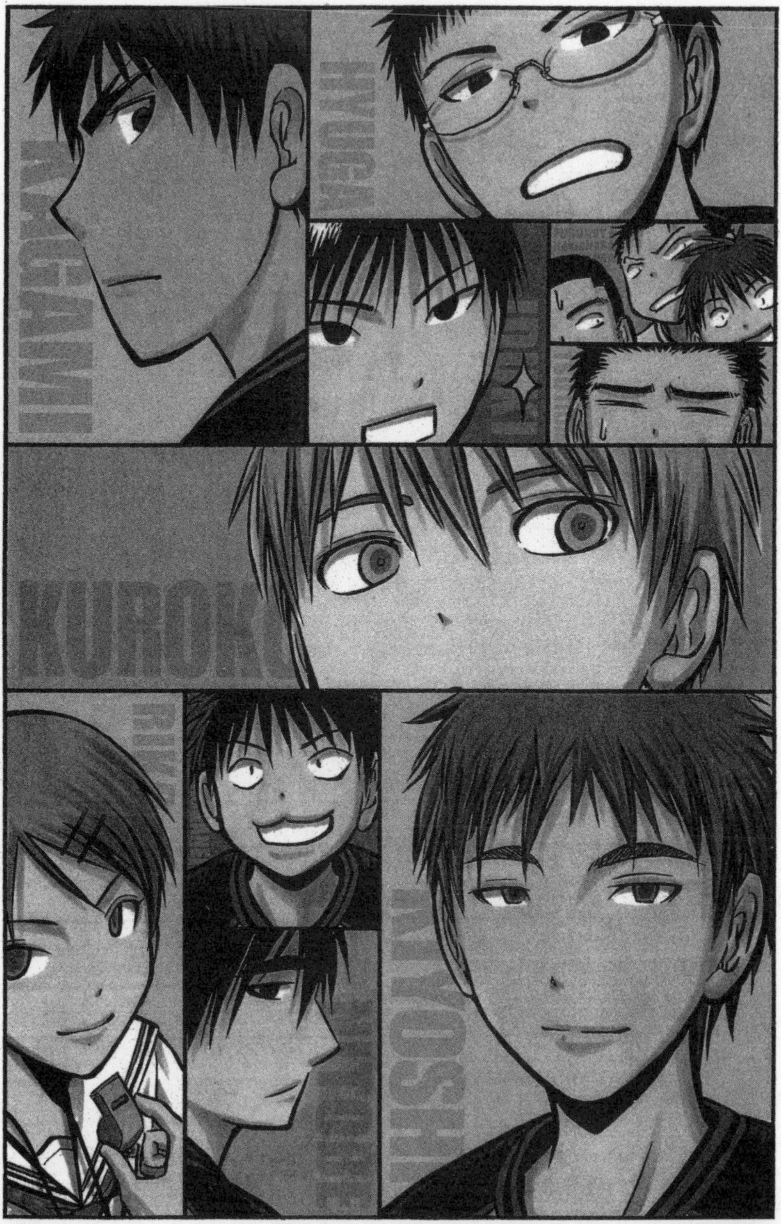
HYUGA
KAGAMI
KUROKO
KIYOSHI

58TH QUARTER: LEAVE IT TO ME!

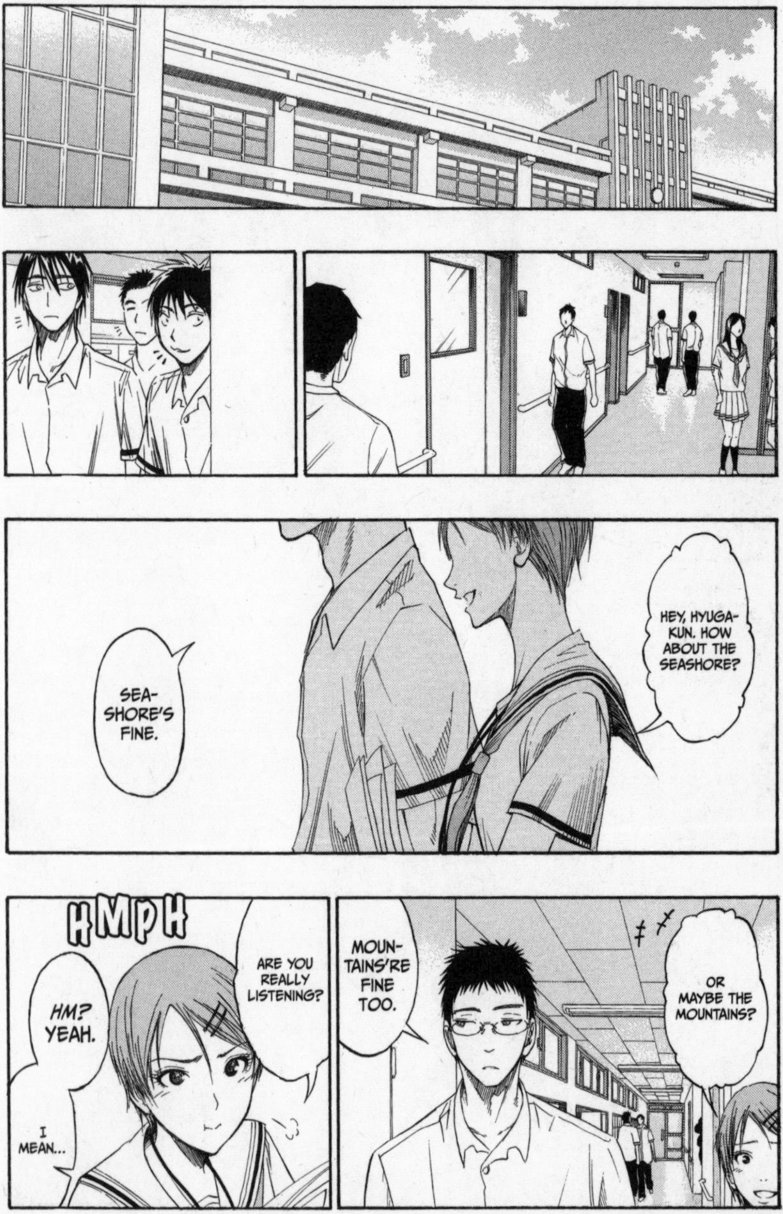
HEY, HYUGA-KUN. HOW ABOUT THE SEASHORE?
SEA-SHORE'S FINE.
OR MAYBE THE MOUNTAINS?
MOUN-TAINS'RE FINE TOO.
ARE YOU REALLY LISTENING?
HMPH
HM? YEAH.
I MEAN...

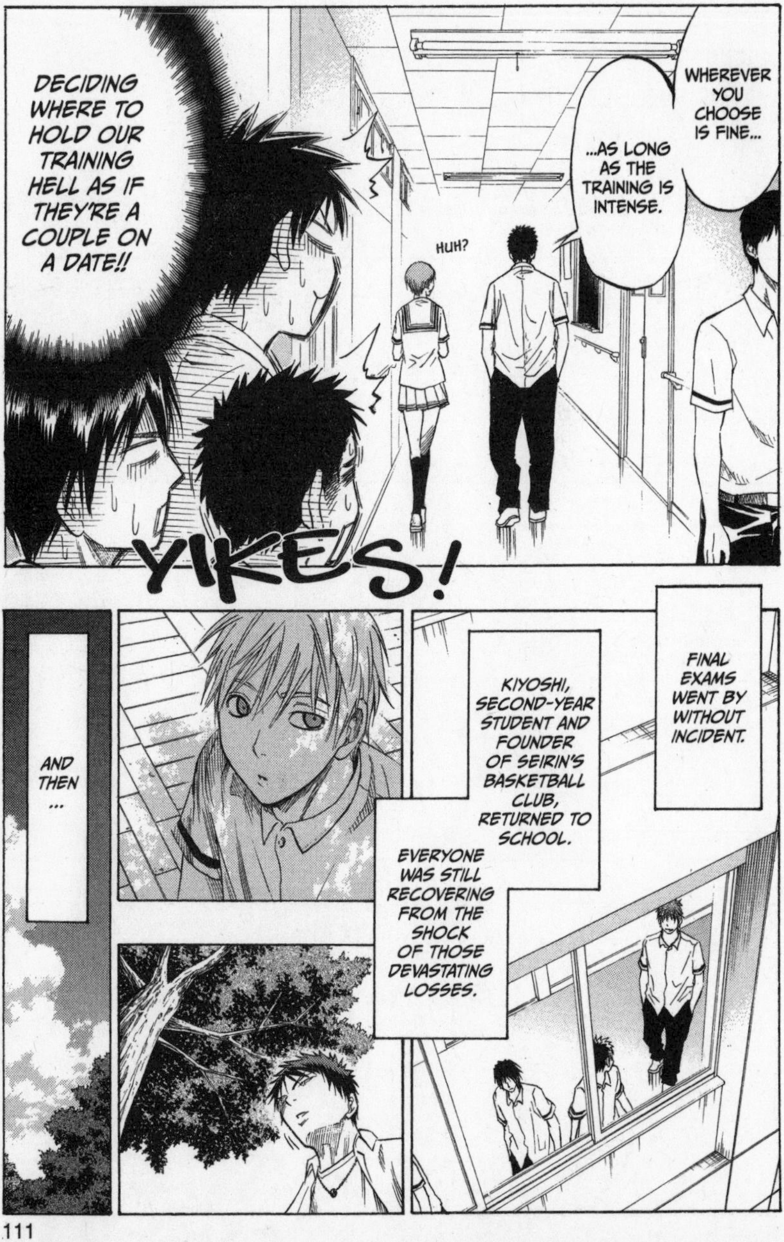
WHEREVER YOU CHOOSE IS FINE...
...AS LONG AS THE TRAINING IS INTENSE.
HUH?
DECIDING WHERE TO HOLD OUR TRAINING HELL AS IF THEY'RE A COUPLE ON A DATE!!
YIKES!
FINAL EXAMS WENT BY WITHOUT INCIDENT.
EVERYONE WAS STILL RECOVERING FROM THE SHOCK OF THOSE DEVASTATING LOSSES.
KIYOSHI, SECOND-YEAR STUDENT AND FOUNDER OF SEIRIN'S BASKETBALL CLUB, RETURNED TO SCHOOL.
AND THEN ...

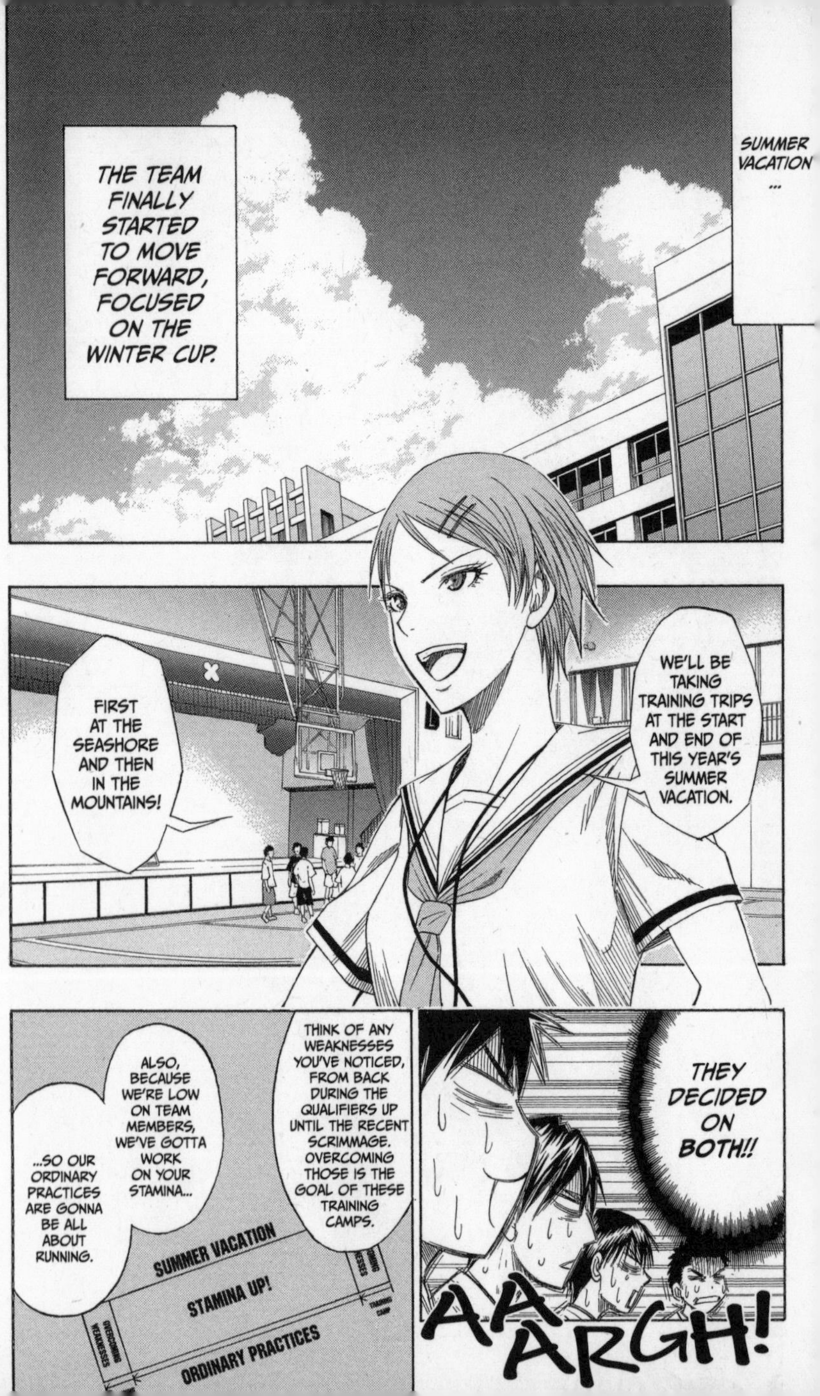
SUMMER VACATION ...
THE TEAM FINALLY STARTED TO MOVE FORWARD, FOCUSED ON THE WINTER CUP.
WE'LL BE TAKING TRAINING TRIPS AT THE START AND END OF THIS YEAR'S SUMMER VACATION.
FIRST AT THE SEASHORE AND THEN IN THE MOUNTAINS!
THEY DECIDED ON BOTH!!
AA ARGH!
THINK OF ANY WEAKNESSES YOU'VE NOTICED, FROM BACK DURING THE QUALIFIERS UP UNTIL THE RECENT SCRIMMAGE. OVERCOMING THOSE IS THE GOAL OF THESE TRAINING CAMPS.
ALSO, BECAUSE WE'RE LOW ON TEAM MEMBERS, WE'VE GOTTA WORK ON YOUR STAMINA...
...SO OUR ORDINARY PRACTICES ARE GONNA BE ALL ABOUT RUNNING.
SUMMER VACATION
STAMINA UP!
ORDINARY PRACTICES

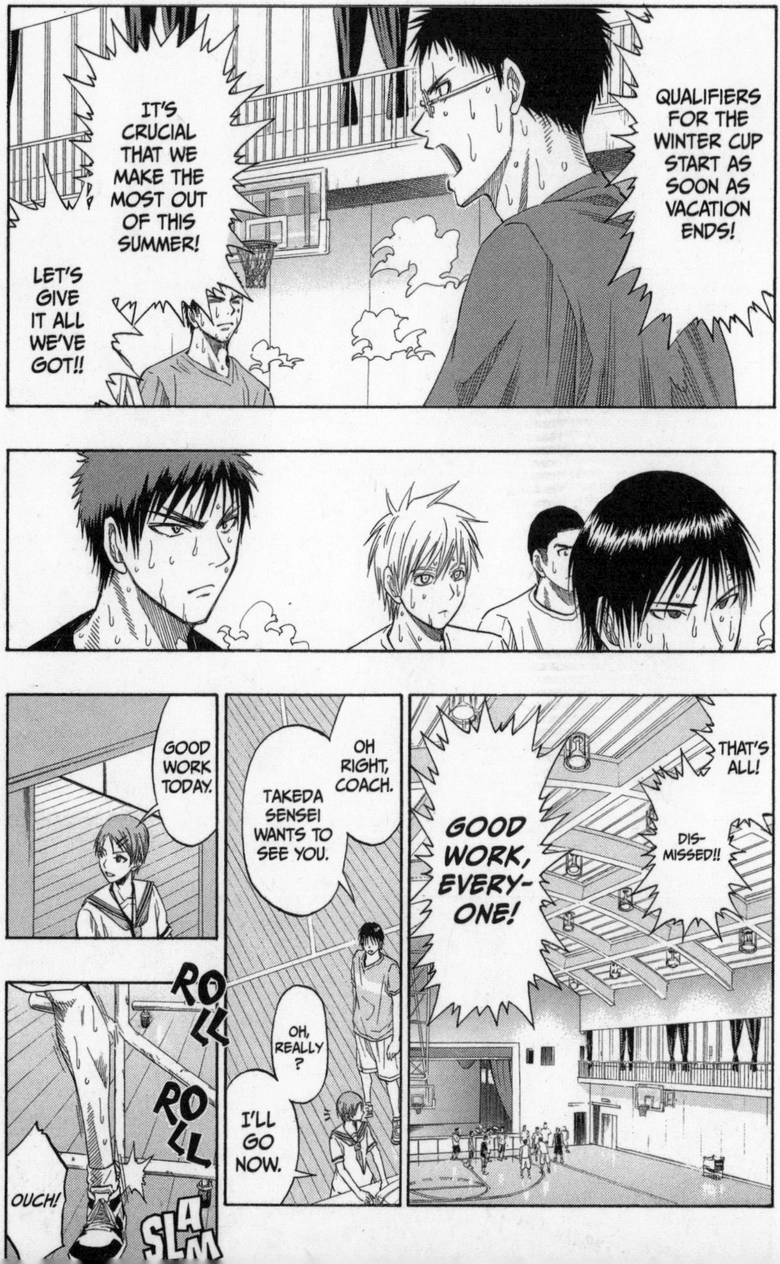
QUALIFIERS FOR THE WINTER CUP START AS SOON AS VACATION ENDS!
IT'S CRUCIAL THAT WE MAKE THE MOST OUT OF THIS SUMMER!
LET'S GIVE IT ALL WE'VE GOT!!
THAT'S ALL!
DIS-MISSED!!
GOOD WORK, EVERY-ONE!
OH RIGHT, COACH.
TAKEDA SENSEI WANTS TO SEE YOU.
OH, REALLY?
I'LL GO NOW.
GOOD WORK TODAY.
ROLL
ROLL
OUCH!
SLAM

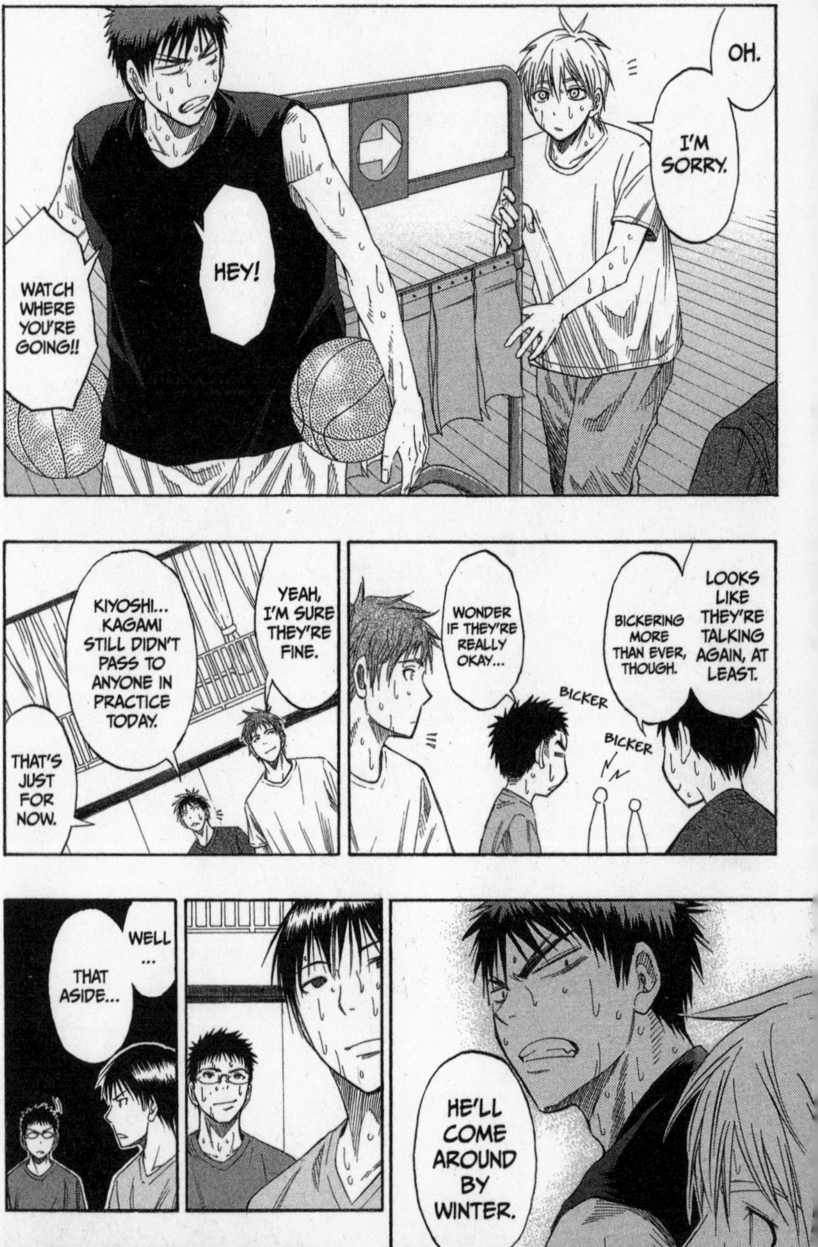
OH.
I'M SORRY.
HEY!
WATCH WHERE YOU'RE GOING!!
LOOKS LIKE THEY'RE TALKING AGAIN, AT LEAST.
BICKERING MORE THAN EVER, THOUGH.
BICKER
BICKER
WONDER IF THEY'RE REALLY OKAY...
YEAH, I'M SURE THEY'RE FINE.
KIYOSHI... KAGAMI STILL DIDN'T PASS TO ANYONE IN PRACTICE TODAY.
THAT'S JUST FOR NOW.
HE'LL COME AROUND BY WINTER.
WELL ...
THAT ASIDE...

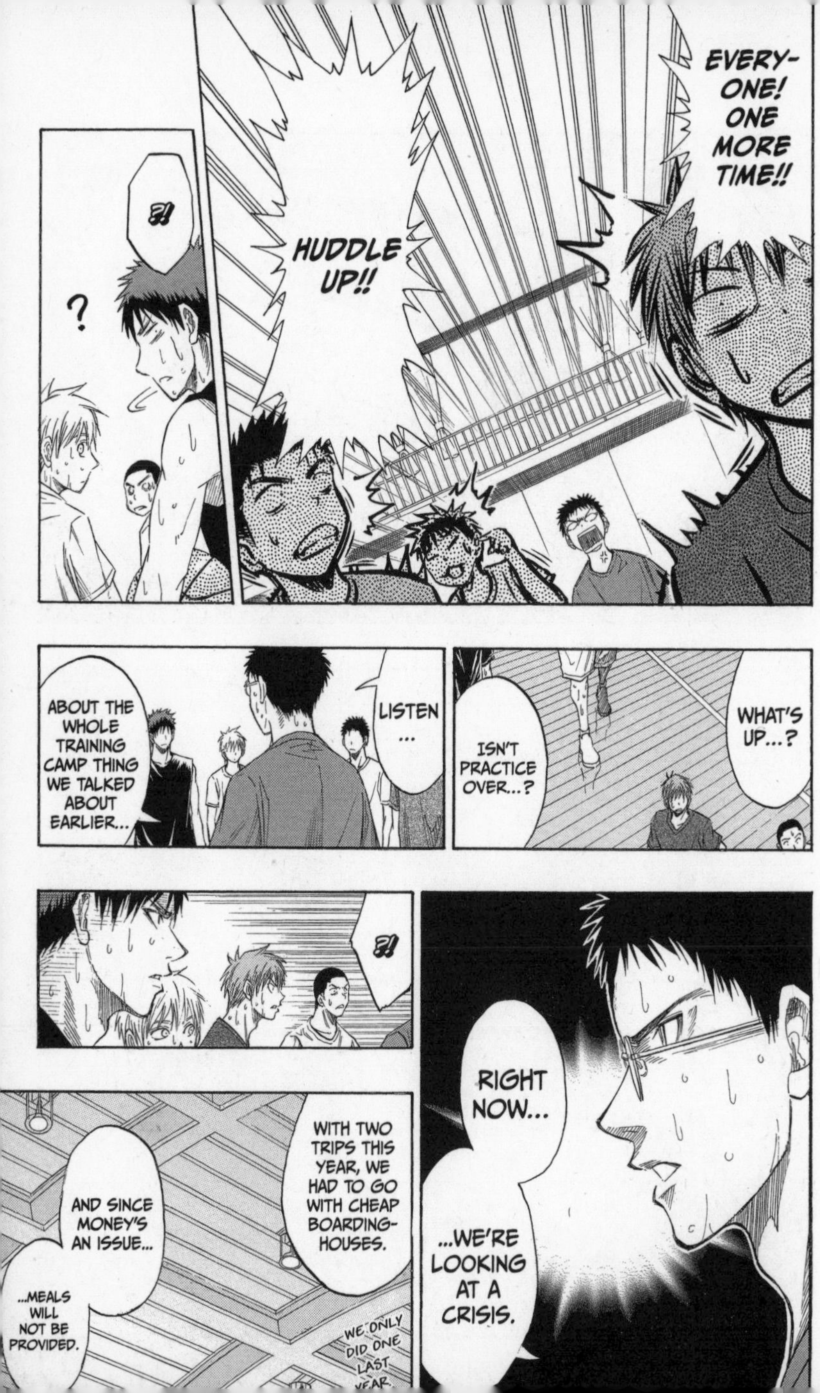
EVERY-ONE! ONE MORE TIME!!
HUDDLE UP!!
?!
?
WHAT'S UP...?
ISN'T PRACTICE OVER...?
LISTEN ...
ABOUT THE WHOLE TRAINING CAMP THING WE TALKED ABOUT EARLIER...
RIGHT NOW...
...WE'RE LOOKING AT A CRISIS.
?!
WITH TWO TRIPS THIS YEAR, WE HAD TO GO WITH CHEAP BOARDING-HOUSES.
WE ONLY DID ONE LAST YEAR.
AND SINCE MONEY'S AN ISSUE...
...MEALS WILL NOT BE PROVIDED.

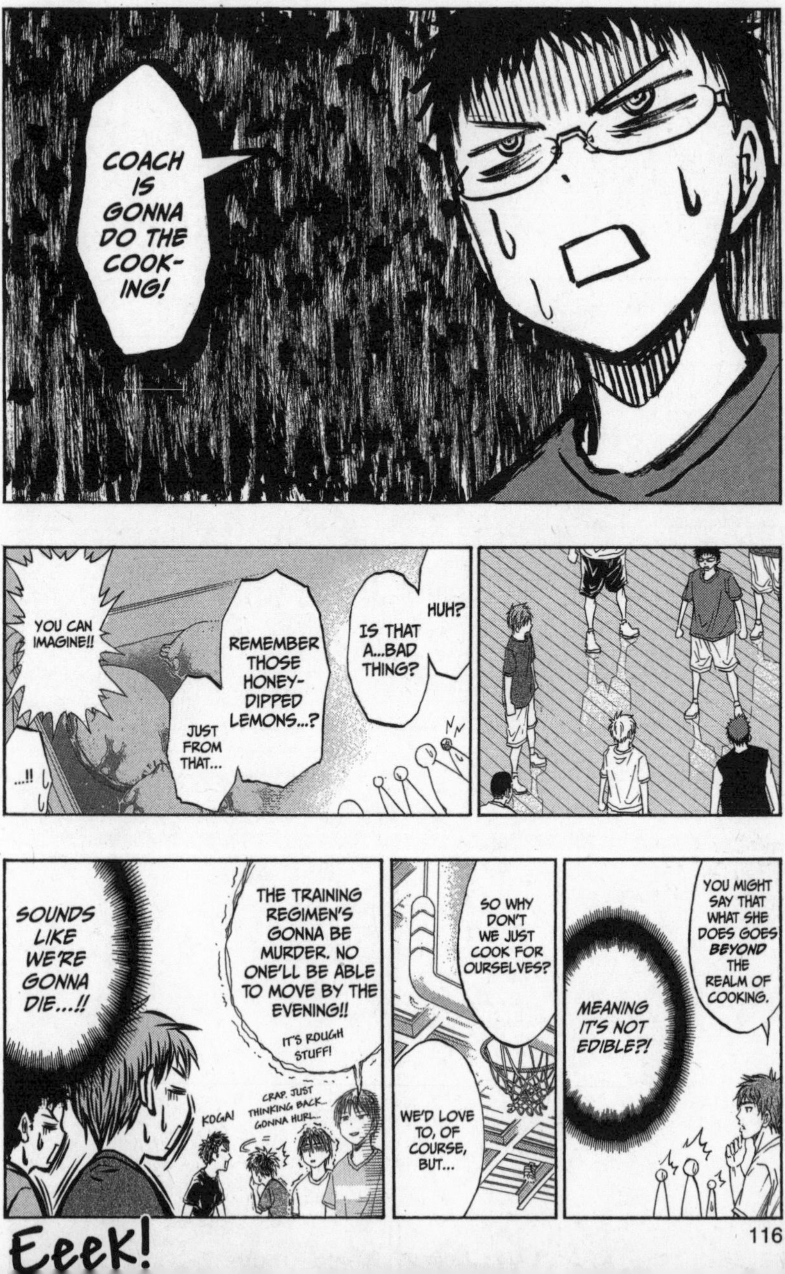
COACH IS GONNA DO THE COOKING!
HUH?
IS THAT A...BAD THING?
REMEMBER THOSE HONEY-DIPPED LEMONS...?
JUST FROM THAT...
YOU CAN IMAGINE!!
...!!
YOU MIGHT SAY THAT WHAT SHE DOES GOES *BEYOND* THE REALM OF COOKING.
MEANING IT'S NOT EDIBLE?!
SO WHY DON'T WE JUST COOK FOR OURSELVES?
WE'D LOVE TO, OF COURSE, BUT...
THE TRAINING REGIMEN'S GONNA BE MURDER. NO ONE'LL BE ABLE TO MOVE BY THE EVENING!!
IT'S ROUGH STUFF!
SOUNDS LIKE WE'RE GONNA DIE...!!
CRAP. JUST THINKING BACK... GONNA HURL...
KOGA!
Eeek!

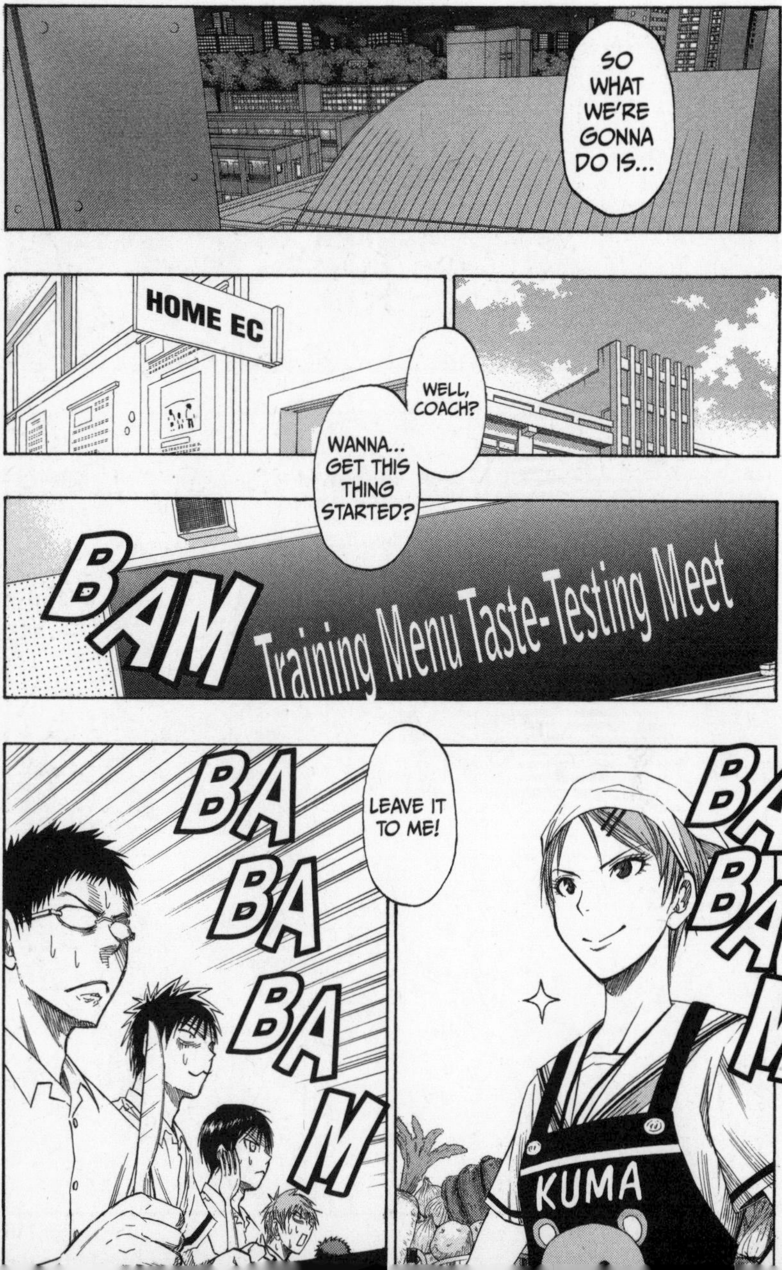
SO WHAT WE'RE GONNA DO IS...
WELL, COACH?
HOME EC
WANNA... GET THIS THING STARTED?
BAM
Training Menu Taste-Testing Meet
LEAVE IT TO ME!
BABABAM
KUMA
BABABABAM

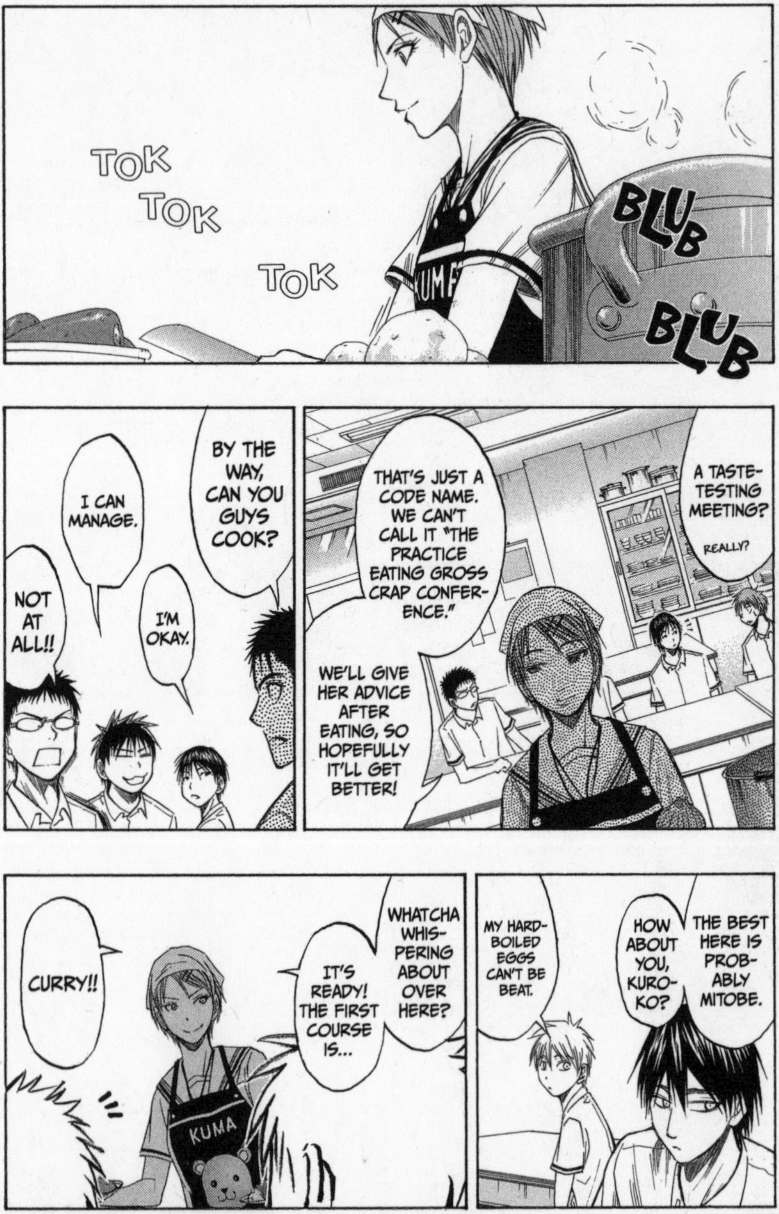
BLUB
BLUB
TOK
TOK
TOK
A TASTE-TESTING MEETING?
REALLY?
THAT'S JUST A CODE NAME. WE CAN'T CALL IT "THE PRACTICE EATING GROSS CRAP CONFERENCE."
WE'LL GIVE HER ADVICE AFTER EATING, SO HOPEFULLY IT'LL GET BETTER!
BY THE WAY, CAN YOU GUYS COOK?
I'M OKAY.
I CAN MANAGE.
NOT AT ALL!!
THE BEST HERE IS PROBABLY MITOBE.
HOW ABOUT YOU, KUROKO?
MY HARD-BOILED EGGS CAN'T BE BEAT.
WHATCHA WHISPERING ABOUT OVER HERE?
IT'S READY! THE FIRST COURSE IS...
CURRY!!
KUMA

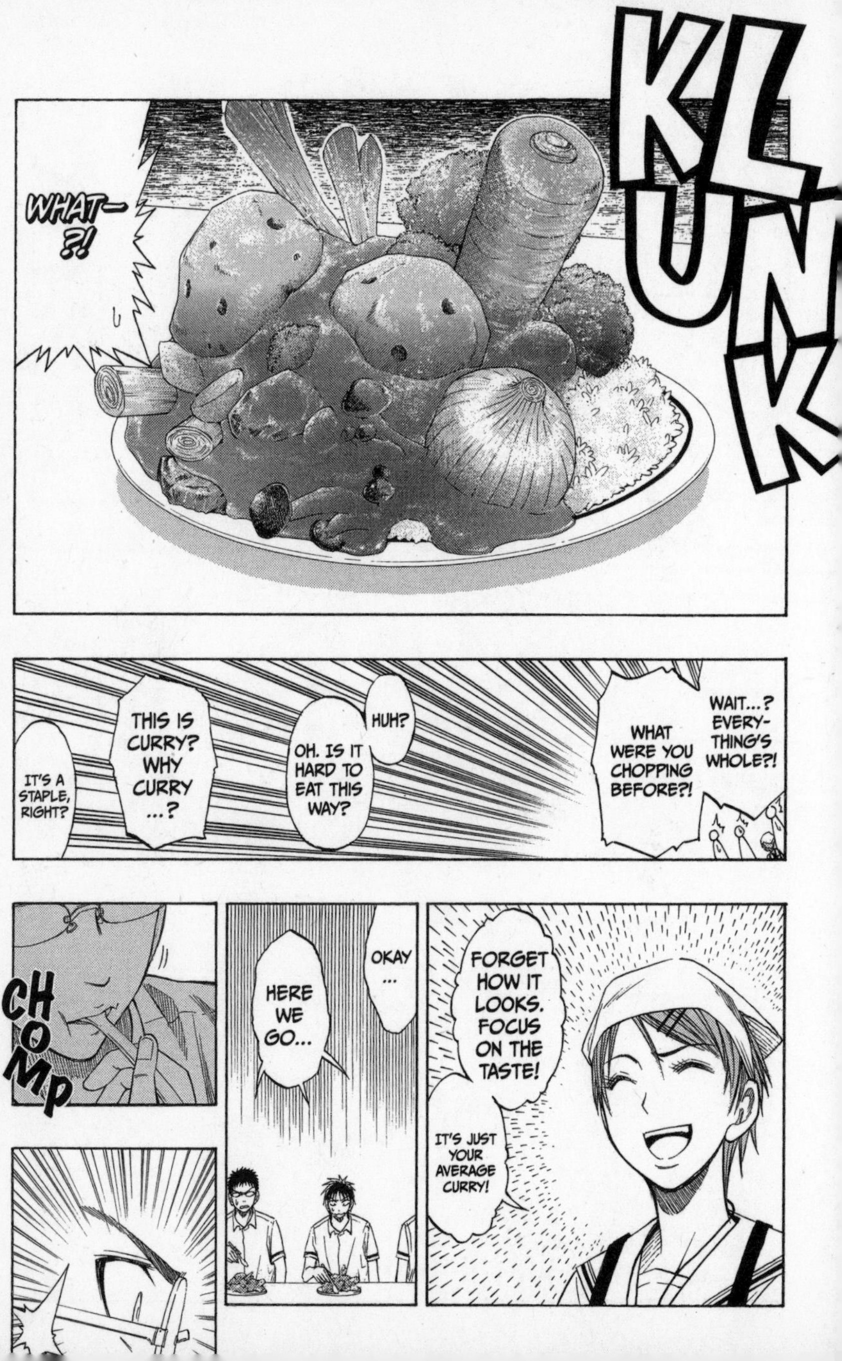
KLUNK
WHAT— ?!
WAIT...? EVERY-THING'S WHOLE?!
WHAT WERE YOU CHOPPING BEFORE?!
HUH?
OH. IS IT HARD TO EAT THIS WAY?
THIS IS CURRY? WHY CURRY ...?
IT'S A STAPLE, RIGHT?
FORGET HOW IT LOOKS. FOCUS ON THE TASTE!
IT'S JUST YOUR AVERAGE CURRY!
OKAY ...
HERE WE GO...
CHOMP

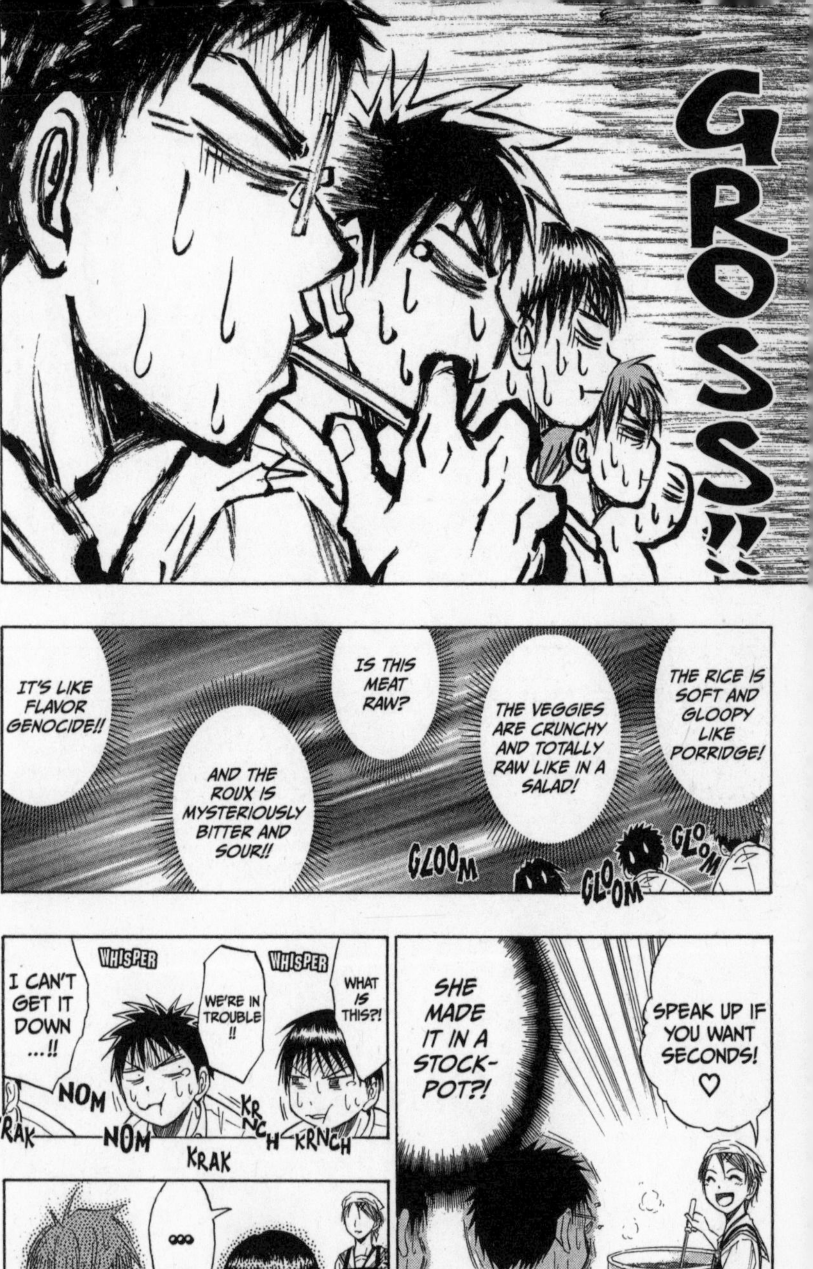
GROSS!!
THE RICE IS SOFT AND GLOOPY LIKE PORRIDGE!
THE VEGGIES ARE CRUNCHY AND TOTALLY RAW LIKE IN A SALAD!
IS THIS MEAT RAW?
AND THE ROUX IS MYSTERIOUSLY BITTER AND SOUR!!
IT'S LIKE FLAVOR GENOCIDE!!
GLOOM
GLOOM
GLOOM
SPEAK UP IF YOU WANT SECONDS! ♡
SHE MADE IT IN A STOCK-POT?!
WHAT IS THIS?!
WHISPER
WE'RE IN TROUBLE!!
WHISPER
I CAN'T GET IT DOWN ...!!
KRNCH
KRNCH
NOM
NOM
KRAK
KRAK
...
KUMA

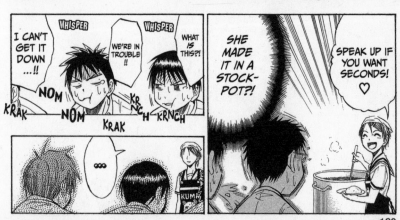

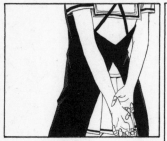

RIGHT. THOUGHT SO...

IT'S NOT... VERY GOOD, IS IT...?

KUMA

...

DELISH.

SHAH

NOM

NOM

CHOMP

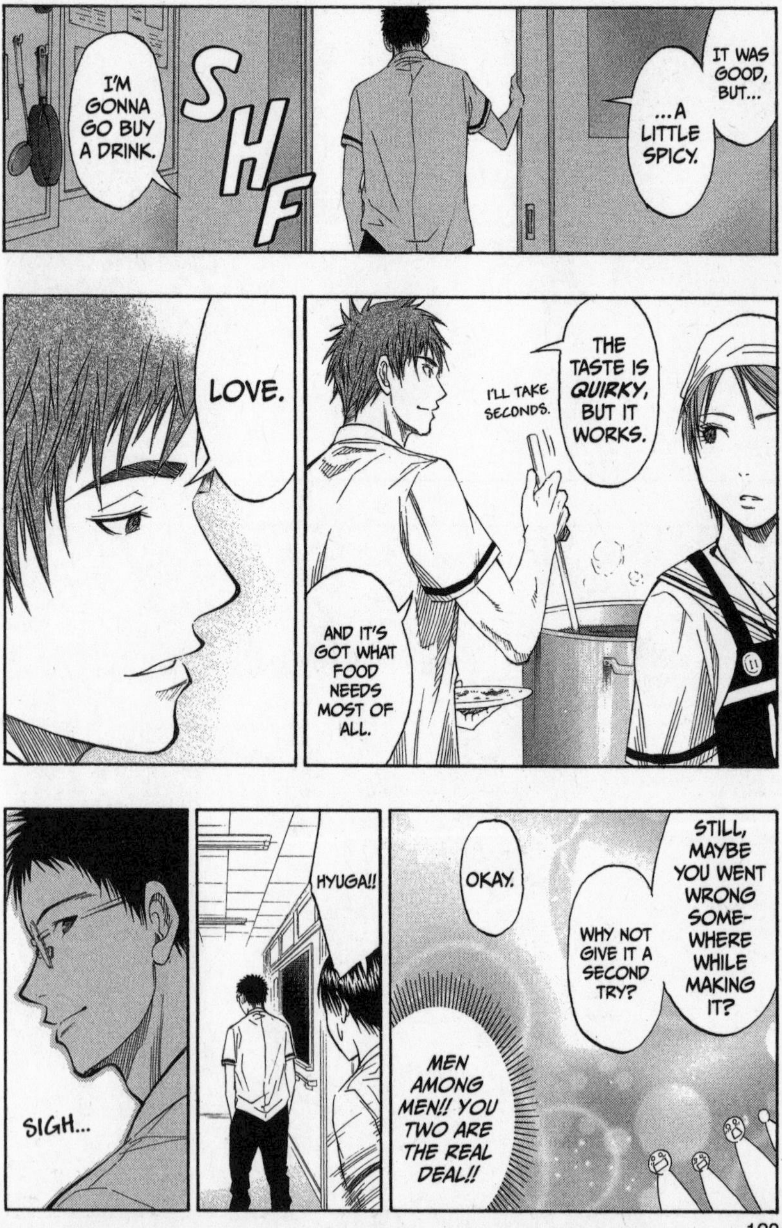
IT WAS GOOD, BUT...
...A LITTLE SPICY.
SHF
I'M GONNA GO BUY A DRINK.
THE TASTE IS QUIRKY, BUT IT WORKS.
I'LL TAKE SECONDS.
AND IT'S GOT WHAT FOOD NEEDS MOST OF ALL.
LOVE.
STILL, MAYBE YOU WENT WRONG SOME-WHERE WHILE MAKING IT?
WHY NOT GIVE IT A SECOND TRY?
OKAY.
MEN AMONG MEN!! YOU TWO ARE THE REAL DEAL!!
HYUGA!!
SIGH...

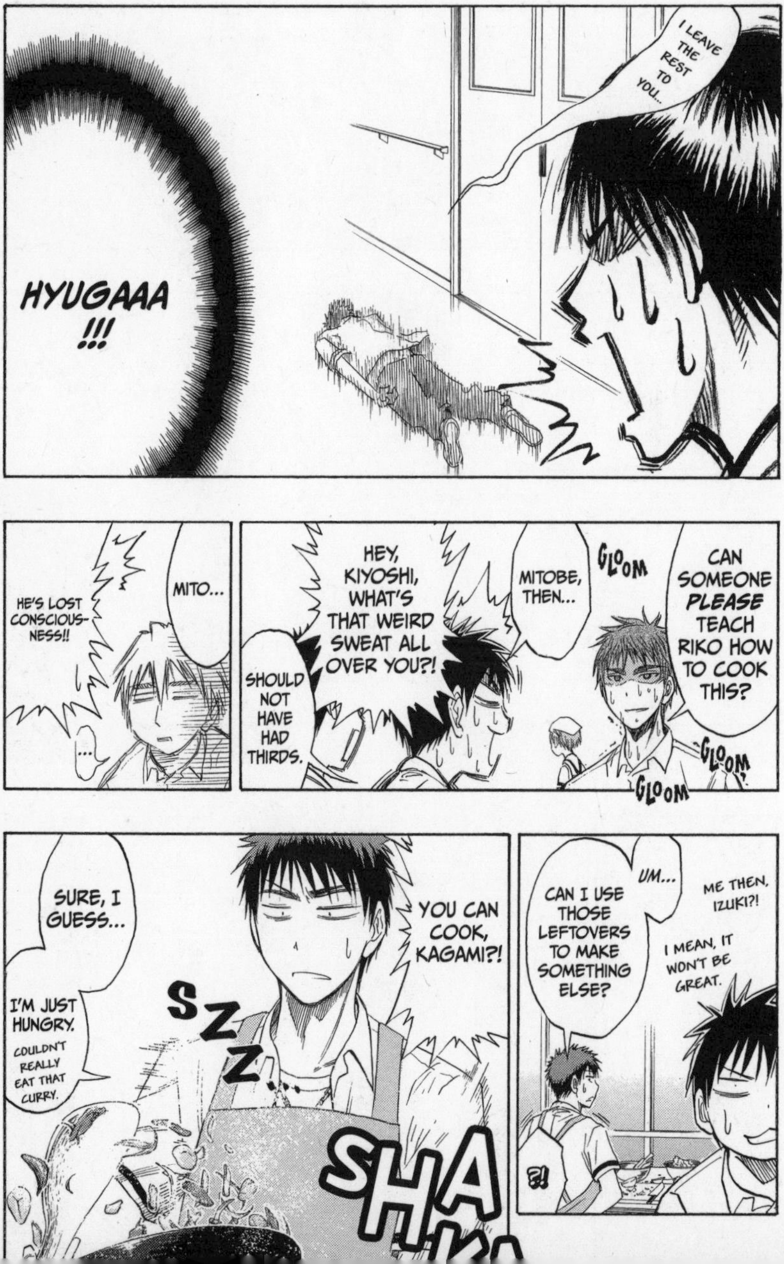
I LEAVE THE REST TO YOU...
HYUGAAA !!!
CAN SOMEONE PLEASE TEACH RIKO HOW TO COOK THIS?
GLOOM
GLOOM
GLOOM
MITOBE, THEN...
HEY, KIYOSHI, WHAT'S THAT WEIRD SWEAT ALL OVER YOU?!
SHOULD NOT HAVE HAD THIRDS.
MITO...
HE'S LOST CONSCIOUS-NESS!!
...
ME THEN, IZUKI?!
I MEAN, IT WON'T BE GREAT.
UM...
CAN I USE THOSE LEFTOVERS TO MAKE SOMETHING ELSE?
?!
YOU CAN COOK, KAGAMI?!
SURE, I GUESS...
I'M JUST HUNGRY.
COULDN'T REALLY EAT THAT CURRY.
SZZ
SHA

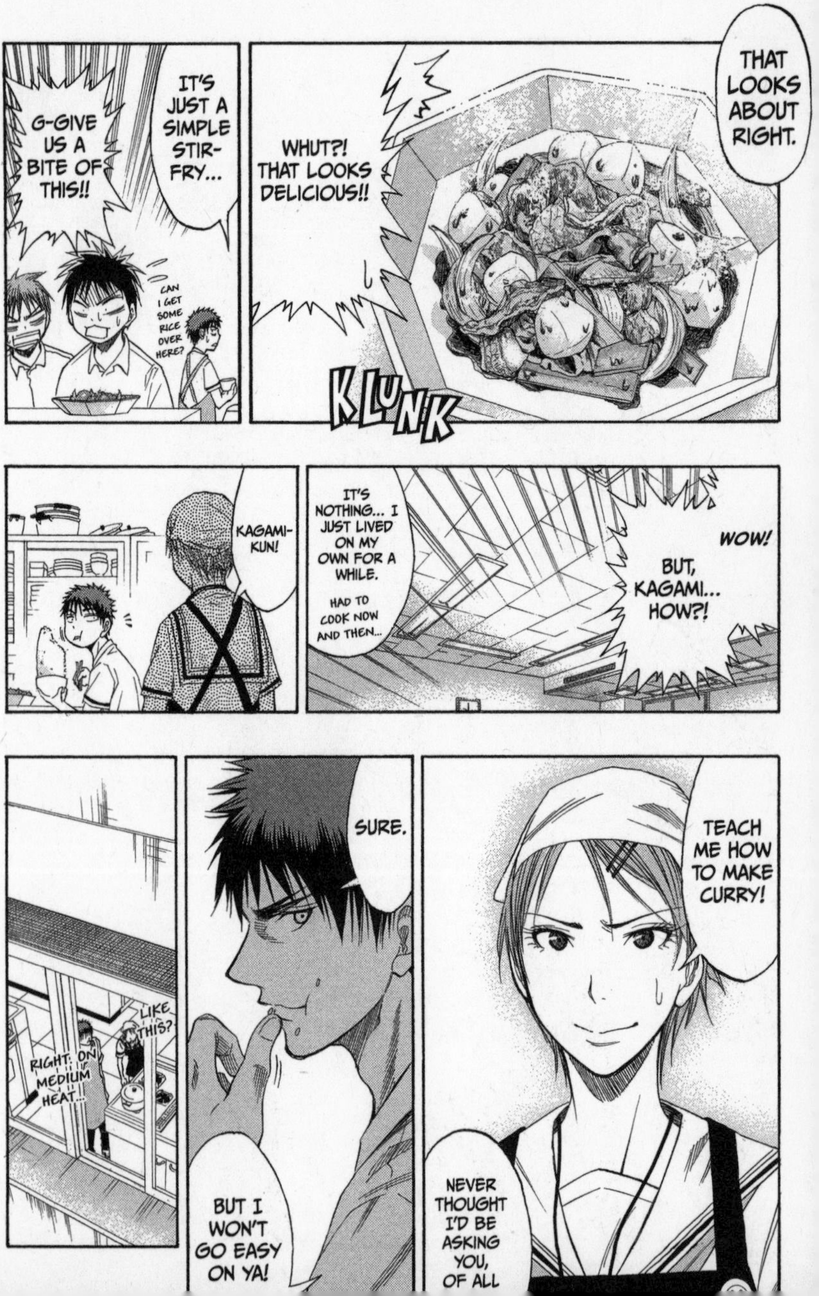
THAT LOOKS ABOUT RIGHT.
WHUT?! THAT LOOKS DELICIOUS!!
KLUNK
IT'S JUST A SIMPLE STIR-FRY...
G-GIVE US A BITE OF THIS!!
CAN I GET SOME RICE OVER HERE?
WOW!
BUT, KAGAMI... HOW?!
IT'S NOTHING... I JUST LIVED ON MY OWN FOR A WHILE.
HAD TO COOK NOW AND THEN...
KAGAMI-KUN!
TEACH ME HOW TO MAKE CURRY!
NEVER THOUGHT I'D BE ASKING YOU, OF ALL
SURE.
BUT I WON'T GO EASY ON YA!
LIKE THIS?
RIGHT. ON MEDIUM HEAT...

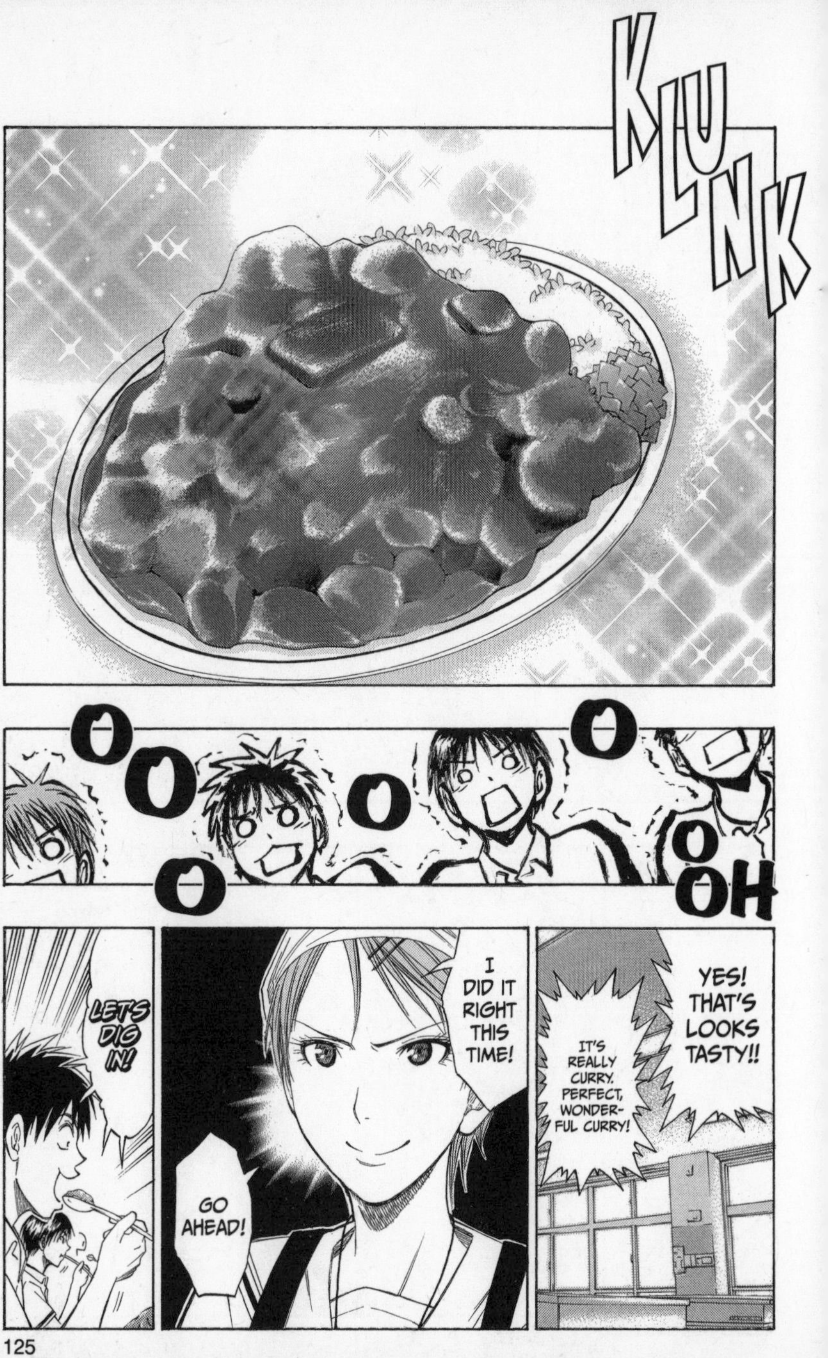
KLUNK
OOOOOOOH
YES! THAT'S LOOKS TASTY!!
IT'S REALLY CURRY. PERFECT, WONDERFUL CURRY!
I DID IT RIGHT THIS TIME!
GO AHEAD!
LET'S DIG IN!

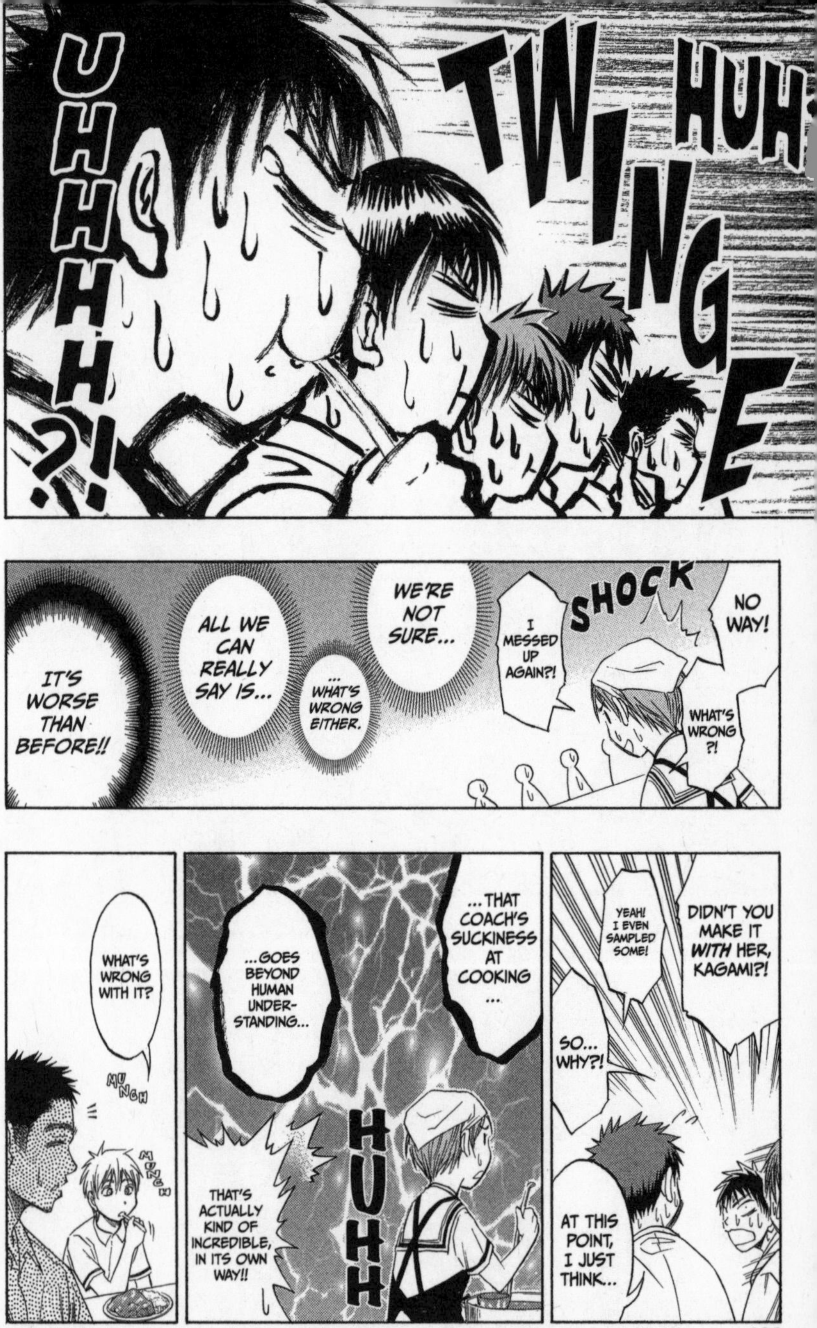
HUH
TWINGE
UHHHHH?!
NO WAY!
WHAT'S WRONG ?!
SHOCK
I MESSED UP AGAIN?!
WE'RE NOT SURE...
...WHAT'S WRONG EITHER.
ALL WE CAN REALLY SAY IS...
IT'S WORSE THAN BEFORE!!
DIDN'T YOU MAKE IT *WITH* HER, KAGAMI?!
YEAH! I EVEN SAMPLED SOME!
SO... WHY?!
AT THIS POINT, I JUST THINK...
...THAT COACH'S SUCKINESS AT COOKING...
...GOES BEYOND HUMAN UNDER-STANDING...
HUHH
THAT'S ACTUALLY KIND OF INCREDIBLE, IN ITS OWN WAY!!
WHAT'S WRONG WITH IT?
MUNCH
MUNCH

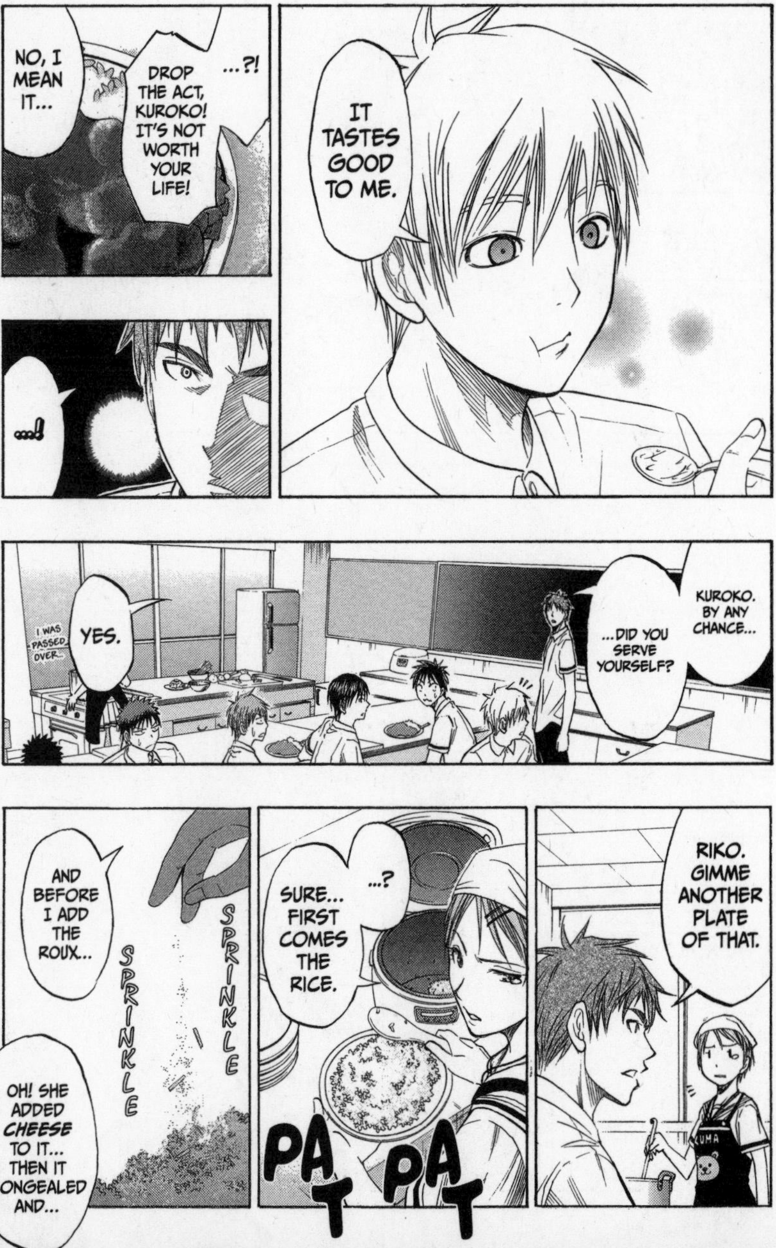
IT TASTES GOOD TO ME.
...?!
DROP THE ACT, KUROKO! IT'S NOT WORTH YOUR LIFE!
NO, I MEAN IT...
...!
KUROKO. BY ANY CHANCE...
...DID YOU SERVE YOURSELF?
YES.
I WAS PASSED OVER...
RIKO. GIMME ANOTHER PLATE OF THAT.
...?
SURE... FIRST COMES THE RICE.
PAT PAT
AND BEFORE I ADD THE ROUX...
SPRINKLE SPRINKLE
OH! SHE ADDED CHEESE TO IT... THEN IT CONGEALED AND...

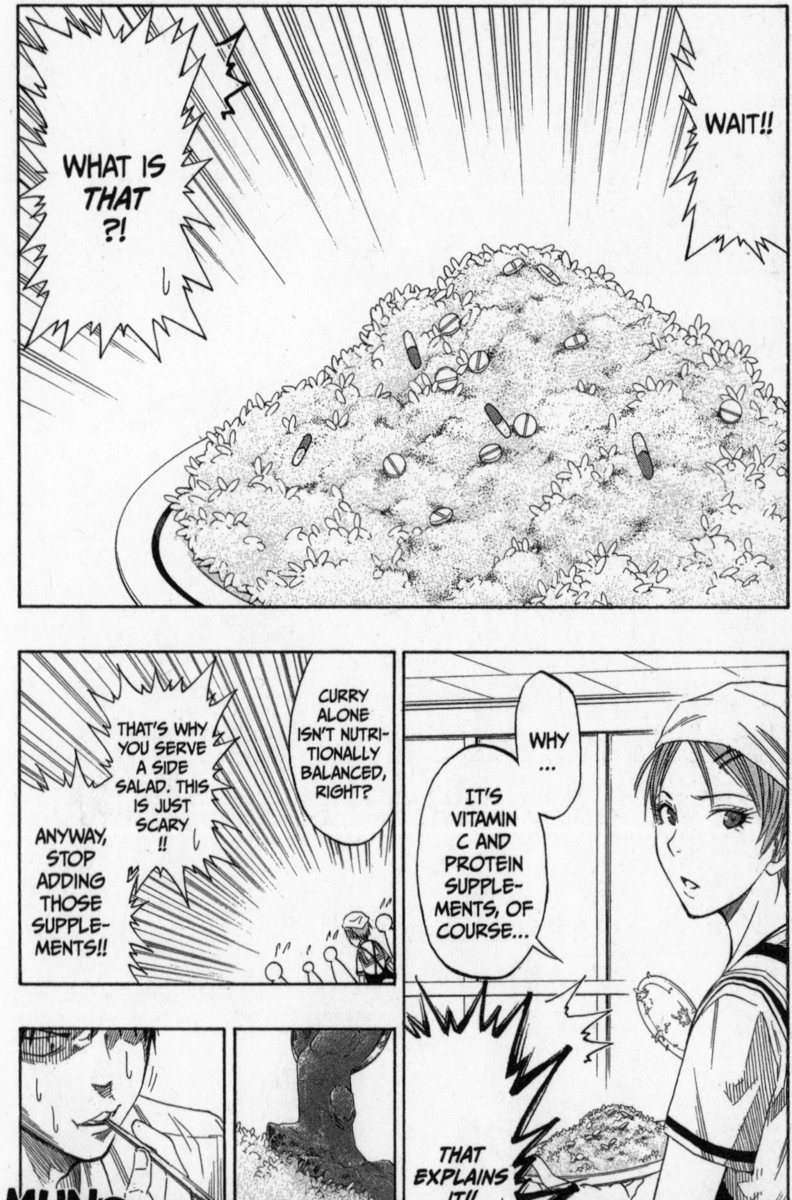
WAIT!!
WHAT IS THAT ?!
WHY ...
IT'S VITAMIN C AND PROTEIN SUPPLEMENTS, OF COURSE...
THAT EXPLAINS IT!!
CURRY ALONE ISN'T NUTRITIONALLY BALANCED, RIGHT?
THAT'S WHY YOU SERVE A SIDE SALAD. THIS IS JUST SCARY !!
ANYWAY, STOP ADDING THOSE SUPPLEMENTS!!
MUNCH

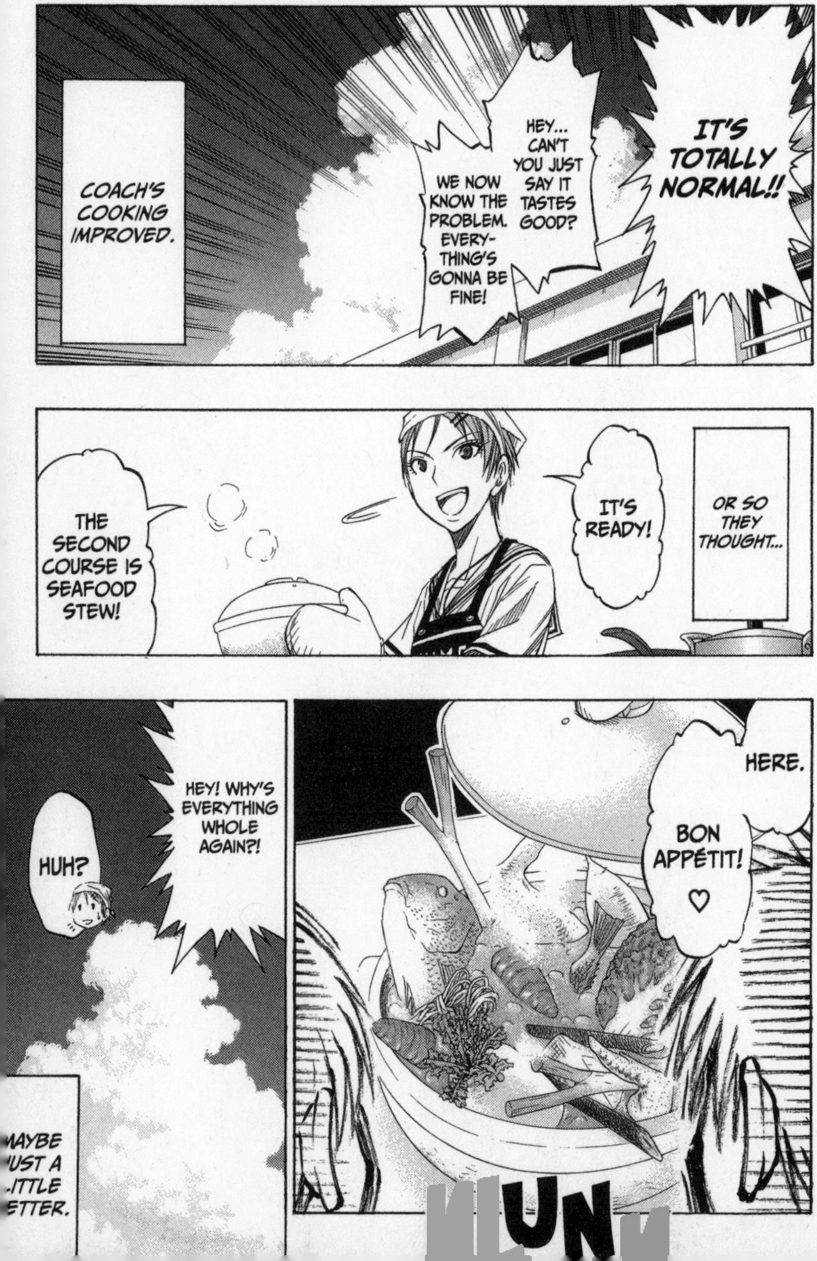
IT'S TOTALLY NORMAL!!
HEY... CAN'T YOU JUST SAY IT TASTES GOOD?
WE NOW KNOW THE PROBLEM. EVERYTHING'S GONNA BE FINE!
COACH'S COOKING IMPROVED.
OR SO THEY THOUGHT...
IT'S READY!
THE SECOND COURSE IS SEAFOOD STEW!
HERE.
BON APPÉTIT! ♡
HEY! WHY'S EVERYTHING WHOLE AGAIN?!
HUH?
MAYBE JUST A LITTLE BETTER.

KUROKO'S BASKETBALL BLOOPERS

TAKE 31

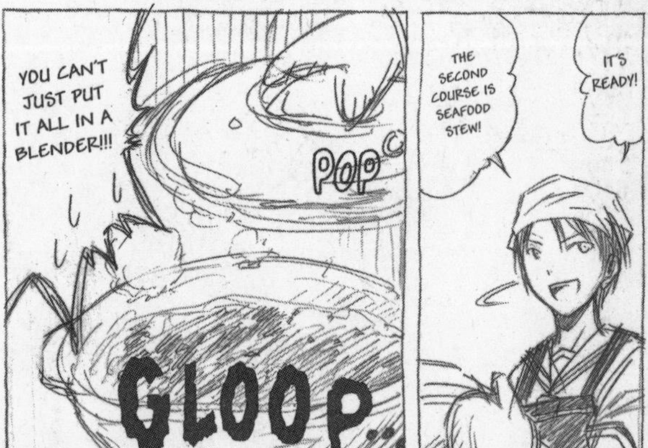
IT'S READY!
THE SECOND COURSE IS SEAFOOD STEW!
YOU CAN'T JUST PUT IT ALL IN A BLENDER!!!
POP
GLOOP..

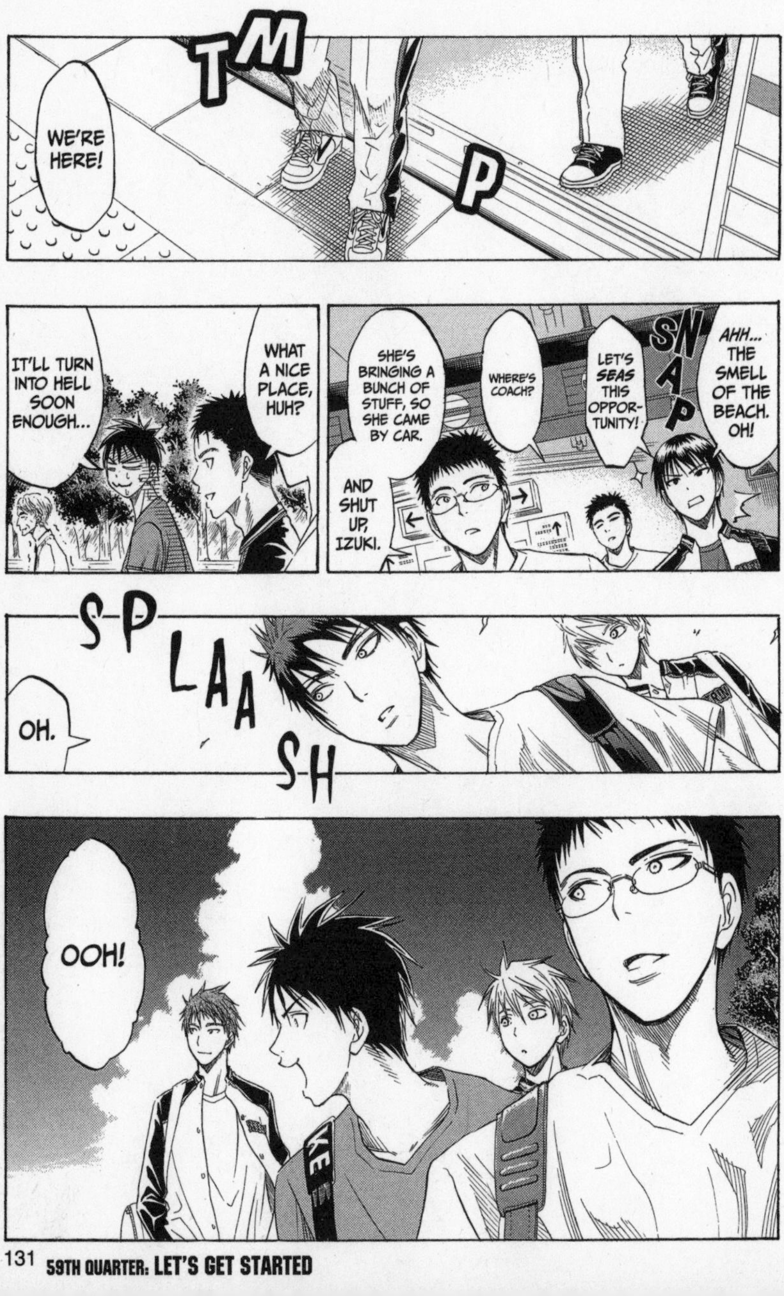
TMP
WE'RE HERE!
AHH... THE SMELL OF THE BEACH. OH!
SNAP
LET'S SEAS THIS OPPORTUNITY!
WHERE'S COACH?
SHE'S BRINGING A BUNCH OF STUFF, SO SHE CAME BY CAR.
AND SHUT UP, IZUKI.
WHAT A NICE PLACE, HUH?
IT'LL TURN INTO HELL SOON ENOUGH...
SPLAASH
OH.
OOH!

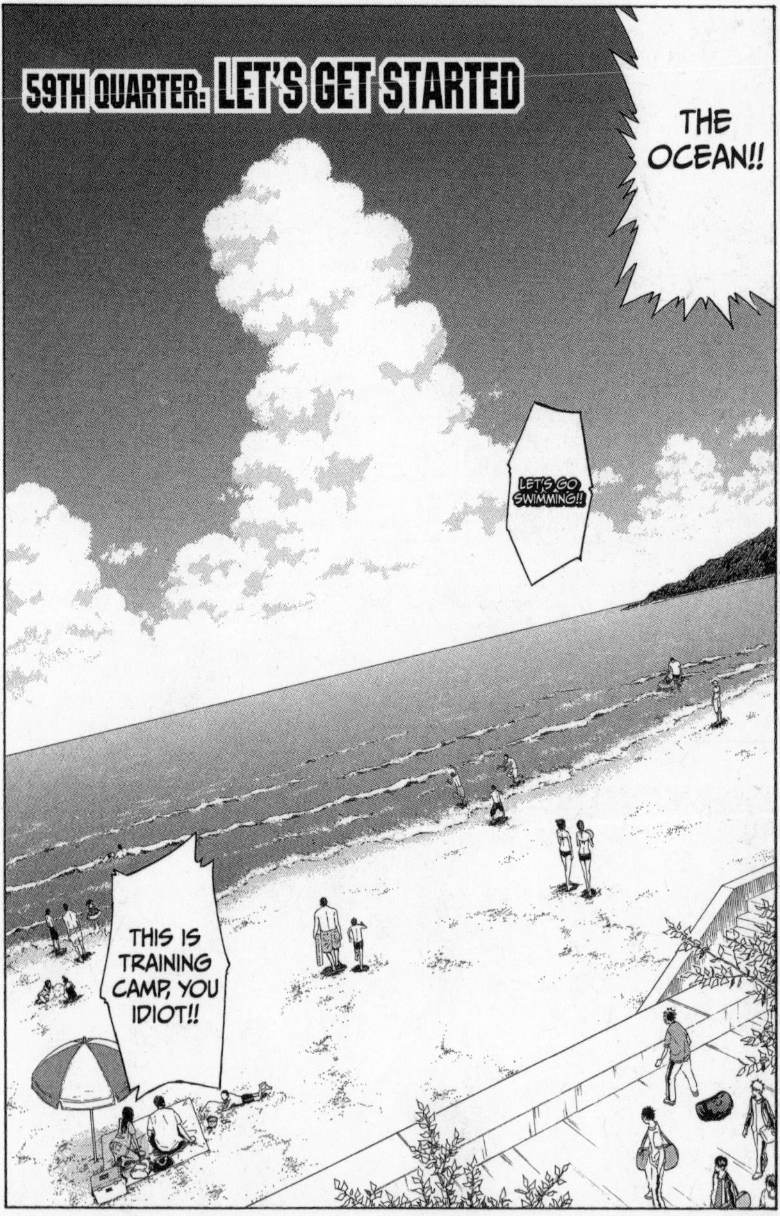
59TH QUARTER: LET'S GET STARTED
THE OCEAN!!
LET'S GO SWIMMING!!
THIS IS TRAINING CAMP, YOU IDIOT!!

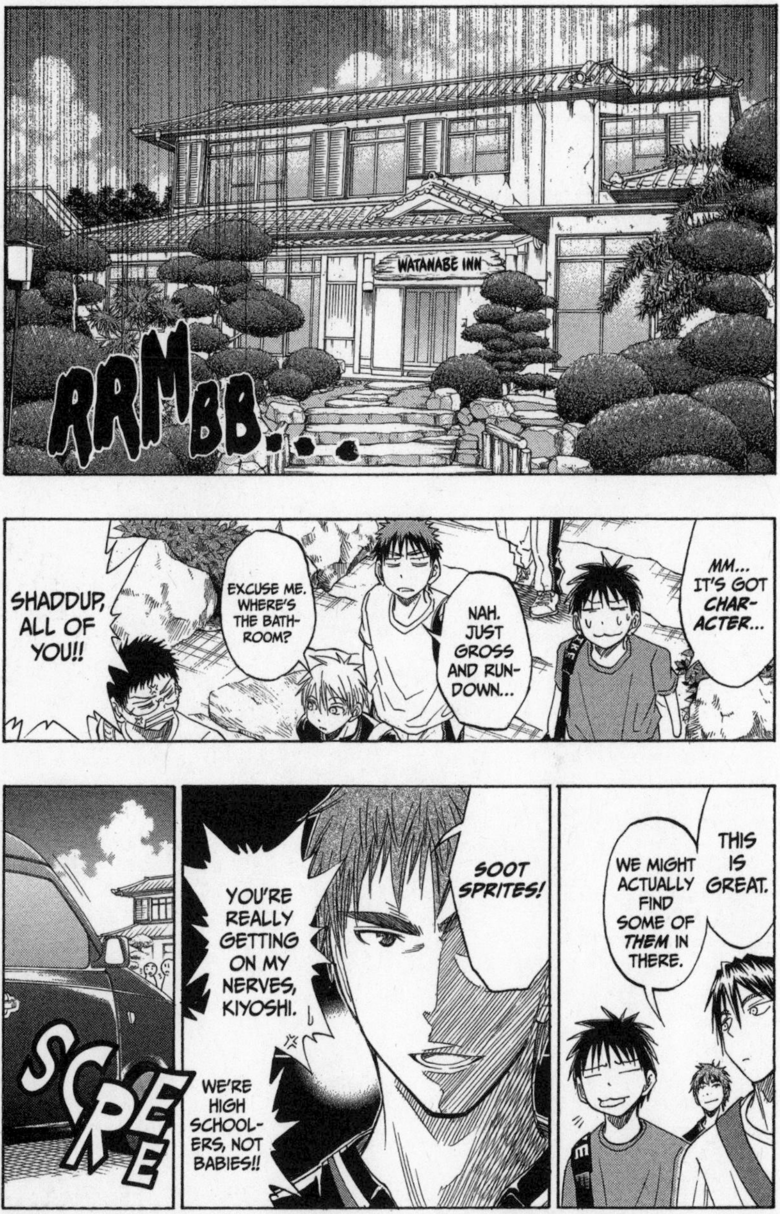
WATANABE INN
RRMBB...
MM... IT'S GOT CHARACTER...
NAH. JUST GROSS AND RUN-DOWN...
EXCUSE ME. WHERE'S THE BATHROOM?
SHADDUP, ALL OF YOU!!
THIS IS GREAT.
WE MIGHT ACTUALLY FIND SOME OF THEM IN THERE.
SOOT SPRITES!
YOU'RE REALLY GETTING ON MY NERVES, KIYOSHI.
WE'RE HIGH SCHOOL-ERS, NOT BABIES!!
SCREE

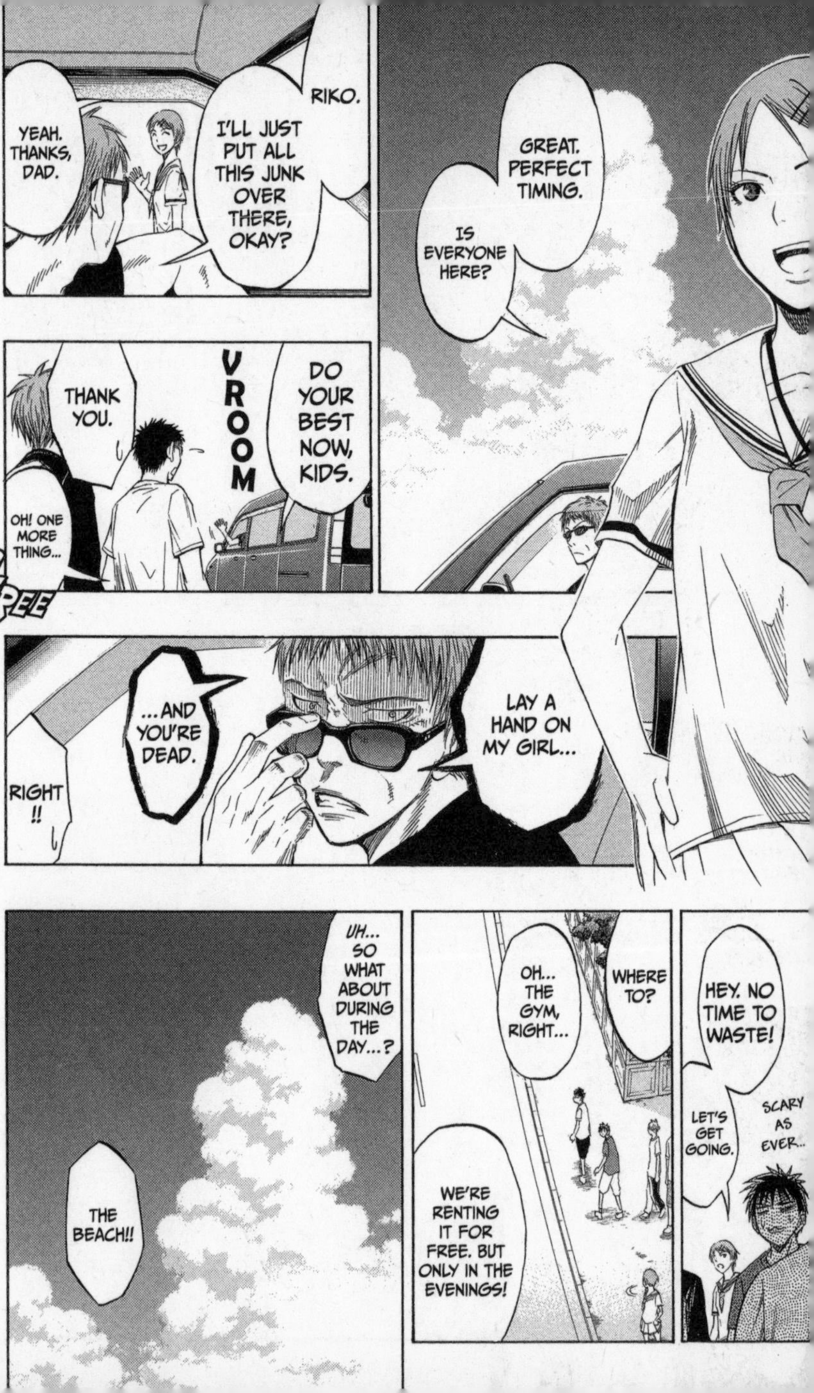
GREAT. PERFECT TIMING.
IS EVERYONE HERE?
RIKO.
I'LL JUST PUT ALL THIS JUNK OVER THERE, OKAY?
YEAH. THANKS, DAD.
DO YOUR BEST NOW, KIDS.
VROOM
THANK YOU.
OH! ONE MORE THING...
SCREE
LAY A HAND ON MY GIRL...
...AND YOU'RE DEAD.
RIGHT!!
HEY. NO TIME TO WASTE!
LET'S GET GOING.
SCARY AS EVER...
WHERE TO?
OH... THE GYM, RIGHT...
WE'RE RENTING IT FOR FREE. BUT ONLY IN THE EVENINGS!
UH... SO WHAT ABOUT DURING THE DAY...?
THE BEACH!!

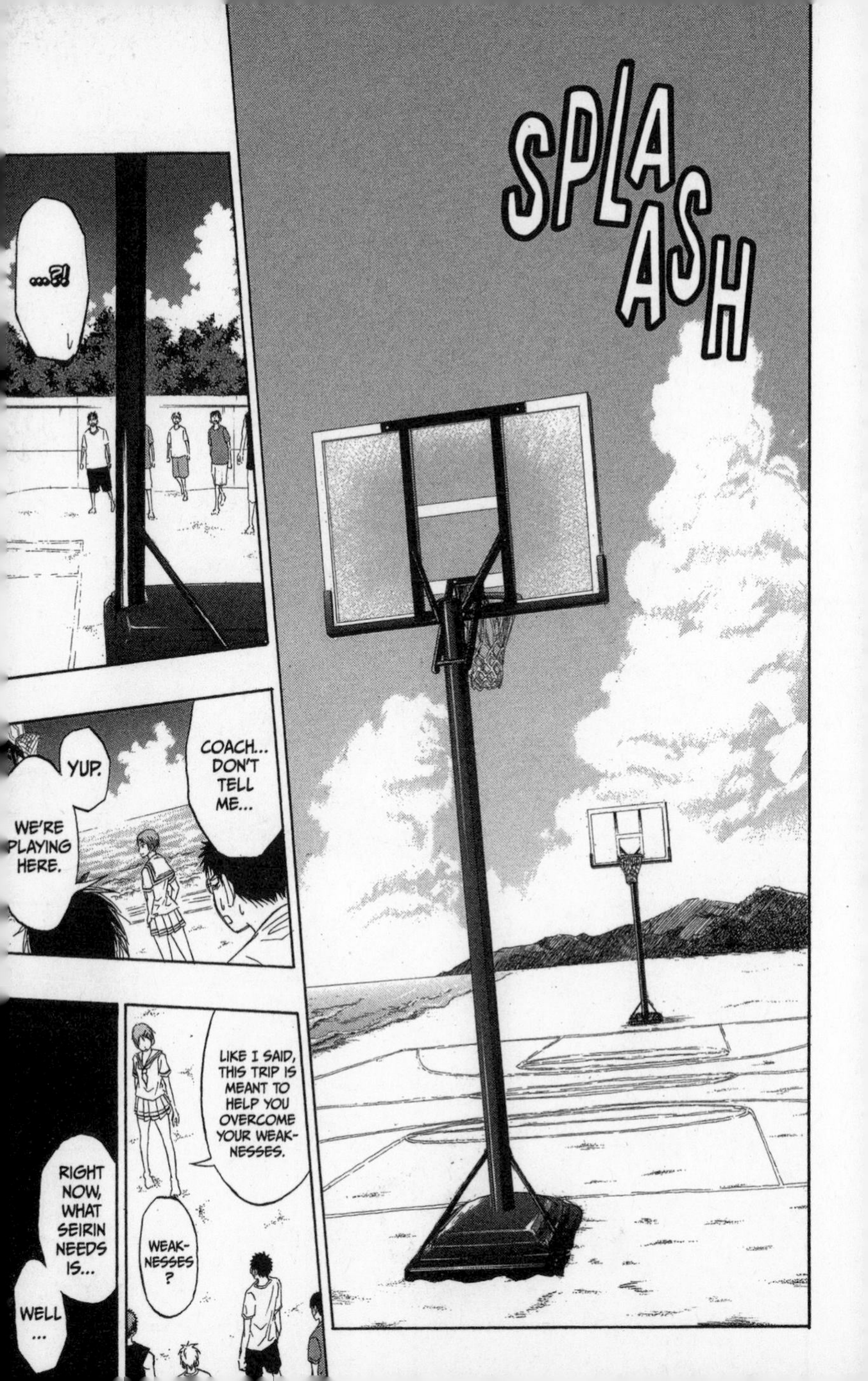
SPLASH
...?!
COACH... DON'T TELL ME...
YUP.
WE'RE PLAYING HERE.
LIKE I SAID, THIS TRIP IS MEANT TO HELP YOU OVERCOME YOUR WEAK-NESSES.
WEAK-NESSES?
RIGHT NOW, WHAT SEIRIN NEEDS IS...
WELL...

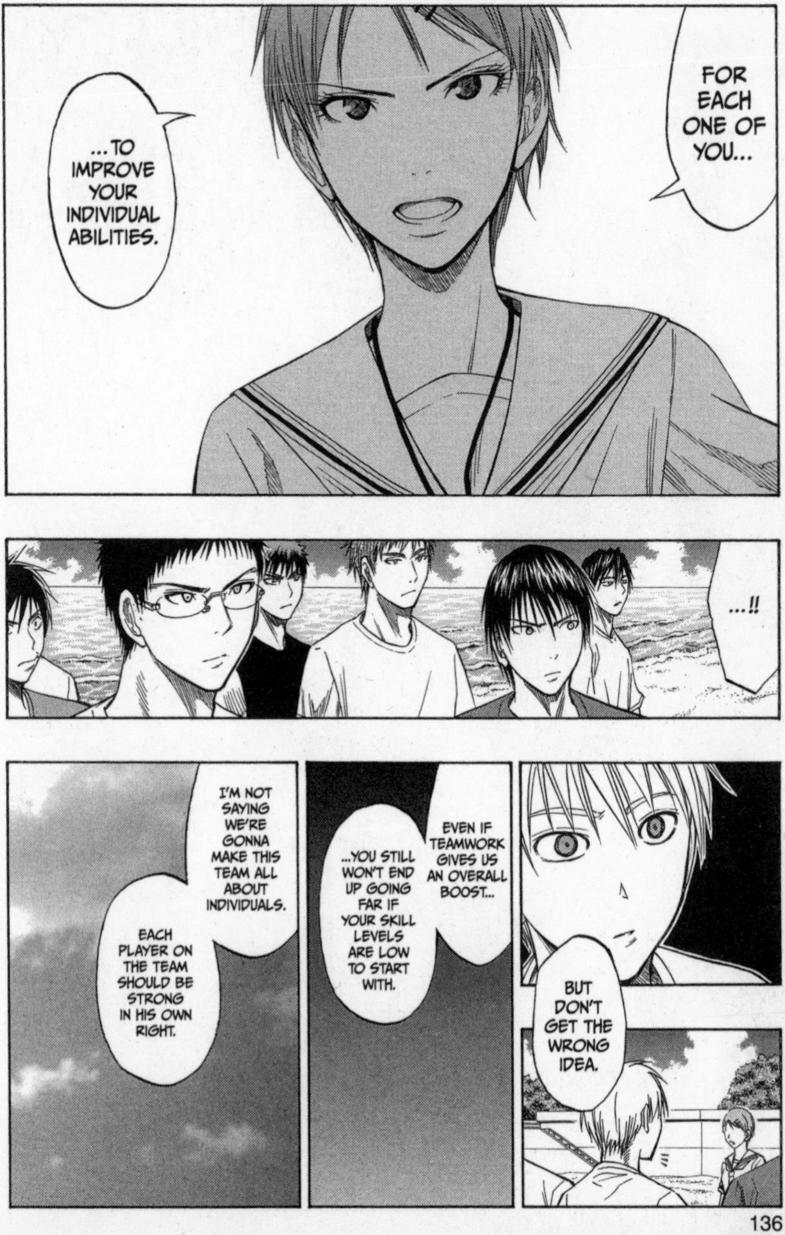

FOR EACH ONE OF YOU...
...TO IMPROVE YOUR INDIVIDUAL ABILITIES.
...!!
BUT DON'T GET THE WRONG IDEA.
EVEN IF TEAMWORK GIVES US AN OVERALL BOOST...
...YOU STILL WON'T END UP GOING FAR IF YOUR SKILL LEVELS ARE LOW TO START WITH.
I'M NOT SAYING WE'RE GONNA MAKE THIS TEAM ALL ABOUT INDIVIDUALS.
EACH PLAYER ON THE TEAM SHOULD BE STRONG IN HIS OWN RIGHT.

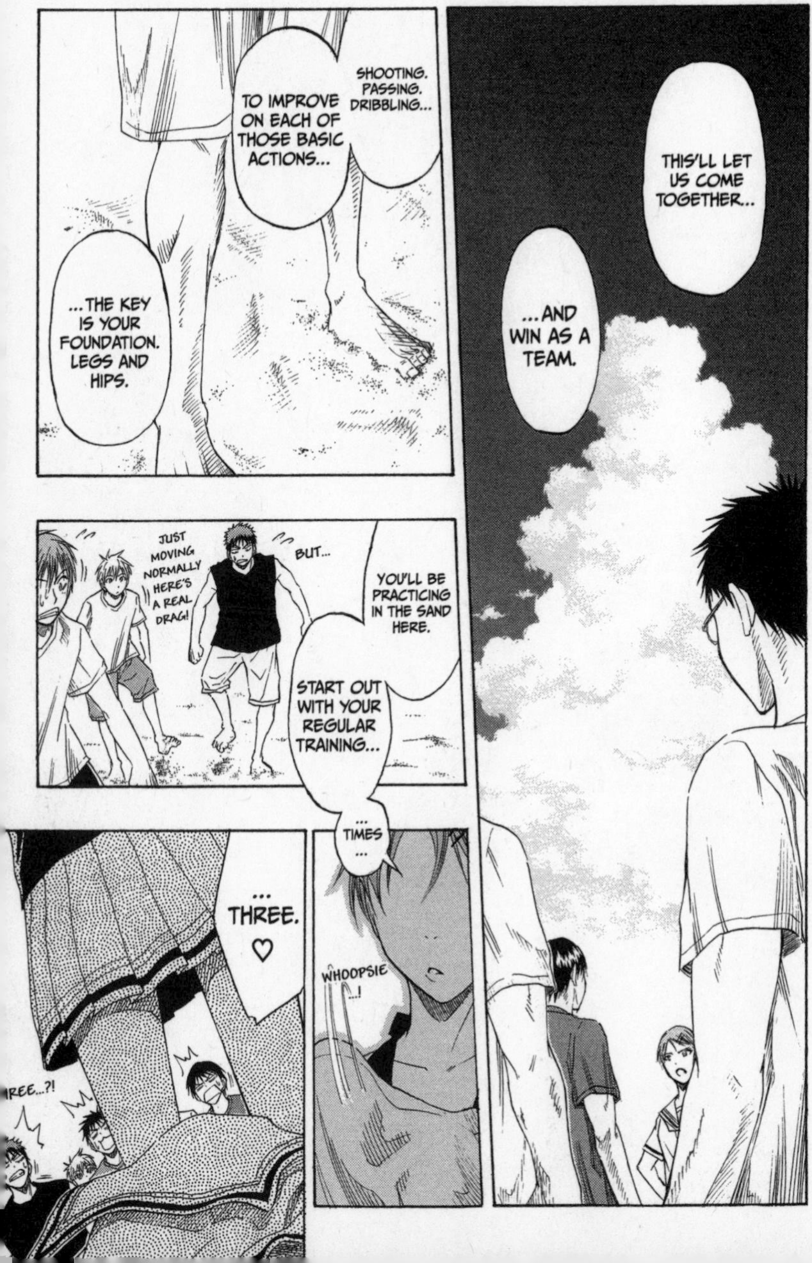
THIS'LL LET US COME TOGETHER...
...AND WIN AS A TEAM.
SHOOTING. PASSING. DRIBBLING...
TO IMPROVE ON EACH OF THOSE BASIC ACTIONS...
...THE KEY IS YOUR FOUNDATION. LEGS AND HIPS.
BUT...
YOU'LL BE PRACTICING IN THE SAND HERE.
START OUT WITH YOUR REGULAR TRAINING...
JUST MOVING NORMALLY HERE'S A REAL DRAG!
...TIMES...
WHOOPSIE ...!
...THREE. ♡
REE...?!

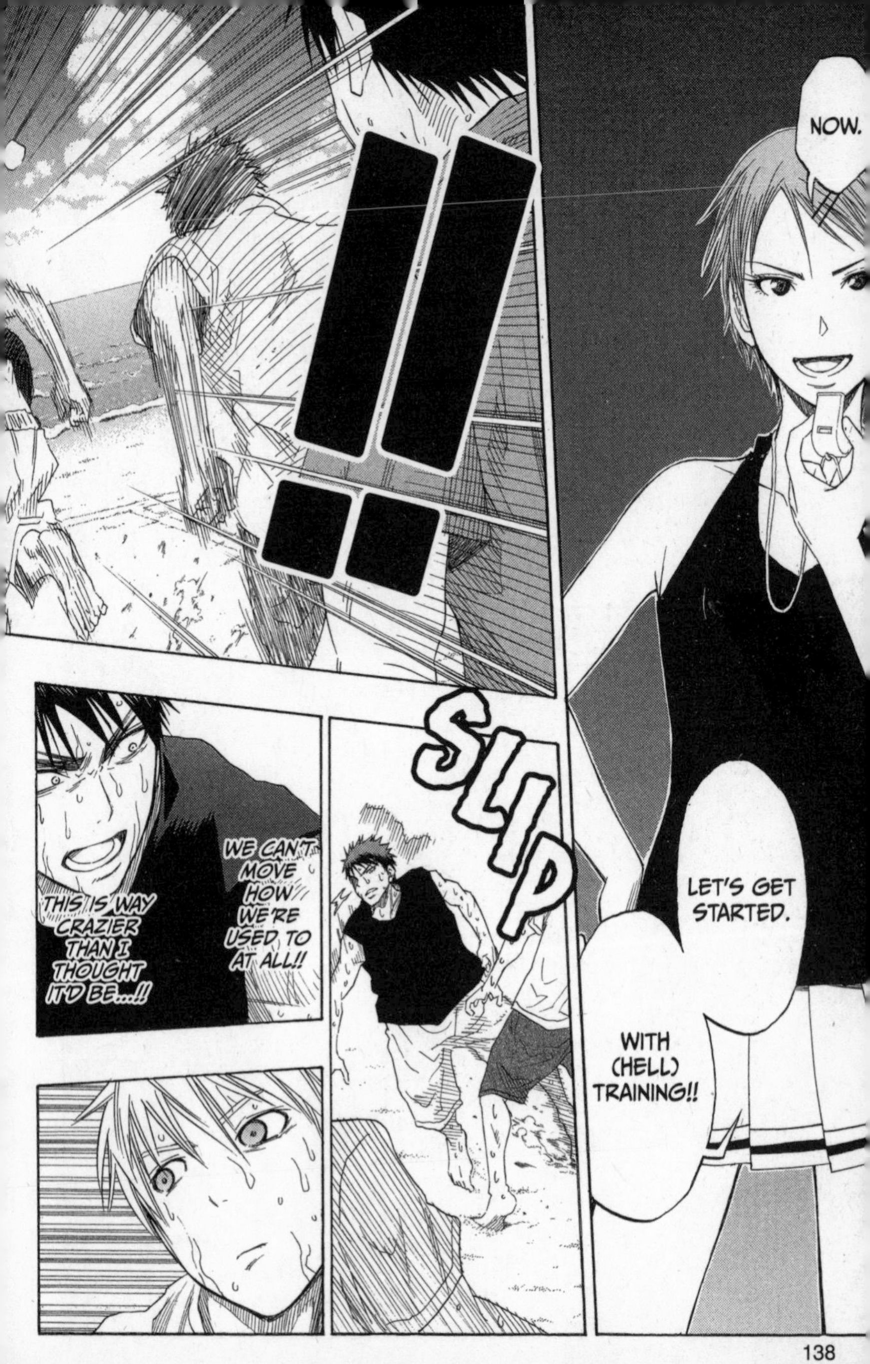
NOW.
LET'S GET STARTED.
WITH (HELL) TRAINING!!
!!
SLIP
WE CAN'T MOVE HOW WE'RE USED TO AT ALL!!
THIS IS WAY CRAZIER THAN I THOUGHT IT'D BE...!!

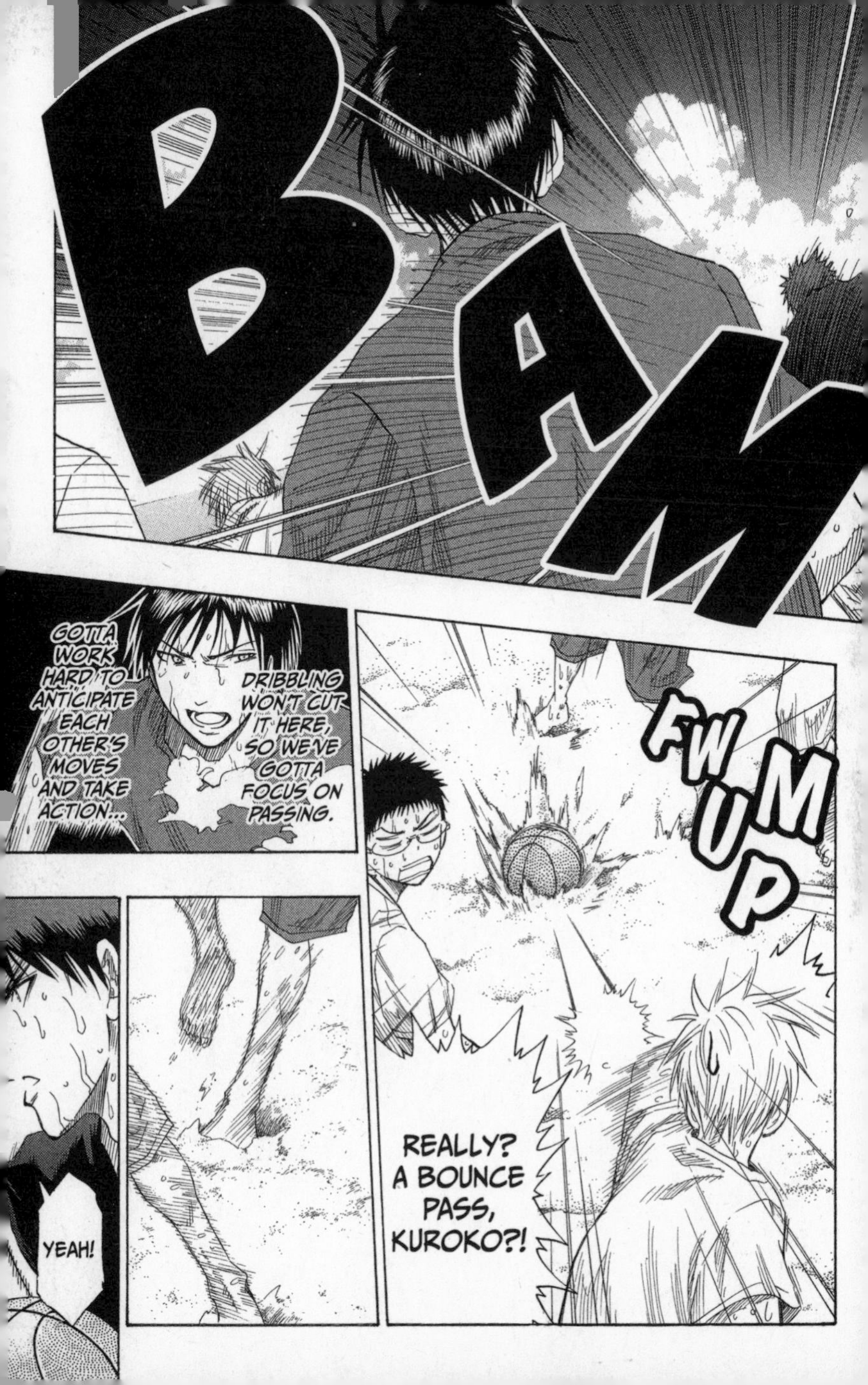
BAM
FWUMP
REALLY? A BOUNCE PASS, KUROKO?!
DRIBBLING WON'T CUT IT HERE, SO WE'VE GOTTA FOCUS ON PASSING.
GOTTA WORK HARD TO ANTICIPATE EACH OTHER'S MOVES AND TAKE ACTION...
YEAH!

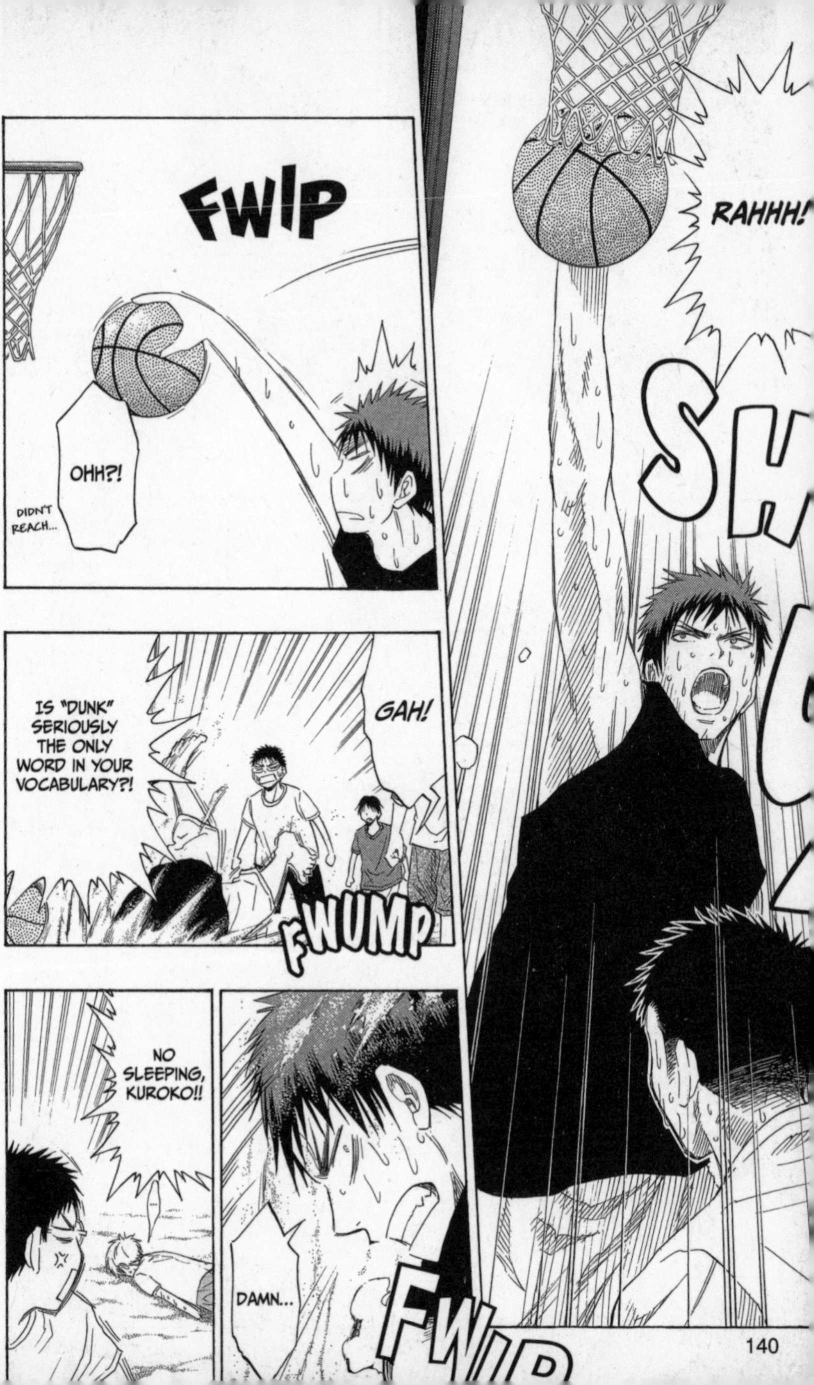
RAHHH!
SH
FWIP
OHH?!
DIDN'T REACH...
GAH!
IS "DUNK" SERIOUSLY THE ONLY WORD IN YOUR VOCABULARY?!
FWUMP
DAMN...
FWI
NO SLEEPING, KUROKO!!
...

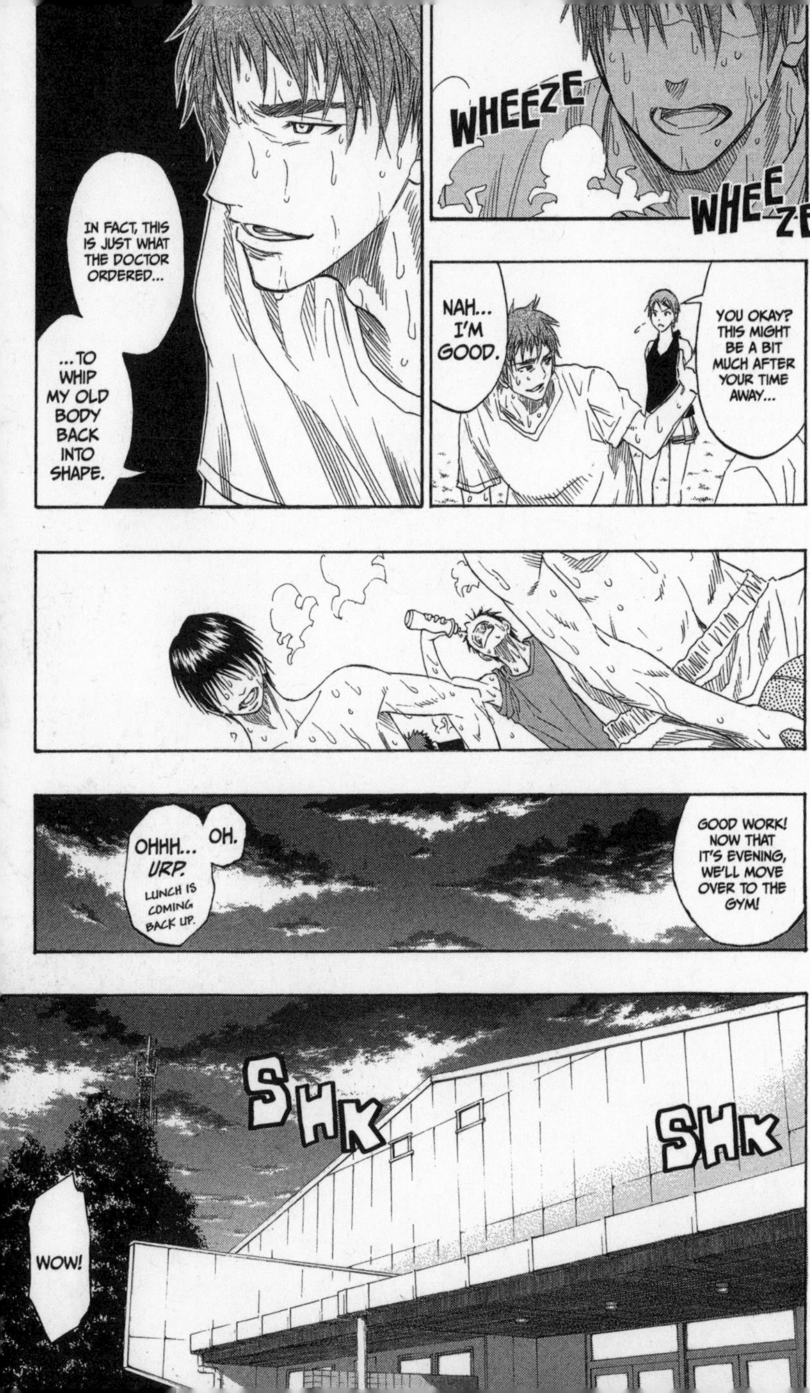
WHEEZE
WHEEZE
YOU OKAY? THIS MIGHT BE A BIT MUCH AFTER YOUR TIME AWAY...
NAH... I'M GOOD.
IN FACT, THIS IS JUST WHAT THE DOCTOR ORDERED...
...TO WHIP MY OLD BODY BACK INTO SHAPE.
GOOD WORK! NOW THAT IT'S EVENING, WE'LL MOVE OVER TO THE GYM!
OH.
OHHH... URP.
LUNCH IS COMING BACK UP.
SHK
SHK
WOW!

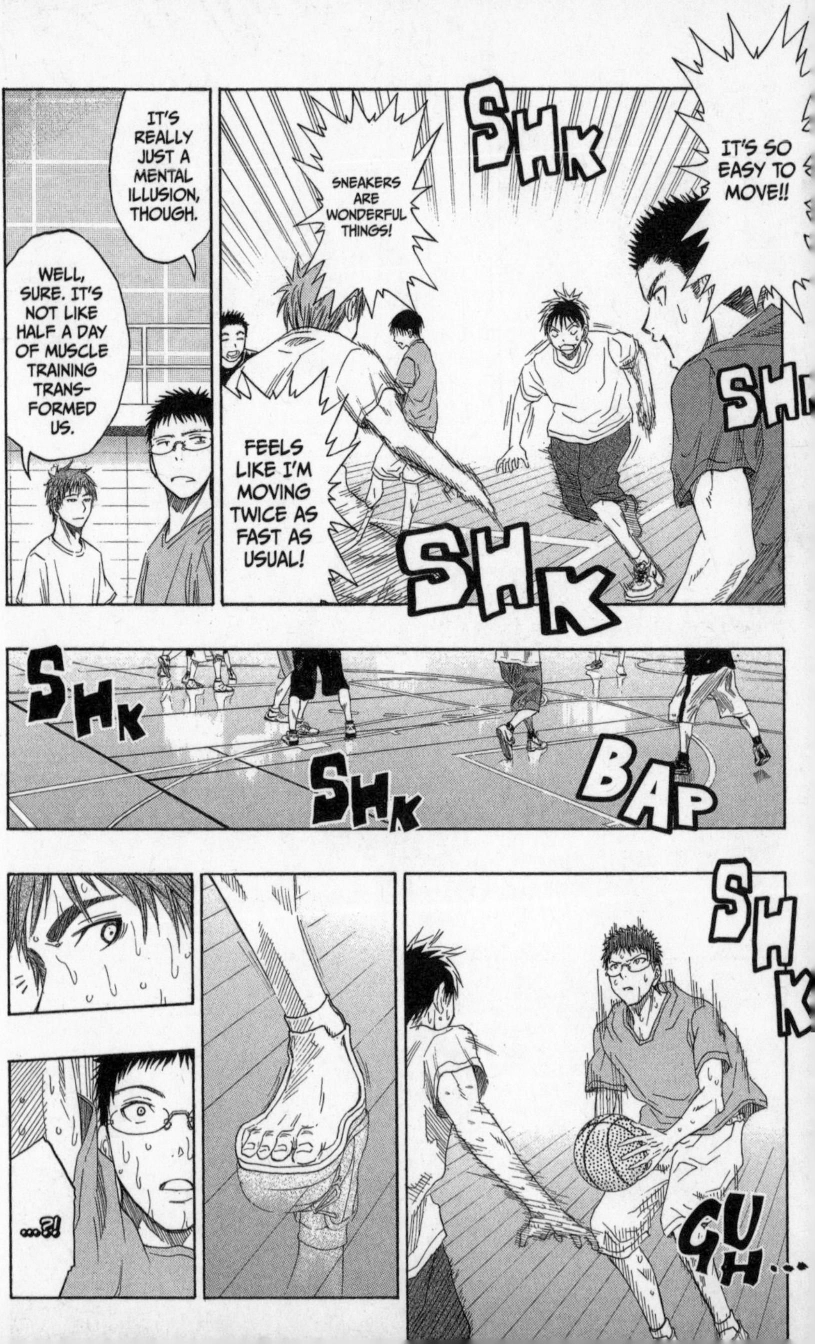
SHK
IT'S SO EASY TO MOVE!!
SNEAKERS ARE WONDERFUL THINGS!
SH
FEELS LIKE I'M MOVING TWICE AS FAST AS USUAL!
SHK
IT'S REALLY JUST A MENTAL ILLUSION, THOUGH.
WELL, SURE. IT'S NOT LIKE HALF A DAY OF MUSCLE TRAINING TRANS-FORMED US.
BAP
SHK
SHK
SHK
GUH...
...?!

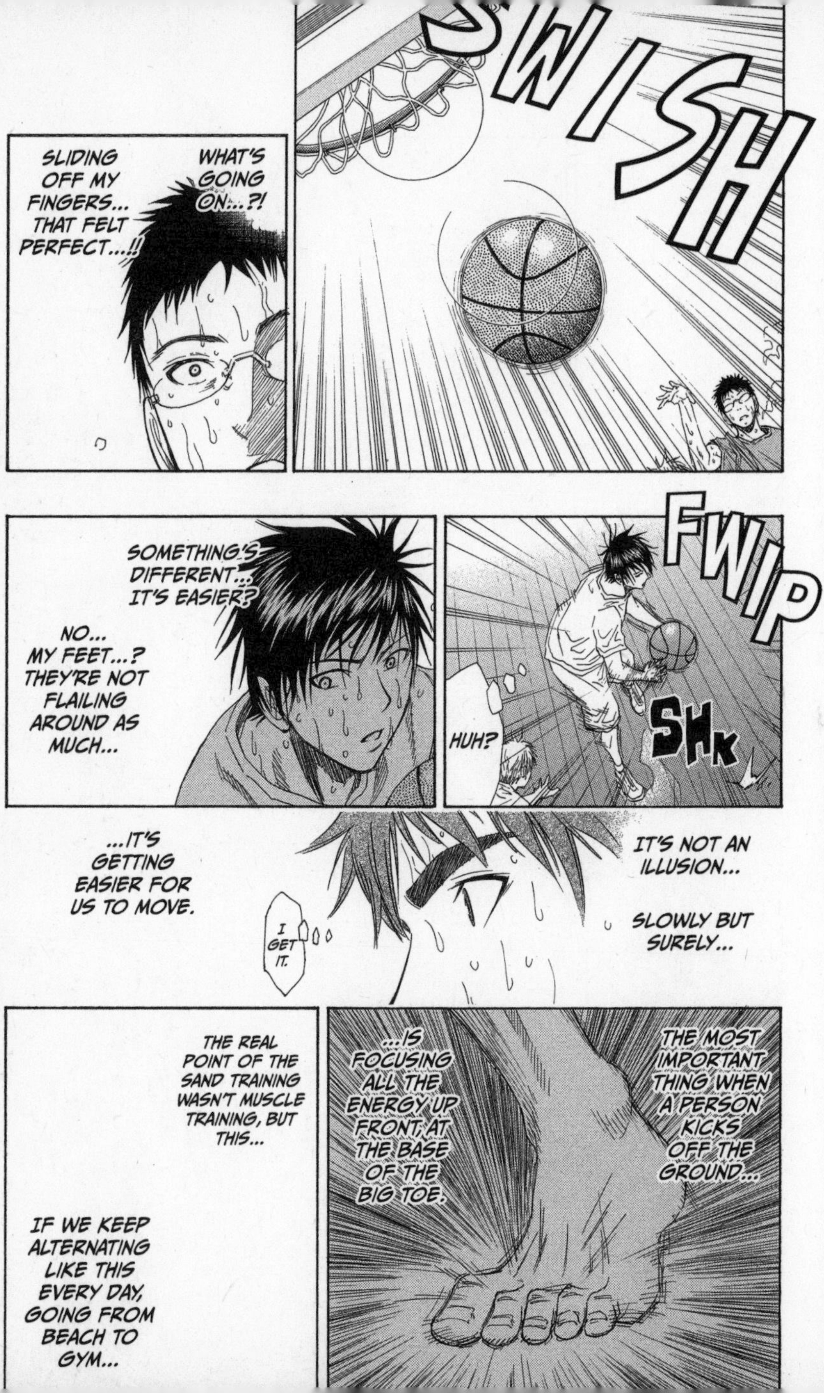
SWISH
WHAT'S GOING ON...?!
SLIDING OFF MY FINGERS... THAT FELT PERFECT...!!
FWIP
SHK
HUH?
SOMETHING'S DIFFERENT... IT'S EASIER?
NO... MY FEET...? THEY'RE NOT FLAILING AROUND AS MUCH...
IT'S NOT AN ILLUSION...
SLOWLY BUT SURELY...
I GET IT.
...IT'S GETTING EASIER FOR US TO MOVE.
THE MOST IMPORTANT THING WHEN A PERSON KICKS OFF THE GROUND...
...IS FOCUSING ALL THE ENERGY UP FRONT, AT THE BASE OF THE BIG TOE.
THE REAL POINT OF THE SAND TRAINING WASN'T MUSCLE TRAINING, BUT THIS...
IF WE KEEP ALTERNATING LIKE THIS EVERY DAY, GOING FROM BEACH TO GYM...

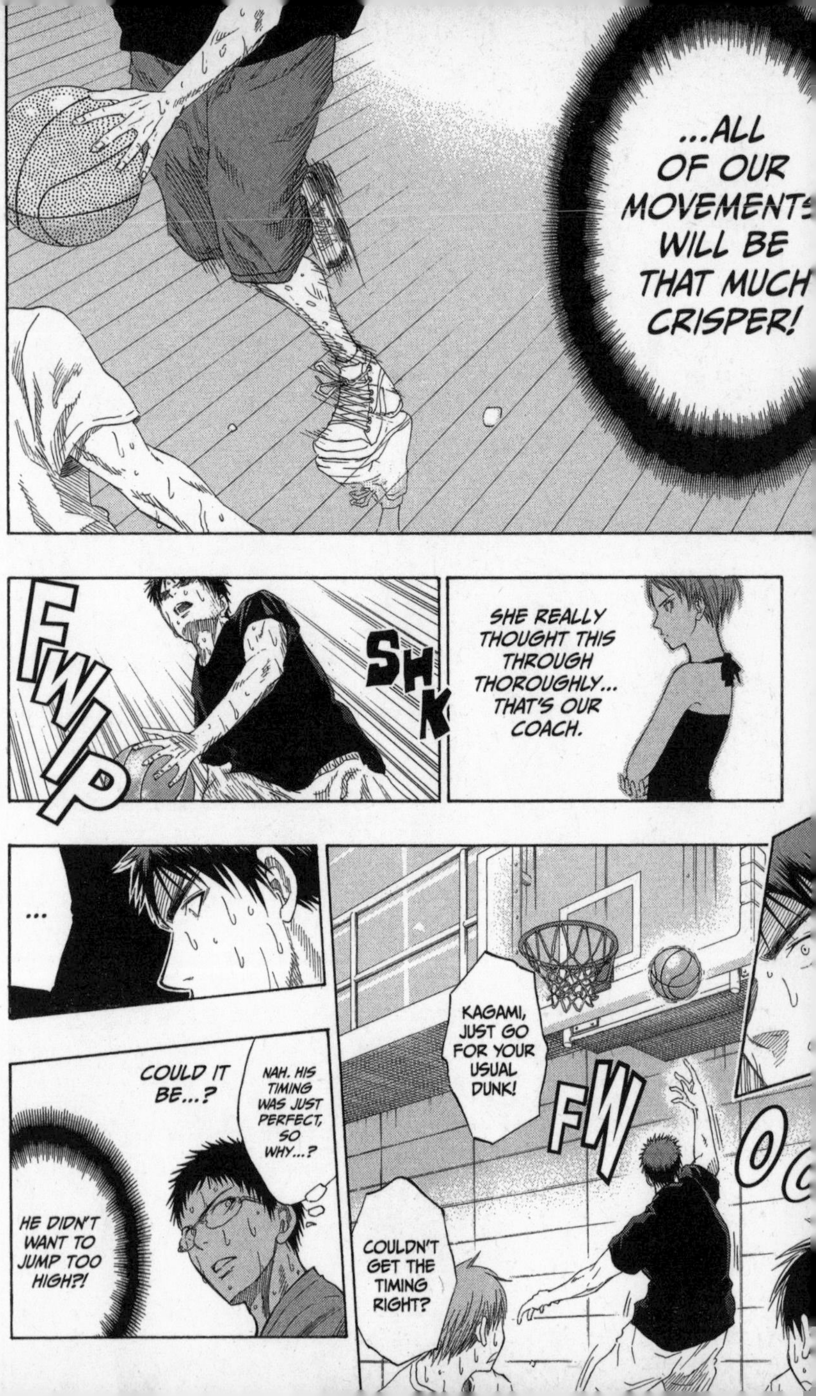

...ALL OF OUR MOVEMENTS WILL BE THAT MUCH CRISPER!
SHE REALLY THOUGHT THIS THROUGH THOROUGHLY... THAT'S OUR COACH.
SHK
FWIP
KAGAMI, JUST GO FOR YOUR USUAL DUNK!
FW
COULDN'T GET THE TIMING RIGHT?
...
COULD IT BE...?
NAH. HIS TIMING WAS JUST PERFECT, SO WHY...?
HE DIDN'T WANT TO JUMP TOO HIGH?!

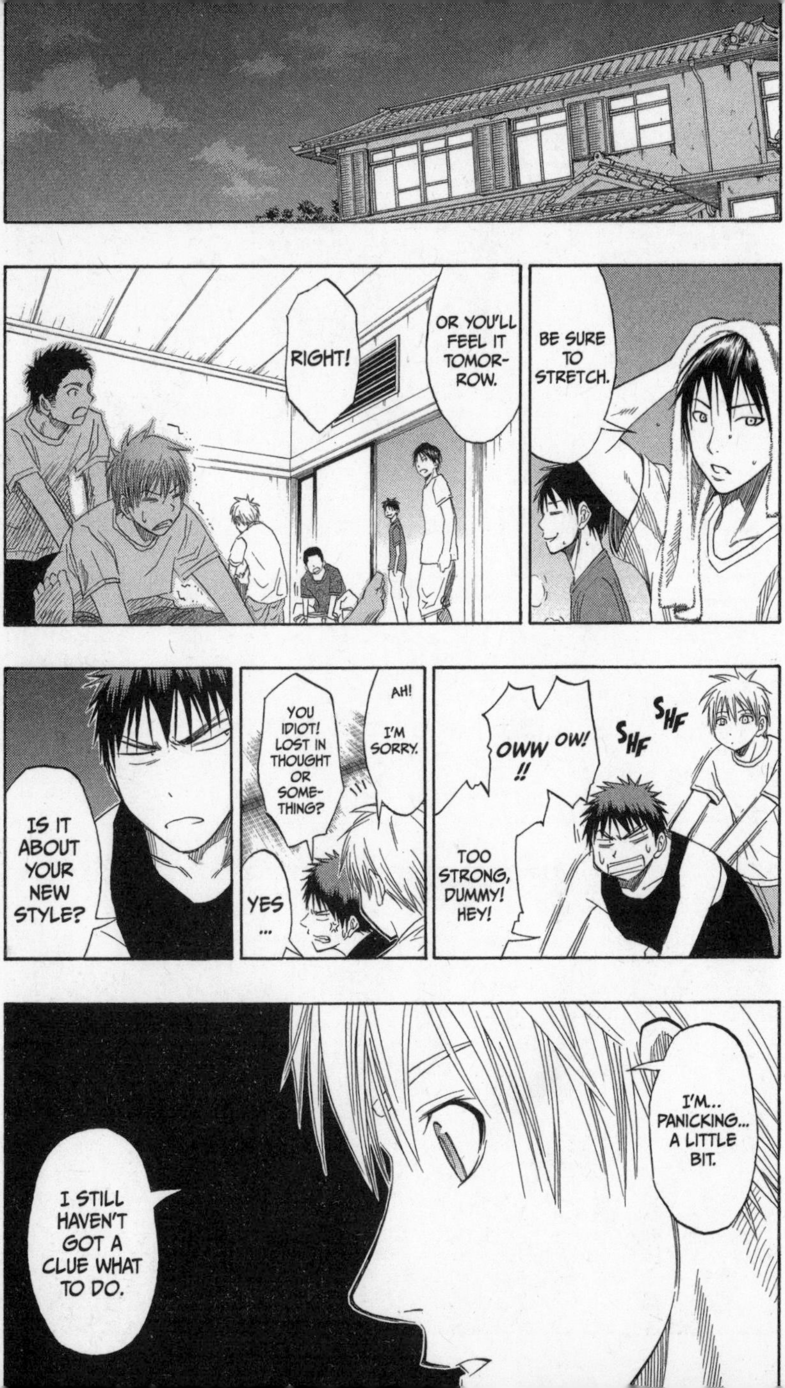
BE SURE TO STRETCH.
OR YOU'LL FEEL IT TOMORROW.
RIGHT!
SHF SHF
OWW OW!!
TOO STRONG, DUMMY! HEY!
AH! I'M SORRY.
YOU IDIOT! LOST IN THOUGHT OR SOMETHING?
YES...
IS IT ABOUT YOUR NEW STYLE?
I'M... PANICKING... A LITTLE BIT.
I STILL HAVEN'T GOT A CLUE WHAT TO DO.

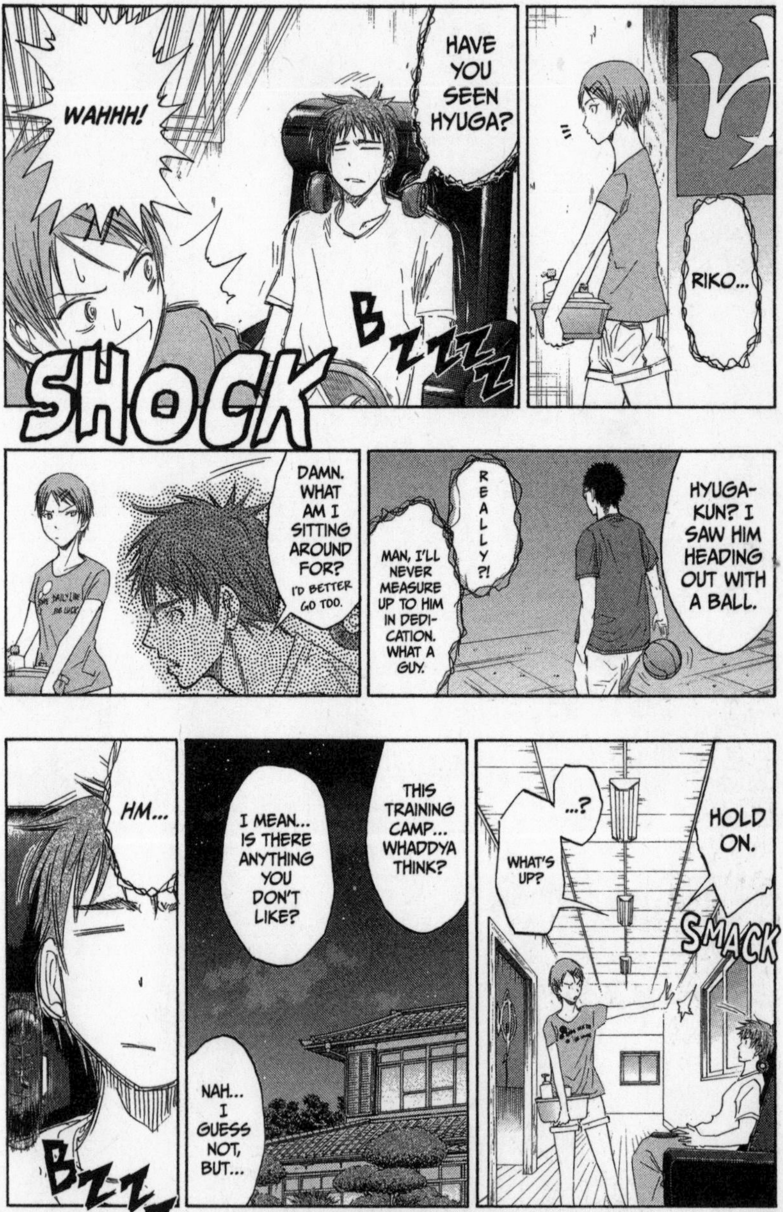
RIKO...
HAVE YOU SEEN HYUGA?
WAHHH!
SHOCK
BZZZZ
HYUGA-KUN? I SAW HIM HEADING OUT WITH A BALL.
REALLY?!
MAN, I'LL NEVER MEASURE UP TO HIM IN DEDICATION. WHAT A GUY.
DAMN. WHAT AM I SITTING AROUND FOR?
I'D BETTER GO TOO.
HOLD ON.
SMACK
...?
WHAT'S UP?
THIS TRAINING CAMP... WHADDYA THINK?
I MEAN... IS THERE ANYTHING YOU DON'T LIKE?
NAH... I GUESS NOT, BUT...
HM...
BZZZ

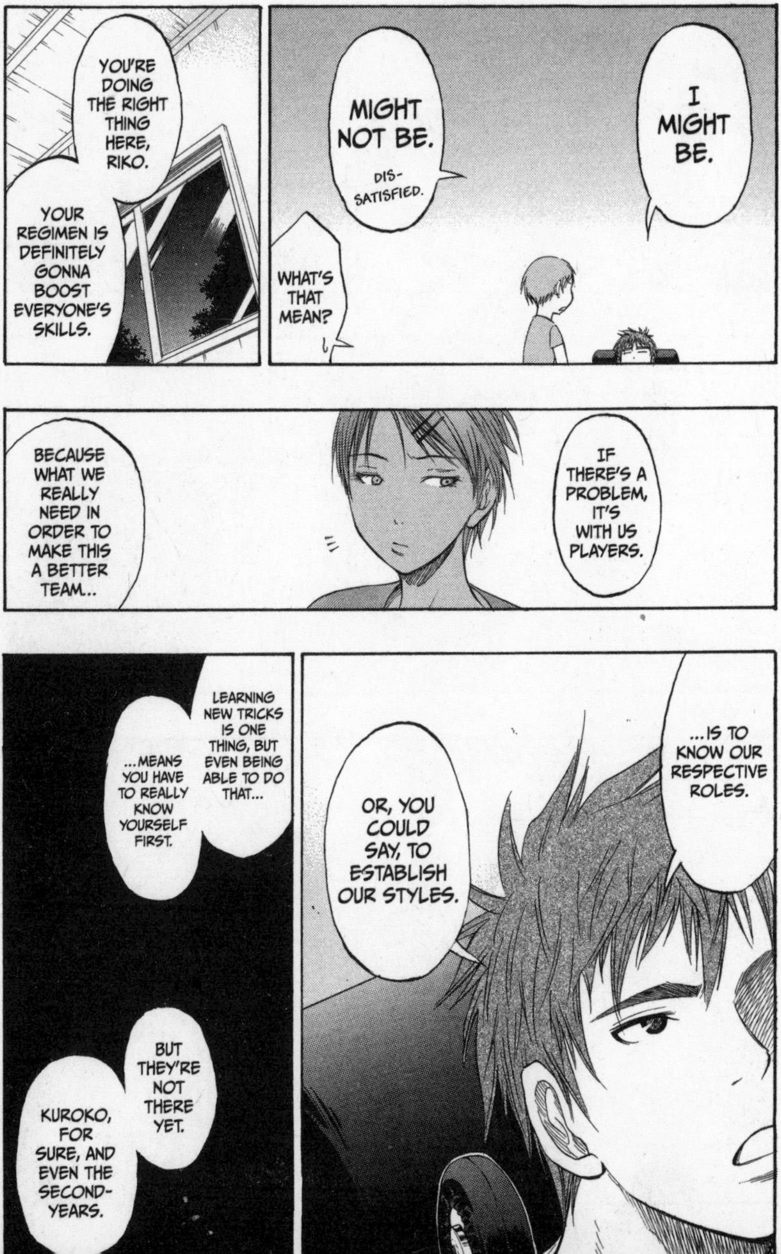
I MIGHT BE.
MIGHT NOT BE.
DIS-SATISFIED.
WHAT'S THAT MEAN?
YOU'RE DOING THE RIGHT THING HERE, RIKO.
YOUR REGIMEN IS DEFINITELY GONNA BOOST EVERYONE'S SKILLS.
IF THERE'S A PROBLEM, IT'S WITH US PLAYERS.
BECAUSE WHAT WE REALLY NEED IN ORDER TO MAKE THIS A BETTER TEAM...
...IS TO KNOW OUR RESPECTIVE ROLES.
OR, YOU COULD SAY, TO ESTABLISH OUR STYLES.
LEARNING NEW TRICKS IS ONE THING, BUT EVEN BEING ABLE TO DO THAT...
...MEANS YOU HAVE TO REALLY KNOW YOURSELF FIRST.
BUT THEY'RE NOT THERE YET.
KUROKO, FOR SURE, AND EVEN THE SECOND-YEARS.

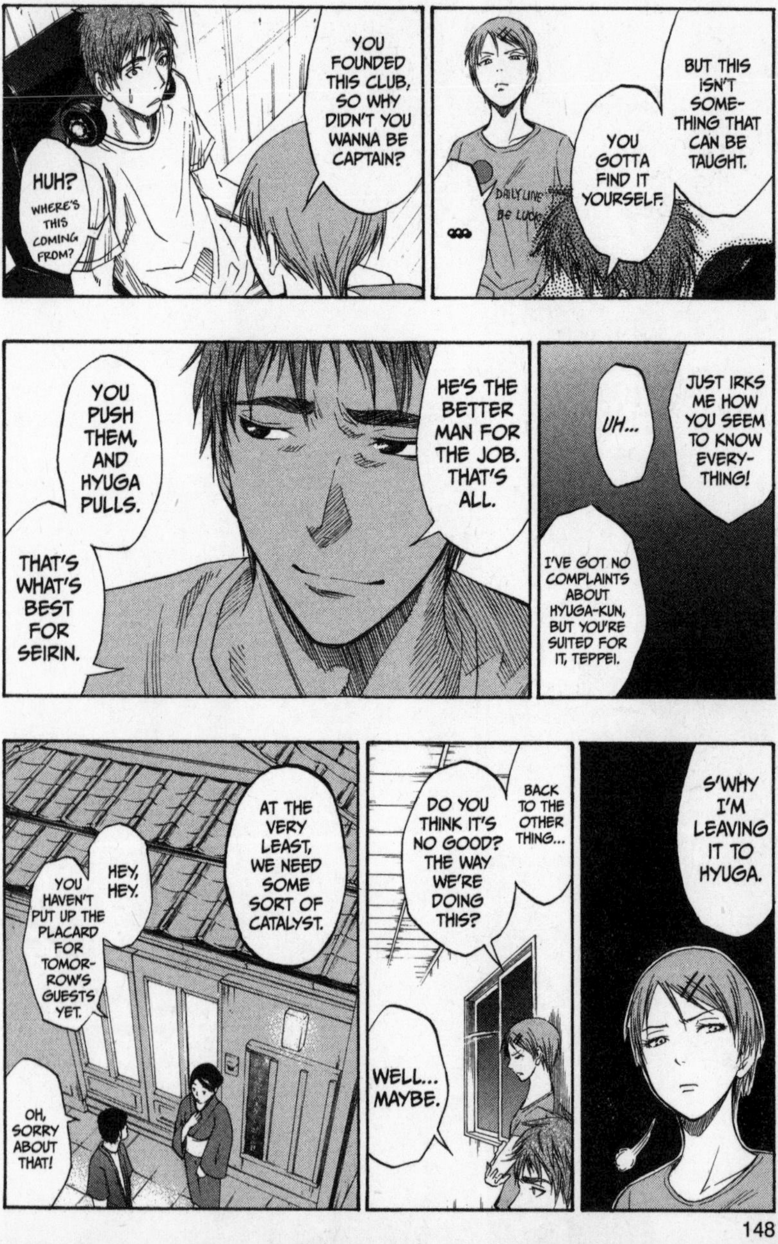
BUT THIS ISN'T SOME-THING THAT CAN BE TAUGHT.
YOU GOTTA FIND IT YOURSELF.
...
YOU FOUNDED THIS CLUB, SO WHY DIDN'T YOU WANNA BE CAPTAIN?
HUH? WHERE'S THIS COMING FROM?
JUST IRKS ME HOW YOU SEEM TO KNOW EVERY-THING!
UH...
I'VE GOT NO COMPLAINTS ABOUT HYUGA-KUN, BUT YOU'RE SUITED FOR IT, TEPPEI.
HE'S THE BETTER MAN FOR THE JOB. THAT'S ALL.
YOU PUSH THEM, AND HYUGA PULLS.
THAT'S WHAT'S BEST FOR SEIRIN.
S'WHY I'M LEAVING IT TO HYUGA.
BACK TO THE OTHER THING...
DO YOU THINK IT'S NO GOOD? THE WAY WE'RE DOING THIS?
WELL... MAYBE.
AT THE VERY LEAST, WE NEED SOME SORT OF CATALYST.
HEY, HEY.
YOU HAVEN'T PUT UP THE PLACARD FOR TOMORROW'S GUESTS YET.
OH, SORRY ABOUT THAT!

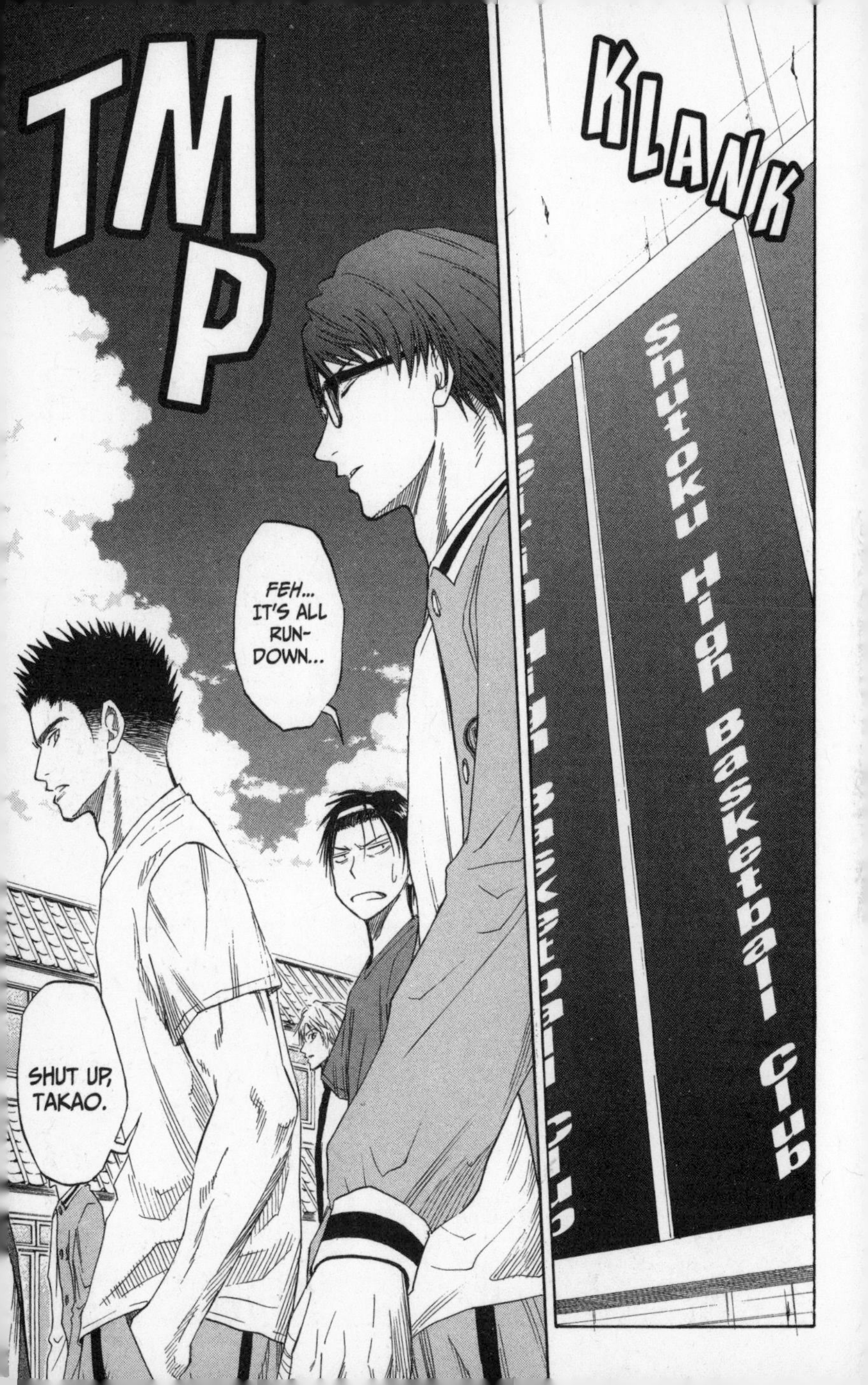
KLANK
Shutoku High Basketball Club
TMP
FEH... IT'S ALL RUN-DOWN...
SHUT UP, TAKAO.

KUROKO'S BASKETBALL BLOOPERS

TAKE 8

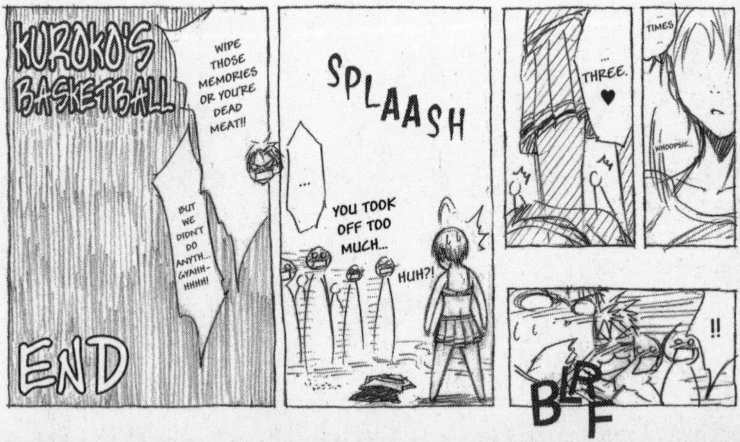

... TIMES ...
WHOOPSIE...
... THREE. ♥
!!
BLRRF
SPLAASH
...
YOU TOOK OFF TOO MUCH...
HUH?!
KUROKO'S BASKETBALL
WIPE THOSE MEMORIES OR YOU'RE DEAD MEAT!!
BUT WE DIDN'T DO ANYTH... GYAHH-HHHH!
END

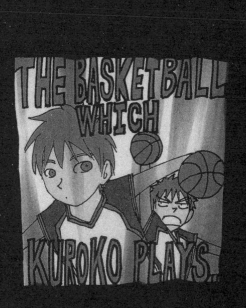

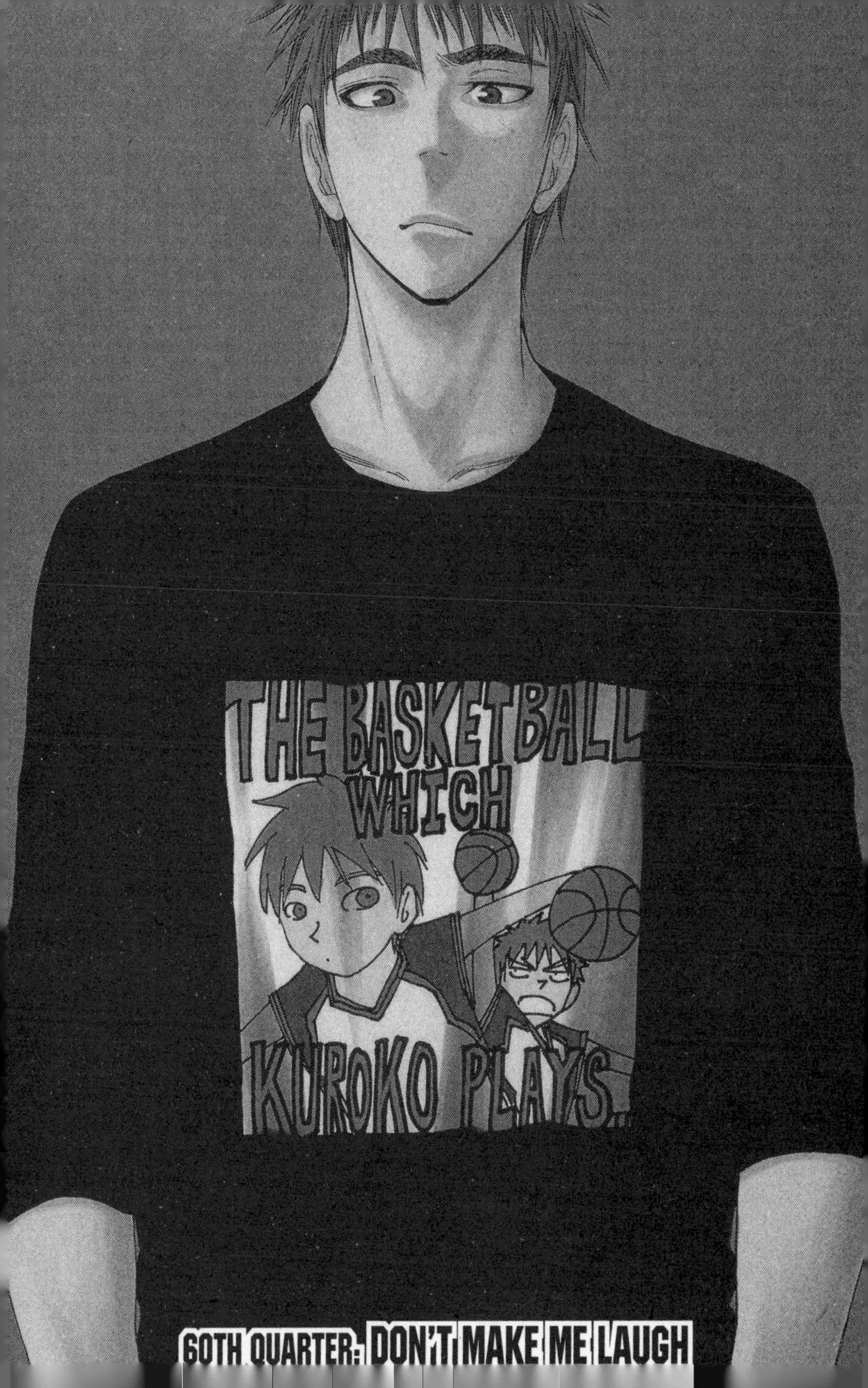

THE BASKETBALL WHICH KUROKO PLAYS...

60TH QUARTER: DON'T MAKE ME LAUGH

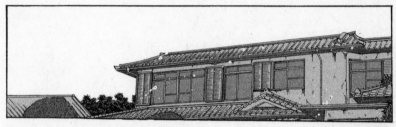

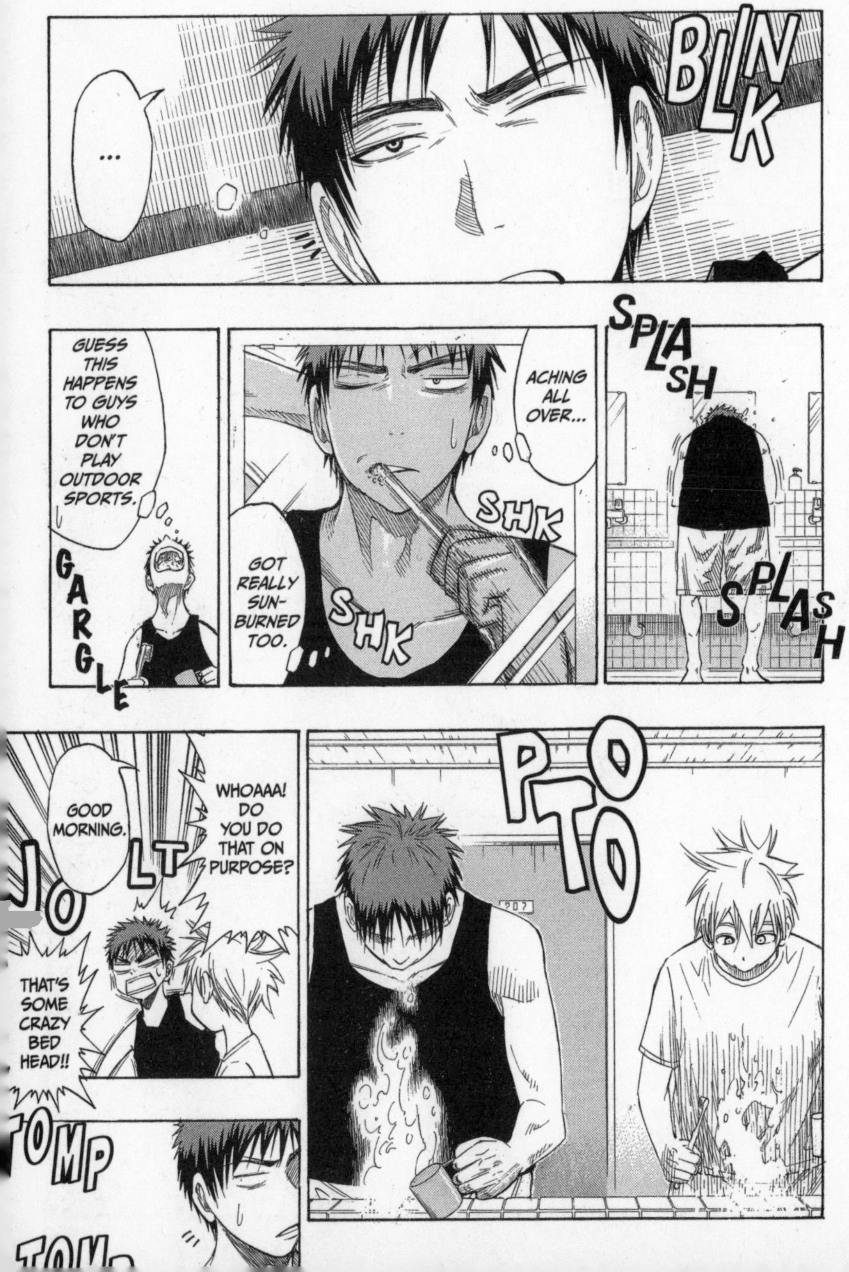
BLINK
...
SPLASH
SPLASH
ACHING ALL OVER...
SHK
SHK
GOT REALLY SUN-BURNED TOO.
GUESS THIS HAPPENS TO GUYS WHO DON'T PLAY OUTDOOR SPORTS.
GARGLE
WHOAAA! DO YOU DO THAT ON PURPOSE?
GOOD MORNING.
JOLT
THAT'S SOME CRAZY BED HEAD!!
TOMP

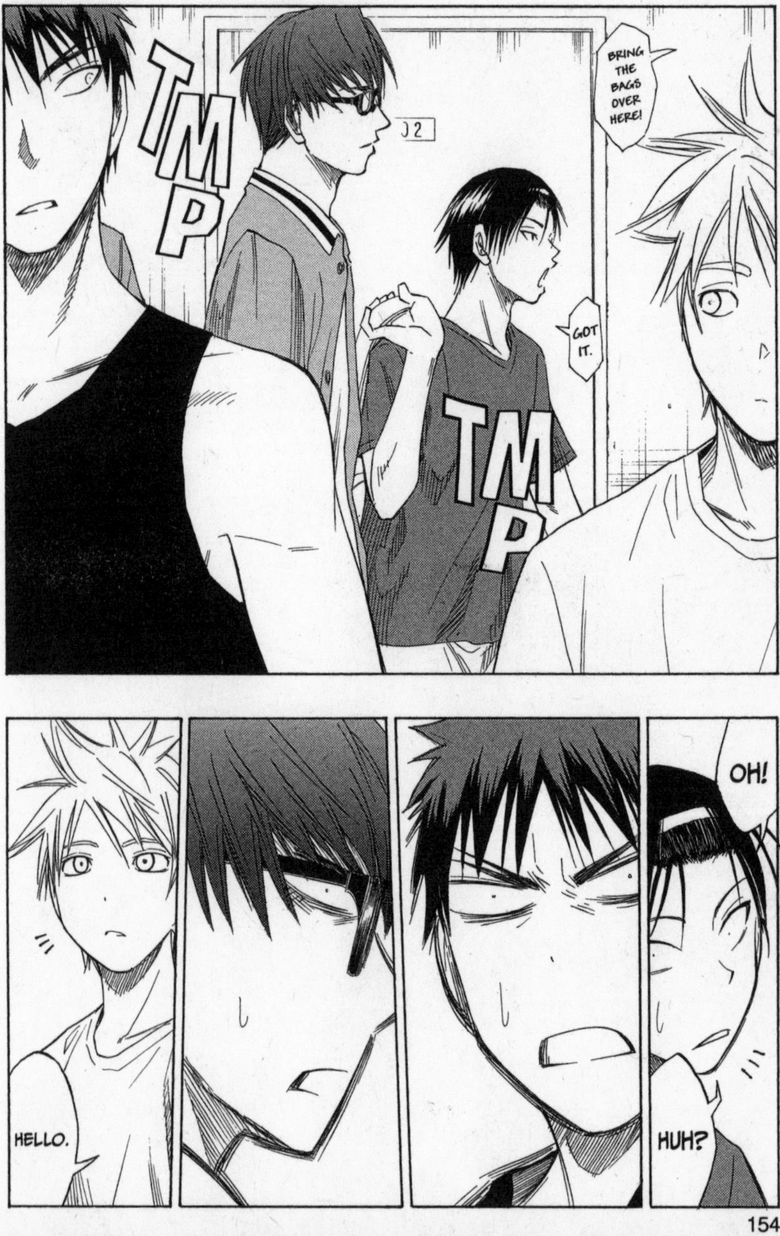
BRING THE BAGS OVER HERE!
TMP
GOT IT.
TMP
OH!
HUH?
HELLO.

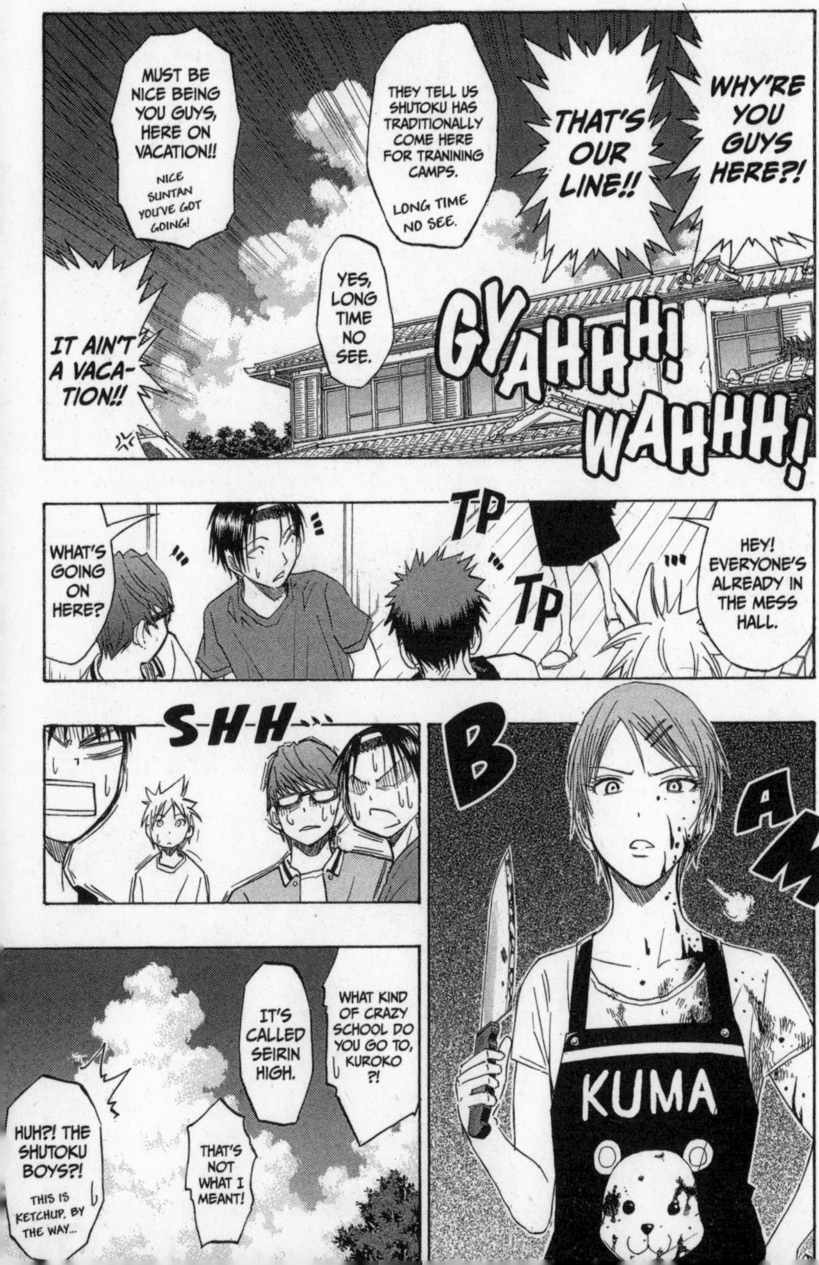
WHY'RE YOU GUYS HERE?!
THAT'S OUR LINE!!
GYAHHH! WAHHH!
THEY TELL US SHUTOKU HAS TRADITIONALLY COME HERE FOR TRANINING CAMPS.
LONG TIME NO SEE.
YES, LONG TIME NO SEE.
MUST BE NICE BEING YOU GUYS, HERE ON VACATION!!
NICE SUNTAN YOU'VE GOT GOING!
IT AIN'T A VACATION!!
HEY! EVERYONE'S ALREADY IN THE MESS HALL.
TP
TP
WHAT'S GOING ON HERE?
BAM
KUMA
S-H-H
WHAT KIND OF CRAZY SCHOOL DO YOU GO TO, KUROKO?!
IT'S CALLED SEIRIN HIGH.
THAT'S NOT WHAT I MEANT!
HUH?! THE SHUTOKU BOYS?!
THIS IS KETCHUP, BY THE WAY...

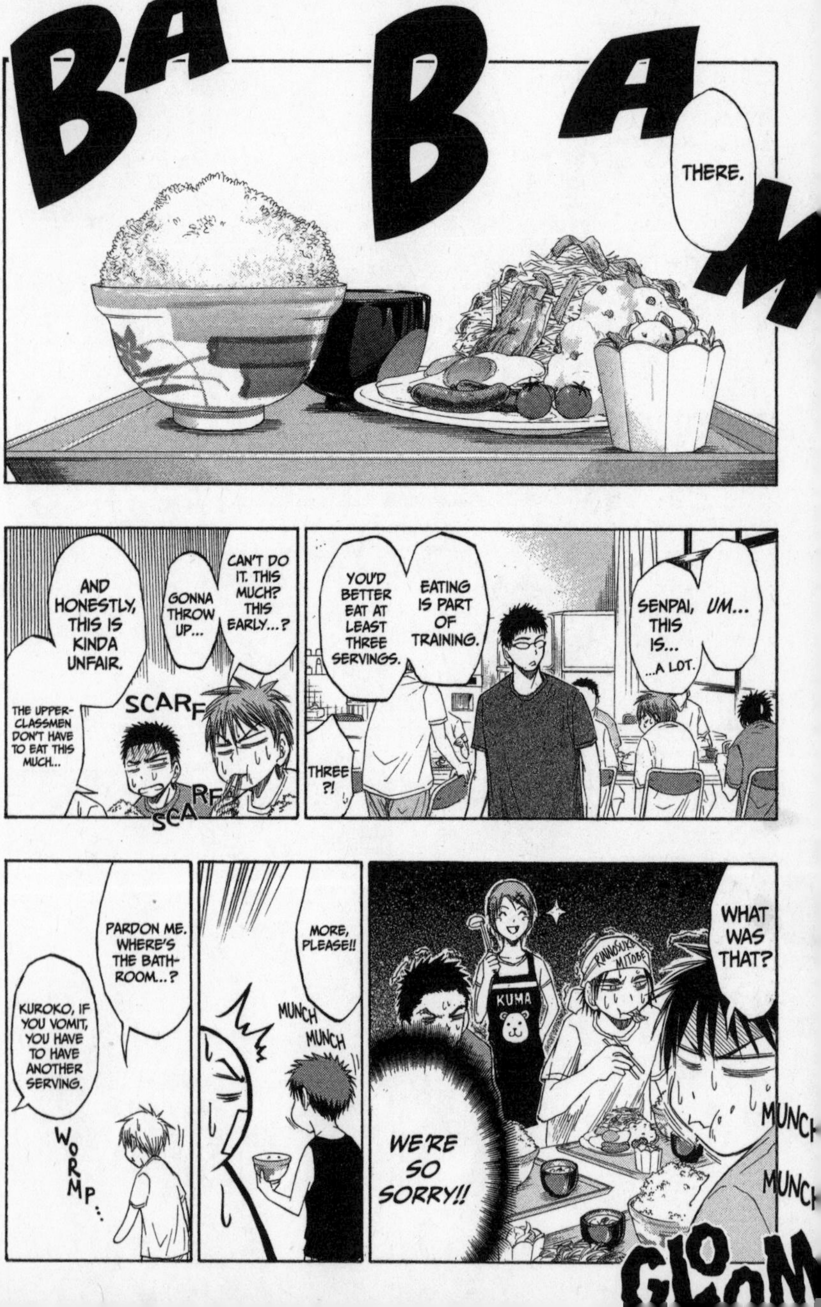
BABAM
THERE.
UM...
SENPAI, THIS IS... ...A LOT.
EATING IS PART OF TRAINING.
YOU'D BETTER EAT AT LEAST THREE SERVINGS.
THREE?!
CAN'T DO IT. THIS MUCH? THIS EARLY...?
GONNA THROW UP...
AND HONESTLY, THIS IS KINDA UNFAIR.
SCARF
SCARF
THE UPPER-CLASSMEN DON'T HAVE TO EAT THIS MUCH...
WHAT WAS THAT?
KUMA
RINNOSUKE MITOBE
WE'RE SO SORRY!!
MUNCH
MUNCH
GLOM
MORE, PLEASE!!
MUNCH
MUNCH
PARDON ME. WHERE'S THE BATH-ROOM...?
KUROKO, IF YOU VOMIT, YOU HAVE TO HAVE ANOTHER SERVING.
WORMP...

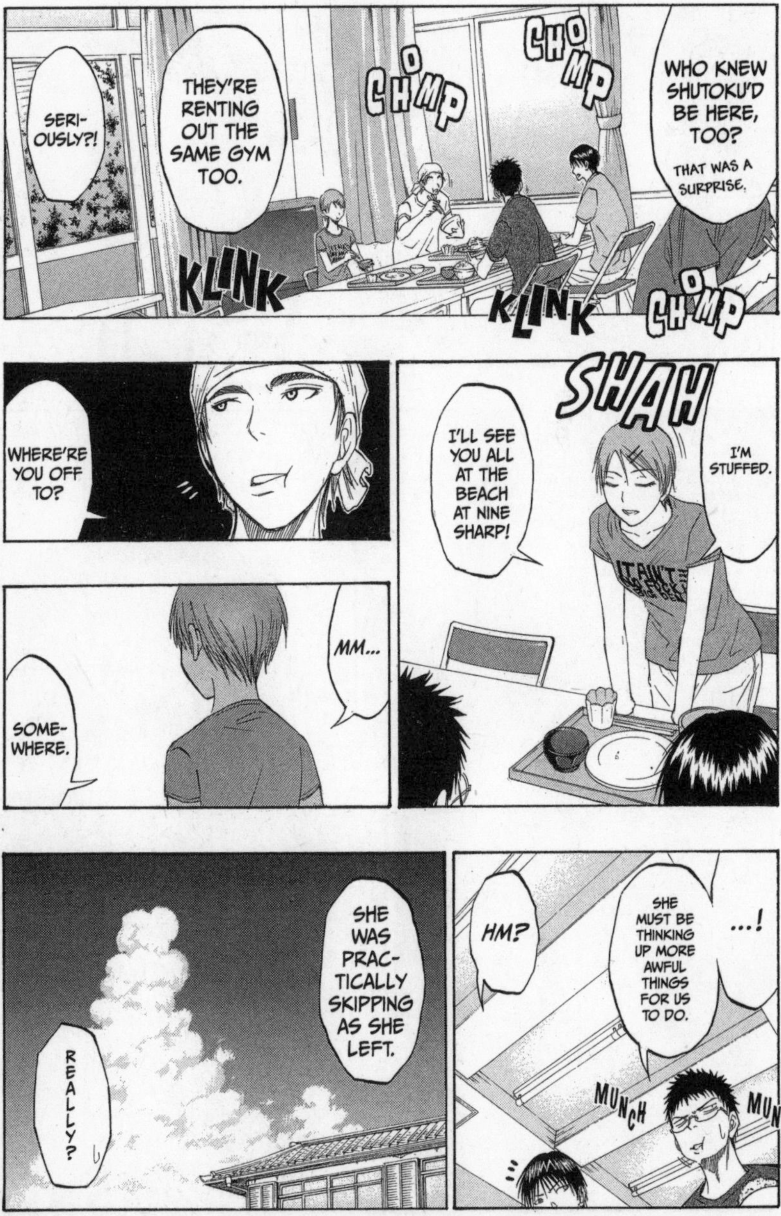
WHO KNEW SHUTOKU'D BE HERE, TOO?
THAT WAS A SURPRISE.
CHOMP
CHOMP
CHOMP
THEY'RE RENTING OUT THE SAME GYM TOO.
SERI-OUSLY?!
KLINK
KLINK
SHAH
I'M STUFFED.
I'LL SEE YOU ALL AT THE BEACH AT NINE SHARP!
WHERE'RE YOU OFF TO?
MM...
SOME-WHERE.
...!
SHE MUST BE THINKING UP MORE AWFUL THINGS FOR US TO DO.
HM?
MUNCH
MUNCH
SHE WAS PRAC-TICALLY SKIPPING AS SHE LEFT.
REALLY?

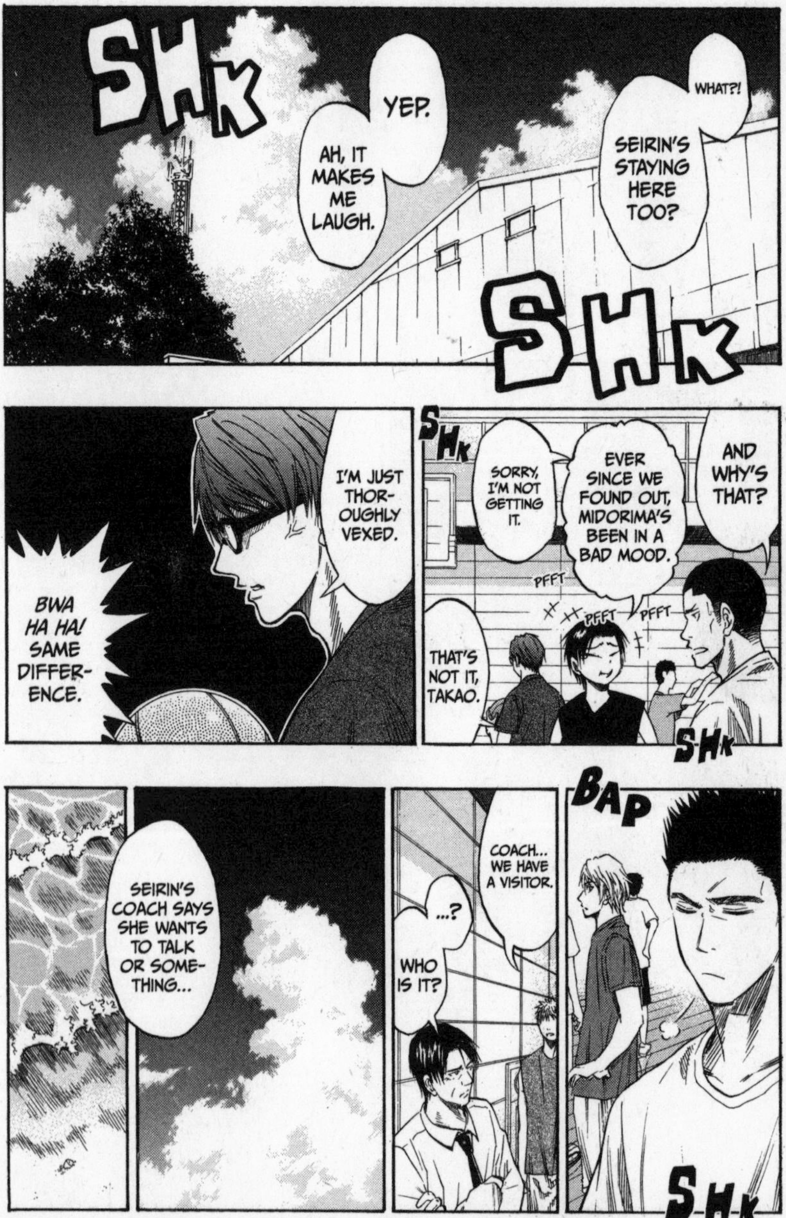
WHAT?!
SEIRIN'S STAYING HERE TOO?
SHK
YEP.
AH, IT MAKES ME LAUGH.
SHK
AND WHY'S THAT?
EVER SINCE WE FOUND OUT, MIDORIMA'S BEEN IN A BAD MOOD.
SORRY, I'M NOT GETTING IT.
SHK
PFFT
PFFT
PFFT
THAT'S NOT IT, TAKAO.
SHK
I'M JUST THOR-OUGHLY VEXED.
BWA HA HA! SAME DIFFER-ENCE.
BAP
SHK
COACH... WE HAVE A VISITOR.
...?
WHO IS IT?
SEIRIN'S COACH SAYS SHE WANTS TO TALK OR SOME-THING...

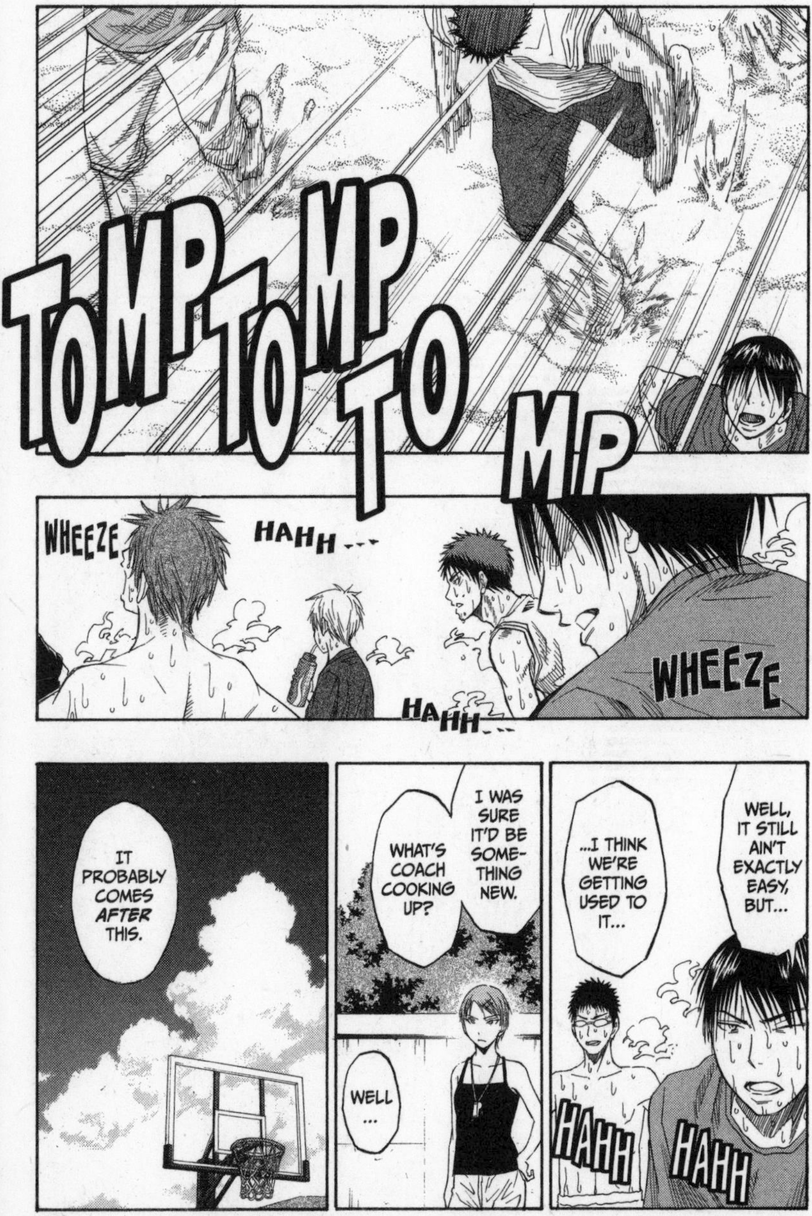
TOMP TOMP TOMP
WHEEZE
HAHH...
HAHH...
WHEEZE
WELL, IT STILL AIN'T EXACTLY EASY, BUT...
...I THINK WE'RE GETTING USED TO IT...
HAHH
HAHH
I WAS SURE IT'D BE SOME-THING NEW.
WHAT'S COACH COOKING UP?
WELL...
IT PROBABLY COMES *AFTER* THIS.

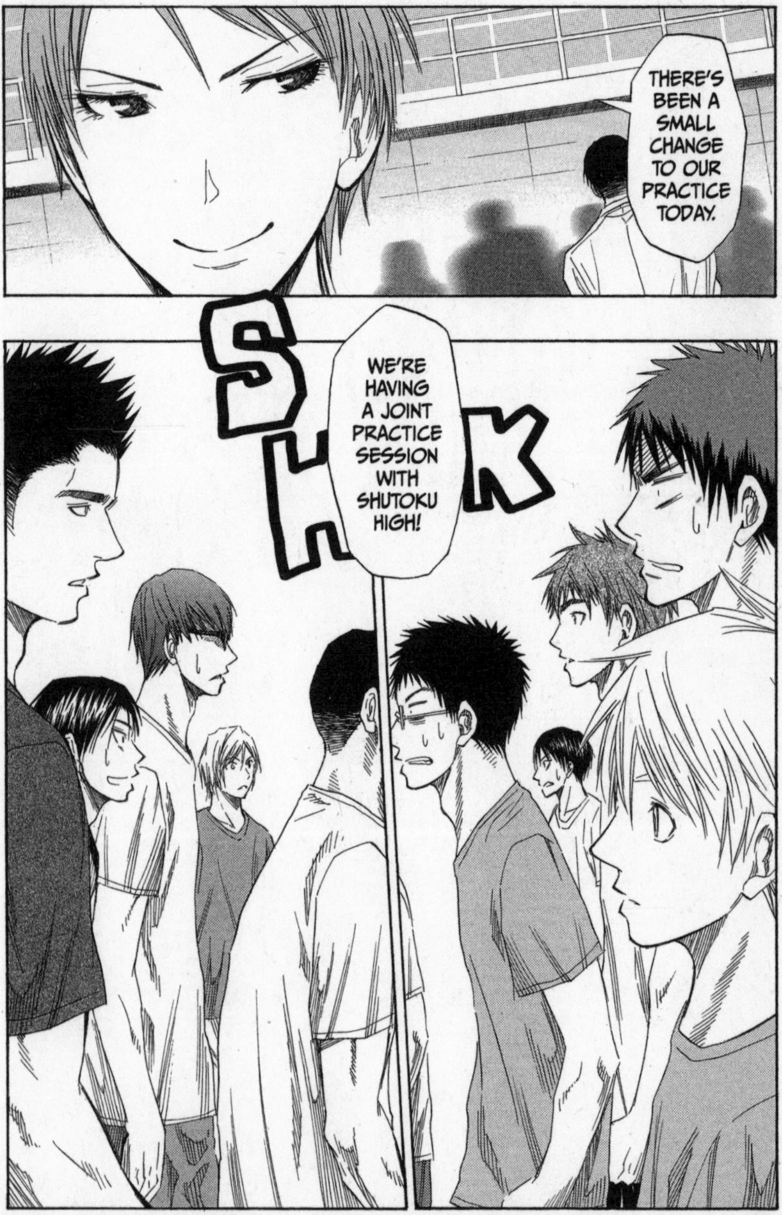
THERE'S BEEN A SMALL CHANGE TO OUR PRACTICE TODAY.
WE'RE HAVING A JOINT PRACTICE SESSION WITH SHUTOKU HIGH!
SHAK

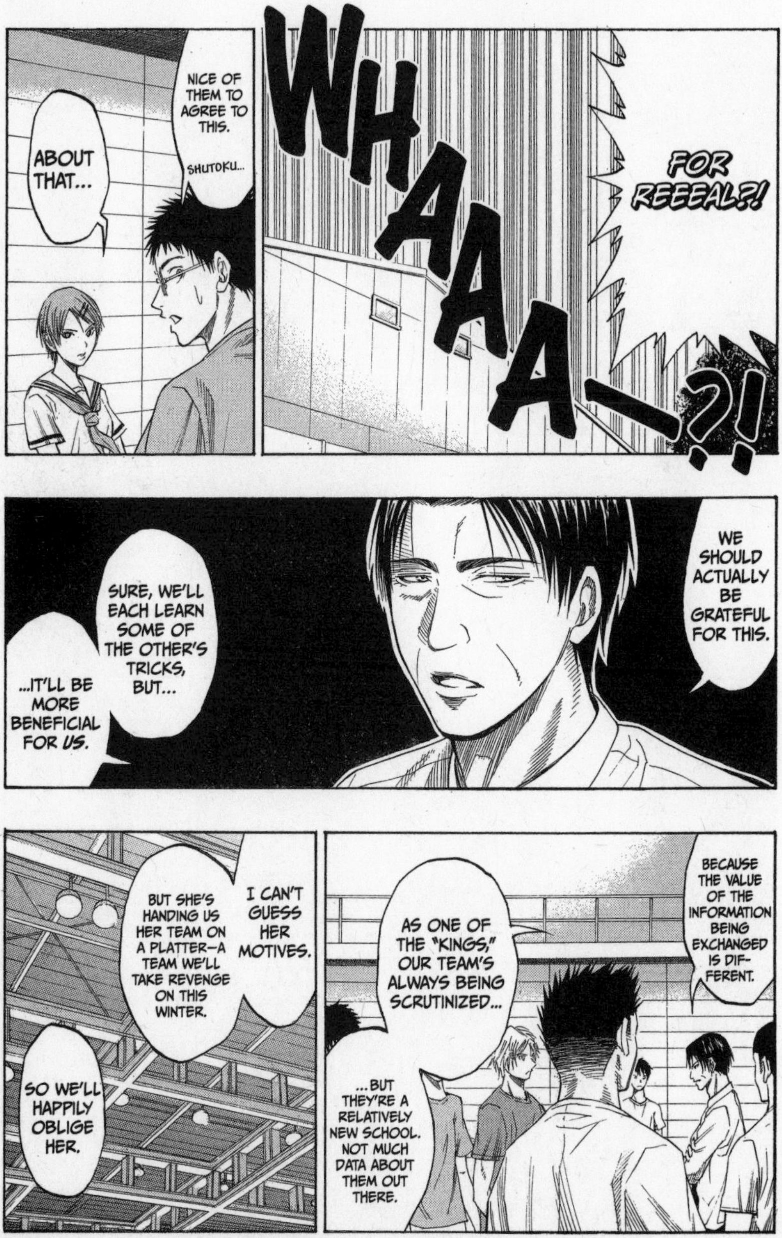
WHAAAA—?!
FOR REEEAL?!
NICE OF THEM TO AGREE TO THIS.
SHUTOKU...
ABOUT THAT...
WE SHOULD ACTUALLY BE GRATEFUL FOR THIS.
SURE, WE'LL EACH LEARN SOME OF THE OTHER'S TRICKS, BUT...
...IT'LL BE MORE BENEFICIAL FOR *US*.
BECAUSE THE VALUE OF THE INFORMATION BEING EXCHANGED IS DIFFERENT.
AS ONE OF THE "KINGS," OUR TEAM'S ALWAYS BEING SCRUTINIZED...
...BUT THEY'RE A RELATIVELY NEW SCHOOL. NOT MUCH DATA ABOUT THEM OUT THERE.
I CAN'T GUESS HER MOTIVES.
BUT SHE'S HANDING US HER TEAM ON A PLATTER—A TEAM WE'LL TAKE REVENGE ON THIS WINTER.
SO WE'LL HAPPILY OBLIGE HER.

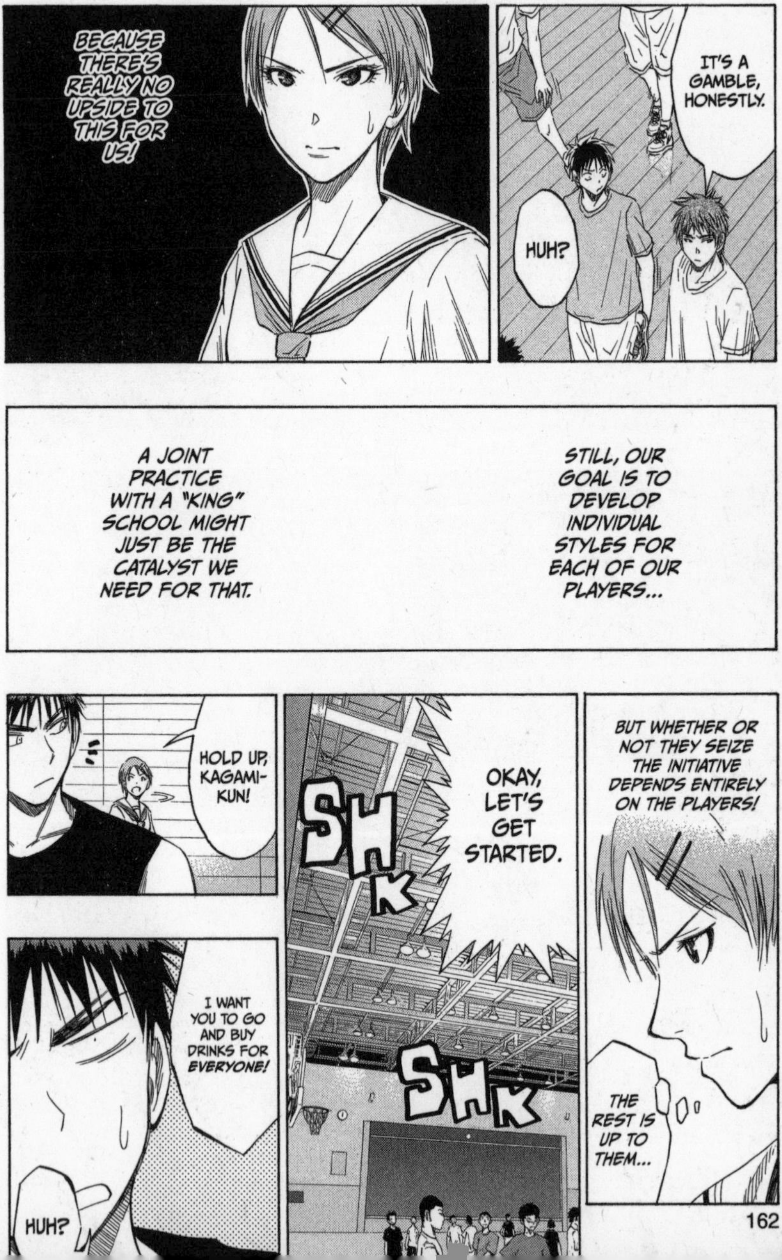
IT'S A GAMBLE, HONESTLY.
HUH?
BECAUSE THERE'S REALLY NO UPSIDE TO THIS FOR US!
STILL, OUR GOAL IS TO DEVELOP INDIVIDUAL STYLES FOR EACH OF OUR PLAYERS...
A JOINT PRACTICE WITH A "KING" SCHOOL MIGHT JUST BE THE CATALYST WE NEED FOR THAT.
BUT WHETHER OR NOT THEY SEIZE THE INITIATIVE DEPENDS ENTIRELY ON THE PLAYERS!
THE REST IS UP TO THEM...
OKAY, LET'S GET STARTED.
SHK
SHK
HOLD UP, KAGAMI-KUN!
I WANT YOU TO GO AND BUY DRINKS FOR *EVERYONE*!
HUH?

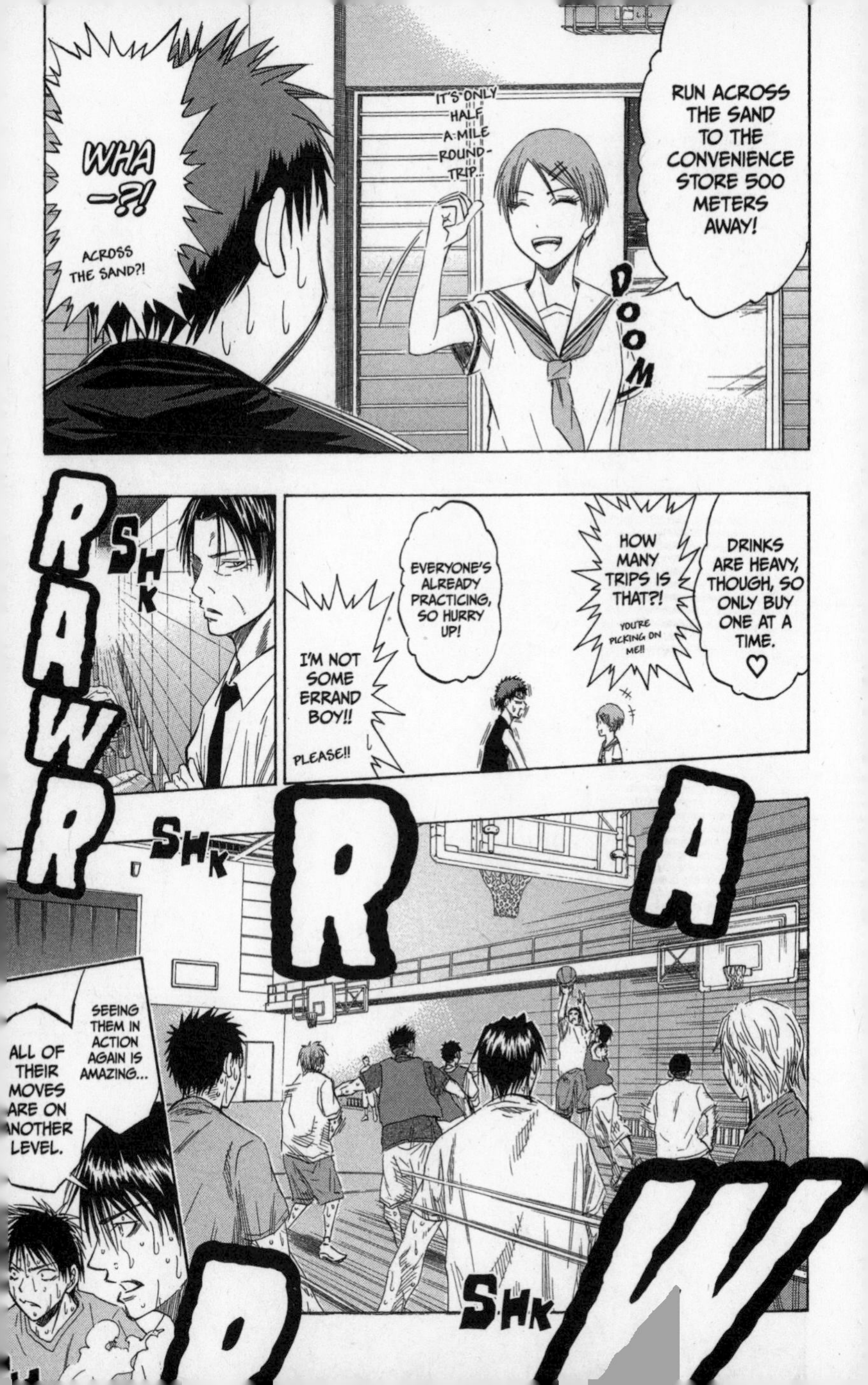

RUN ACROSS THE SAND TO THE CONVENIENCE STORE 500 METERS AWAY!
IT'S ONLY HALF A MILE ROUND-TRIP...
DOOM
WHA—?!
ACROSS THE SAND?!
DRINKS ARE HEAVY, THOUGH, SO ONLY BUY ONE AT A TIME. ♡
HOW MANY TRIPS IS THAT?!
YOU'RE PICKING ON ME!!
EVERYONE'S ALREADY PRACTICING, SO HURRY UP!
I'M NOT SOME ERRAND BOY!!
PLEASE!!
SHK
SHK
RAWR
SHK
RAW
SHK
SEEING THEM IN ACTION AGAIN IS AMAZING...
ALL OF THEIR MOVES ARE ON ANOTHER LEVEL.

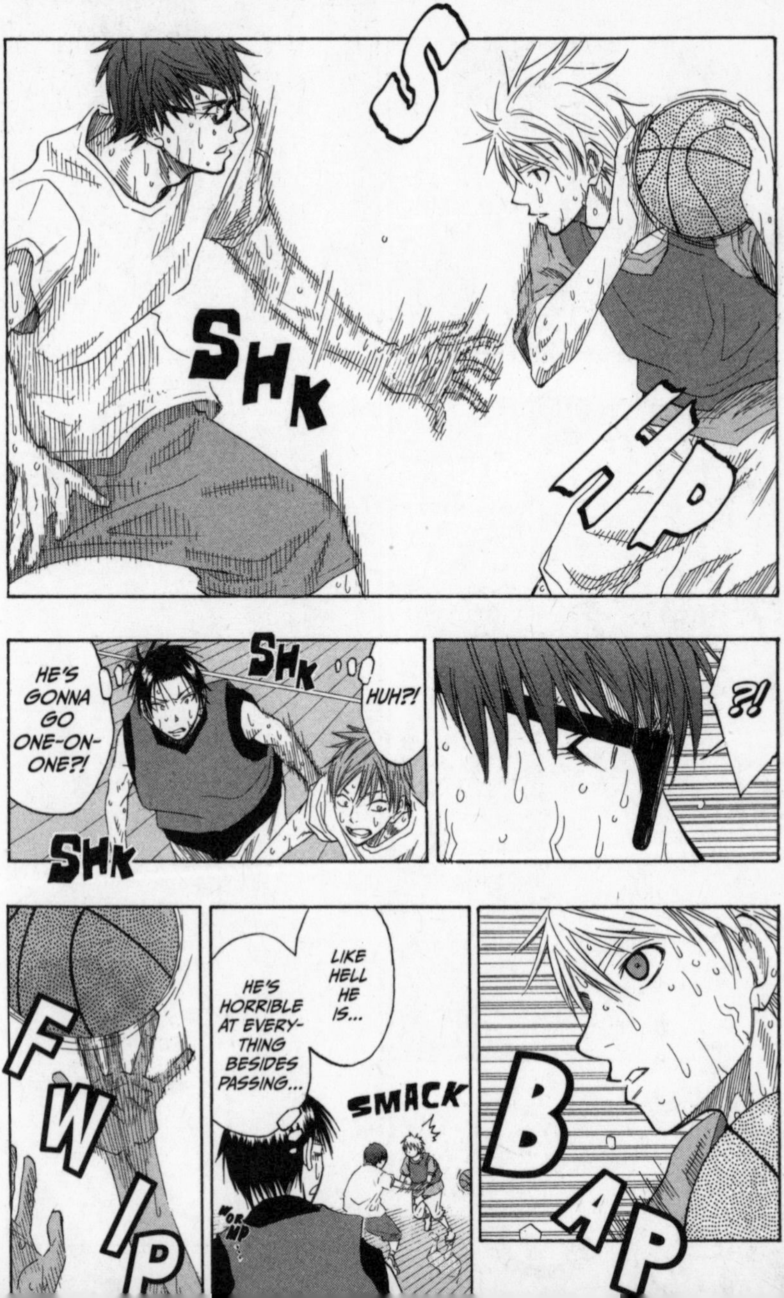
SHK
?!
HUH?!
SHK
HE'S GONNA GO ONE-ON-ONE?!
SHK
BAP
LIKE HELL HE IS...
HE'S HORRIBLE AT EVERY-THING BESIDES PASSING...
SMACK
FWIP

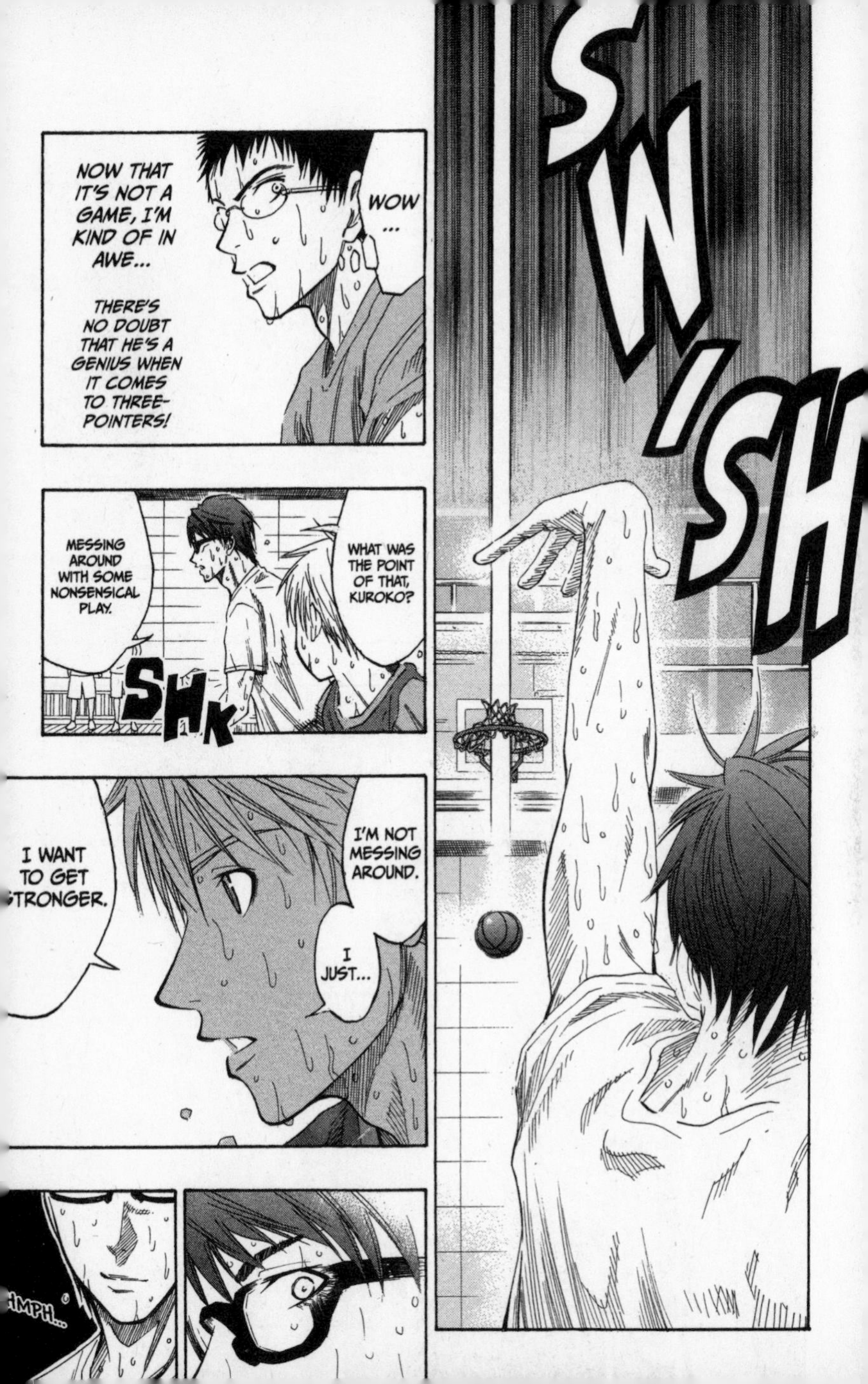
SWISH
WOW...
NOW THAT IT'S NOT A GAME, I'M KIND OF IN AWE...
THERE'S NO DOUBT THAT HE'S A GENIUS WHEN IT COMES TO THREE-POINTERS!
WHAT WAS THE POINT OF THAT, KUROKO?
MESSING AROUND WITH SOME NONSENSICAL PLAY.
SHK
I'M NOT MESSING AROUND.
I JUST...
I WANT TO GET STRONGER.
HMPH...

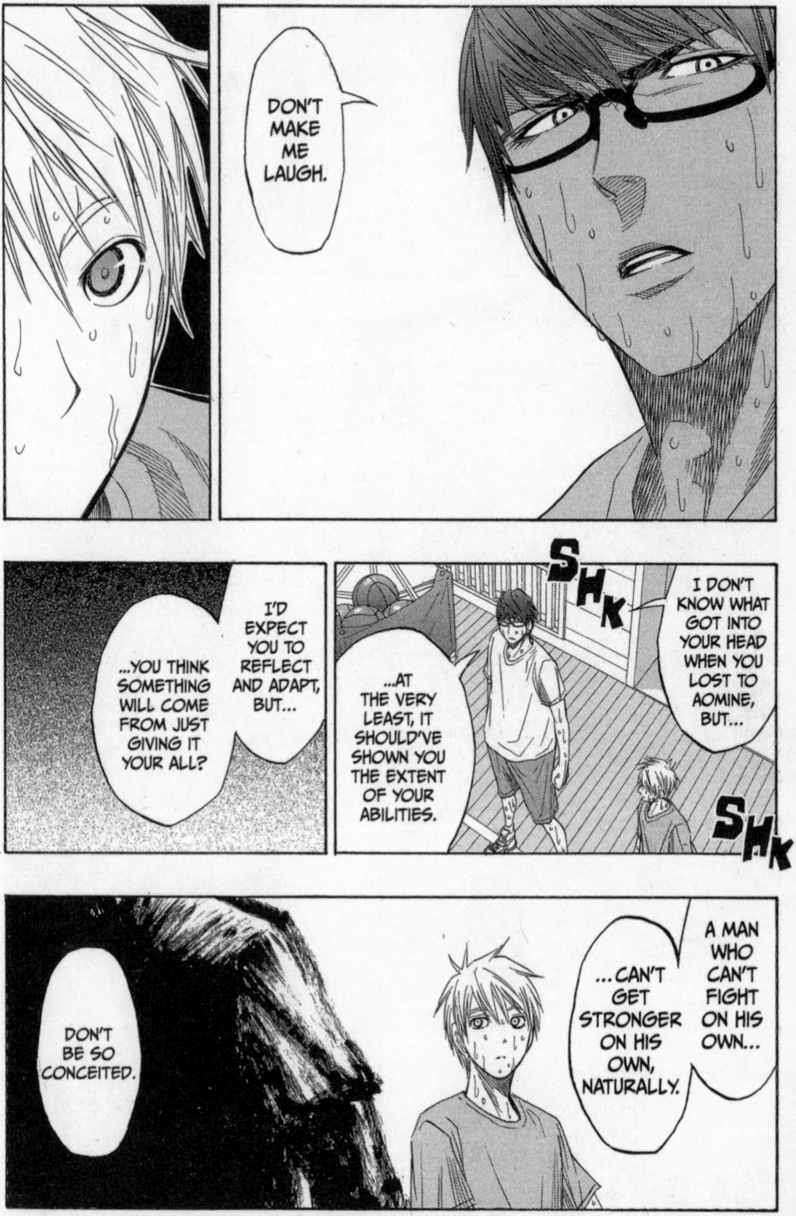
DON'T MAKE ME LAUGH.
SHK
I DON'T KNOW WHAT GOT INTO YOUR HEAD WHEN YOU LOST TO AOMINE, BUT...
...AT THE VERY LEAST, IT SHOULD'VE SHOWN YOU THE EXTENT OF YOUR ABILITIES.
SHK
I'D EXPECT YOU TO REFLECT AND ADAPT, BUT...
...YOU THINK SOMETHING WILL COME FROM JUST GIVING IT YOUR ALL?
A MAN WHO CAN'T FIGHT ON HIS OWN...
...CAN'T GET STRONGER ON HIS OWN, NATURALLY.
DON'T BE SO CONCEITED.

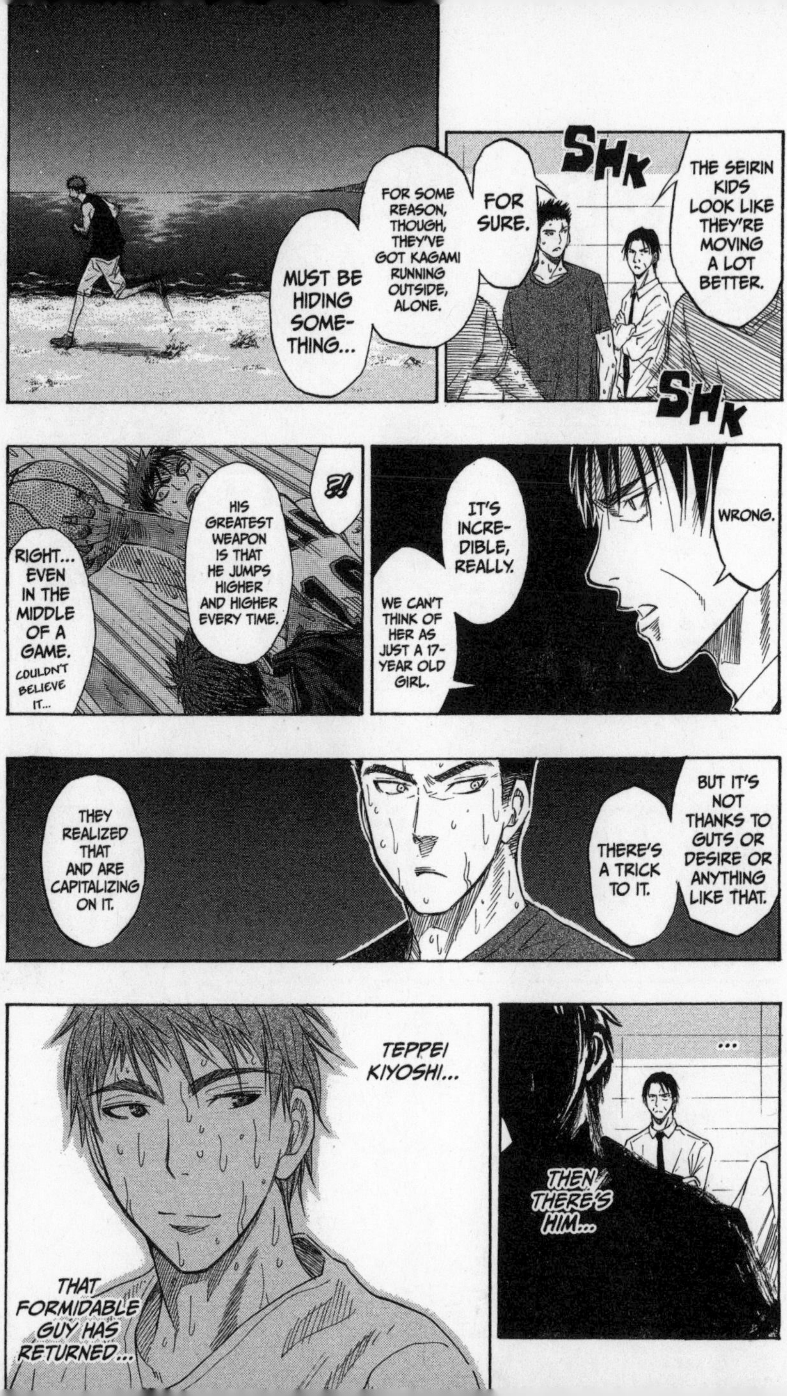
SHK
THE SEIRIN KIDS LOOK LIKE THEY'RE MOVING A LOT BETTER.
FOR SURE.
SHK
FOR SOME REASON, THOUGH, THEY'VE GOT KAGAMI RUNNING OUTSIDE, ALONE.
MUST BE HIDING SOME-THING...
WRONG.
IT'S INCRE-DIBLE, REALLY.
WE CAN'T THINK OF HER AS JUST A 17-YEAR OLD GIRL.
?!
HIS GREATEST WEAPON IS THAT HE JUMPS HIGHER AND HIGHER EVERY TIME.
RIGHT... EVEN IN THE MIDDLE OF A GAME.
COULDN'T BELIEVE IT...
BUT IT'S NOT THANKS TO GUTS OR DESIRE OR ANYTHING LIKE THAT.
THERE'S A TRICK TO IT.
THEY REALIZED THAT AND ARE CAPITALIZING ON IT.
...
THEN THERE'S HIM...
TEPPEI KIYOSHI...
THAT FORMIDABLE GUY HAS RETURNED...

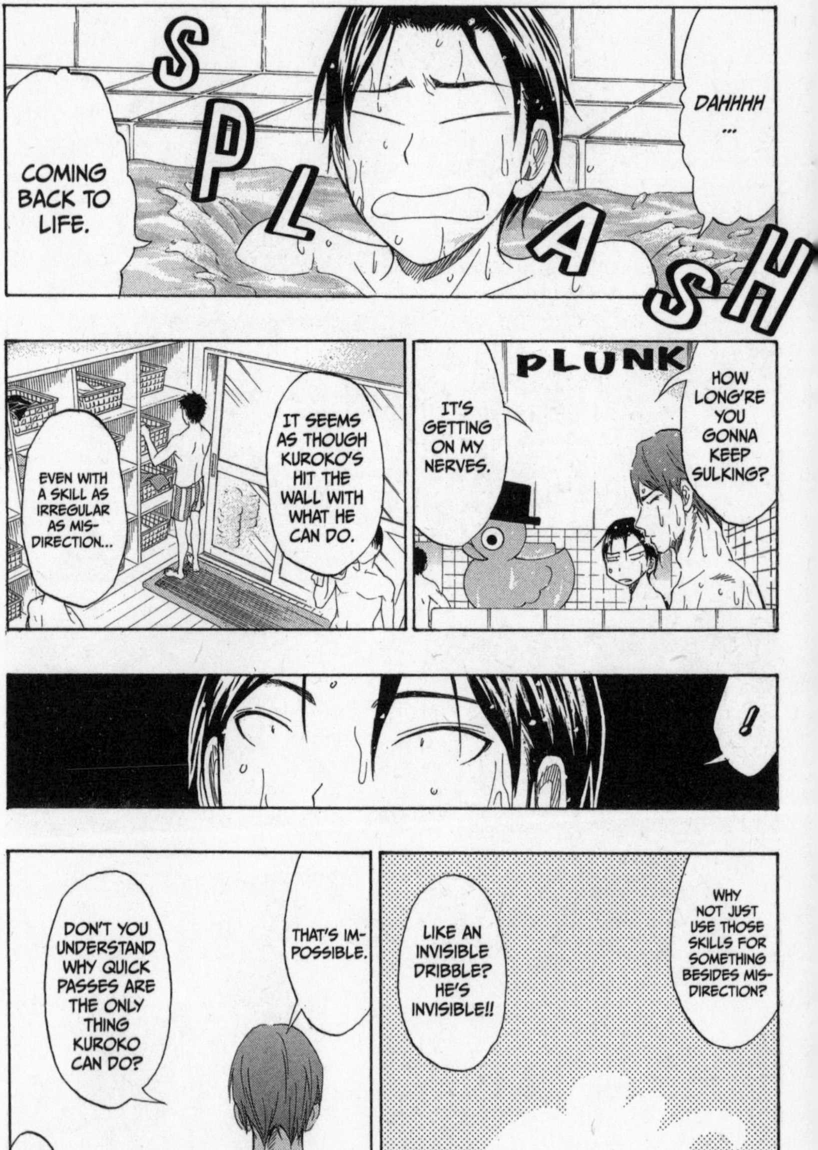
DAHHHH ...
SPLASH
COMING BACK TO LIFE.
HOW LONG'RE YOU GONNA KEEP SULKING?
PLUNK
IT'S GETTING ON MY NERVES.
IT SEEMS AS THOUGH KUROKO'S HIT THE WALL WITH WHAT HE CAN DO.
EVEN WITH A SKILL AS IRREGULAR AS MIS-DIRECTION...
!
WHY NOT JUST USE THOSE SKILLS FOR SOMETHING BESIDES MIS-DIRECTION?
LIKE AN INVISIBLE DRIBBLE? HE'S INVISIBLE!!
THAT'S IM-POSSIBLE.
DON'T YOU UNDERSTAND WHY QUICK PASSES ARE THE ONLY THING KUROKO CAN DO?
?

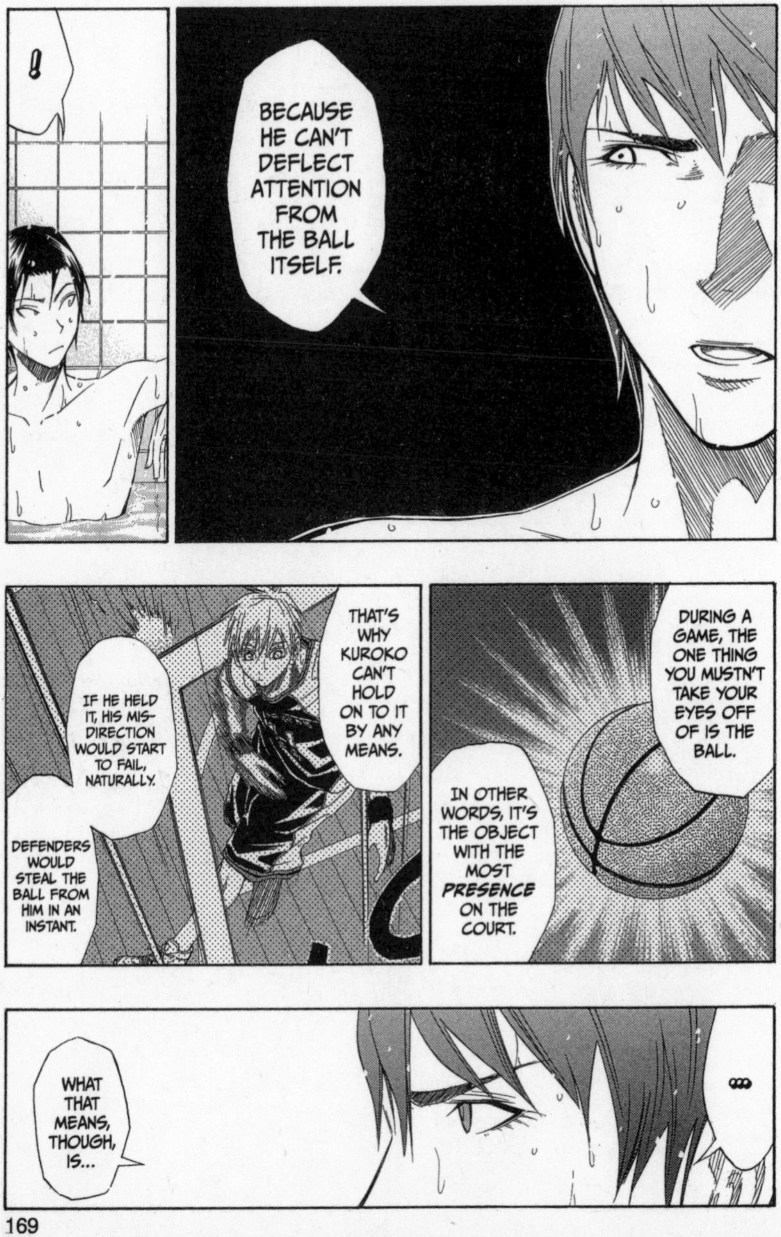
BECAUSE HE CAN'T DEFLECT ATTENTION FROM THE BALL ITSELF.
!
DURING A GAME, THE ONE THING YOU MUSTN'T TAKE YOUR EYES OFF OF IS THE BALL.
IN OTHER WORDS, IT'S THE OBJECT WITH THE MOST *PRESENCE* ON THE COURT.
THAT'S WHY KUROKO CAN'T HOLD ON TO IT BY ANY MEANS.
IF HE HELD IT, HIS MIS-DIRECTION WOULD START TO FAIL, NATURALLY.
DEFENDERS WOULD STEAL THE BALL FROM HIM IN AN INSTANT.
...
WHAT THAT MEANS, THOUGH, IS...

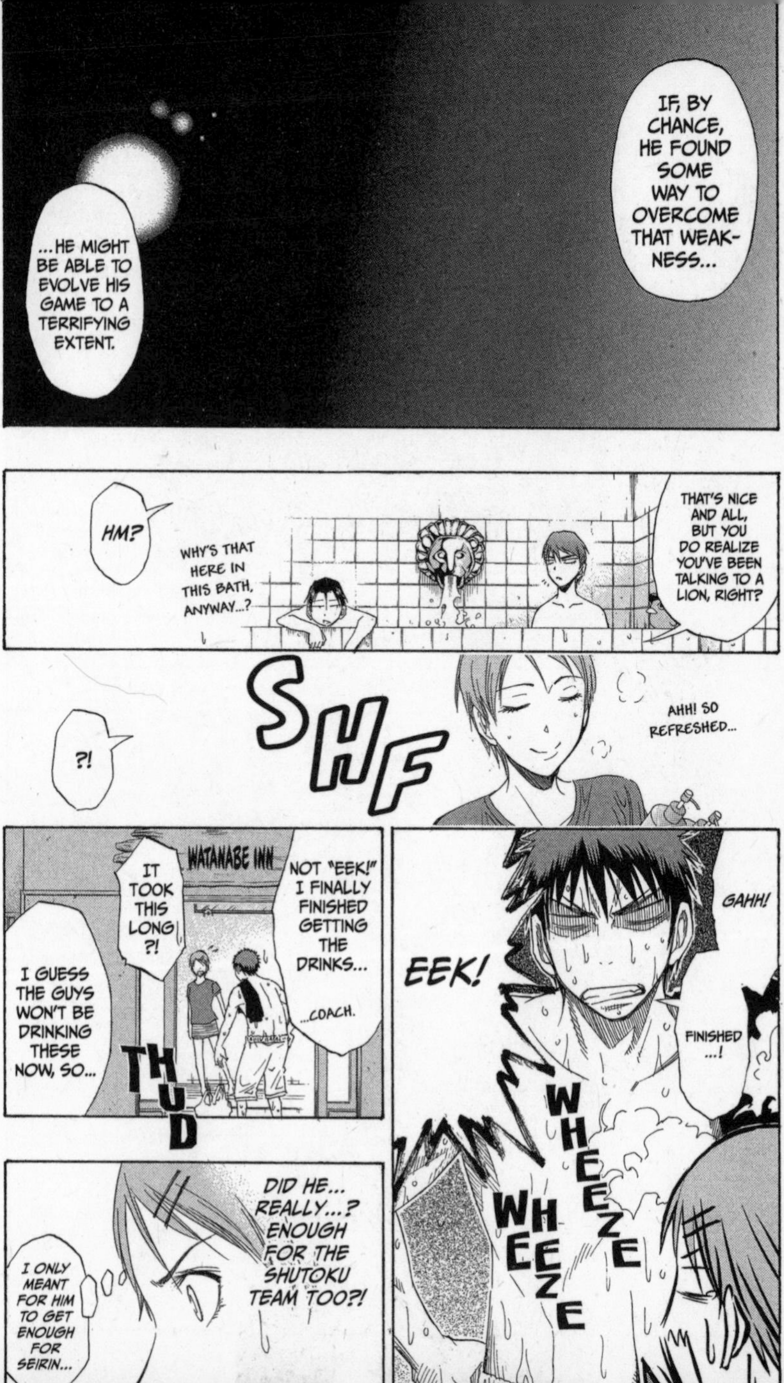
IF, BY CHANCE, HE FOUND SOME WAY TO OVERCOME THAT WEAKNESS...
...HE MIGHT BE ABLE TO EVOLVE HIS GAME TO A TERRIFYING EXTENT.
THAT'S NICE AND ALL, BUT YOU DO REALIZE YOU'VE BEEN TALKING TO A LION, RIGHT?
WHY'S THAT HERE IN THIS BATH, ANYWAY...?
HM?
AHH! SO REFRESHED...
SHF
?!
GAHH!
EEK!
FINISHED ...!
WHEEZE
WHEEZE
NOT "EEK!" I FINALLY FINISHED GETTING THE DRINKS...
...COACH.
WATANABE INN
IT TOOK THIS LONG?!
I GUESS THE GUYS WON'T BE DRINKING THESE NOW, SO...
THUD
DID HE... REALLY...? ENOUGH FOR THE SHUTOKU TEAM TOO?!
I ONLY MEANT FOR HIM TO GET ENOUGH FOR SEIRIN...

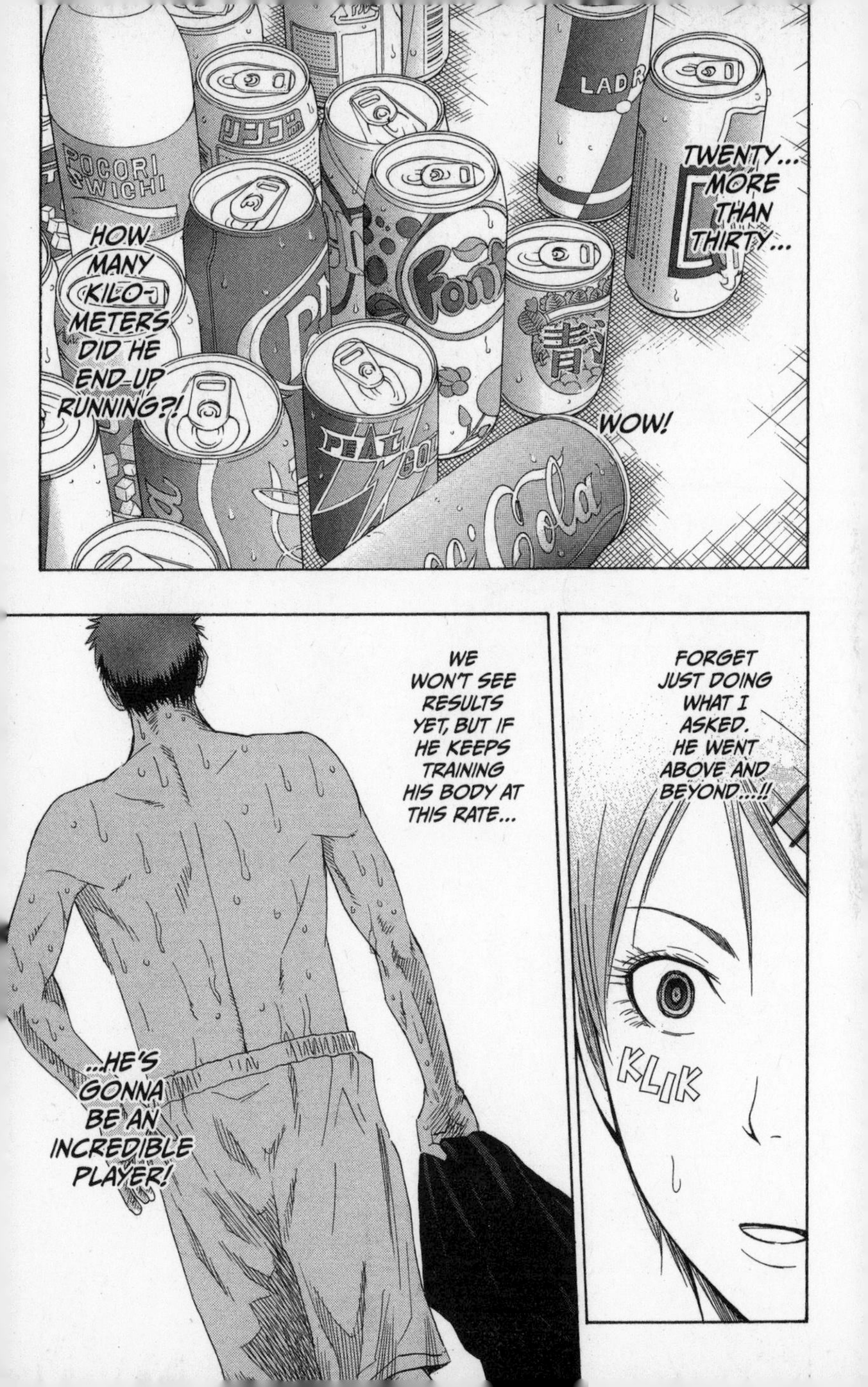
TWENTY... MORE THAN THIRTY...
WOW!
HOW MANY KILOMETERS DID HE END UP RUNNING?!
FORGET JUST DOING WHAT I ASKED. HE WENT ABOVE AND BEYOND...!!
KLIK
WE WON'T SEE RESULTS YET, BUT IF HE KEEPS TRAINING HIS BODY AT THIS RATE...
...HE'S GONNA BE AN INCREDIBLE PLAYER!

KUROKO'S BASKETBALL BLOOPERS

TAKE 5

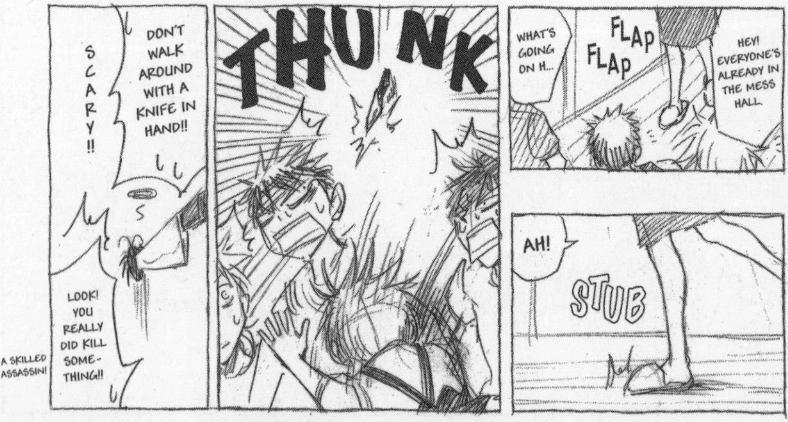
HEY! EVERYONE'S ALREADY IN THE MESS HALL.
FLAP FLAP
WHAT'S GOING ON H...
AH!
STUB
THUNK
DON'T WALK AROUND WITH A KNIFE IN HAND!!
SCARY!!
LOOK! YOU REALLY DID KILL SOME-THING!!
A SKILLED ASSASSIN!

61ST QUARTER: TRY JUMPING

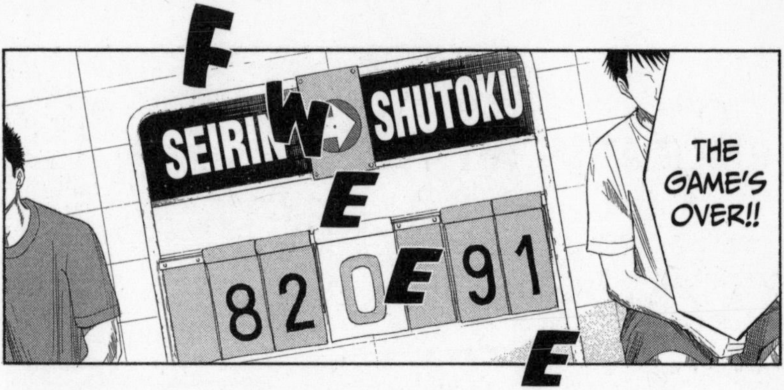
THE GAME'S OVER!!
FWEEE
SEIRIN
SHUTOKU
82
91

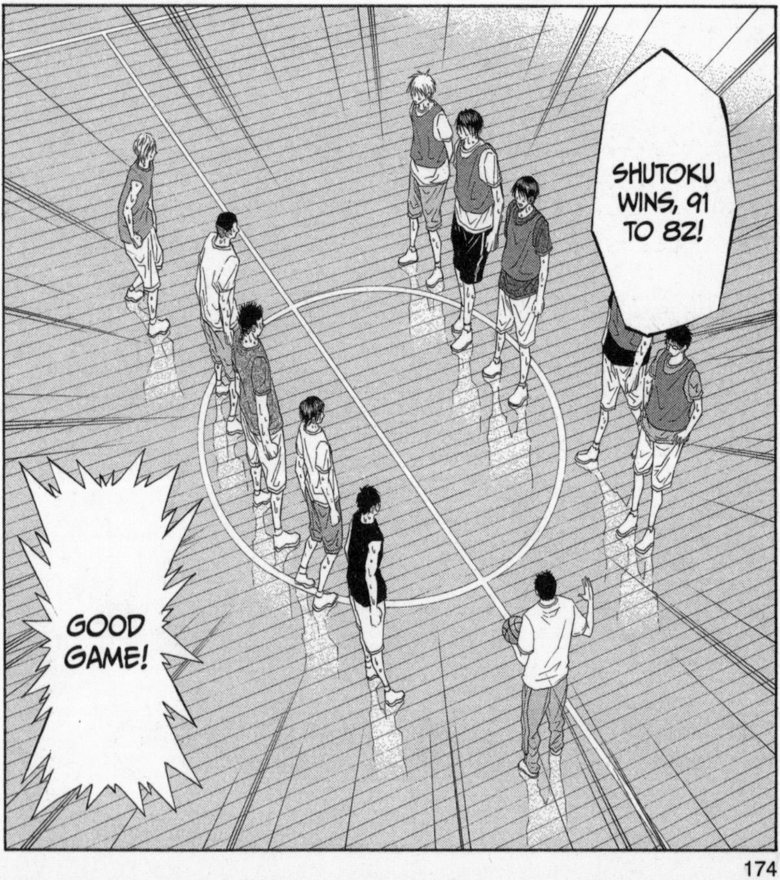
SHUTOKU WINS, 91 TO 82!
GOOD GAME!

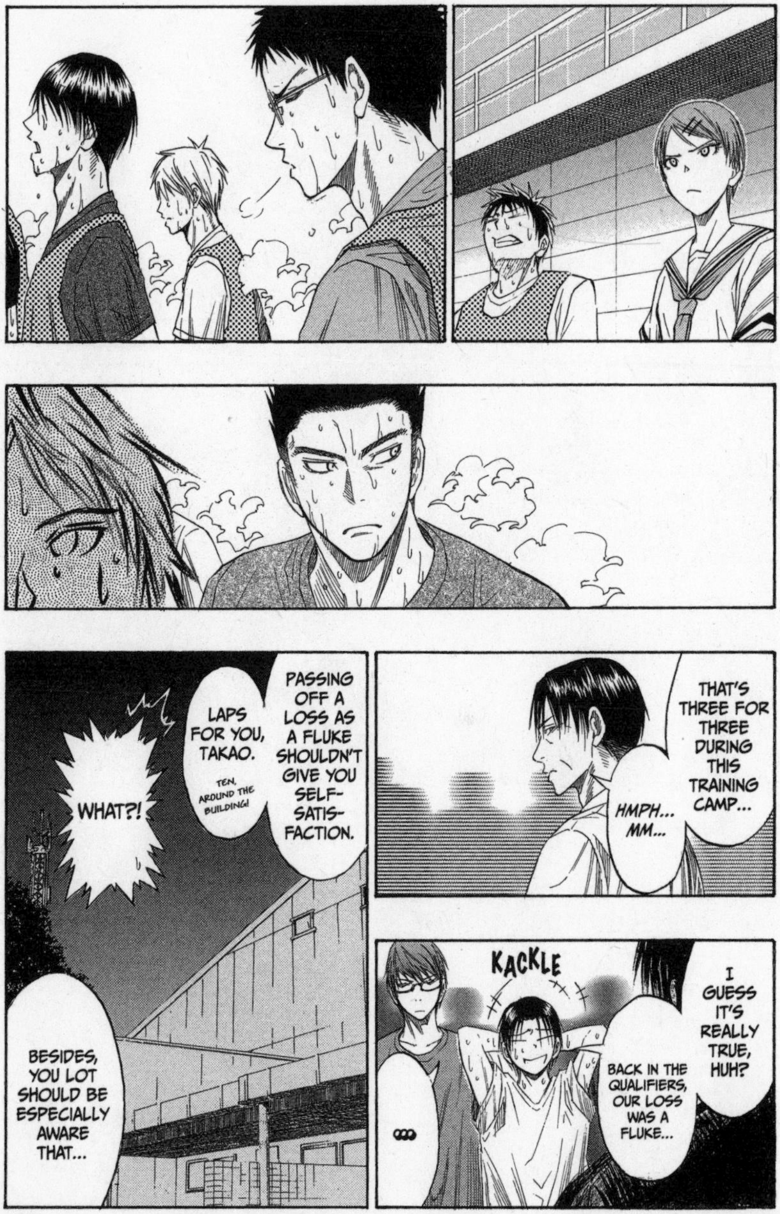
THAT'S THREE FOR THREE DURING THIS TRAINING CAMP...
HMPH... MM...
KACKLE
I GUESS IT'S REALLY TRUE, HUH?
BACK IN THE QUALIFIERS, OUR LOSS WAS A FLUKE...
...
PASSING OFF A LOSS AS A FLUKE SHOULDN'T GIVE YOU SELF-SATISFACTION.
LAPS FOR YOU, TAKAO.
TEN, AROUND THE BUILDING!
WHAT?!
BESIDES, YOU LOT SHOULD BE ESPECIALLY AWARE THAT...

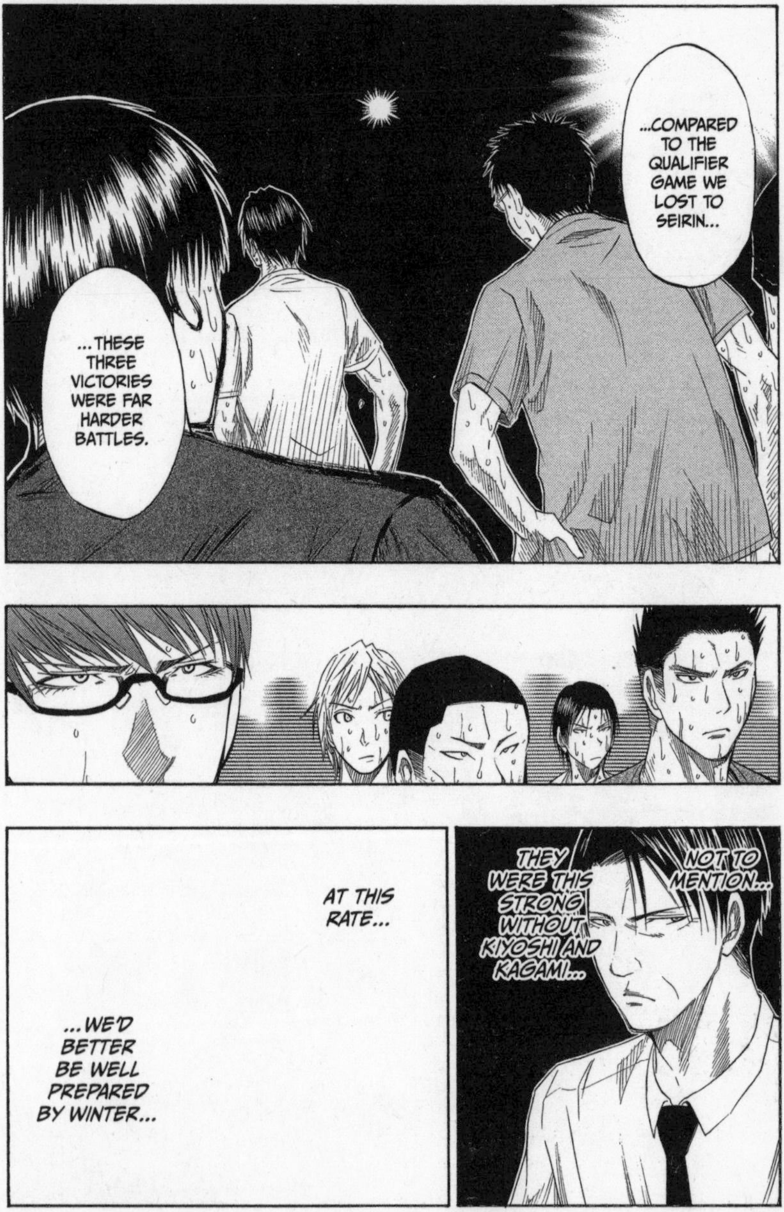
...COMPARED TO THE QUALIFIER GAME WE LOST TO SEIRIN...
...THESE THREE VICTORIES WERE FAR HARDER BATTLES.
NOT TO MENTION...
THEY WERE THIS STRONG WITHOUT KIYOSHI AND KAGAMI...
AT THIS RATE...
...WE'D BETTER BE WELL PREPARED BY WINTER...

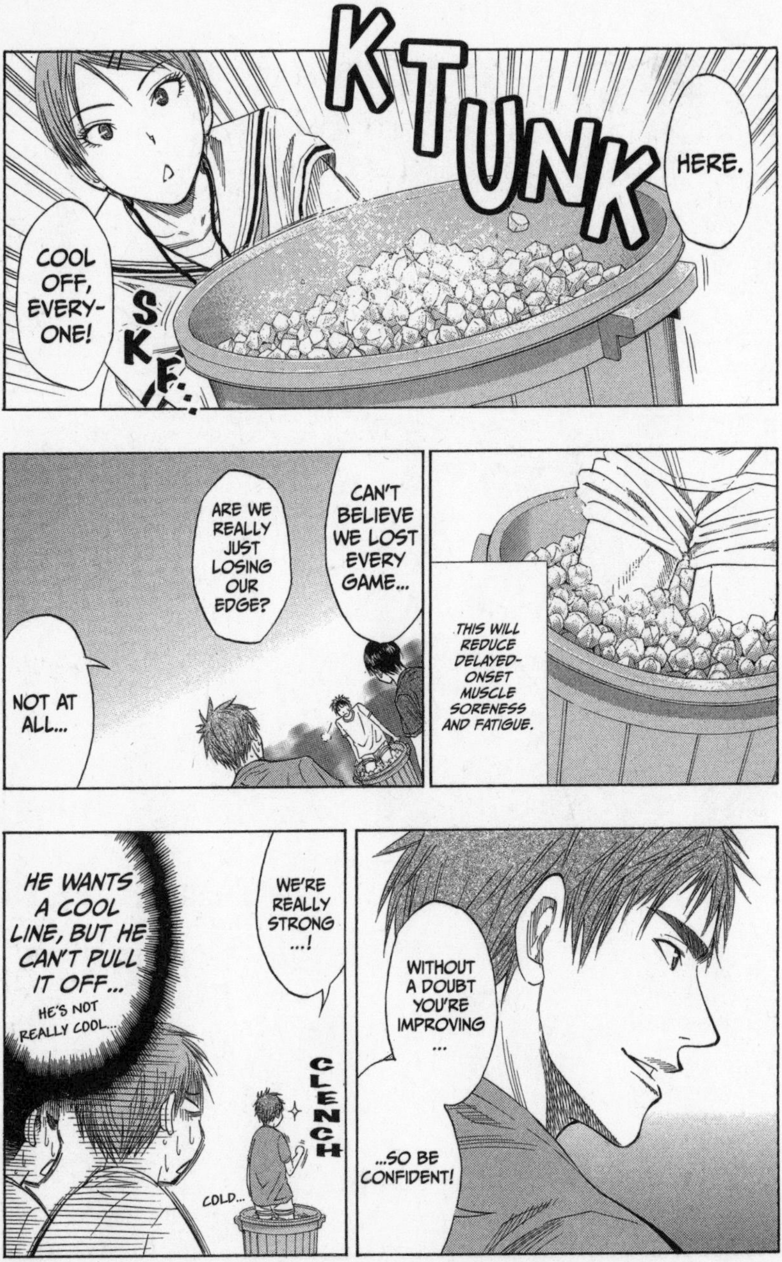
KTUNK
HERE.
COOL OFF, EVERY-ONE!
SKF...
THIS WILL REDUCE DELAYED-ONSET MUSCLE SORENESS AND FATIGUE.
CAN'T BELIEVE WE LOST EVERY GAME...
ARE WE REALLY JUST LOSING OUR EDGE?
NOT AT ALL...
WITHOUT A DOUBT YOU'RE IMPROVING...
...SO BE CONFIDENT!
WE'RE REALLY STRONG...!
CLENCH
HE WANTS A COOL LINE, BUT HE CAN'T PULL IT OFF...
HE'S NOT REALLY COOL...
COLD...

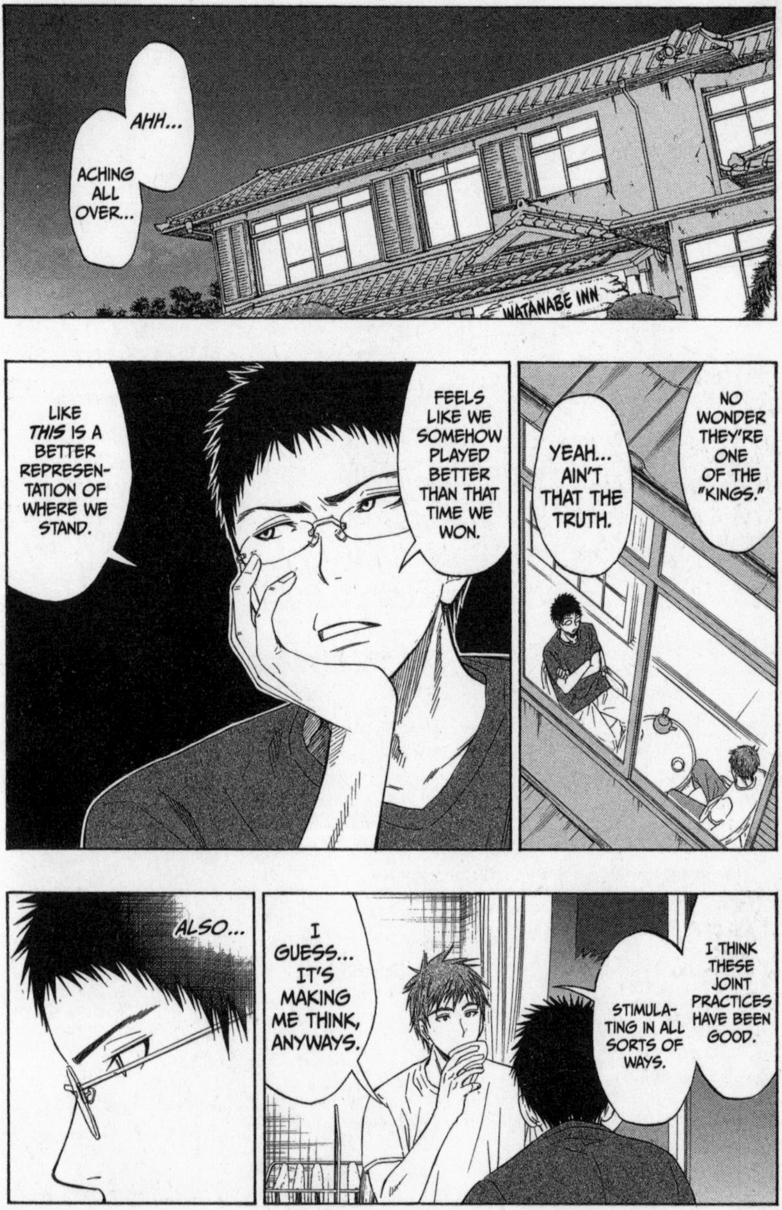
AHH...
ACHING ALL OVER...
WATANABE INN
NO WONDER THEY'RE ONE OF THE "KINGS."
YEAH... AIN'T THAT THE TRUTH.
FEELS LIKE WE SOMEHOW PLAYED BETTER THAN THAT TIME WE WON.
LIKE *THIS* IS A BETTER REPRESENTATION OF WHERE WE STAND.
I THINK THESE JOINT PRACTICES HAVE BEEN GOOD.
STIMULATING IN ALL SORTS OF WAYS.
I GUESS... IT'S MAKING ME THINK, ANYWAYS.
ALSO...

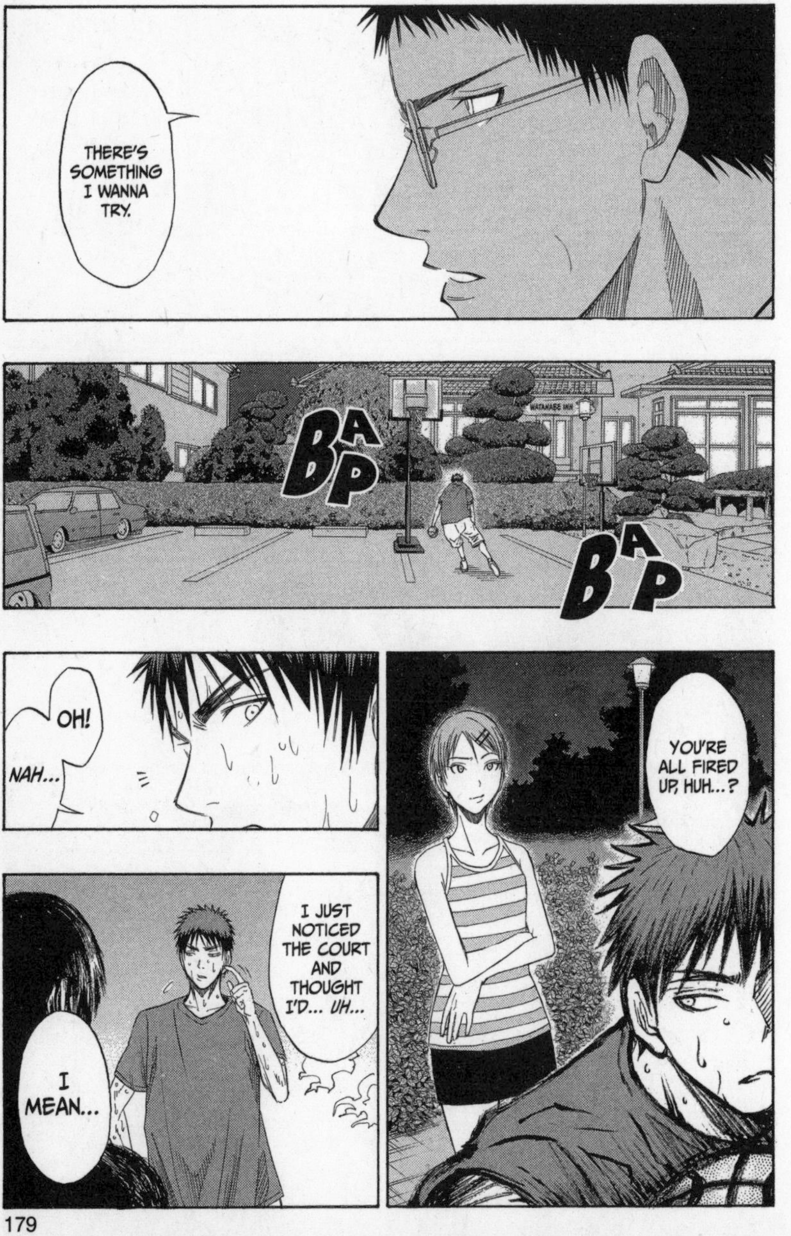
THERE'S SOMETHING I WANNA TRY.
BAP
BAP
YOU'RE ALL FIRED UP, HUH...?
OH!
NAH...
I JUST NOTICED THE COURT AND THOUGHT I'D... UH...
I MEAN...

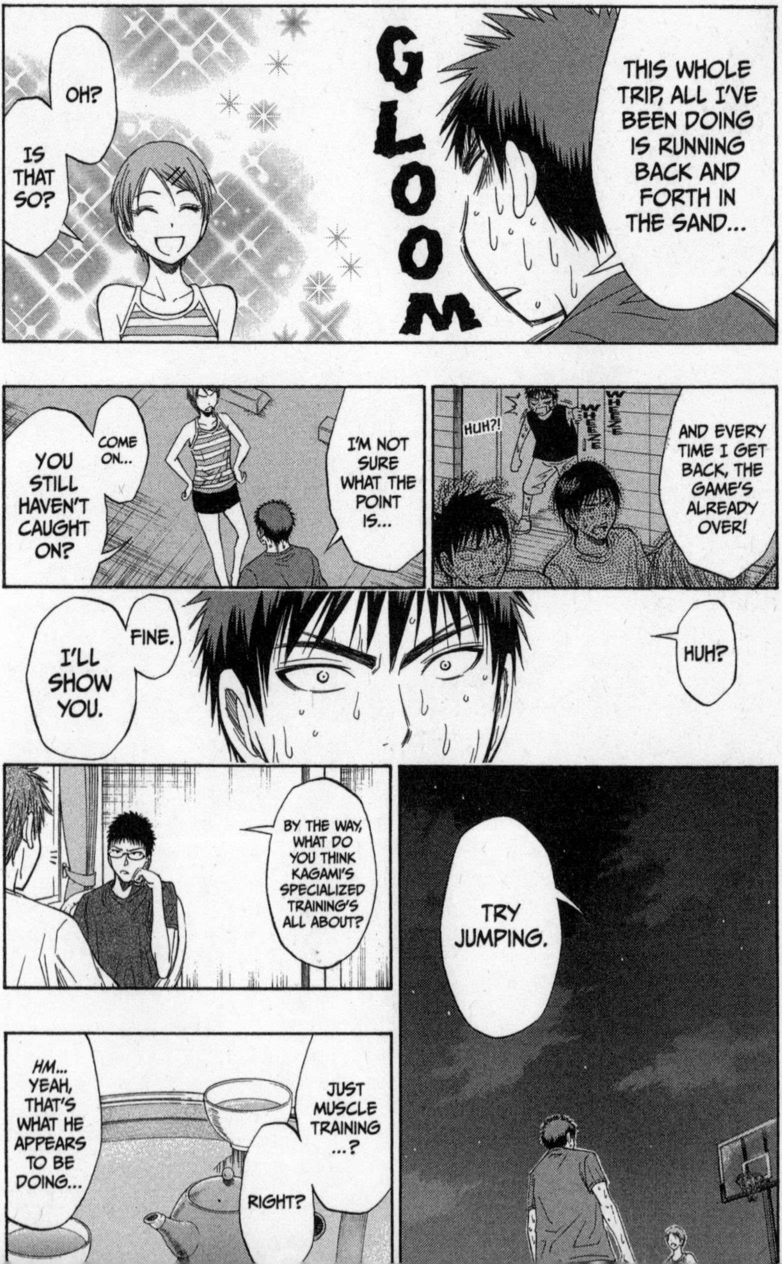
THIS WHOLE TRIP, ALL I'VE BEEN DOING IS RUNNING BACK AND FORTH IN THE SAND...
GLOOM
OH?
IS THAT SO?
AND EVERY TIME I GET BACK, THE GAME'S ALREADY OVER!
WHEEZE
WHEEZE
HUH?!
I'M NOT SURE WHAT THE POINT IS...
COME ON...
YOU STILL HAVEN'T CAUGHT ON?
HUH?
FINE.
I'LL SHOW YOU.
TRY JUMPING.
BY THE WAY, WHAT DO YOU THINK KAGAMI'S SPECIALIZED TRAINING'S ALL ABOUT?
JUST MUSCLE TRAINING ...?
RIGHT?
HM... YEAH, THAT'S WHAT HE APPEARS TO BE DOING...

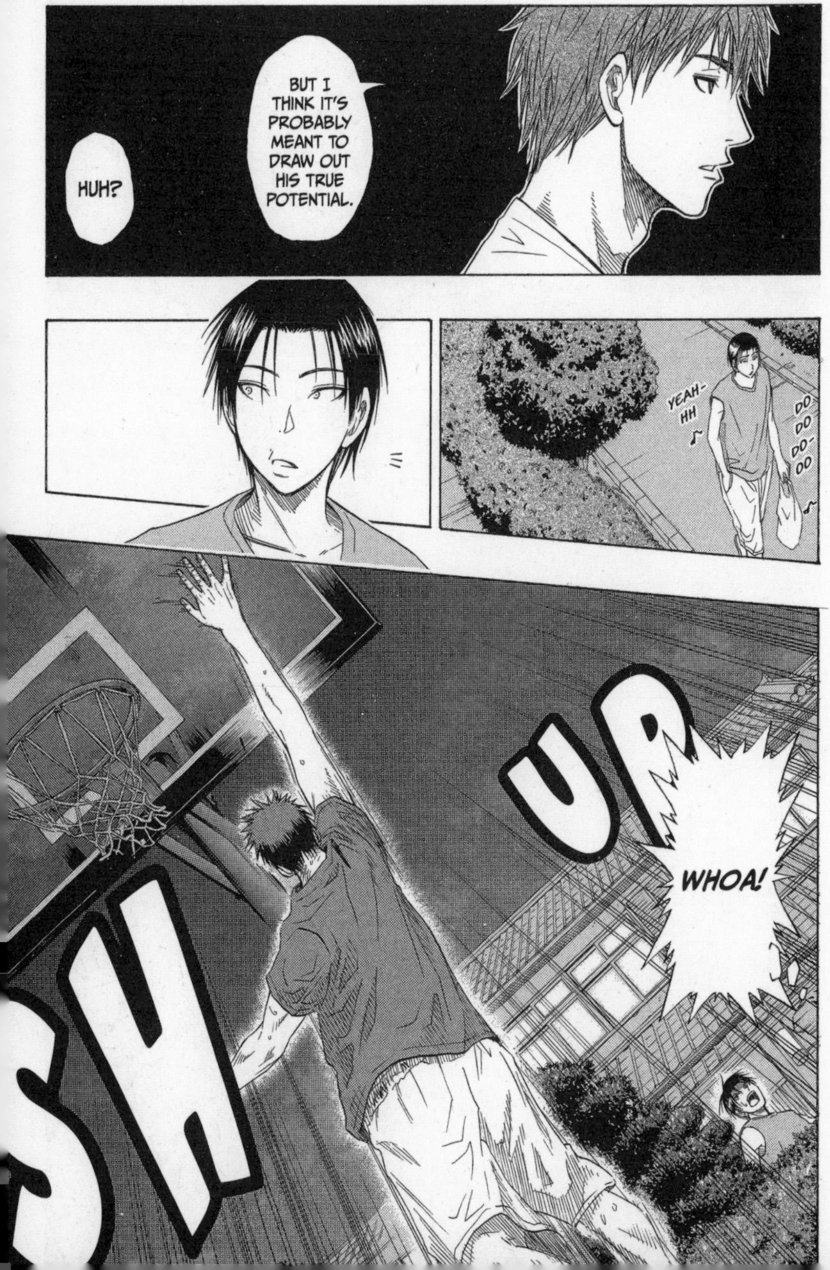
BUT I THINK IT'S PROBABLY MEANT TO DRAW OUT HIS TRUE POTENTIAL.
HUH?
YEAH-HH ♪
DO DO DO-DO ♪
UP
WHOA!
SH

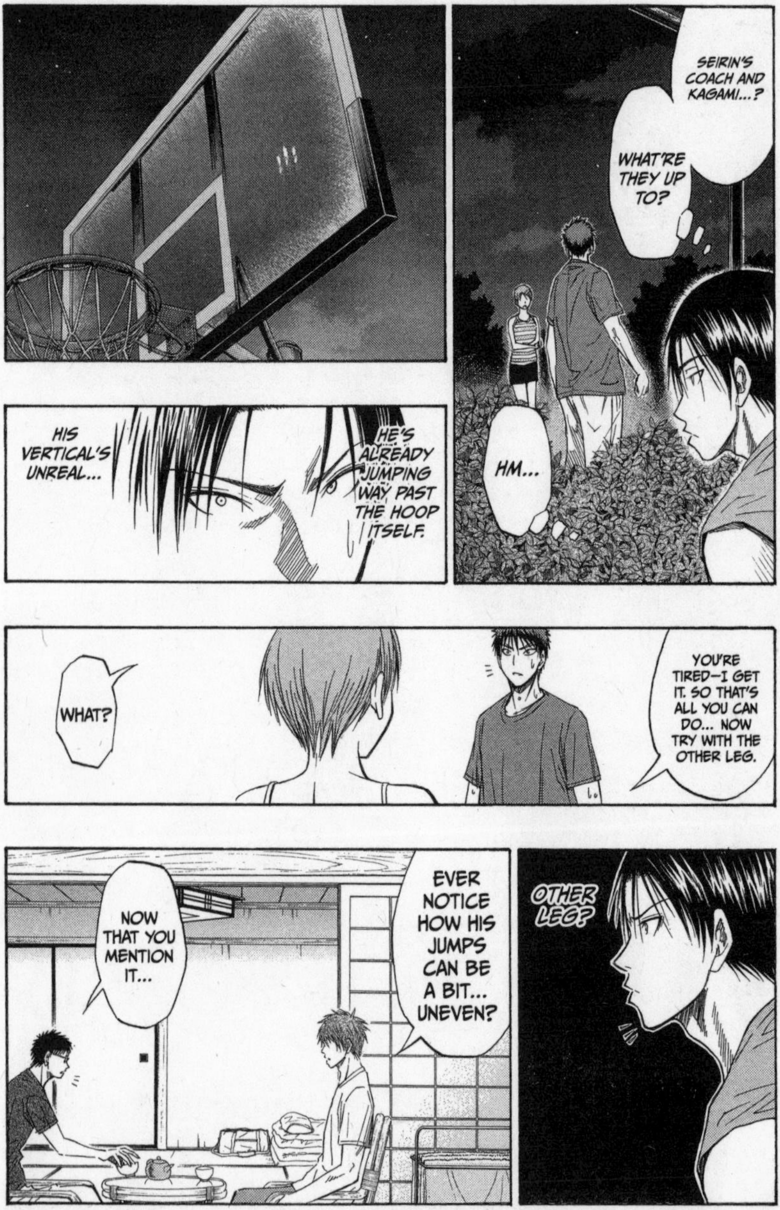
SEIRIN'S COACH AND KAGAMI...?
WHAT'RE THEY UP TO?
HM...
HE'S ALREADY JUMPING WAY PAST THE HOOP ITSELF.
HIS VERTICAL'S UNREAL...
YOU'RE TIRED—I GET IT. SO THAT'S ALL YOU CAN DO... NOW TRY WITH THE OTHER LEG.
WHAT?
OTHER LEG?
EVER NOTICE HOW HIS JUMPS CAN BE A BIT... UNEVEN?
NOW THAT YOU MENTION IT...

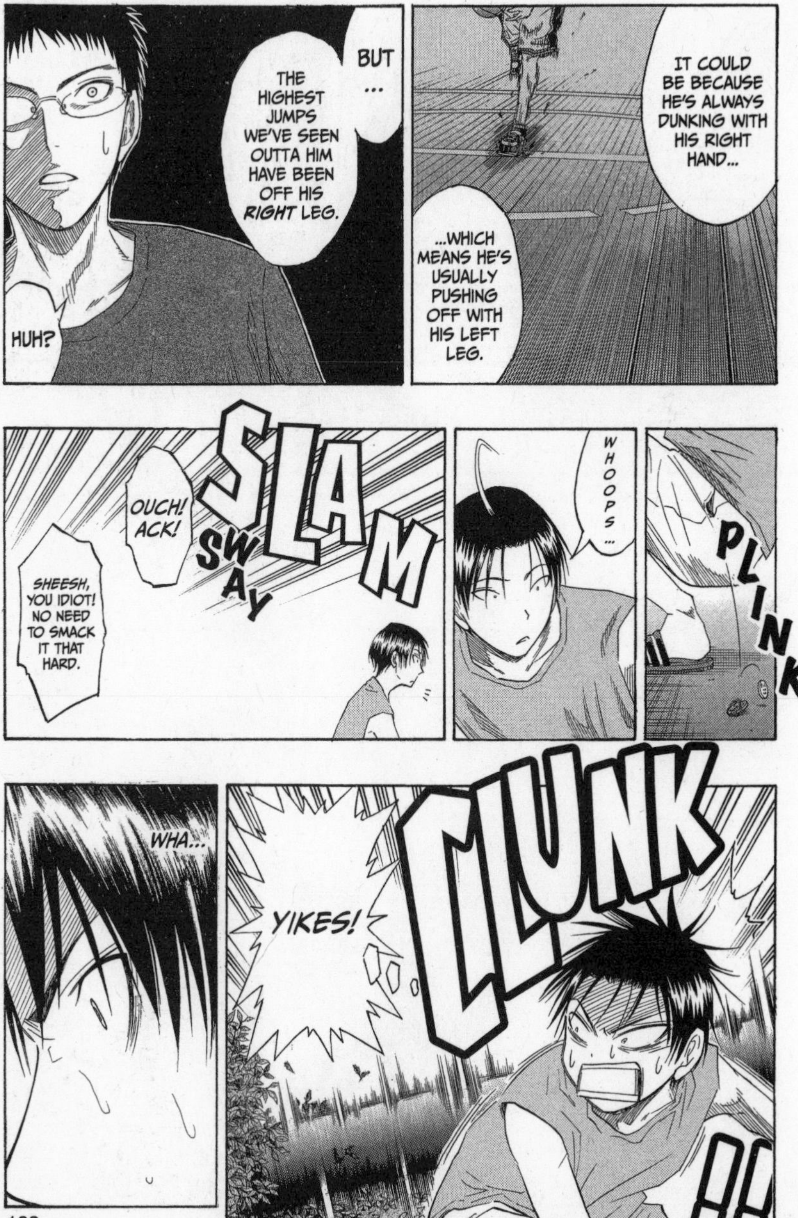
IT COULD BE BECAUSE HE'S ALWAYS DUNKING WITH HIS RIGHT HAND...
...WHICH MEANS HE'S USUALLY PUSHING OFF WITH HIS LEFT LEG.
BUT ...
THE HIGHEST JUMPS WE'VE SEEN OUTTA HIM HAVE BEEN OFF HIS RIGHT LEG.
HUH?
PLINK
WHOOPS...
SLAM
OUCH! ACK!
SWAY
SHEESH, YOU IDIOT! NO NEED TO SMACK IT THAT HARD.
CLUNK
YIKES!
!!
WHA...

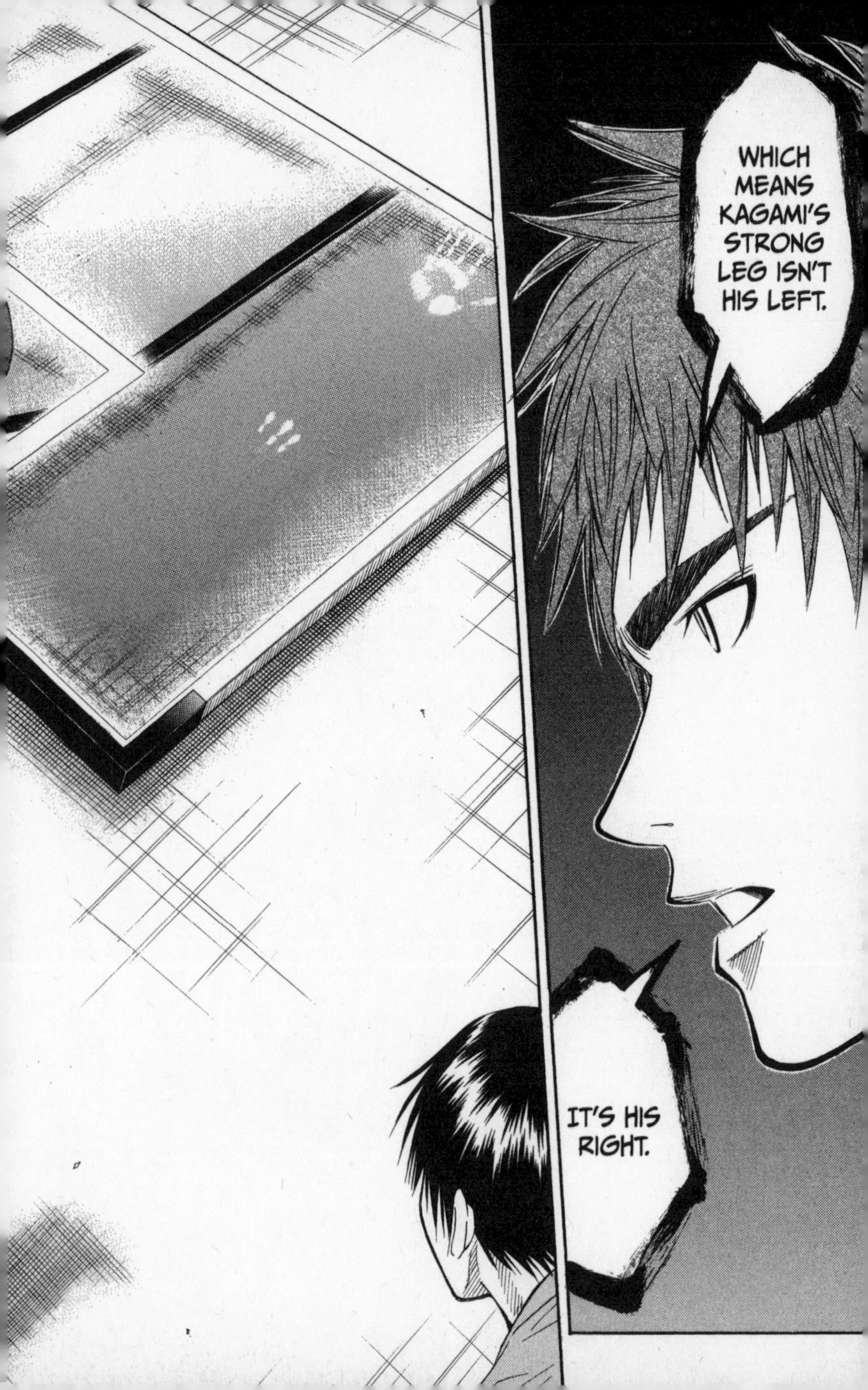
WHICH MEANS KAGAMI'S STRONG LEG ISN'T HIS LEFT.
IT'S HIS RIGHT.

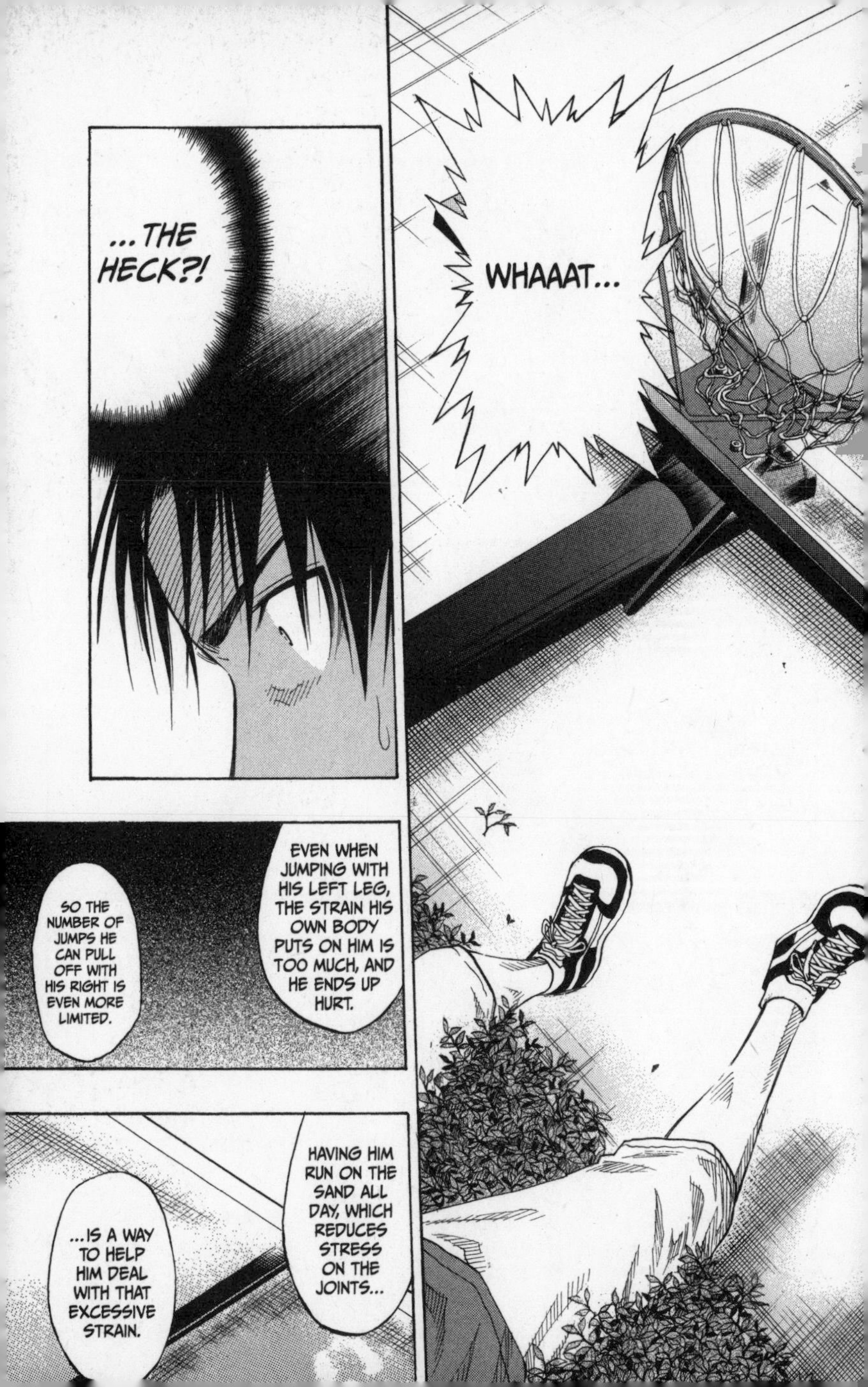
WHAAAT...
...THE HECK?!
EVEN WHEN JUMPING WITH HIS LEFT LEG, THE STRAIN HIS OWN BODY PUTS ON HIM IS TOO MUCH, AND HE ENDS UP HURT.
SO THE NUMBER OF JUMPS HE CAN PULL OFF WITH HIS RIGHT IS EVEN MORE LIMITED.
HAVING HIM RUN ON THE SAND ALL DAY, WHICH REDUCES STRESS ON THE JOINTS...
...IS A WAY TO HELP HIM DEAL WITH THAT EXCESSIVE STRAIN.

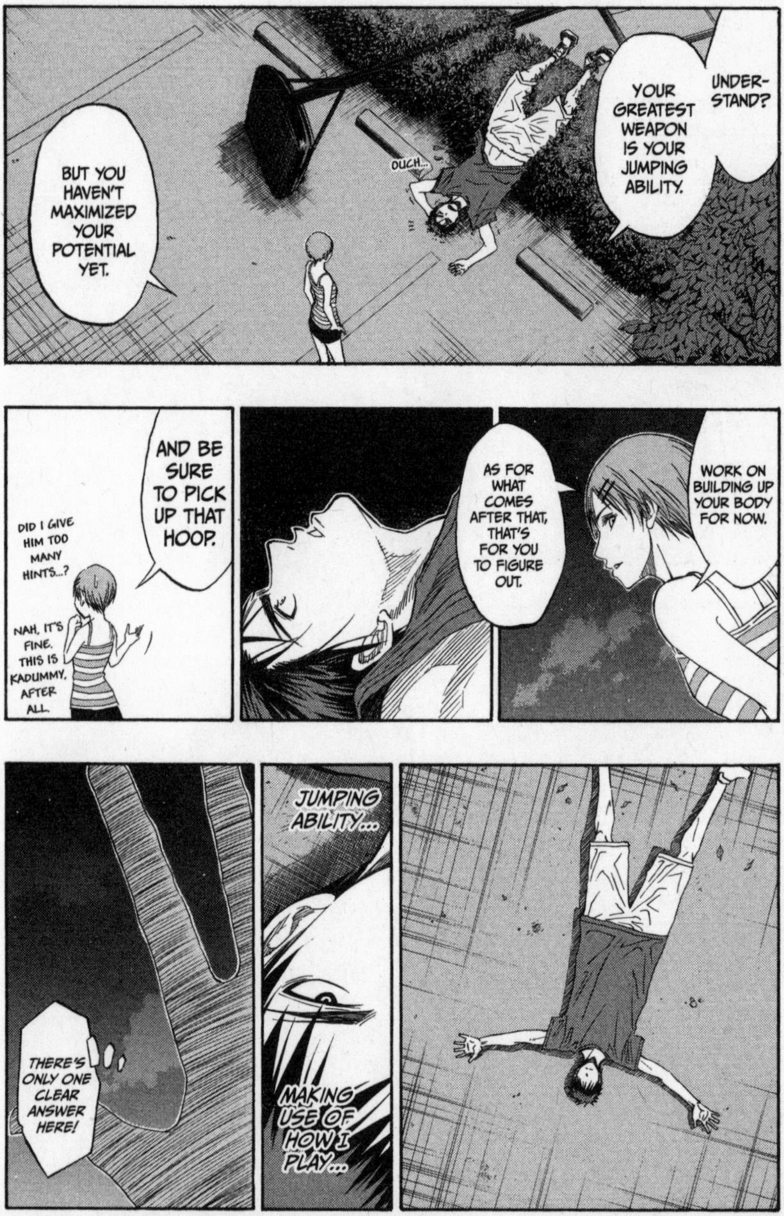
UNDER-STAND?
YOUR GREATEST WEAPON IS YOUR JUMPING ABILITY.
OUCH...
BUT YOU HAVEN'T MAXIMIZED YOUR POTENTIAL YET.
WORK ON BUILDING UP YOUR BODY FOR NOW.
AS FOR WHAT COMES AFTER THAT, THAT'S FOR YOU TO FIGURE OUT.
AND BE SURE TO PICK UP THAT HOOP.
DID I GIVE HIM TOO MANY HINTS...?
NAH, IT'S FINE. THIS IS KADUMMY, AFTER ALL.
JUMPING ABILITY...
MAKING USE OF HOW I PLAY...
THERE'S ONLY ONE CLEAR ANSWER HERE!

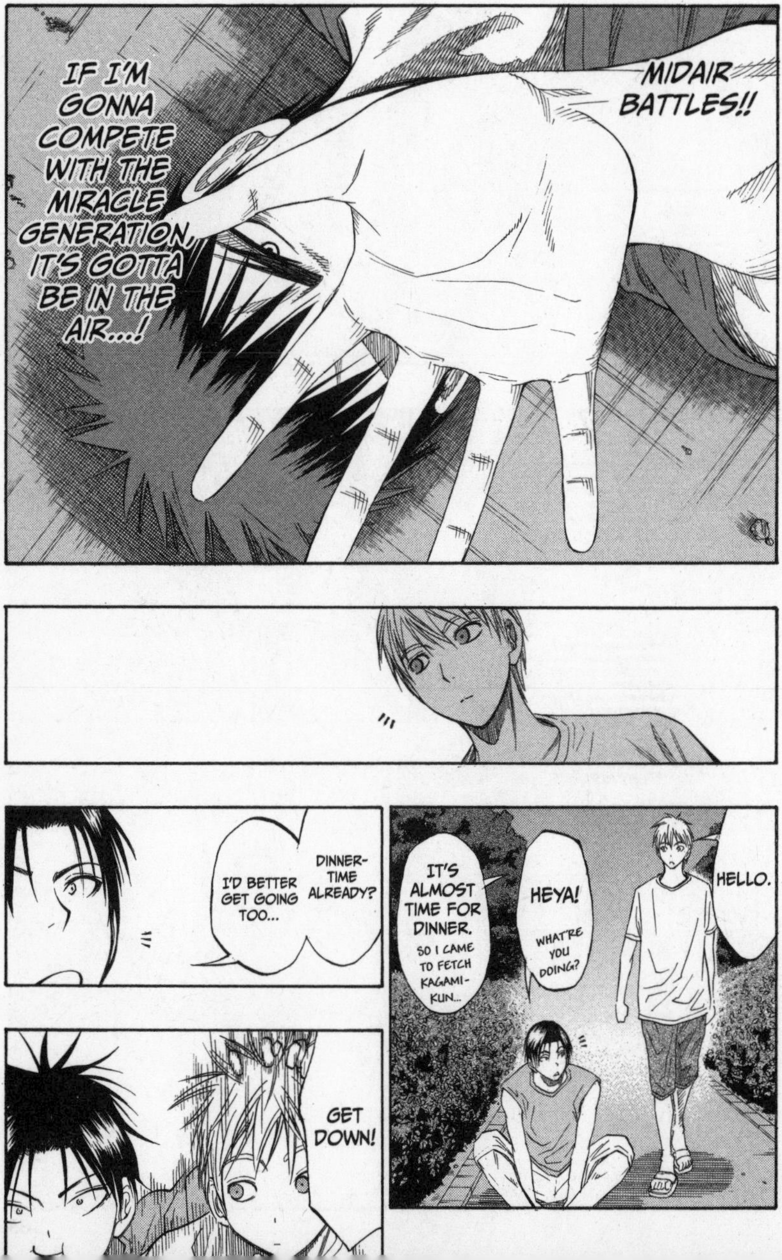
MIDAIR BATTLES!!
IF I'M GONNA COMPETE WITH THE MIRACLE GENERATION, IT'S GOTTA BE IN THE AIR...!
HELLO.
HEYA! WHAT'RE YOU DOING?
IT'S ALMOST TIME FOR DINNER. SO I CAME TO FETCH KAGAMI-KUN...
DINNER-TIME ALREADY?
I'D BETTER GET GOING TOO...
GET DOWN!

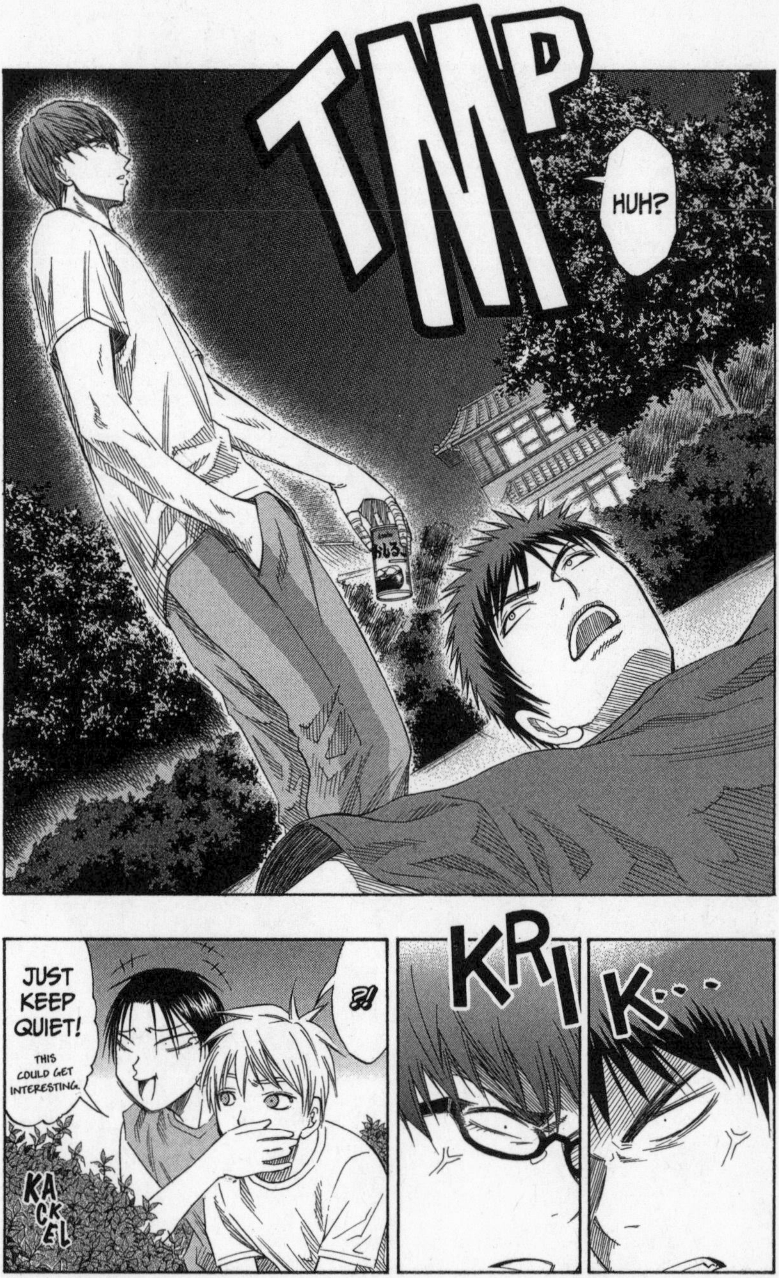
TMP
HUH?
KRIK...
?!
JUST KEEP QUIET!
THIS COULD GET INTERESTING.
KACKEL

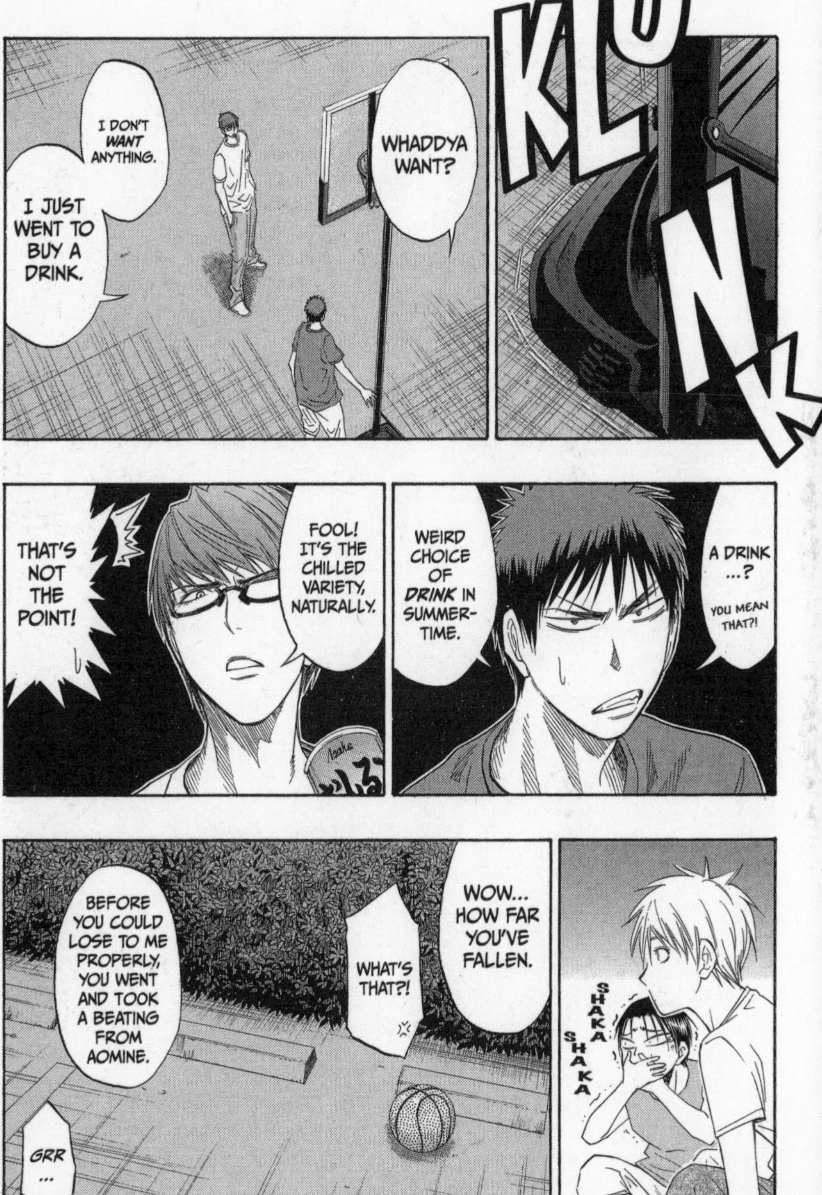
KLUNK
WHADDYA WANT?
I DON'T *WANT* ANYTHING.
I JUST WENT TO BUY A DRINK.
A DRINK ...? YOU MEAN THAT?!
WEIRD CHOICE OF *DRINK* IN SUMMERTIME.
FOOL! IT'S THE CHILLED VARIETY, NATURALLY.
THAT'S NOT THE POINT!
SHAKA SHAKA
WOW... HOW FAR YOU'VE FALLEN.
WHAT'S THAT?!
BEFORE YOU COULD LOSE TO ME PROPERLY, YOU WENT AND TOOK A BEATING FROM AOMINE.
GRR ...

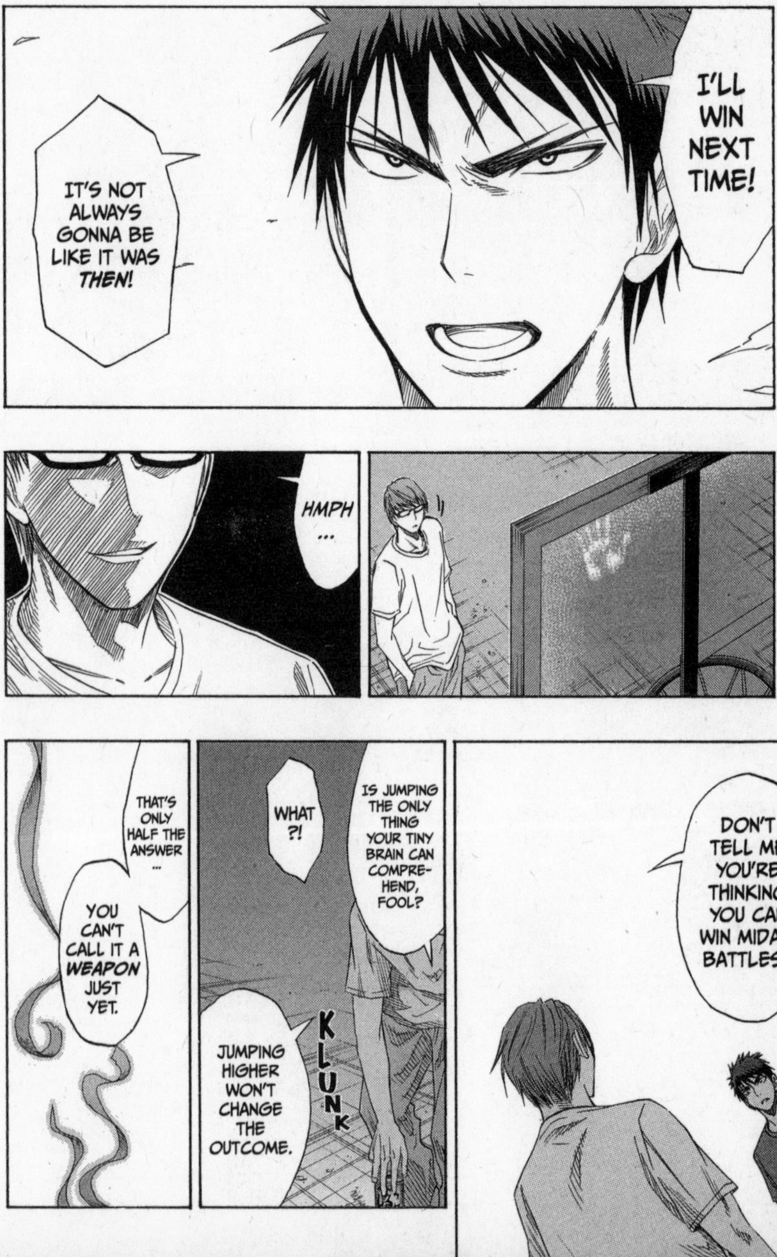
I'LL WIN NEXT TIME!
IT'S NOT ALWAYS GONNA BE LIKE IT WAS *THEN!*
HMPH ...
DON'T TELL ME YOU'RE THINKING YOU CAN WIN MIDAIR BATTLES?
IS JUMPING THE ONLY THING YOUR TINY BRAIN CAN COMPRE-HEND, FOOL?
WHAT?!
KLUNK
JUMPING HIGHER WON'T CHANGE THE OUTCOME.
THAT'S ONLY HALF THE ANSWER ...
YOU CAN'T CALL IT A *WEAPON* JUST YET.

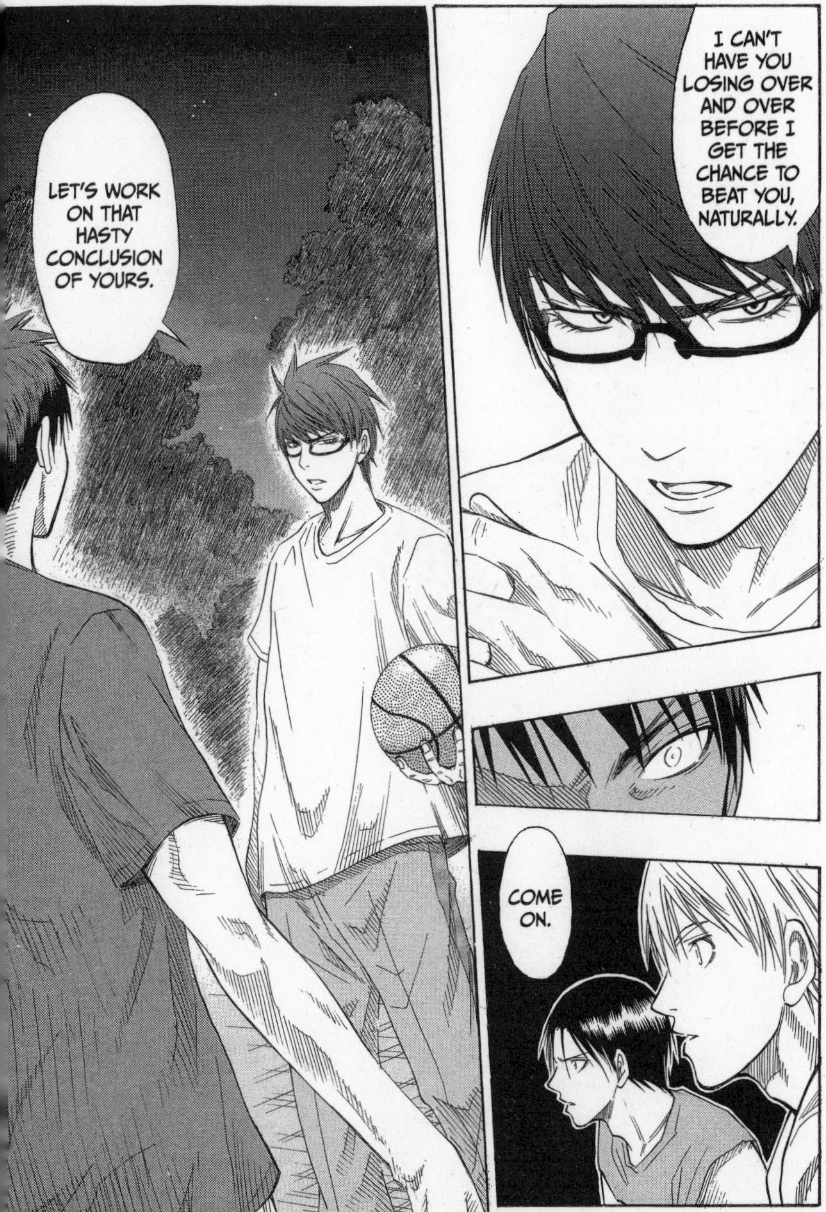
I CAN'T HAVE YOU LOSING OVER AND OVER BEFORE I GET THE CHANCE TO BEAT YOU, NATURALLY.
COME ON.
LET'S WORK ON THAT HASTY CONCLUSION OF YOURS.

KUROKO'S BASKETBALL BLOOPERS

TAKE 12

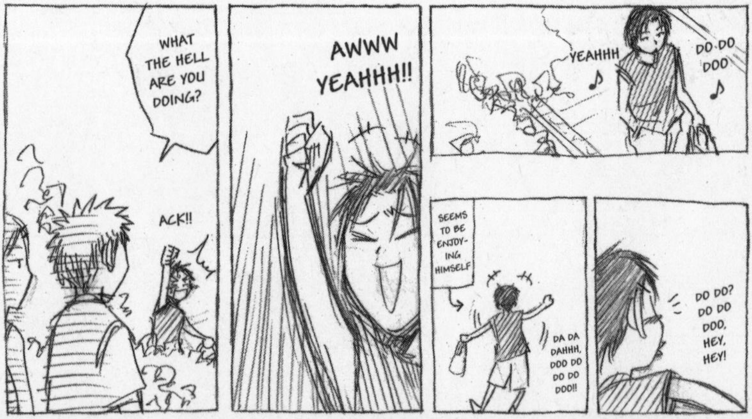
DO DO DOO ♪
YEAHHH ♪
DO DO? DO DO DOO, HEY, HEY!
SEEMS TO BE ENJOY-ING HIMSELF
DA DA DAHHH, DOO DO DO DO DOO!!
AWWW YEAHHH!!
WHAT THE HELL ARE YOU DOING?
ACK!!

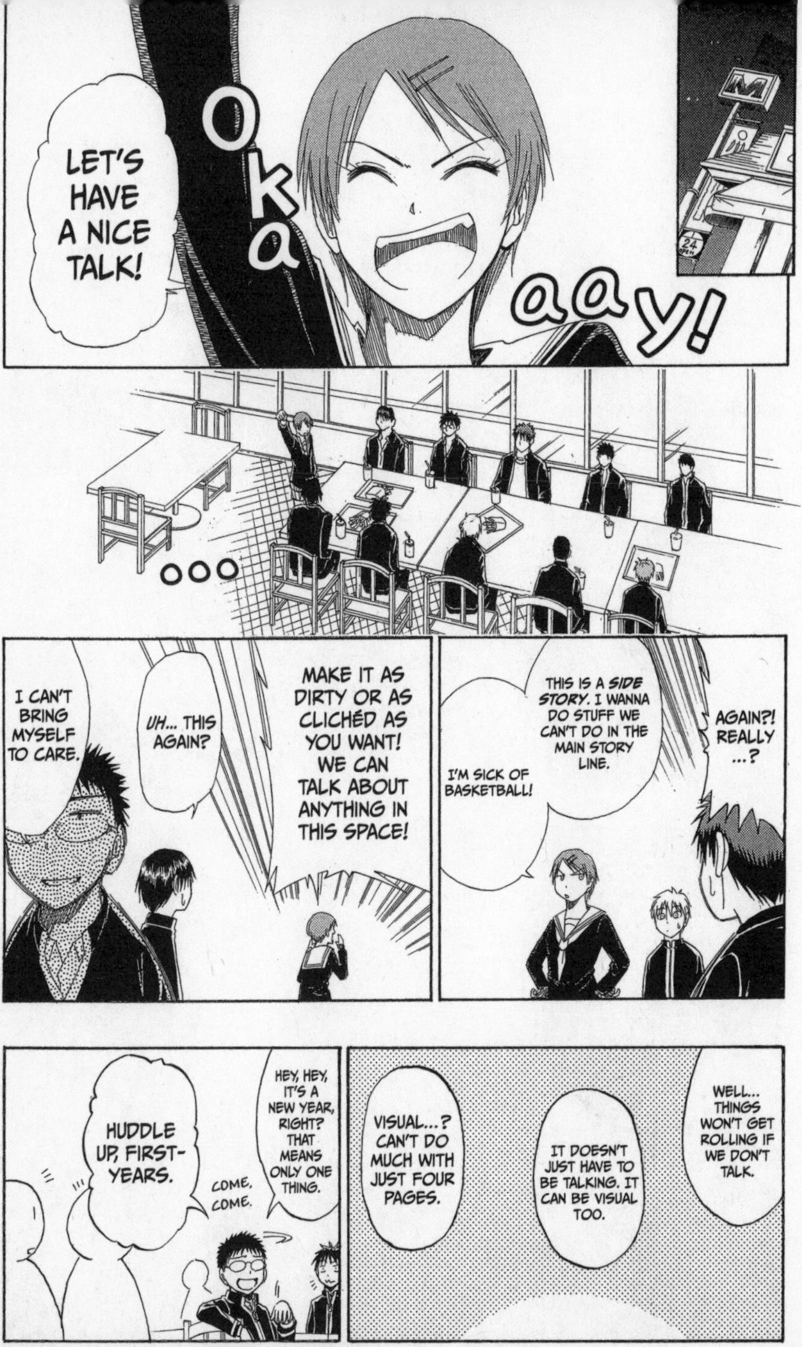
24
Okaaay!
LET'S HAVE A NICE TALK!
OOO
AGAIN?! REALLY ...?
THIS IS A *SIDE STORY*. I WANNA DO STUFF WE CAN'T DO IN THE MAIN STORY LINE.
I'M SICK OF BASKETBALL!
MAKE IT AS DIRTY OR AS CLICHÉD AS YOU WANT! WE CAN TALK ABOUT ANYTHING IN THIS SPACE!
UH... THIS AGAIN?
I CAN'T BRING MYSELF TO CARE.
WELL... THINGS WON'T GET ROLLING IF WE DON'T TALK.
IT DOESN'T JUST HAVE TO BE TALKING. IT CAN BE VISUAL TOO.
VISUAL...? CAN'T DO MUCH WITH JUST FOUR PAGES.
HEY, HEY, IT'S A NEW YEAR, RIGHT? THAT MEANS ONLY ONE THING.
COME, COME.
HUDDLE UP, FIRST-YEARS.

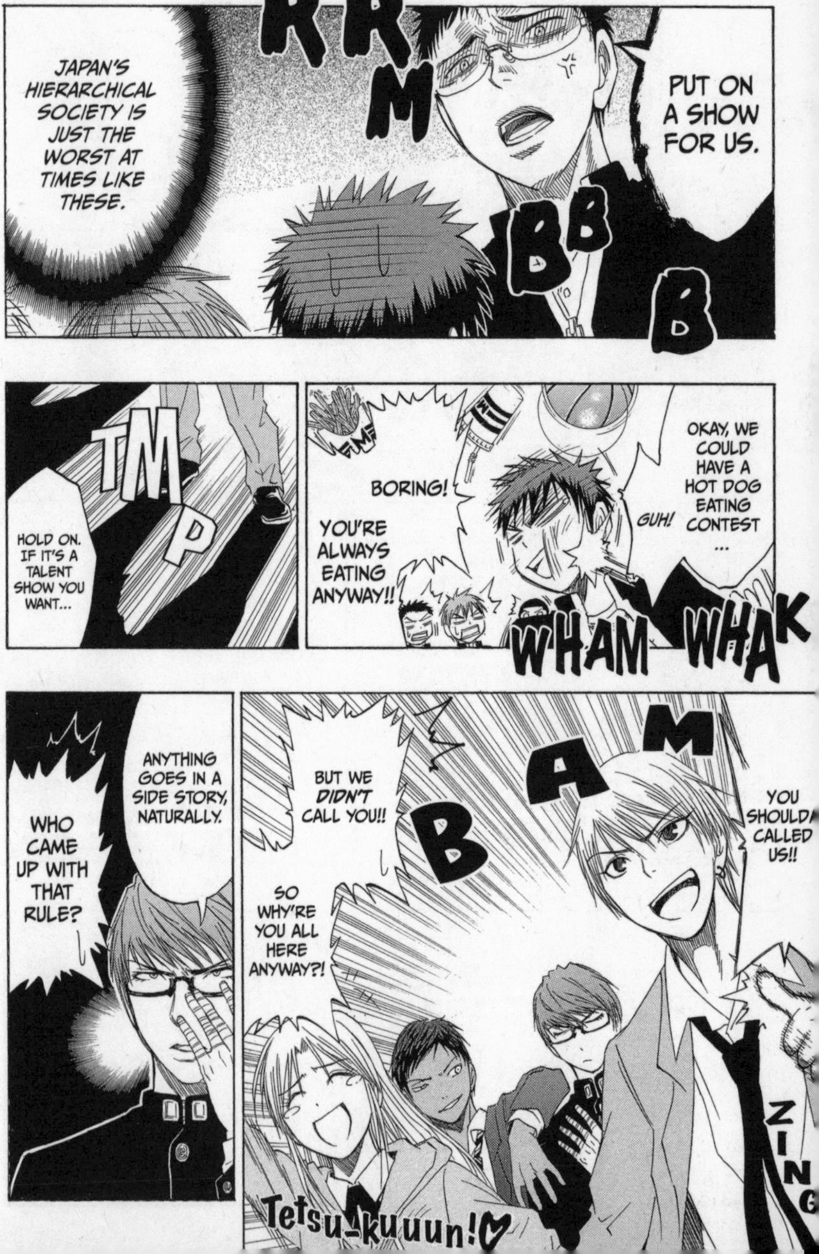
PUT ON A SHOW FOR US.
RRM
BBB
JAPAN'S HIERARCHICAL SOCIETY IS JUST THE WORST AT TIMES LIKE THESE.
OKAY, WE COULD HAVE A HOT DOG EATING CONTEST...
GUH!
BORING!
YOU'RE ALWAYS EATING ANYWAY!!
WHAM
WHAK
TMP
HOLD ON. IF IT'S A TALENT SHOW YOU WANT...
YOU SHOULD CALLED US!!
BAM
BUT WE *DIDN'T* CALL YOU!!
SO WHY'RE YOU ALL HERE ANYWAY?!
ZING
Tetsu-kuuun!♡
ANYTHING GOES IN A SIDE STORY, NATURALLY.
WHO CAME UP WITH THAT RULE?

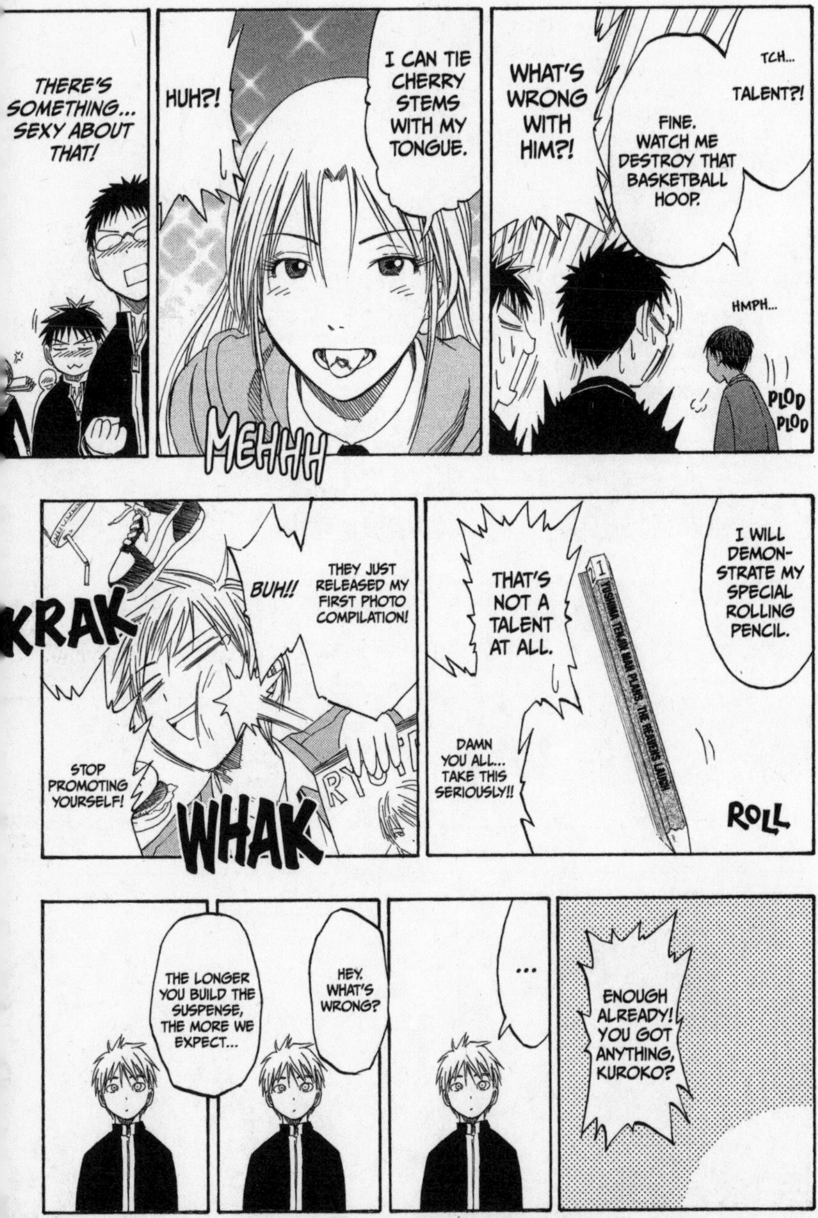
TCH...
TALENT?!
FINE. WATCH ME DESTROY THAT BASKETBALL HOOP.
WHAT'S WRONG WITH HIM?!
HMPH...
PLOD PLOD
I CAN TIE CHERRY STEMS WITH MY TONGUE.
HUH?!
MEHHHH
THERE'S SOMETHING... SEXY ABOUT THAT!
I WILL DEMON-STRATE MY SPECIAL ROLLING PENCIL.
THAT'S NOT A TALENT AT ALL.
DAMN YOU ALL... TAKE THIS SERIOUSLY!!
ROLL
THEY JUST RELEASED MY FIRST PHOTO COMPILATION!
BUH!!
KRAK
STOP PROMOTING YOURSELF!
WHAK
ENOUGH ALREADY! YOU GOT ANYTHING, KUROKO?
...
HEY. WHAT'S WRONG?
THE LONGER YOU BUILD THE SUSPENSE, THE MORE WE EXPECT...

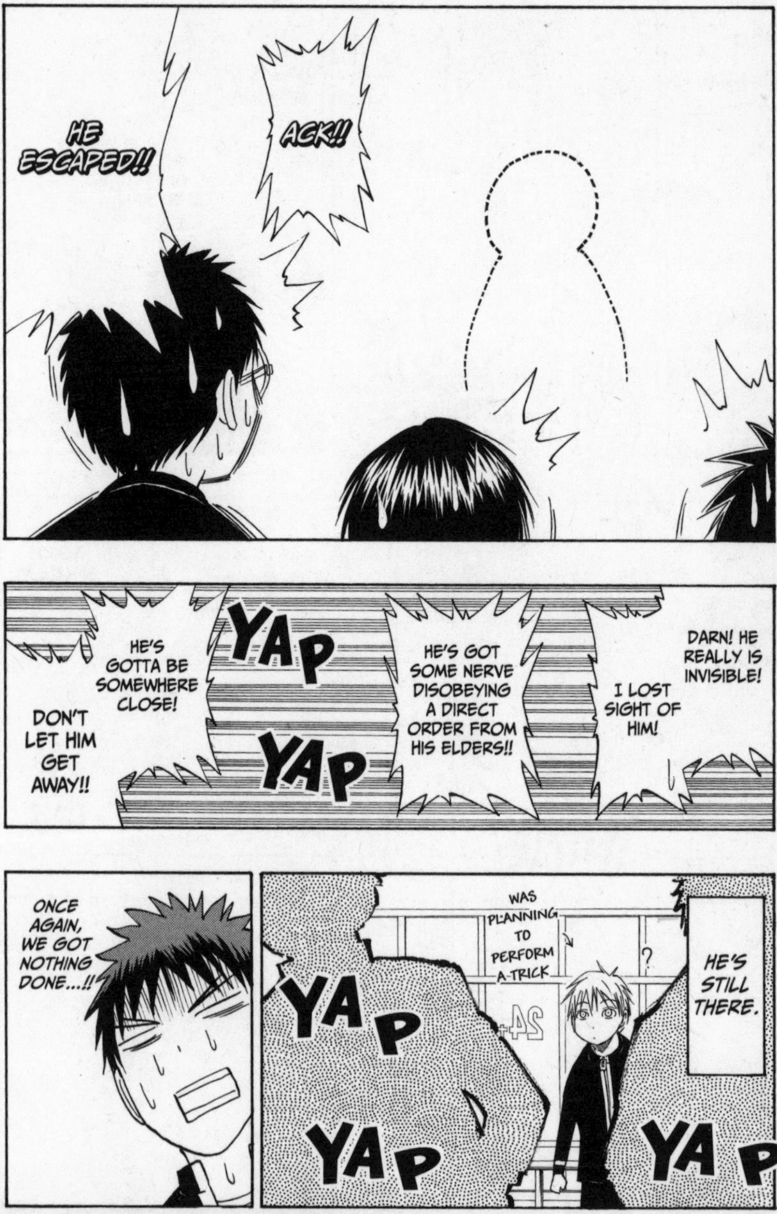

ACK!!
HE ESCAPED!!
DARN! HE REALLY IS INVISIBLE!
I LOST SIGHT OF HIM!
HE'S GOT SOME NERVE DISOBEYING A DIRECT ORDER FROM HIS ELDERS!!
YAP
YAP
HE'S GOTTA BE SOMEWHERE CLOSE!
DON'T LET HIM GET AWAY!!
HE'S STILL THERE.
?
WAS PLANNING TO PERFORM A TRICK
YAP
YAP
YAP
YAP
ONCE AGAIN, WE GOT NOTHING DONE...!!

KUROKO'S BASKETBALL: SIDE STORY (END)

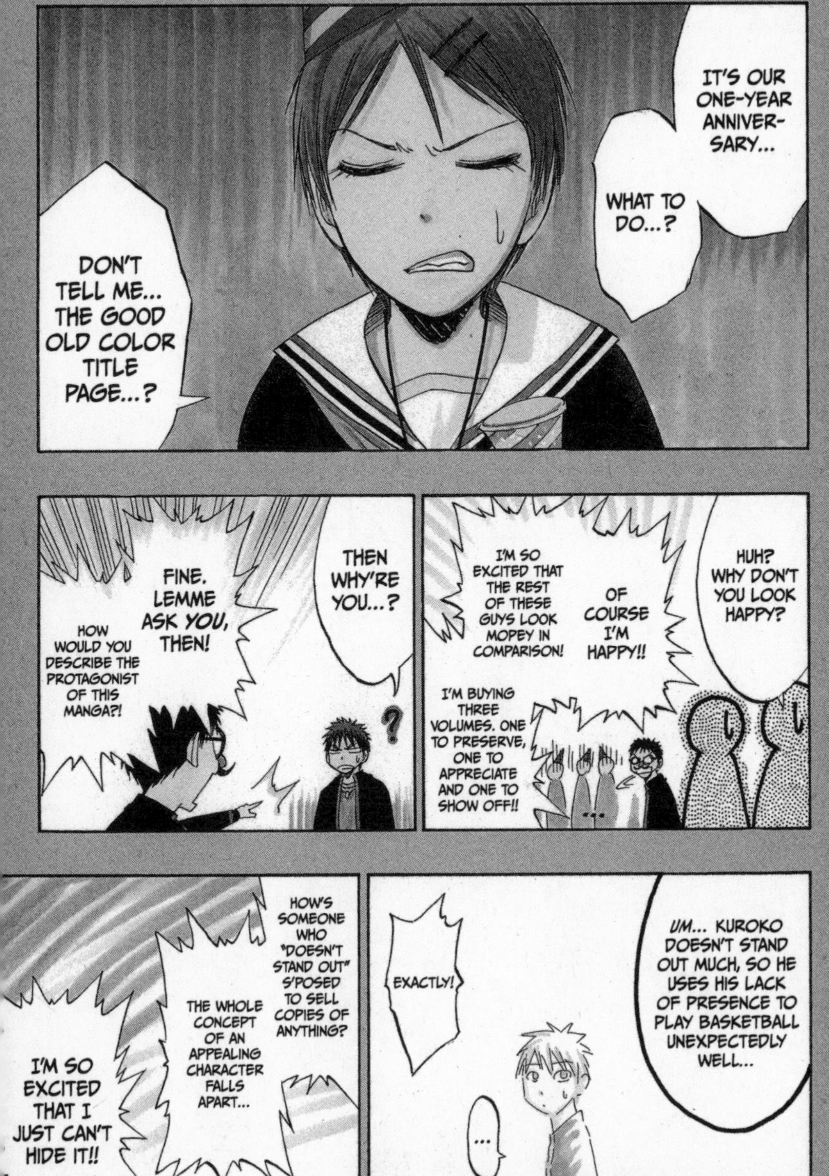
IT'S OUR ONE-YEAR ANNIVER-SARY...
WHAT TO DO...?
DON'T TELL ME... THE GOOD OLD COLOR TITLE PAGE...?
HUH? WHY DON'T YOU LOOK HAPPY?
OF COURSE I'M HAPPY!!
I'M SO EXCITED THAT THE REST OF THESE GUYS LOOK MOPEY IN COMPARISON!
I'M BUYING THREE VOLUMES. ONE TO PRESERVE, ONE TO APPRECIATE AND ONE TO SHOW OFF!!
...
THEN WHY'RE YOU...?
?
FINE. LEMME ASK *YOU*, THEN!
HOW WOULD YOU DESCRIBE THE PROTAGONIST OF THIS MANGA?!
UM... KUROKO DOESN'T STAND OUT MUCH, SO HE USES HIS LACK OF PRESENCE TO PLAY BASKETBALL UNEXPECTEDLY WELL...
EXACTLY!
...
HOW'S SOMEONE WHO "DOESN'T STAND OUT" S'POSED TO SELL COPIES OF ANYTHING?
THE WHOLE CONCEPT OF AN APPEALING CHARACTER FALLS APART...
I'M SO EXCITED THAT I JUST CAN'T HIDE IT!!

*Note: This feature originally appeared in color in *Weekly Shonen Jump* 2010, issue #7

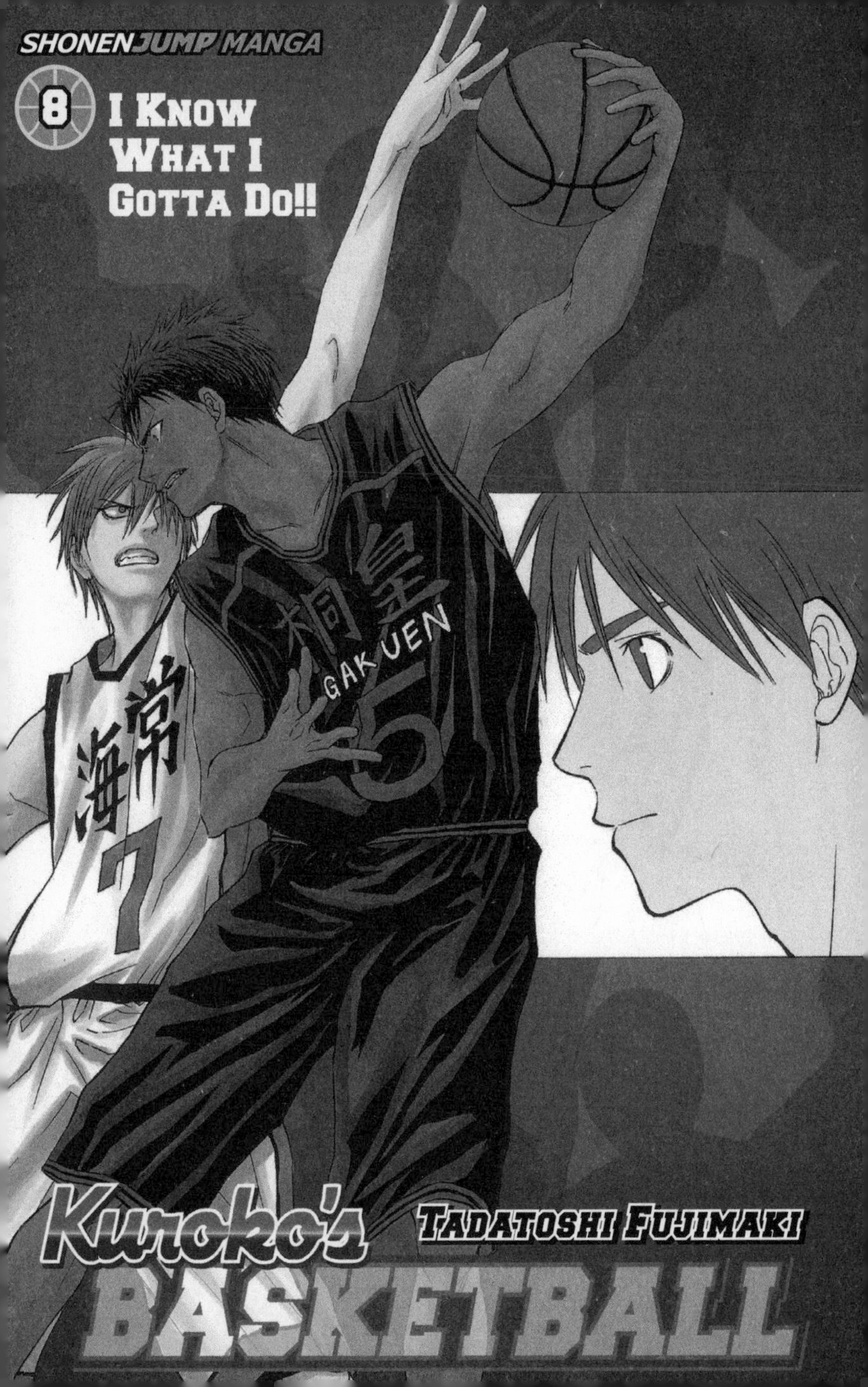
SHONEN JUMP MANGA
8
I KNOW WHAT I GOTTA DO!!
桐皇
GAKUEN
5
海常
7
TADATOSHI FUJIMAKI
Kuroko's BASKETBALL

TADATOSHI FUJIMAKI

I always seriously stress about what to write here. Without some kind of twist, it's just not very interesting. I want to say something insightful that makes me look cool. Annnd now I feel like I've already blown that chance.

—2010

62ND QUARTER: I KNOW WHAT I GOTTA DO!!

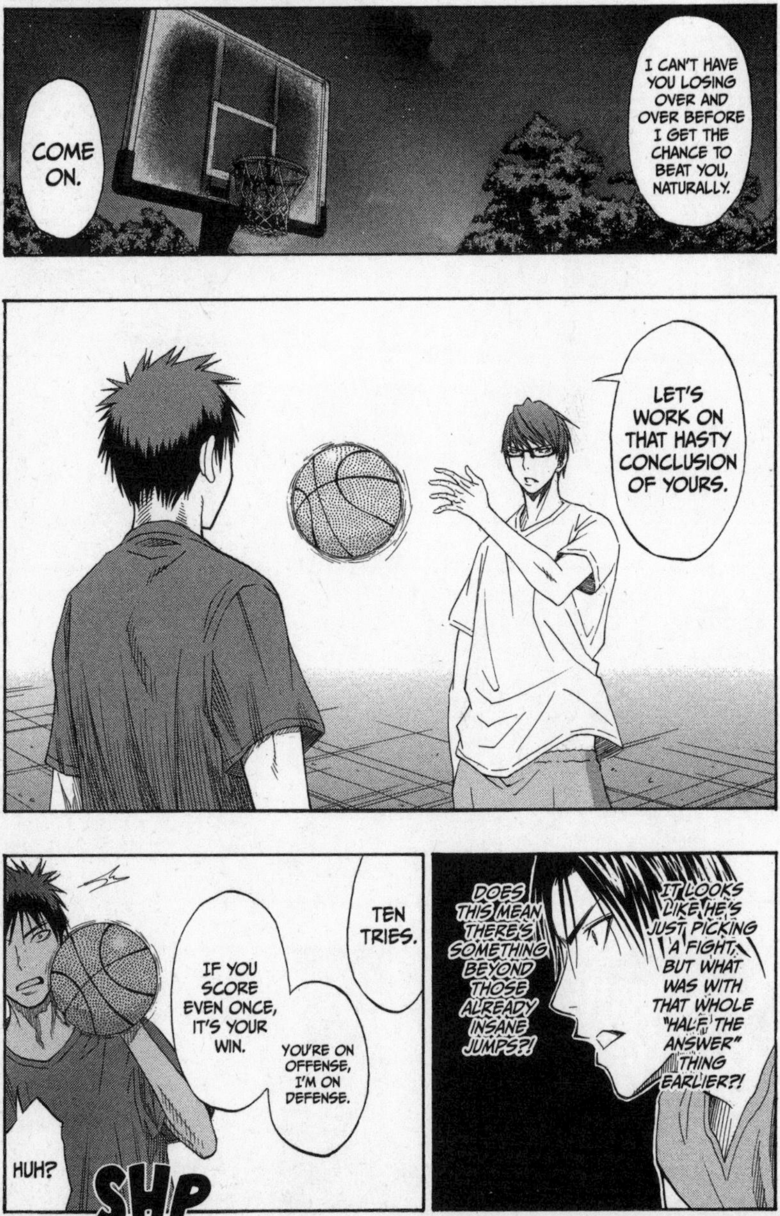

I CAN'T HAVE YOU LOSING OVER AND OVER BEFORE I GET THE CHANCE TO BEAT YOU, NATURALLY.
COME ON.
LET'S WORK ON THAT HASTY CONCLUSION OF YOURS.
IT LOOKS LIKE HE'S JUST PICKING A FIGHT, BUT WHAT WAS WITH THAT WHOLE "HALF THE ANSWER" THING EARLIER?!
DOES THIS MEAN THERE'S SOMETHING BEYOND THOSE ALREADY INSANE JUMPS?!
TEN TRIES.
IF YOU SCORE EVEN ONCE, IT'S YOUR WIN.
YOU'RE ON OFFENSE, I'M ON DEFENSE.
HUH?
SHP

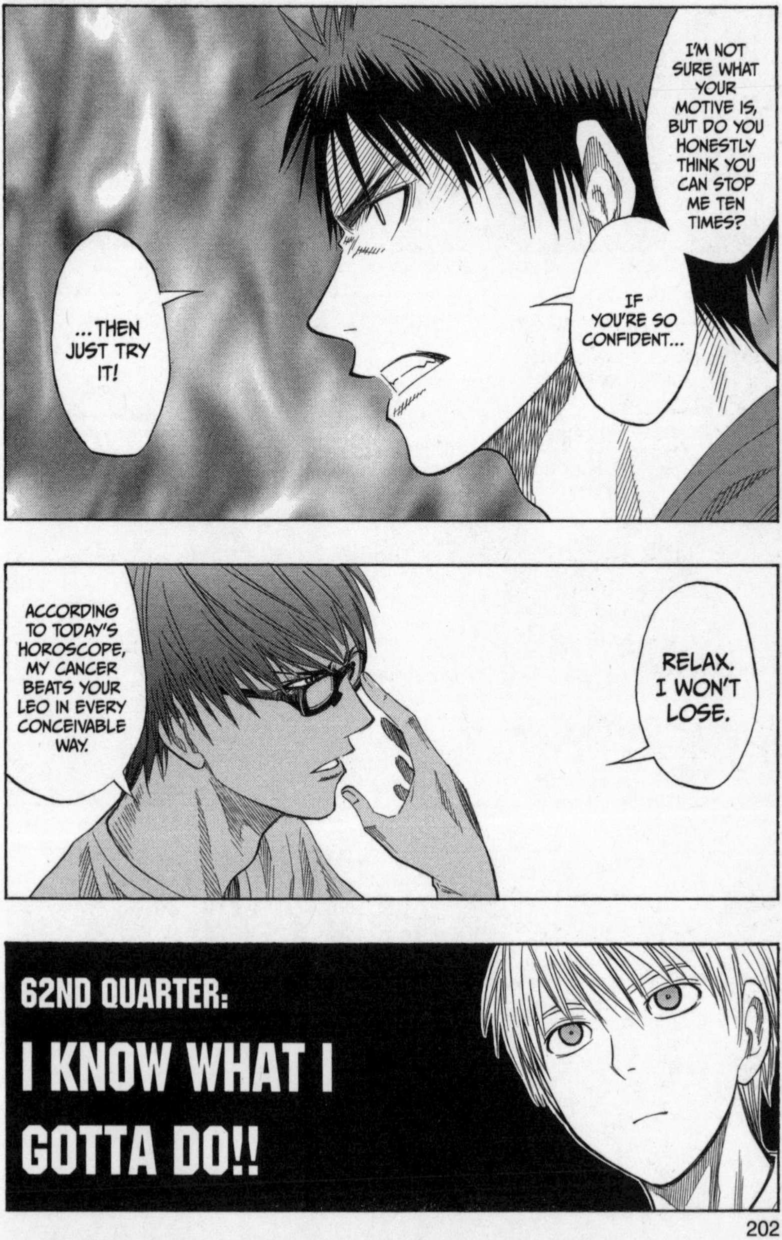
I'M NOT SURE WHAT YOUR MOTIVE IS, BUT DO YOU HONESTLY THINK YOU CAN STOP ME TEN TIMES?
IF YOU'RE SO CONFIDENT...
...THEN JUST TRY IT!
RELAX. I WON'T LOSE.
ACCORDING TO TODAY'S HOROSCOPE, MY CANCER BEATS YOUR LEO IN EVERY CONCEIVABLE WAY.
62ND QUARTER:
I KNOW WHAT I GOTTA DO!!

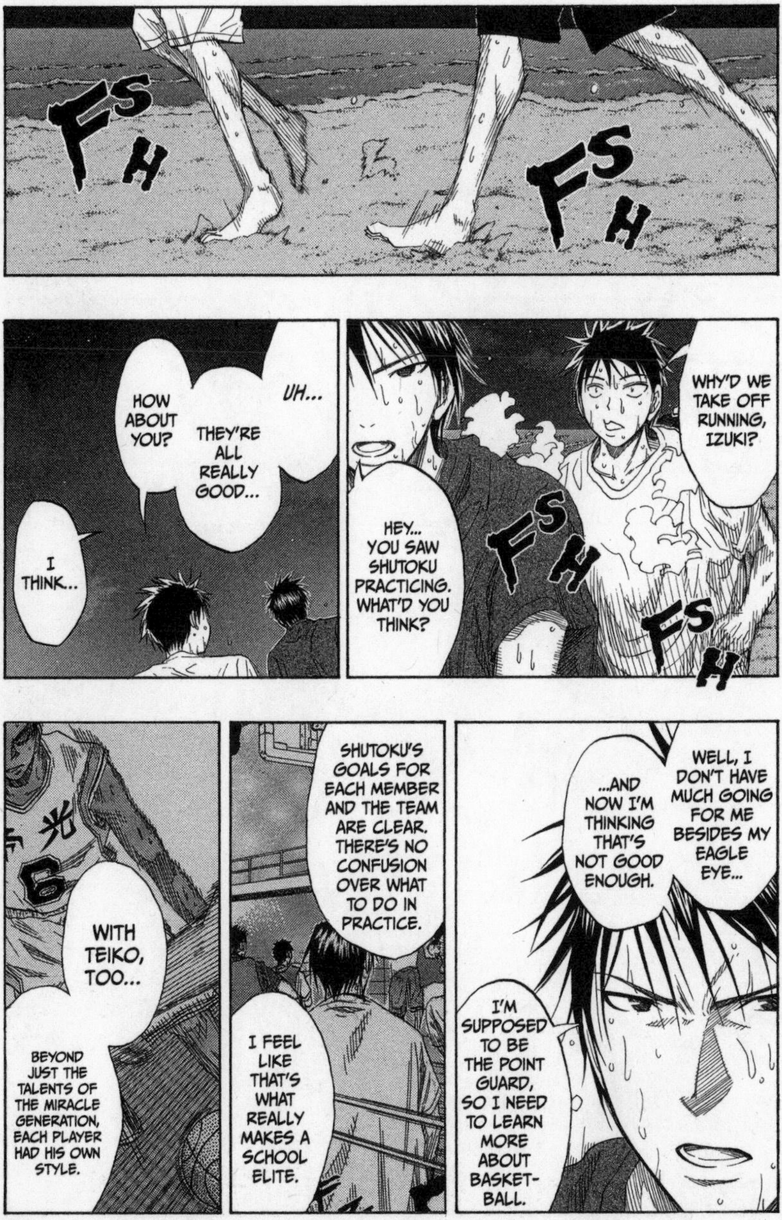
FSH
FSH
WHY'D WE TAKE OFF RUNNING, IZUKI?
HEY... YOU SAW SHUTOKU PRACTICING. WHAT'D YOU THINK?
FSH
FSH
UH...
THEY'RE ALL REALLY GOOD...
HOW ABOUT YOU?
I THINK...
WELL, I DON'T HAVE MUCH GOING FOR ME BESIDES MY EAGLE EYE...
...AND NOW I'M THINKING THAT'S NOT GOOD ENOUGH.
I'M SUPPOSED TO BE THE POINT GUARD, SO I NEED TO LEARN MORE ABOUT BASKET-BALL.
SHUTOKU'S GOALS FOR EACH MEMBER AND THE TEAM ARE CLEAR. THERE'S NO CONFUSION OVER WHAT TO DO IN PRACTICE.
I FEEL LIKE THAT'S WHAT REALLY MAKES A SCHOOL ELITE.
WITH TEIKO, TOO...
BEYOND JUST THE TALENTS OF THE MIRACLE GENERATION, EACH PLAYER HAD HIS OWN STYLE.

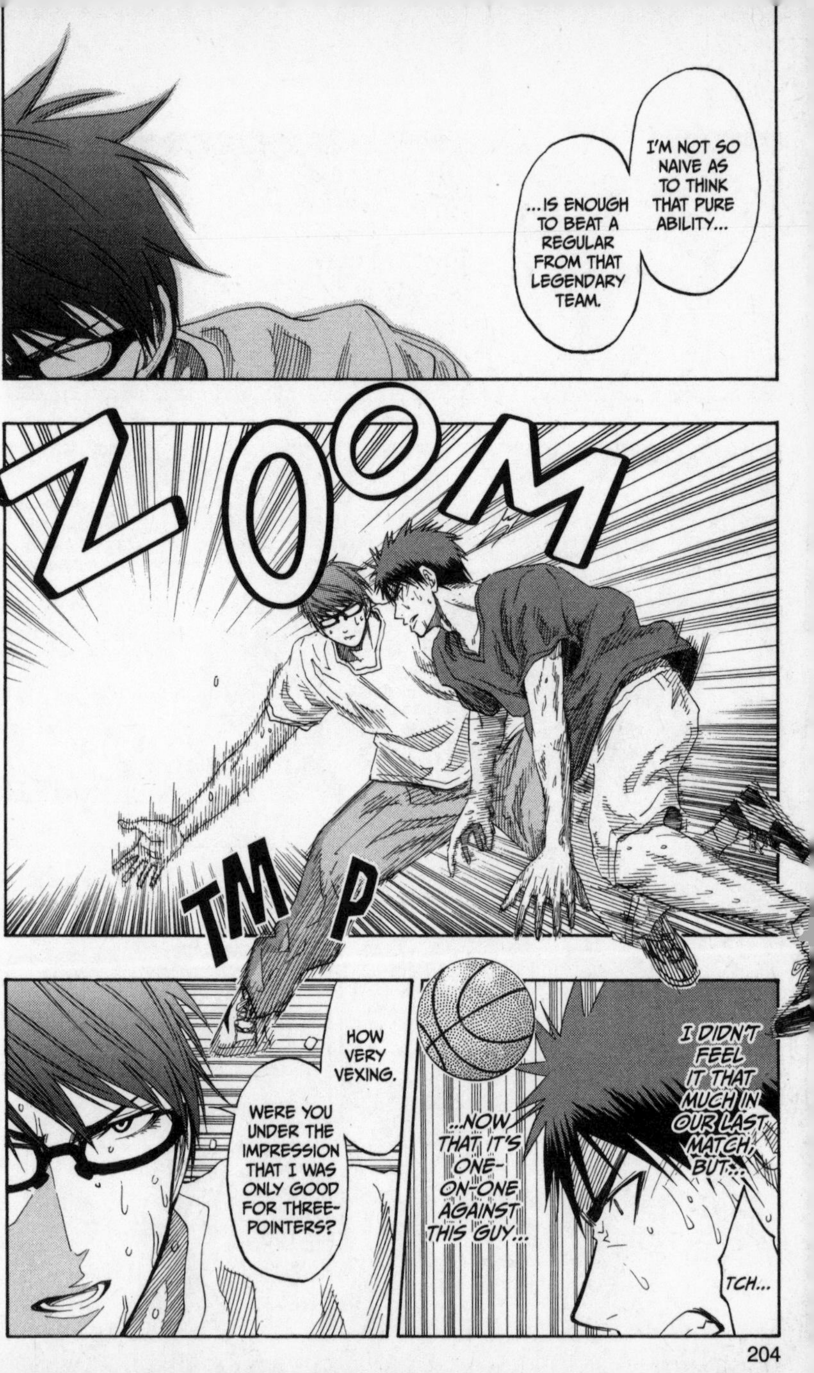
I'M NOT SO NAIVE AS TO THINK THAT PURE ABILITY...
...IS ENOUGH TO BEAT A REGULAR FROM THAT LEGENDARY TEAM.
ZOOM
TMP
I DIDN'T FEEL IT THAT MUCH IN OUR LAST MATCH, BUT...
...NOW THAT IT'S ONE-ON-ONE AGAINST THIS GUY...
TCH...
HOW VERY VEXING.
WERE YOU UNDER THE IMPRESSION THAT I WAS ONLY GOOD FOR THREE-POINTERS?

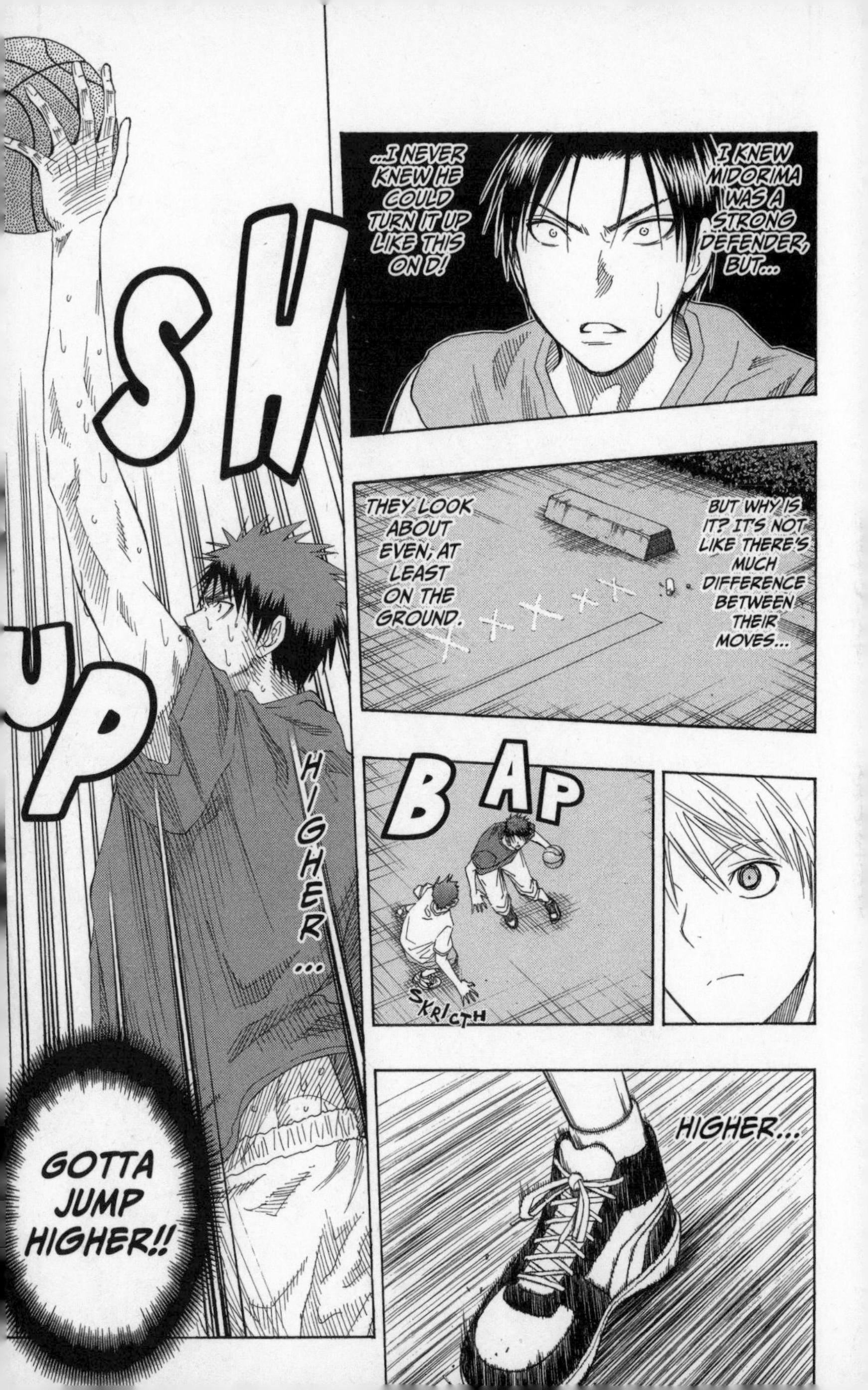
I KNEW MIDORIMA WAS A STRONG DEFENDER, BUT...
...I NEVER KNEW HE COULD TURN IT UP LIKE THIS ON D!
BUT WHY IS IT? IT'S NOT LIKE THERE'S MUCH DIFFERENCE BETWEEN THEIR MOVES...
THEY LOOK ABOUT EVEN, AT LEAST ON THE GROUND.
BAP
SKRICTH
HIGHER...
SH
UP
HIGHER...
GOTTA JUMP HIGHER!!

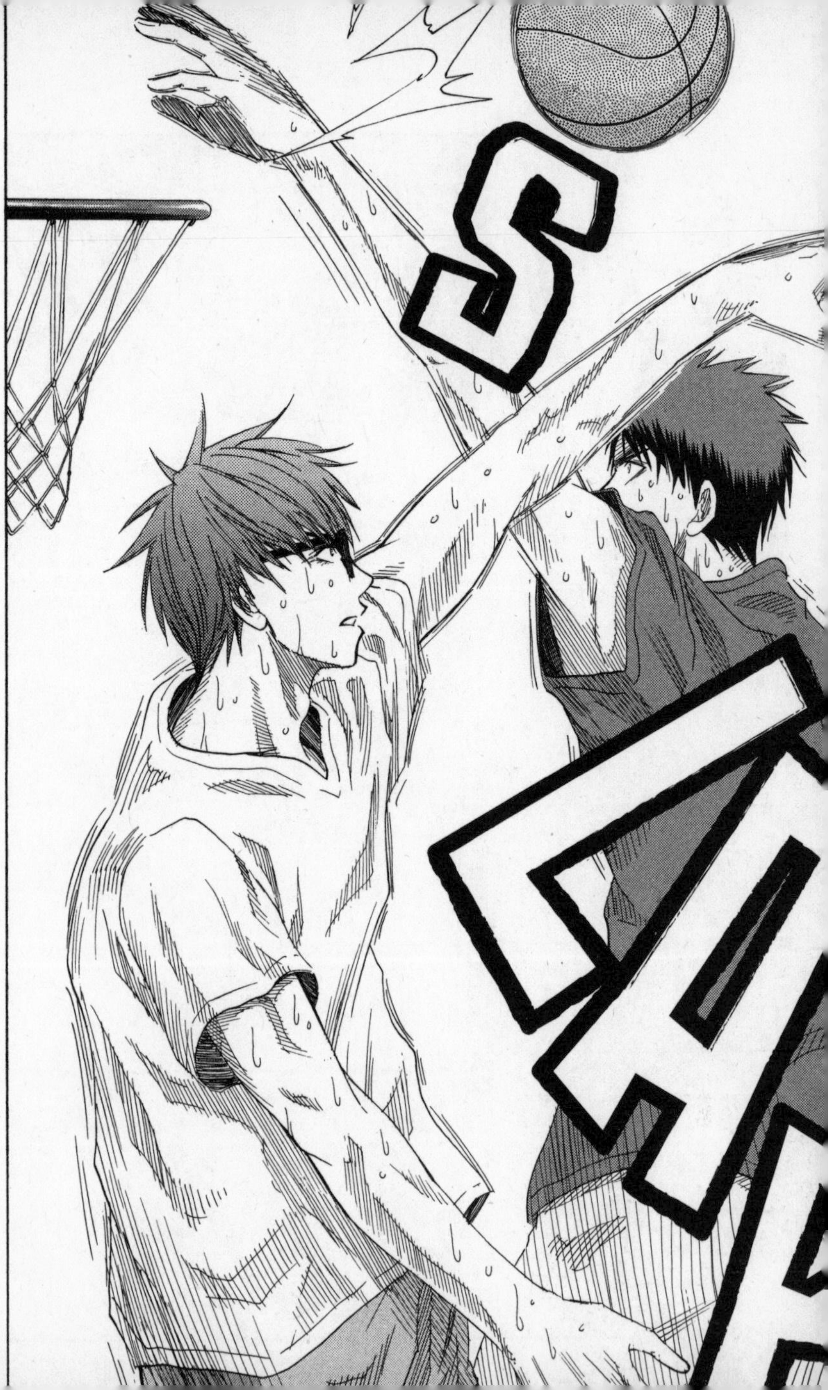

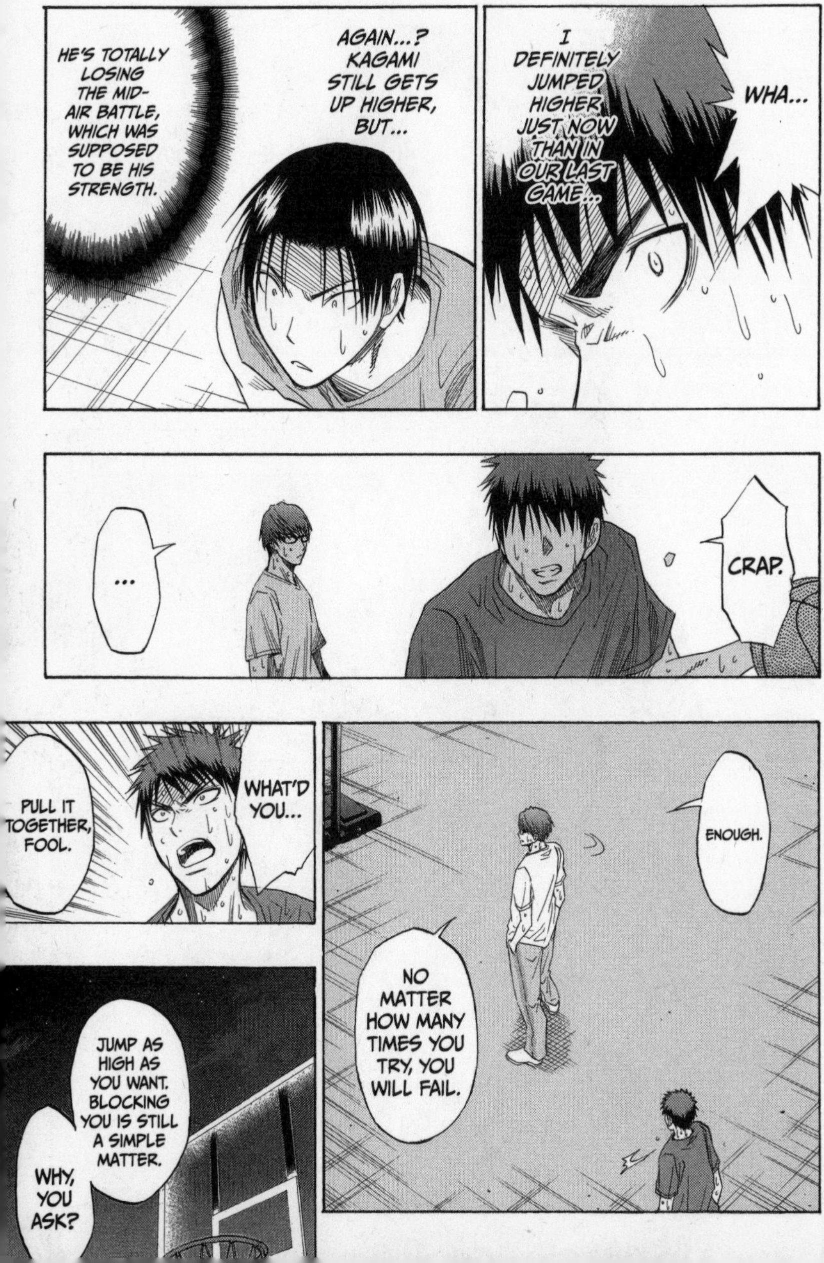

WHA...
I DEFINITELY JUMPED HIGHER JUST NOW THAN IN OUR LAST GAME...
AGAIN...? KAGAMI STILL GETS UP HIGHER, BUT...
HE'S TOTALLY LOSING THE MID-AIR BATTLE, WHICH WAS SUPPOSED TO BE HIS STRENGTH.
CRAP.
...
ENOUGH.
NO MATTER HOW MANY TIMES YOU TRY, YOU WILL FAIL.
PULL IT TOGETHER, FOOL.
WHAT'D YOU...
JUMP AS HIGH AS YOU WANT. BLOCKING YOU IS STILL A SIMPLE MATTER.
WHY, YOU ASK?

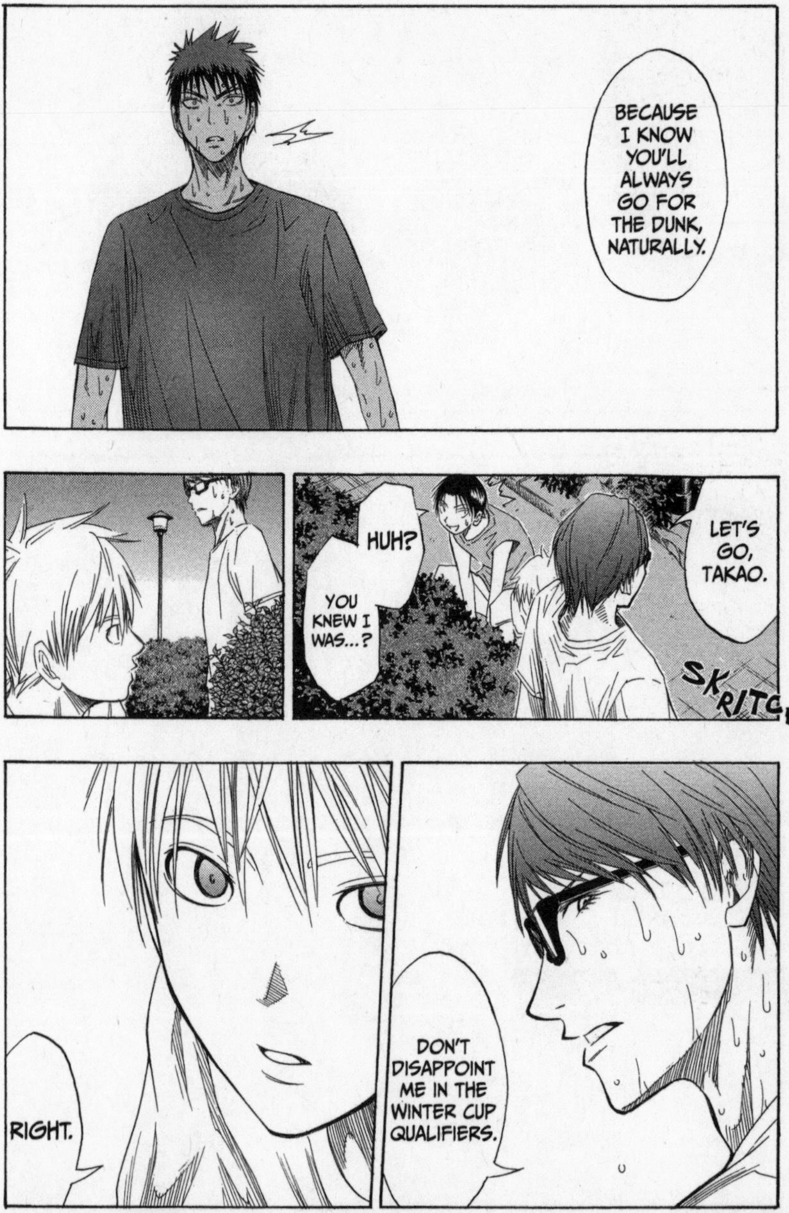
BECAUSE I KNOW YOU'LL ALWAYS GO FOR THE DUNK, NATURALLY.
LET'S GO, TAKAO.
SKRITCH
HUH?
YOU KNEW I WAS...?
DON'T DISAPPOINT ME IN THE WINTER CUP QUALIFIERS.
RIGHT.

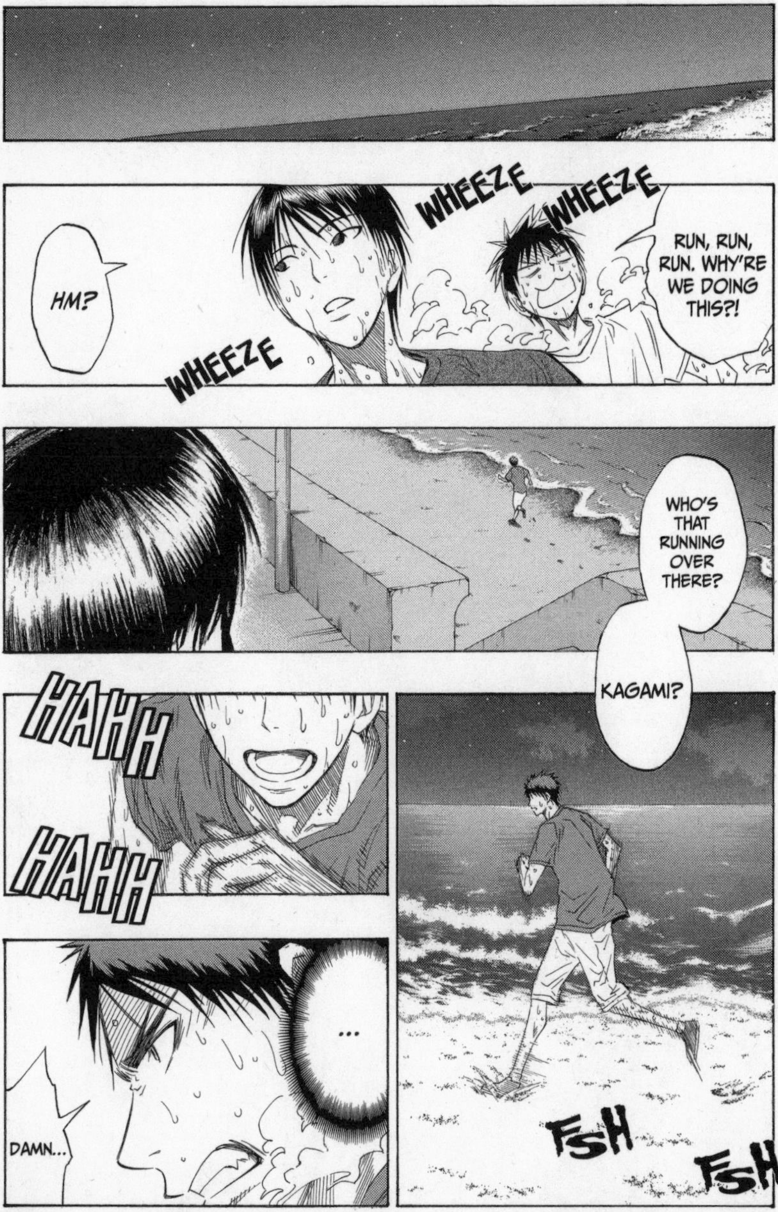
WHEEZE
WHEEZE
RUN, RUN, RUN. WHY'RE WE DOING THIS?!
WHEEZE
HM?
WHO'S THAT RUNNING OVER THERE?
KAGAMI?
FSH
FSH
HAHH
HAHH
...
DAMN...

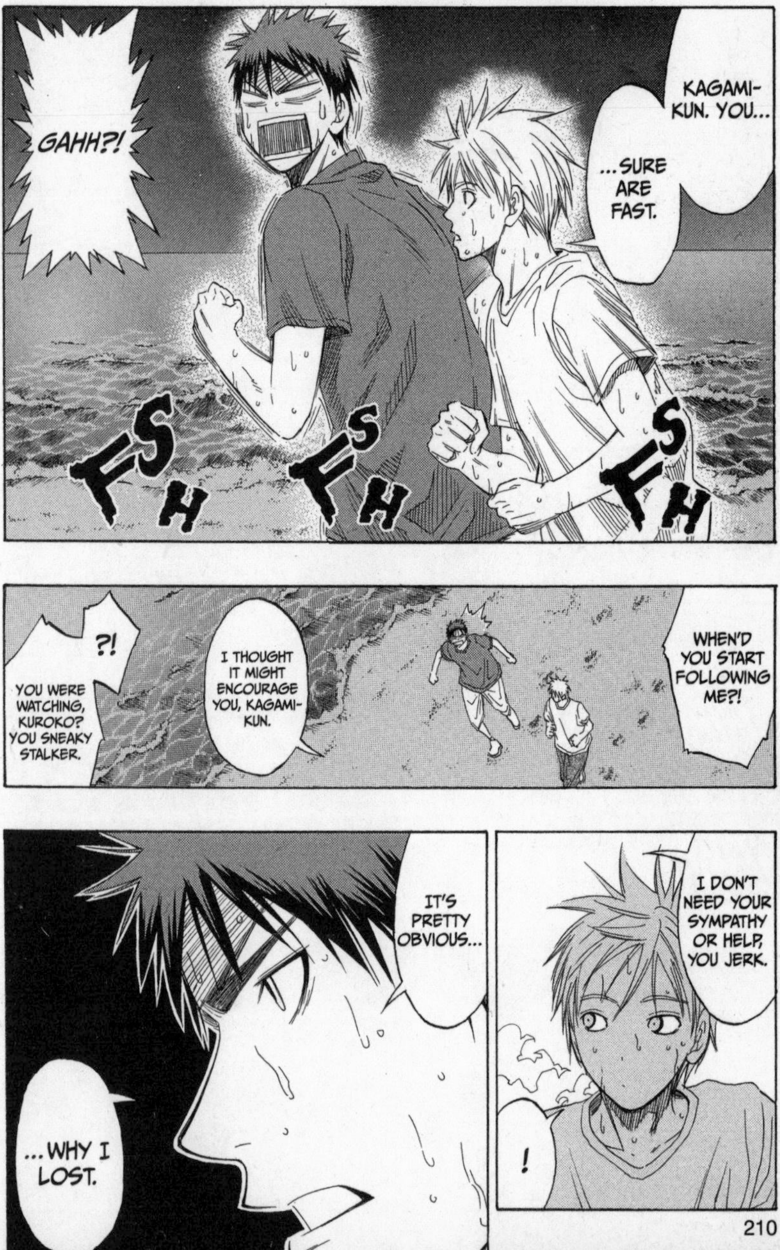
KAGAMI-KUN. YOU...
...SURE ARE FAST.
GAHH?!
FSH
FSH
FSH
WHEN'D YOU START FOLLOWING ME?!
I THOUGHT IT MIGHT ENCOURAGE YOU, KAGAMI-KUN.
?!
YOU WERE WATCHING, KUROKO? YOU SNEAKY STALKER.
I DON'T NEED YOUR SYMPATHY OR HELP, YOU JERK.
!
IT'S PRETTY OBVIOUS...
...WHY I LOST.

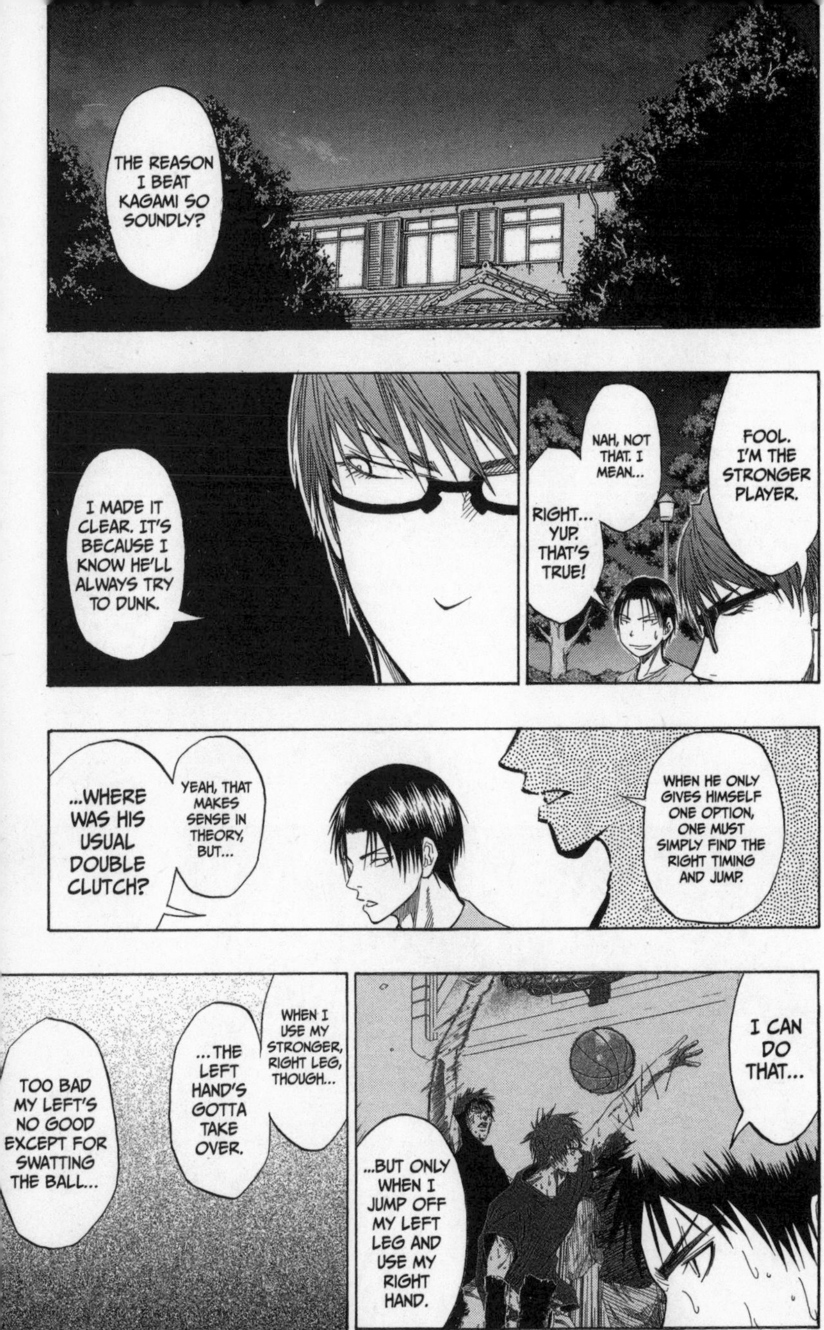
THE REASON I BEAT KAGAMI SO SOUNDLY?
FOOL. I'M THE STRONGER PLAYER.
NAH, NOT THAT. I MEAN...
RIGHT... YUP. THAT'S TRUE!
I MADE IT CLEAR. IT'S BECAUSE I KNOW HE'LL ALWAYS TRY TO DUNK.
WHEN HE ONLY GIVES HIMSELF ONE OPTION, ONE MUST SIMPLY FIND THE RIGHT TIMING AND JUMP.
YEAH, THAT MAKES SENSE IN THEORY, BUT...
...WHERE WAS HIS USUAL DOUBLE CLUTCH?
I CAN DO THAT...
...BUT ONLY WHEN I JUMP OFF MY LEFT LEG AND USE MY RIGHT HAND.
WHEN I USE MY STRONGER, RIGHT LEG, THOUGH...
...THE LEFT HAND'S GOTTA TAKE OVER.
TOO BAD MY LEFT'S NO GOOD EXCEPT FOR SWATTING THE BALL...

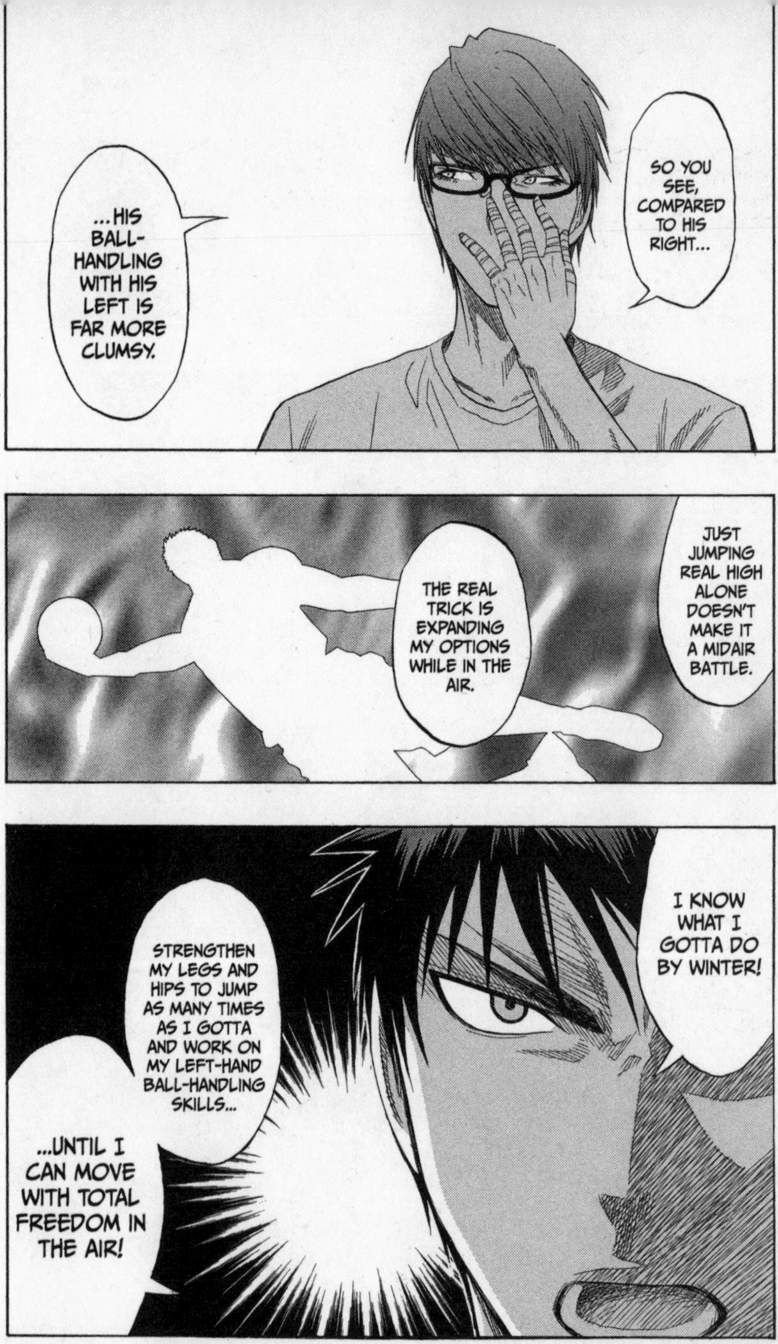

SO YOU SEE, COMPARED TO HIS RIGHT...
...HIS BALL-HANDLING WITH HIS LEFT IS FAR MORE CLUMSY.
JUST JUMPING REAL HIGH ALONE DOESN'T MAKE IT A MIDAIR BATTLE.
THE REAL TRICK IS EXPANDING MY OPTIONS WHILE IN THE AIR.
I KNOW WHAT I GOTTA DO BY WINTER!
STRENGTHEN MY LEGS AND HIPS TO JUMP AS MANY TIMES AS I GOTTA AND WORK ON MY LEFT-HAND BALL-HANDLING SKILLS...
...UNTIL I CAN MOVE WITH TOTAL FREEDOM IN THE AIR!

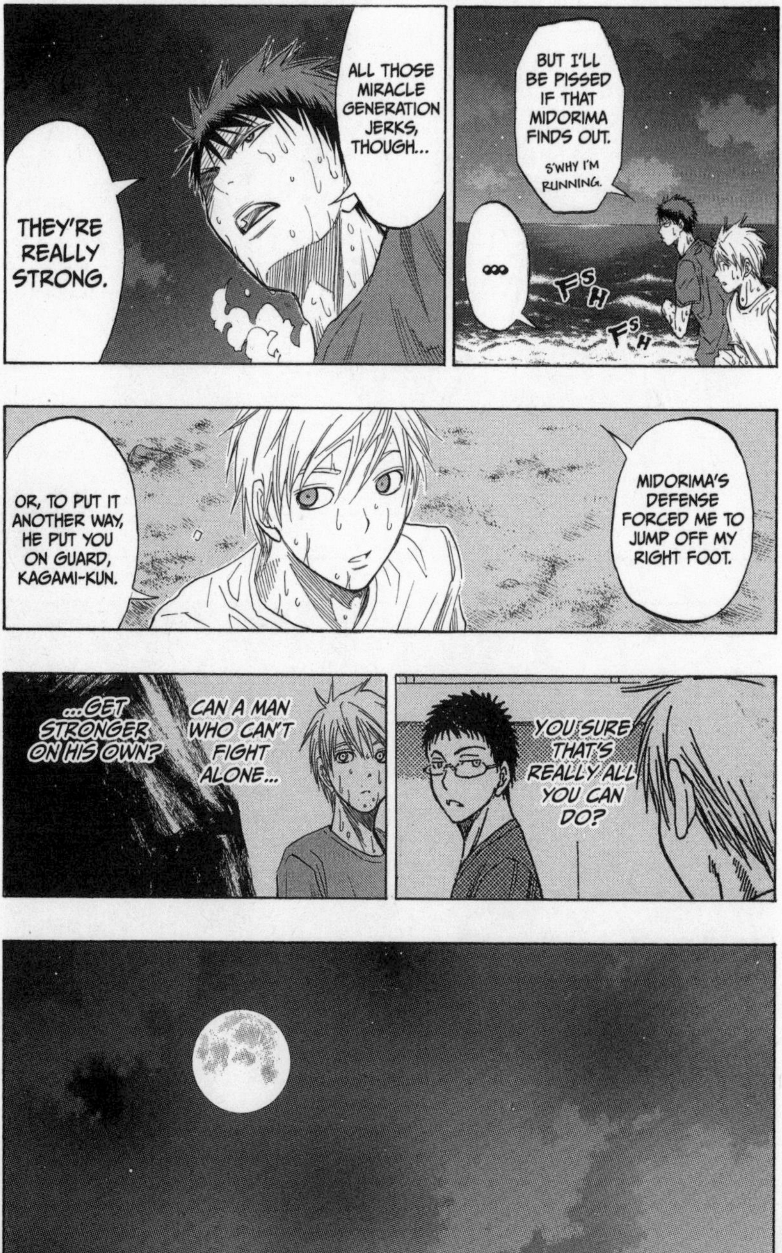
BUT I'LL BE PISSED IF THAT MIDORIMA FINDS OUT.
S'WHY I'M RUNNING.
...
FSH
FSH
ALL THOSE MIRACLE GENERATION JERKS, THOUGH...
THEY'RE REALLY STRONG.
MIDORIMA'S DEFENSE FORCED ME TO JUMP OFF MY RIGHT FOOT.
OR, TO PUT IT ANOTHER WAY, HE PUT YOU ON GUARD, KAGAMI-KUN.
YOU SURE THAT'S REALLY ALL YOU CAN DO?
CAN A MAN WHO CAN'T FIGHT ALONE...
...GET STRONGER ON HIS OWN?

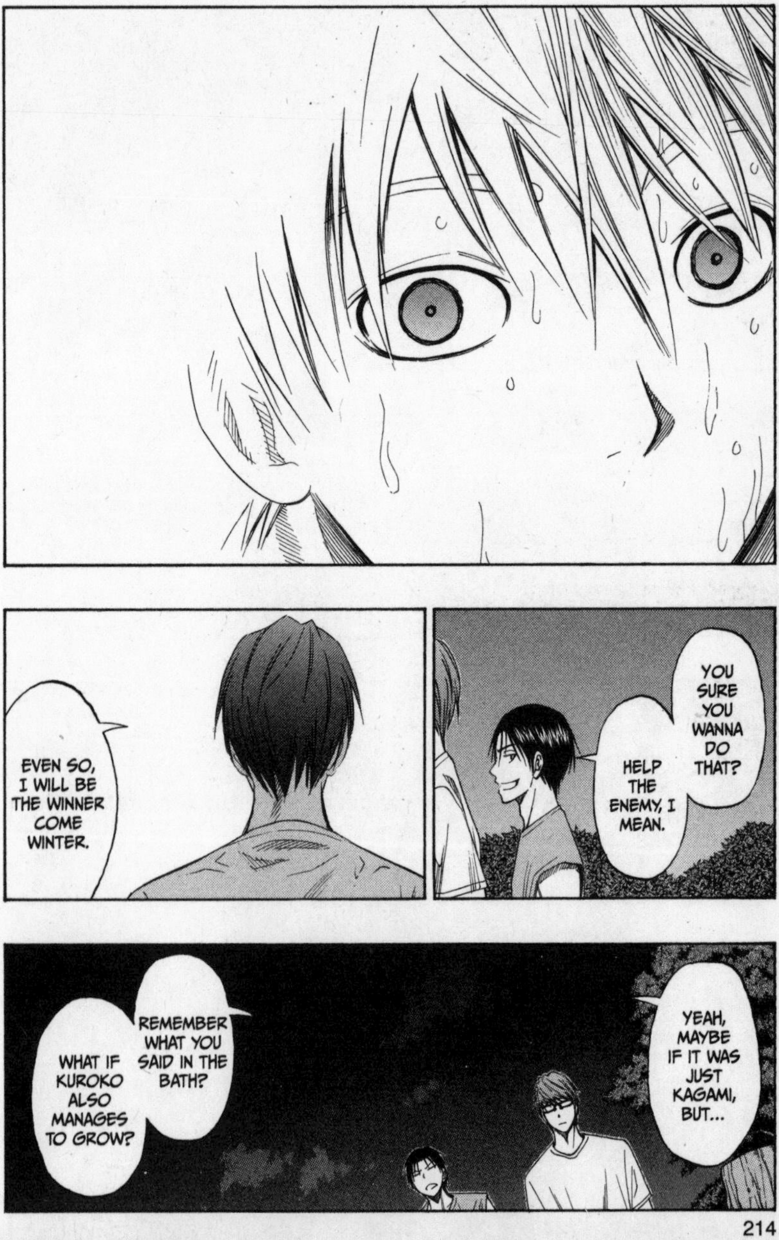
YOU SURE YOU WANNA DO THAT?
HELP THE ENEMY, I MEAN.
EVEN SO, I WILL BE THE WINNER COME WINTER.
YEAH, MAYBE IF IT WAS JUST KAGAMI, BUT...
REMEMBER WHAT YOU SAID IN THE BATH?
WHAT IF KUROKO ALSO MANAGES TO GROW?

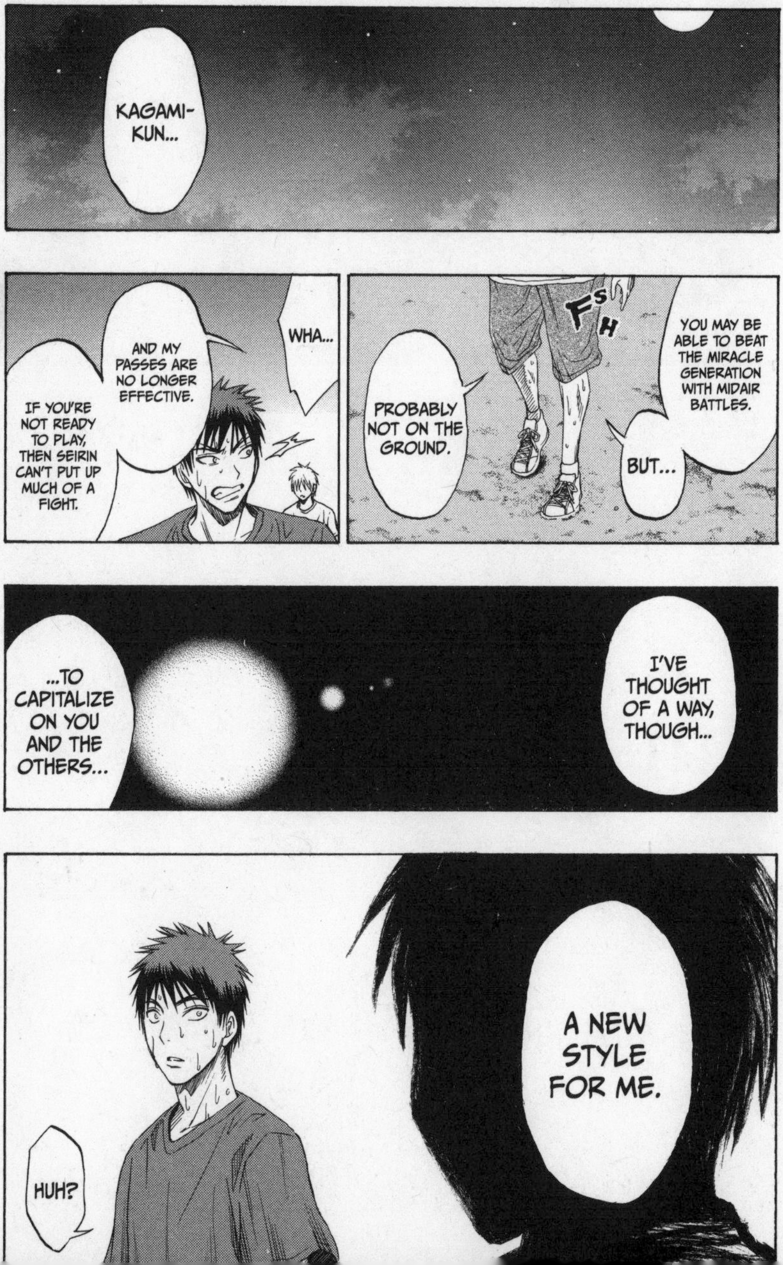
KAGAMI-KUN...
YOU MAY BE ABLE TO BEAT THE MIRACLE GENERATION WITH MIDAIR BATTLES.
FSH
BUT...
PROBABLY NOT ON THE GROUND.
WHA...
AND MY PASSES ARE NO LONGER EFFECTIVE.
IF YOU'RE NOT READY TO PLAY, THEN SEIRIN CAN'T PUT UP MUCH OF A FIGHT.
I'VE THOUGHT OF A WAY, THOUGH...
...TO CAPITALIZE ON YOU AND THE OTHERS...
A NEW STYLE FOR ME.
HUH?

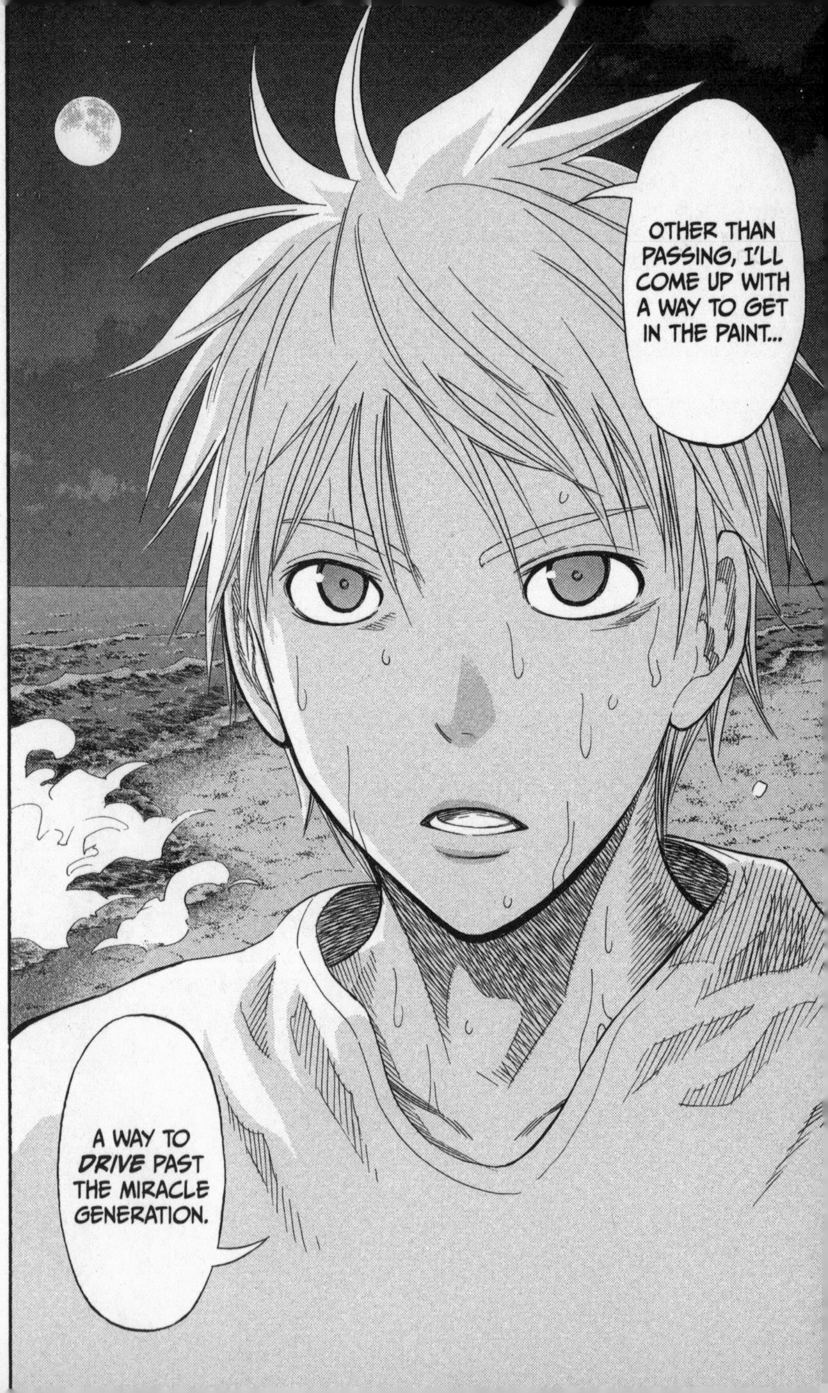
OTHER THAN PASSING, I'LL COME UP WITH A WAY TO GET IN THE PAINT...
A WAY TO *DRIVE* PAST THE MIRACLE GENERATION.

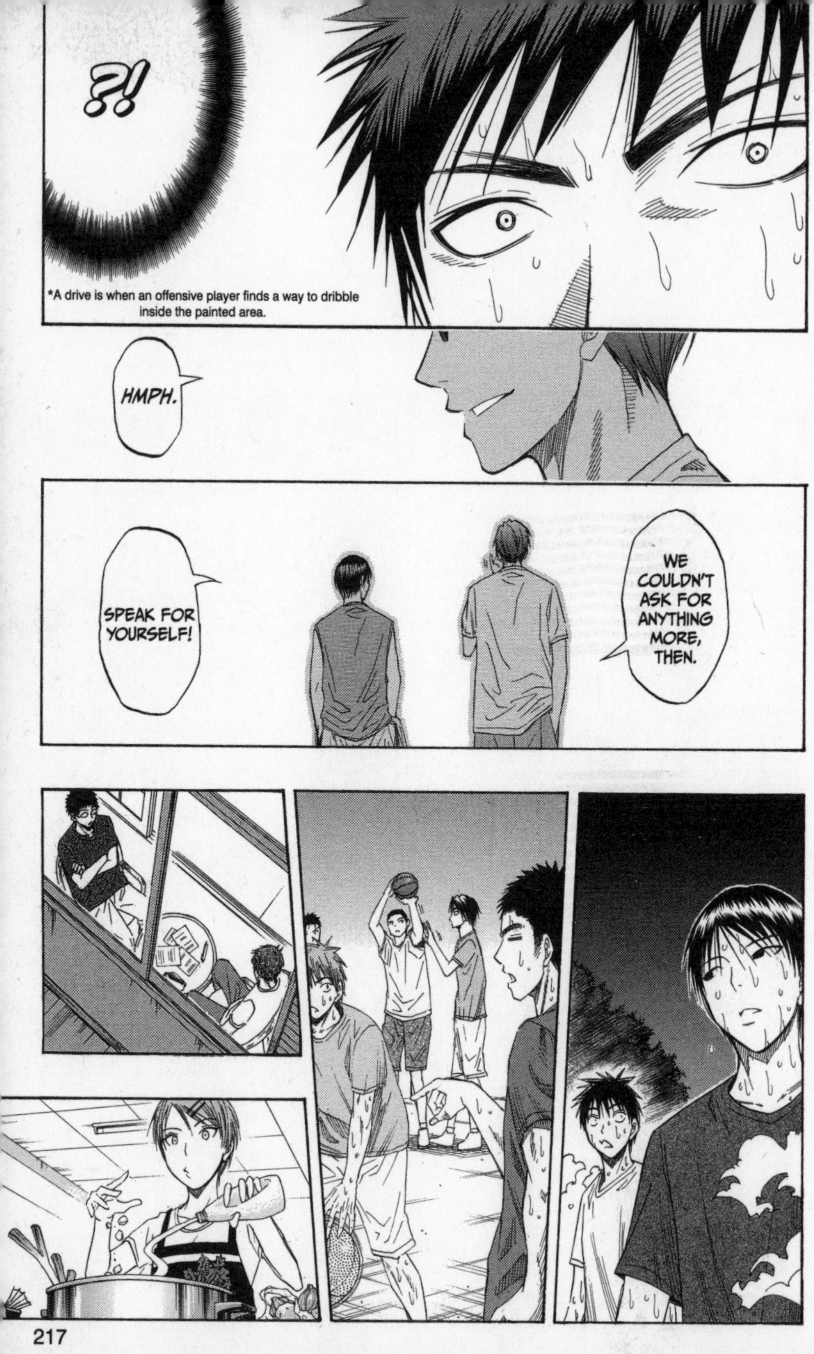
?!
*A drive is when an offensive player finds a way to dribble inside the painted area.
HMPH.
WE COULDN'T ASK FOR ANYTHING MORE, THEN.
SPEAK FOR YOURSELF!

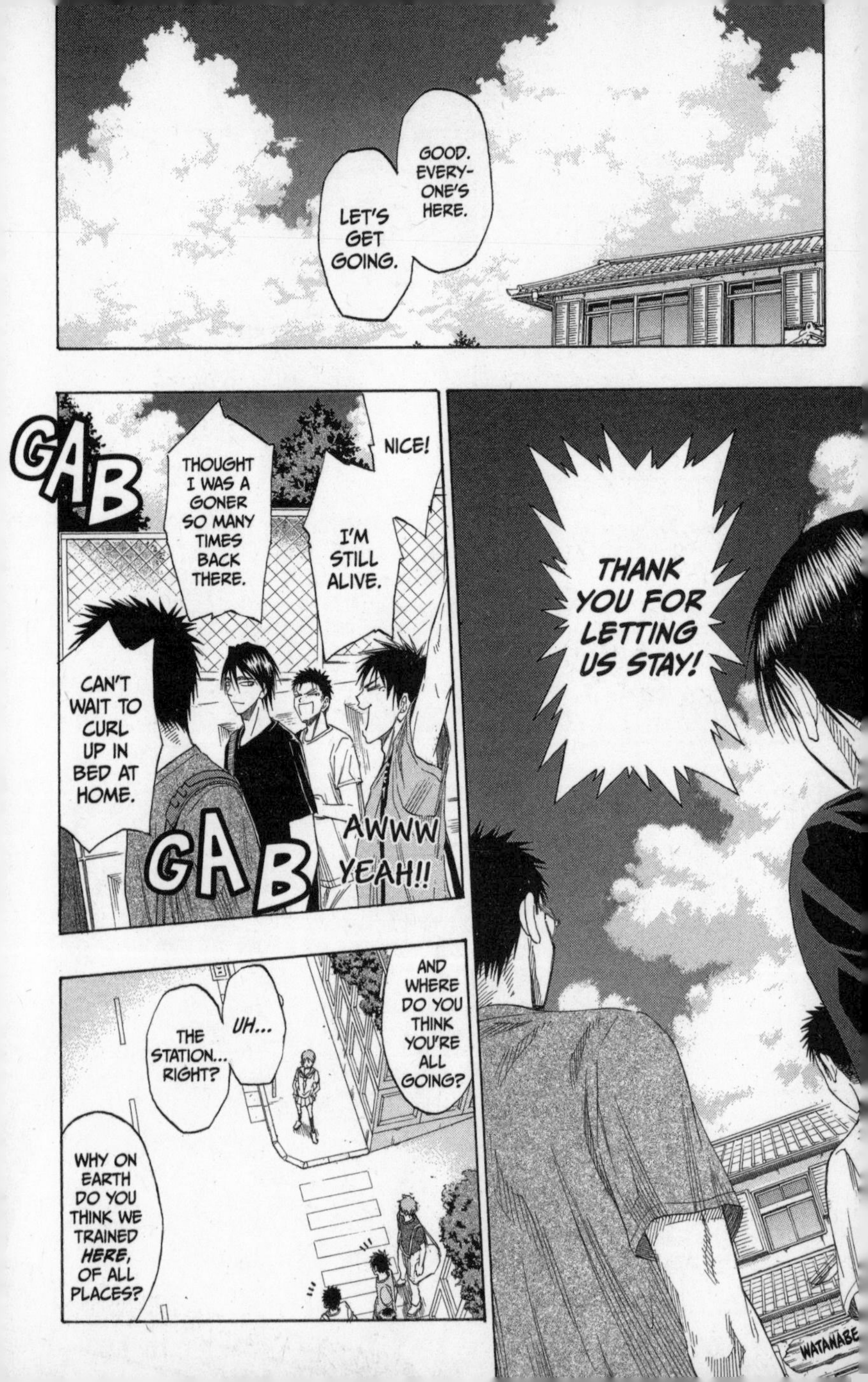
GOOD. EVERY-ONE'S HERE.
LET'S GET GOING.
THANK YOU FOR LETTING US STAY!
WATANABE
NICE!
I'M STILL ALIVE.
THOUGHT I WAS A GONER SO MANY TIMES BACK THERE.
GAB
CAN'T WAIT TO CURL UP IN BED AT HOME.
AWWW YEAH!!
GAB
AND WHERE DO YOU THINK YOU'RE ALL GOING?
UH...
THE STATION... RIGHT?
WHY ON EARTH DO YOU THINK WE TRAINED *HERE*, OF ALL PLACES?

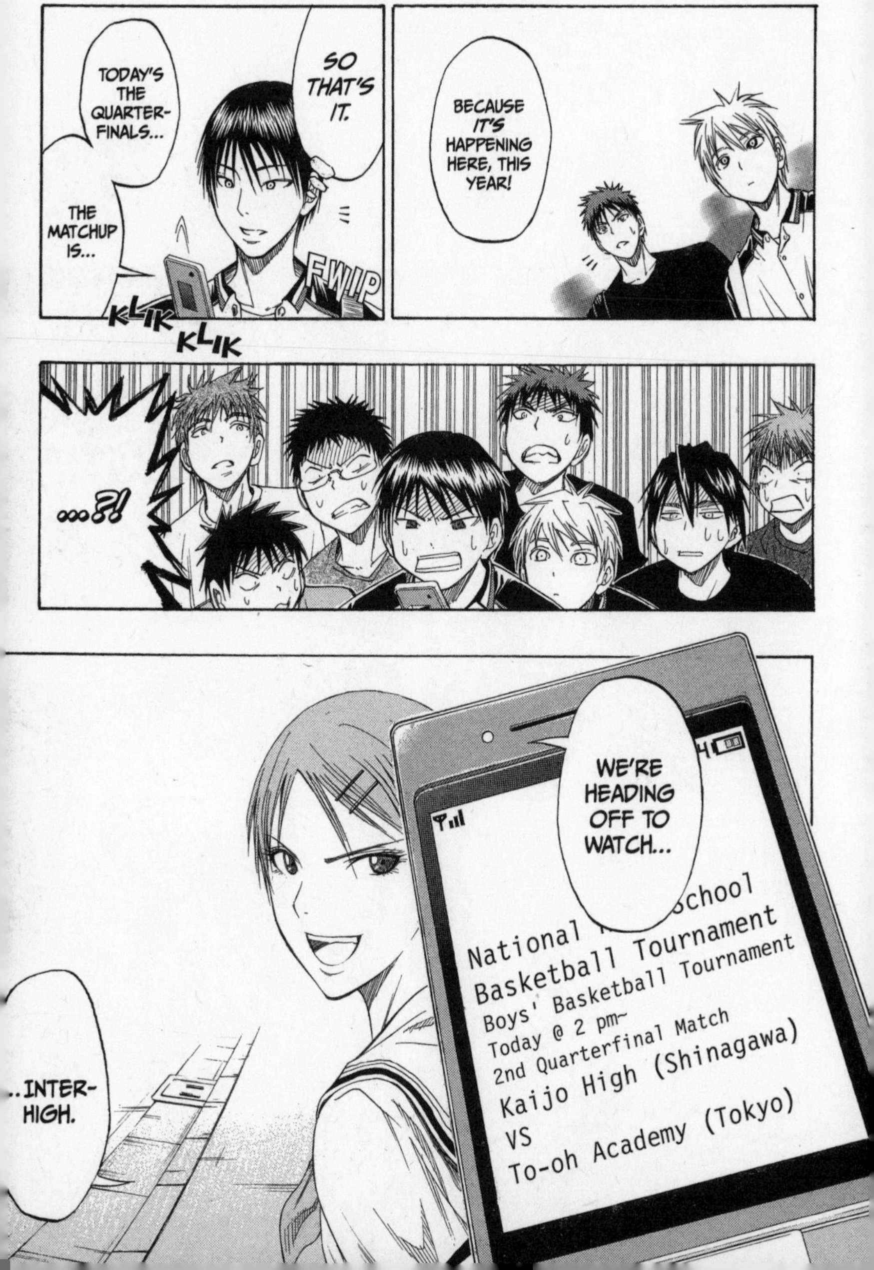
BECAUSE IT'S HAPPENING HERE, THIS YEAR!
SO THAT'S IT.
TODAY'S THE QUARTER-FINALS...
THE MATCHUP IS...
FWIP
KLIK KLIK
...?!
WE'RE HEADING OFF TO WATCH...
National
School
Basketball Tournament
Boys' Basketball Tournament
Today @ 2 pm~
2nd Quarterfinal Match
Kaijo High (Shinagawa)
VS
To-oh Academy (Tokyo)
...INTER-HIGH.

KUROKO'S BASKETBALL BLOOPERS TAKE 23

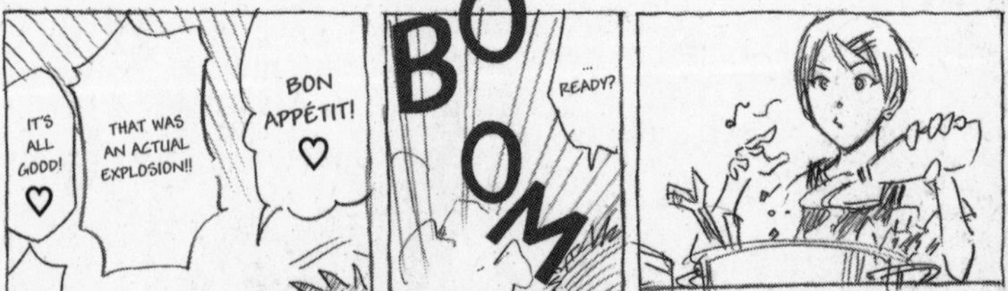
HEY, COACH. IS THE FOOD...
SHF
...READY?
BOOM
BON APPÉTIT! ♡
THAT WAS AN ACTUAL EXPLOSION!!
IT'S ALL GOOD! ♡
LIKE HELL IT IS!!

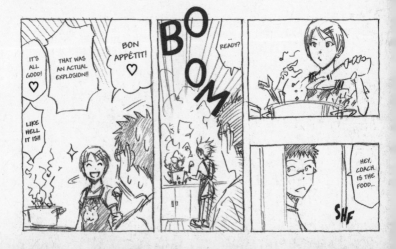

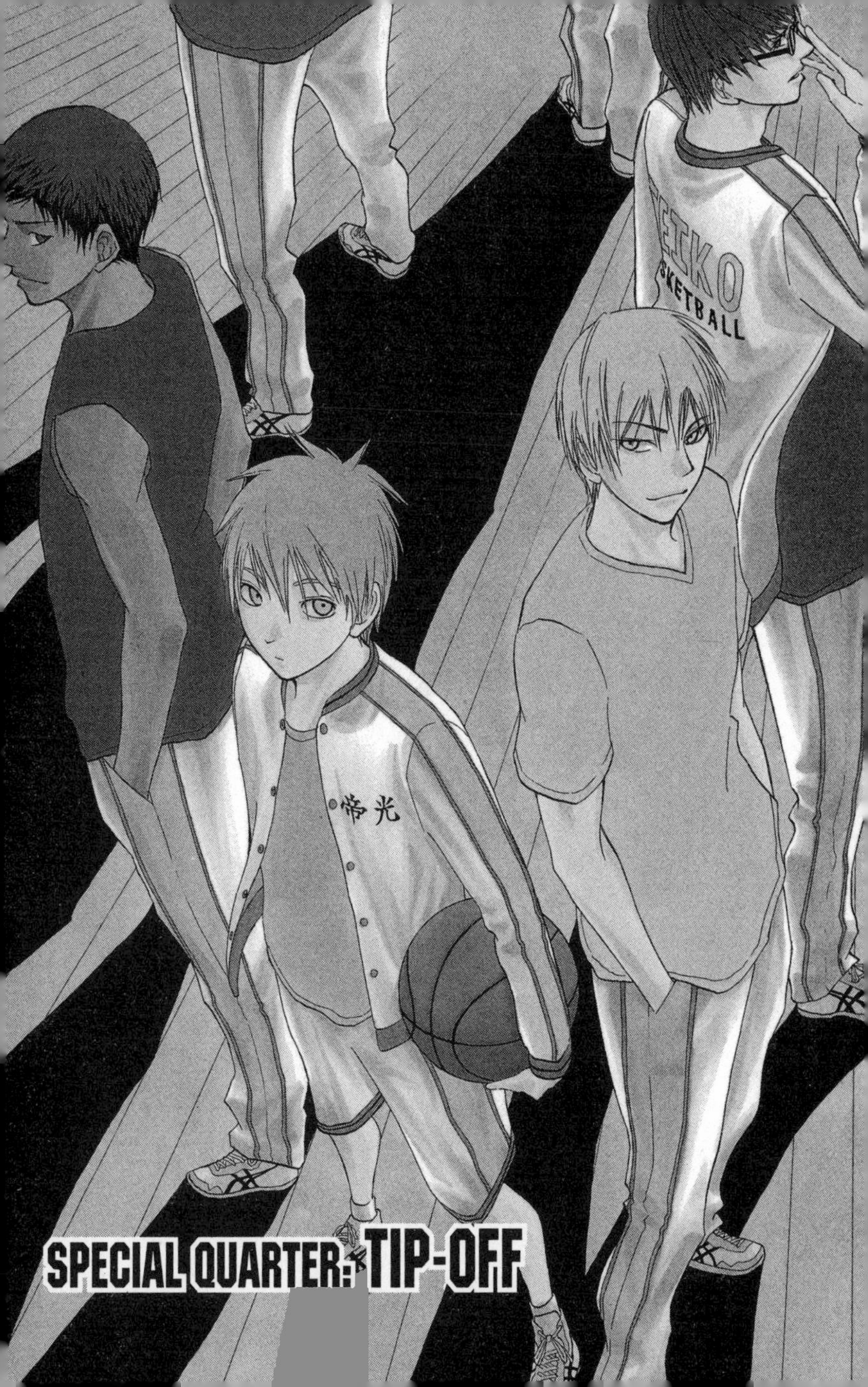
帝光
SPECIAL QUARTER: TIP-OFF

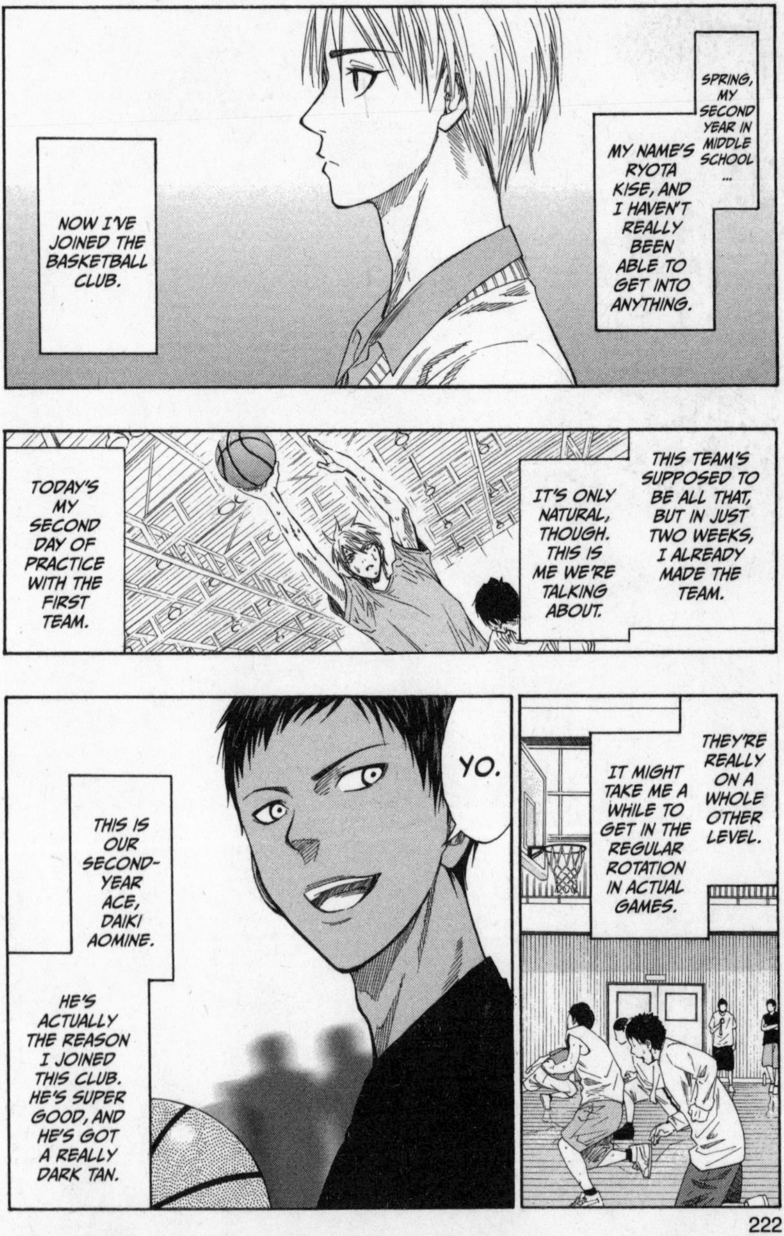
SPRING, MY SECOND YEAR IN MIDDLE SCHOOL...
MY NAME'S RYOTA KISE, AND I HAVEN'T REALLY BEEN ABLE TO GET INTO ANYTHING.
NOW I'VE JOINED THE BASKETBALL CLUB.
THIS TEAM'S SUPPOSED TO BE ALL THAT, BUT IN JUST TWO WEEKS, I ALREADY MADE THE TEAM.
IT'S ONLY NATURAL, THOUGH. THIS IS ME WE'RE TALKING ABOUT.
TODAY'S MY SECOND DAY OF PRACTICE WITH THE FIRST TEAM.
THEY'RE REALLY ON A WHOLE OTHER LEVEL.
IT MIGHT TAKE ME A WHILE TO GET IN THE REGULAR ROTATION IN ACTUAL GAMES.
YO.
THIS IS OUR SECOND-YEAR ACE, DAIKI AOMINE.
HE'S ACTUALLY THE REASON I JOINED THIS CLUB. HE'S SUPER GOOD, AND HE'S GOT A REALLY DARK TAN.

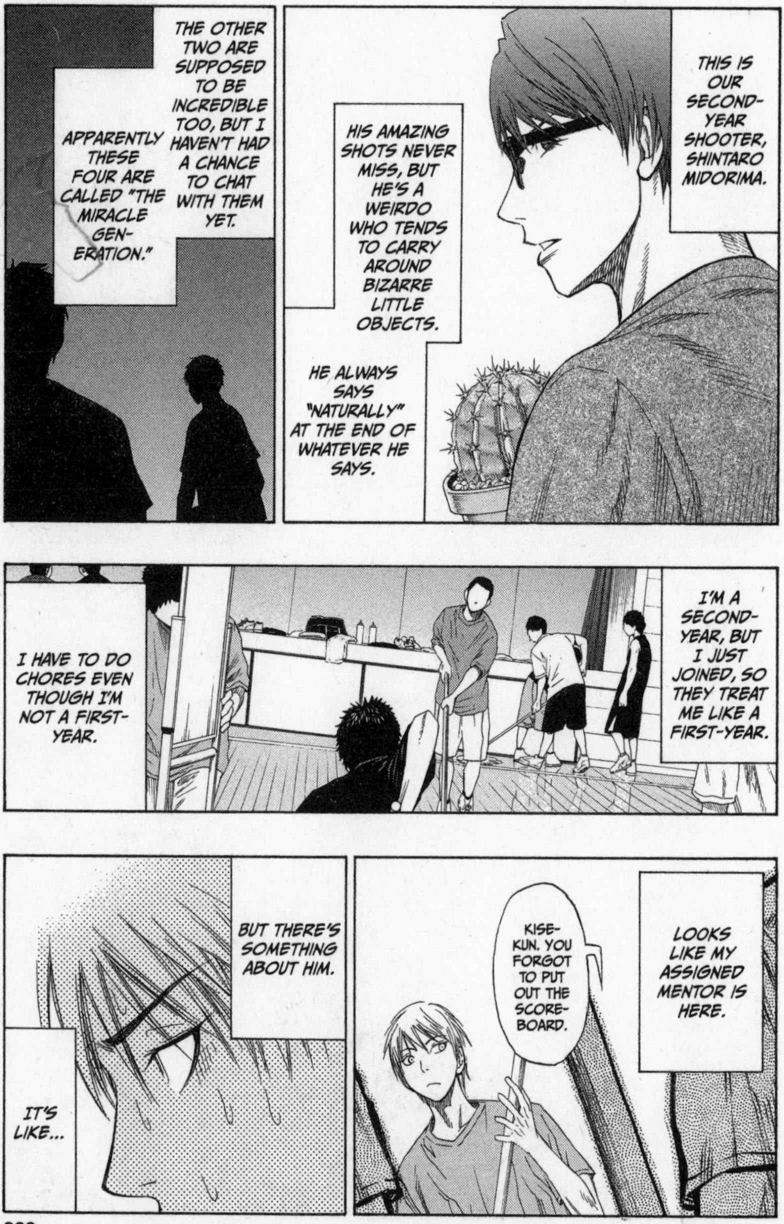
THIS IS OUR SECOND-YEAR SHOOTER, SHINTARO MIDORIMA.
HIS AMAZING SHOTS NEVER MISS, BUT HE'S A WEIRDO WHO TENDS TO CARRY AROUND BIZARRE LITTLE OBJECTS.
HE ALWAYS SAYS "NATURALLY" AT THE END OF WHATEVER HE SAYS.
THE OTHER TWO ARE SUPPOSED TO BE INCREDIBLE TOO, BUT I HAVEN'T HAD A CHANCE TO CHAT WITH THEM YET.
APPARENTLY THESE FOUR ARE CALLED "THE MIRACLE GENERATION."
I'M A SECOND-YEAR, BUT I JUST JOINED, SO THEY TREAT ME LIKE A FIRST-YEAR.
I HAVE TO DO CHORES EVEN THOUGH I'M NOT A FIRST-YEAR.
LOOKS LIKE MY ASSIGNED MENTOR IS HERE.
KISE-KUN. YOU FORGOT TO PUT OUT THE SCOREBOARD.
BUT THERE'S SOMETHING ABOUT HIM.
IT'S LIKE...

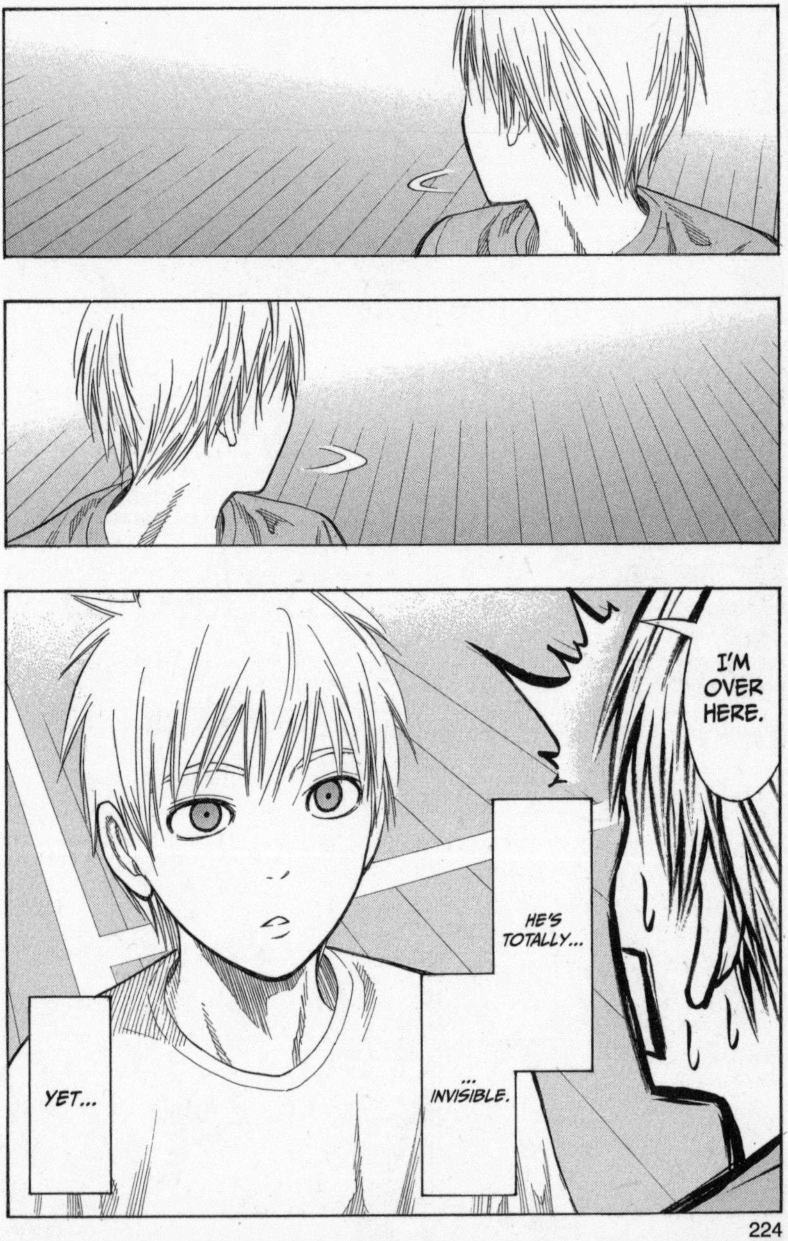
I'M OVER HERE.
HE'S TOTALLY...
...INVISIBLE.
YET...

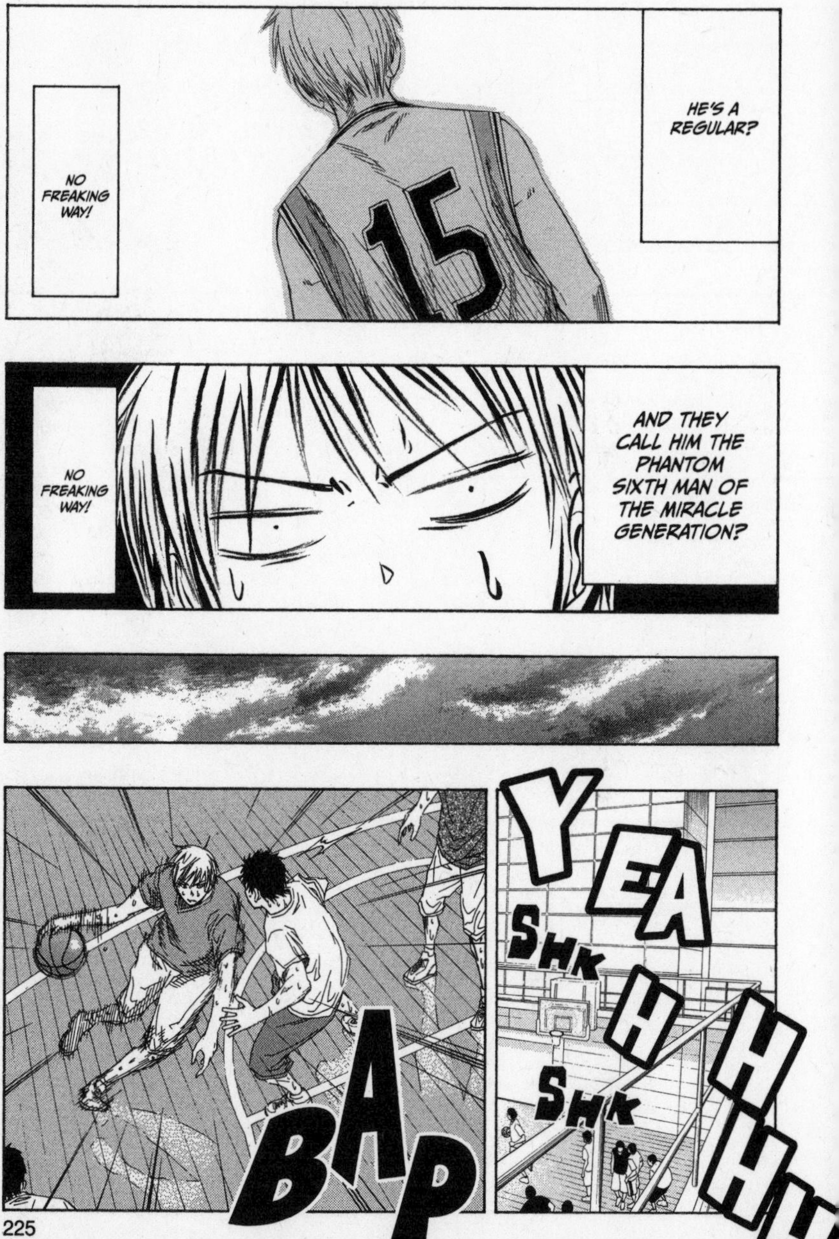

HE'S A REGULAR?
NO FREAKING WAY!
AND THEY CALL HIM THE PHANTOM SIXTH MAN OF THE MIRACLE GENERATION?
NO FREAKING WAY!
YEAHHHHH
SHK
SHK
BAP

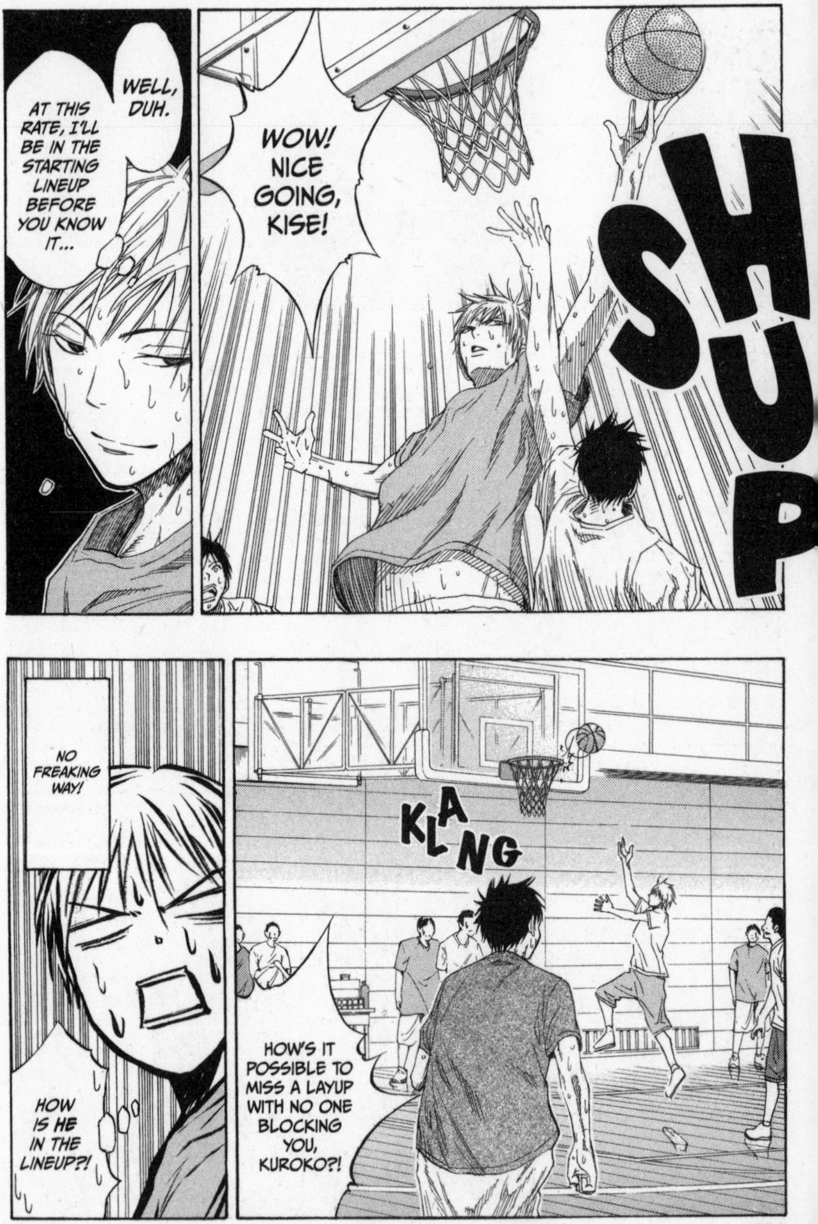
SHUP
WOW! NICE GOING, KISE!
WELL, DUH.
AT THIS RATE, I'LL BE IN THE STARTING LINEUP BEFORE YOU KNOW IT...
KLANG
HOW'S IT POSSIBLE TO MISS A LAYUP WITH NO ONE BLOCKING YOU, KUROKO?!
NO FREAKING WAY!
HOW IS HE IN THE LINEUP?!

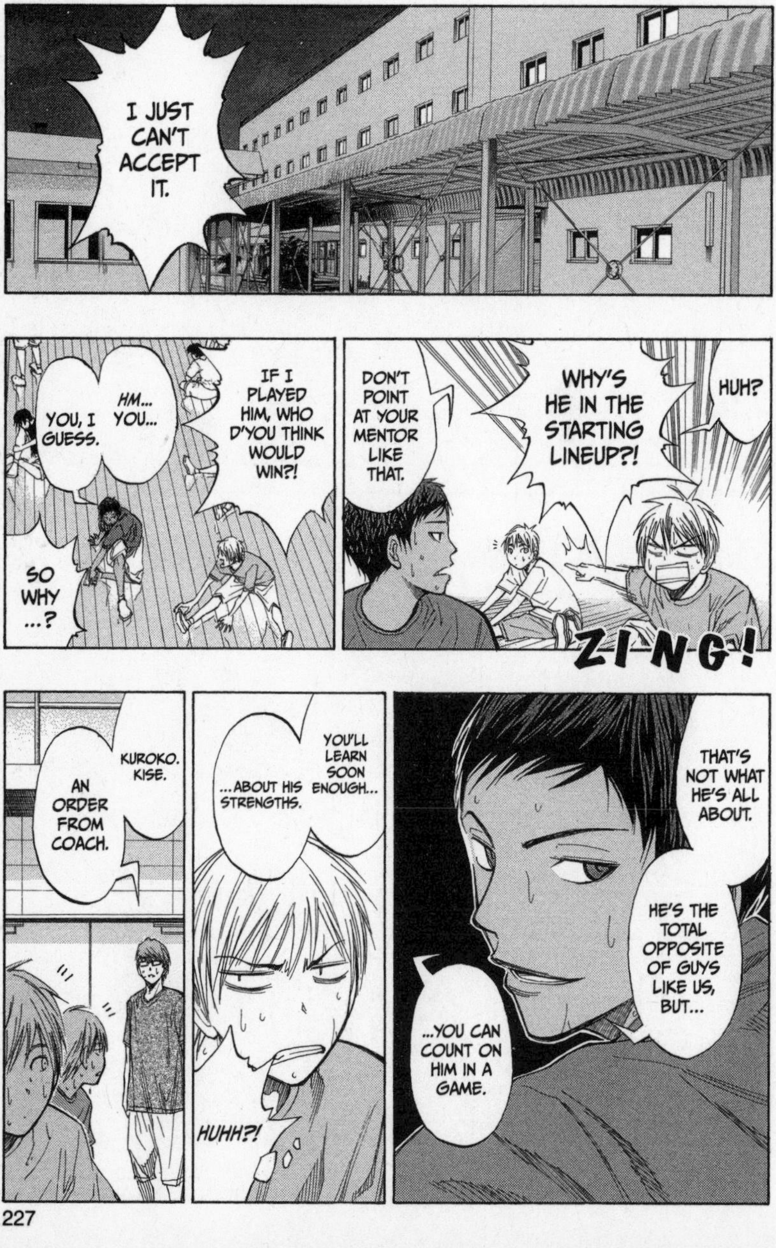
I JUST CAN'T ACCEPT IT.
HUH?
WHY'S HE IN THE STARTING LINEUP?!
DON'T POINT AT YOUR MENTOR LIKE THAT.
ZING!
IF I PLAYED HIM, WHO D'YOU THINK WOULD WIN?!
HM... YOU...
YOU, I GUESS.
SO WHY ...?
THAT'S NOT WHAT HE'S ALL ABOUT.
HE'S THE TOTAL OPPOSITE OF GUYS LIKE US, BUT...
...YOU CAN COUNT ON HIM IN A GAME.
YOU'LL LEARN SOON ENOUGH...
...ABOUT HIS STRENGTHS.
HUHH?!
KUROKO. KISE.
AN ORDER FROM COACH.

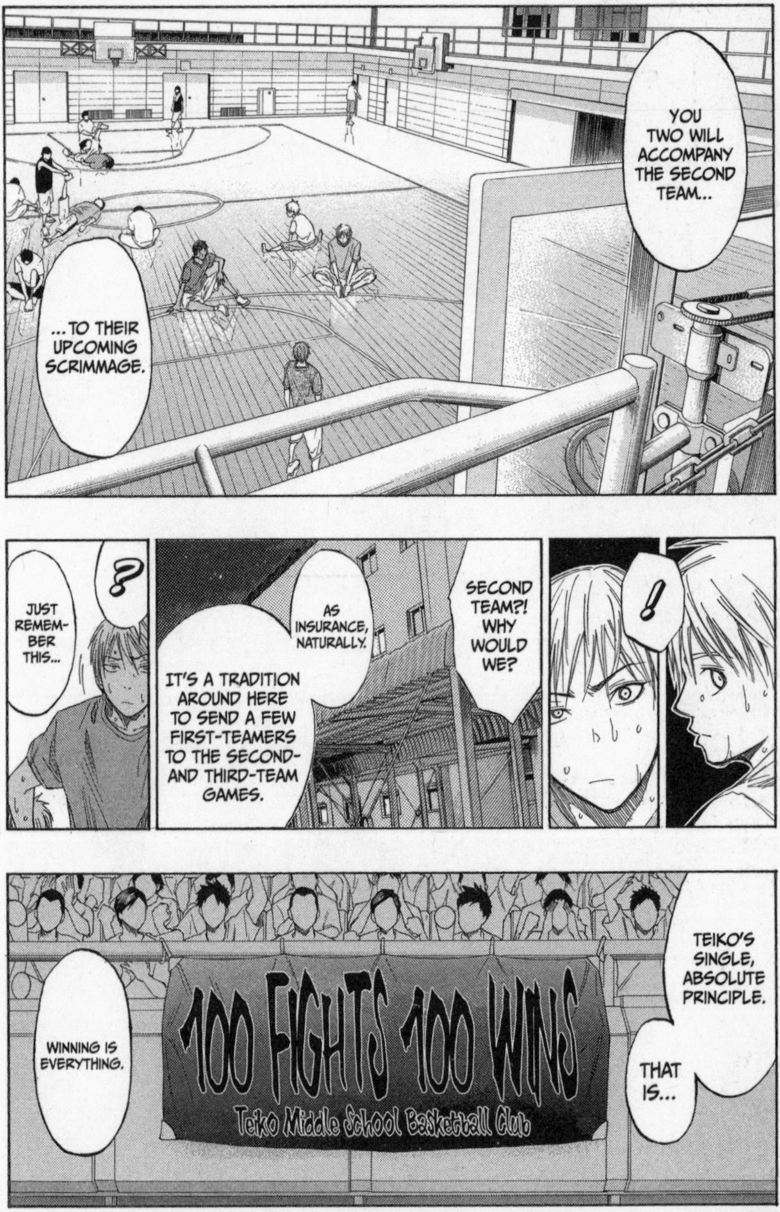
YOU TWO WILL ACCOMPANY THE SECOND TEAM...
...TO THEIR UPCOMING SCRIMMAGE.
!
SECOND TEAM?! WHY WOULD WE?
AS INSURANCE, NATURALLY.
IT'S A TRADITION AROUND HERE TO SEND A FEW FIRST-TEAMERS TO THE SECOND- AND THIRD-TEAM GAMES.
?
JUST REMEMBER THIS...
TEIKO'S SINGLE, ABSOLUTE PRINCIPLE.
THAT IS...
100 FIGHTS 100 WINS
Teiko Middle School Basketball Club
WINNING IS EVERYTHING.

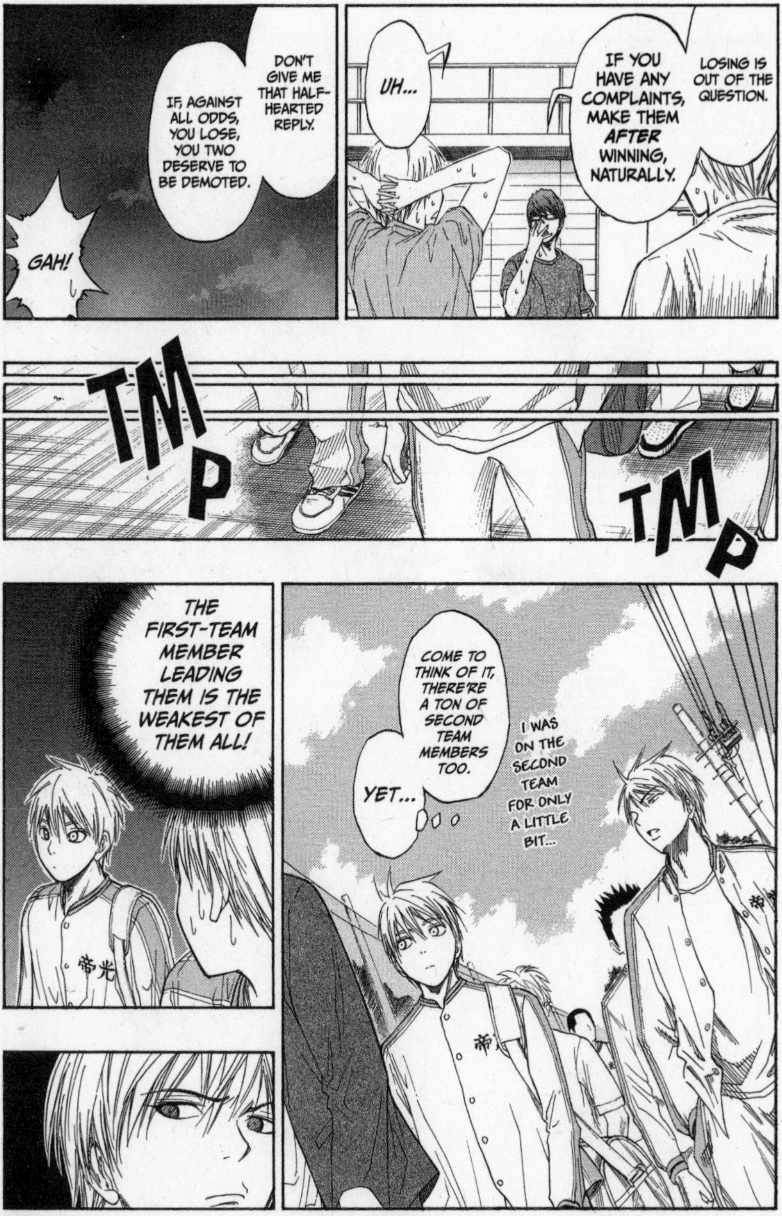
LOSING IS OUT OF THE QUESTION.
IF YOU HAVE ANY COMPLAINTS, MAKE THEM AFTER WINNING, NATURALLY.
UH...
DON'T GIVE ME THAT HALF-HEARTED REPLY.
IF, AGAINST ALL ODDS, YOU LOSE, YOU TWO DESERVE TO BE DEMOTED.
GAH!
TMP
TMP
I WAS ON THE SECOND TEAM FOR ONLY A LITTLE BIT...
COME TO THINK OF IT, THERE'RE A TON OF SECOND TEAM MEMBERS TOO.
YET...
THE FIRST-TEAM MEMBER LEADING THEM IS THE WEAKEST OF THEM ALL!

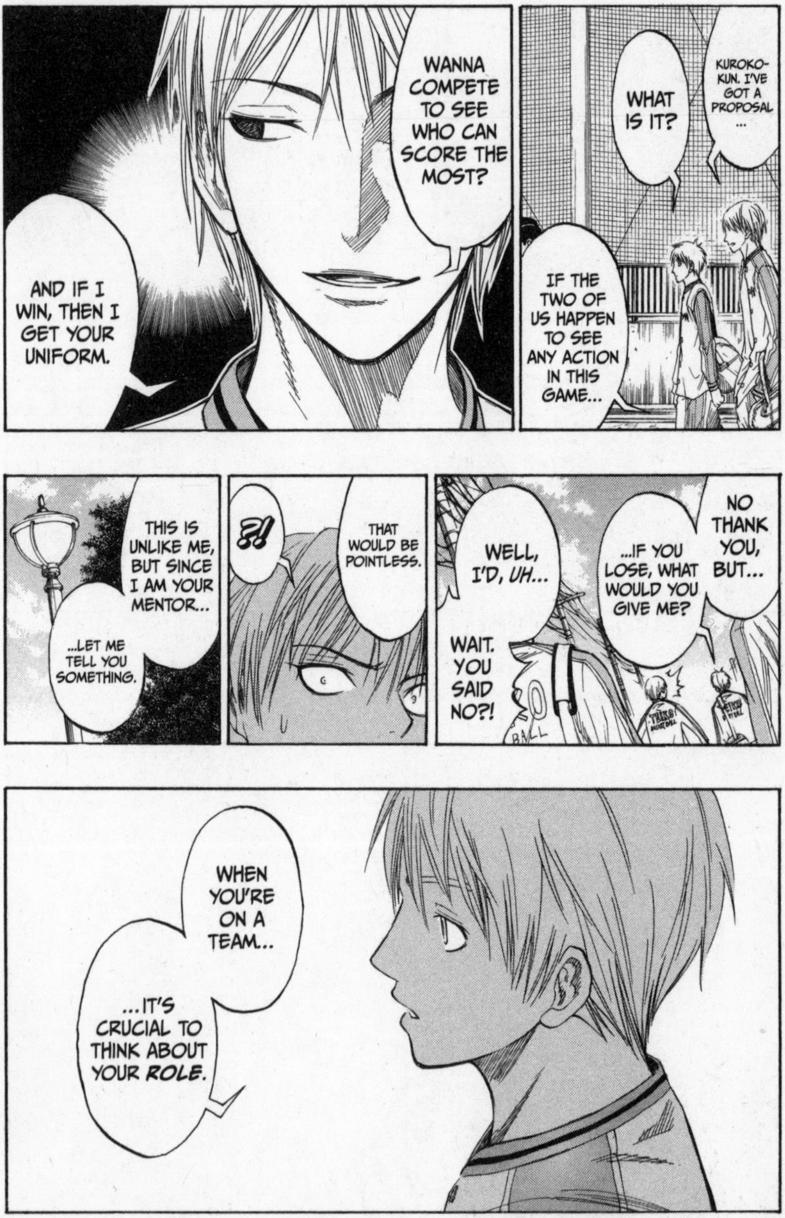
KUROKO-KUN. I'VE GOT A PROPOSAL ...
WHAT IS IT?
IF THE TWO OF US HAPPEN TO SEE ANY ACTION IN THIS GAME...
WANNA COMPETE TO SEE WHO CAN SCORE THE MOST?
AND IF I WIN, THEN I GET YOUR UNIFORM.
NO THANK YOU, BUT...
...IF YOU LOSE, WHAT WOULD YOU GIVE ME?
WELL, I'D, *UH*...
WAIT. YOU SAID NO?!
THAT WOULD BE POINTLESS.
?!
THIS IS UNLIKE ME, BUT SINCE I AM YOUR MENTOR...
...LET ME TELL YOU SOMETHING.
WHEN YOU'RE ON A TEAM...
...IT'S CRUCIAL TO THINK ABOUT YOUR **ROLE**.

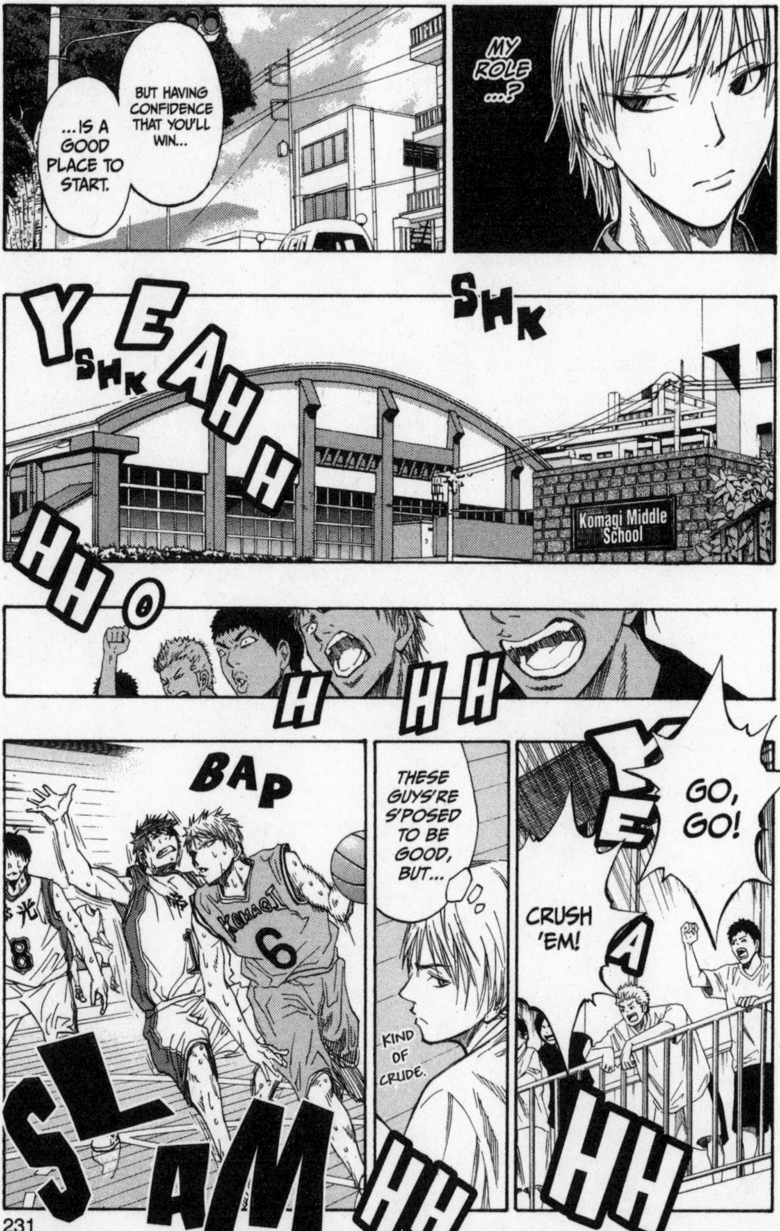
MY ROLE ...?
BUT HAVING CONFIDENCE THAT YOU'LL WIN...
...IS A GOOD PLACE TO START.
SHK
YEAHHHHHO
SHK
Komagi Middle School
HHHH
YEAHHH
GO, GO!
CRUSH 'EM!
THESE GUYS'RE S'POSED TO BE GOOD, BUT...
KIND OF CRUDE.
BAP
SLAM

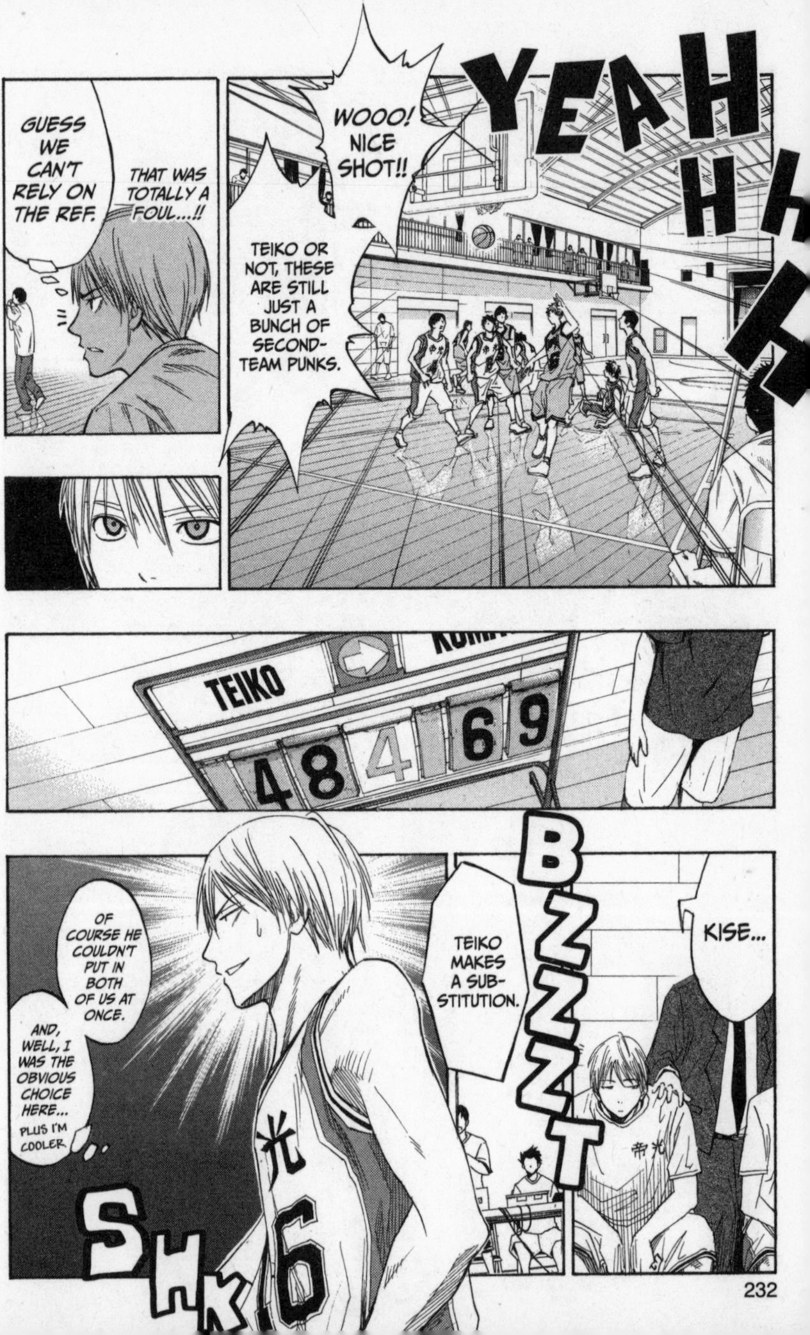
YEAHHHH
WOOO! NICE SHOT!!
TEIKO OR NOT, THESE ARE STILL JUST A BUNCH OF SECOND-TEAM PUNKS.
THAT WAS TOTALLY A FOUL...!!
GUESS WE CAN'T RELY ON THE REF.
TEIKO
48
69
KISE...
TEIKO MAKES A SUB-STITUTION.
BZZZZT
OF COURSE HE COULDN'T PUT IN BOTH OF US AT ONCE.
AND, WELL, I WAS THE OBVIOUS CHOICE HERE...
PLUS I'M COOLER
SHK

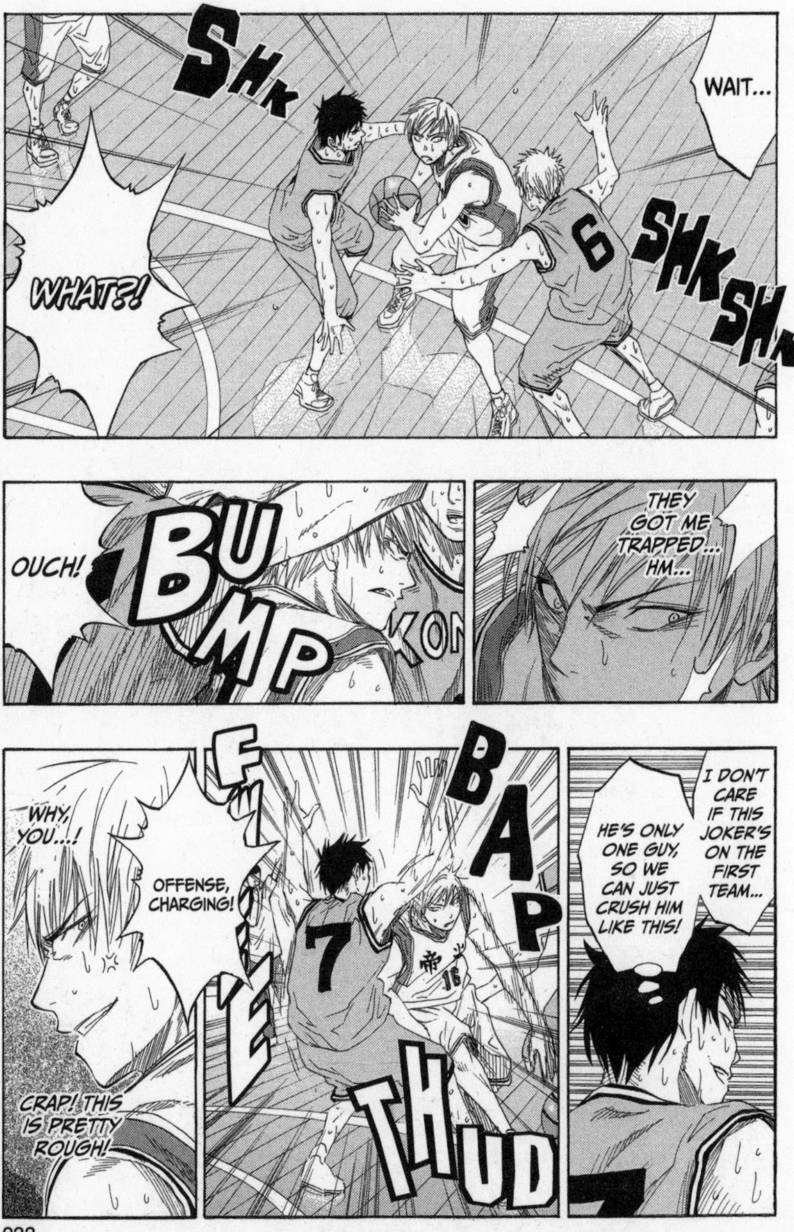
WAIT...
SHK
SHKSHKSHK
WHAT?!
THEY GOT ME TRAPPED... HM...
BUMP
OUCH!
I DON'T CARE IF THIS JOKER'S ON THE FIRST TEAM...
HE'S ONLY ONE GUY, SO WE CAN JUST CRUSH HIM LIKE THIS!
BAP
F 'E
OFFENSE, CHARGING!
THUD
WHY, YOU...!
CRAP! THIS IS PRETTY ROUGH!

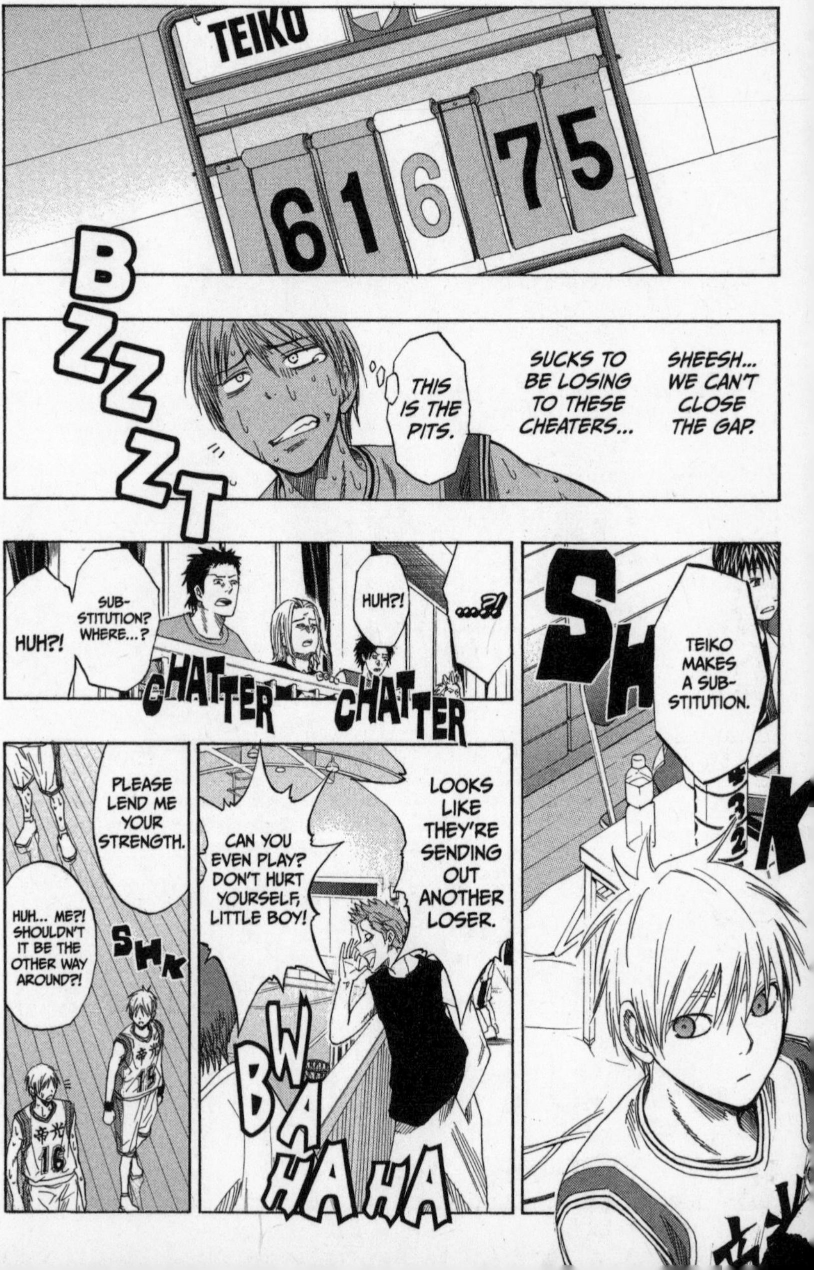
TEIKO
61
6
75
BZZZT
SHEESH... WE CAN'T CLOSE THE GAP.
SUCKS TO BE LOSING TO THESE CHEATERS...
THIS IS THE PITS.
SHK
TEIKO MAKES A SUB-STITUTION.
...?!
HUH?!
SUB-STITUTION? WHERE...?
HUH?!
CHATTER CHATTER
LOOKS LIKE THEY'RE SENDING OUT ANOTHER LOSER.
CAN YOU EVEN PLAY? DON'T HURT YOURSELF, LITTLE BOY!
BWAHAHAHA
PLEASE LEND ME YOUR STRENGTH.
HUH... ME?! SHOULDN'T IT BE THE OTHER WAY AROUND?!
SHK

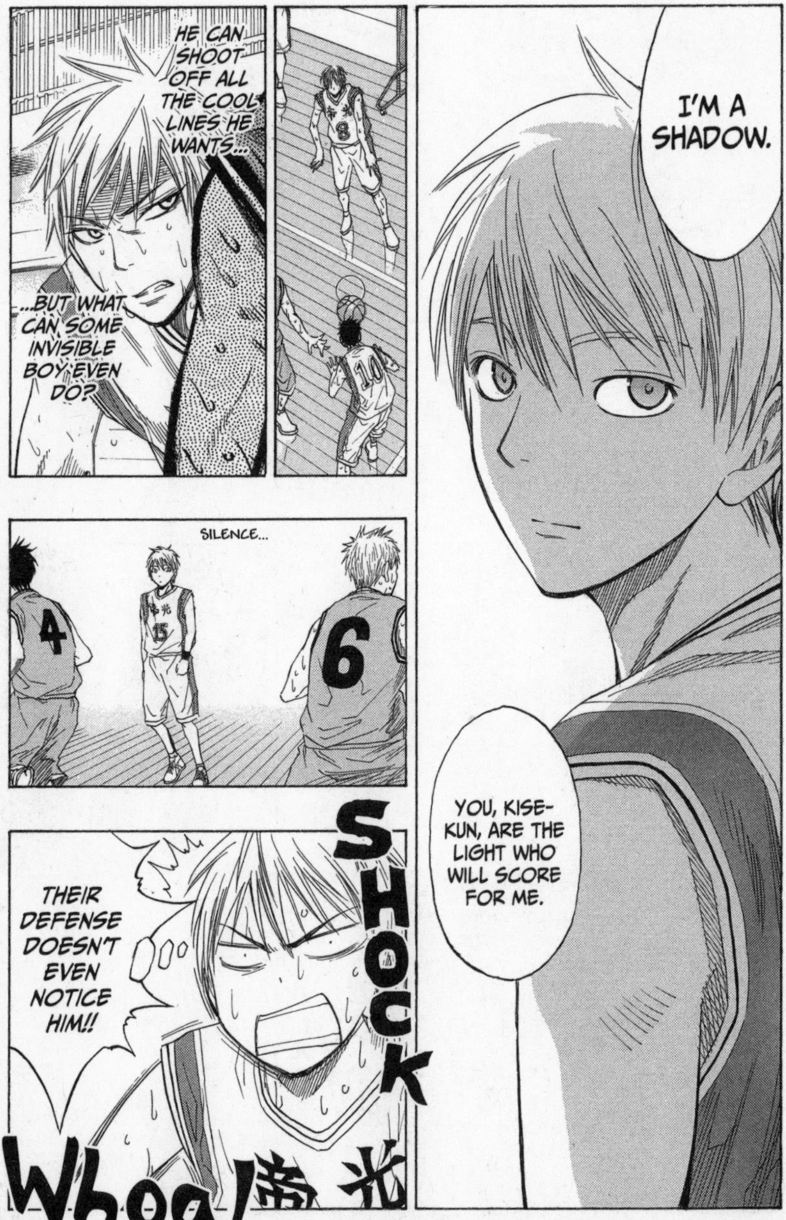
I'M A SHADOW.
YOU, KISE-KUN, ARE THE LIGHT WHO WILL SCORE FOR ME.
HE CAN SHOOT OFF ALL THE COOL LINES HE WANTS...
...BUT WHAT CAN SOME INVISIBLE BOY EVEN DO?
SILENCE...
SHOCK
THEIR DEFENSE DOESN'T EVEN NOTICE HIM!!
Whoa! 帝光

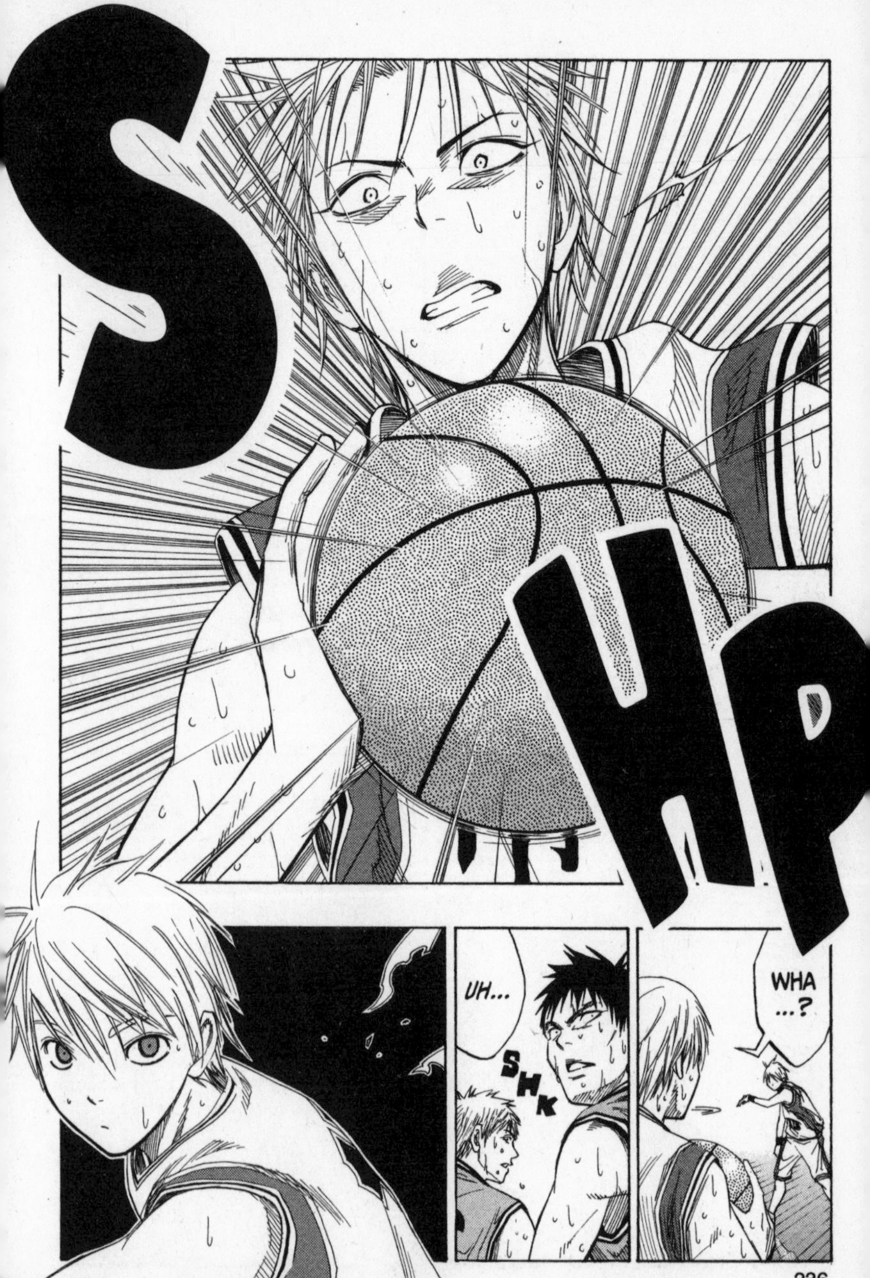
SHP
WHA ...?
UH...
SHK

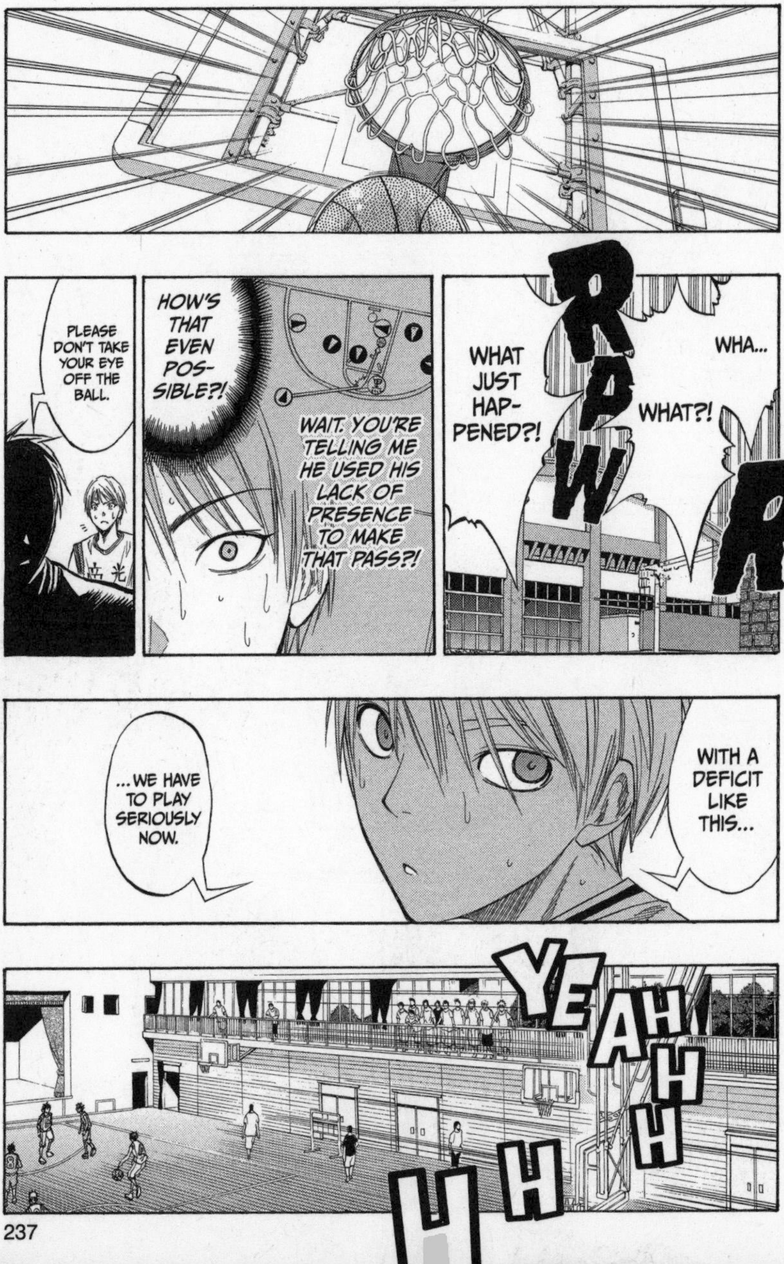
WHA...
WHAT?!
WHAT JUST HAP-PENED?!
HOW'S THAT EVEN POS-SIBLE?!
WAIT. YOU'RE TELLING ME HE USED HIS LACK OF PRESENCE TO MAKE THAT PASS?!
PLEASE DON'T TAKE YOUR EYE OFF THE BALL.
WITH A DEFICIT LIKE THIS...
...WE HAVE TO PLAY SERIOUSLY NOW.
YEAHHHHH

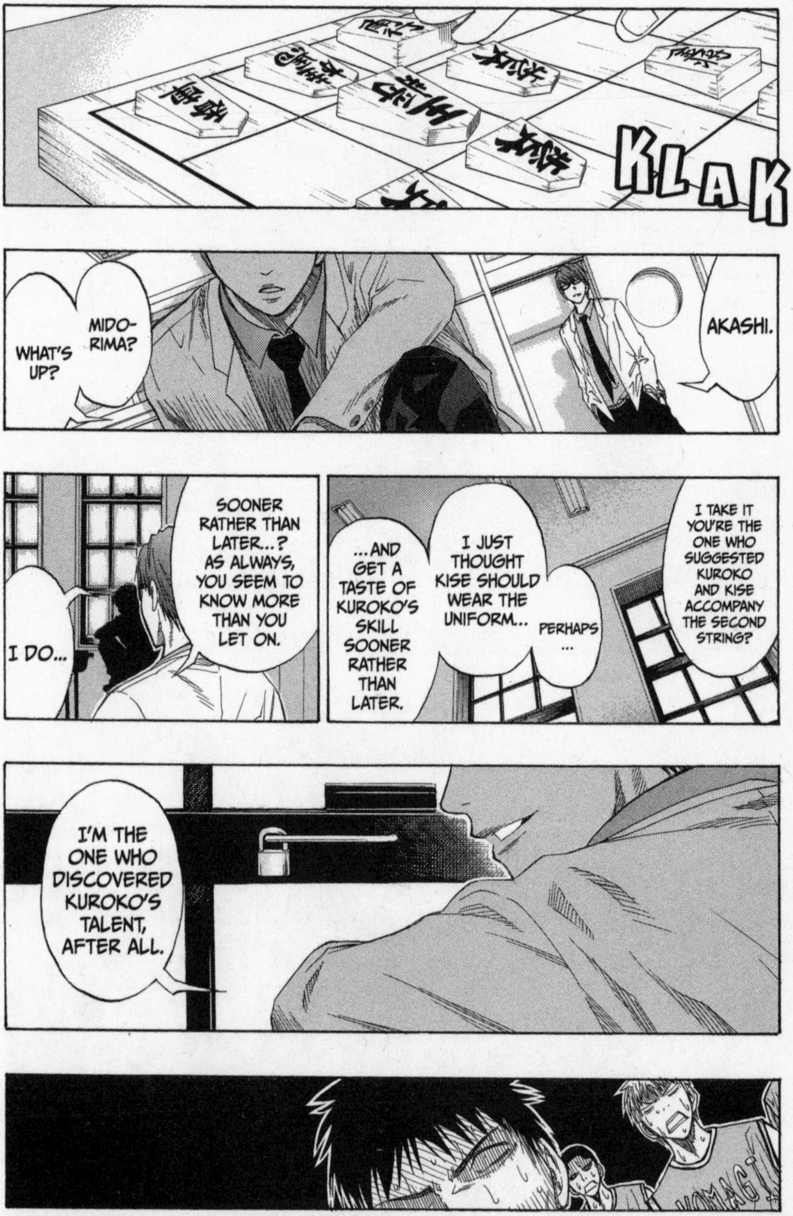
KLAK
AKASHI.
MIDO-RIMA?
WHAT'S UP?
I TAKE IT YOU'RE THE ONE WHO SUGGESTED KUROKO AND KISE ACCOMPANY THE SECOND STRING?
PERHAPS...
I JUST THOUGHT KISE SHOULD WEAR THE UNIFORM...
...AND GET A TASTE OF KUROKO'S SKILL SOONER RATHER THAN LATER.
SOONER RATHER THAN LATER...? AS ALWAYS, YOU SEEM TO KNOW MORE THAN YOU LET ON.
I DO...
I'M THE ONE WHO DISCOVERED KUROKO'S TALENT, AFTER ALL.

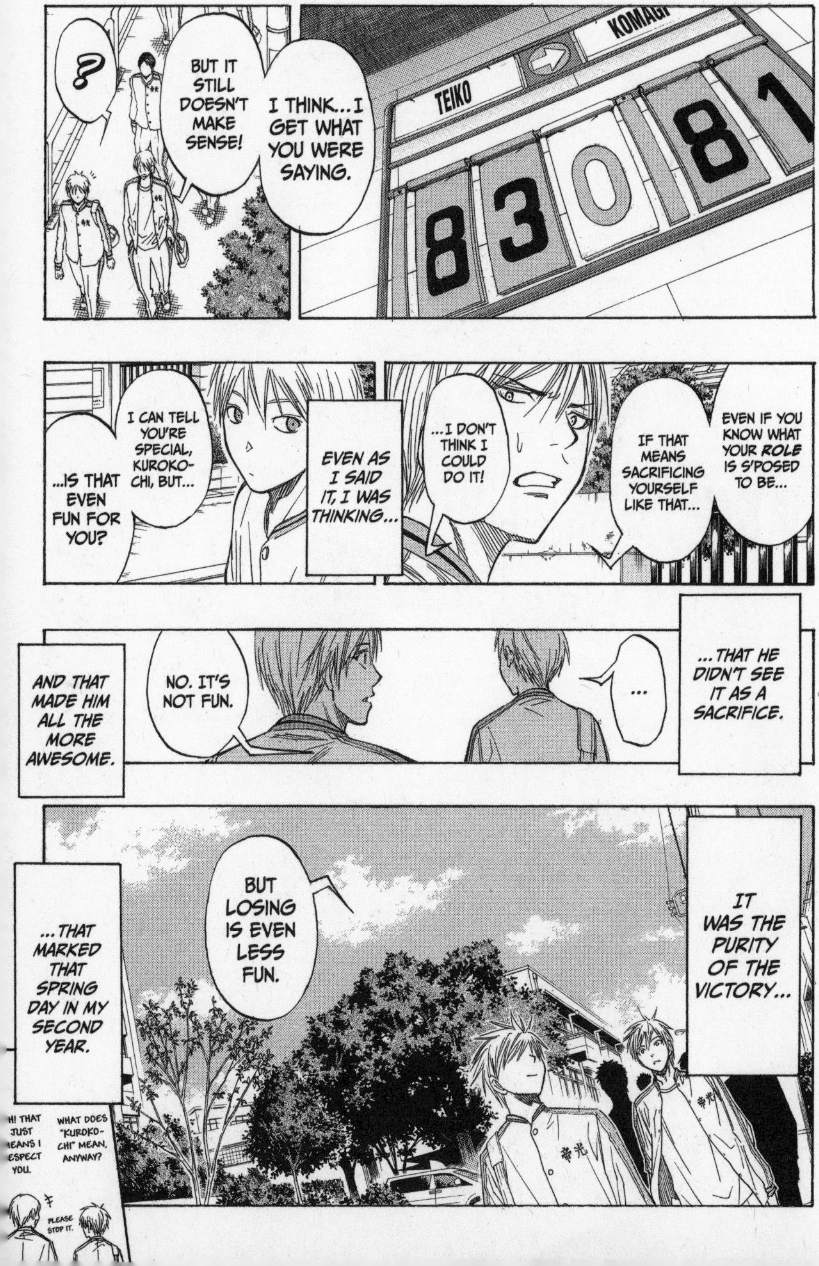
KOMAGI
TEIKO
83
81
I THINK...I GET WHAT YOU WERE SAYING.
BUT IT STILL DOESN'T MAKE SENSE!
?
EVEN IF YOU KNOW WHAT YOUR ROLE IS S'POSED TO BE...
IF THAT MEANS SACRIFICING YOURSELF LIKE THAT...
...I DON'T THINK I COULD DO IT!
EVEN AS I SAID IT, I WAS THINKING...
I CAN TELL YOU'RE SPECIAL, KUROKO-CHI, BUT...
...IS THAT EVEN FUN FOR YOU?
...THAT HE DIDN'T SEE IT AS A SACRIFICE.
...
NO. IT'S NOT FUN.
AND THAT MADE HIM ALL THE MORE AWESOME.
IT WAS THE PURITY OF THE VICTORY...
BUT LOSING IS EVEN LESS FUN.
...THAT MARKED THAT SPRING DAY IN MY SECOND YEAR.
WHAT DOES "KUROKO-CHI" MEAN, ANYWAY?
H! THAT JUST EANS I ESPECT YOU.
PLEASE STOP IT.

KUROKO'S BASKETBALL BLOOPERS

TAKE 1

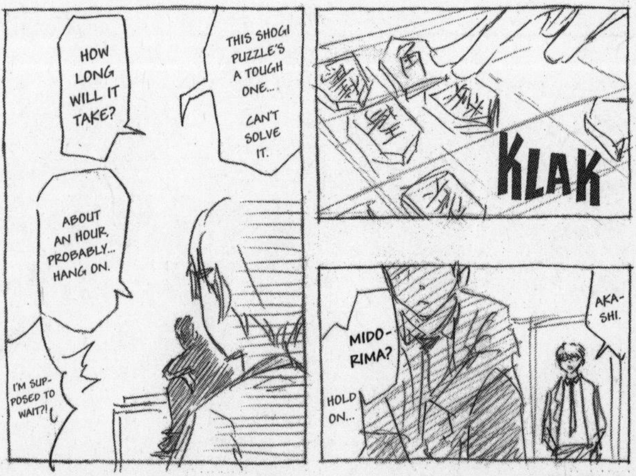
KLAK
AKA-SHI.
MIDO-RIMA?
HOLD ON...
THIS SHOGI PUZZLE'S A TOUGH ONE...
CAN'T SOLVE IT.
HOW LONG WILL IT TAKE?
ABOUT AN HOUR, PROBABLY... HANG ON.
I'M SUP-POSED TO WAIT?!

63RD QUARTER: I'LL WIN EVEN IF IT KILLS ME

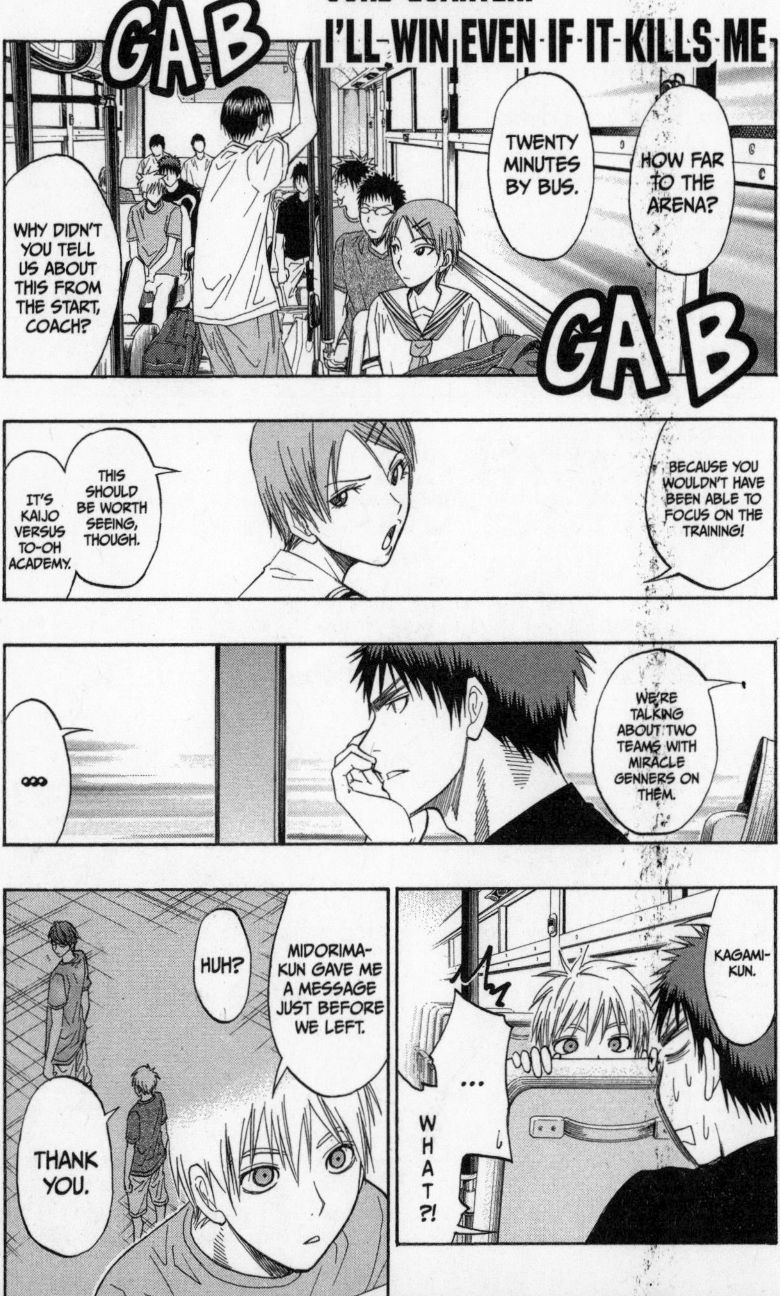

GAB
HOW FAR TO THE ARENA?
TWENTY MINUTES BY BUS.
WHY DIDN'T YOU TELL US ABOUT THIS FROM THE START, COACH?
GAB
BECAUSE YOU WOULDN'T HAVE BEEN ABLE TO FOCUS ON THE TRAINING!
THIS SHOULD BE WORTH SEEING, THOUGH.
IT'S KAIJO VERSUS TO-OH ACADEMY.
WE'RE TALKING ABOUT TWO TEAMS WITH MIRACLE GENNERS ON THEM.
...
KAGAMI-KUN.
...
WHAT?!
MIDORIMA-KUN GAVE ME A MESSAGE JUST BEFORE WE LEFT.
HUH?
THANK YOU.

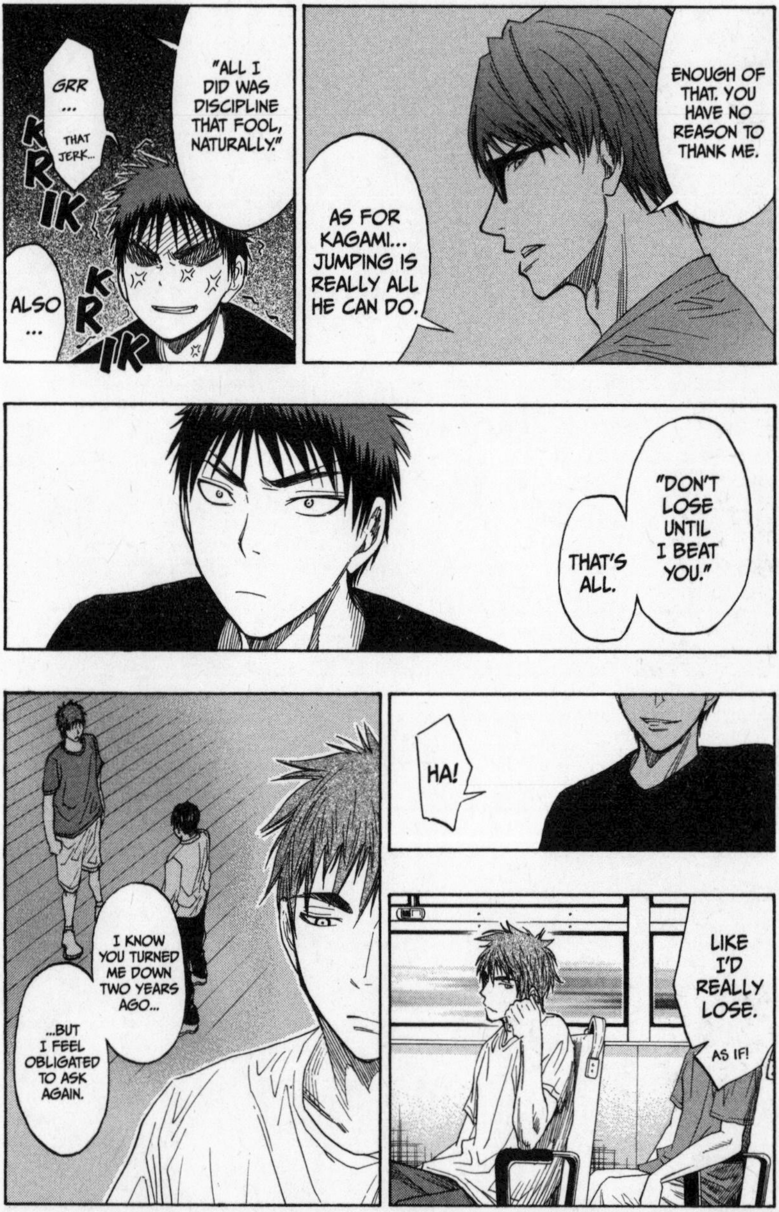
ENOUGH OF THAT. YOU HAVE NO REASON TO THANK ME.
AS FOR KAGAMI... JUMPING IS REALLY ALL HE CAN DO.
"ALL I DID WAS DISCIPLINE THAT FOOL, NATURALLY."
GRR ...
THAT JERK...
KRIK
KRIK
ALSO ...
"DON'T LOSE UNTIL I BEAT YOU."
THAT'S ALL.
HA!
LIKE I'D REALLY LOSE.
AS IF!
I KNOW YOU TURNED ME DOWN TWO YEARS AGO...
...BUT I FEEL OBLIGATED TO ASK AGAIN.

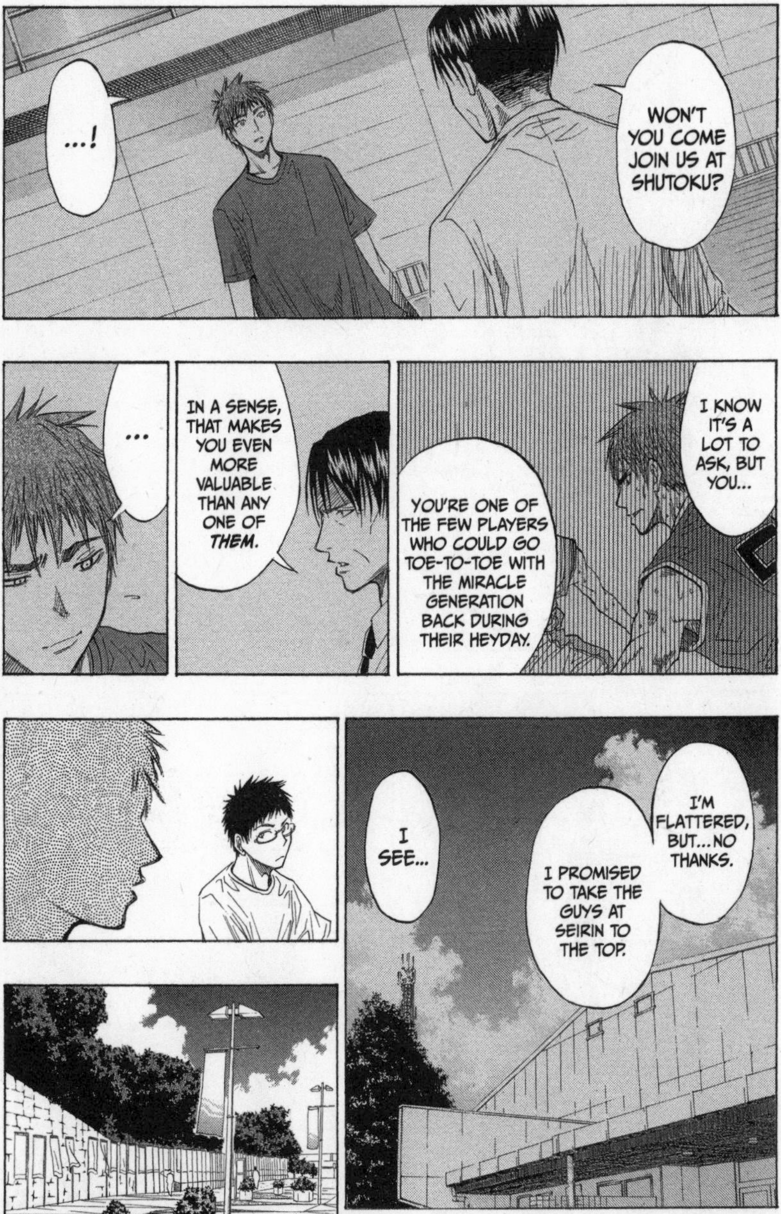
WON'T YOU COME JOIN US AT SHUTOKU?
...!
I KNOW IT'S A LOT TO ASK, BUT YOU...
YOU'RE ONE OF THE FEW PLAYERS WHO COULD GO TOE-TO-TOE WITH THE MIRACLE GENERATION BACK DURING THEIR HEYDAY.
IN A SENSE, THAT MAKES YOU EVEN MORE VALUABLE THAN ANY ONE OF *THEM*.
...
I'M FLATTERED, BUT...NO THANKS.
I PROMISED TO TAKE THE GUYS AT SEIRIN TO THE TOP.
I SEE...

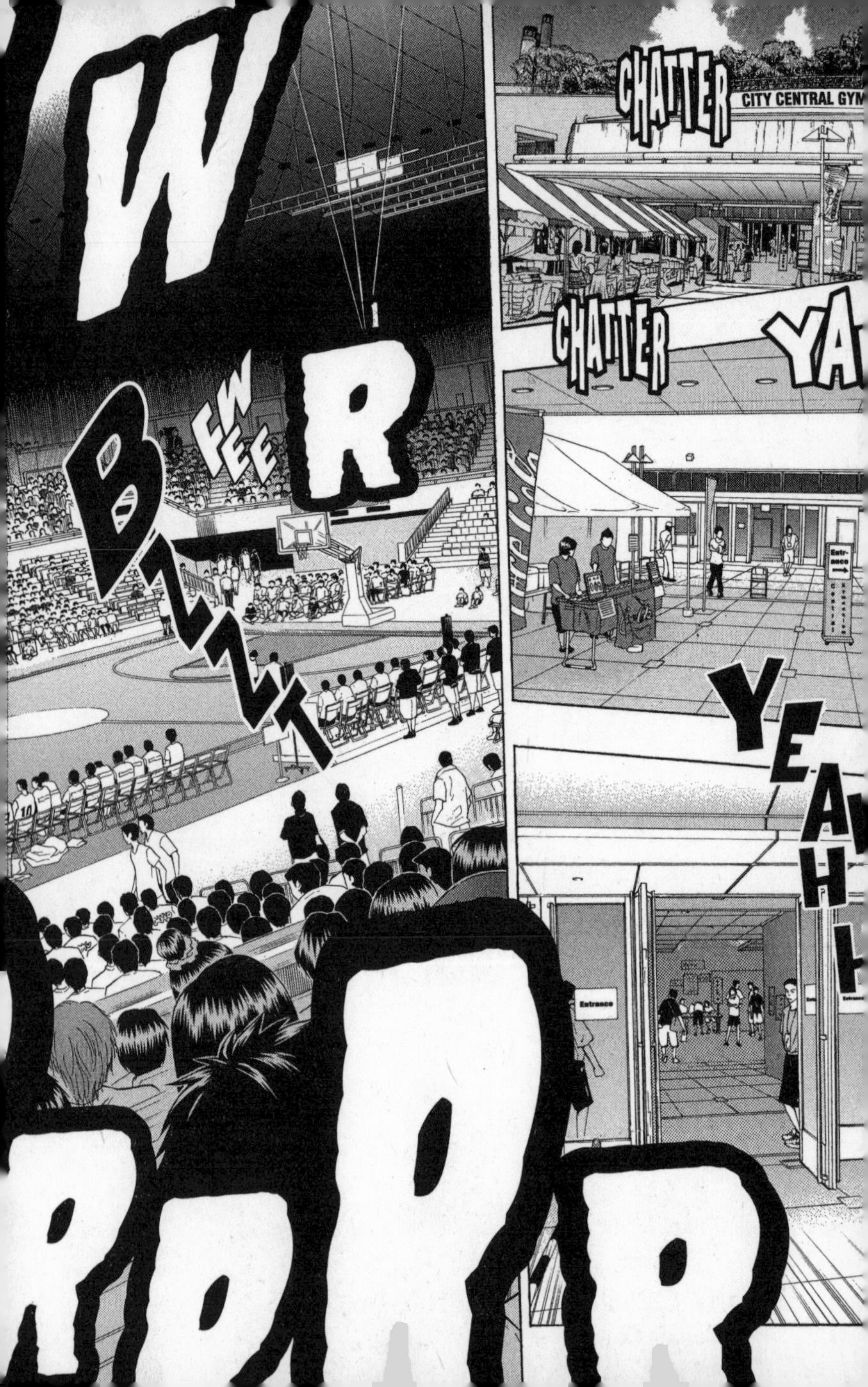
CHATTER
CITY CENTRAL GYM
CHATTER
YEAH
Entrance
FWEEER
BZZZT

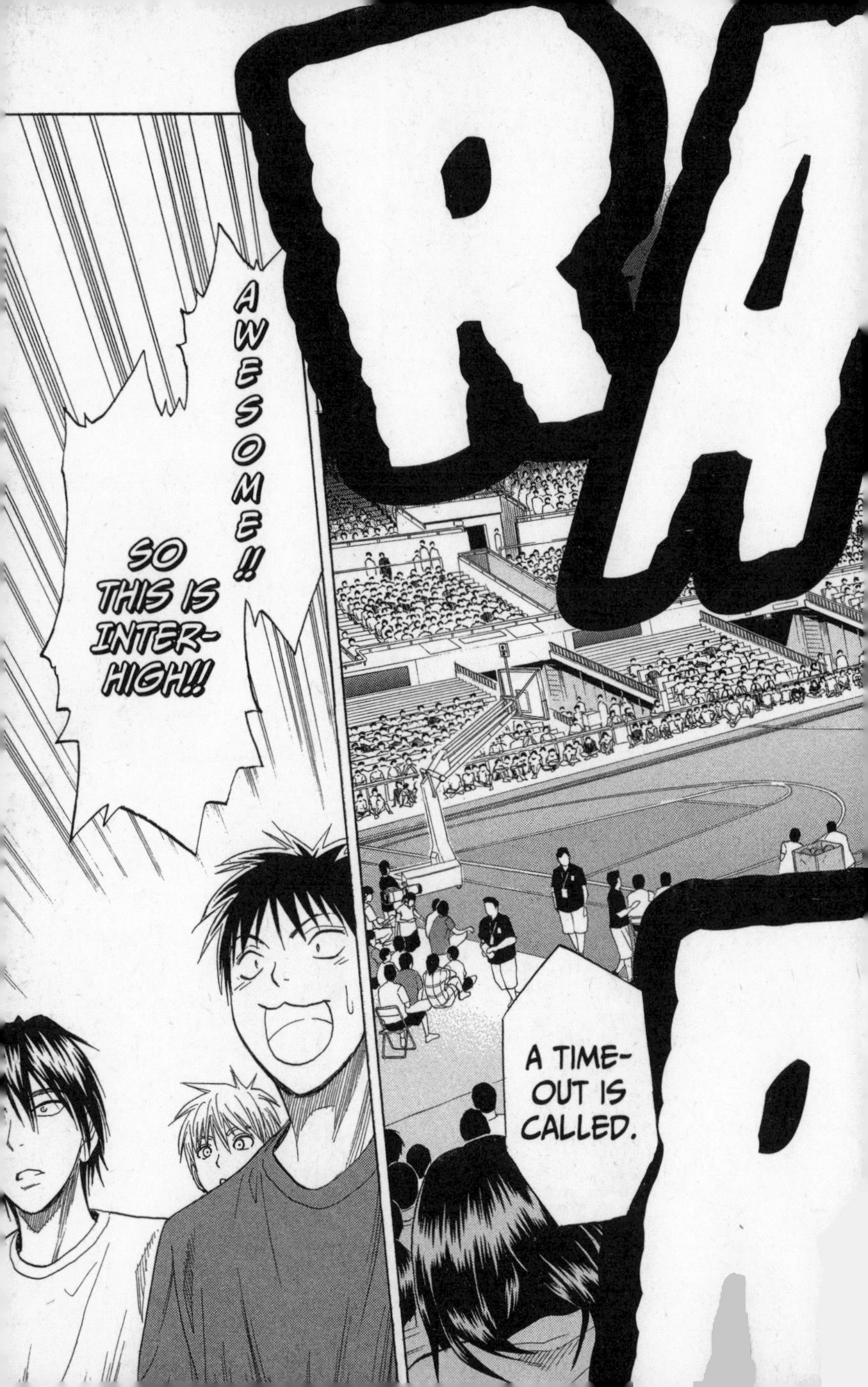
A TIME-OUT IS CALLED.
AWESOME!!
SO THIS IS INTER-HIGH!!

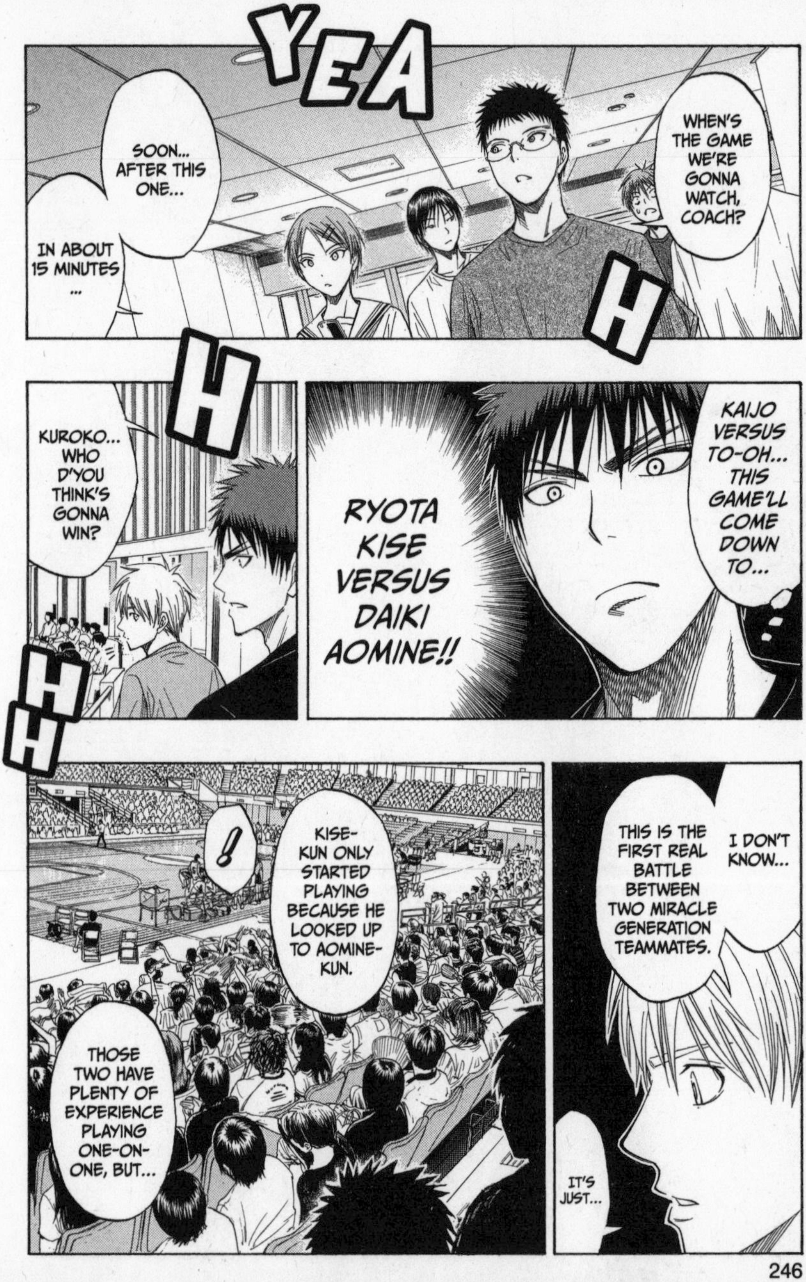
YEAHHHH
WHEN'S THE GAME WE'RE GONNA WATCH, COACH?
SOON... AFTER THIS ONE...
IN ABOUT 15 MINUTES...
KAIJO VERSUS TO-OH... THIS GAME'LL COME DOWN TO...
RYOTA KISE VERSUS DAIKI AOMINE!!
KUROKO... WHO D'YOU THINK'S GONNA WIN?
I DON'T KNOW...
THIS IS THE FIRST REAL BATTLE BETWEEN TWO MIRACLE GENERATION TEAMMATES.
IT'S JUST...
!
KISE-KUN ONLY STARTED PLAYING BECAUSE HE LOOKED UP TO AOMINE-KUN.
THOSE TWO HAVE PLENTY OF EXPERIENCE PLAYING ONE-ON-ONE, BUT...

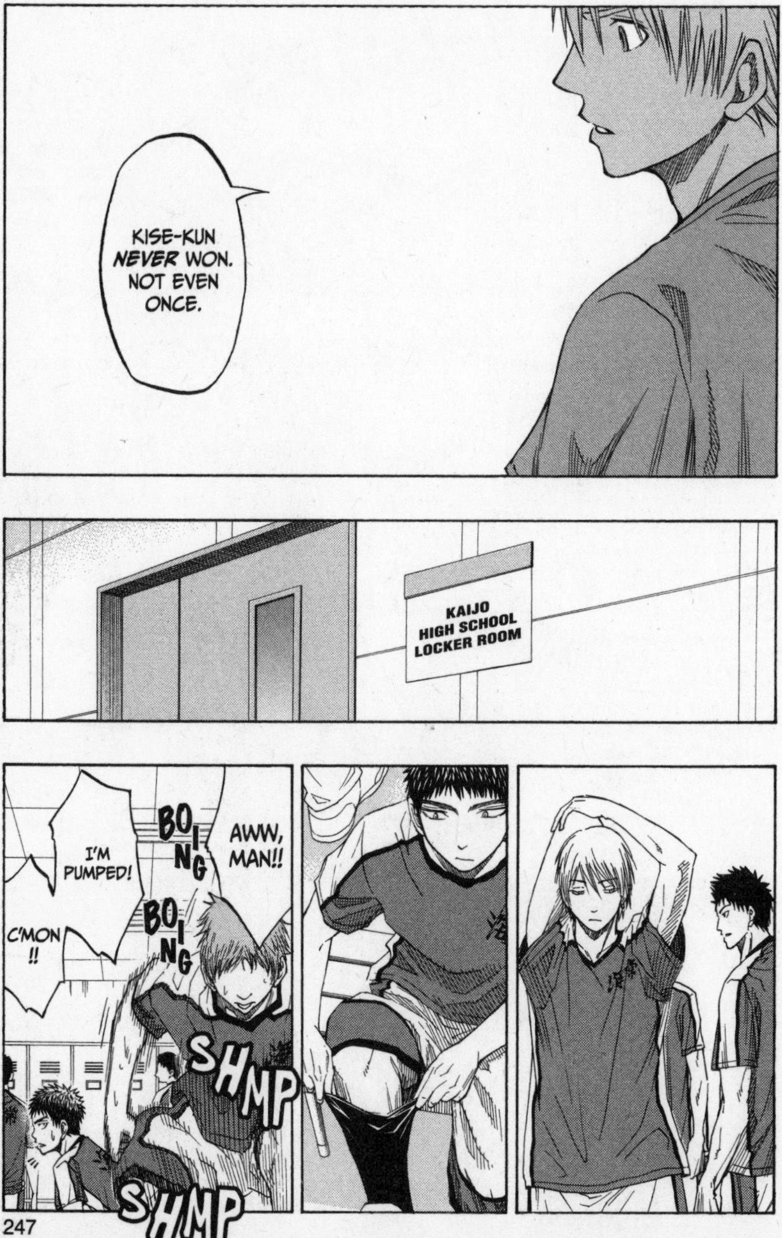
KISE-KUN *NEVER* WON. NOT EVEN ONCE.
KAIJO HIGH SCHOOL LOCKER ROOM
AWW, MAN!!
BOING
BOING
I'M PUMPED!
C'MON !!
SHMP
SHMP

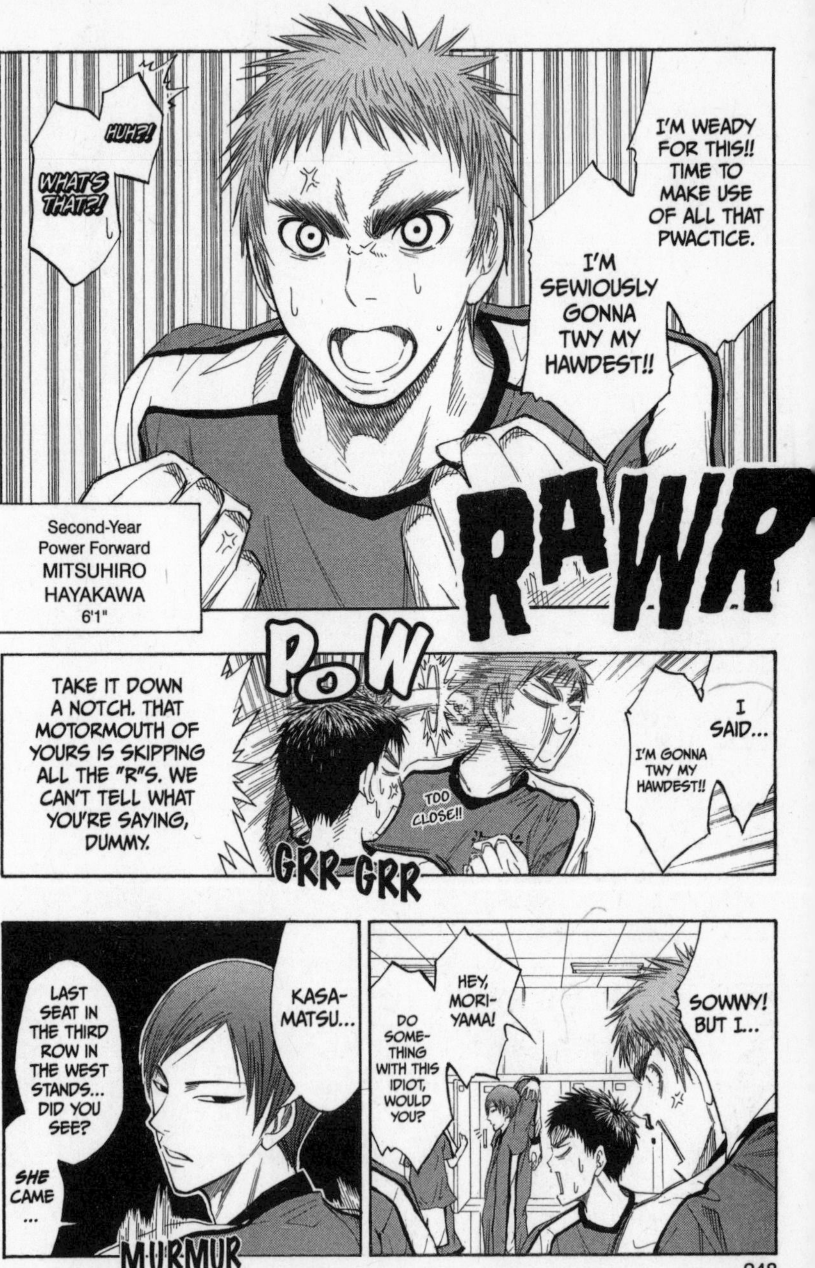
I'M WEADY FOR THIS!! TIME TO MAKE USE OF ALL THAT PWACTICE.
I'M SEWIOUSLY GONNA TWY MY HAWDEST!!
RAWR
HUH?!
WHAT'S THAT?!
Second-Year Power Forward MITSUHIRO HAYAKAWA 6'1"
I SAID...
I'M GONNA TWY MY HAWDEST!!
POW
TOO CLOSE!!
GRR GRR
TAKE IT DOWN A NOTCH. THAT MOTORMOUTH OF YOURS IS SKIPPING ALL THE "R"S. WE CAN'T TELL WHAT YOU'RE SAYING, DUMMY.
SOWWY! BUT I...
HEY, MORI-YAMA!
DO SOME-THING WITH THIS IDIOT, WOULD YOU?
KASA-MATSU...
LAST SEAT IN THE THIRD ROW IN THE WEST STANDS... DID YOU SEE?
SHE CAME...
MURMUR

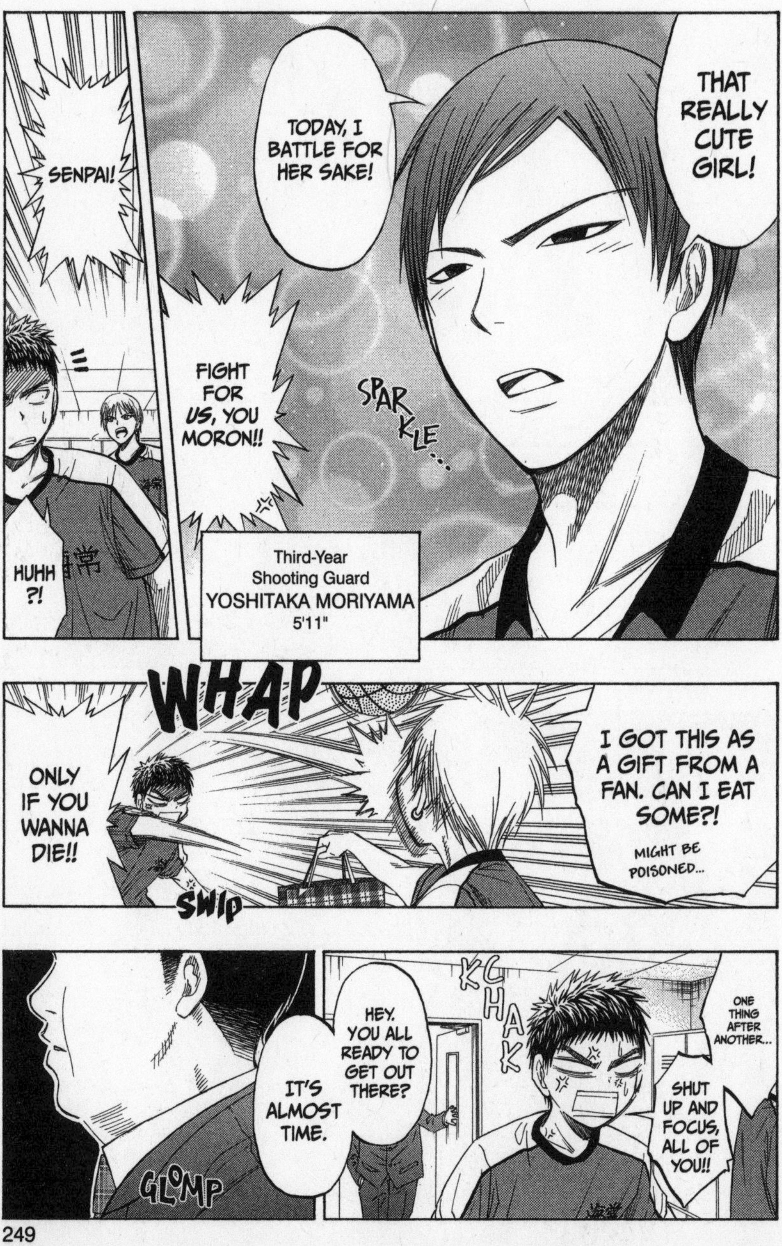
THAT REALLY CUTE GIRL!
TODAY, I BATTLE FOR HER SAKE!
SPARKLE...
FIGHT FOR *US*, YOU MORON!!
Third-Year Shooting Guard YOSHITAKA MORIYAMA 5'11"
SENPAI!
HUHH ?!
I GOT THIS AS A GIFT FROM A FAN. CAN I EAT SOME?!
MIGHT BE POISONED...
WHAP
ONLY IF YOU WANNA DIE!!
SWIP
ONE THING AFTER ANOTHER...
SHUT UP AND FOCUS, ALL OF YOU!!
KCHAK
HEY. YOU ALL READY TO GET OUT THERE?
IT'S ALMOST TIME.
GLOMP

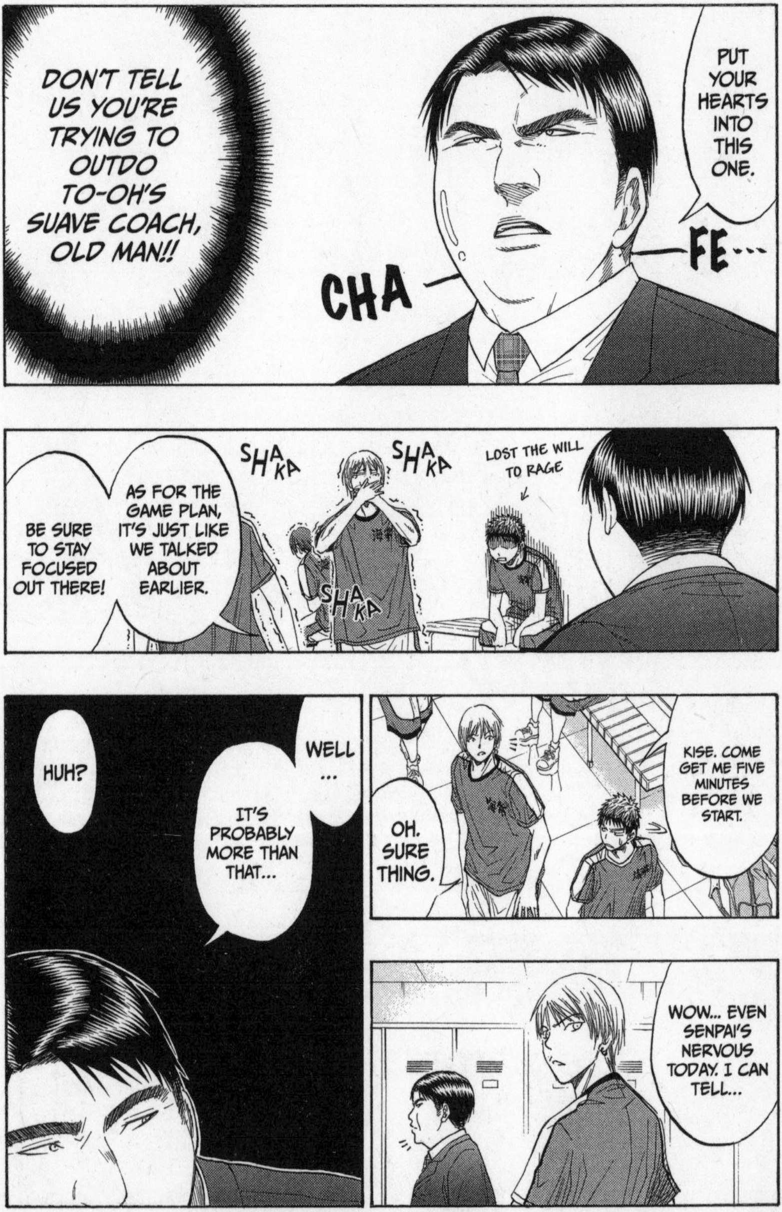
PUT YOUR HEARTS INTO THIS ONE.
FE...
CHA
DON'T TELL US YOU'RE TRYING TO OUTDO TO-OH'S SUAVE COACH, OLD MAN!!
LOST THE WILL TO RAGE
SHAKA
SHAKA
SHAKA
AS FOR THE GAME PLAN, IT'S JUST LIKE WE TALKED ABOUT EARLIER.
BE SURE TO STAY FOCUSED OUT THERE!
KISE. COME GET ME FIVE MINUTES BEFORE WE START.
OH. SURE THING.
WOW... EVEN SENPAI'S NERVOUS TODAY. I CAN TELL...
WELL ...
IT'S PROBABLY MORE THAN THAT...
HUH?

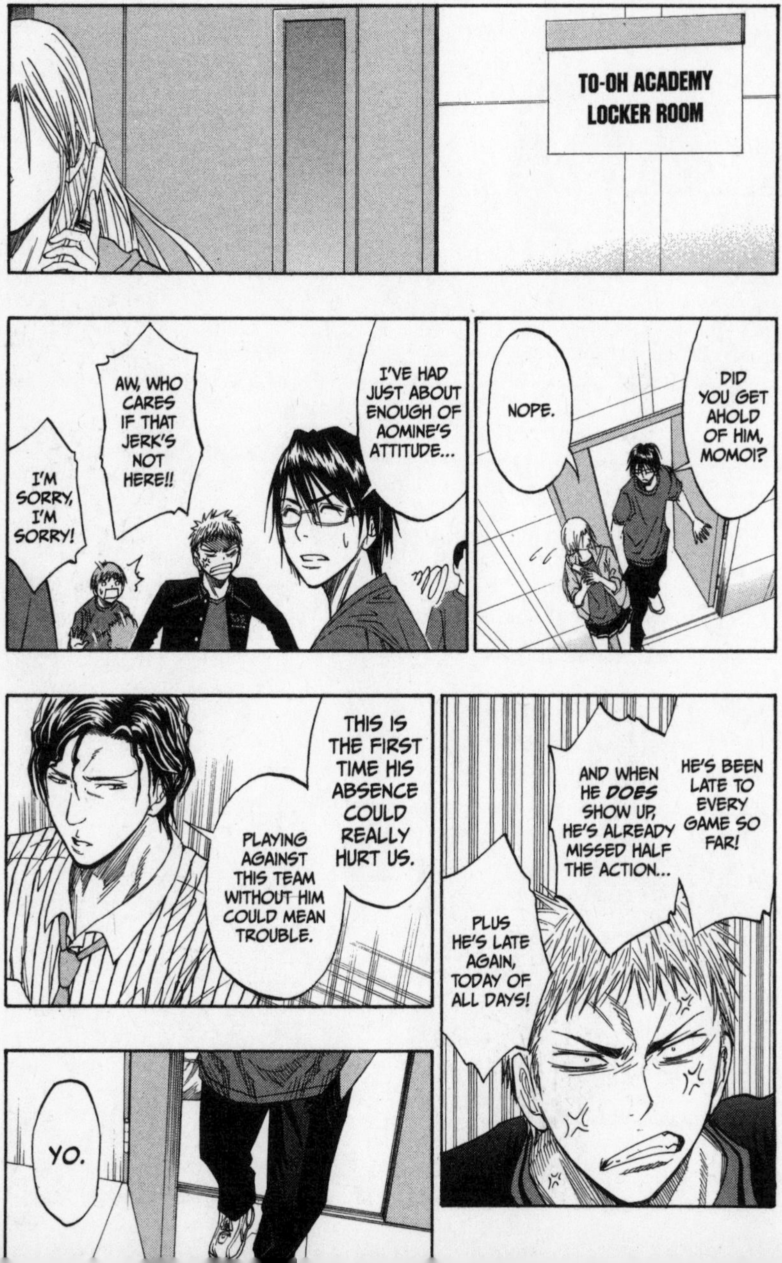
TO-OH ACADEMY LOCKER ROOM
DID YOU GET AHOLD OF HIM, MOMOI?
NOPE.
I'VE HAD JUST ABOUT ENOUGH OF AOMINE'S ATTITUDE...
AW, WHO CARES IF THAT JERK'S NOT HERE!!
I'M SORRY, I'M SORRY!
HE'S BEEN LATE TO EVERY GAME SO FAR!
AND WHEN HE *DOES* SHOW UP, HE'S ALREADY MISSED HALF THE ACTION...
PLUS HE'S LATE AGAIN, TODAY OF ALL DAYS!
THIS IS THE FIRST TIME HIS ABSENCE COULD REALLY HURT US.
PLAYING AGAINST THIS TEAM WITHOUT HIM COULD MEAN TROUBLE.
YO.

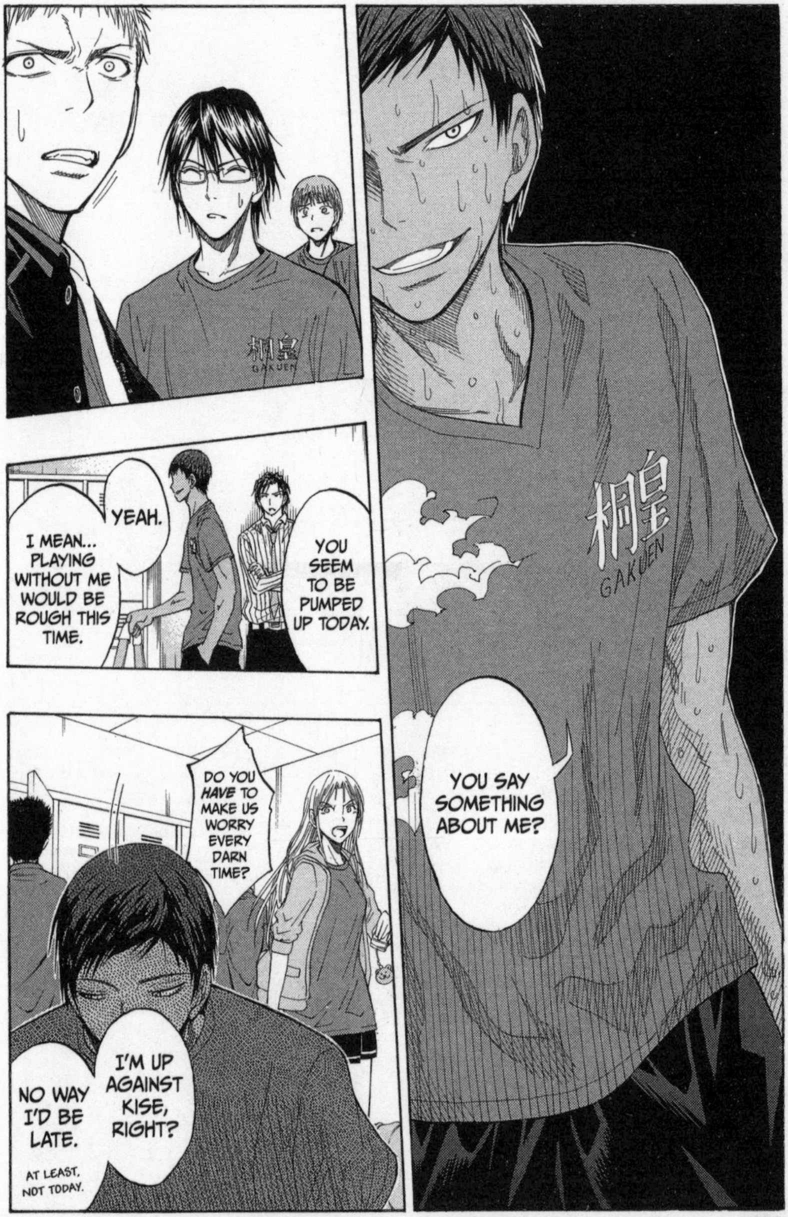
YOU SAY SOMETHING ABOUT ME?
YOU SEEM TO BE PUMPED UP TODAY.
YEAH.
I MEAN... PLAYING WITHOUT ME WOULD BE ROUGH THIS TIME.
DO YOU *HAVE* TO MAKE US WORRY EVERY DARN TIME?
I'M UP AGAINST KISE, RIGHT?
NO WAY I'D BE LATE.
AT LEAST, NOT TODAY.

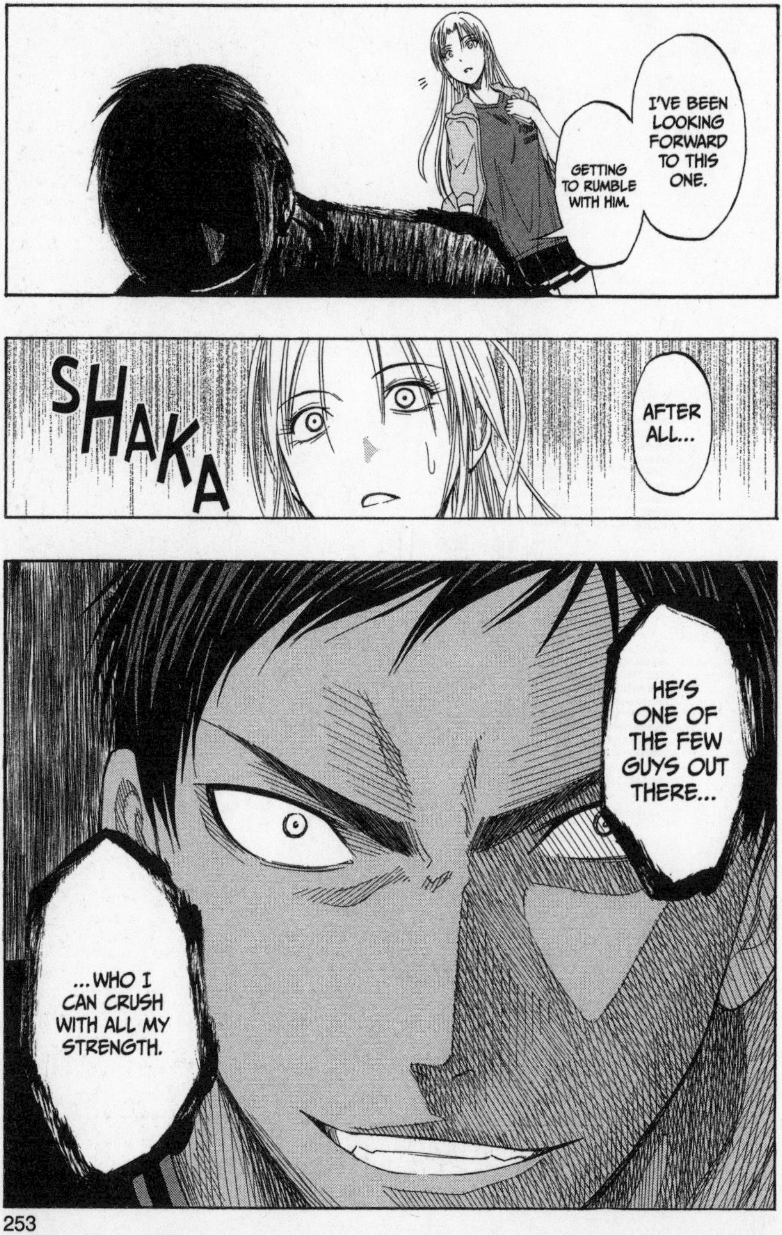
I'VE BEEN LOOKING FORWARD TO THIS ONE.
GETTING TO RUMBLE WITH HIM.
AFTER ALL...
SHAKA
HE'S ONE OF THE FEW GUYS OUT THERE...
...WHO I CAN CRUSH WITH ALL MY STRENGTH.

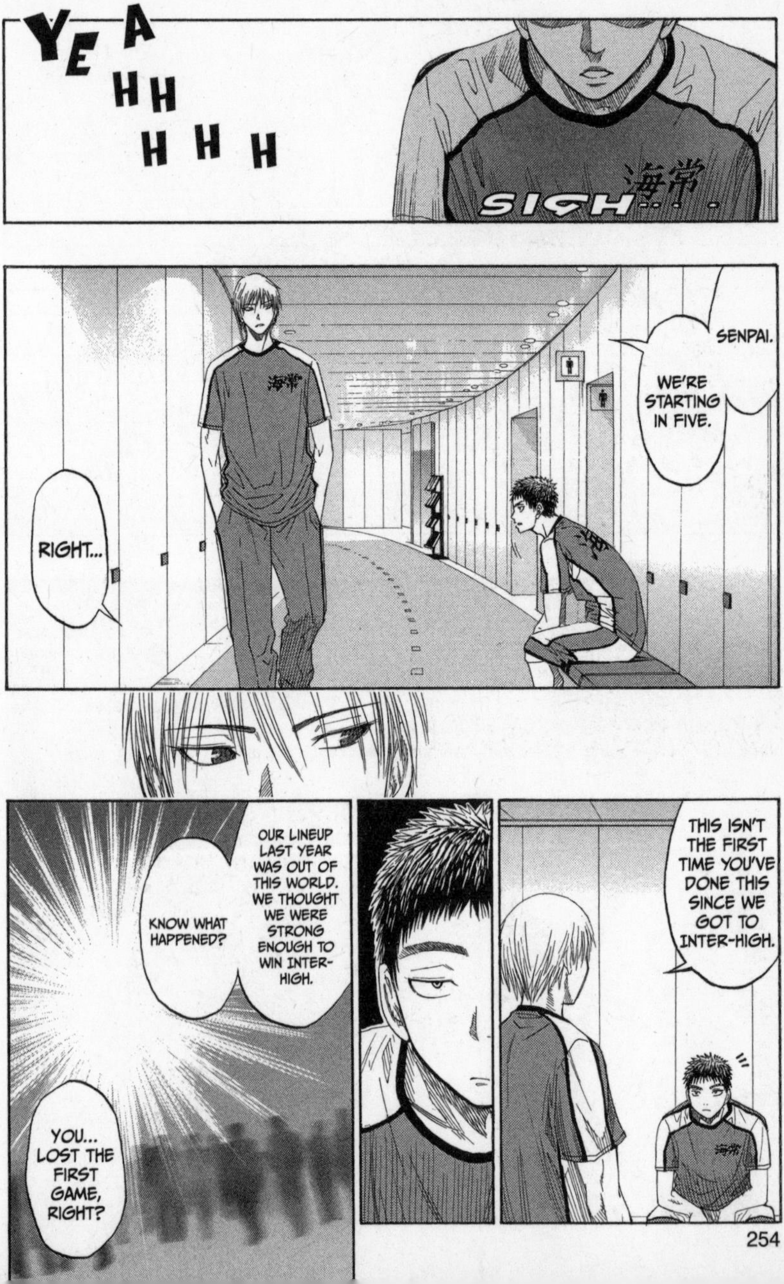
YEAHHHHHH
SIGH...
SENPAI.
WE'RE STARTING IN FIVE.
RIGHT...
THIS ISN'T THE FIRST TIME YOU'VE DONE THIS SINCE WE GOT TO INTER-HIGH.
OUR LINEUP LAST YEAR WAS OUT OF THIS WORLD. WE THOUGHT WE WERE STRONG ENOUGH TO WIN INTER-HIGH.
KNOW WHAT HAPPENED?
YOU... LOST THE FIRST GAME, RIGHT?

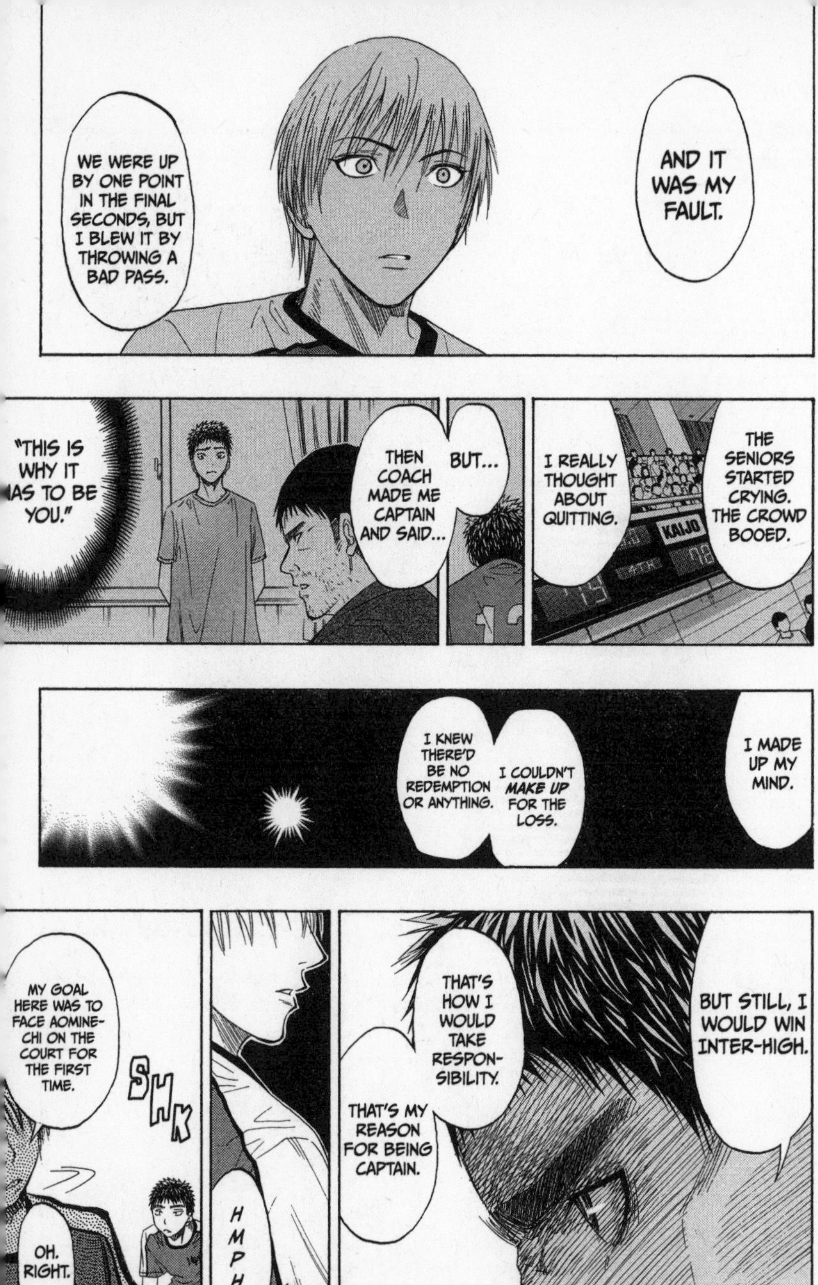
AND IT WAS MY FAULT.
WE WERE UP BY ONE POINT IN THE FINAL SECONDS, BUT I BLEW IT BY THROWING A BAD PASS.
THE SENIORS STARTED CRYING. THE CROWD BOOED.
I REALLY THOUGHT ABOUT QUITTING.
KAIJO
BUT...
THEN COACH MADE ME CAPTAIN AND SAID...
"THIS IS WHY IT HAS TO BE YOU."
I MADE UP MY MIND.
I COULDN'T *MAKE UP* FOR THE LOSS.
I KNEW THERE'D BE NO REDEMPTION OR ANYTHING.
BUT STILL, I WOULD WIN INTER-HIGH.
THAT'S HOW I WOULD TAKE RESPONSIBILITY.
THAT'S MY REASON FOR BEING CAPTAIN.
HMPH...
MY GOAL HERE WAS TO FACE AOMINE-CHI ON THE COURT FOR THE FIRST TIME.
SHK
OH. RIGHT.

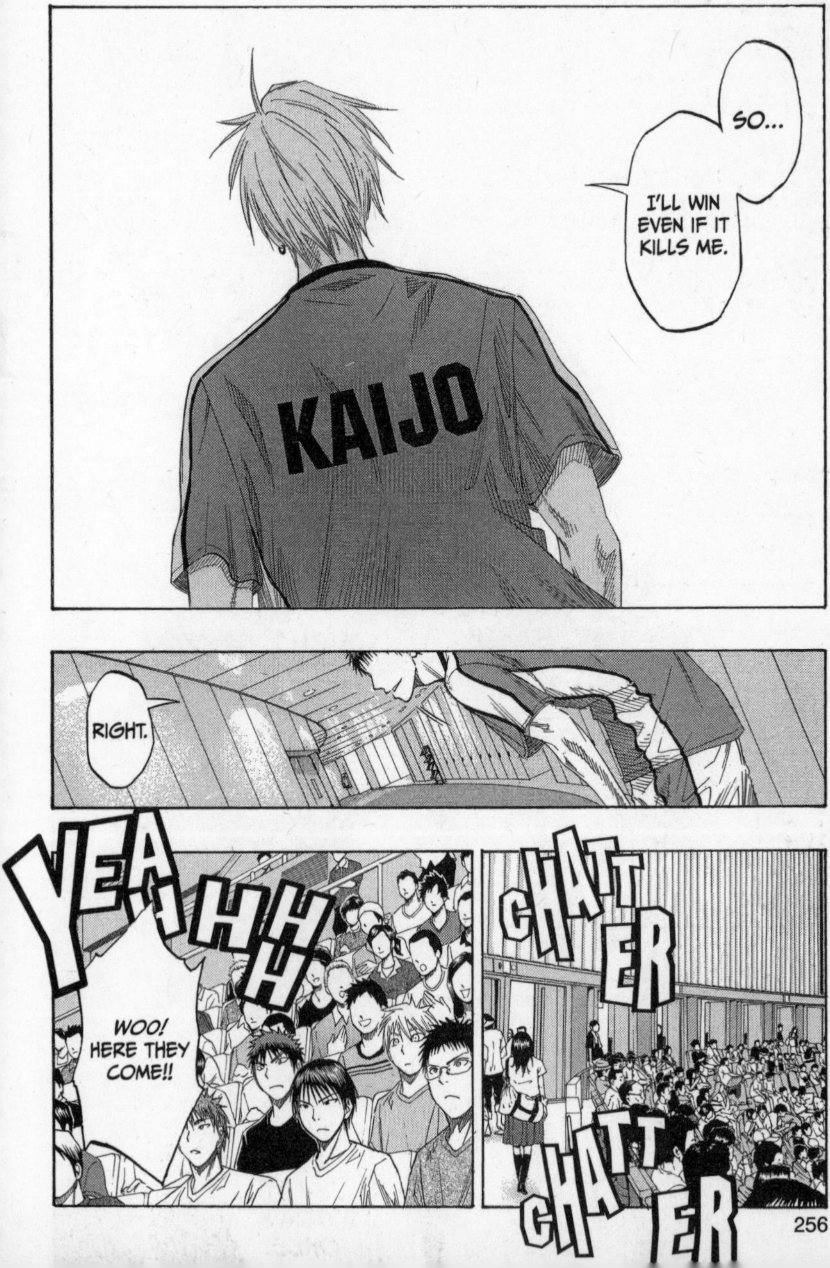
SO...
I'LL WIN EVEN IF IT KILLS ME.
KAIJO
RIGHT.
CHATTER
CHATTER
YEAHHHH
WOO! HERE THEY COME!!

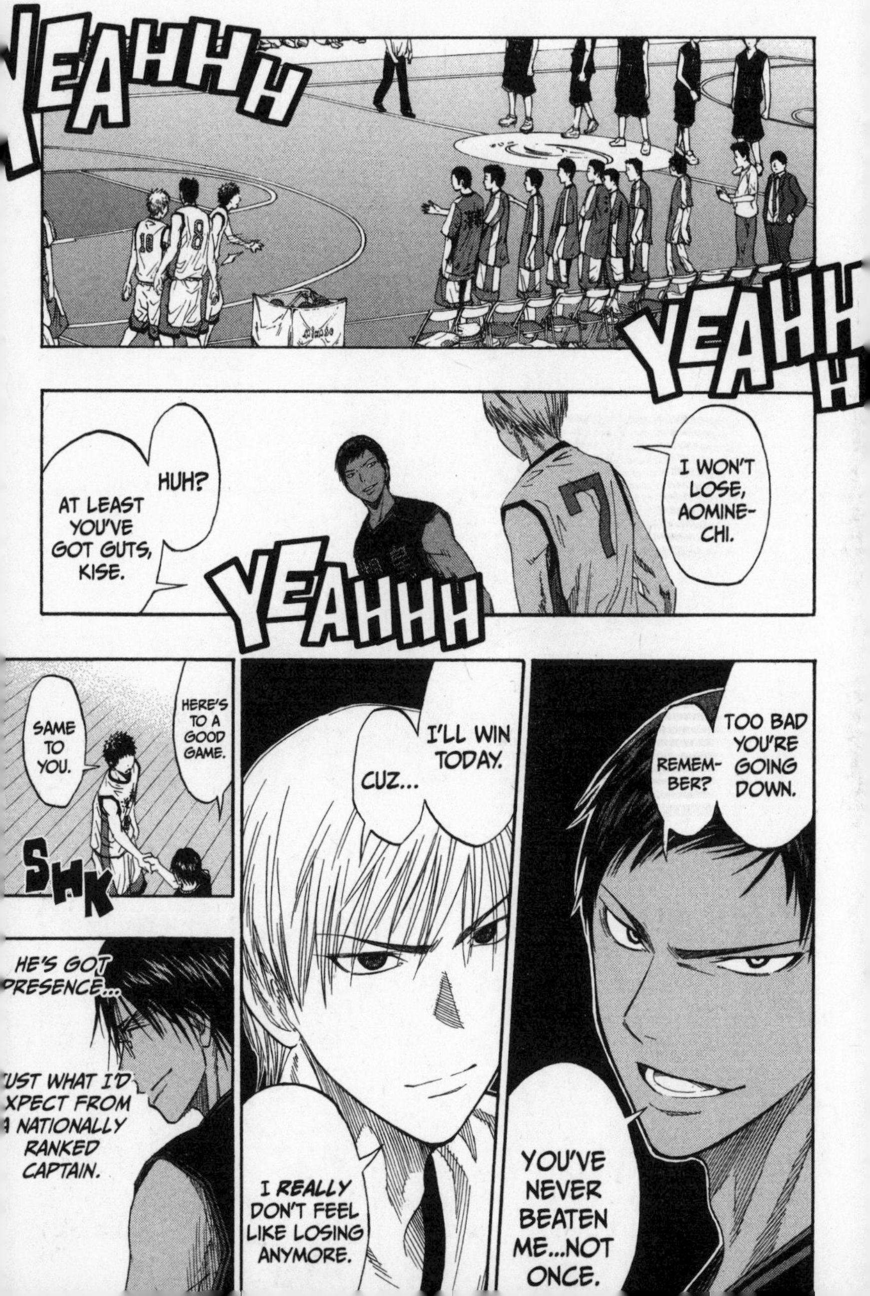
YEAHHH
YEAHHH
I WON'T LOSE, AOMINE-CHI.
HUH? AT LEAST YOU'VE GOT GUTS, KISE.
YEAHHH
TOO BAD YOU'RE GOING DOWN.
REMEMBER?
YOU'VE NEVER BEATEN ME...NOT ONCE.
I'LL WIN TODAY.
CUZ...
I *REALLY* DON'T FEEL LIKE LOSING ANYMORE.
HERE'S TO A GOOD GAME.
SAME TO YOU.
SHK
HE'S GOT PRESENCE...
JUST WHAT I'D EXPECT FROM A NATIONALLY RANKED CAPTAIN.

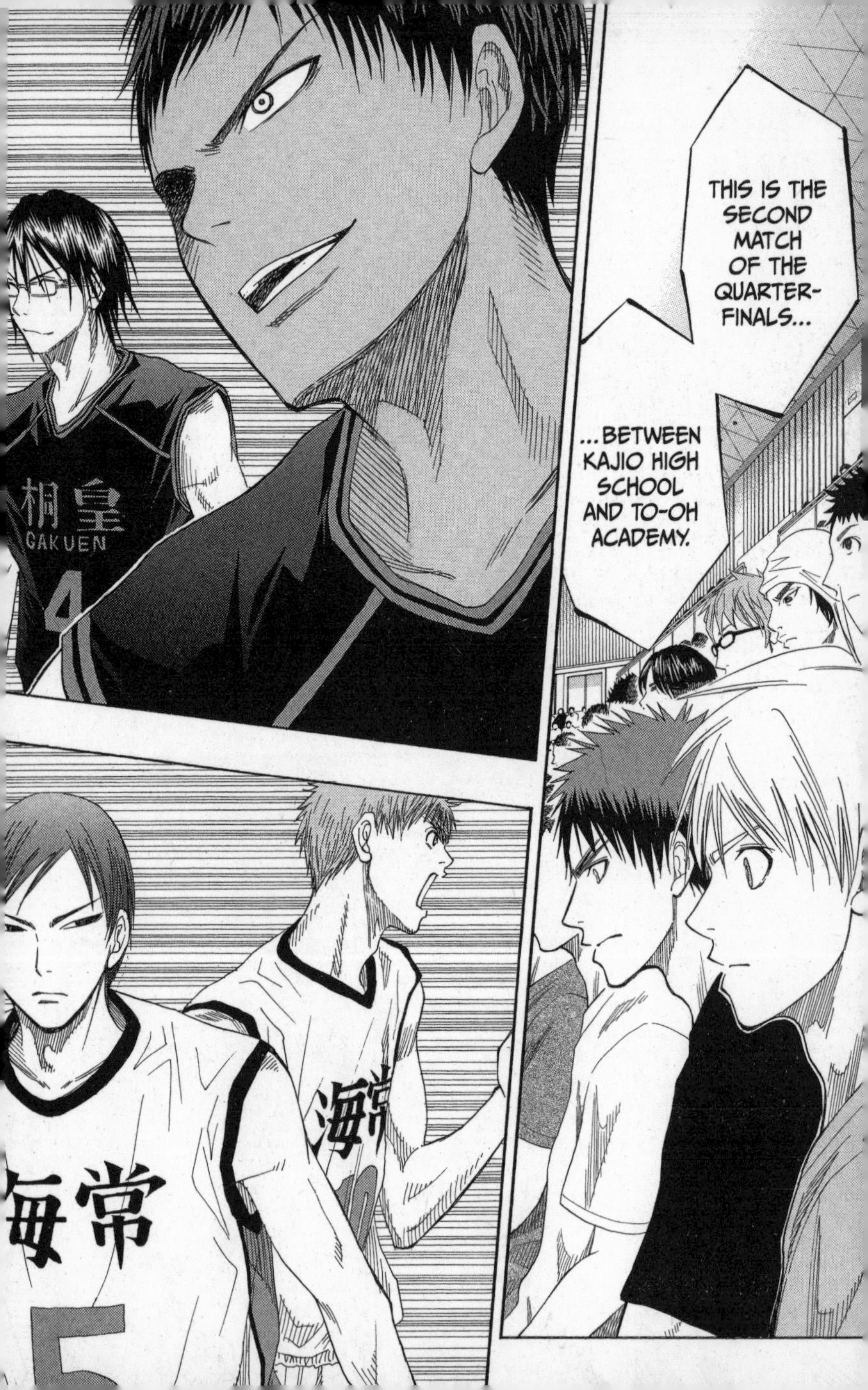
THIS IS THE SECOND MATCH OF THE QUARTER-FINALS...
...BETWEEN KAJIO HIGH SCHOOL AND TO-OH ACADEMY.
桐皇
GAKUEN
海常
海常

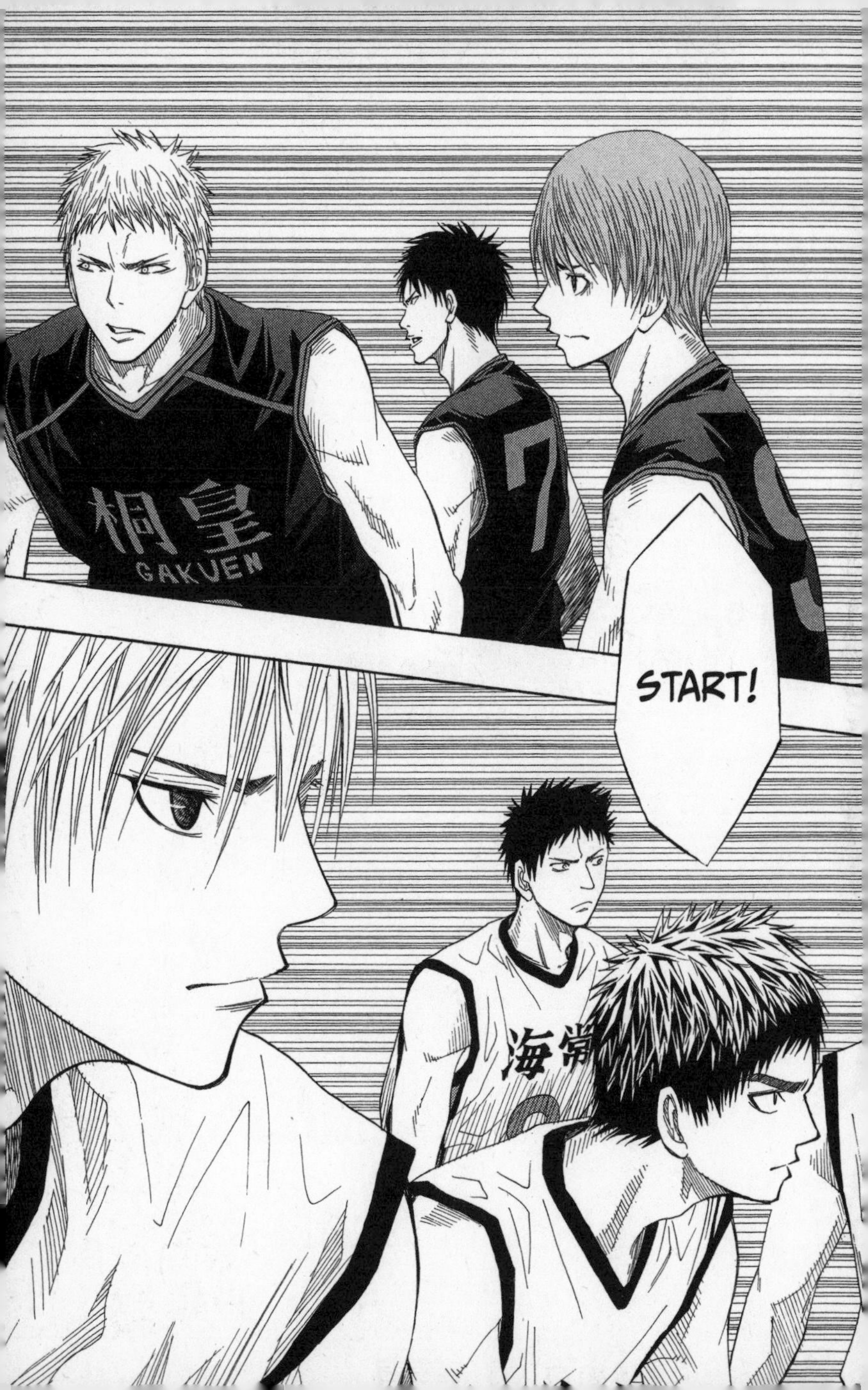
桐皇
GAKUEN
START!
海常

KUROKO'S BASKETBALL BLOOPERS

TAKE 2

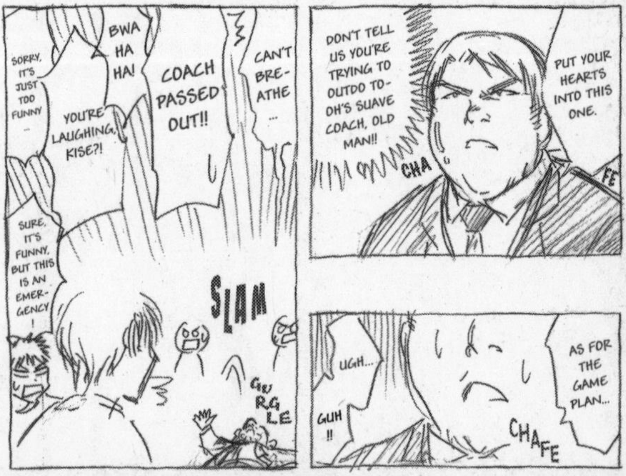
PUT YOUR HEARTS INTO THIS ONE.
DON'T TELL US YOU'RE TRYING TO OUTDO TO-OH'S SUAVE COACH, OLD MAN!!
CHA
FE
AS FOR THE GAME PLAN...
CHAFE
UGH...
GUH!!
CAN'T BRE-ATHE...
BWA HA HA!
COACH PASSED OUT!!
SORRY, IT'S JUST TOO FUNNY...
YOU'RE LAUGHING, KISE?!
SLAM
GURGLE
SURE, IT'S FUNNY, BUT THIS IS AN EMER-GENCY!

*AFTER THIS, THE COACH REMOVED HIS JACKET AND TIE.

64TH QUARTER: NOT THAT MATURE!

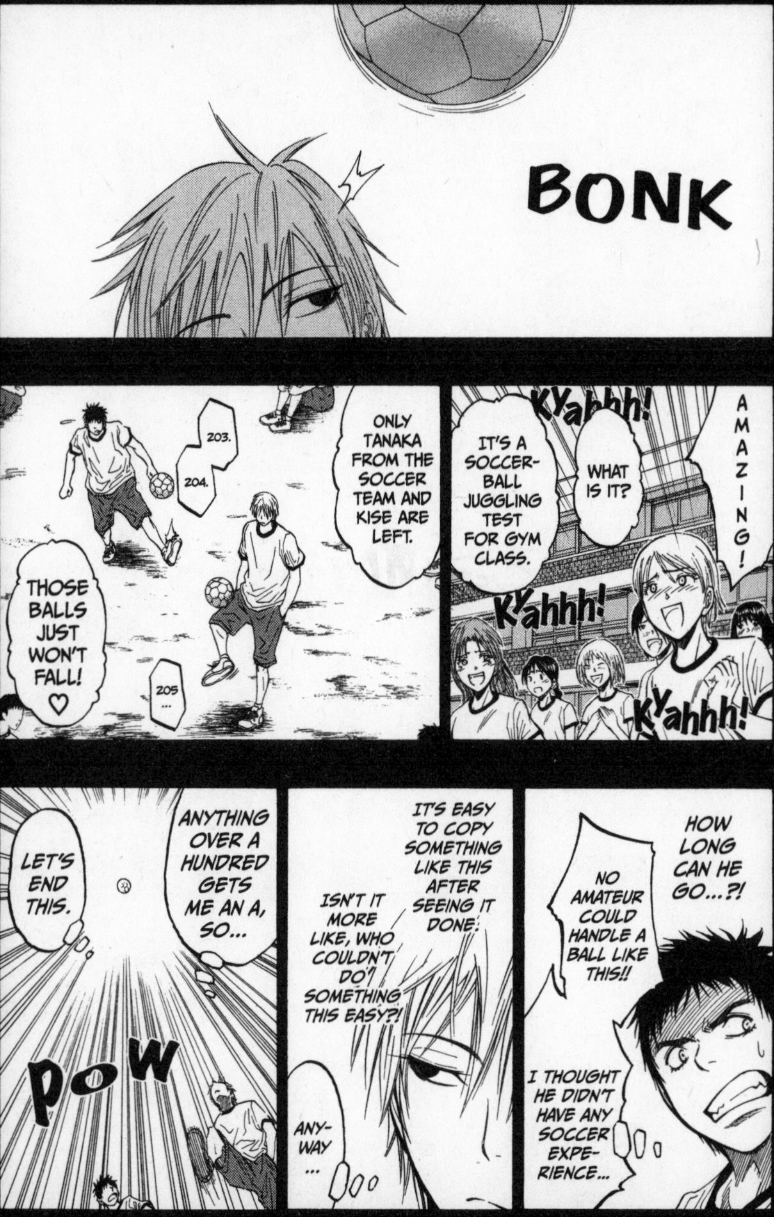
BONK
AMAZING!
Kyahhh!
WHAT IS IT?
IT'S A SOCCER-BALL JUGGLING TEST FOR GYM CLASS.
Kyahhh!
Kyahhh!
ONLY TANAKA FROM THE SOCCER TEAM AND KISE ARE LEFT.
203.
204.
THOSE BALLS JUST WON'T FALL! ♡
205 ...
HOW LONG CAN HE GO...?!
NO AMATEUR COULD HANDLE A BALL LIKE THIS!!
I THOUGHT HE DIDN'T HAVE ANY SOCCER EXPE-RIENCE...
IT'S EASY TO COPY SOMETHING LIKE THIS AFTER SEEING IT DONE.
ISN'T IT MORE LIKE, WHO COULDN'T DO SOMETHING THIS EASY?!
ANY-WAY ...
ANYTHING OVER A HUNDRED GETS ME AN A, SO...
LET'S END THIS.
POW

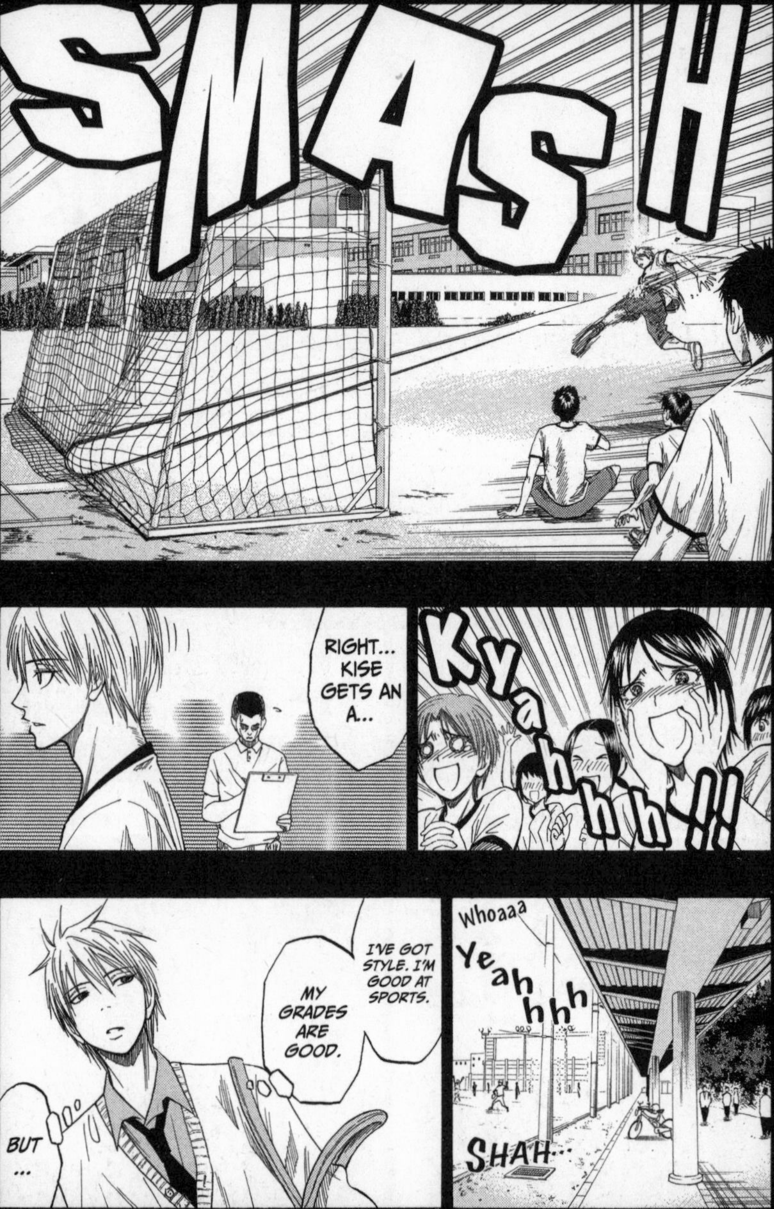
SMASH
Kyahhhh!!
RIGHT... KISE GETS AN A...
Whoaaa
Yeahhhh
SHAH...
I'VE GOT STYLE. I'M GOOD AT SPORTS.
MY GRADES ARE GOOD.
BUT ...

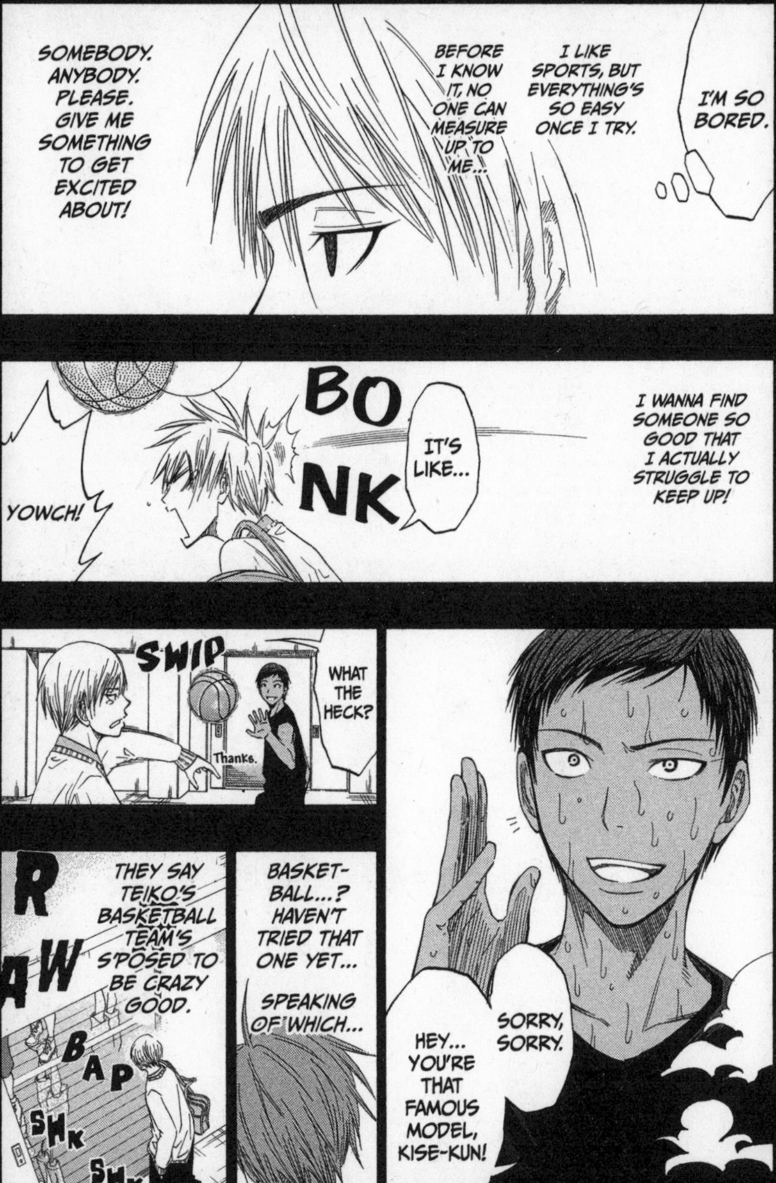
I'M SO BORED.
I LIKE SPORTS, BUT EVERYTHING'S SO EASY ONCE I TRY.
BEFORE I KNOW IT, NO ONE CAN MEASURE UP TO ME...
SOMEBODY. ANYBODY. PLEASE. GIVE ME SOMETHING TO GET EXCITED ABOUT!
I WANNA FIND SOMEONE SO GOOD THAT I ACTUALLY STRUGGLE TO KEEP UP!
IT'S LIKE...
BONK
YOWCH!
SORRY, SORRY.
HEY... YOU'RE THAT FAMOUS MODEL, KISE-KUN!
WHAT THE HECK?
SWIP
Thanks.
BASKET-BALL...? HAVEN'T TRIED THAT ONE YET...
SPEAKING OF WHICH...
THEY SAY TEIKO'S BASKETBALL TEAM'S S'POSED TO BE CRAZY GOOD.
RAW
BAP
SHK
SHK

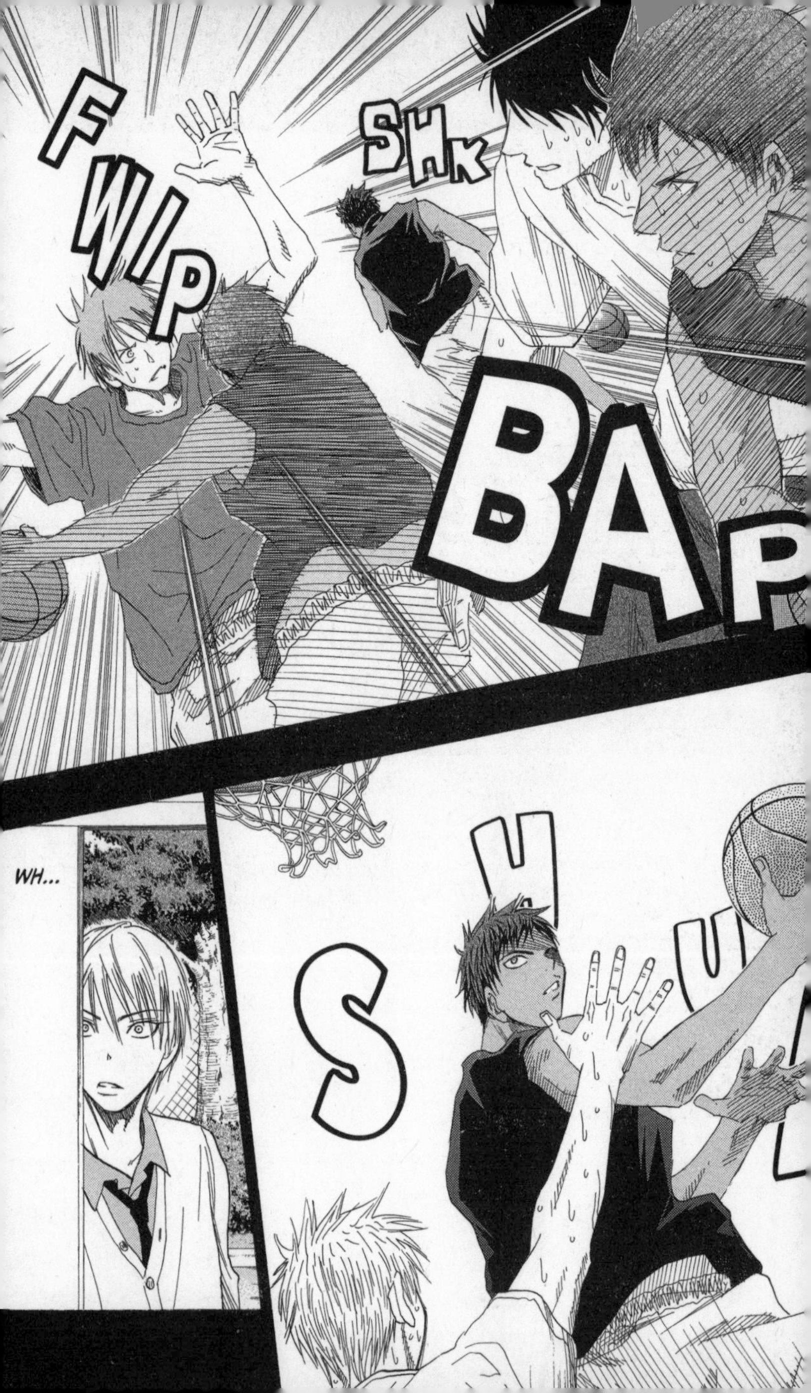
SHK
BAP
FWIP
WH...

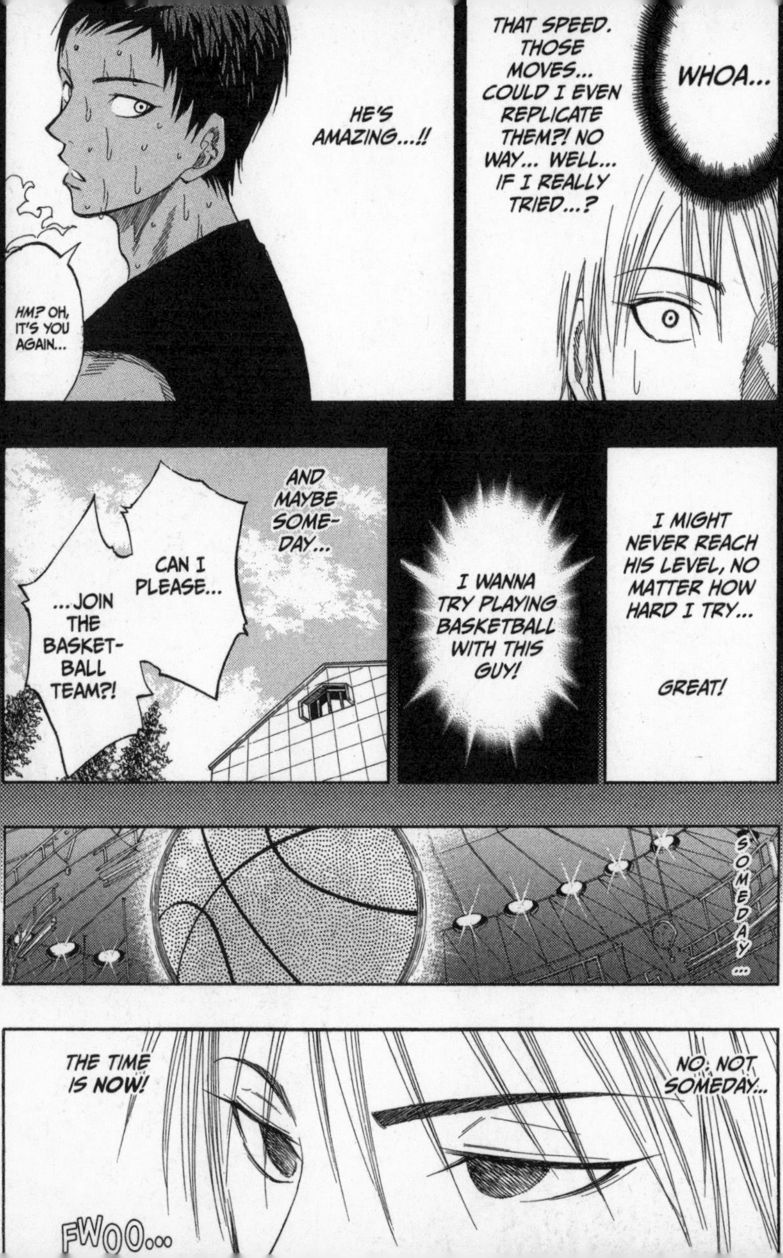
WHOA...
THAT SPEED. THOSE MOVES... COULD I EVEN REPLICATE THEM?! NO WAY... WELL... IF I REALLY TRIED...?
HE'S AMAZING...!!
HM? OH, IT'S YOU AGAIN...
I MIGHT NEVER REACH HIS LEVEL, NO MATTER HOW HARD I TRY...
GREAT!
I WANNA TRY PLAYING BASKETBALL WITH THIS GUY!
AND MAYBE SOMEDAY...
CAN I PLEASE...
...JOIN THE BASKETBALL TEAM?!
SOMEDAY...
NO. NOT SOMEDAY...
THE TIME IS NOW!
FWOO...

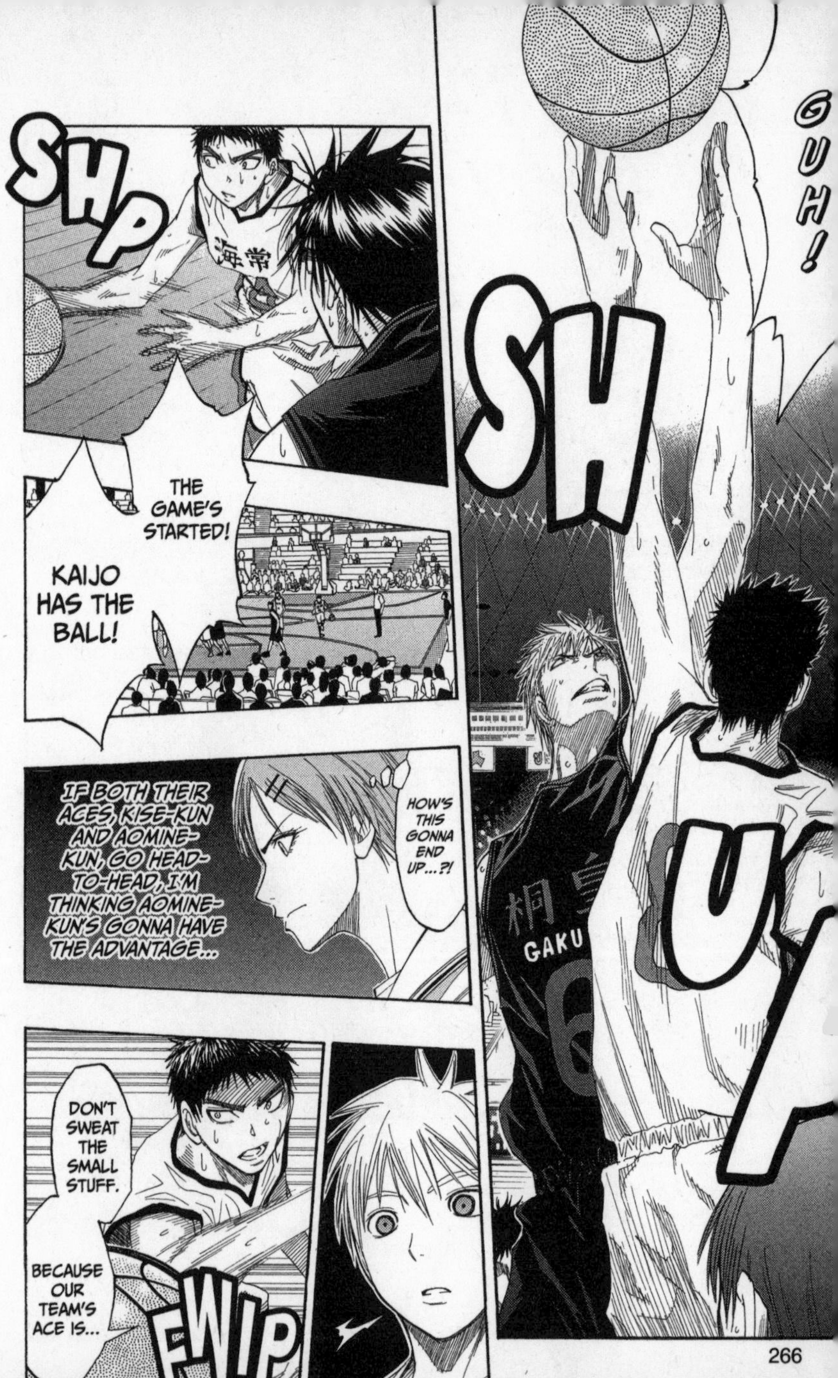
GUH!
SHU
GAKU
SHP
海常
THE GAME'S STARTED!
KAIJO HAS THE BALL!
HOW'S THIS GONNA END UP...?!
IF BOTH THEIR ACES, KISE-KUN AND AOMINE-KUN, GO HEAD-TO-HEAD, I'M THINKING AOMINE-KUN'S GONNA HAVE THE ADVANTAGE...
DON'T SWEAT THE SMALL STUFF.
BECAUSE OUR TEAM'S ACE IS...
FWIP

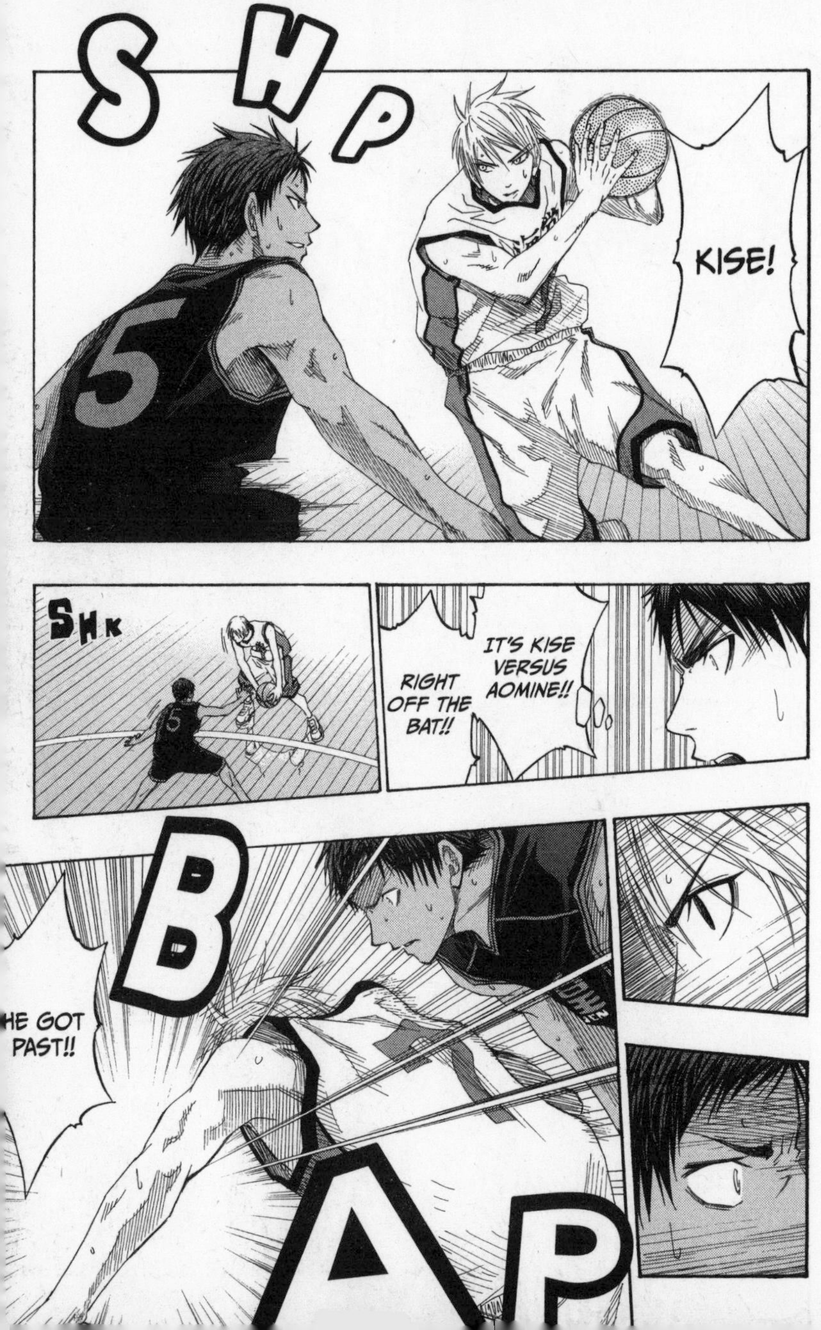
KISE!
SHP
IT'S KISE VERSUS AOMINE!!
RIGHT OFF THE BAT!!
SHK
BAP
HE GOT PAST!!

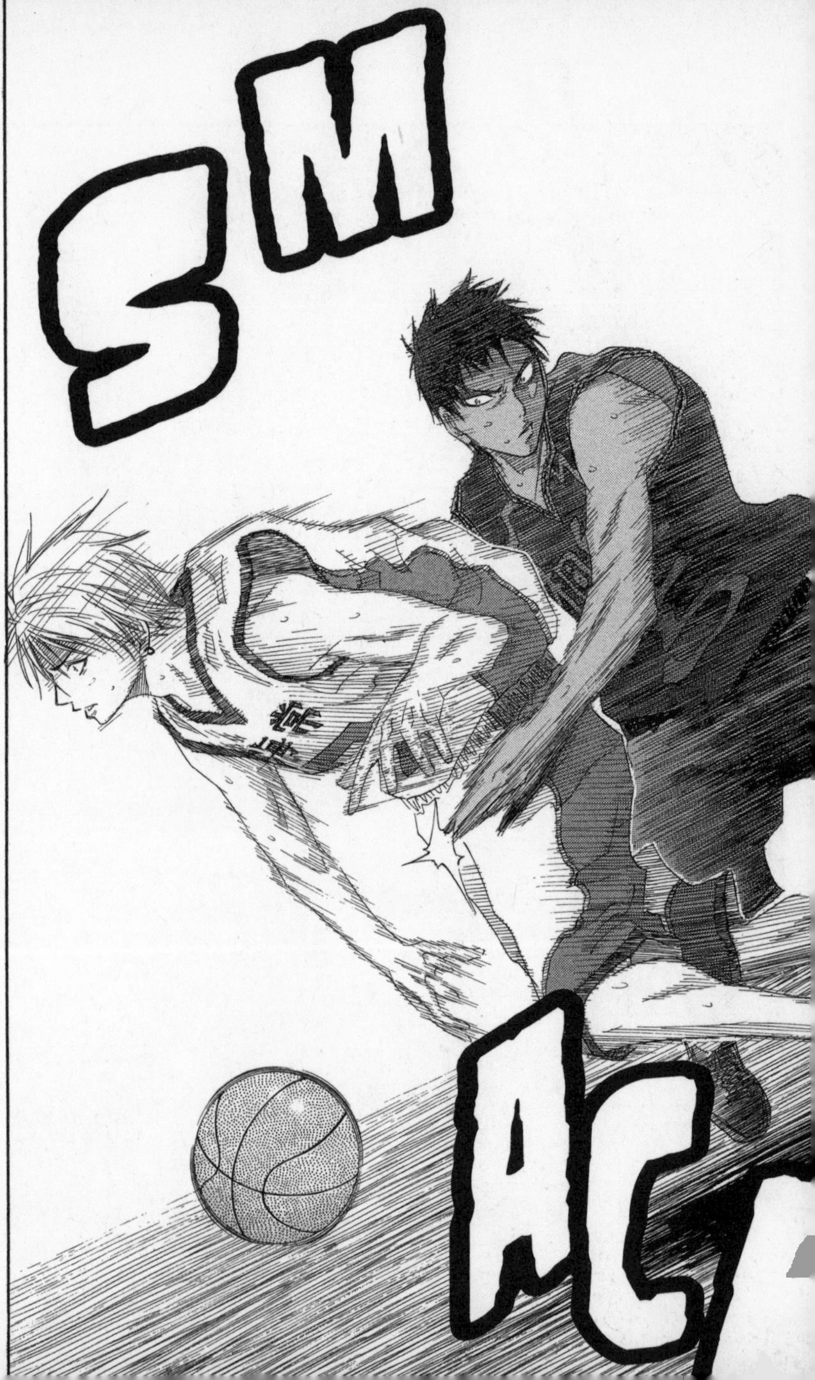
SM
AC

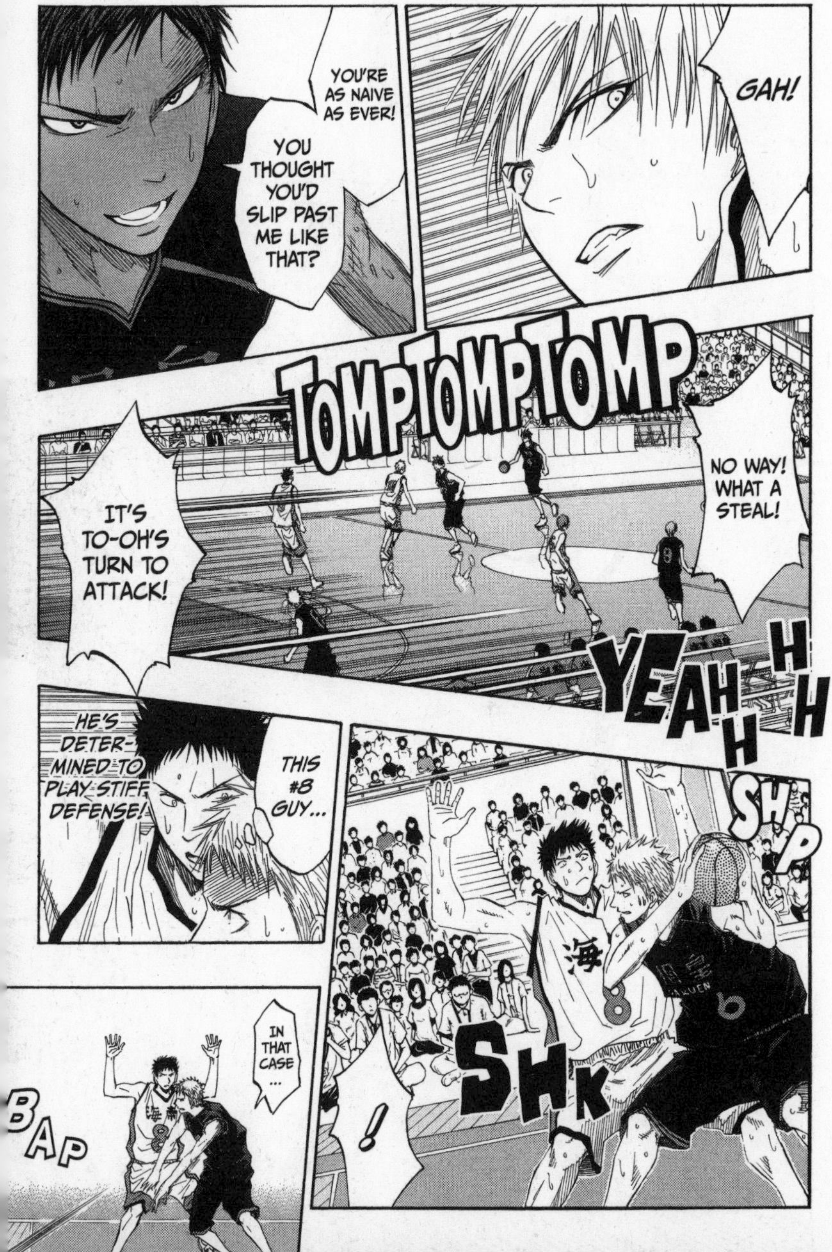
GAH!
YOU'RE AS NAIVE AS EVER!
YOU THOUGHT YOU'D SLIP PAST ME LIKE THAT?
TOMP TOMP TOMP
NO WAY! WHAT A STEAL!
IT'S TO-OH'S TURN TO ATTACK!
YEAHHHHH
SHP
SHK
!
THIS #8 GUY...
HE'S DETERMINED TO PLAY STIFF DEFENSE!
IN THAT CASE...
BAP

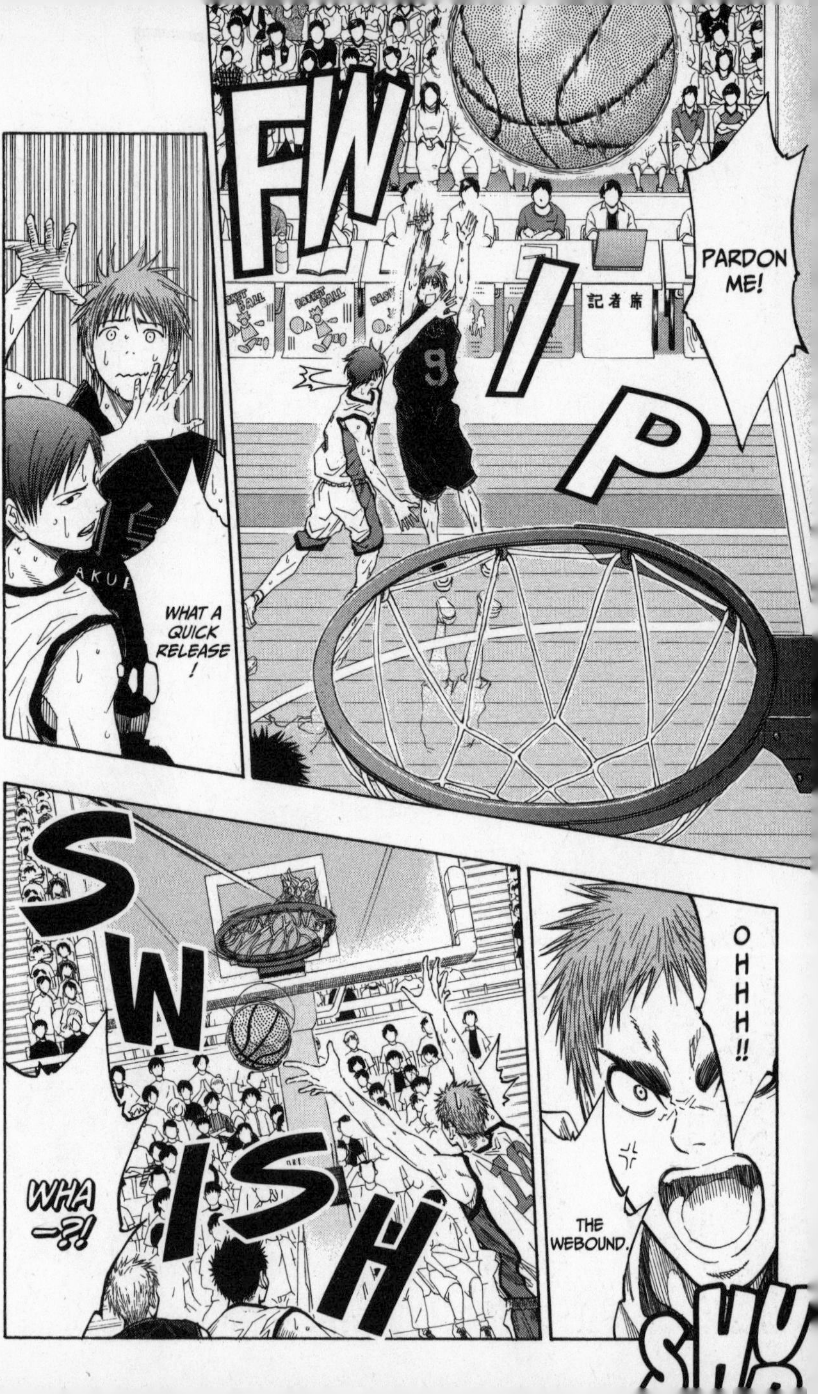
FWIP
PARDON ME!
記者席
WHAT A QUICK RELEASE!
OHHH!!
THE WEBOUND.
SHU
SWISH
WHA—?!

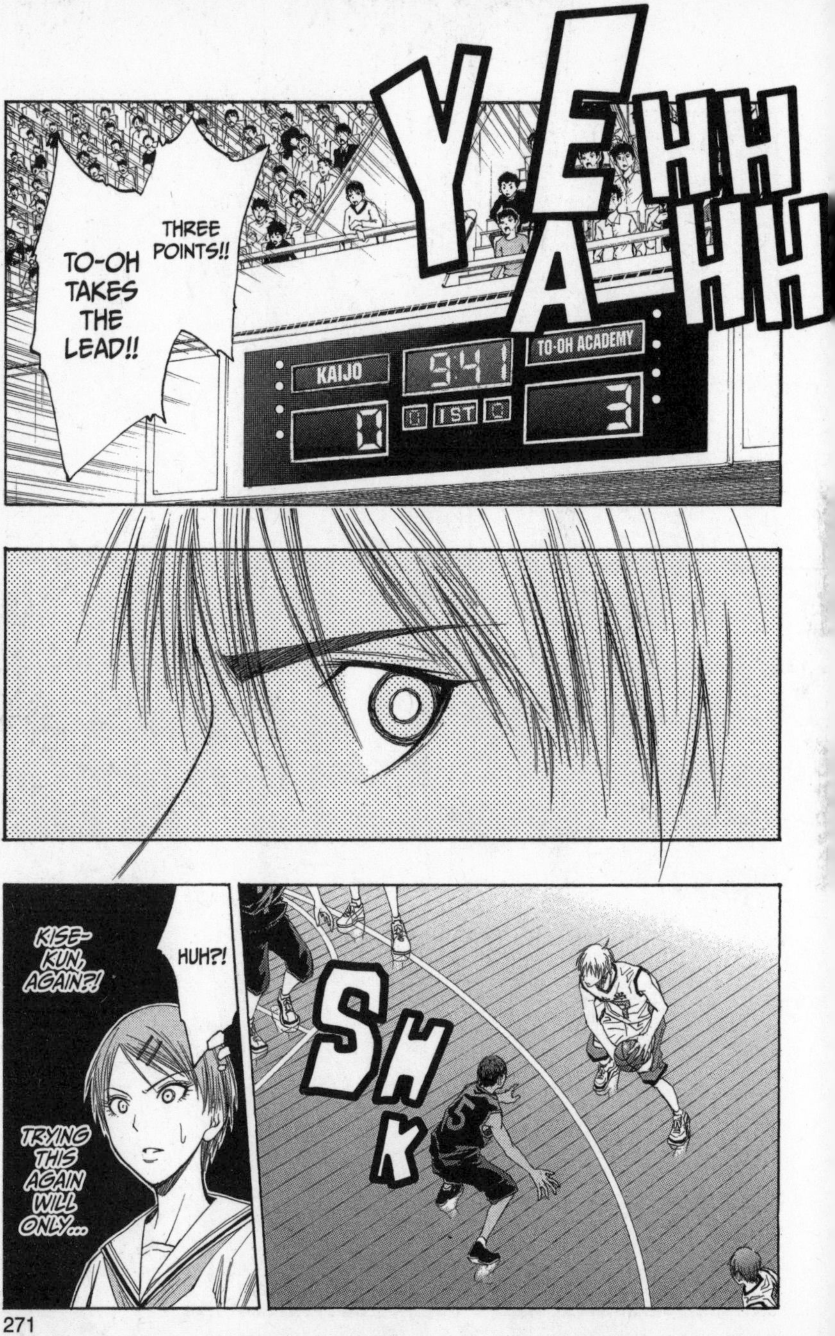
YEAHHH
AHHH
THREE POINTS!!
TO-OH TAKES THE LEAD!!
KAIJO
TO-OH ACADEMY
9:41
1ST Q
0
3
SHK
HUH?!
KISE-KUN, AGAIN?!
TRYING THIS AGAIN WILL ONLY...

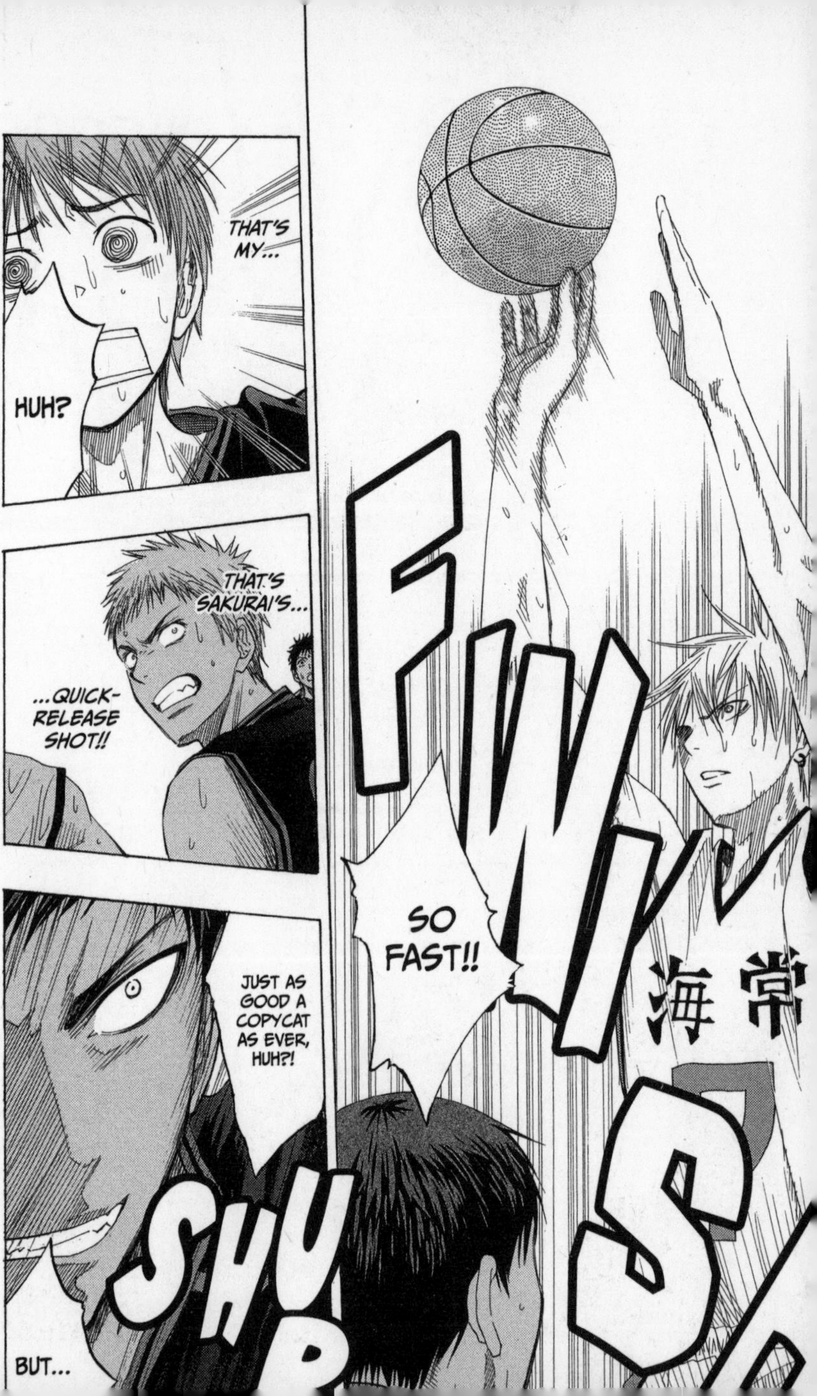
FWIS
SO FAST!!
SHU
THAT'S MY...
HUH?
THAT'S SAKURAI'S...
...QUICK-RELEASE SHOT!!
JUST AS GOOD A COPYCAT AS EVER, HUH?!
BUT...

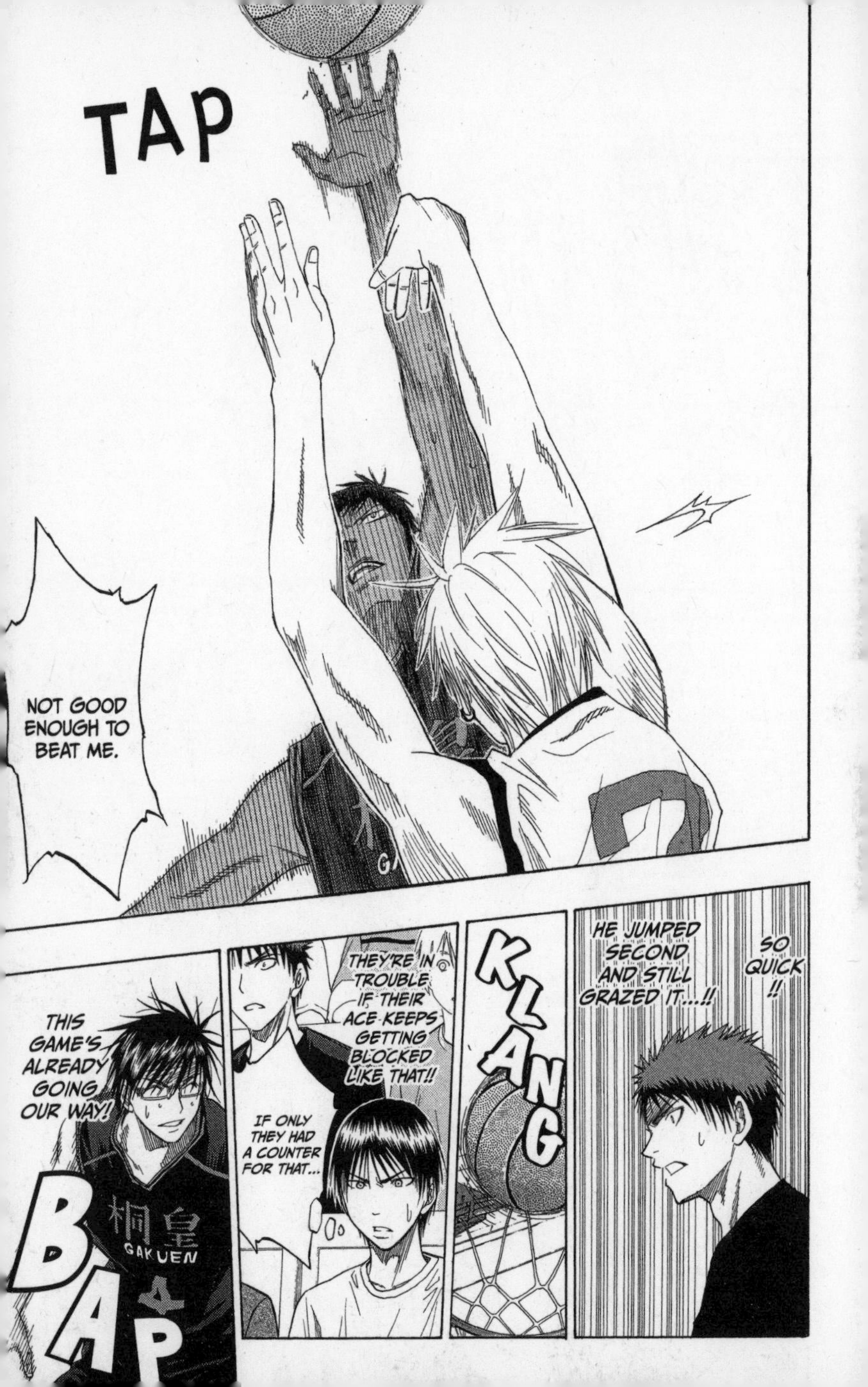
TAP
NOT GOOD ENOUGH TO BEAT ME.
SO QUICK!!
HE JUMPED SECOND AND STILL GRAZED IT...!!
KLANG
THEY'RE IN TROUBLE IF THEIR ACE KEEPS GETTING BLOCKED LIKE THAT!!
IF ONLY THEY HAD A COUNTER FOR THAT...
THIS GAME'S ALREADY GOING OUR WAY!
BAP
桐皇
GAKUEN

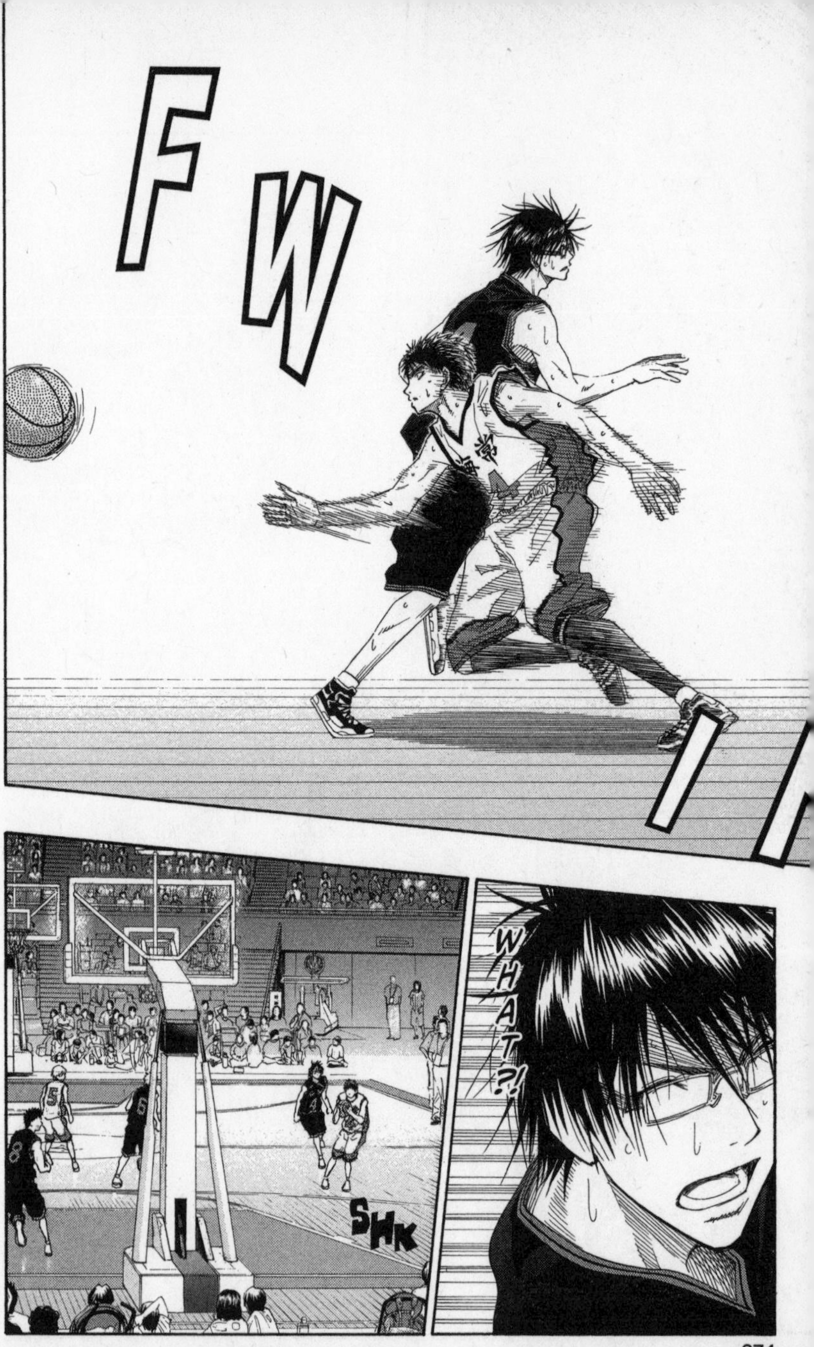
FW
WHAT?!
SHK

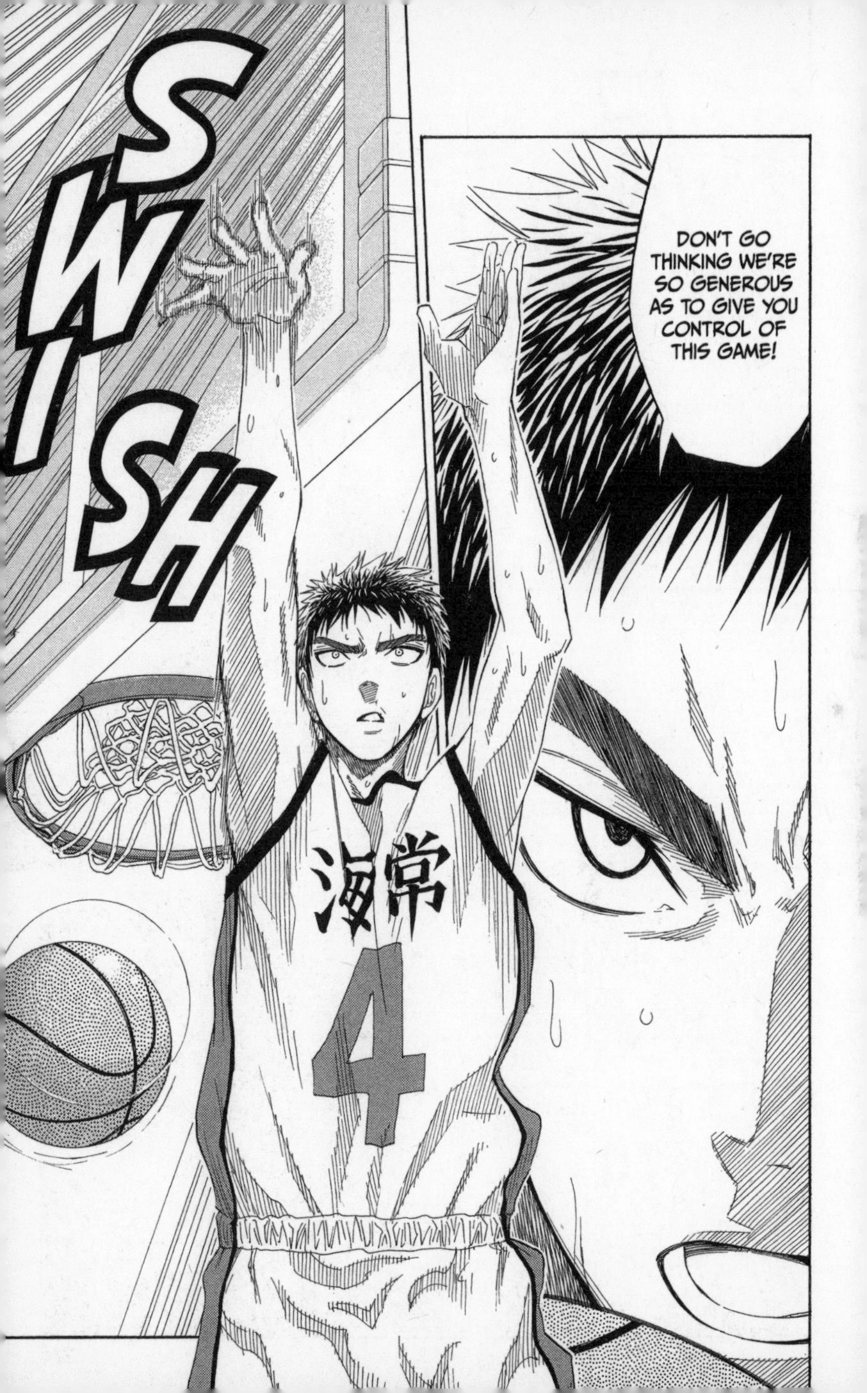
DON'T GO THINKING WE'RE SO GENEROUS AS TO GIVE YOU CONTROL OF THIS GAME!
SWISH

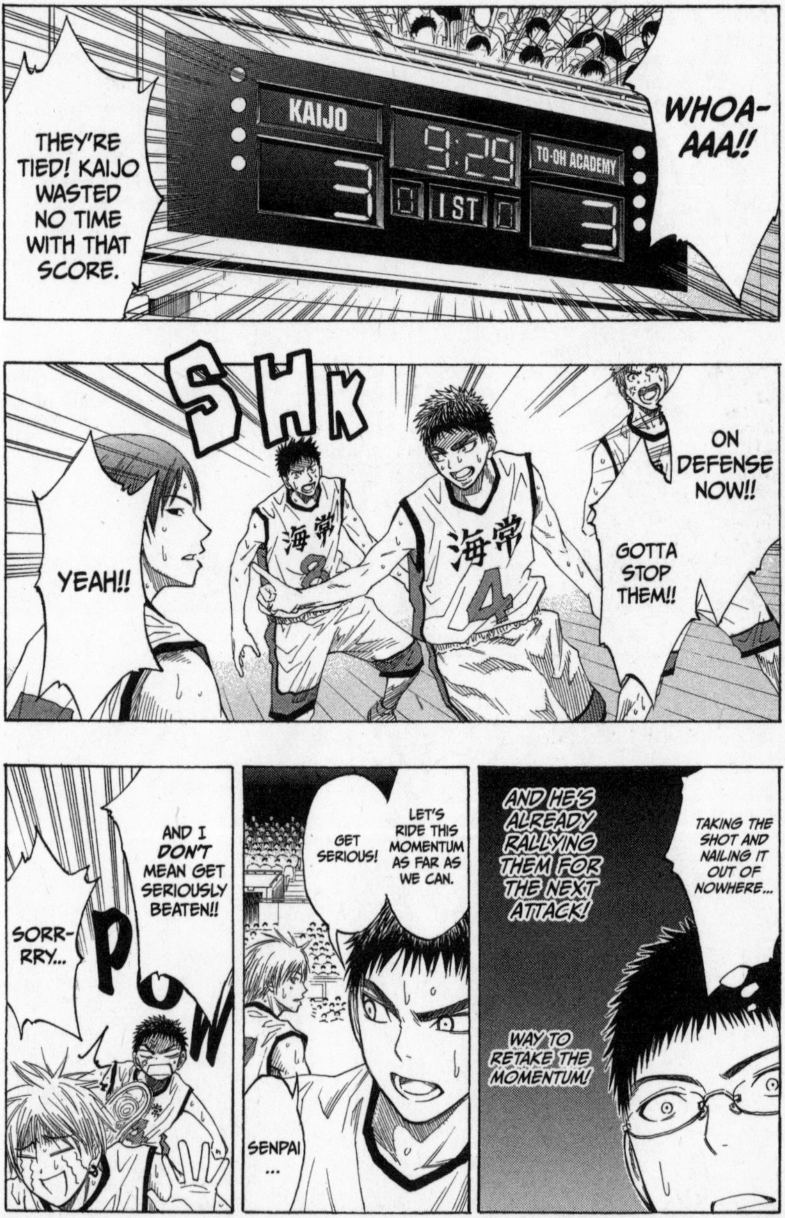
WHOA-AAA!!
KAIJO
9:29
TO-OH ACADEMY
3
1ST
3
THEY'RE TIED! KAIJO WASTED NO TIME WITH THAT SCORE.
ON DEFENSE NOW!!
SHK
GOTTA STOP THEM!!
YEAH!!
TAKING THE SHOT AND NAILING IT OUT OF NOWHERE...
AND HE'S ALREADY RALLYING THEM FOR THE NEXT ATTACK!
WAY TO RETAKE THE MOMENTUM!
LET'S RIDE THIS MOMENTUM AS FAR AS WE CAN.
GET SERIOUS!
SENPAI ...
AND I *DON'T* MEAN GET SERIOUSLY BEATEN!!
SORR-RRY...
POW

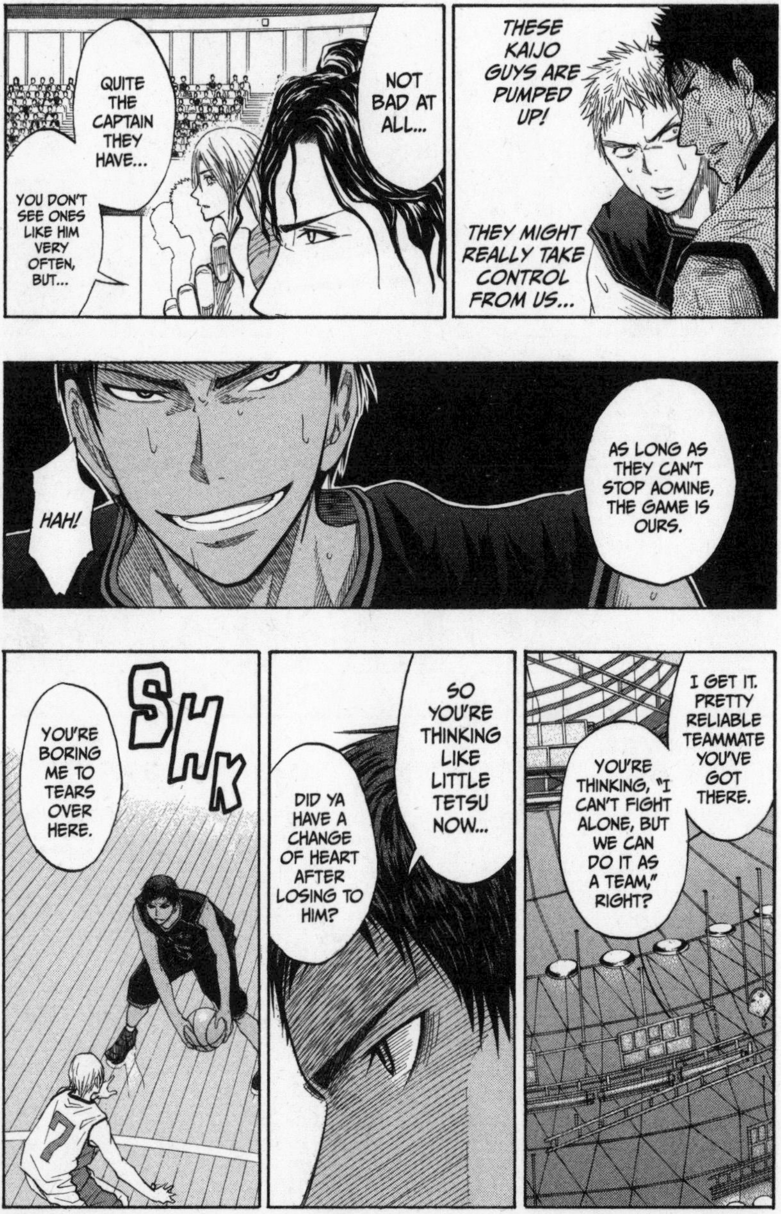
THESE KAIJO GUYS ARE PUMPED UP!
THEY MIGHT REALLY TAKE CONTROL FROM US...
NOT BAD AT ALL...
QUITE THE CAPTAIN THEY HAVE...
YOU DON'T SEE ONES LIKE HIM VERY OFTEN, BUT...
AS LONG AS THEY CAN'T STOP AOMINE, THE GAME IS OURS.
HAH!
I GET IT. PRETTY RELIABLE TEAMMATE YOU'VE GOT THERE.
YOU'RE THINKING, "I CAN'T FIGHT ALONE, BUT WE CAN DO IT AS A TEAM," RIGHT?
SO YOU'RE THINKING LIKE LITTLE TETSU NOW...
DID YA HAVE A CHANGE OF HEART AFTER LOSING TO HIM?
SHK
YOU'RE BORING ME TO TEARS OVER HERE.

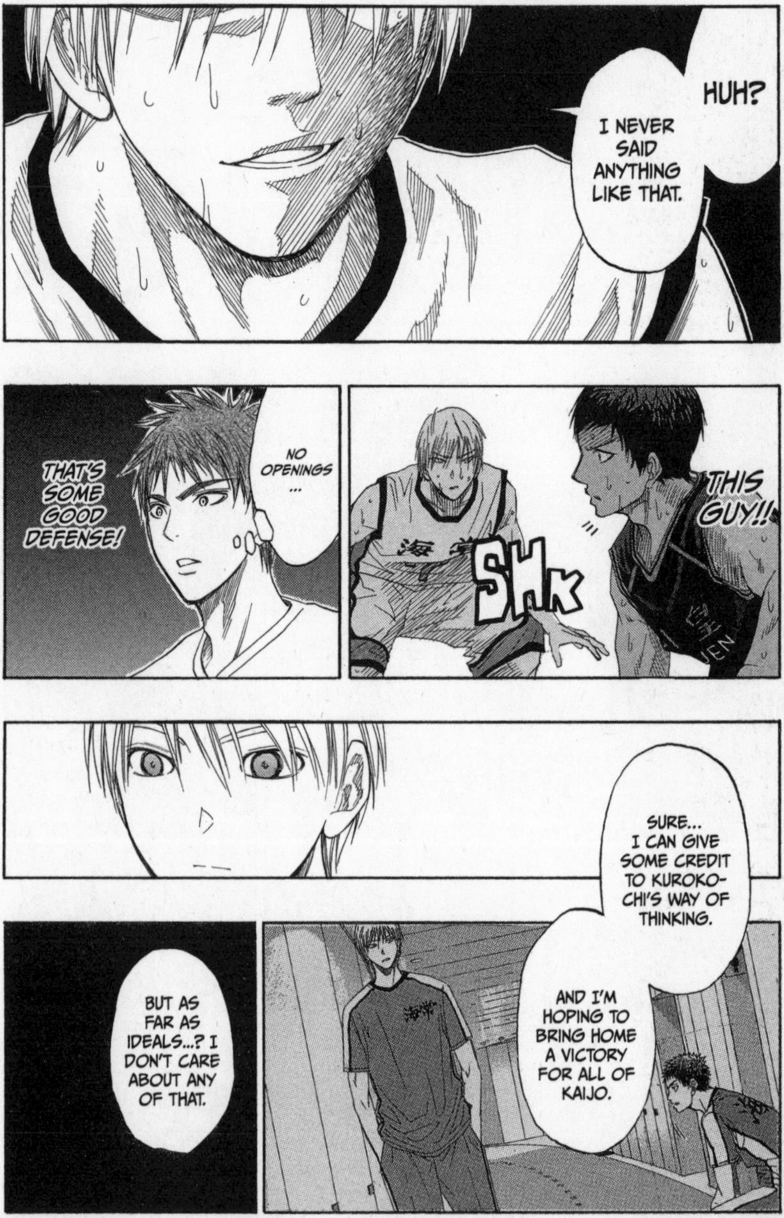
HUH?
I NEVER SAID ANYTHING LIKE THAT.
THIS GUY!!
SHK
NO OPENINGS ...
THAT'S SOME GOOD DEFENSE!
SURE... I CAN GIVE SOME CREDIT TO KUROKO-CHI'S WAY OF THINKING.
AND I'M HOPING TO BRING HOME A VICTORY FOR ALL OF KAIJO.
BUT AS FAR AS IDEALS...? I DON'T CARE ABOUT ANY OF THAT.

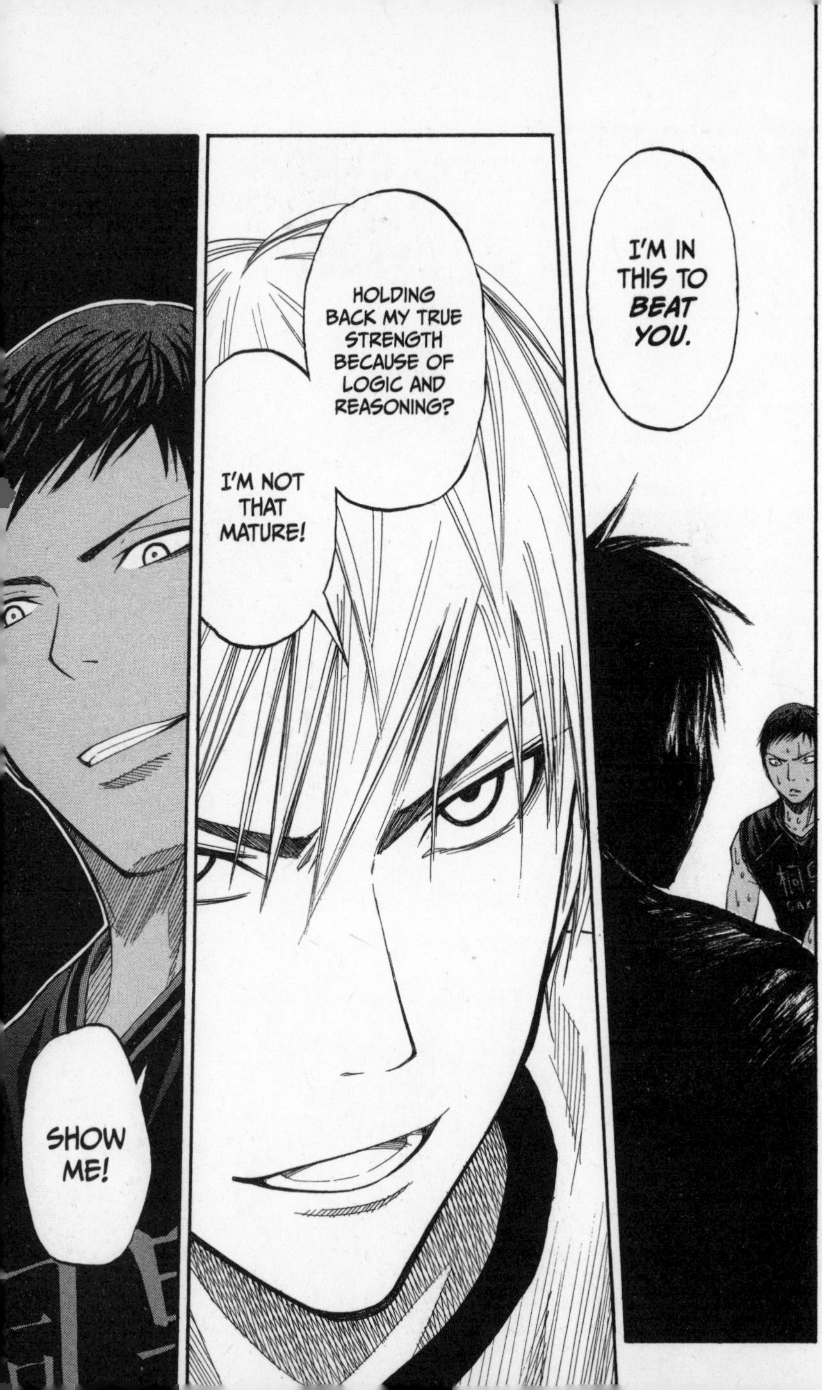
I'M IN THIS TO *BEAT YOU.*
HOLDING BACK MY TRUE STRENGTH BECAUSE OF LOGIC AND REASONING?
I'M NOT THAT MATURE!
SHOW ME!

KUROKO'S BASKETBALL BLOOPERS

TAKE 9

ANYTHING OVER A HUNDRED GETS ME AN A, SO...
LET'S END THIS.
POW
FWOSH
SMASH
KLINK
AH! HE'S RUNNING...
SO FAST!!
WHOOSH

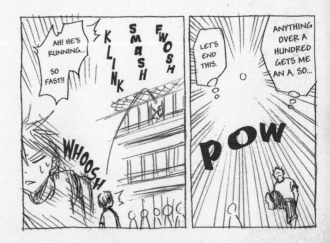

65TH QUARTER: WHO DO YOU THINK IT WAS?

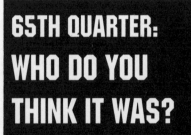

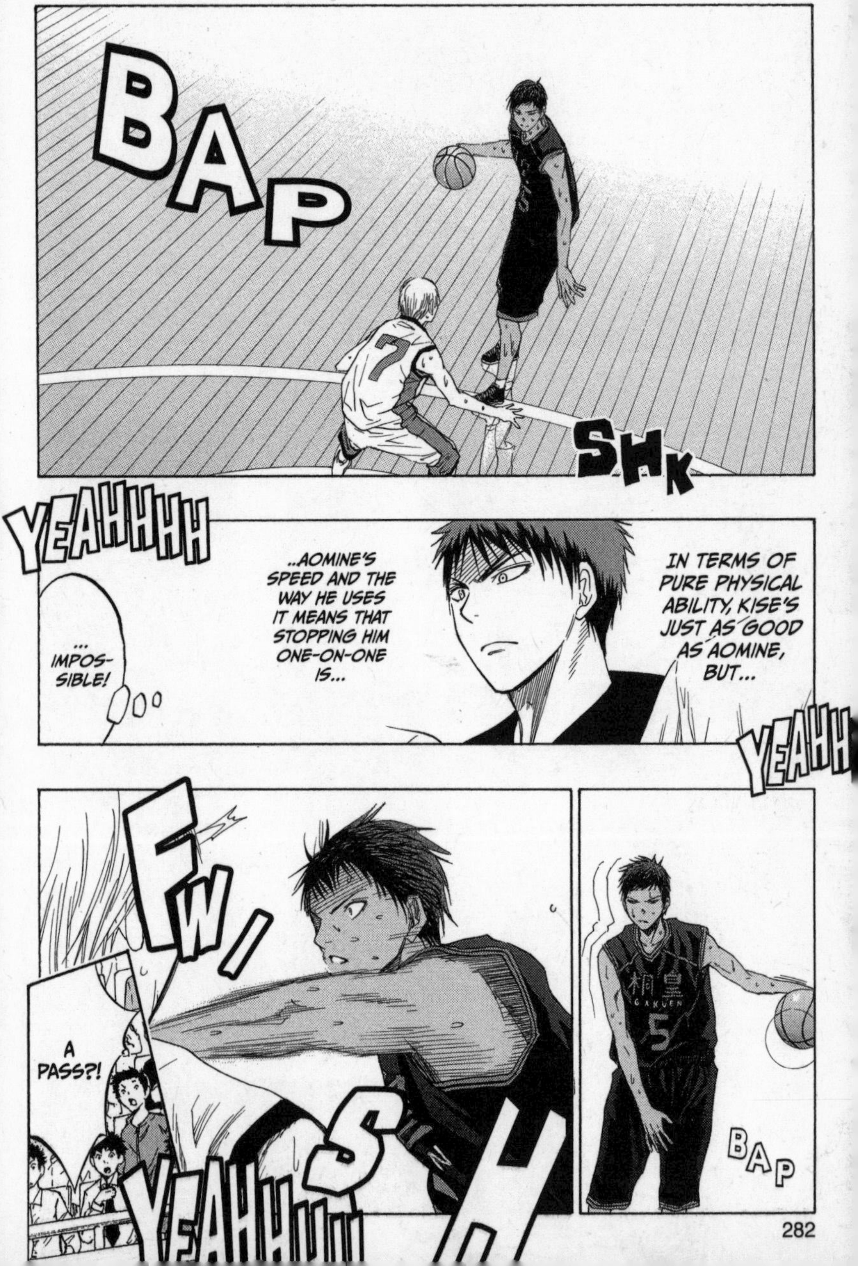
BAP
SHK
YEAHHH
IN TERMS OF PURE PHYSICAL ABILITY, KISE'S JUST AS GOOD AS AOMINE, BUT...
...AOMINE'S SPEED AND THE WAY HE USES IT MEANS THAT STOPPING HIM ONE-ON-ONE IS...
...IMPOSSIBLE!
YEAHHHH
BAP
FWI
SH
A PASS?!
YEAHHHH

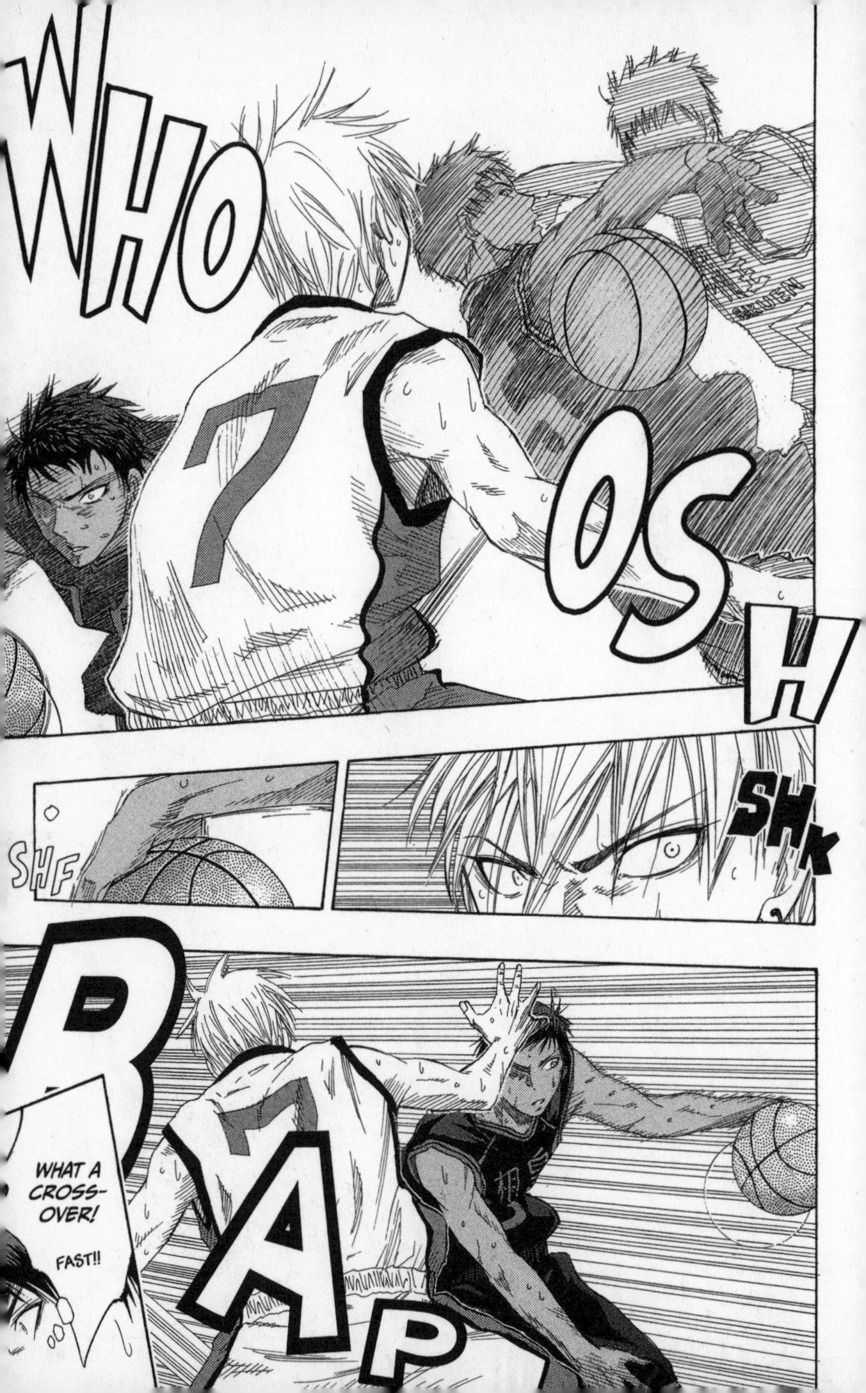
WHOOSH
SHK
SHF
BRAP
WHAT A CROSS-OVER!
FAST!!

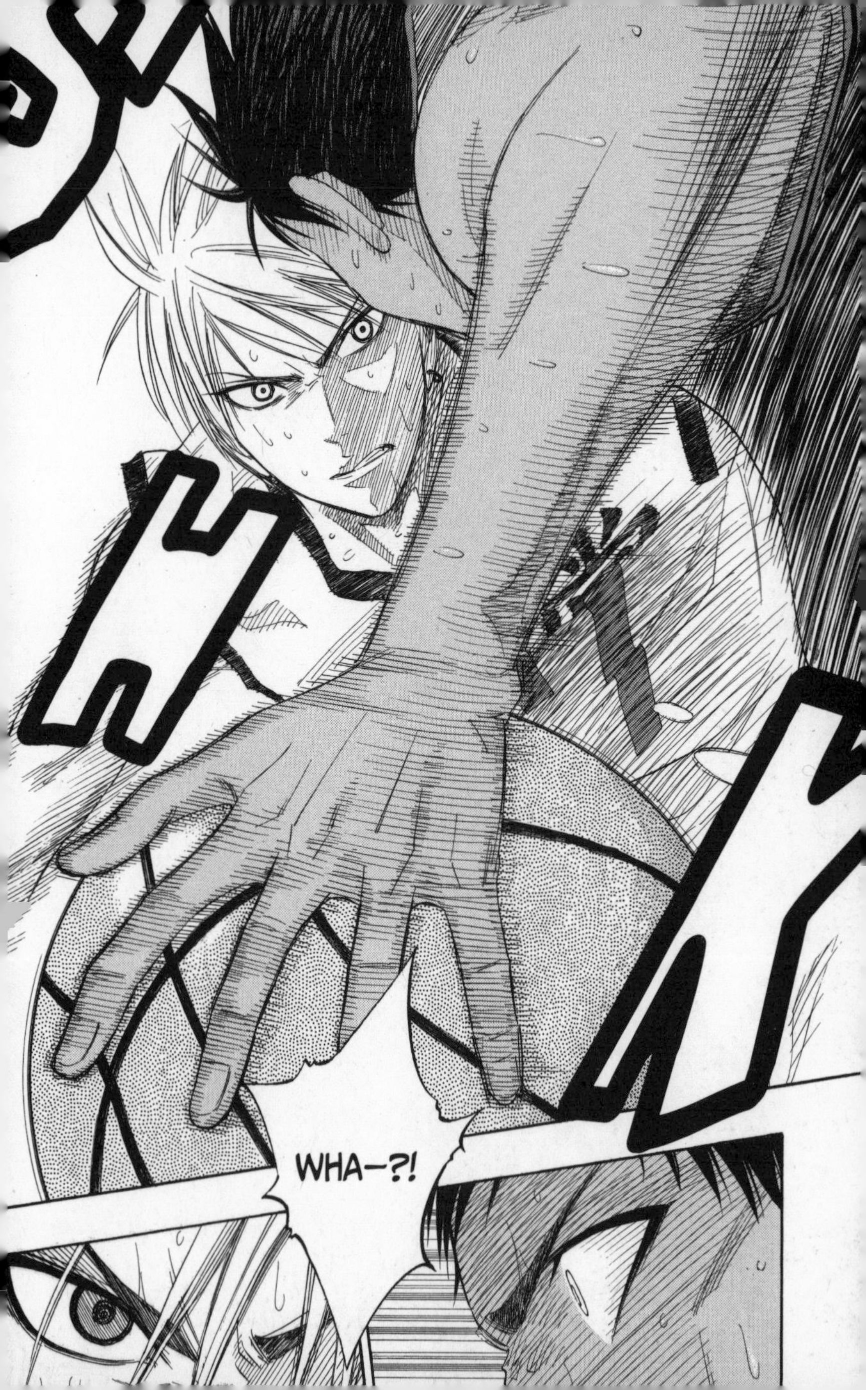
WHA-?!

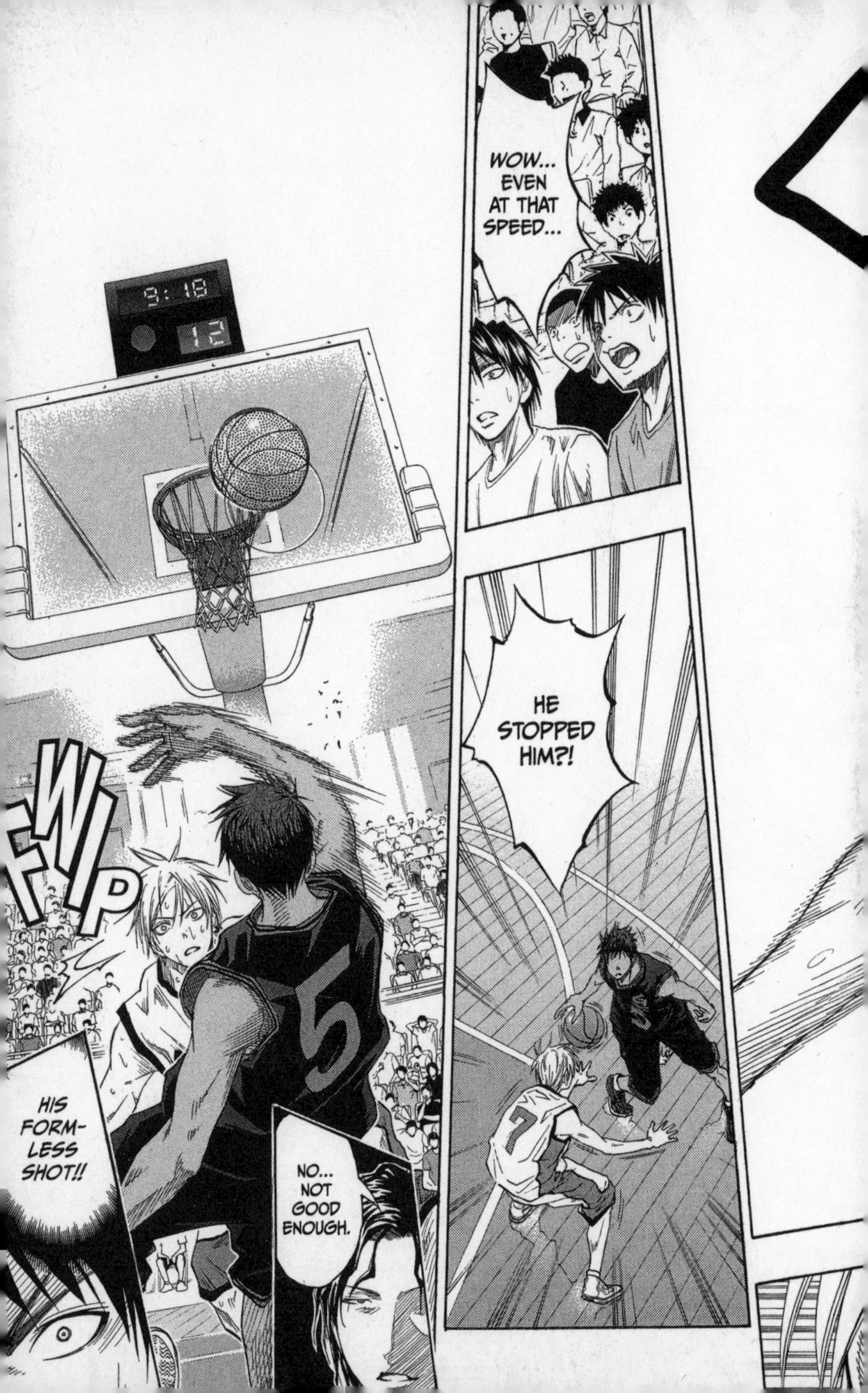
WOW... EVEN AT THAT SPEED...
HE STOPPED HIM?!
9:18
12
FWIP
HIS FORM-LESS SHOT!!
NO... NOT GOOD ENOUGH.

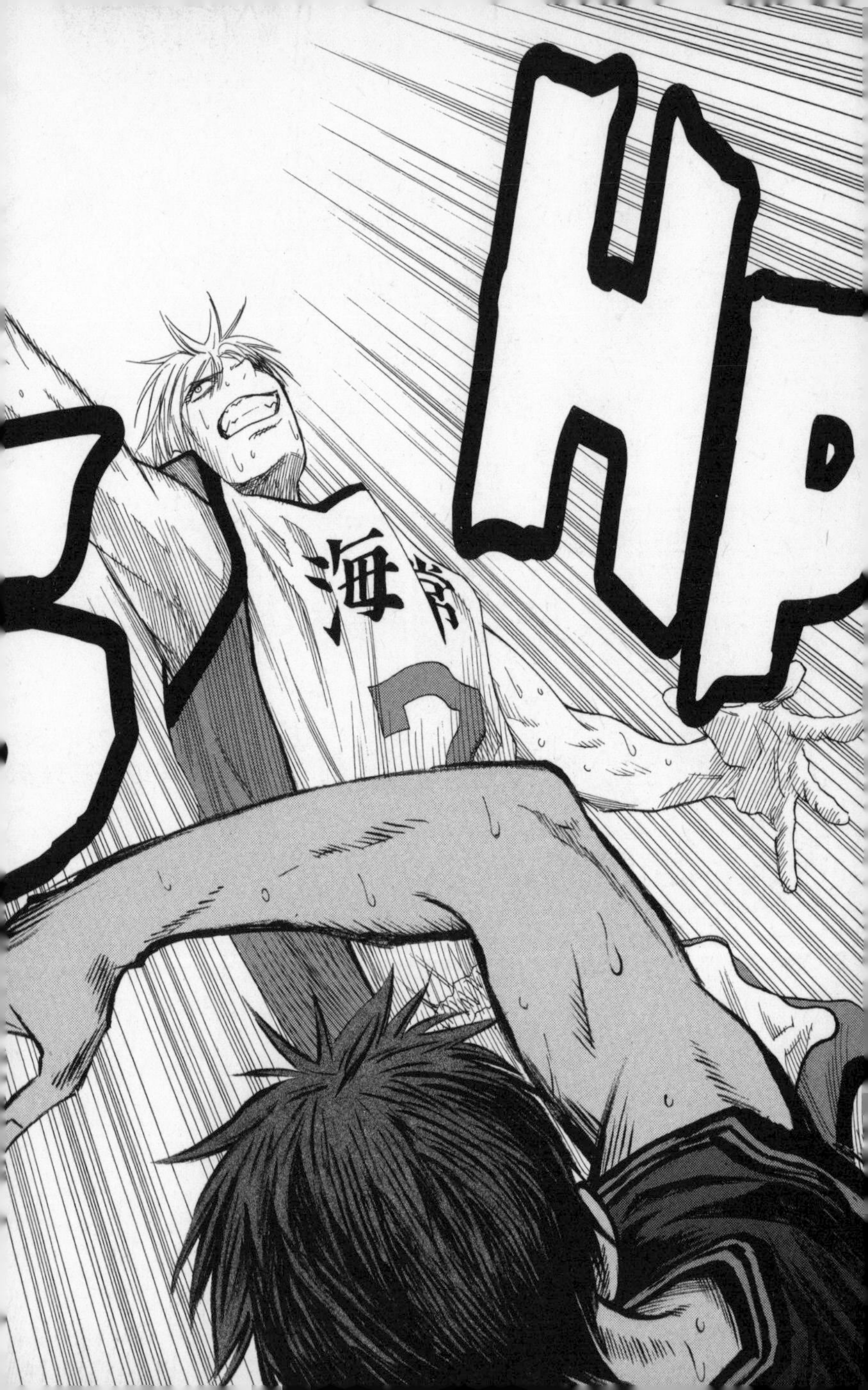
海常

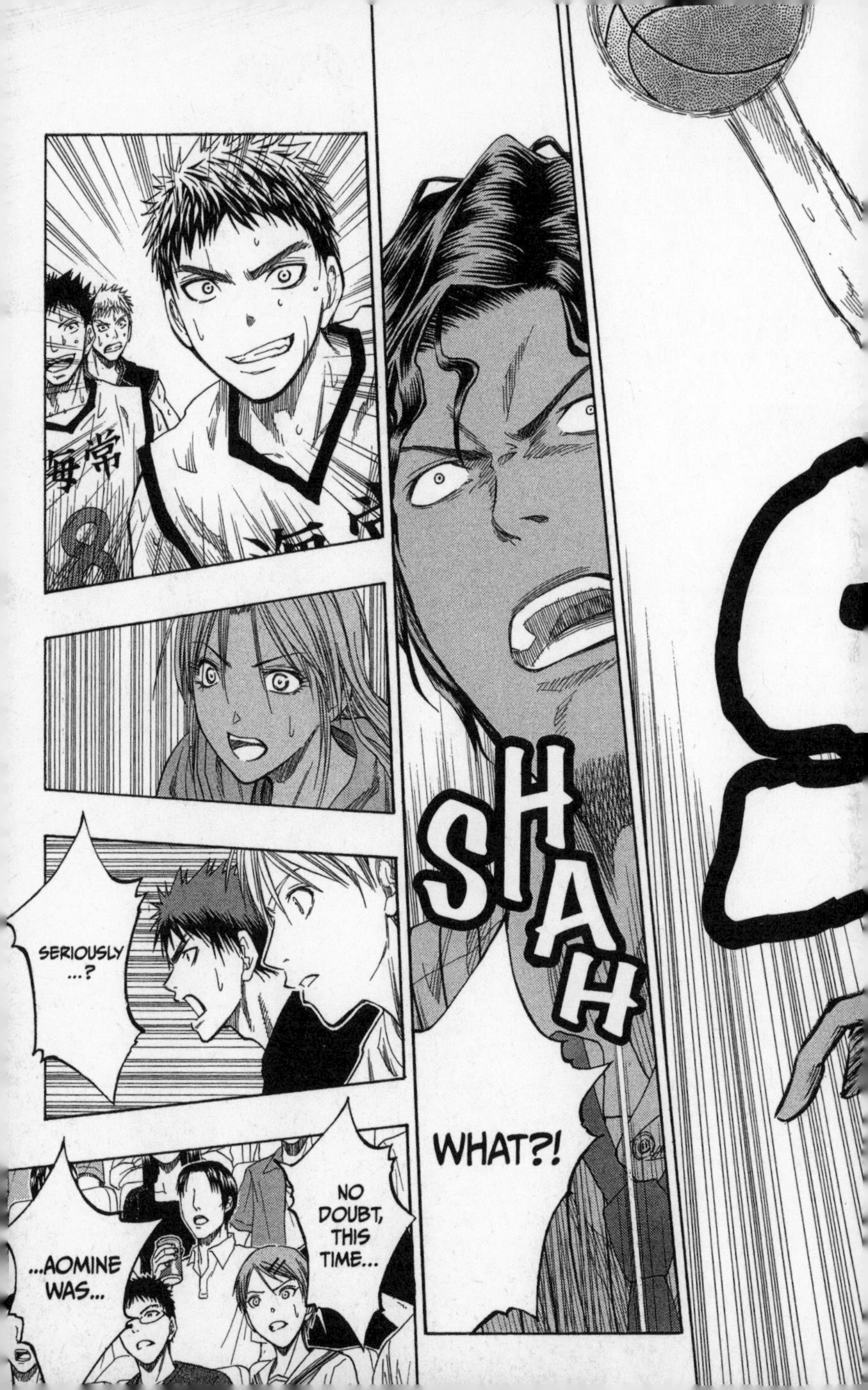
SHAH
WHAT?!
SERIOUSLY ...?
NO DOUBT, THIS TIME...
...AOMINE WAS...

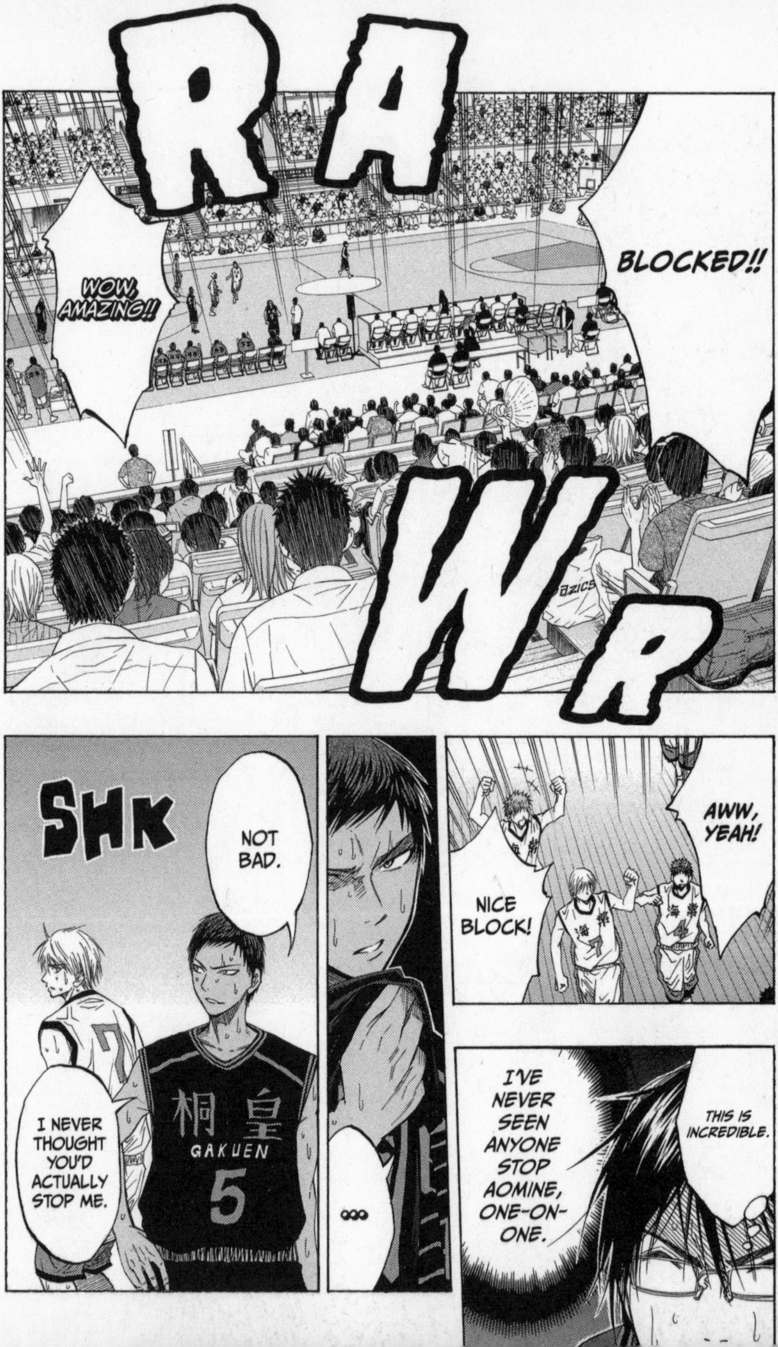
RAWR
BLOCKED!!
WOW, AMAZING!!
AWW, YEAH!
NICE BLOCK!
THIS IS INCREDIBLE.
I'VE NEVER SEEN ANYONE STOP AOMINE, ONE-ON-ONE.
...
SHK
NOT BAD.
I NEVER THOUGHT YOU'D ACTUALLY STOP ME.
桐皇
GAKUEN
5

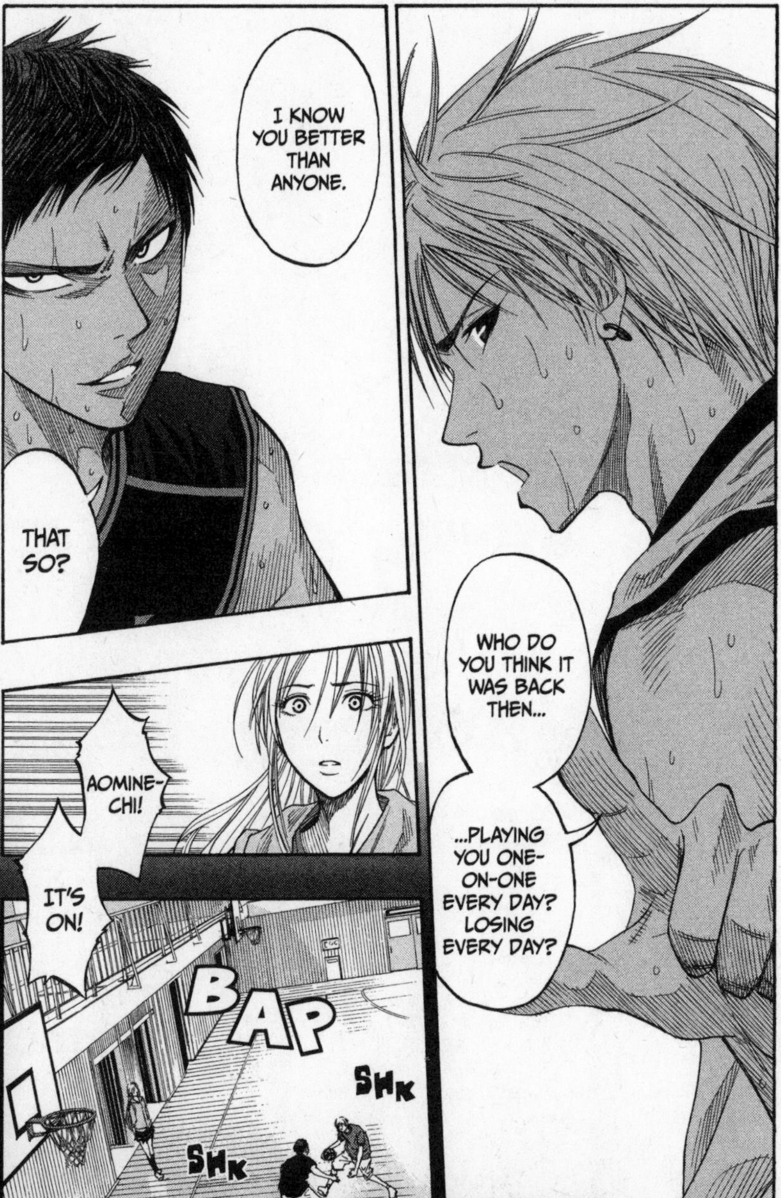
WHO DO YOU THINK IT WAS BACK THEN...
...PLAYING YOU ONE-ON-ONE EVERY DAY? LOSING EVERY DAY?
I KNOW YOU BETTER THAN ANYONE.
THAT SO?
AOMINE-CHI!
IT'S ON!
BAP
SHK
SHK

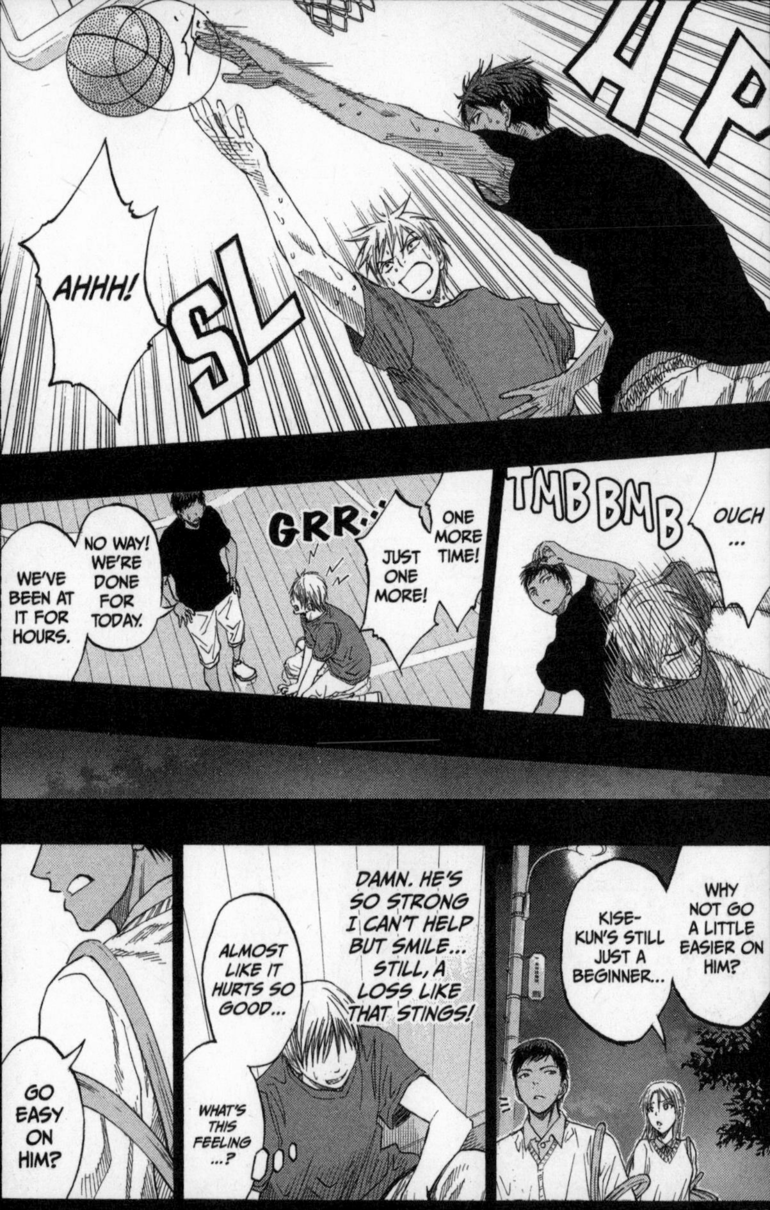
AP
SL
AHHH!
TMB BMB
OUCH ...
ONE MORE TIME!
JUST ONE MORE!
GRR...
NO WAY! WE'RE DONE FOR TODAY.
WE'VE BEEN AT IT FOR HOURS.
WHY NOT GO A LITTLE EASIER ON HIM?
KISE-KUN'S STILL JUST A BEGINNER...
DAMN. HE'S SO STRONG I CAN'T HELP BUT SMILE... STILL, A LOSS LIKE THAT STINGS!
ALMOST LIKE IT HURTS SO GOOD...
WHAT'S THIS FEELING ...?
GO EASY ON HIM?

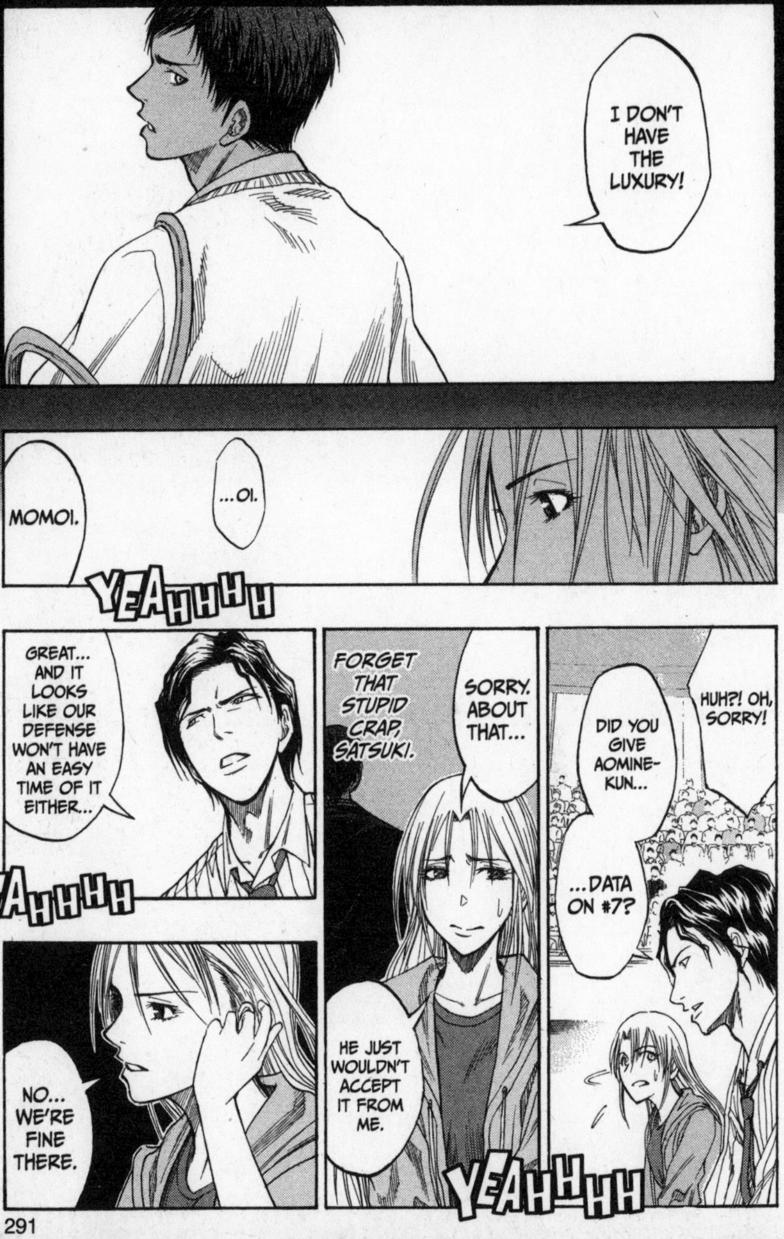
I DON'T HAVE THE LUXURY!
...OI.
MOMOI.
YEAHHHHH
HUH?! OH, SORRY!
DID YOU GIVE AOMINE-KUN...
...DATA ON #7?
SORRY. ABOUT THAT...
FORGET THAT STUPID CRAP, SATSUKI.
HE JUST WOULDN'T ACCEPT IT FROM ME.
YEAHHHHH
GREAT... AND IT LOOKS LIKE OUR DEFENSE WON'T HAVE AN EASY TIME OF IT EITHER...
YEAHHHHH
NO... WE'RE FINE THERE.

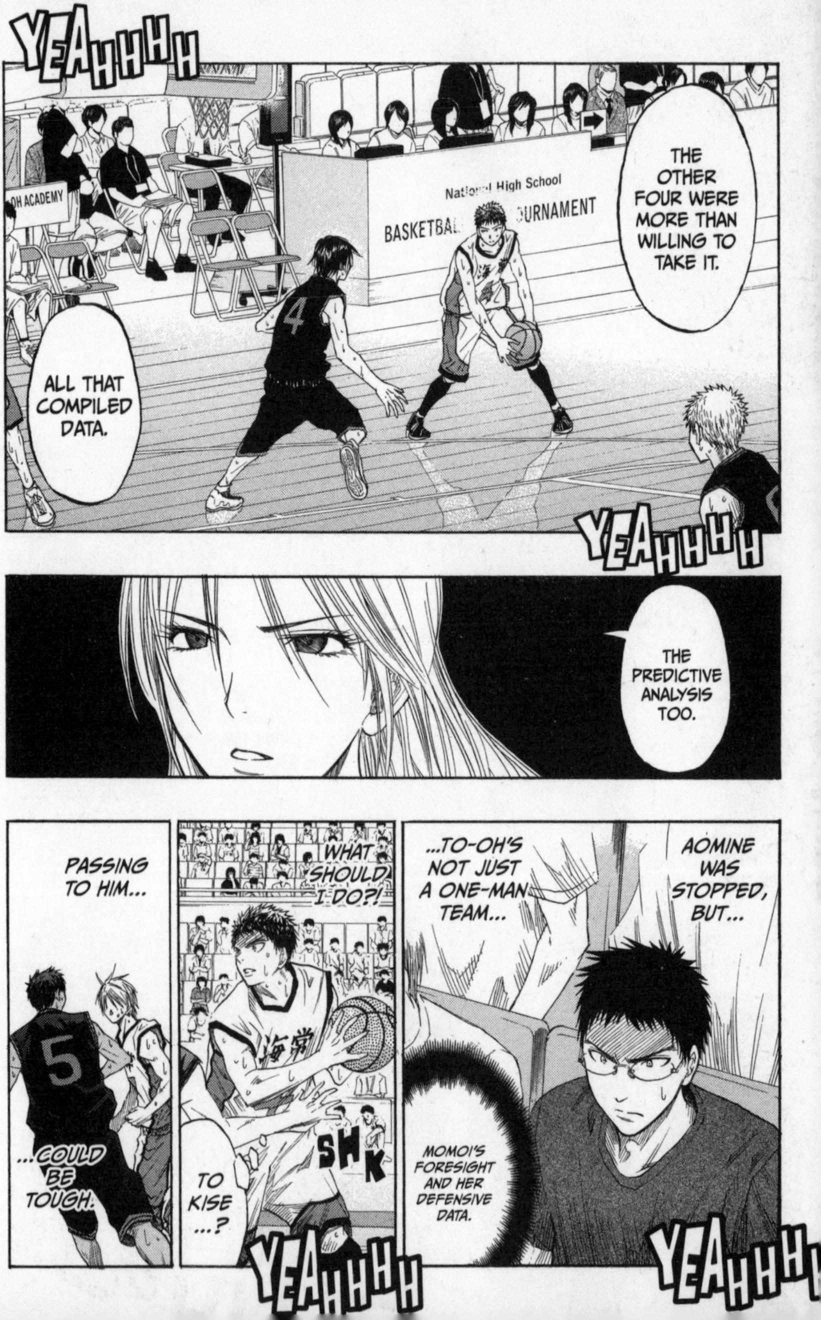
YEAHHHH
THE OTHER FOUR WERE MORE THAN WILLING TO TAKE IT.
National High School
ALL THAT COMPILED DATA.
YEAHHHH
THE PREDICTIVE ANALYSIS TOO.
AOMINE WAS STOPPED, BUT...
...TO-OH'S NOT JUST A ONE-MAN TEAM...
MOMOI'S FORESIGHT AND HER DEFENSIVE DATA.
YEAHHHH
WHAT SHOULD I DO?!
SHK
TO KISE ...?
YEAHHHH
PASSING TO HIM...
...COULD BE TOUGH.

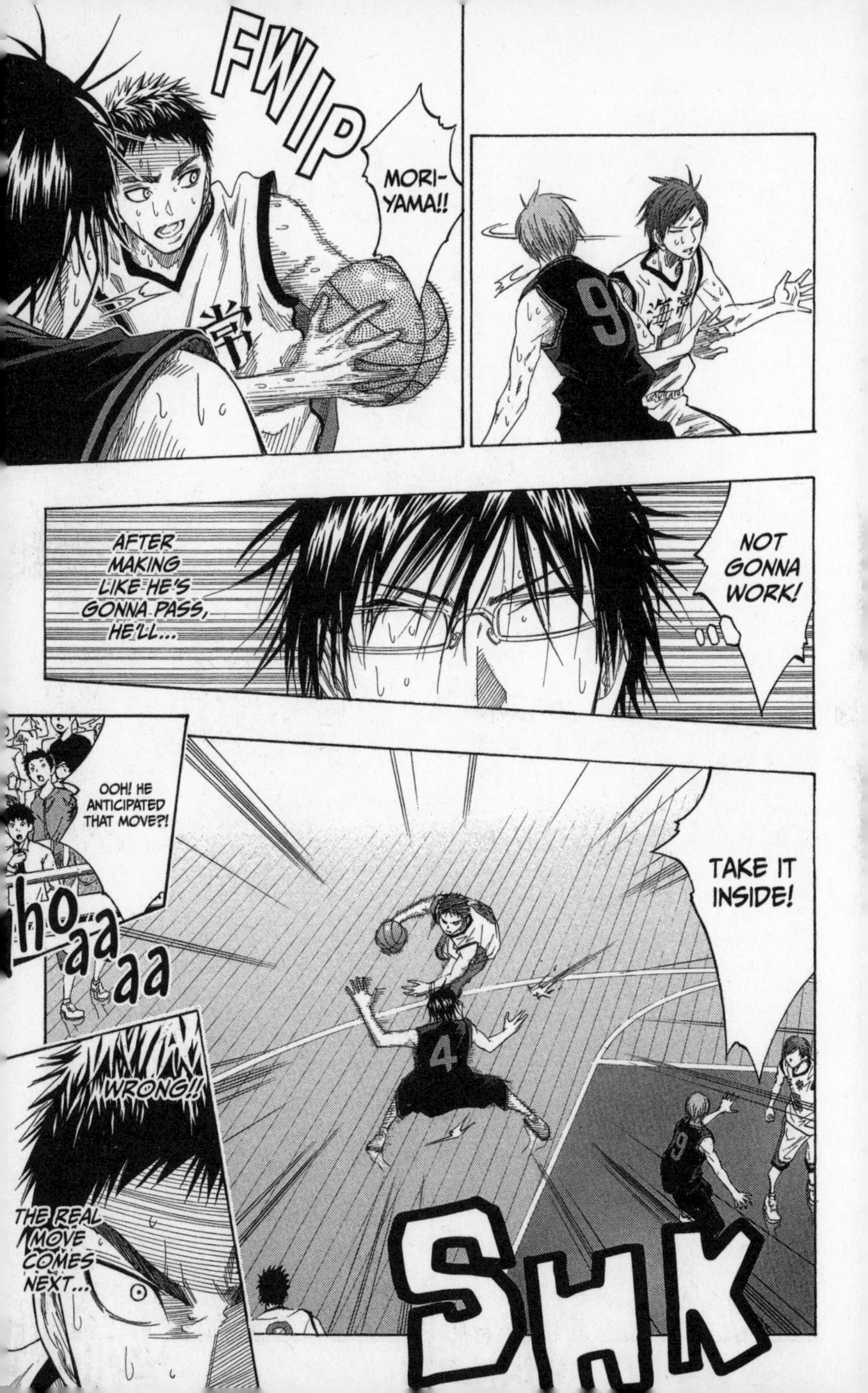
MORI-YAMA!!
FWIP
NOT GONNA WORK!
AFTER MAKING LIKE HE'S GONNA PASS, HE'LL...
TAKE IT INSIDE!
OOH! HE ANTICIPATED THAT MOVE?!
hoaaaaa
SHK
WRONG!!
THE REAL MOVE COMES NEXT...

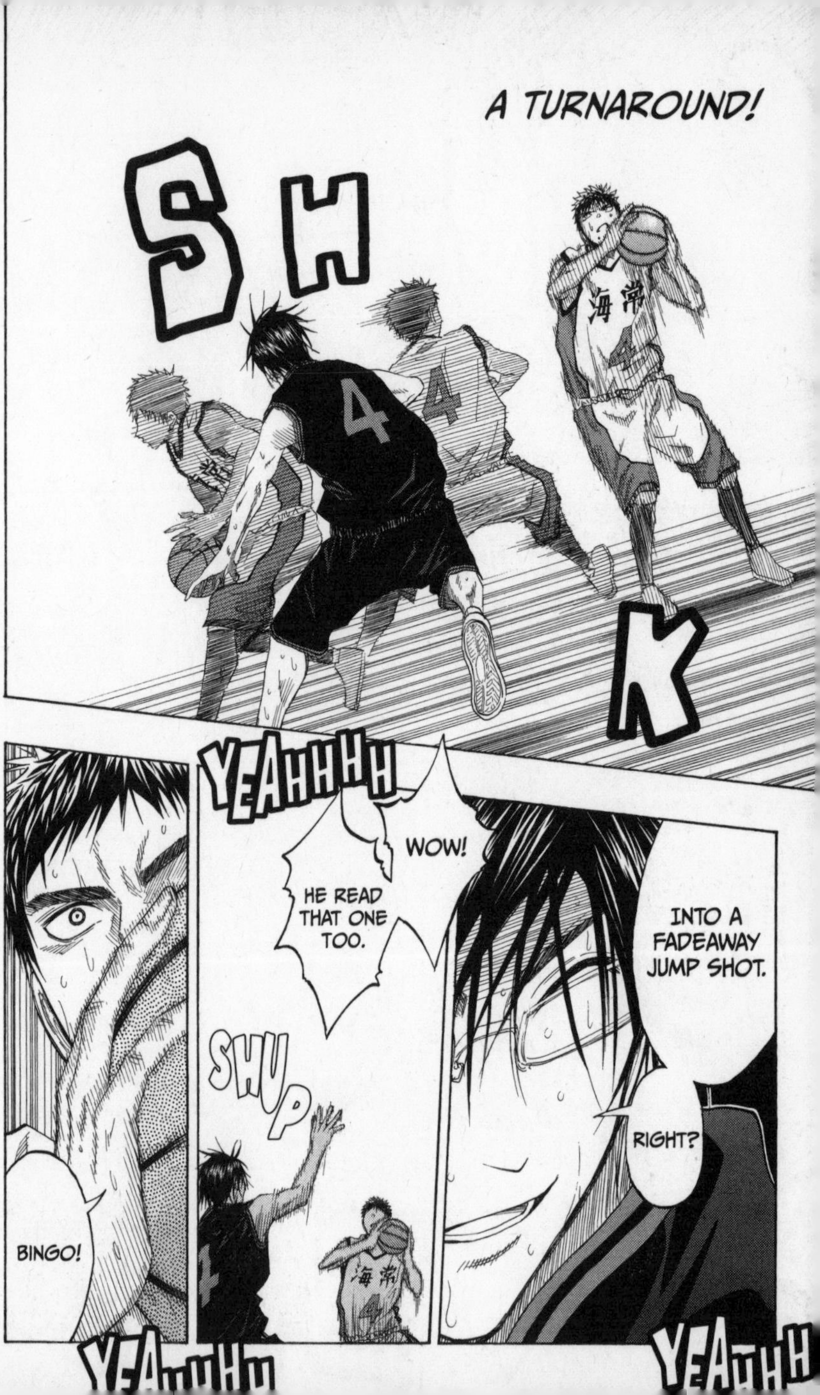
A TURNAROUND!
SHK
INTO A FADEAWAY JUMP SHOT.
RIGHT?
YEAHHH
YEAHHHHH
WOW!
HE READ THAT ONE TOO.
SHUP
BINGO!
YEAHHHH

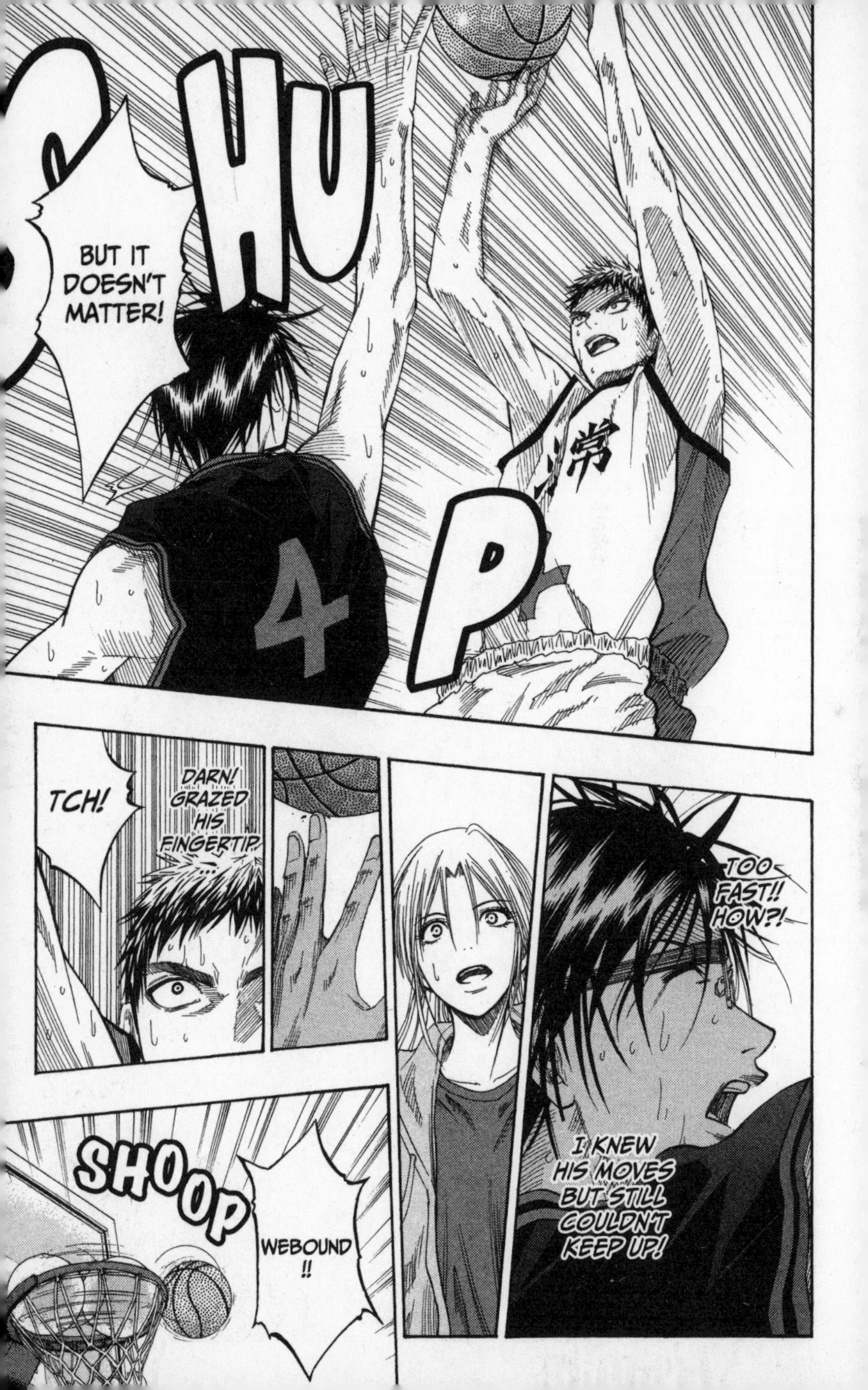
SHUP
BUT IT DOESN'T MATTER!
TOO FAST!! HOW?!
I KNEW HIS MOVES BUT STILL COULDN'T KEEP UP!
DARN! GRAZED HIS FINGERTIP
TCH!
SHOOP
WEBOUND !!

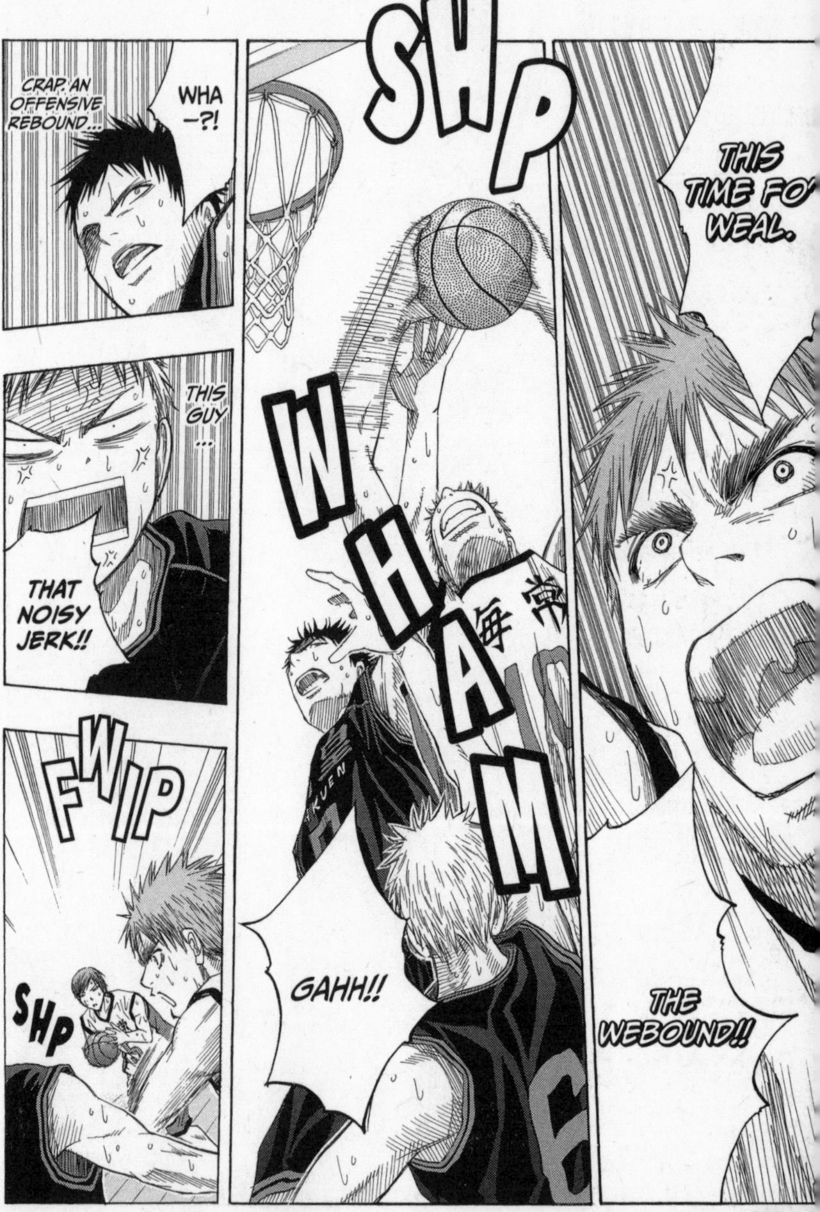
THIS TIME FO' WEAL.
THE WEBOUND!!
SHP
WHAM
GAHH!!
WHA —?!
CRAP. AN OFFENSIVE REBOUND...
THIS GUY ...
THAT NOISY JERK!!
FWIP
SHP

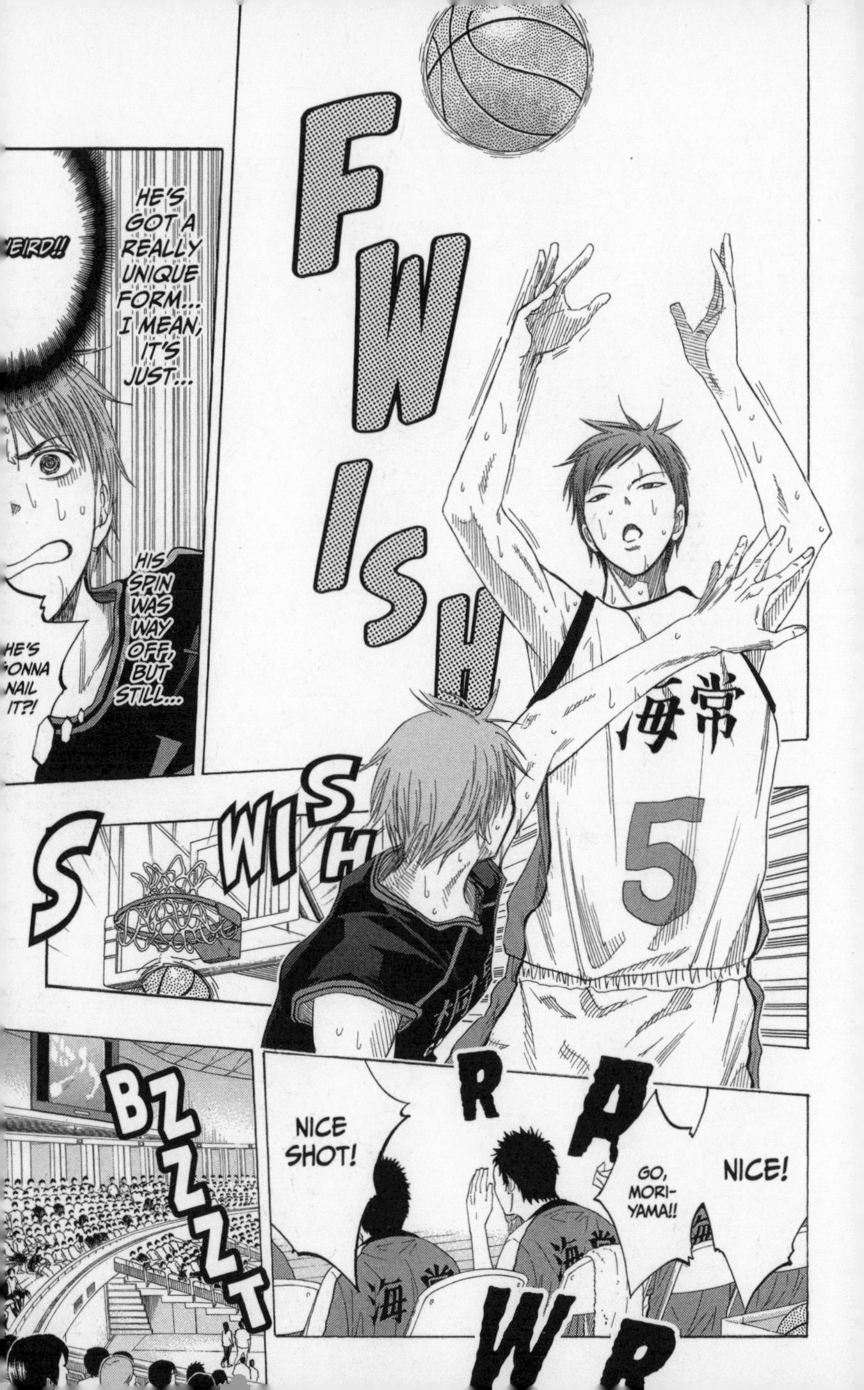
FWISH
HE'S GOT A REALLY UNIQUE FORM... I MEAN, IT'S JUST...
EIRD!!
HIS SPIN WAS WAY OFF, BUT STILL...
HE'S GONNA NAIL IT?!
SWISH
RAWR
NICE!
GO, MORI-YAMA!!
NICE SHOT!
BZZZZT

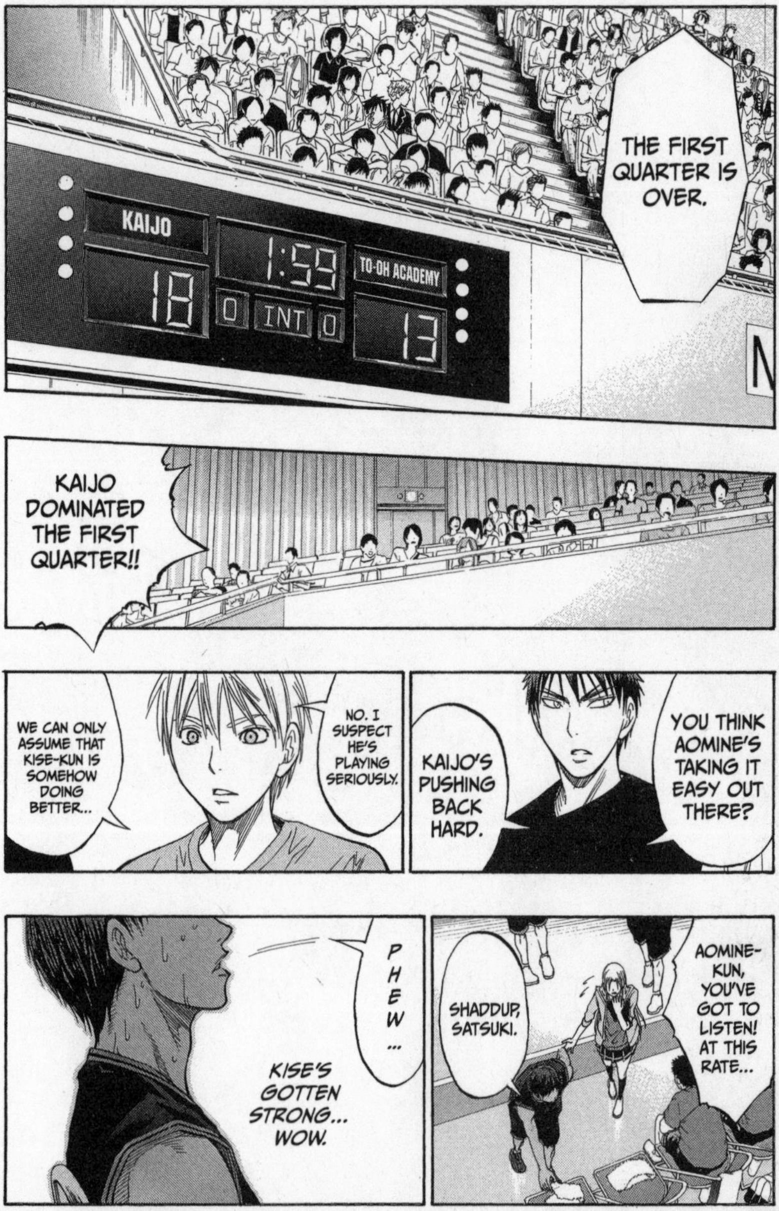
THE FIRST QUARTER IS OVER.
KAIJO
1:59
TO-OH ACADEMY
18
0 INT 0
13
KAIJO DOMINATED THE FIRST QUARTER!!
YOU THINK AOMINE'S TAKING IT EASY OUT THERE?
KAIJO'S PUSHING BACK HARD.
NO. I SUSPECT HE'S PLAYING SERIOUSLY.
WE CAN ONLY ASSUME THAT KISE-KUN IS SOMEHOW DOING BETTER...
AOMINE-KUN, YOU'VE GOT TO LISTEN! AT THIS RATE...
SHADDUP, SATSUKI.
PHEW...
KISE'S GOTTEN STRONG... WOW.

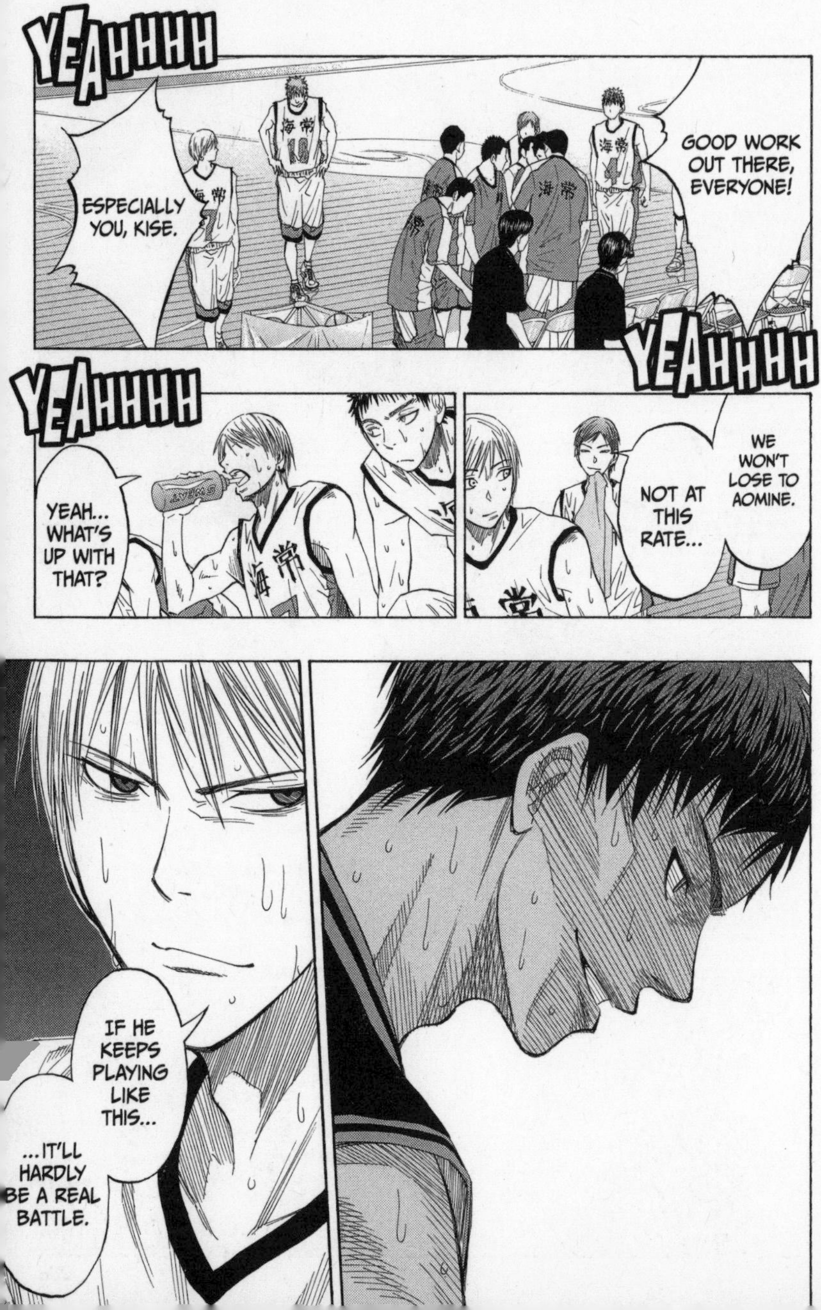
GOOD WORK OUT THERE, EVERYONE!
ESPECIALLY YOU, KISE.
YEAHHHH
YEAHHHH
WE WON'T LOSE TO AOMINE.
NOT AT THIS RATE...
YEAHHHH
YEAH... WHAT'S UP WITH THAT?
IF HE KEEPS PLAYING LIKE THIS...
...IT'LL HARDLY BE A REAL BATTLE.

KUROKO'S BASKETBALL BLOOPERS

TAKE 7

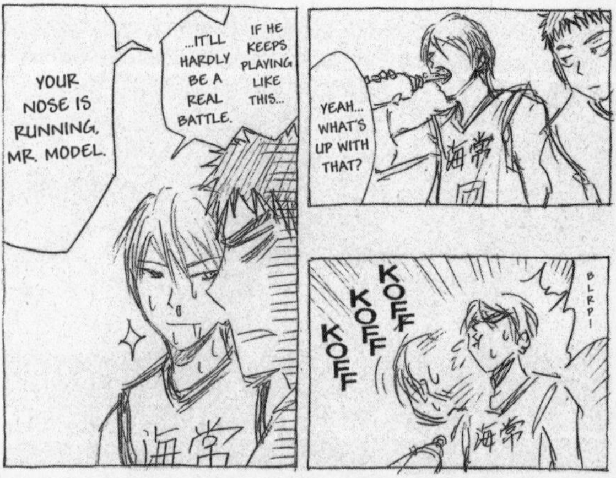

YEAH... WHAT'S UP WITH THAT?
BLRP!
KOFF
KOFF
KOFF
IF HE KEEPS PLAYING LIKE THIS...
...IT'LL HARDLY BE A REAL BATTLE.
YOUR NOSE IS RUNNING, MR. MODEL.

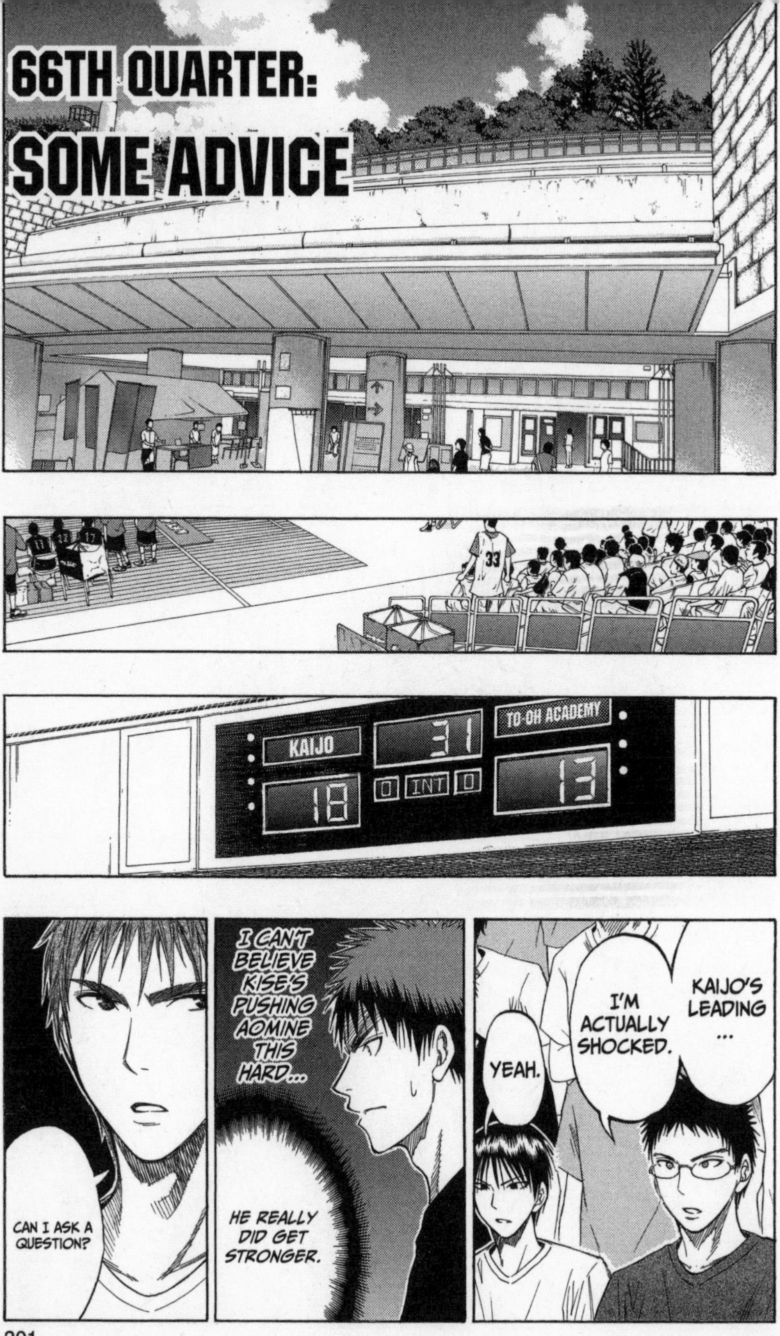
66TH QUARTER:
SOME ADVICE
TO OH ACADEMY
31
KAIJO
18
0
INT
0
13
KAIJO'S LEADING ...
I'M ACTUALLY SHOCKED.
YEAH.
I CAN'T BELIEVE KISE'S PUSHING AOMINE THIS HARD...
HE REALLY DID GET STRONGER.
CAN I ASK A QUESTION?

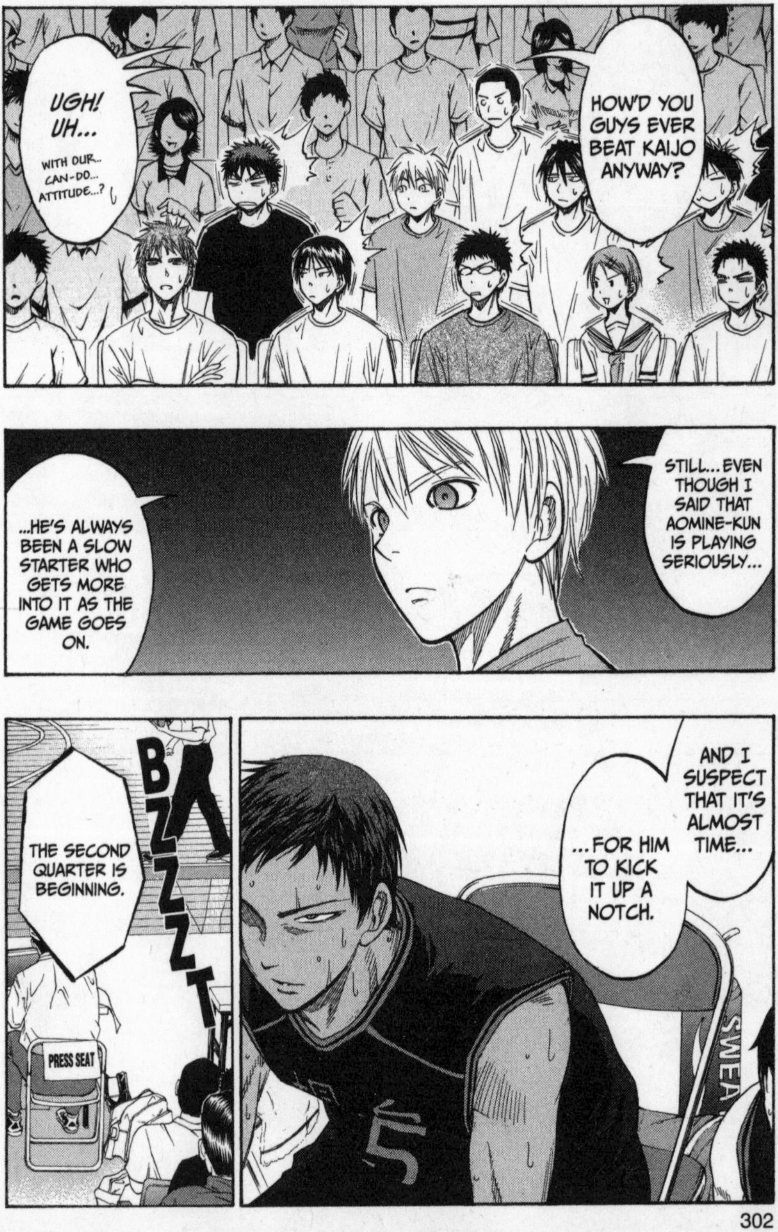
HOW'D YOU GUYS EVER BEAT KAIJO ANYWAY?
UGH! UH...
WITH OUR... CAN-DO... ATTITUDE...?
STILL... EVEN THOUGH I SAID THAT AOMINE-KUN IS PLAYING SERIOUSLY...
...HE'S ALWAYS BEEN A SLOW STARTER WHO GETS MORE INTO IT AS THE GAME GOES ON.
AND I SUSPECT THAT IT'S ALMOST TIME...
...FOR HIM TO KICK IT UP A NOTCH.
BZZZT
THE SECOND QUARTER IS BEGINNING.
PRESS SEAT

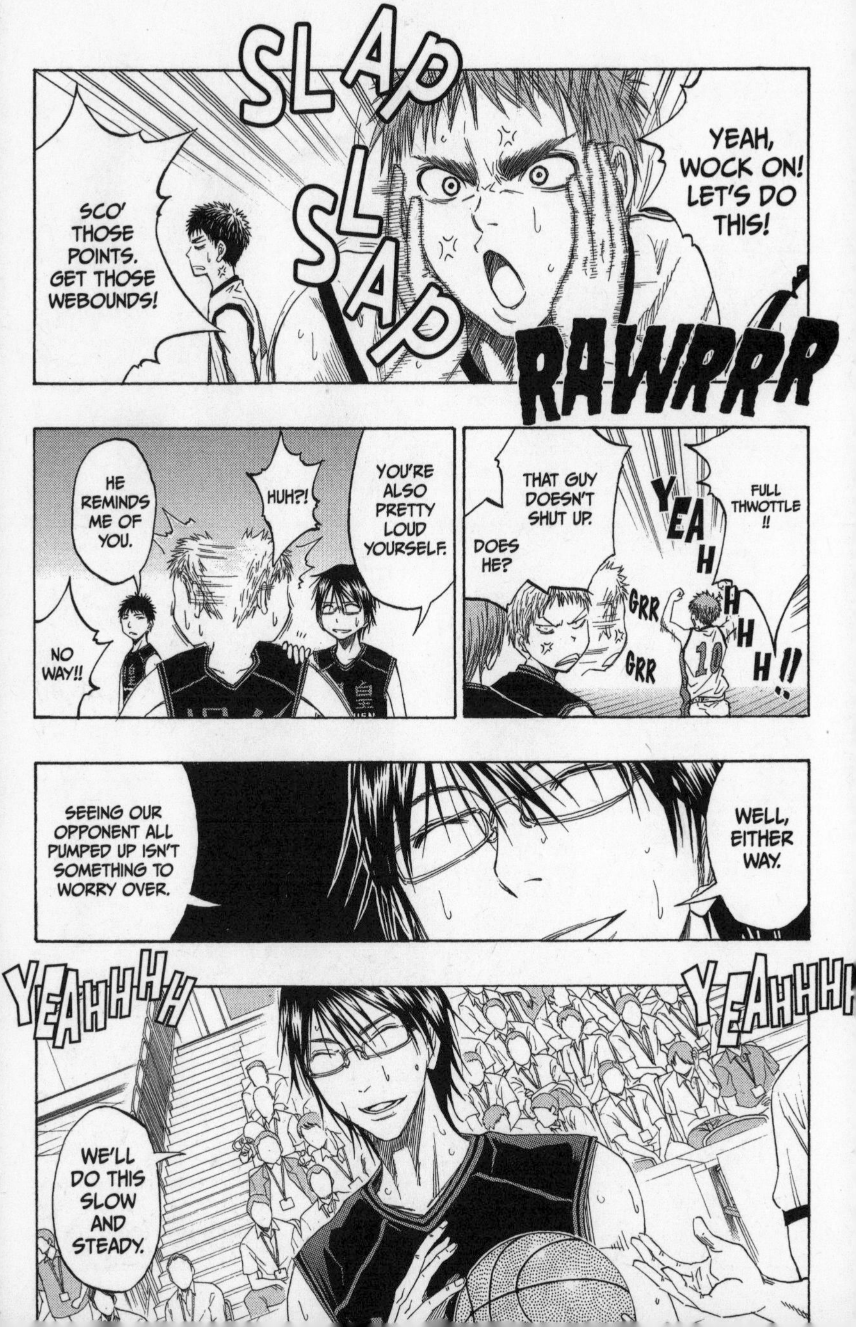
SLAP
YEAH, WOCK ON! LET'S DO THIS!
SLAP
SCO' THOSE POINTS. GET THOSE WEBOUNDS!
RAWRRR
FULL THWOTTLE!!
YEAHHHHH!!
THAT GUY DOESN'T SHUT UP.
GRR
GRR
DOES HE?
YOU'RE ALSO PRETTY LOUD YOURSELF.
HUH?!
HE REMINDS ME OF YOU.
NO WAY!!
WELL, EITHER WAY.
SEEING OUR OPPONENT ALL PUMPED UP ISN'T SOMETHING TO WORRY OVER.
YEAHHHH
YEAHHHHH
WE'LL DO THIS SLOW AND STEADY.

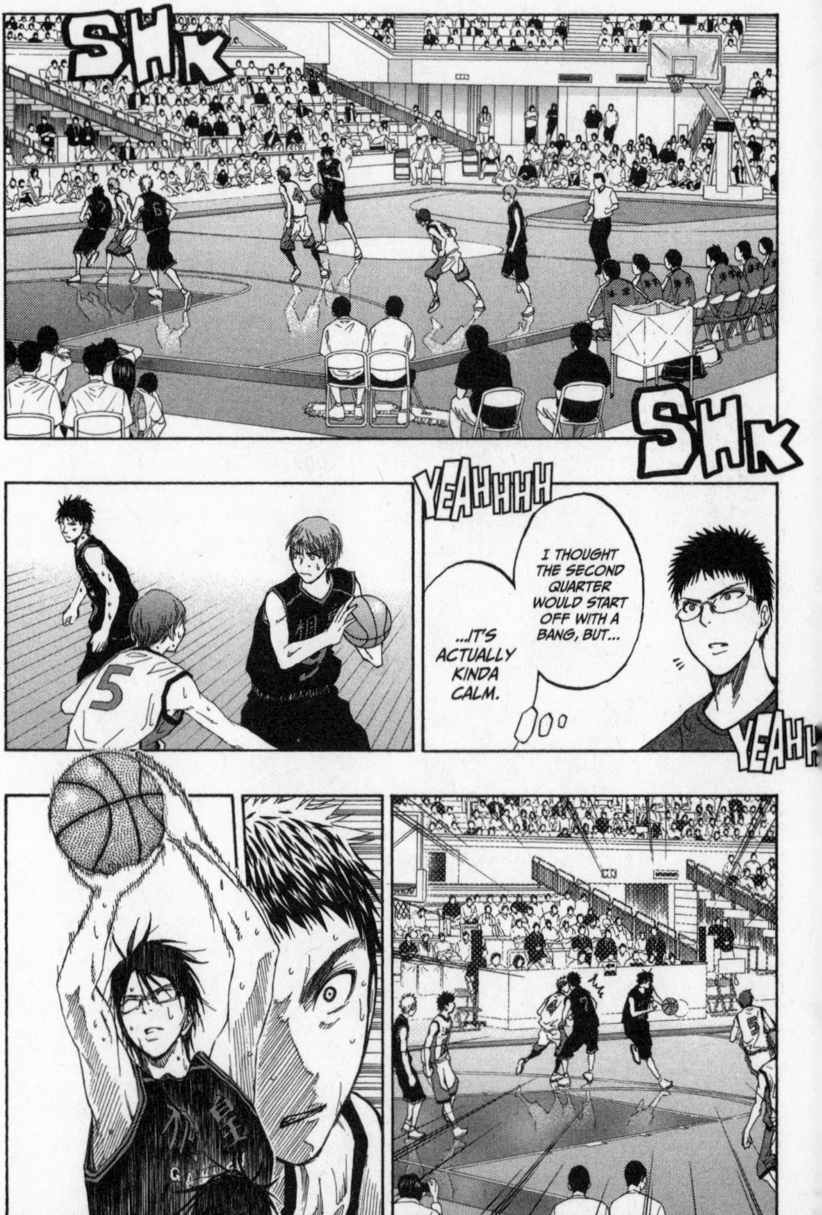
SHK
SHK
YEAHHHH
I THOUGHT THE SECOND QUARTER WOULD START OFF WITH A BANG, BUT...
...IT'S ACTUALLY KINDA CALM.
YEAHH

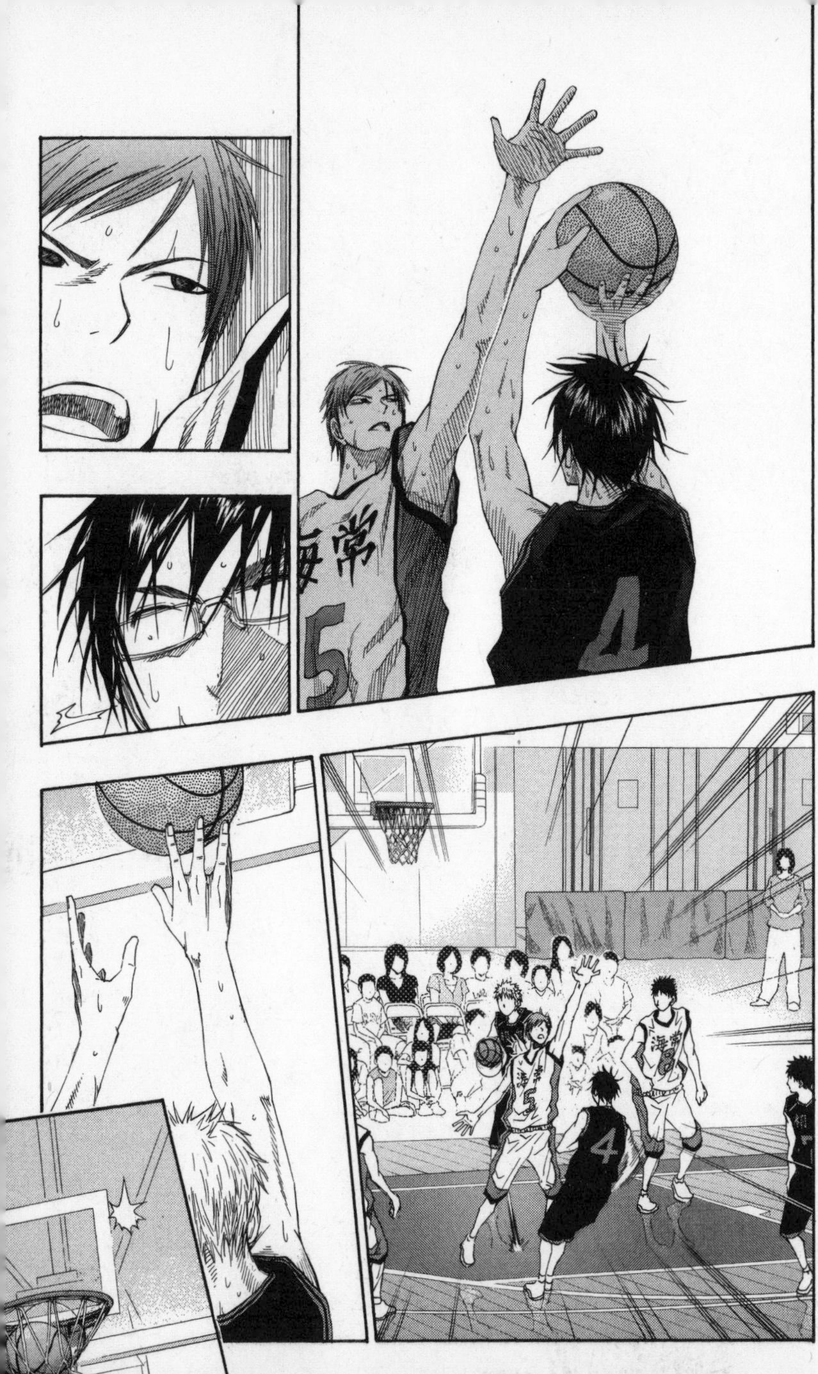

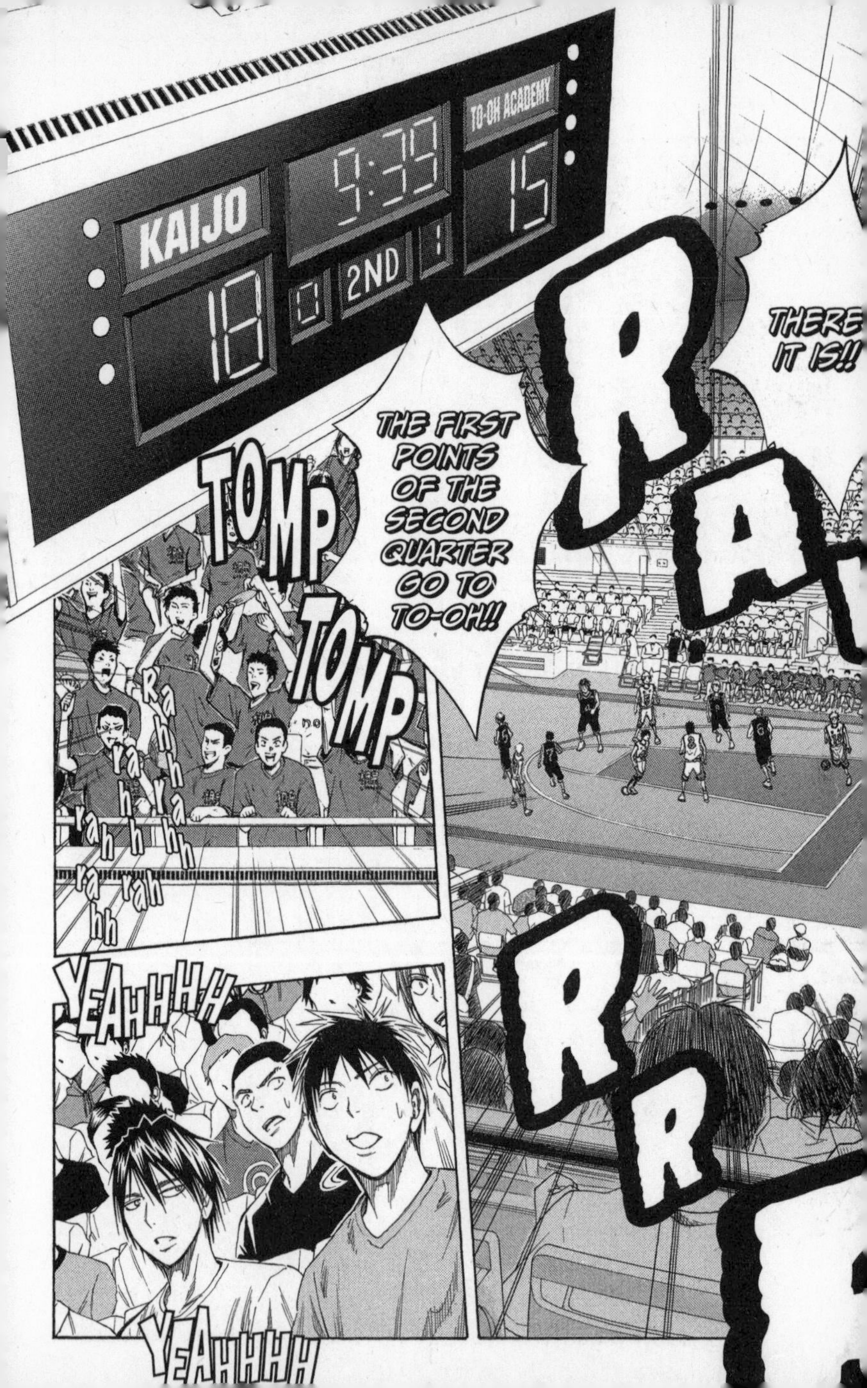
KAIJO
9:39
2ND
TO-OH ACADEMY
18
15
THERE IT IS!!
RA
THE FIRST POINTS OF THE SECOND QUARTER GO TO TO-OH!!
TOMP
TOMP
rah
rah
RR
YEAHHHH
YEAHHHH

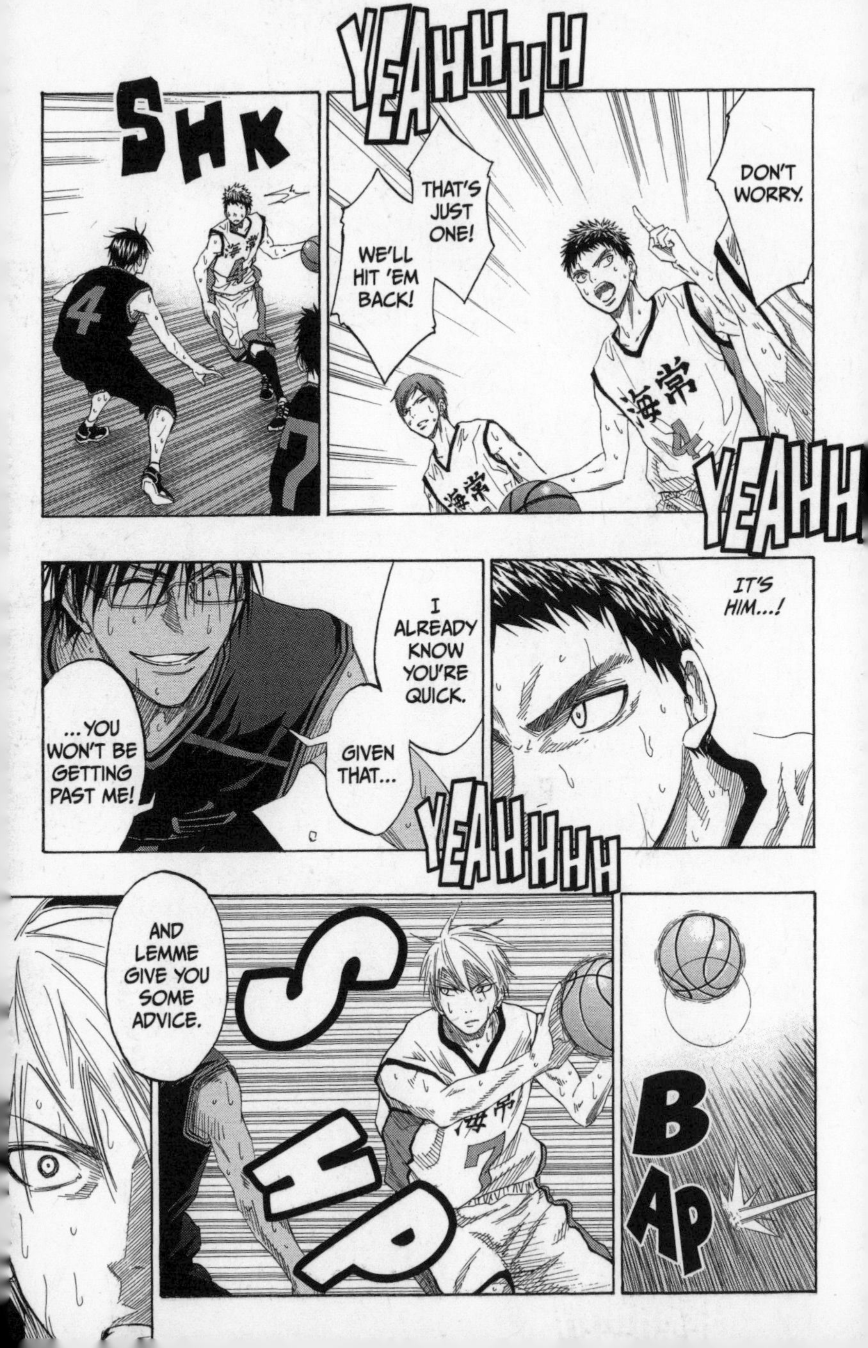
YEAHHHHH
DON'T WORRY.
THAT'S JUST ONE!
WE'LL HIT 'EM BACK!
YEAHH
SHK
IT'S HIM...!
I ALREADY KNOW YOU'RE QUICK.
GIVEN THAT...
...YOU WON'T BE GETTING PAST ME!
YEAHHHHH
BAP
AND LEMME GIVE YOU SOME ADVICE.
SHP

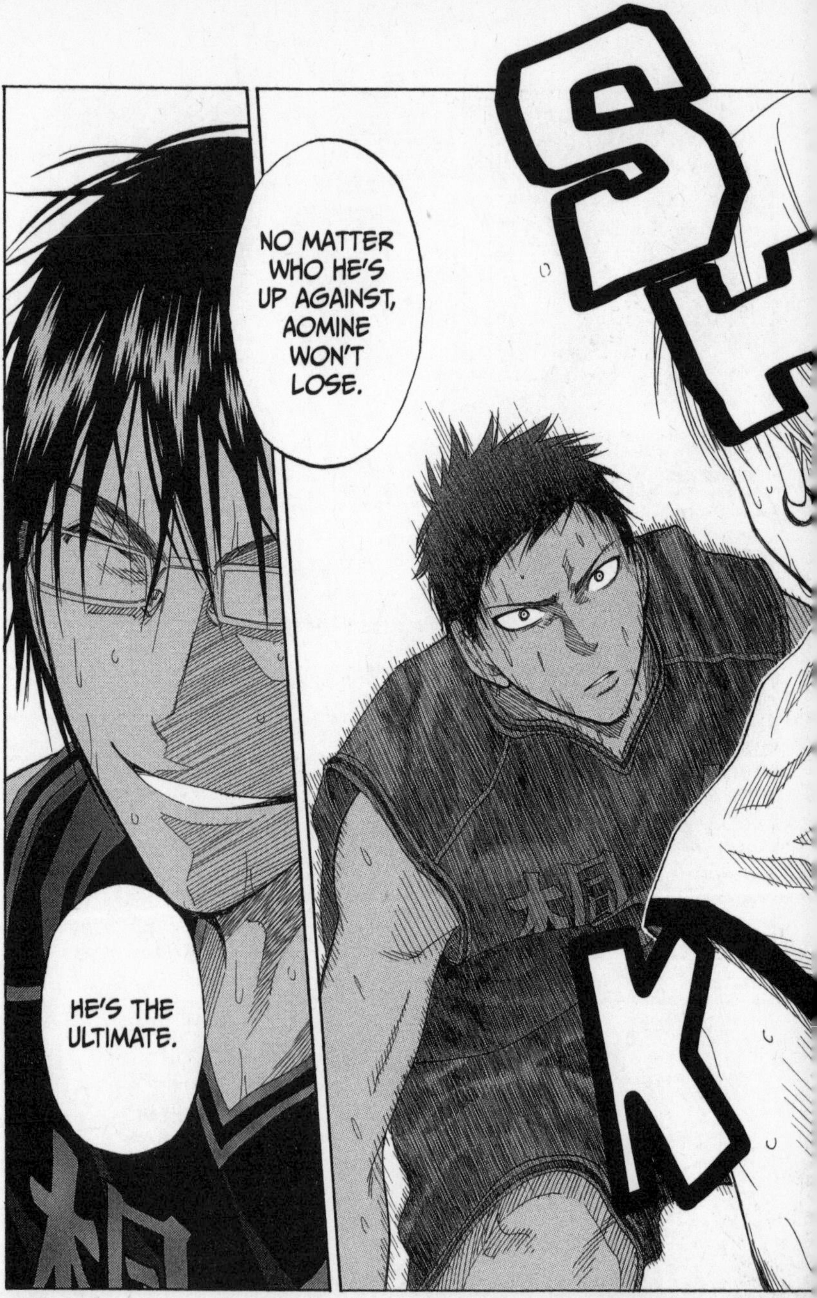
NO MATTER WHO HE'S UP AGAINST, AOMINE WON'T LOSE.
HE'S THE ULTIMATE.

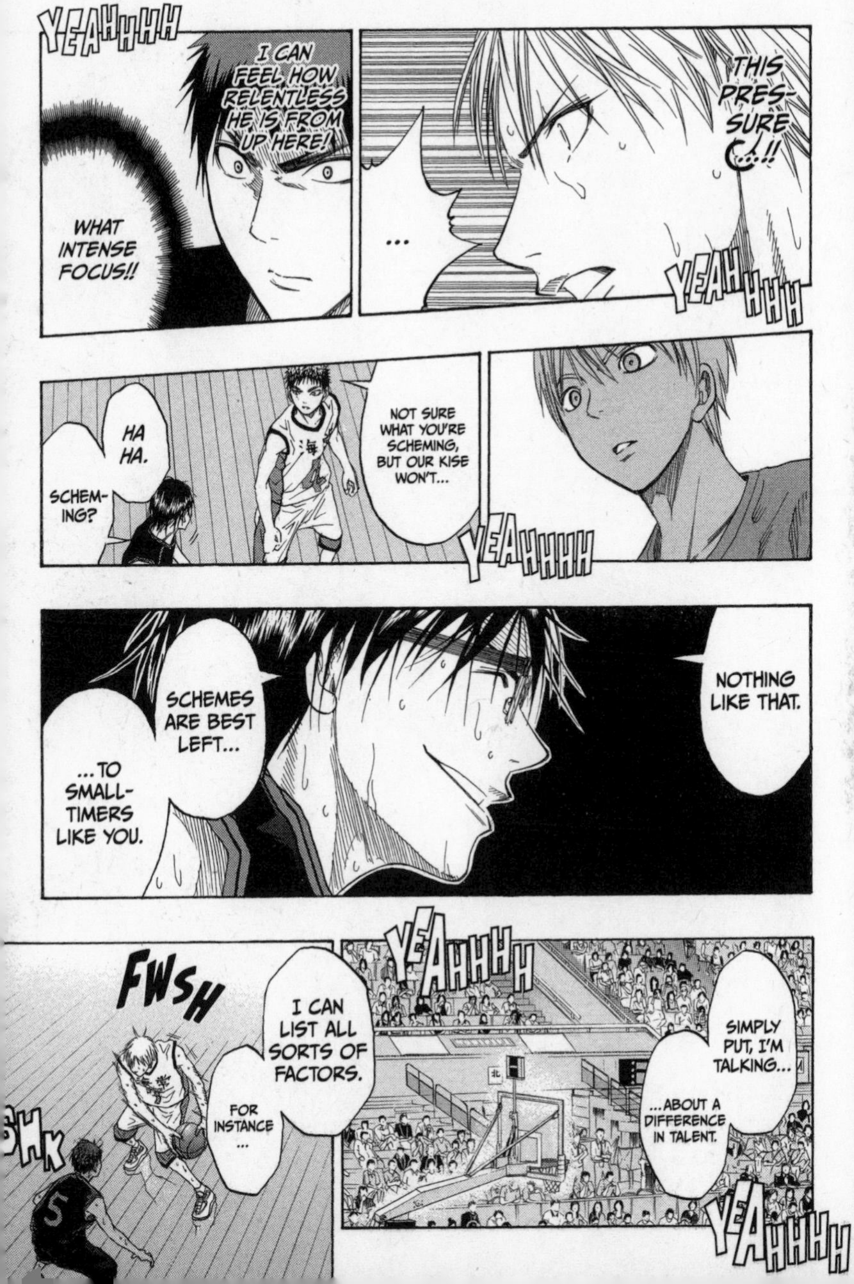
THIS PRESSURE...!!
...
YEAHHHH
YEAHHHH
I CAN FEEL HOW RELENTLESS HE IS FROM UP HERE!
WHAT INTENSE FOCUS!!
YEAHHHH
NOT SURE WHAT YOU'RE SCHEMING, BUT OUR KISE WON'T...
HA HA.
SCHEMING?
NOTHING LIKE THAT.
SCHEMES ARE BEST LEFT...
...TO SMALL-TIMERS LIKE YOU.
YEAHHHH
SIMPLY PUT, I'M TALKING...
...ABOUT A DIFFERENCE IN TALENT.
YEAHHHH
FWSH
I CAN LIST ALL SORTS OF FACTORS.
FOR INSTANCE...
SHK

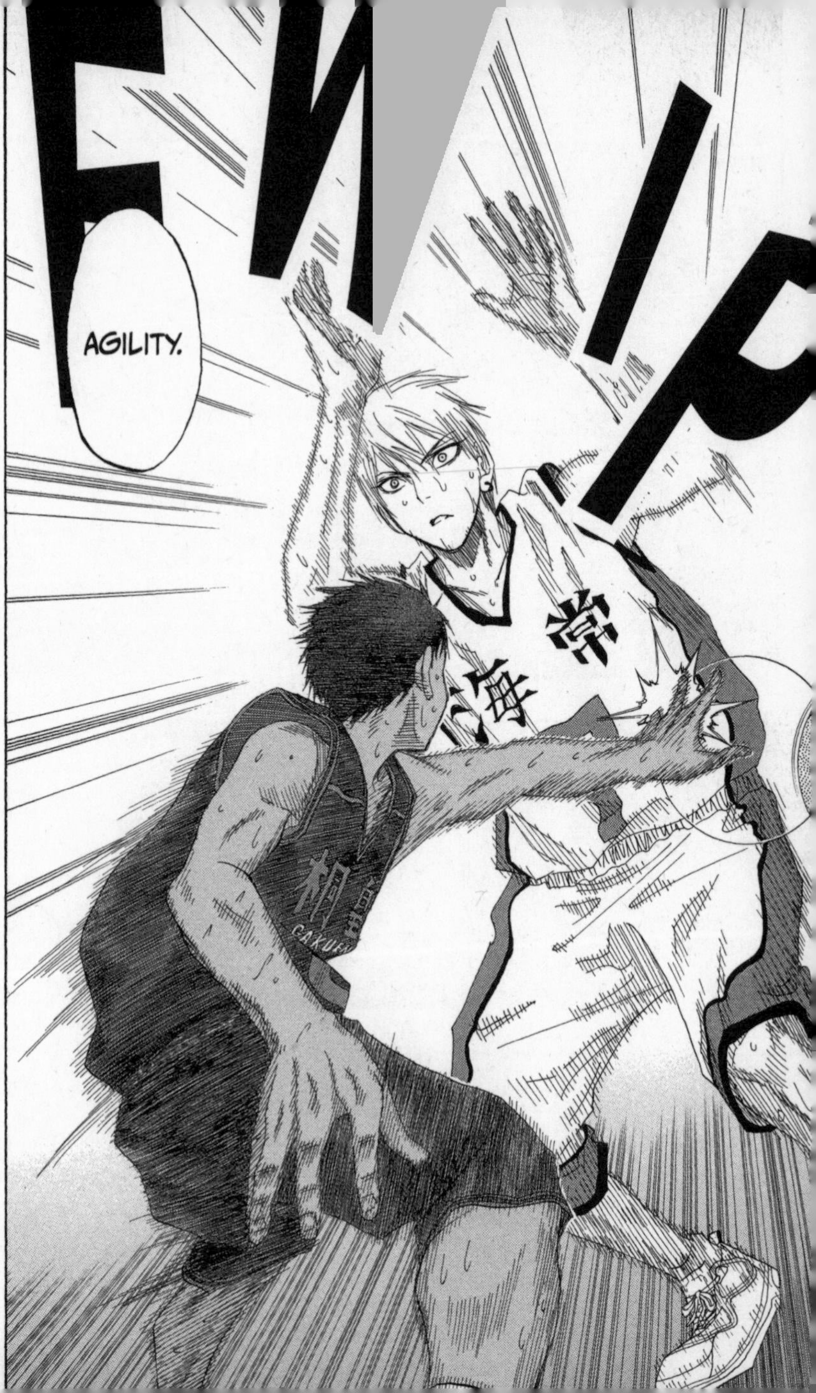
AGILITY.

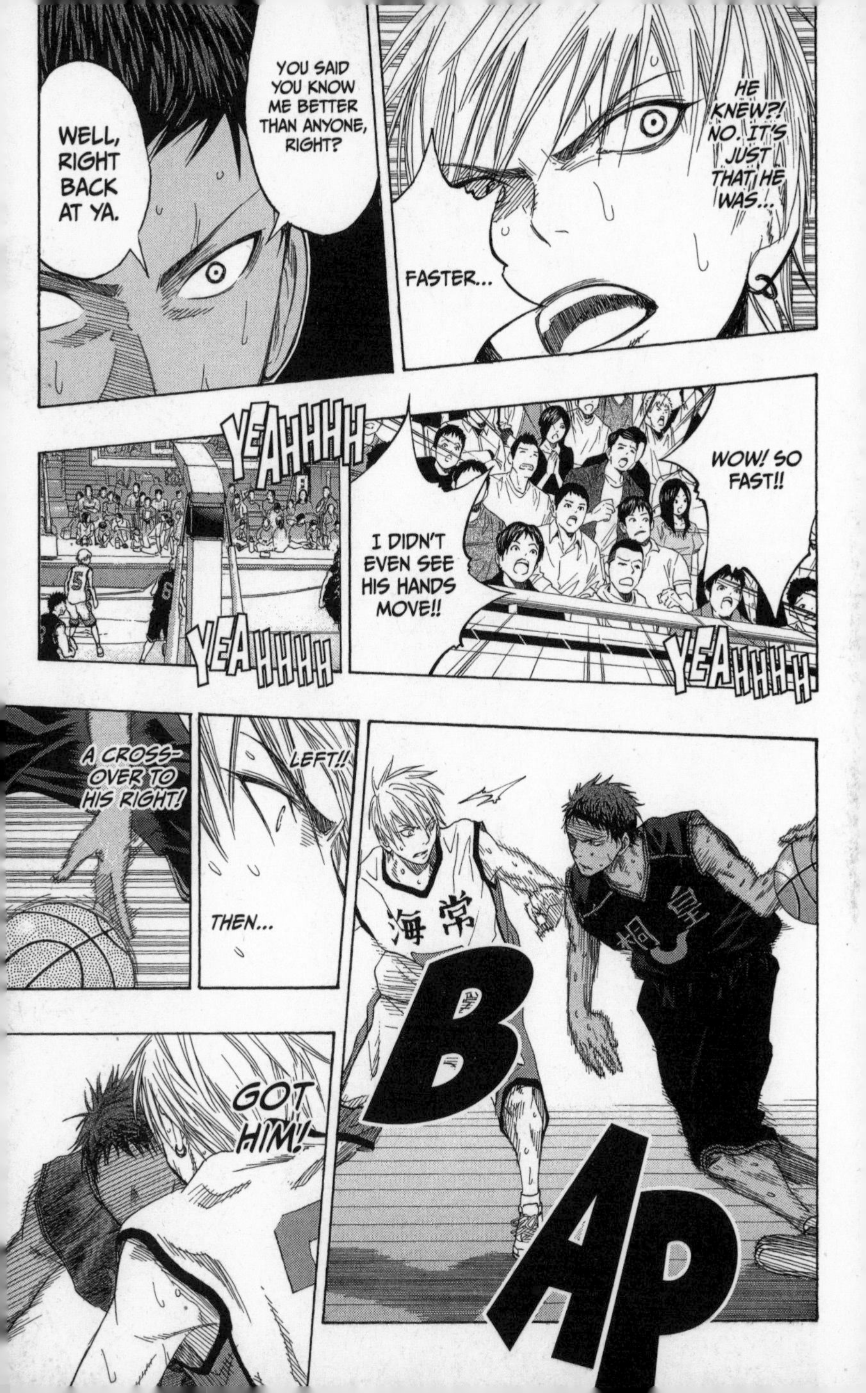
HE KNEW?! NO. IT'S JUST THAT HE WAS...
FASTER...
YOU SAID YOU KNOW ME BETTER THAN ANYONE, RIGHT?
WELL, RIGHT BACK AT YA.
WOW! SO FAST!!
I DIDN'T EVEN SEE HIS HANDS MOVE!!
YEAHHHHH
YEAHHHH
YEAHHHHH
BAP
LEFT!!
THEN...
A CROSS-OVER TO HIS RIGHT!
GOT HIM!

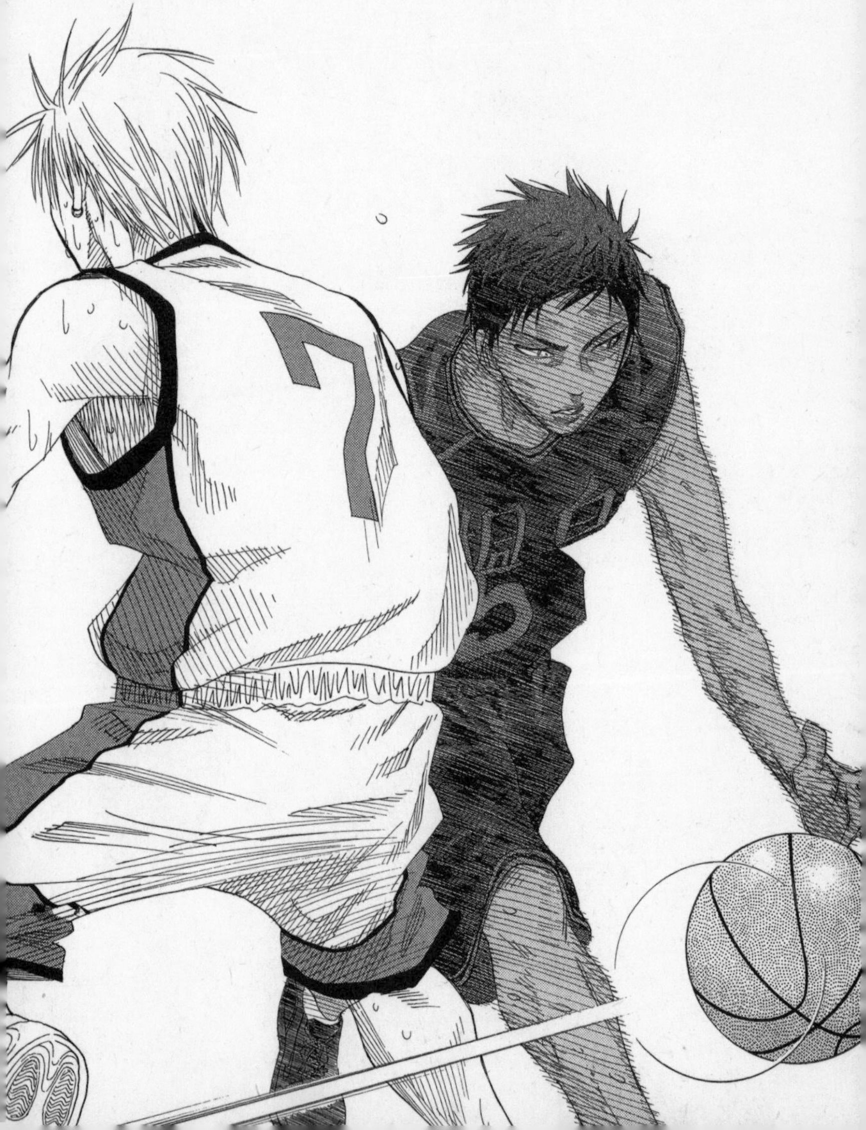

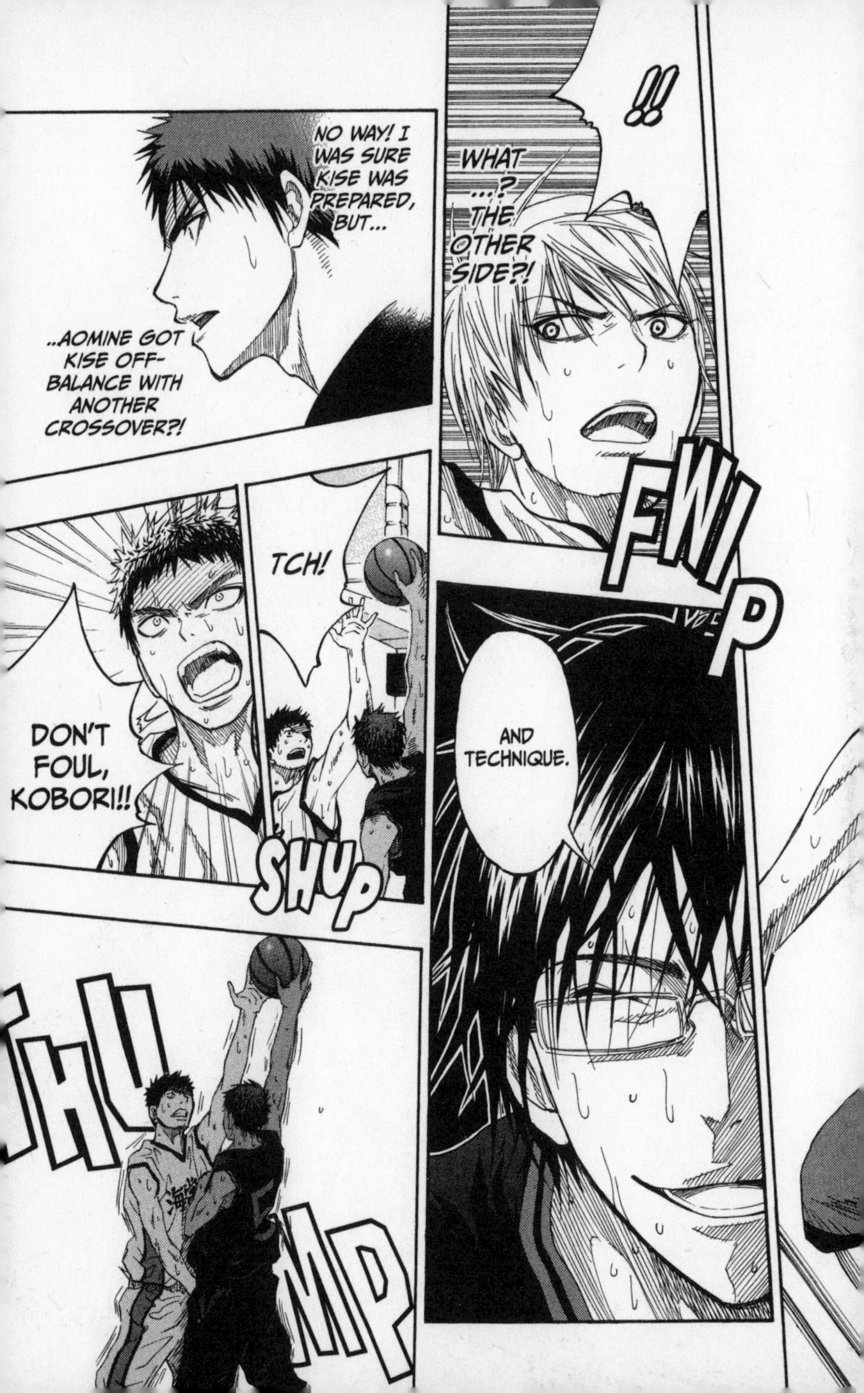
!!
WHAT ...? THE OTHER SIDE?!
FWIP
NO WAY! I WAS SURE KISE WAS PREPARED, BUT...
...AOMINE GOT KISE OFF-BALANCE WITH ANOTHER CROSSOVER?!
AND TECHNIQUE.
TCH!
SHUP
DON'T FOUL, KOBORI!!
THUMP

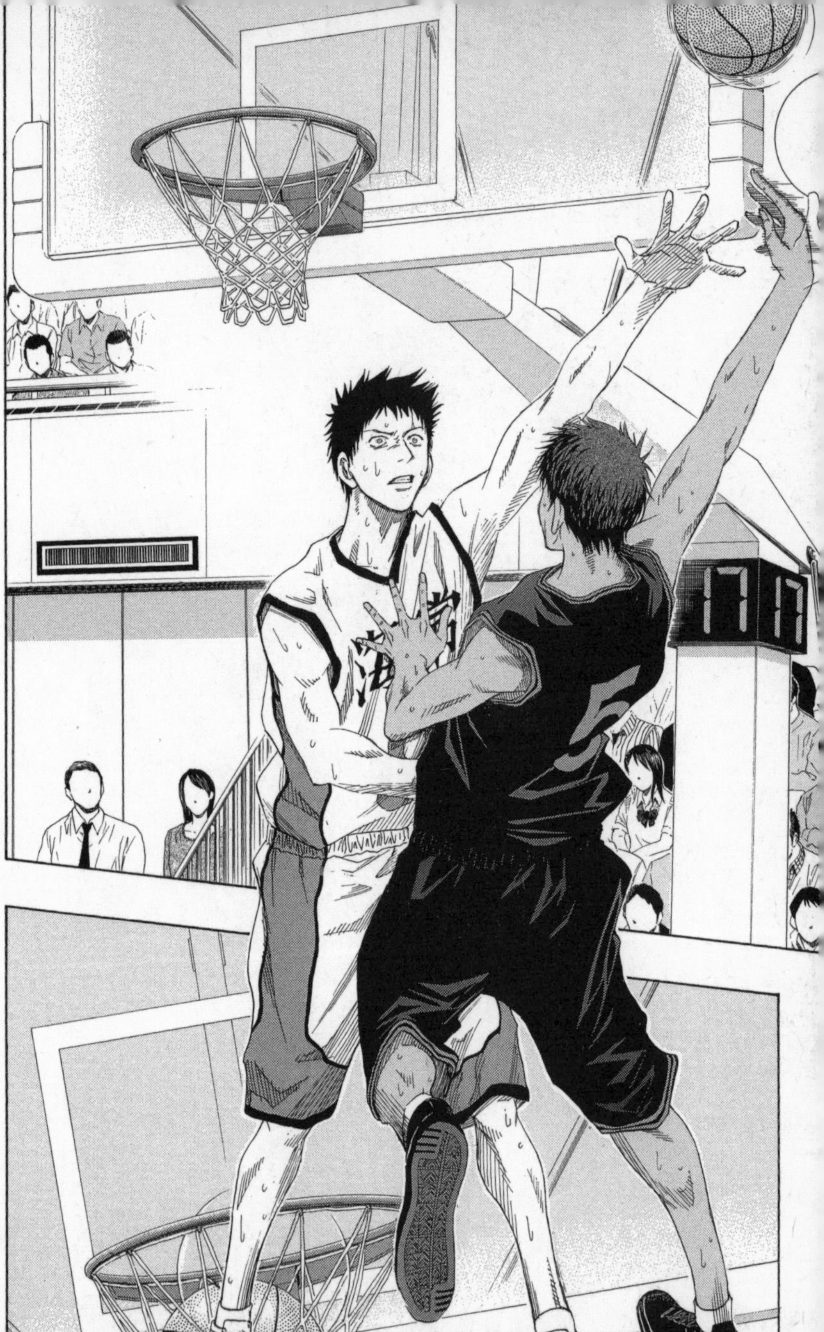

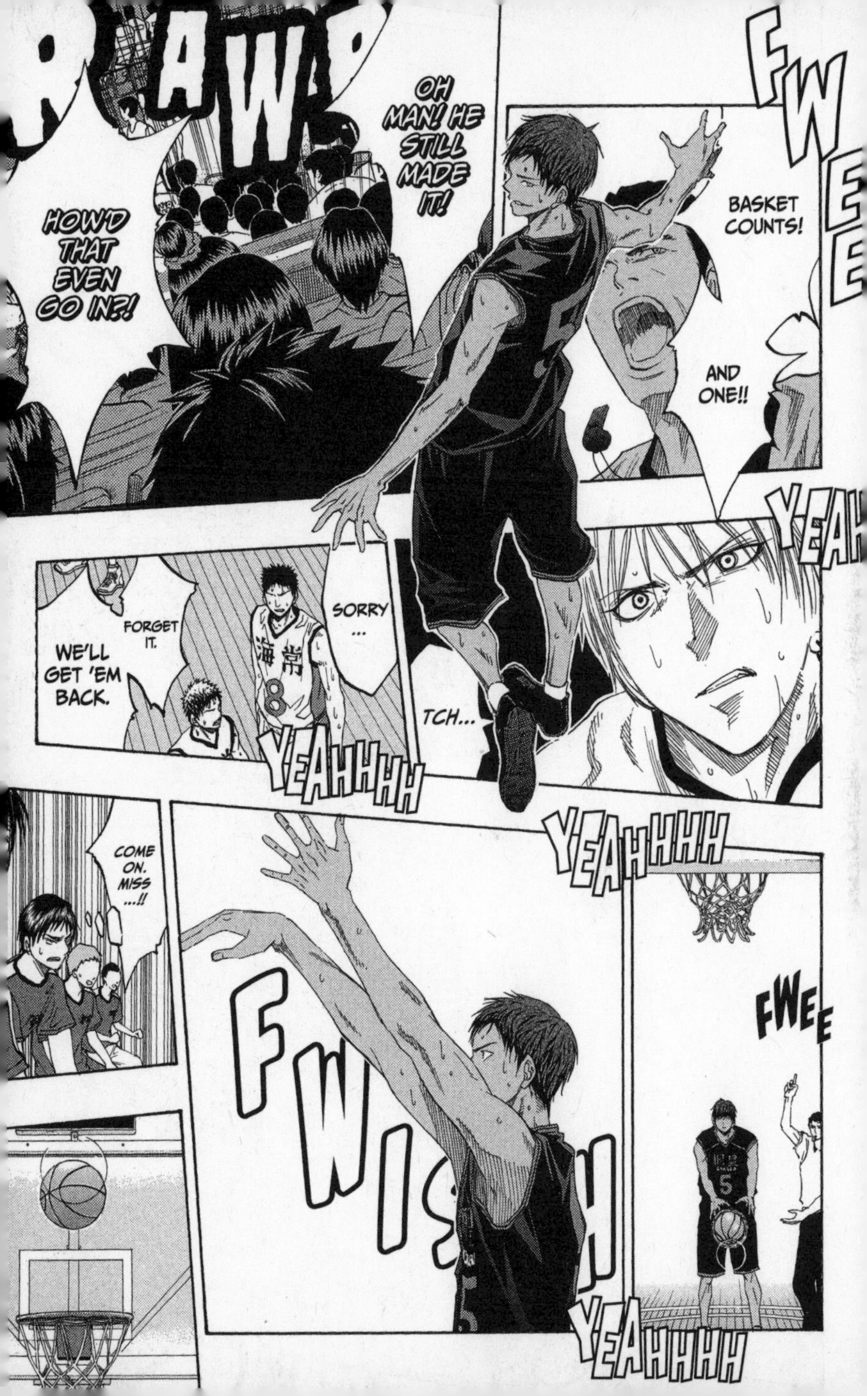
FWEE
BASKET COUNTS!
AND ONE!!
OH MAN! HE STILL MADE IT!
HOW'D THAT EVEN GO IN?!
YEAH
TCH...
SORRY ...
FORGET IT.
WE'LL GET 'EM BACK.
YEAHHHH
YEAHHHH
FWEE
FWISH
YEAHHHH
COME ON. MISS ...!!

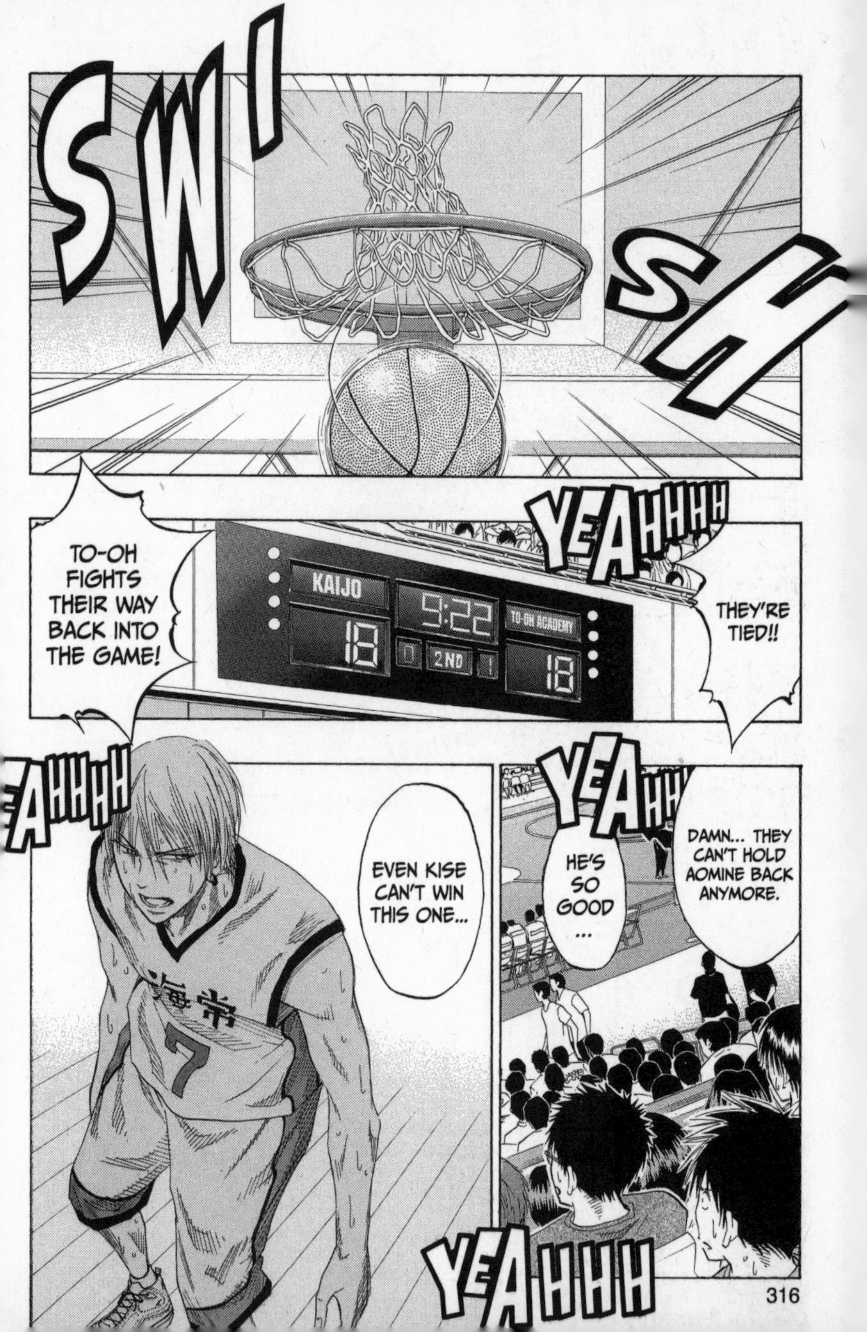
SWISH
YEAHHHH
KAIJO
9:22
TO-OH ACADEMY
18
2ND
18
THEY'RE TIED!!
TO-OH FIGHTS THEIR WAY BACK INTO THE GAME!
YEAHHHH
DAMN... THEY CAN'T HOLD AOMINE BACK ANYMORE.
HE'S SO GOOD ...
EVEN KISE CAN'T WIN THIS ONE...
海常
7
YEAHHHH
YEAHHH

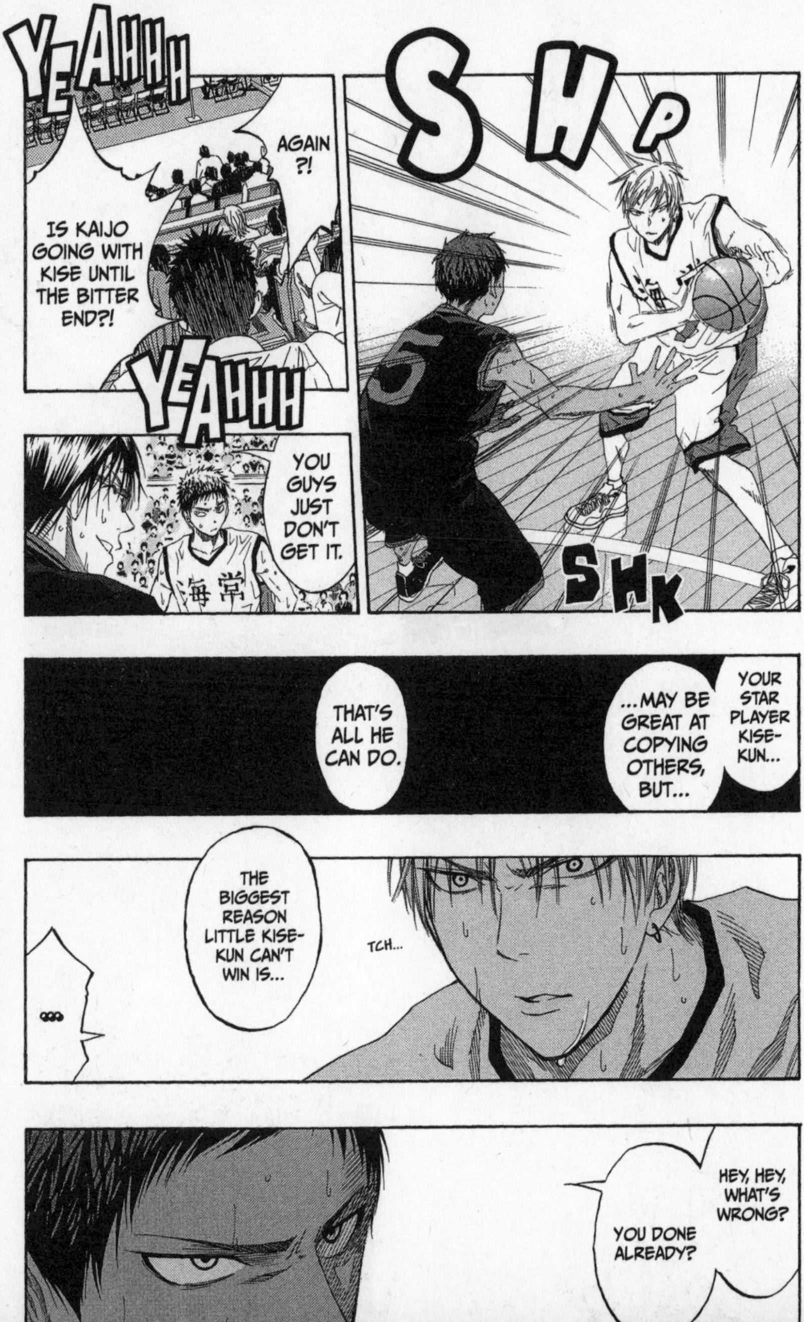
SHP
SHK
YEAHHH
AGAIN?!
IS KAIJO GOING WITH KISE UNTIL THE BITTER END?!
YEAHHH
YOU GUYS JUST DON'T GET IT.
YOUR STAR PLAYER KISE-KUN...
...MAY BE GREAT AT COPYING OTHERS, BUT...
THAT'S ALL HE CAN DO.
TCH...
THE BIGGEST REASON LITTLE KISE-KUN CAN'T WIN IS...
...
HEY, HEY, WHAT'S WRONG?
YOU DONE ALREADY?

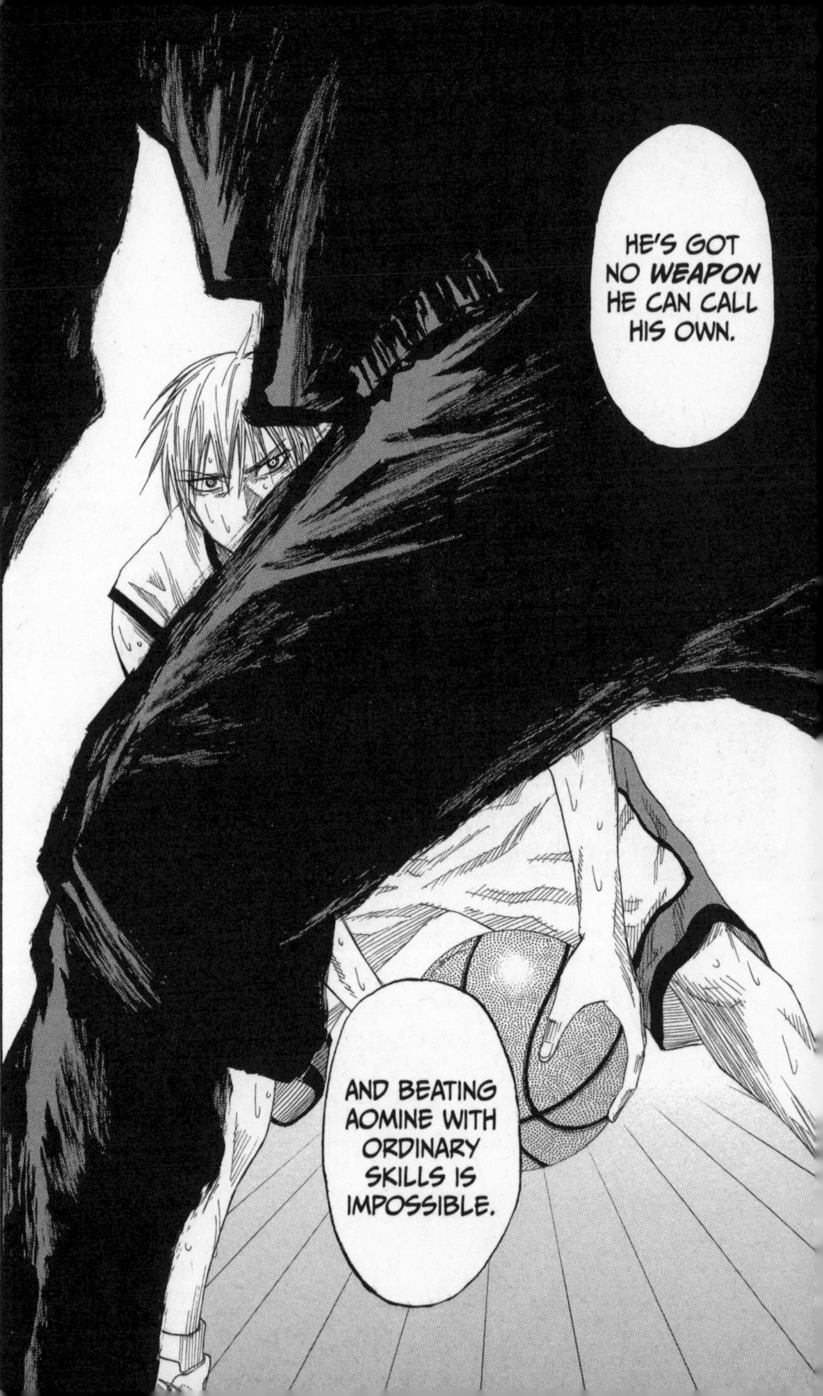
HE'S GOT NO *WEAPON* HE CAN CALL HIS OWN.
AND BEATING AOMINE WITH ORDINARY SKILLS IS IMPOSSIBLE.

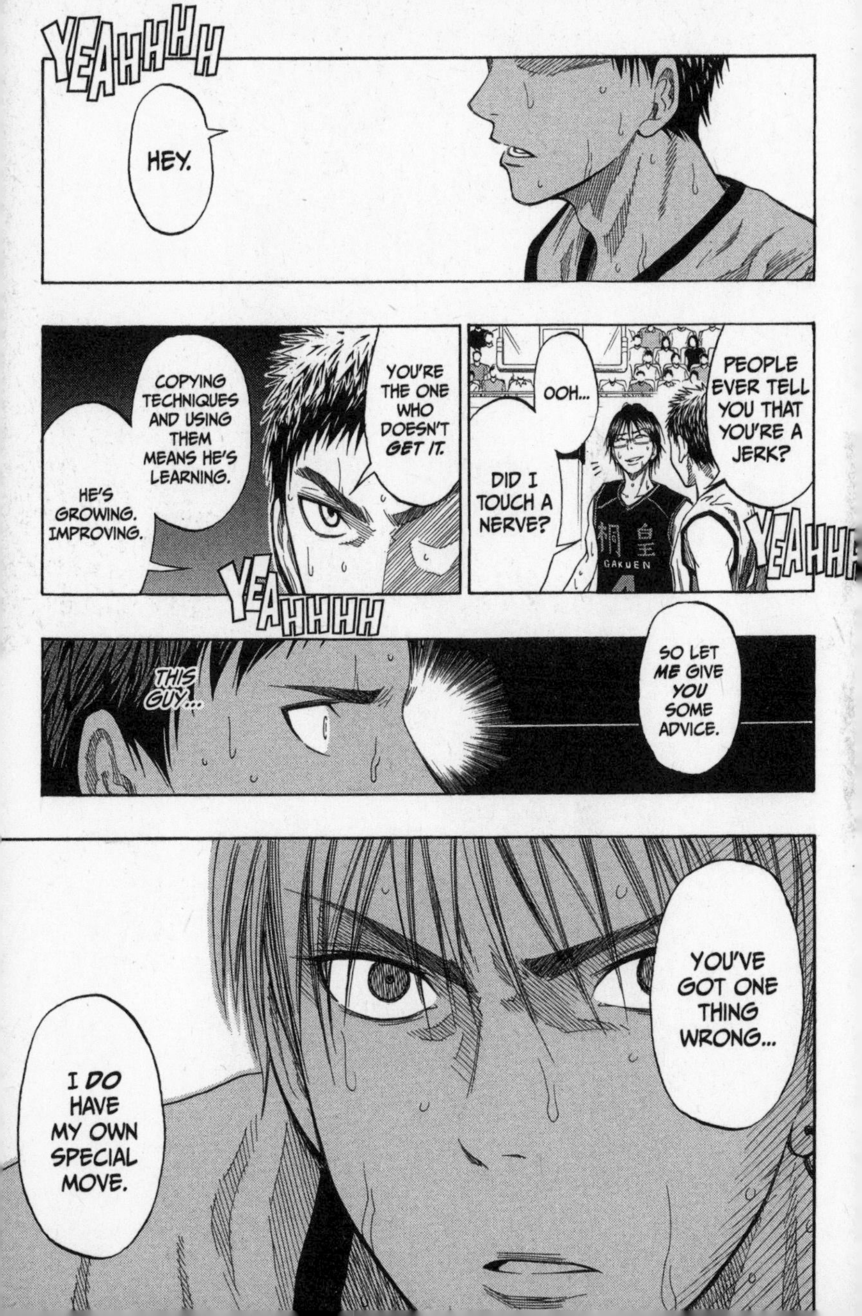
YEAHHHH
HEY.
PEOPLE EVER TELL YOU THAT YOU'RE A JERK?
OOH...
DID I TOUCH A NERVE?
GAKUEN
YOU'RE THE ONE WHO DOESN'T *GET IT.*
COPYING TECHNIQUES AND USING THEM MEANS HE'S LEARNING.
HE'S GROWING. IMPROVING.
YEAHHHH
SO LET *ME* GIVE *YOU* SOME ADVICE.
THIS GUY...
YOU'VE GOT ONE THING WRONG...
I *DO* HAVE MY OWN SPECIAL MOVE.

KUROKO'S BASKETBALL BLOOPERS
TAKE 12

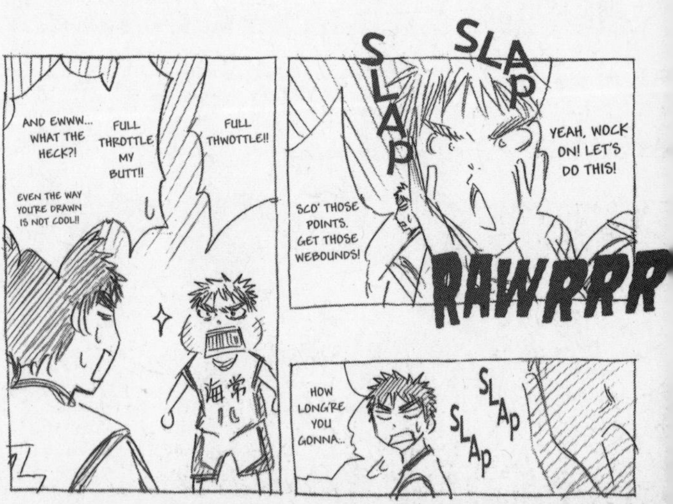
SLAP
YEAH, WOCK ON! LET'S DO THIS!
SLAP
SCO' THOSE POINTS. GET THOSE WEBOUNDS!
RAWRRR
SLAP SLAP
HOW LONG'RE YOU GONNA...
FULL THWOTTLE!!
FULL THROTTLE MY BUTT!!
AND EWWW... WHAT THE HECK?!
EVEN THE WAY YOU'RE DRAWN IS NOT COOL!!

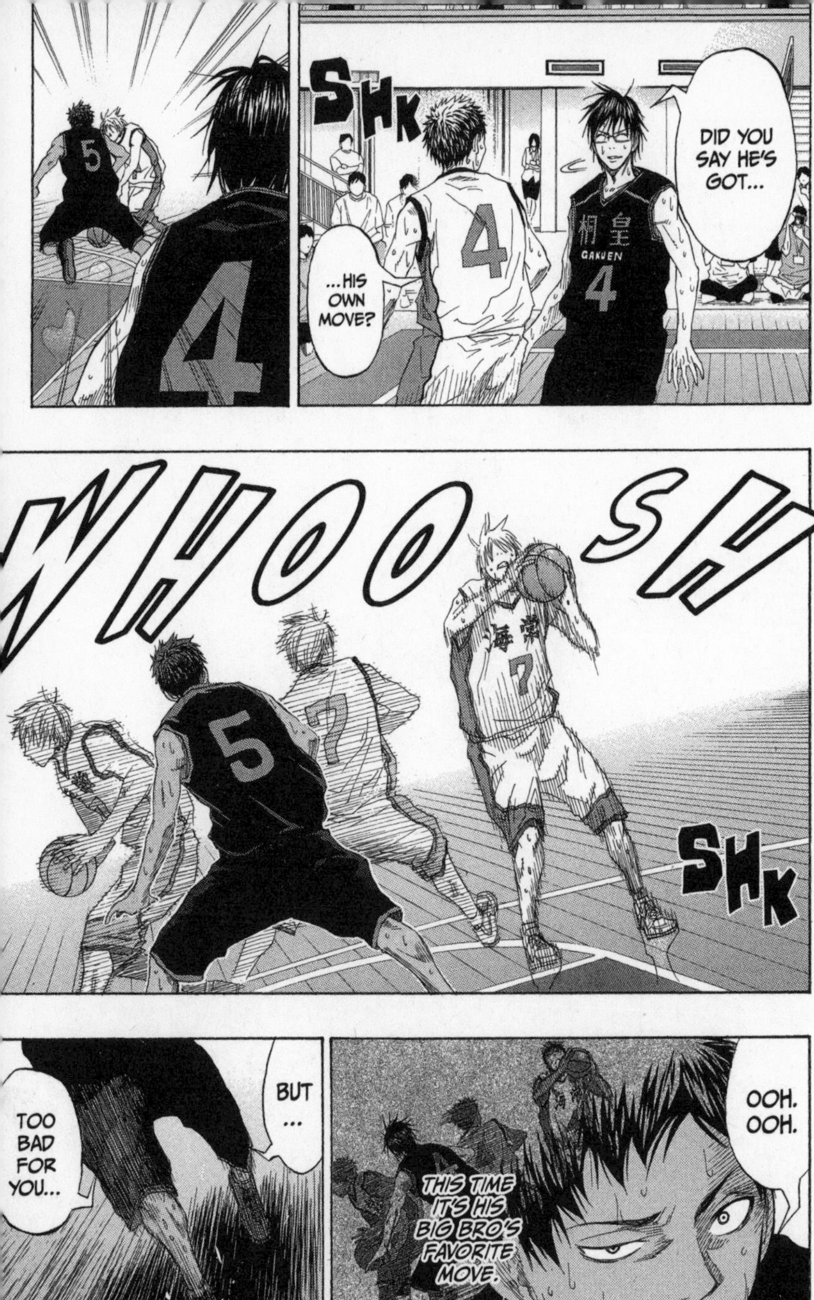
DID YOU SAY HE'S GOT...
SHK
...HIS OWN MOVE?
WHOOSH
SHK
OOH. OOH.
THIS TIME IT'S HIS BIG BRO'S FAVORITE MOVE.
BUT ...
TOO BAD FOR YOU...

67TH QUARTER: GOTTA STOP

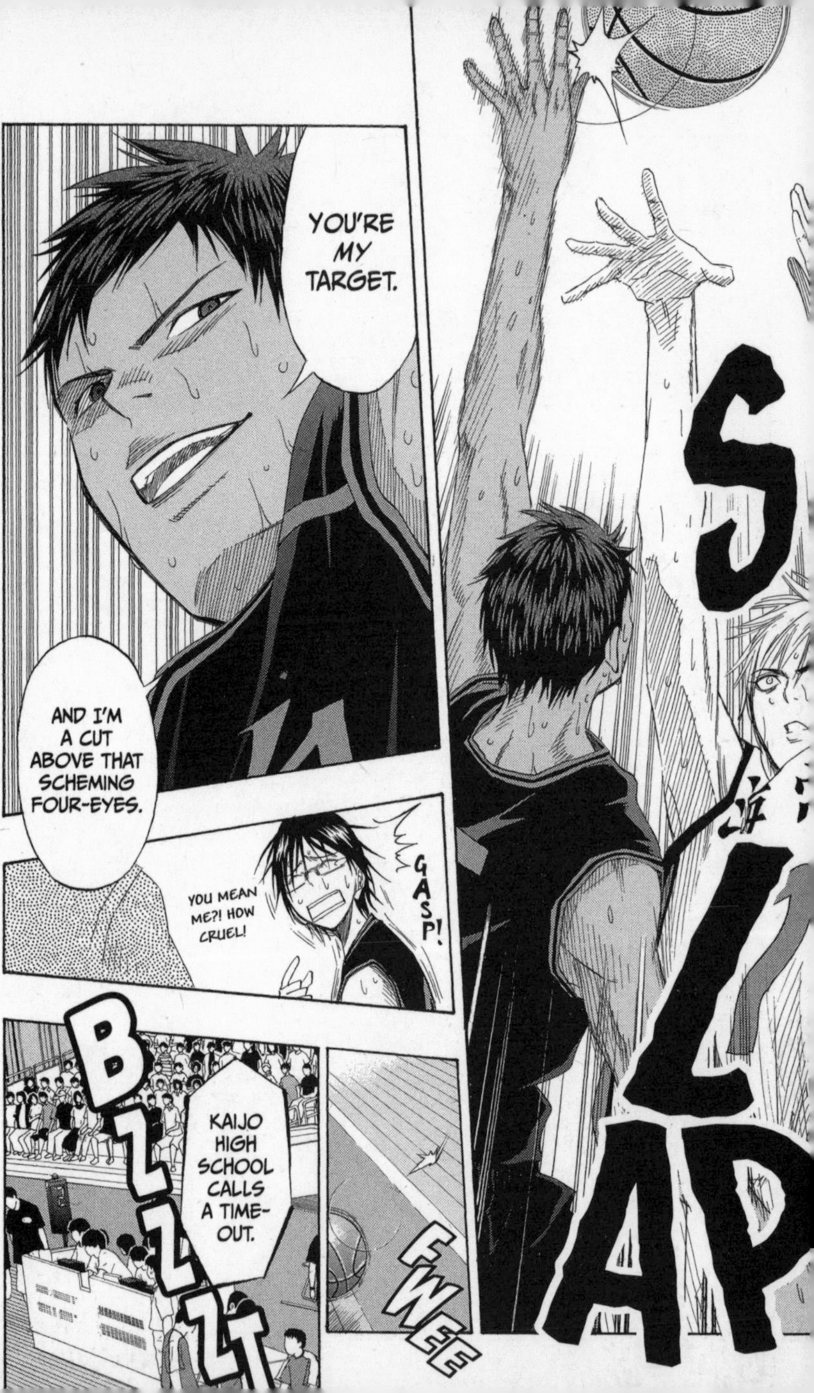
SLAP
YOU'RE MY TARGET.
AND I'M A CUT ABOVE THAT SCHEMING FOUR-EYES.
GASP!
YOU MEAN ME?! HOW CRUEL!
FWEE
KAIJO HIGH SCHOOL CALLS A TIME-OUT.
BZZZT

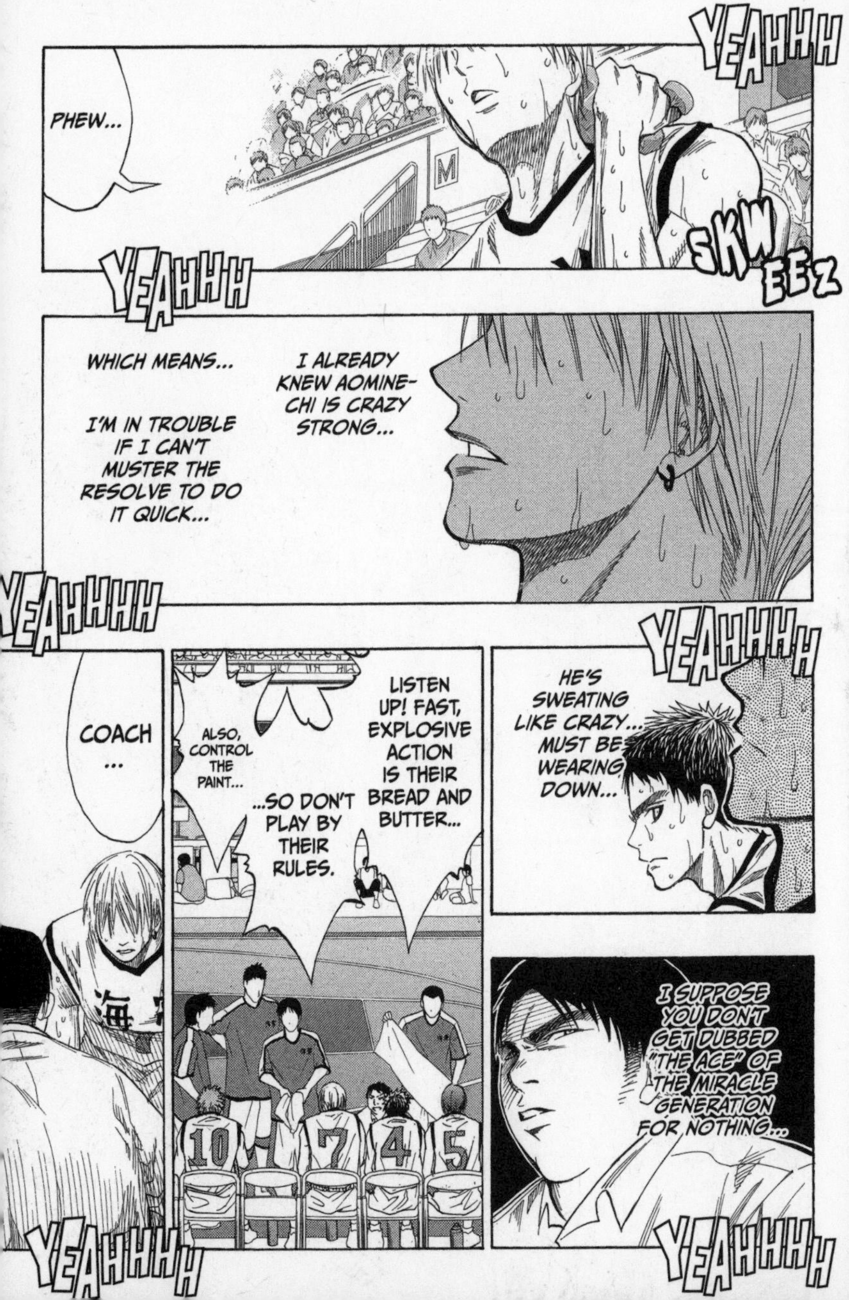
YEAHHH
SKWEEZ
PHEW...
YEAHHH
I ALREADY KNEW AOMINE-CHI IS CRAZY STRONG...
WHICH MEANS...
I'M IN TROUBLE IF I CAN'T MUSTER THE RESOLVE TO DO IT QUICK...
YEAHHHH
YEAHHHH
HE'S SWEATING LIKE CRAZY... MUST BE WEARING DOWN...
I SUPPOSE YOU DON'T GET DUBBED "THE ACE" OF THE MIRACLE GENERATION FOR NOTHING...
YEAHHHH
LISTEN UP! FAST, EXPLOSIVE ACTION IS THEIR BREAD AND BUTTER...
...SO DON'T PLAY BY THEIR RULES.
ALSO, CONTROL THE PAINT...
COACH...
YEAHHHH

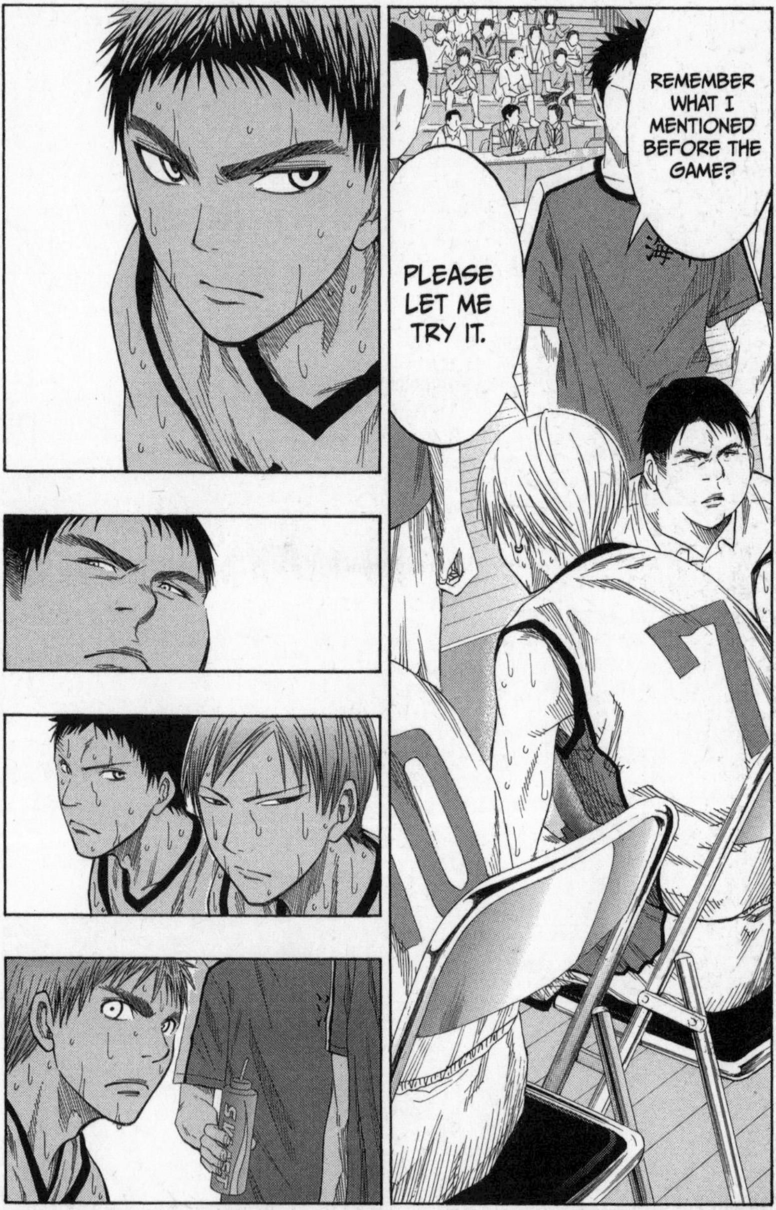
REMEMBER WHAT I MENTIONED BEFORE THE GAME?
PLEASE LET ME TRY IT.

67TH QUARTER: GOTTA STOP

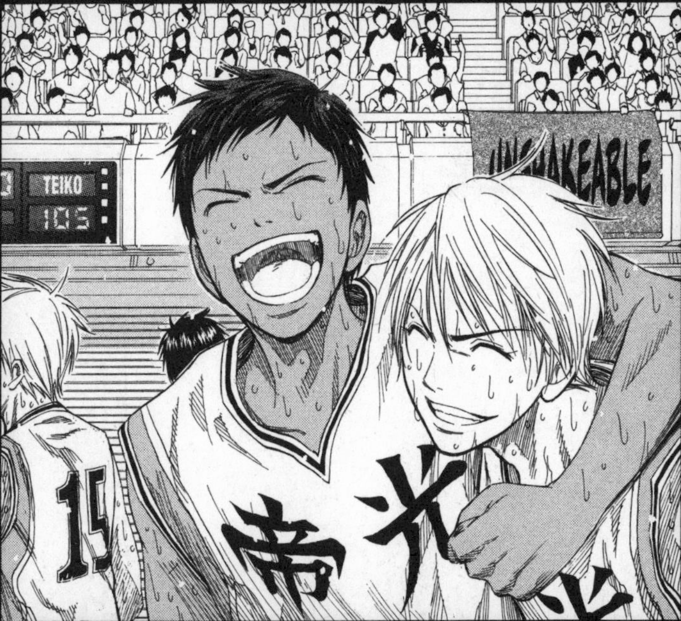
TEIKO
103
UNSHAKEABLE

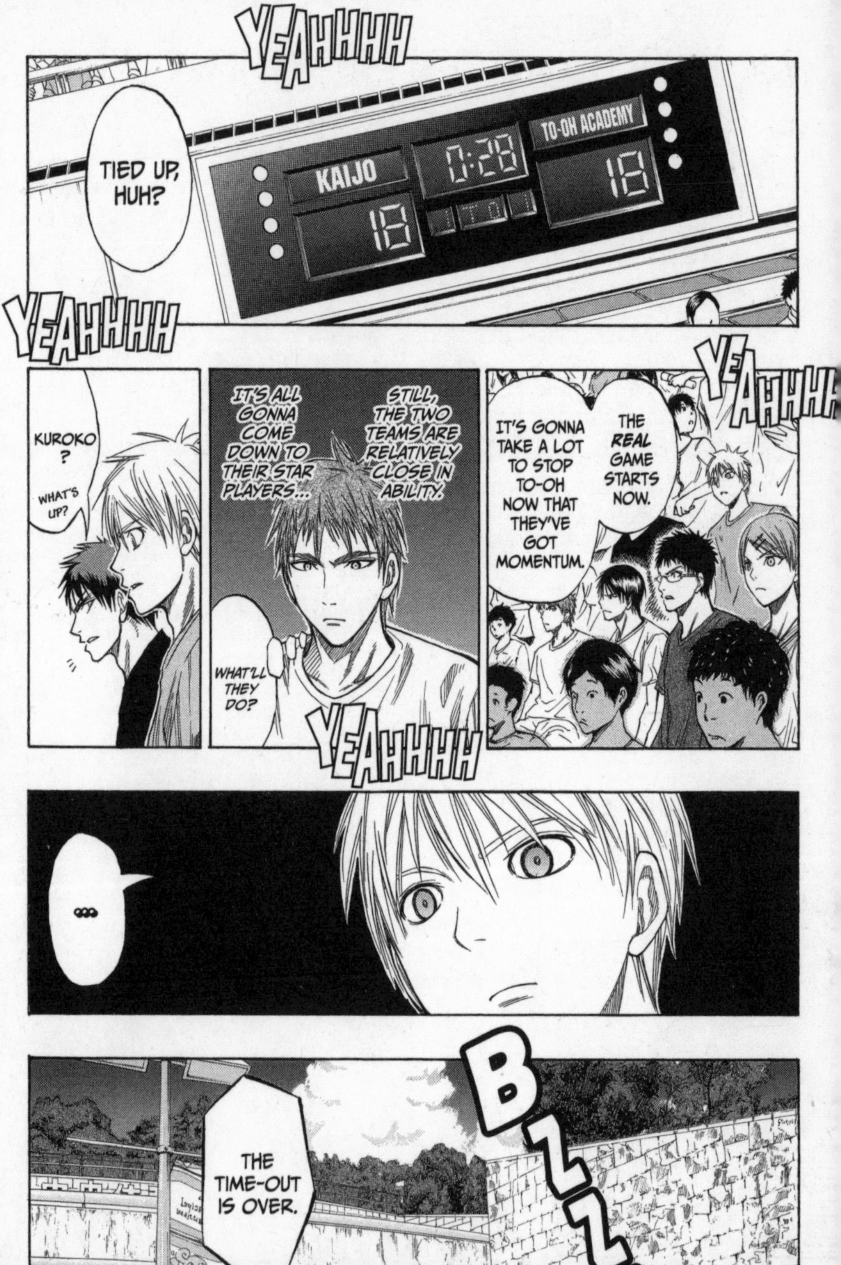
YEAHHHH
TO-OH ACADEMY
0:28
KAIJO
18
18
TIED UP, HUH?
YEAHHHH
YEAHHHH
THE REAL GAME STARTS NOW.
IT'S GONNA TAKE A LOT TO STOP TO-OH NOW THAT THEY'VE GOT MOMENTUM.
STILL, THE TWO TEAMS ARE RELATIVELY CLOSE IN ABILITY.
IT'S ALL GONNA COME DOWN TO THEIR STAR PLAYERS...
WHAT'LL THEY DO?
YEAHHHH
KUROKO?
WHAT'S UP?
...
B
THE TIME-OUT IS OVER.

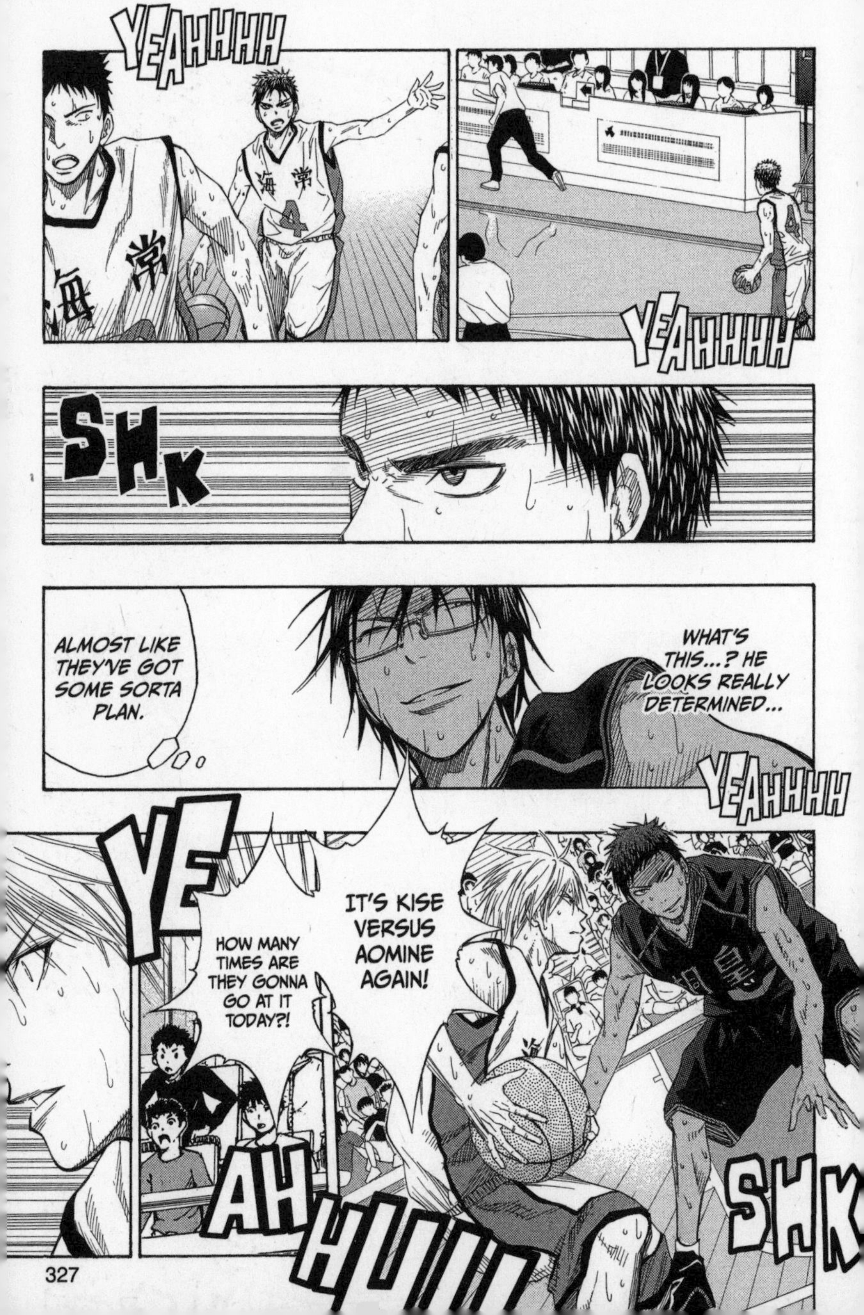
YEAHHHH
YEAHHHH
SHK
WHAT'S THIS...? HE LOOKS REALLY DETERMINED...
ALMOST LIKE THEY'VE GOT SOME SORTA PLAN.
YEAHHHH
SHK
IT'S KISE VERSUS AOMINE AGAIN!
HOW MANY TIMES ARE THEY GONNA GO AT IT TODAY?!
YE
AH

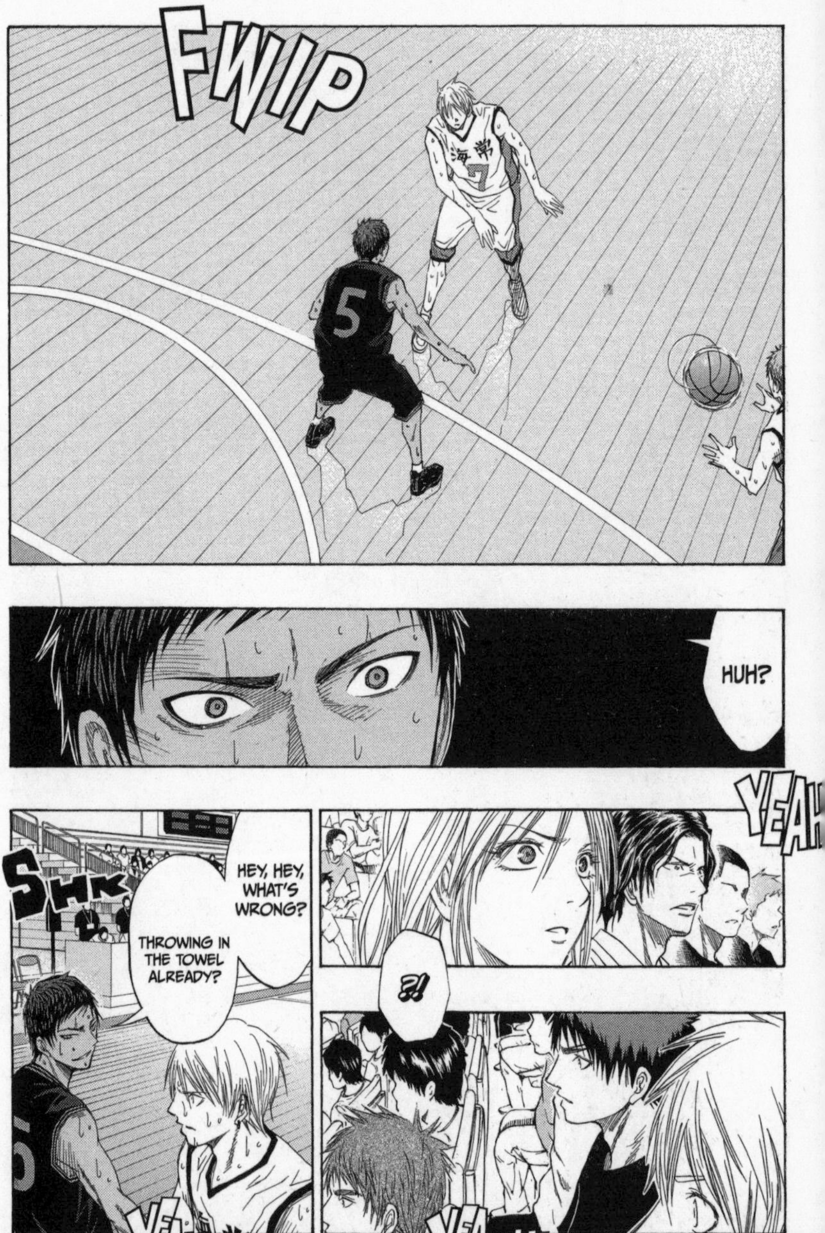
FWIP
HUH?
YEAH
?!
YEAHHHH
SHK
HEY, HEY, WHAT'S WRONG?
THROWING IN THE TOWEL ALREADY?
YEAHHHH

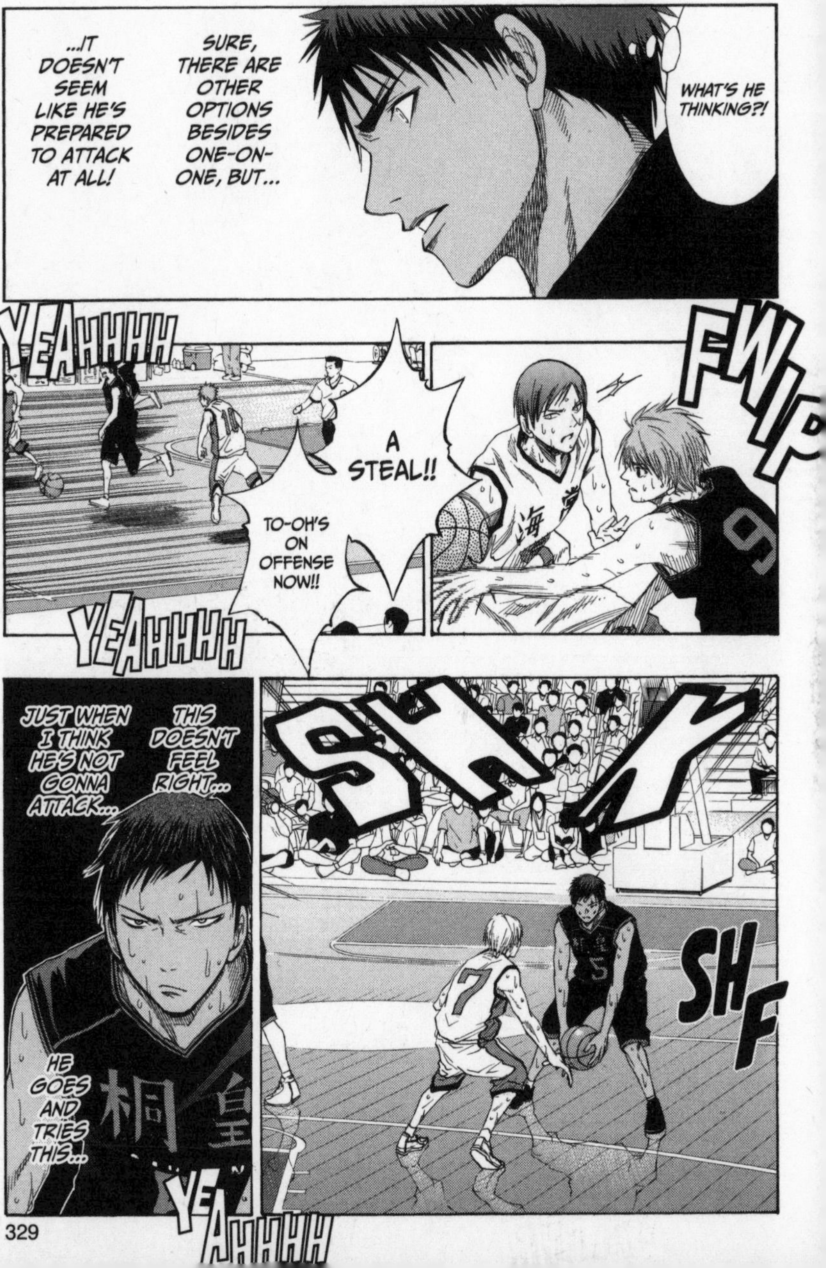
WHAT'S HE THINKING?!
SURE, THERE ARE OTHER OPTIONS BESIDES ONE-ON-ONE, BUT...
...IT DOESN'T SEEM LIKE HE'S PREPARED TO ATTACK AT ALL!
FWIP
YEAHHHH
A STEAL!!
TO-OH'S ON OFFENSE NOW!!
YEAHHHH
SHK
SHF
YEAHHHH
THIS DOESN'T FEEL RIGHT...
JUST WHEN I THINK HE'S NOT GONNA ATTACK...
HE GOES AND TRIES THIS...

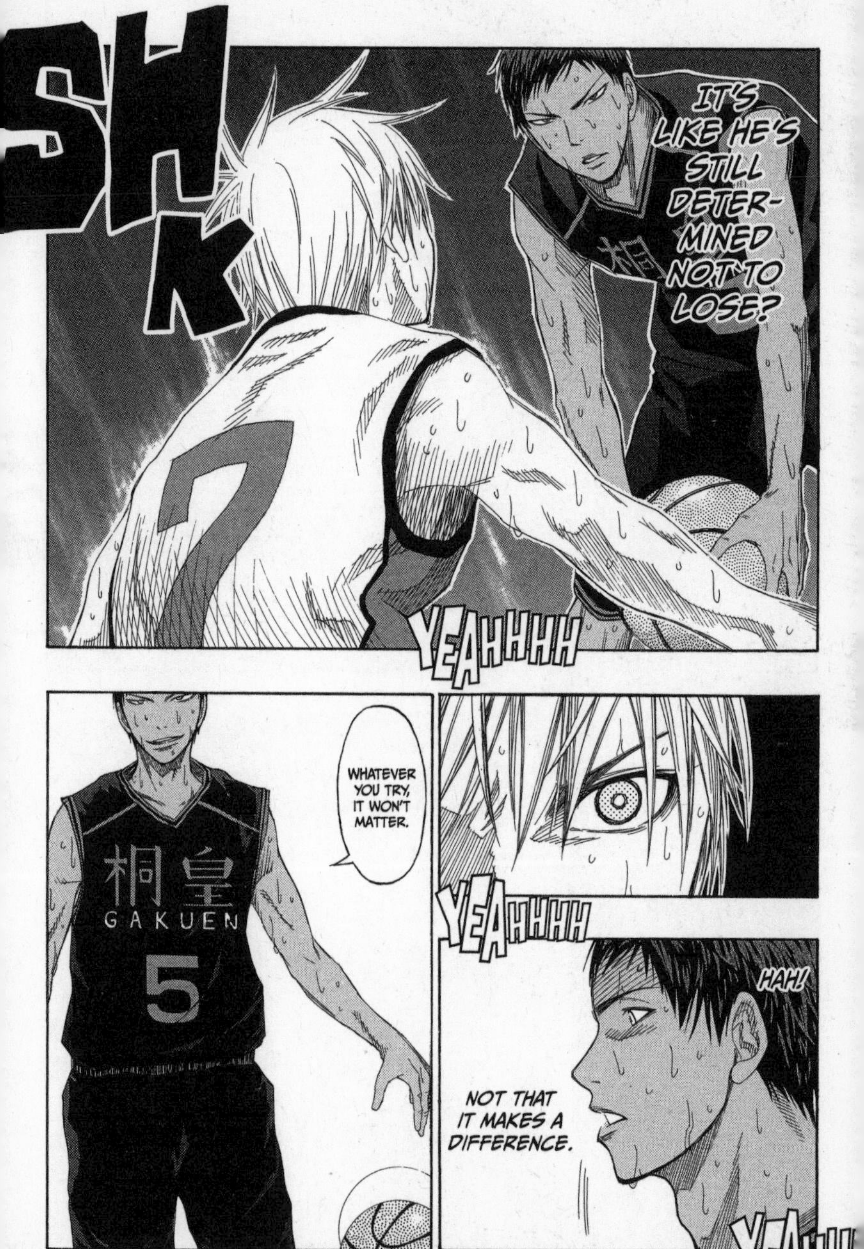
IT'S LIKE HE'S STILL DETER-MINED NOT TO LOSE?
SHK
YEAHHHH
YEAHHHH
HAH!
NOT THAT IT MAKES A DIFFERENCE.
YEAHH
WHATEVER YOU TRY, IT WON'T MATTER.
桐皇
GAKUEN
5

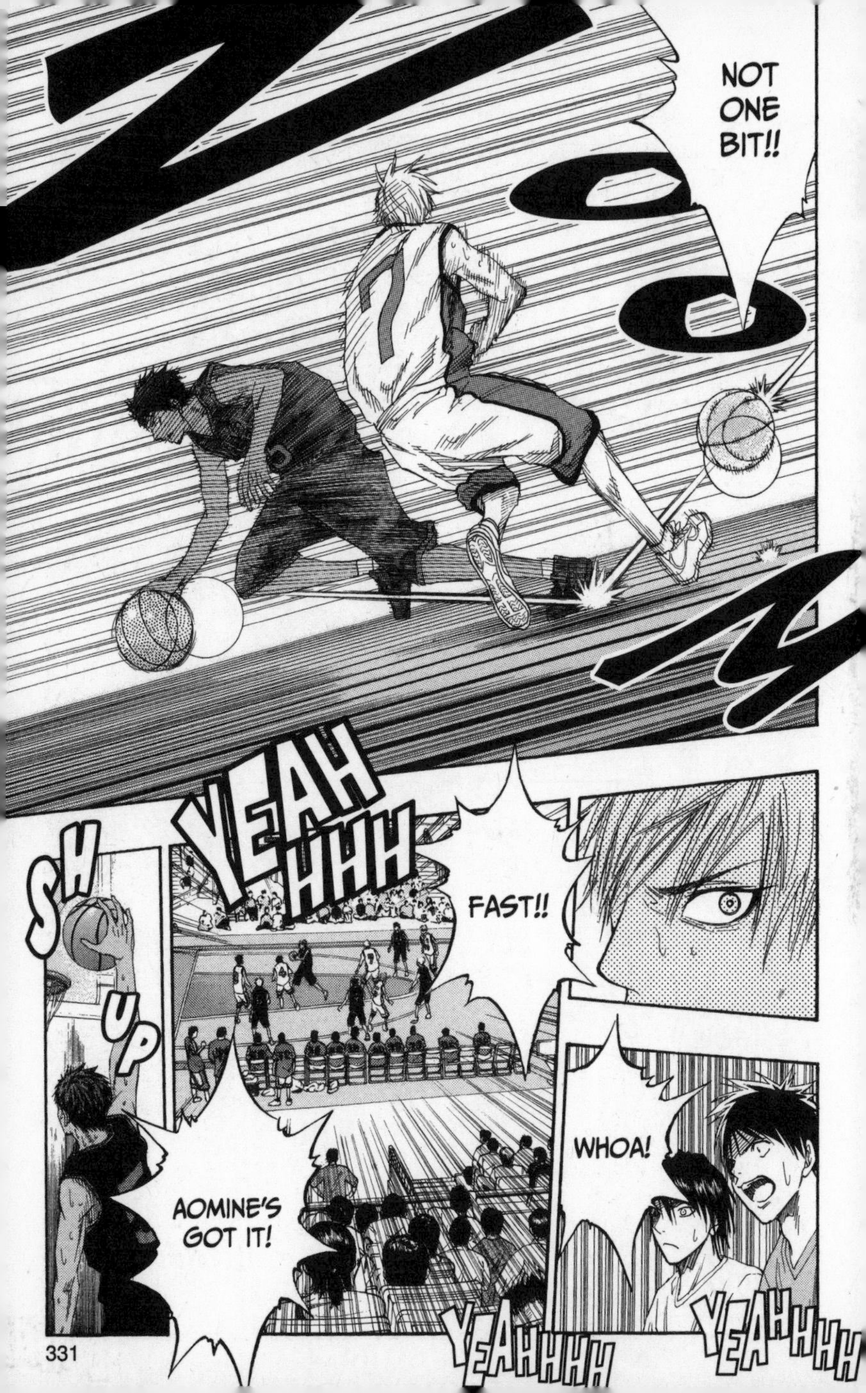
NOT ONE BIT!!
FAST!!
WHOA!
YEAHHHH
YEAH HHH
AOMINE'S GOT IT!
YEAHHHH
SH UP

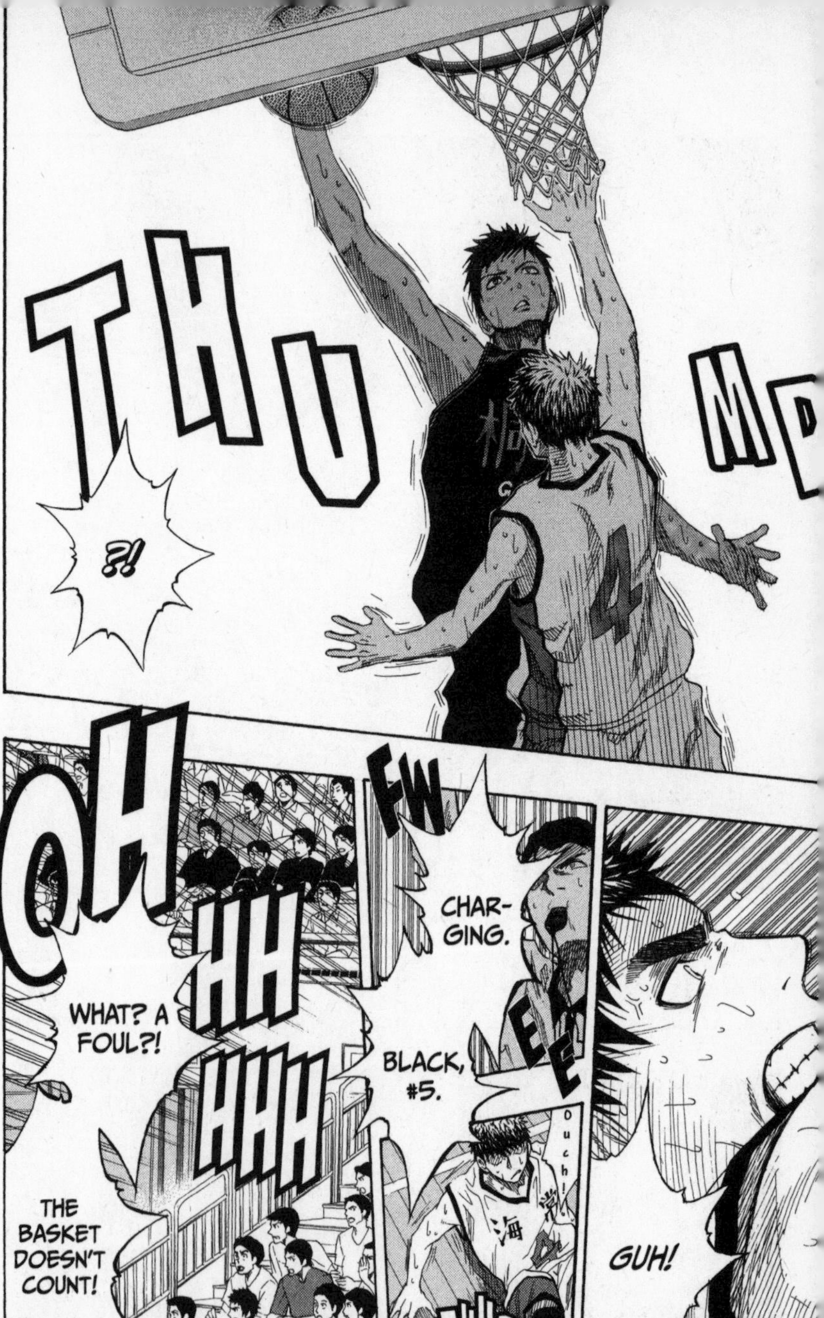
THUMP
?!
GUH!
FW
CHAR-GING.
BLACK, #5.
EEE
Ouch!
THUD
OHHHHHH
WHAT? A FOUL?!
THE BASKET DOESN'T COUNT!

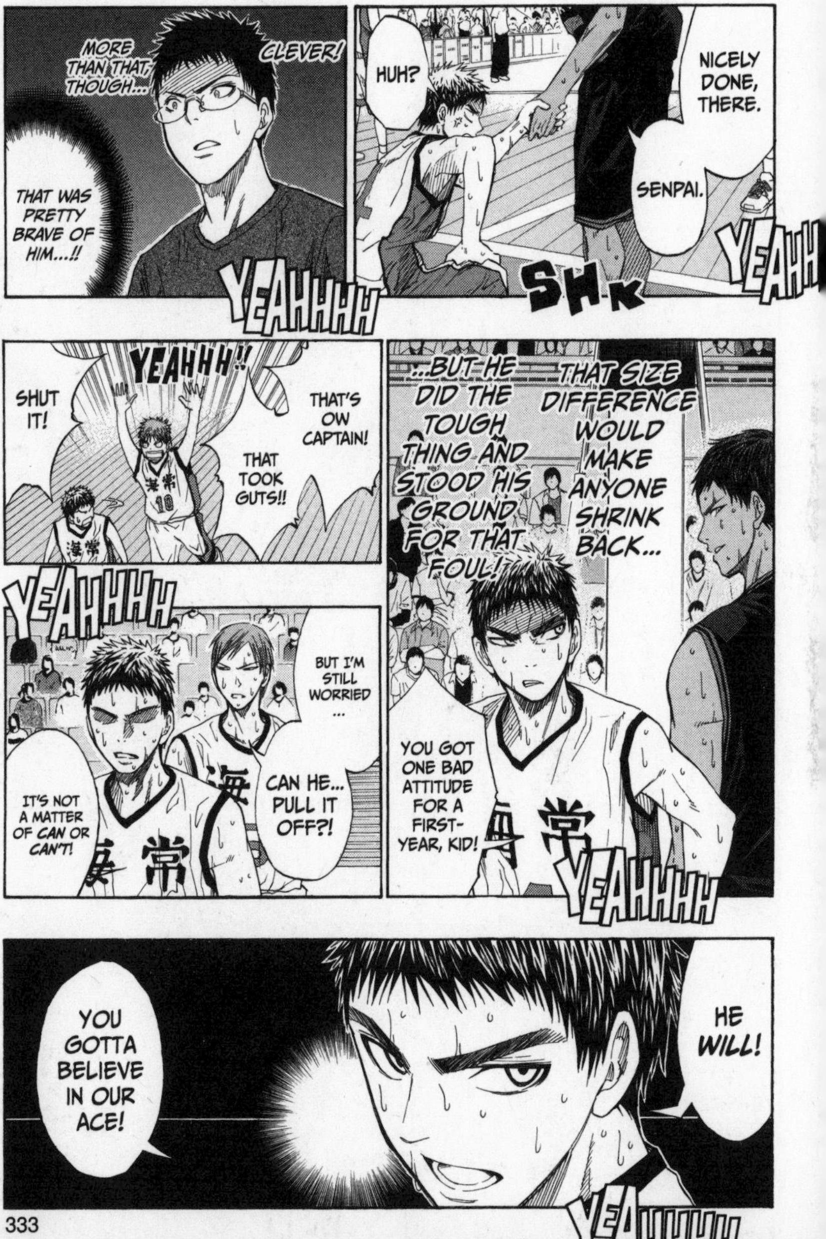
HUH?
NICELY DONE, THERE.
SENPAI.
SHK
YEAHH
CLEVER!
MORE THAN THAT, THOUGH...
THAT WAS PRETTY BRAVE OF HIM...!!
YEAHHHH
THAT SIZE DIFFERENCE WOULD MAKE ANYONE SHRINK BACK...
...BUT HE DID THE TOUGH THING AND STOOD HIS GROUND FOR THAT FOUL!
YOU GOT ONE BAD ATTITUDE FOR A FIRST-YEAR, KID!
YEAHHHH
YEAHHH!!
THAT'S OW CAPTAIN!
THAT TOOK GUTS!!
SHUT IT!
YEAHHHH
BUT I'M STILL WORRIED ...
CAN HE... PULL IT OFF?!
IT'S NOT A MATTER OF CAN OR CAN'T!
HE WILL!
YOU GOTTA BELIEVE IN OUR ACE!
YEAHHHH

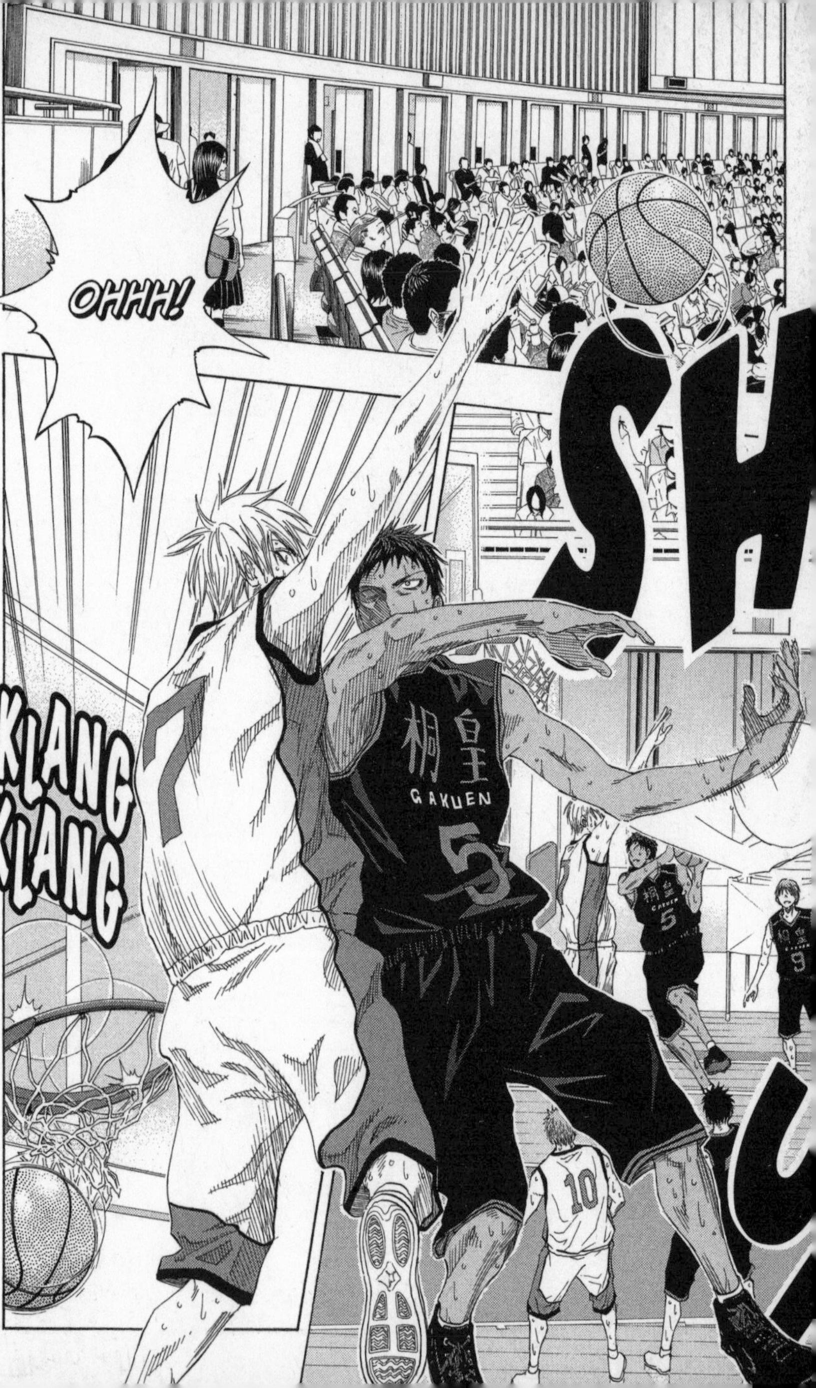
OHHH!
KLANG
KLANG
桐皇
GAKUEN

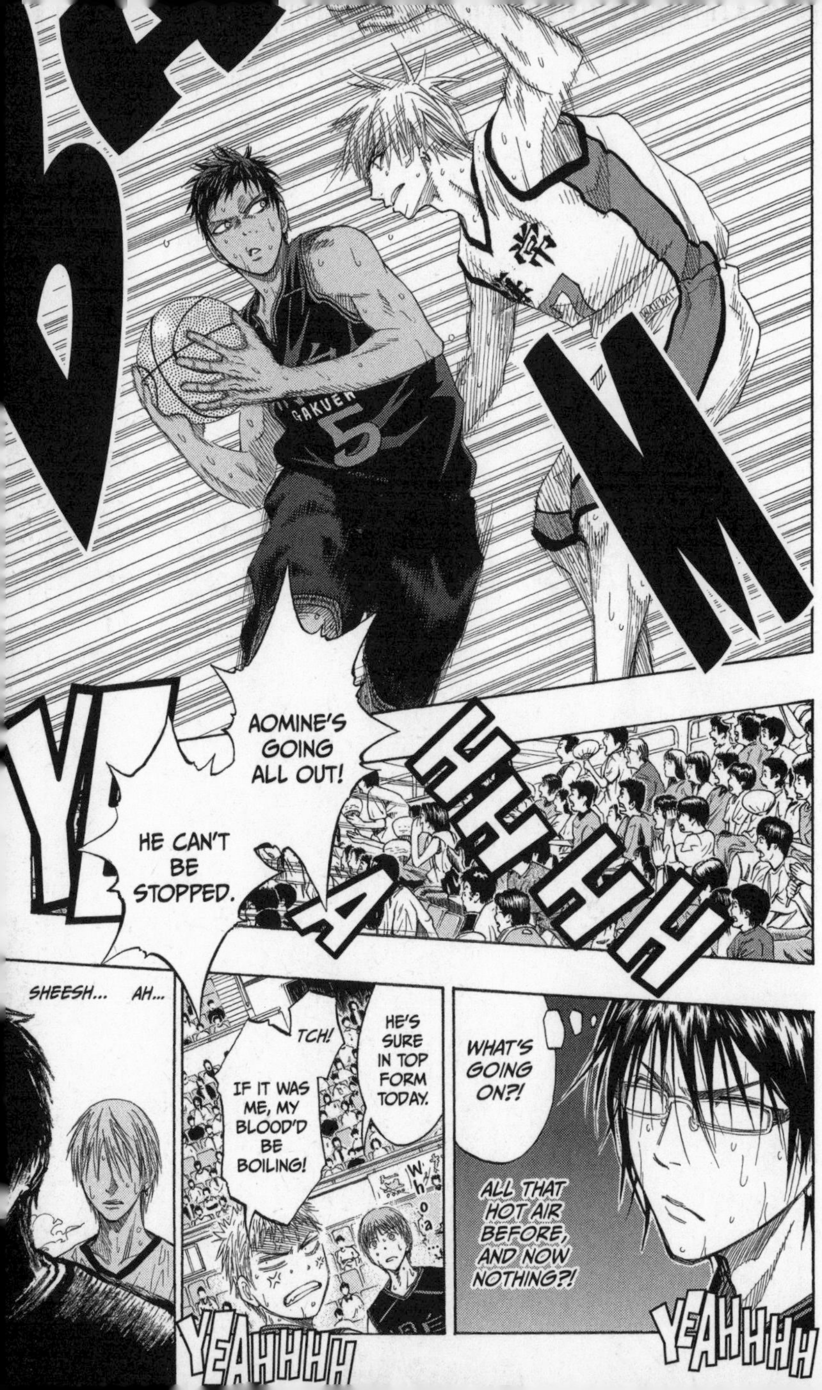
AOMINE'S GOING ALL OUT!
HE CAN'T BE STOPPED.
WHAT'S GOING ON?!
ALL THAT HOT AIR BEFORE, AND NOW NOTHING?!
YEAHHHHH
HE'S SURE IN TOP FORM TODAY.
TCH!
IF IT WAS ME, MY BLOOD'D BE BOILING!
YEAHHHHH
SHEESH... AH...

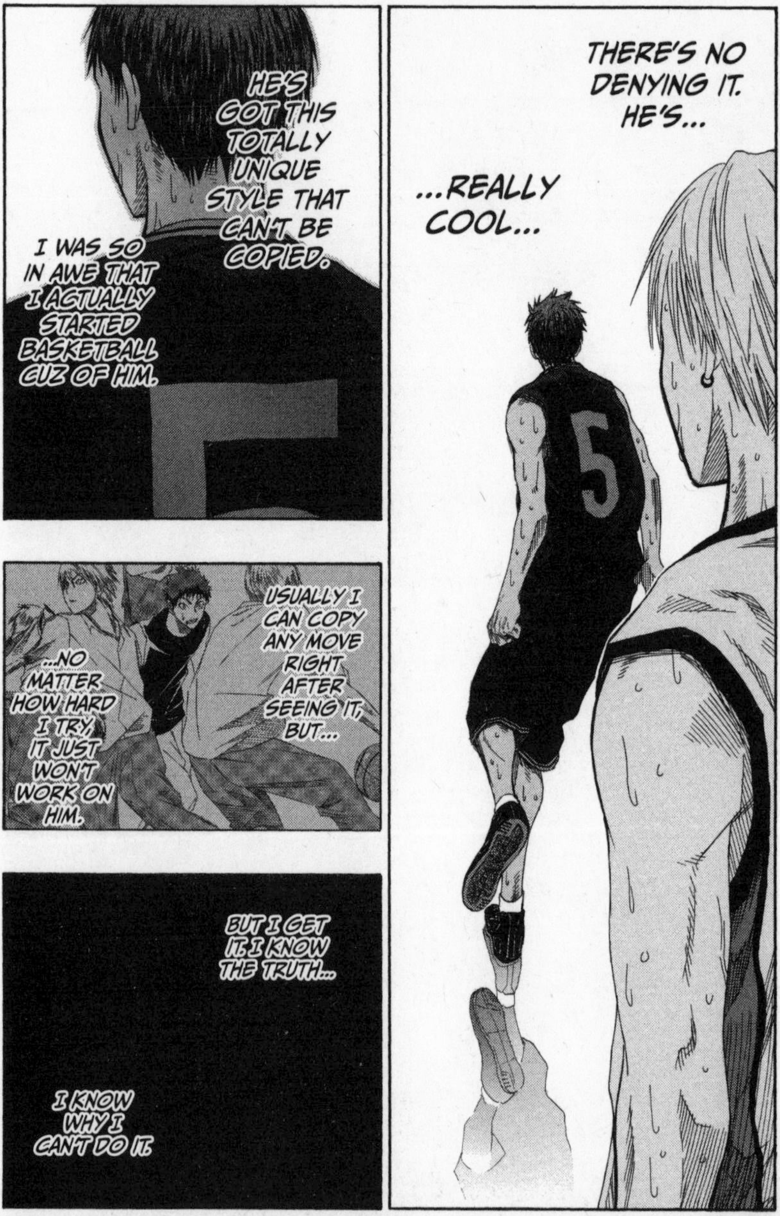
THERE'S NO DENYING IT. HE'S...
...REALLY COOL...
HE'S GOT THIS TOTALLY UNIQUE STYLE THAT CAN'T BE COPIED.
I WAS SO IN AWE THAT I ACTUALLY STARTED BASKETBALL CUZ OF HIM.
USUALLY I CAN COPY ANY MOVE RIGHT AFTER SEEING IT, BUT...
...NO MATTER HOW HARD I TRY, IT JUST WON'T WORK ON HIM.
BUT I GET IT. I KNOW THE TRUTH...
I KNOW WHY I CAN'T DO IT.

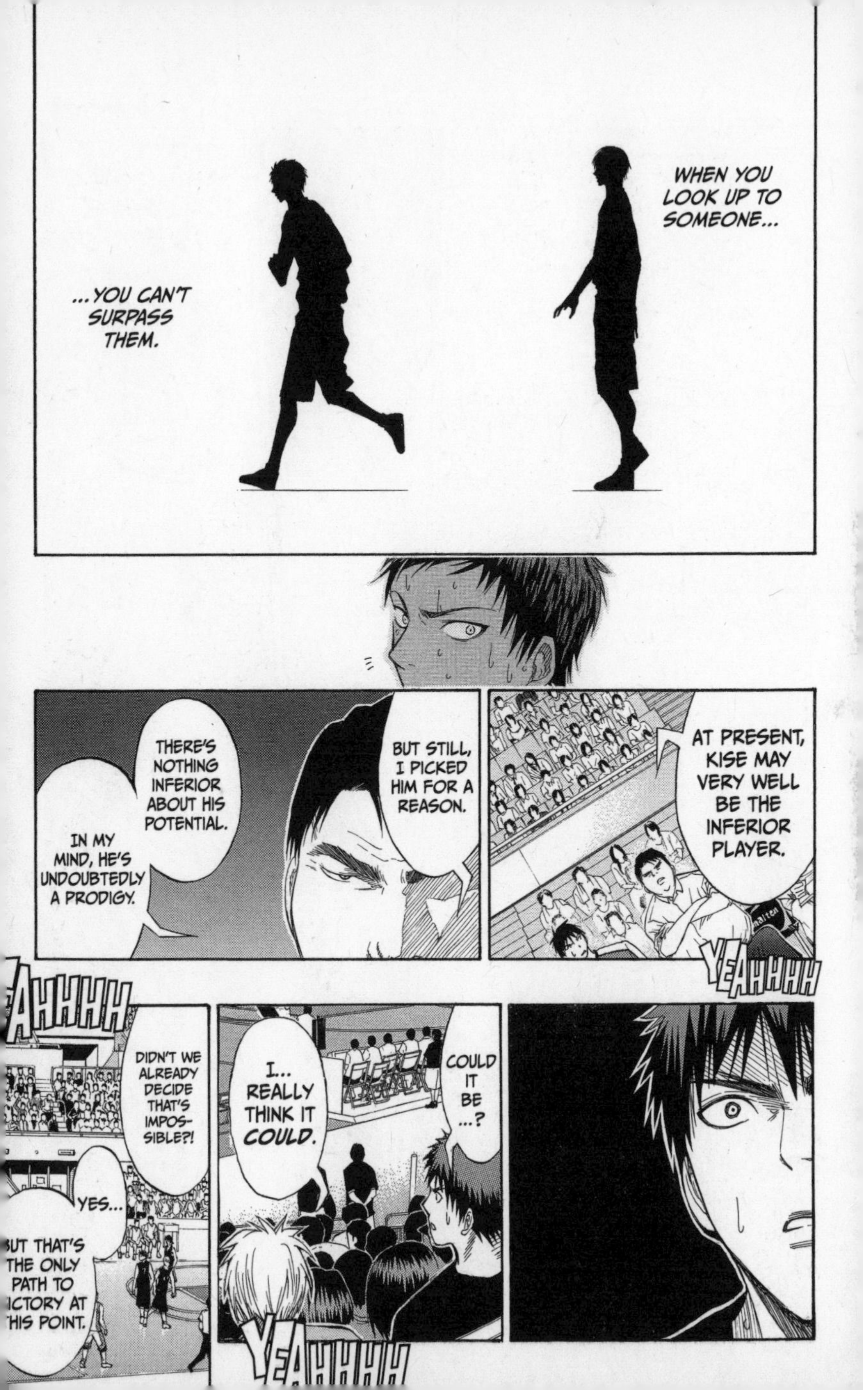
WHEN YOU LOOK UP TO SOMEONE...
...YOU CAN'T SURPASS THEM.
AT PRESENT, KISE MAY VERY WELL BE THE INFERIOR PLAYER.
YEAHHHH
BUT STILL, I PICKED HIM FOR A REASON.
THERE'S NOTHING INFERIOR ABOUT HIS POTENTIAL.
IN MY MIND, HE'S UNDOUBTEDLY A PRODIGY.
COULD IT BE ...?
I... REALLY THINK IT COULD.
YEAHHHH
EAHHHH
DIDN'T WE ALREADY DECIDE THAT'S IMPOSSIBLE?!
YES...
UT THAT'S THE ONLY PATH TO ICTORY AT HIS POINT.

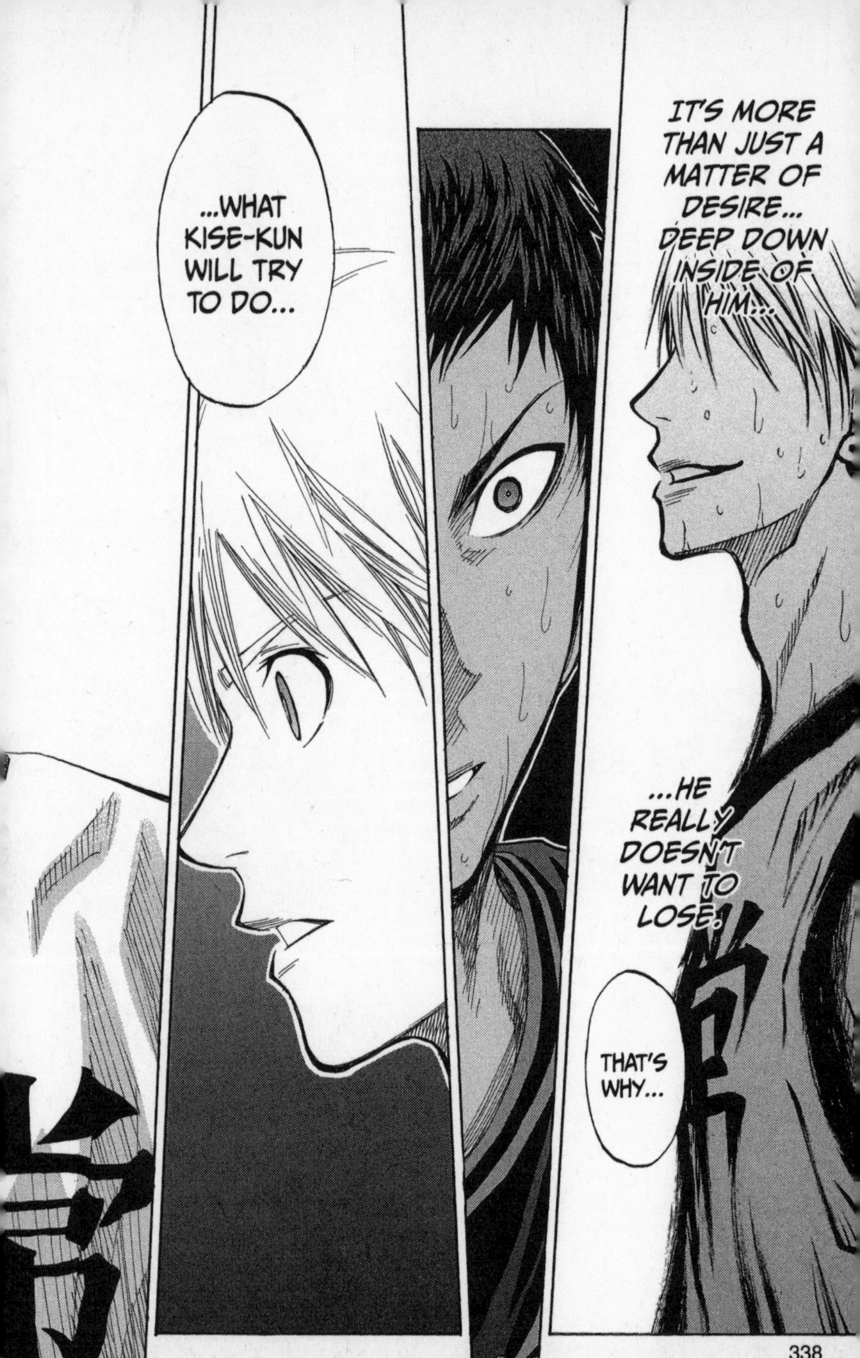
IT'S MORE THAN JUST A MATTER OF DESIRE... DEEP DOWN INSIDE OF HIM...
...HE REALLY DOESN'T WANT TO LOSE.
THAT'S WHY...
...WHAT KISE-KUN WILL TRY TO DO...

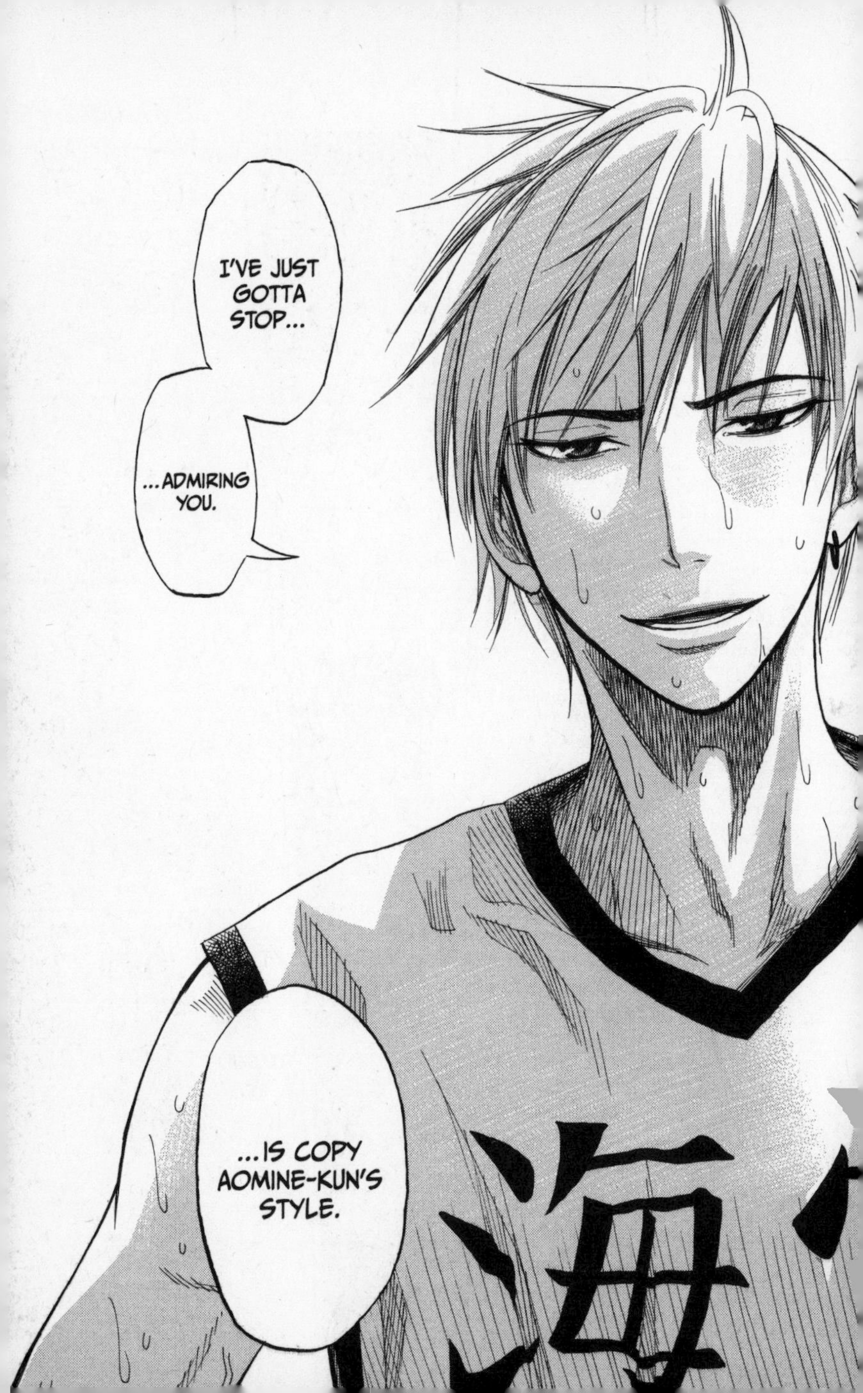
I'VE JUST GOTTA STOP...
...ADMIRING YOU.
...IS COPY AOMINE-KUN'S STYLE.
海

KUROKO'S BASKETBALL BLOOPERS
TAKE 5

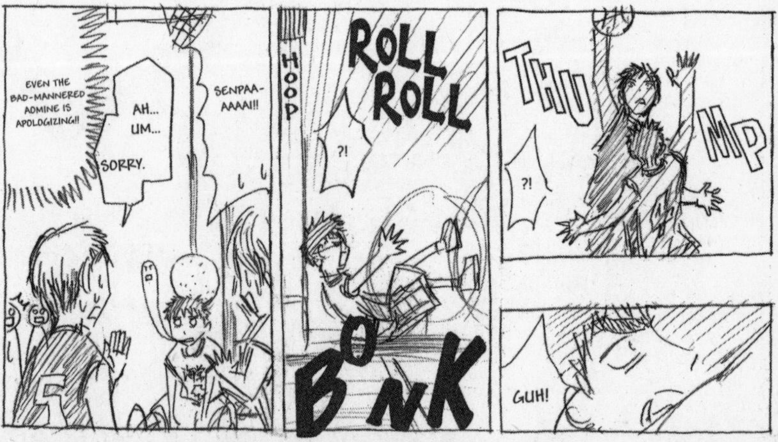
THUMP
?!
GUH!
ROLL ROLL
HOOP
?!
BONK
SENPAA-AAAI!!
AH... UM...
SORRY.
EVEN THE BAD-MANNERED ADMINE IS APOLOGIZING!!

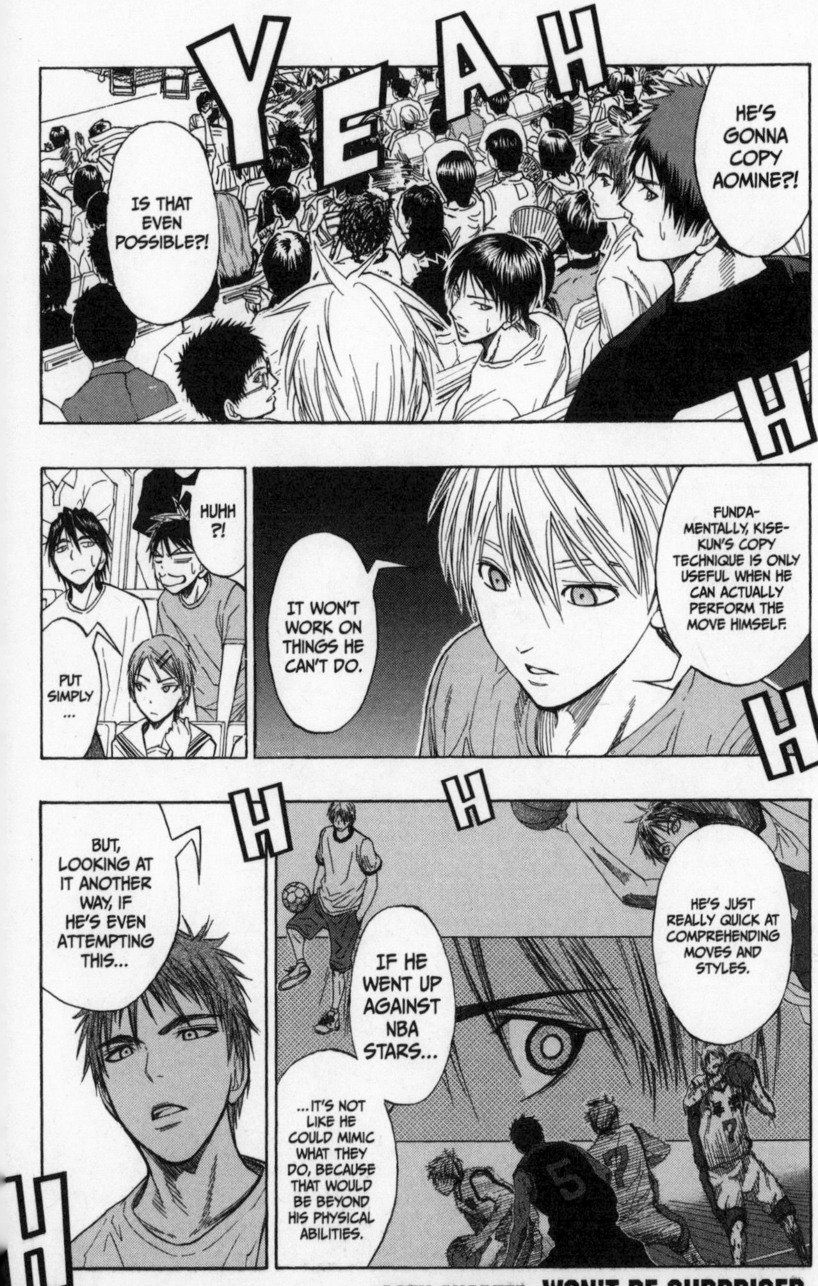
YEAHHHHH
HE'S GONNA COPY AOMINE?!
IS THAT EVEN POSSIBLE?!
FUNDA-MENTALLY, KISE-KUN'S COPY TECHNIQUE IS ONLY USEFUL WHEN HE CAN ACTUALLY PERFORM THE MOVE HIMSELF.
IT WON'T WORK ON THINGS HE CAN'T DO.
HUHH ?!
PUT SIMPLY ...
HE'S JUST REALLY QUICK AT COMPREHENDING MOVES AND STYLES.
IF HE WENT UP AGAINST NBA STARS...
...IT'S NOT LIKE HE COULD MIMIC WHAT THEY DO, BECAUSE THAT WOULD BE BEYOND HIS PHYSICAL ABILITIES.
BUT, LOOKING AT IT ANOTHER WAY, IF HE'S EVEN ATTEMPTING THIS...

68TH QUARTER: WON'T BE SURPRISED

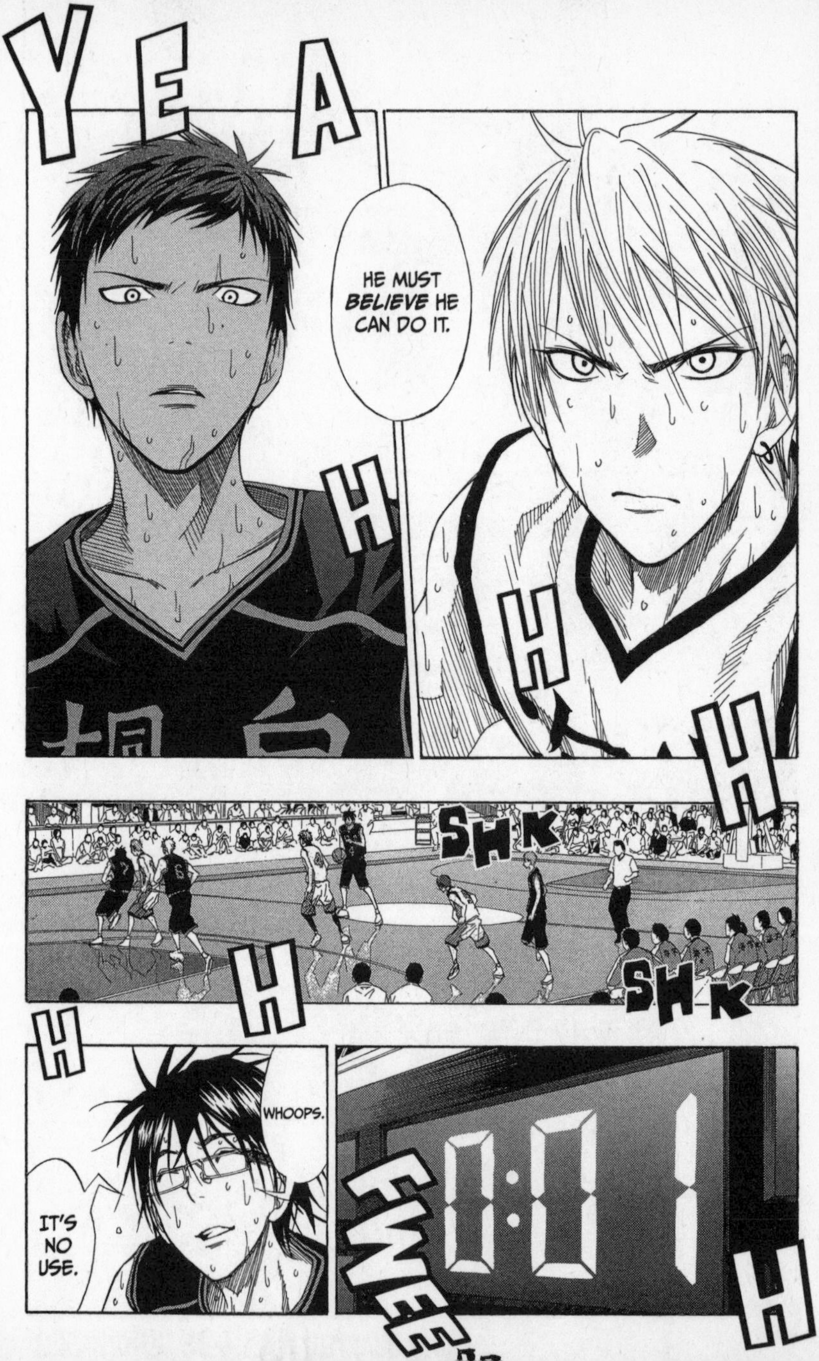
YEA
HE MUST BELIEVE HE CAN DO IT.
HHHHHHH
SHK
SHK
FWEEE
0:01
WHOOPS.
IT'S NO USE.

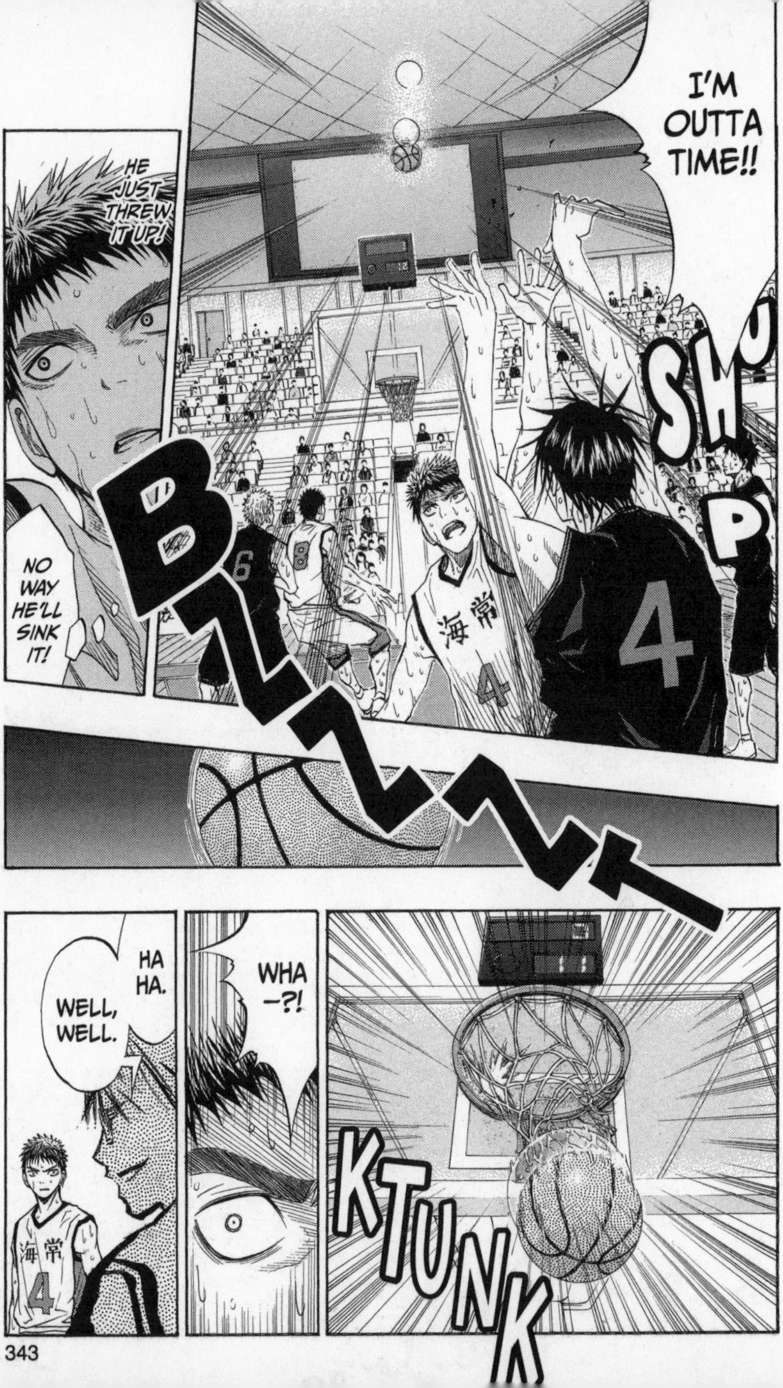
I'M OUTTA TIME!!
SHUP
HE JUST THREW IT UP!
NO WAY HE'LL SINK IT!
KTUNK
WHA—?!
HA HA.
WELL, WELL.

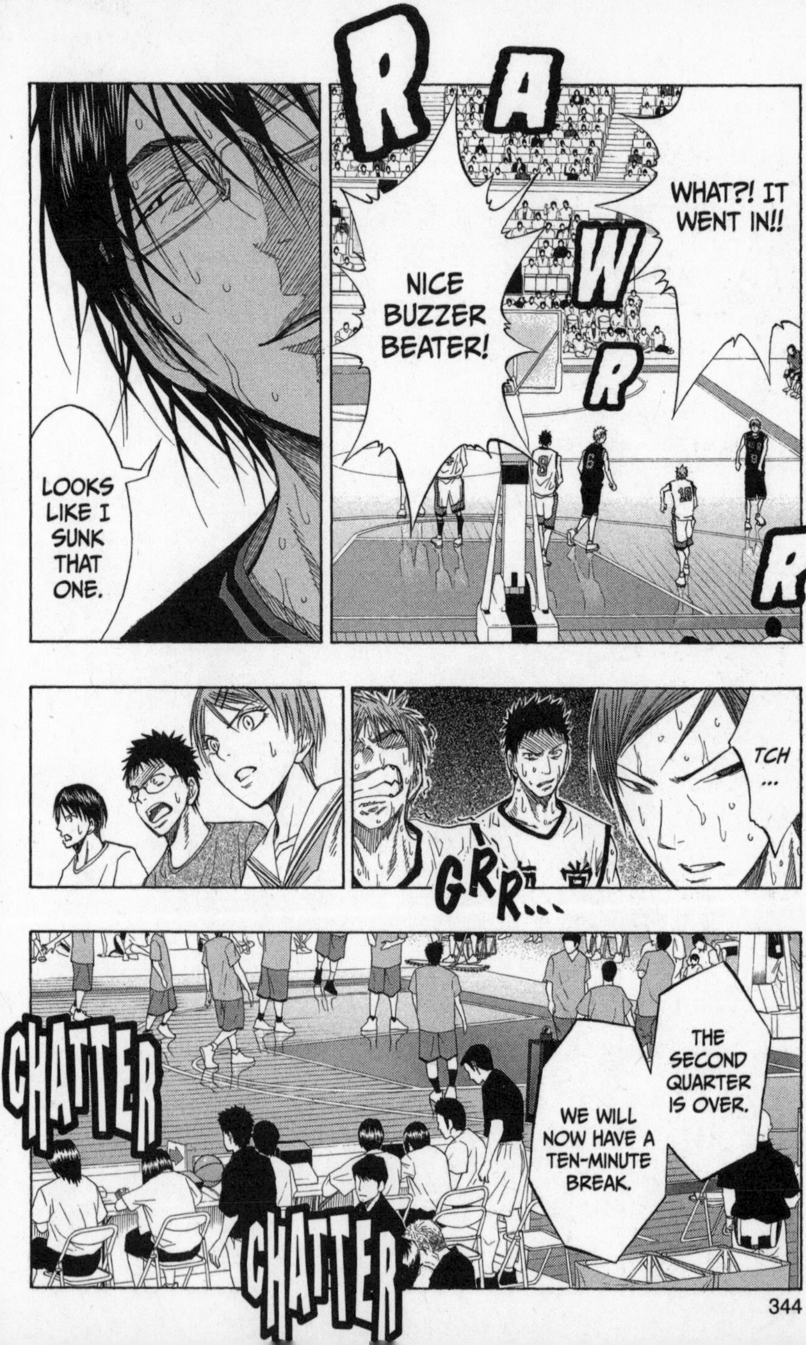
RAWRR
WHAT?! IT WENT IN!!
NICE BUZZER BEATER!
LOOKS LIKE I SUNK THAT ONE.
TCH ...
GRR...
THE SECOND QUARTER IS OVER.
WE WILL NOW HAVE A TEN-MINUTE BREAK.
CHATTER
CHATTER

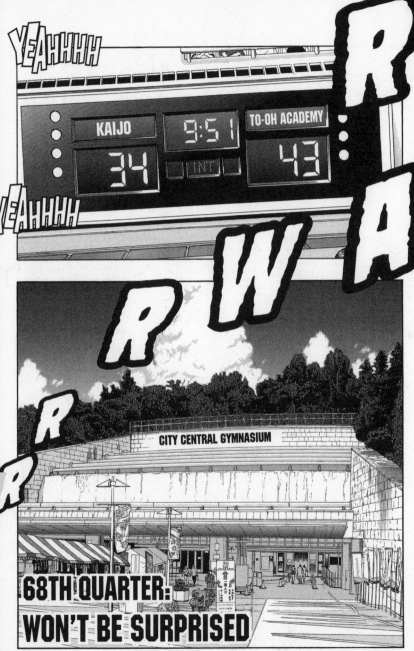

YEAHHHH

RRRWA

KAIJO 9:51 TO-OH ACADEMY
34 INT. 43

YEAHHHH

CITY CENTRAL GYMNASIUM

68TH QUARTER:
WON'T BE SURPRISED

345

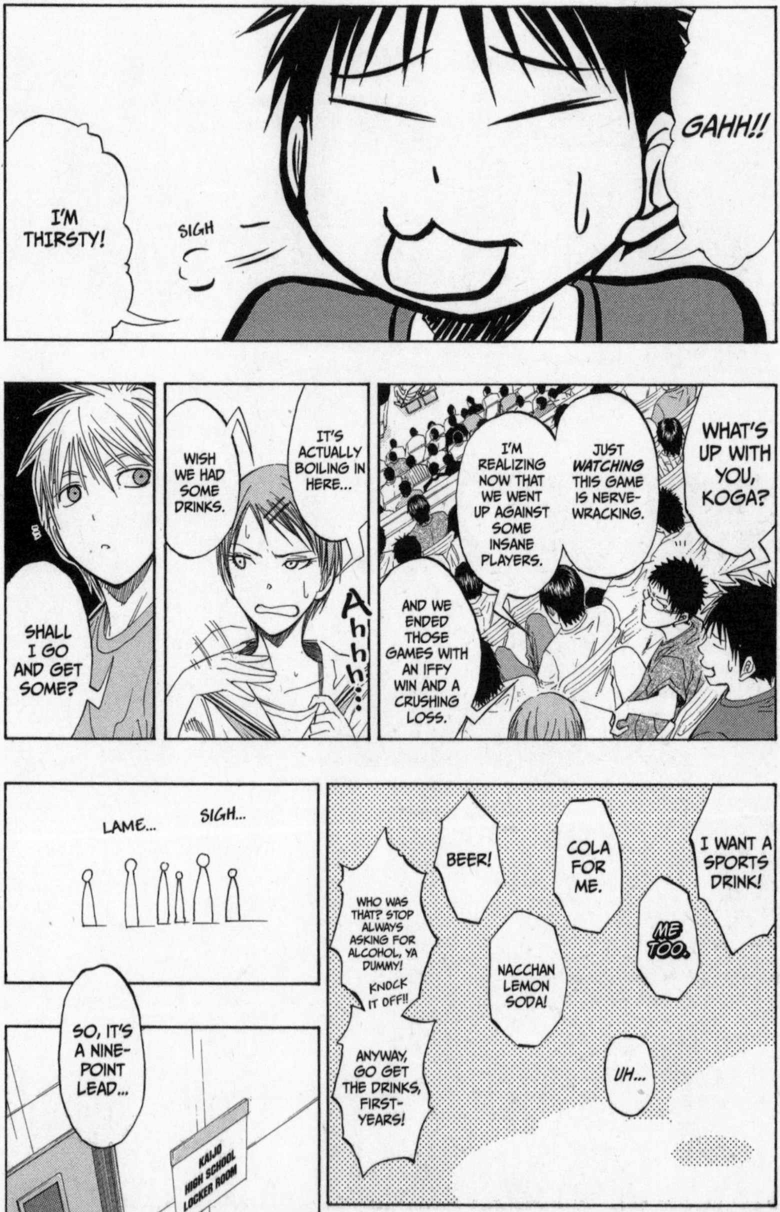
GAHH!!
SIGH
I'M THIRSTY!
WHAT'S UP WITH YOU, KOGA?
JUST *WATCHING* THIS GAME IS NERVE-WRACKING.
I'M REALIZING NOW THAT WE WENT UP AGAINST SOME INSANE PLAYERS.
AND WE ENDED THOSE GAMES WITH AN IFFY WIN AND A CRUSHING LOSS.
IT'S ACTUALLY BOILING IN HERE...
Ahhh...
WISH WE HAD SOME DRINKS.
SHALL I GO AND GET SOME?
I WANT A SPORTS DRINK!
ME TOO.
COLA FOR ME.
BEER!
NACCHAN LEMON SODA!
WHO WAS THAT? STOP ALWAYS ASKING FOR ALCOHOL, YA DUMMY!
KNOCK IT OFF!!
UH...
ANYWAY, GO GET THE DRINKS, FIRST-YEARS!
SIGH...
LAME...
SO, IT'S A NINE-POINT LEAD...
KAIJO HIGH SCHOOL LOCKER ROOM

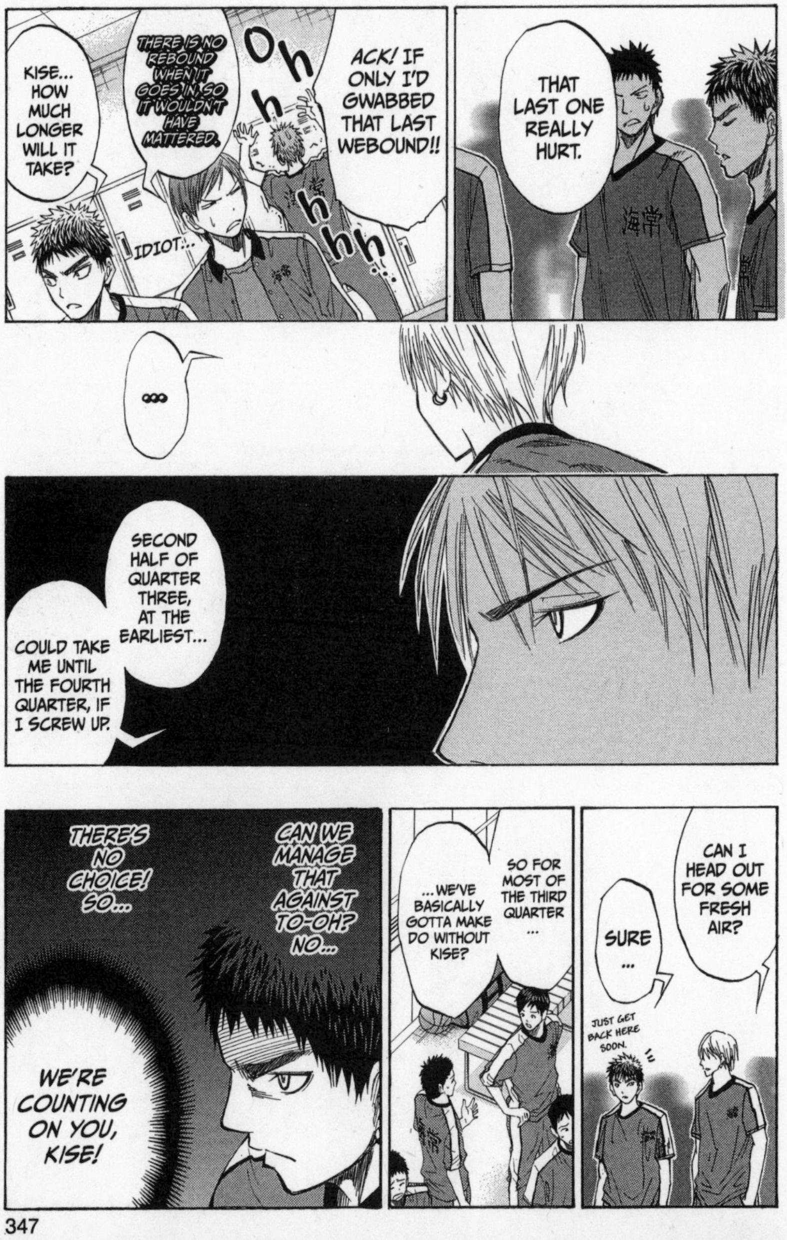
THAT LAST ONE REALLY HURT.
ACK! IF ONLY I'D GWABBED THAT LAST WEBOUND!!
Ohhhhhh
THERE IS NO REBOUND WHEN IT GOES IN, SO IT WOULDN'T HAVE MATTERED.
IDIOT...
KISE... HOW MUCH LONGER WILL IT TAKE?
...
SECOND HALF OF QUARTER THREE, AT THE EARLIEST...
COULD TAKE ME UNTIL THE FOURTH QUARTER, IF I SCREW UP.
CAN I HEAD OUT FOR SOME FRESH AIR?
SURE...
JUST GET BACK HERE SOON.
SO FOR MOST OF THE THIRD QUARTER...
...WE'VE BASICALLY GOTTA MAKE DO WITHOUT KISE?
CAN WE MANAGE THAT AGAINST TO-OH? NO...
THERE'S NO CHOICE! SO...
WE'RE COUNTING ON YOU, KISE!

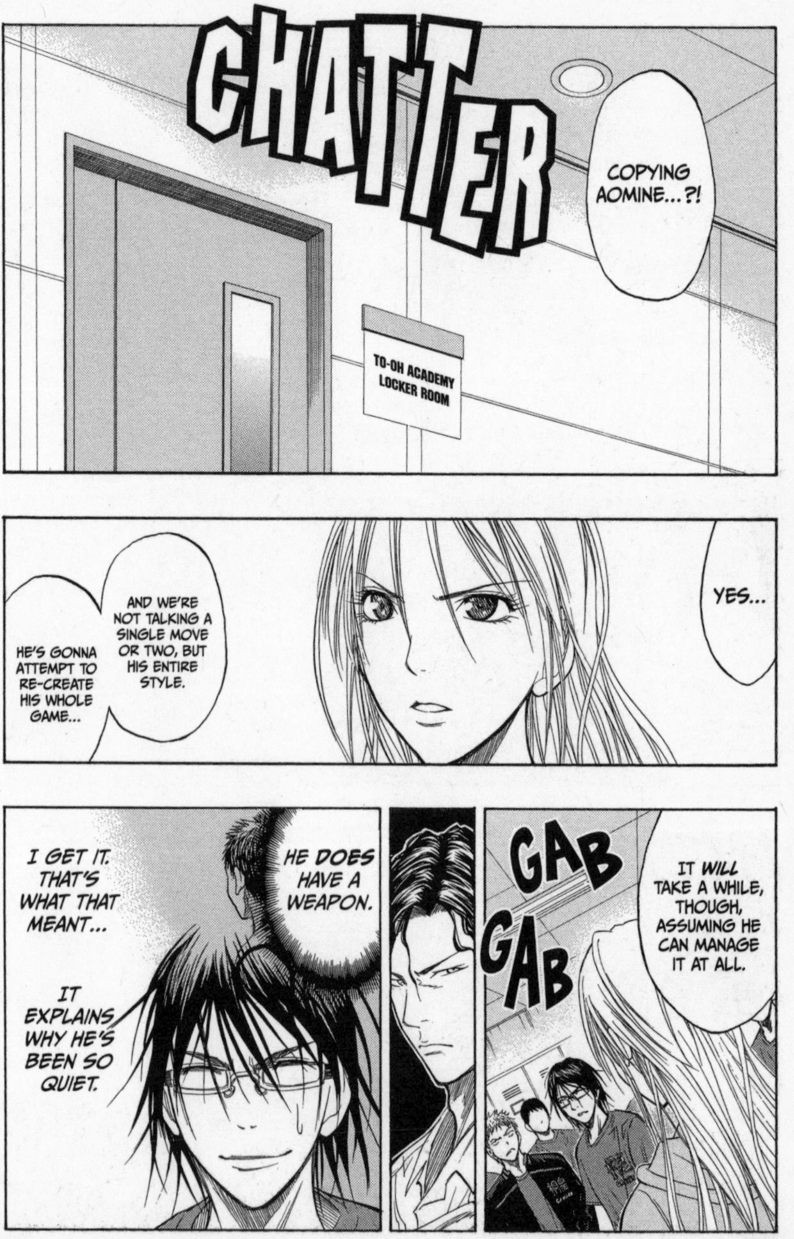
CHATTER
COPYING AOMINE...?!
TO-OH ACADEMY LOCKER ROOM
YES...
AND WE'RE NOT TALKING A SINGLE MOVE OR TWO, BUT HIS ENTIRE STYLE.
HE'S GONNA ATTEMPT TO RE-CREATE HIS WHOLE GAME...
GAB GAB
IT *WILL* TAKE A WHILE, THOUGH, ASSUMING HE CAN MANAGE IT AT ALL.
HE DOES HAVE A WEAPON.
I GET IT. THAT'S WHAT THAT MEANT...
IT EXPLAINS WHY HE'S BEEN SO QUIET.

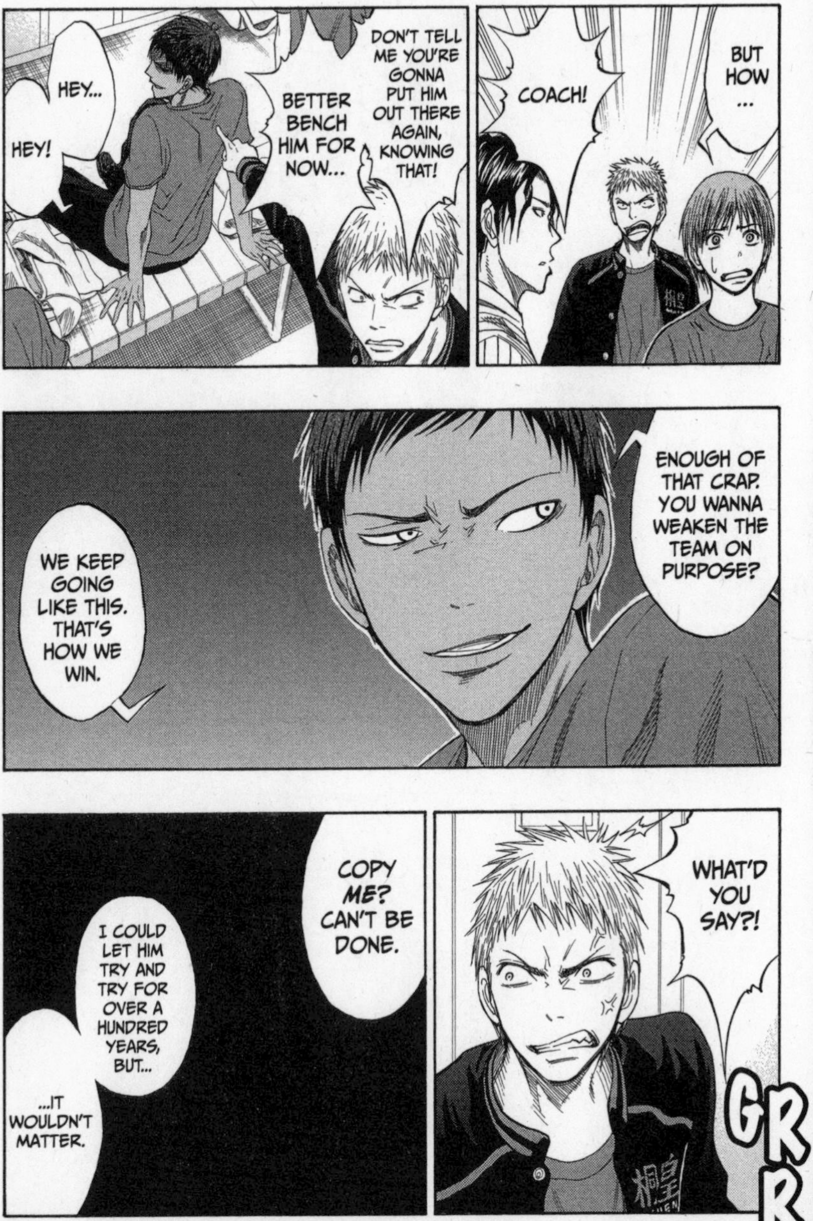
BUT HOW ...
COACH!
DON'T TELL ME YOU'RE GONNA PUT HIM OUT THERE AGAIN, KNOWING THAT!
BETTER BENCH HIM FOR NOW...
HEY...
HEY!
ENOUGH OF THAT CRAP. YOU WANNA WEAKEN THE TEAM ON PURPOSE?
WE KEEP GOING LIKE THIS. THAT'S HOW WE WIN.
WHAT'D YOU SAY?!
GRR
COPY *ME*? CAN'T BE DONE.
I COULD LET HIM TRY AND TRY FOR OVER A HUNDRED YEARS, BUT...
...IT WOULDN'T MATTER.

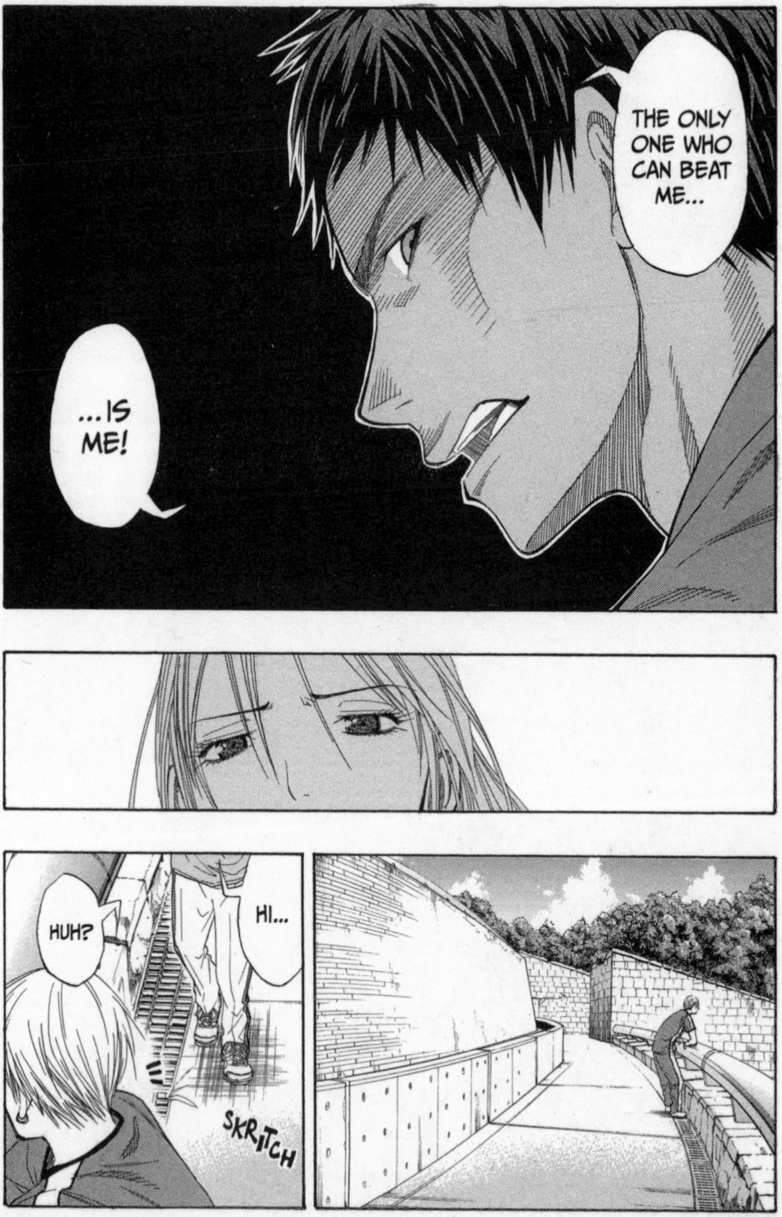
THE ONLY ONE WHO CAN BEAT ME...
...IS ME!
HI...
HUH?
SKRITCH

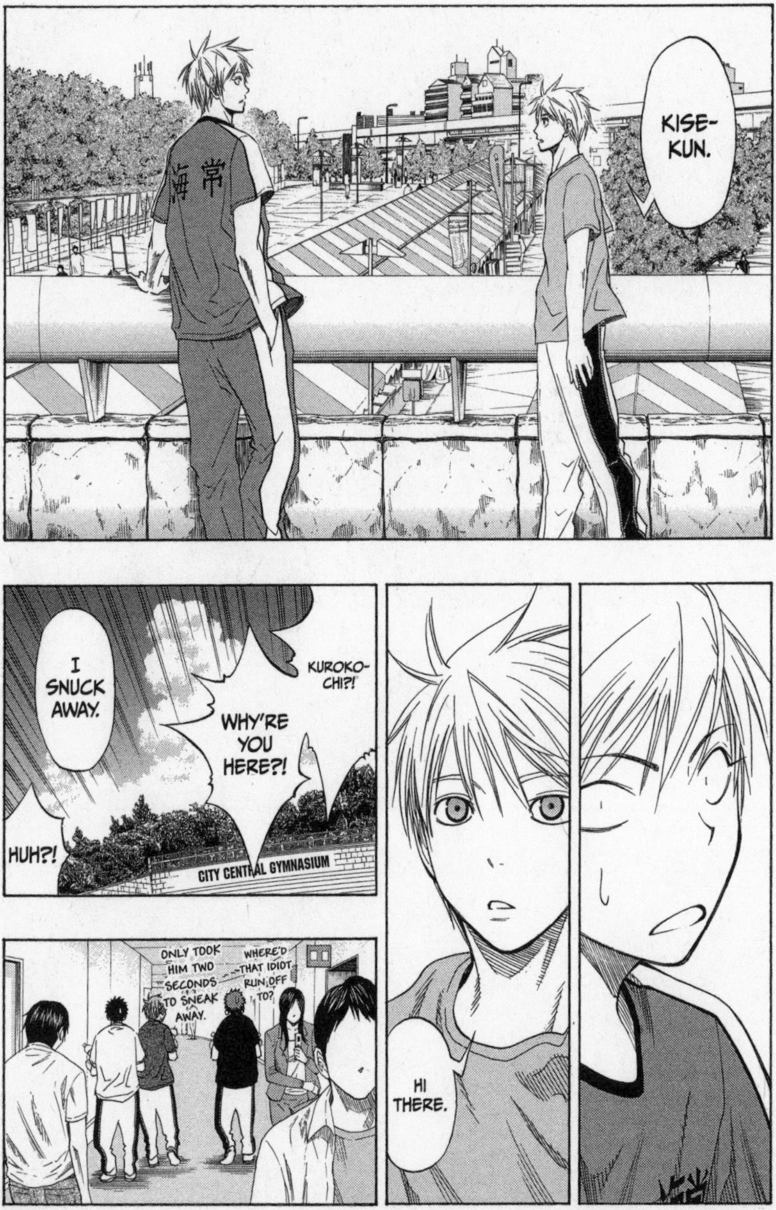
KISE-KUN.
HI THERE.
KUROKO-CHI?!
WHY'RE YOU HERE?!
I SNUCK AWAY.
HUH?!
CITY CENTRAL GYMNASIUM
WHERE'D THAT IDIOT RUN OFF TO?
ONLY TOOK HIM TWO SECONDS TO SNEAK AWAY.

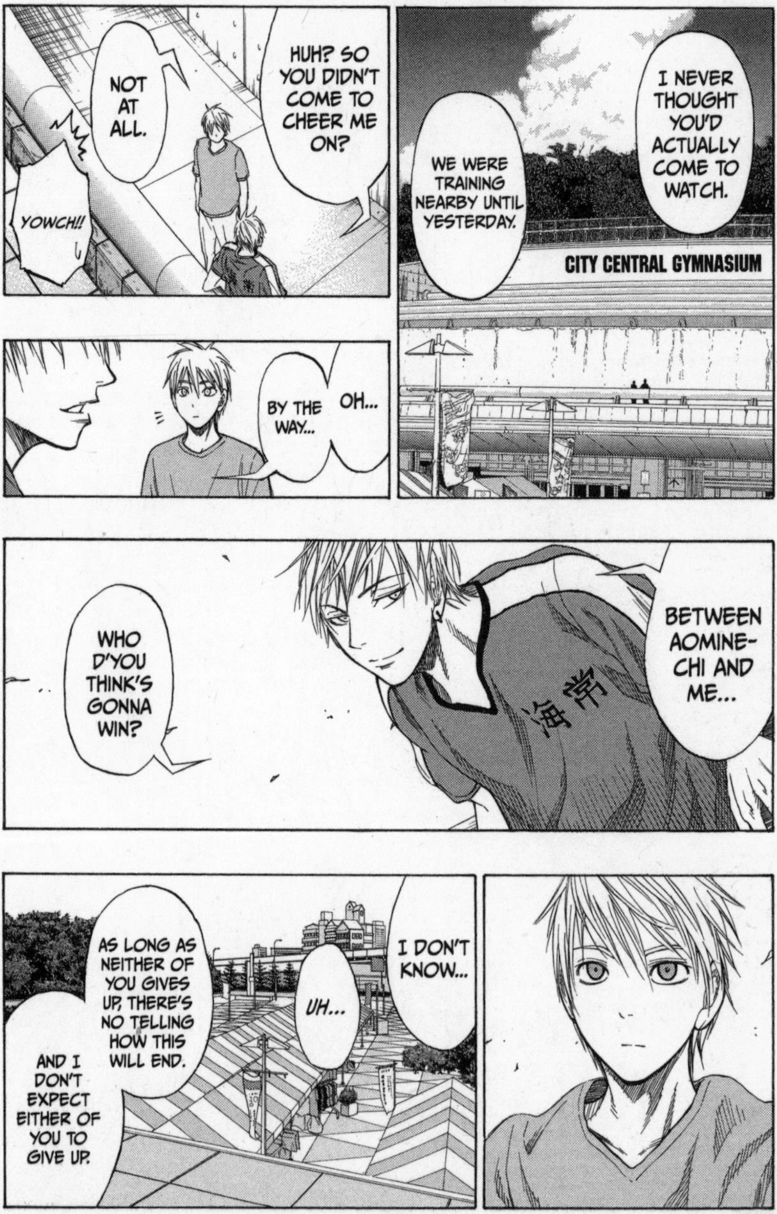
I NEVER THOUGHT YOU'D ACTUALLY COME TO WATCH.
WE WERE TRAINING NEARBY UNTIL YESTERDAY.
CITY CENTRAL GYMNASIUM
HUH? SO YOU DIDN'T COME TO CHEER ME ON?
NOT AT ALL.
YOWCH!!
OH...
BY THE WAY...
BETWEEN AOMINE-CHI AND ME...
海常
WHO D'YOU THINK'S GONNA WIN?
I DON'T KNOW...
UH...
AS LONG AS NEITHER OF YOU GIVES UP, THERE'S NO TELLING HOW THIS WILL END.
AND I DON'T EXPECT EITHER OF YOU TO GIVE UP.

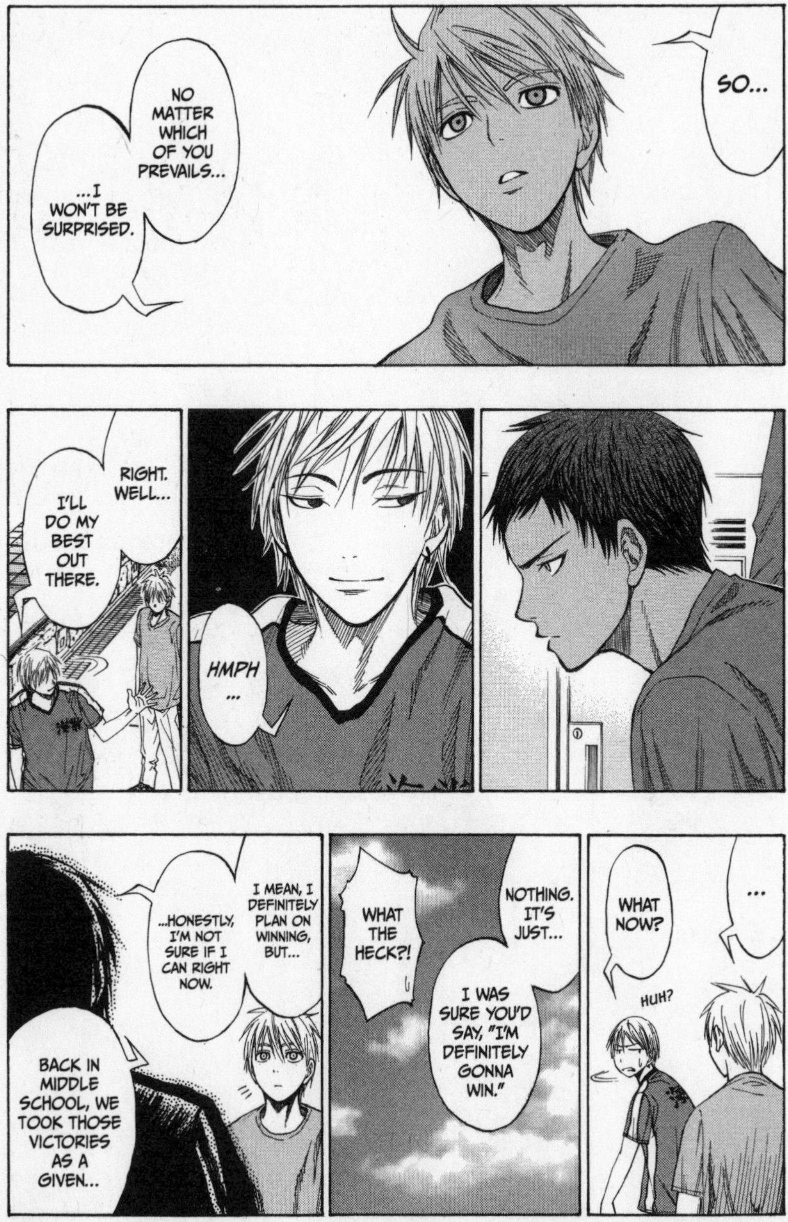
SO...
NO MATTER WHICH OF YOU PREVAILS...
...I WON'T BE SURPRISED.
HMPH...
RIGHT. WELL...
I'LL DO MY BEST OUT THERE.
...
WHAT NOW?
HUH?
NOTHING. IT'S JUST...
WHAT THE HECK?!
I WAS SURE YOU'D SAY, "I'M DEFINITELY GONNA WIN."
I MEAN, I DEFINITELY PLAN ON WINNING, BUT...
...HONESTLY, I'M NOT SURE IF I CAN RIGHT NOW.
BACK IN MIDDLE SCHOOL, WE TOOK THOSE VICTORIES AS A GIVEN...

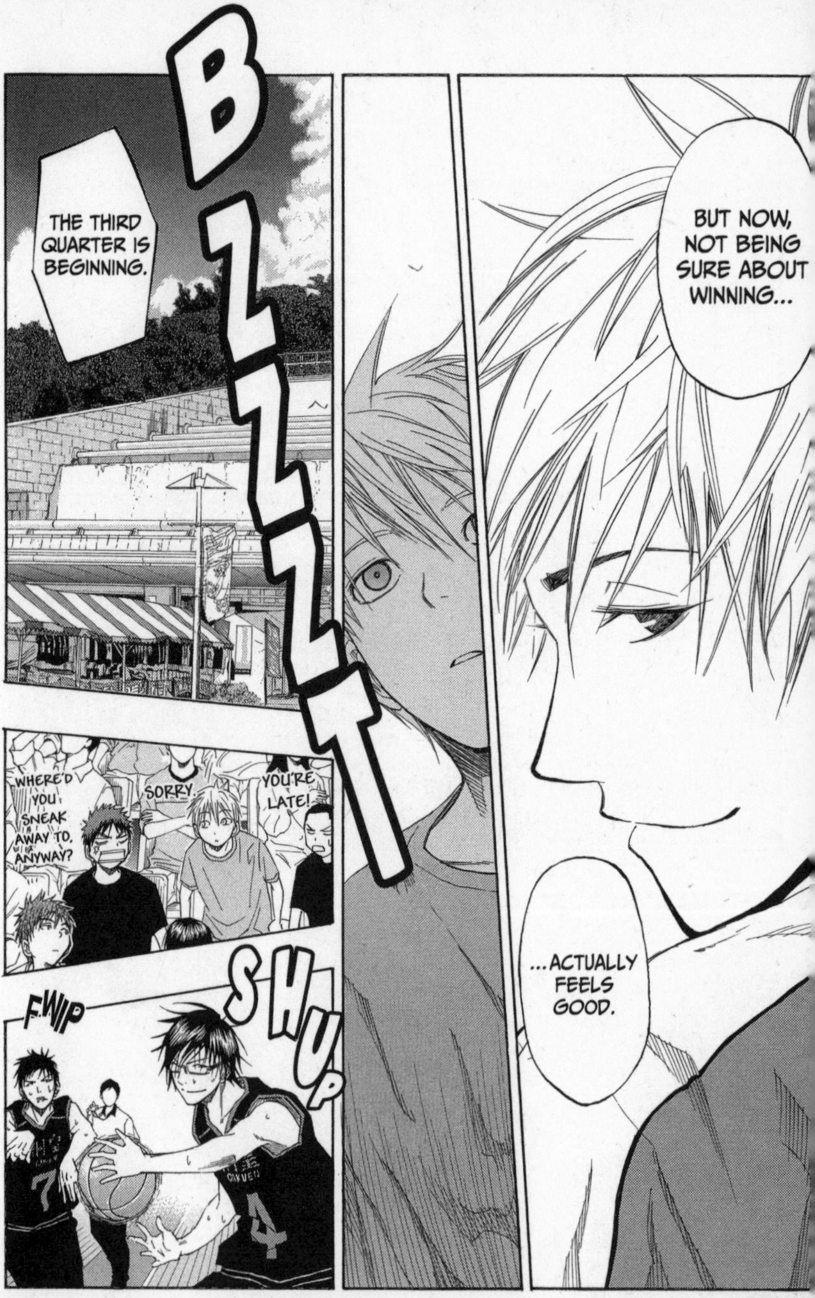
BUT NOW, NOT BEING SURE ABOUT WINNING...
...ACTUALLY FEELS GOOD.
BZZZZT
THE THIRD QUARTER IS BEGINNING.
YOU'RE LATE!
SORRY.
WHERE'D YOU SNEAK AWAY TO, ANYWAY?
SHUP
FWIP

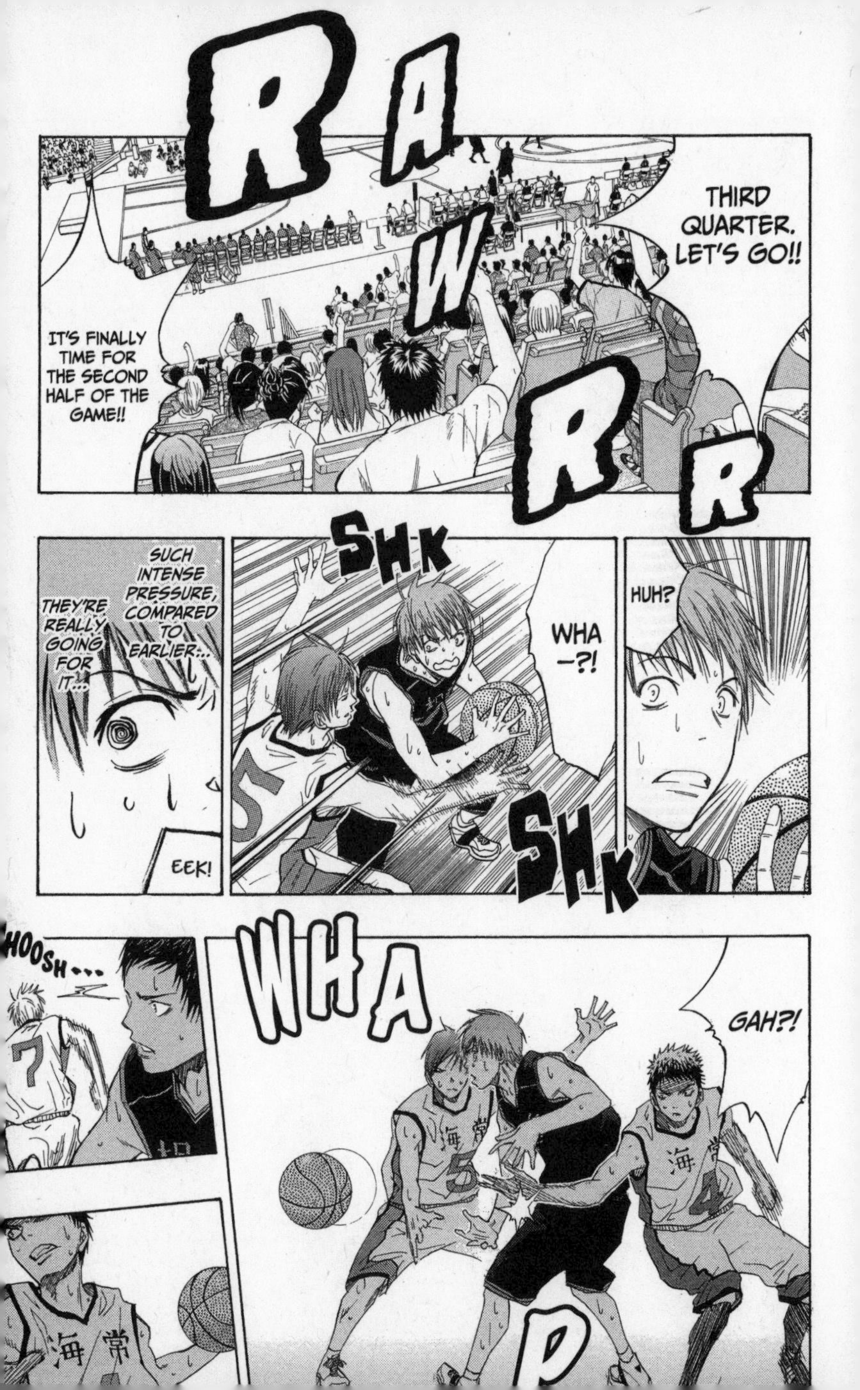
RAWRR
THIRD QUARTER. LET'S GO!!
IT'S FINALLY TIME FOR THE SECOND HALF OF THE GAME!!
HUH?
SHK
WHA-?!
SHK
SUCH INTENSE PRESSURE, COMPARED TO EARLIER...
THEY'RE REALLY GOING FOR IT...
EEK!
WHAP
GAH?!
HOOSH...

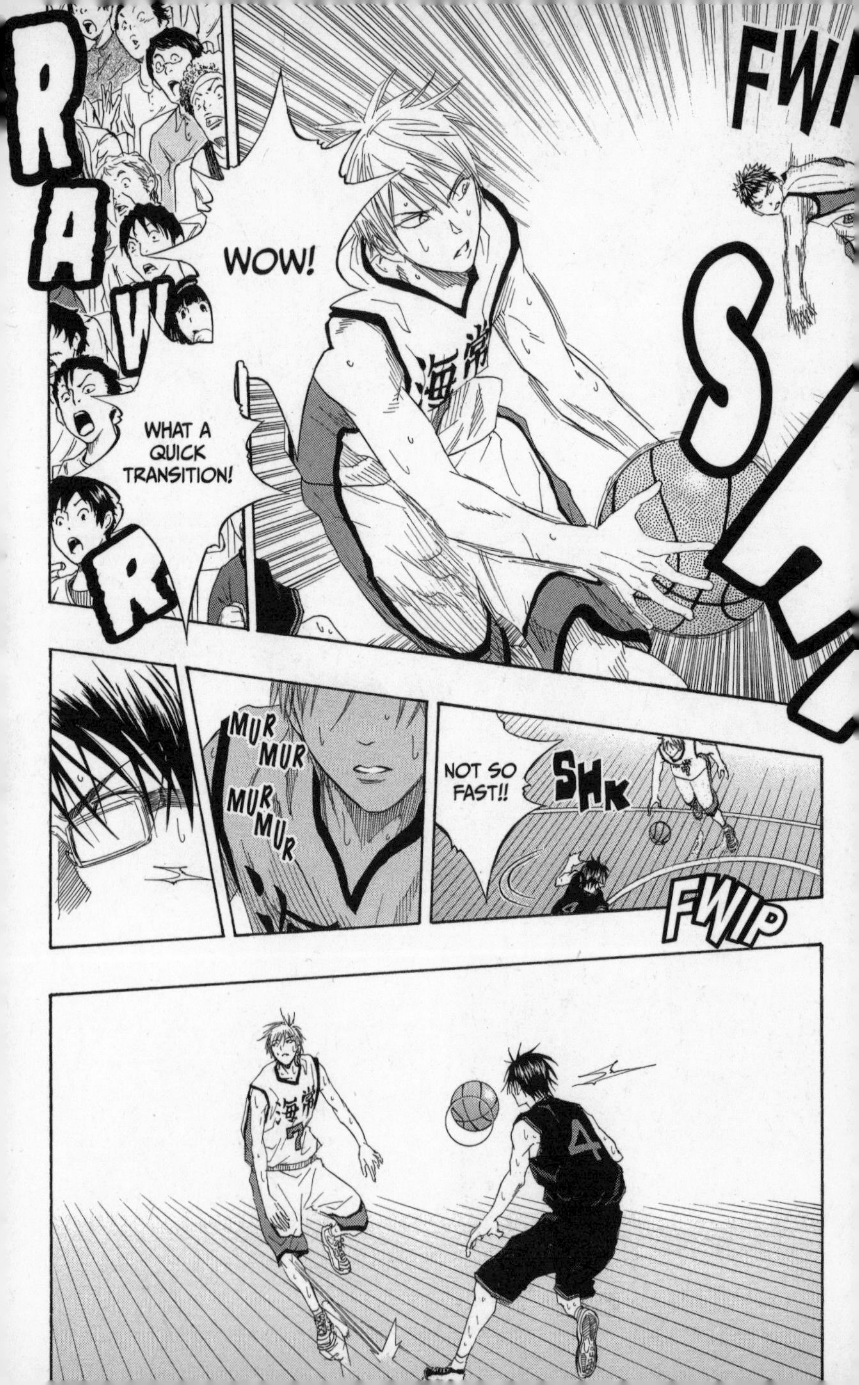
RAWR
WOW!
WHAT A QUICK TRANSITION!
NOT SO FAST!!
SHK
FWIP
MUR MUR
MUR MUR

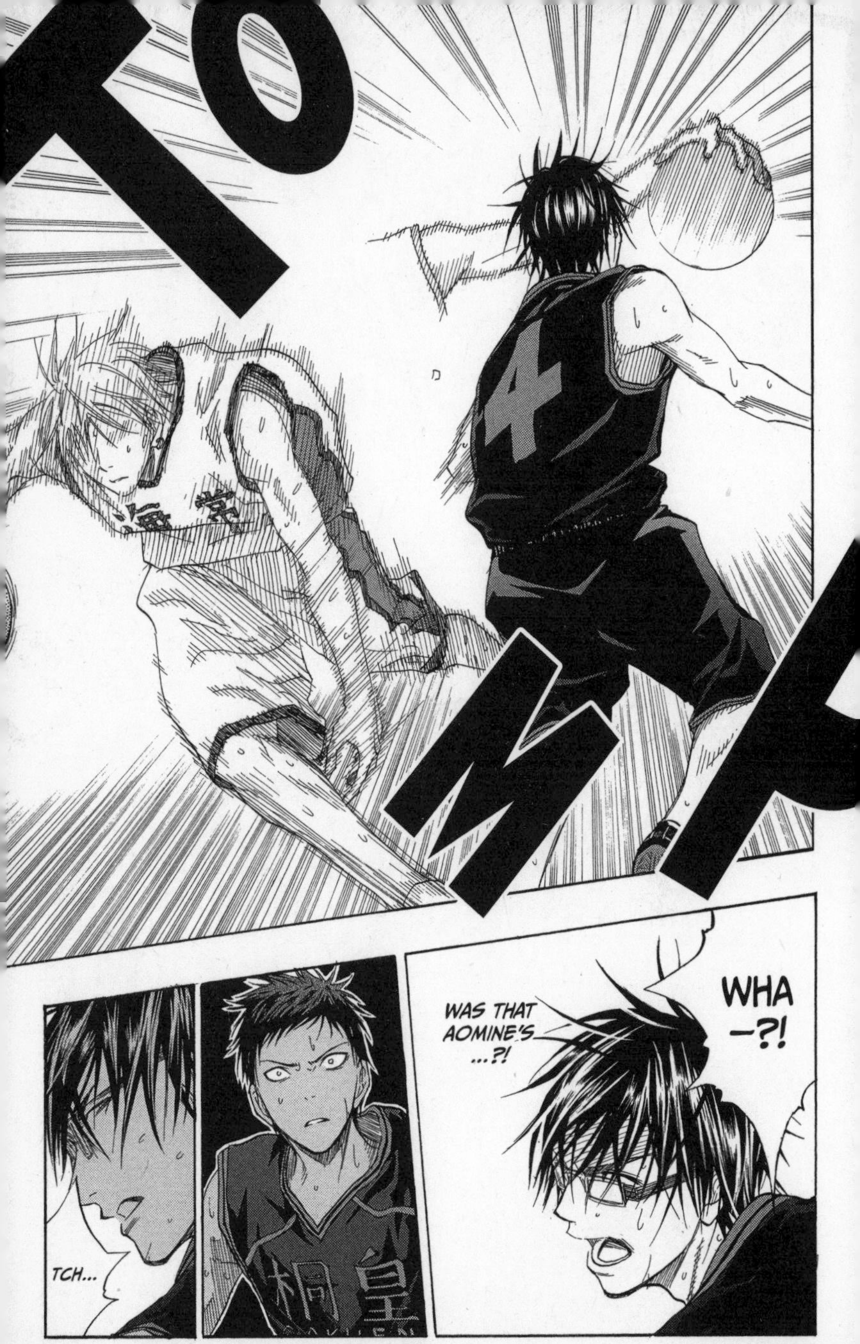
WHA —?!
WAS THAT AOMINE'S ...?!
TCH...

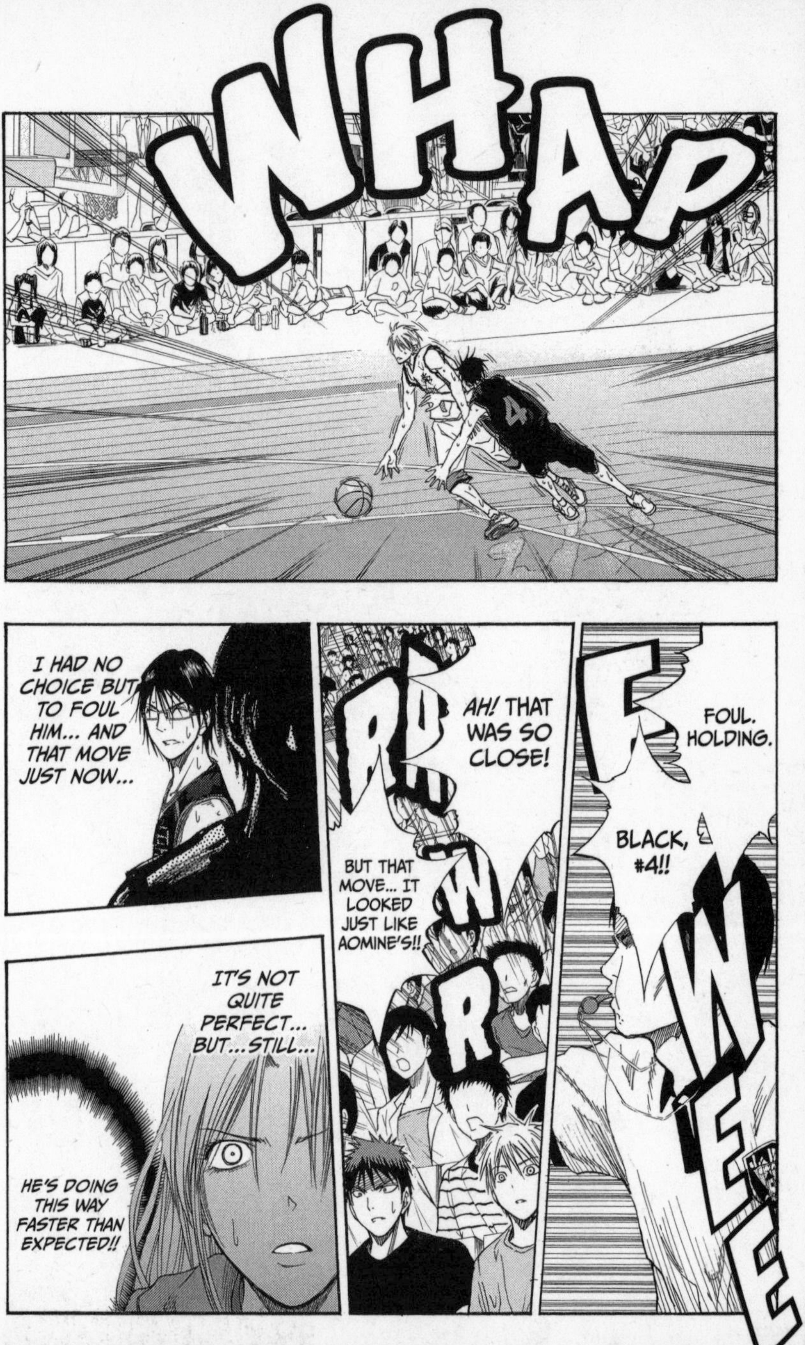
WHAP
FOUL. HOLDING.
BLACK, #4!!
AH! THAT WAS SO CLOSE!
BUT THAT MOVE... IT LOOKED JUST LIKE AOMINE'S!!
I HAD NO CHOICE BUT TO FOUL HIM... AND THAT MOVE JUST NOW...
IT'S NOT QUITE PERFECT... BUT...STILL...
HE'S DOING THIS WAY FASTER THAN EXPECTED!!

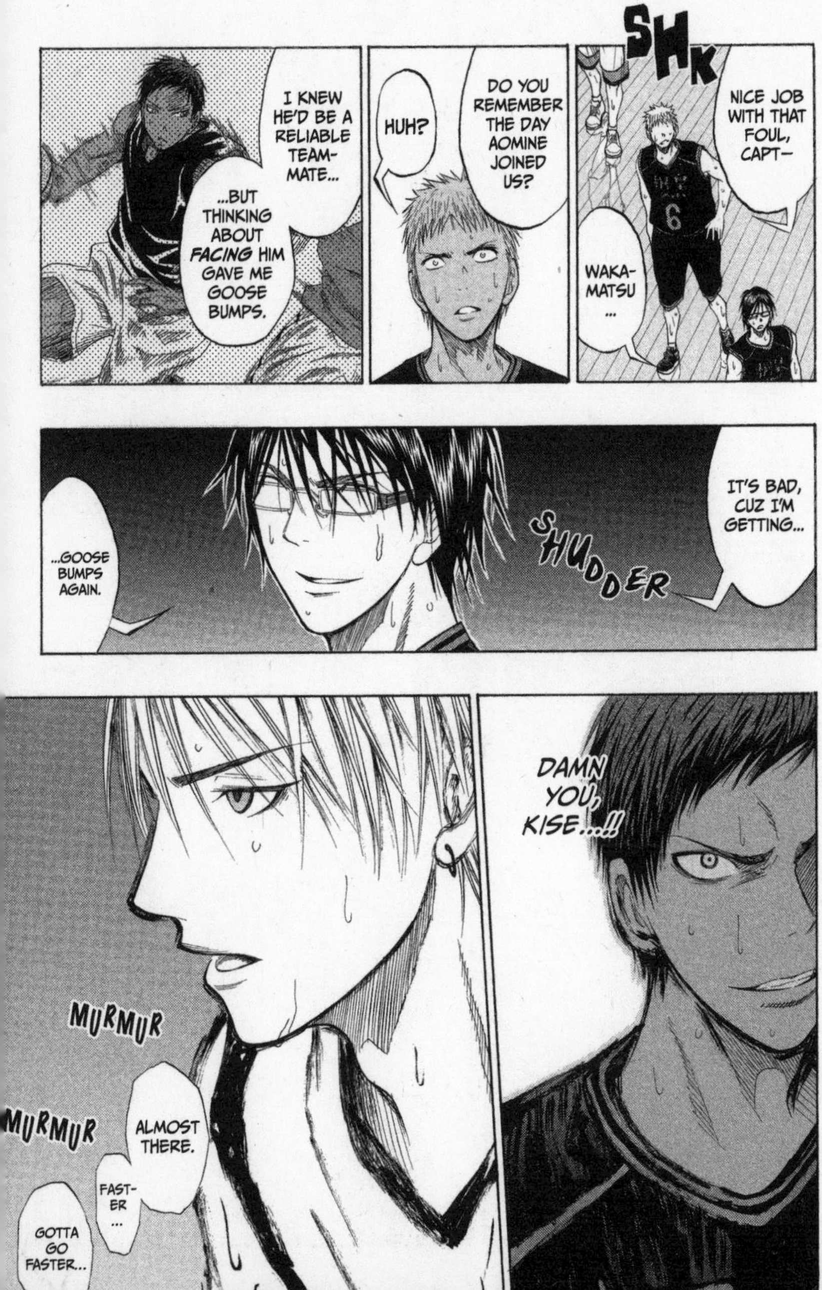
SHK
NICE JOB WITH THAT FOUL, CAPT—
WAKAMATSU...
DO YOU REMEMBER THE DAY AOMINE JOINED US?
HUH?
I KNEW HE'D BE A RELIABLE TEAMMATE...
...BUT THINKING ABOUT *FACING* HIM GAVE ME GOOSE BUMPS.
IT'S BAD, CUZ I'M GETTING...
SHUDDER
...GOOSE BUMPS AGAIN.
DAMN YOU, KISE...!!
MURMUR
MURMUR
ALMOST THERE.
FASTER...
GOTTA GO FASTER...

KUROKO'S BASKETBALL BLOOPERS

TAKE 3

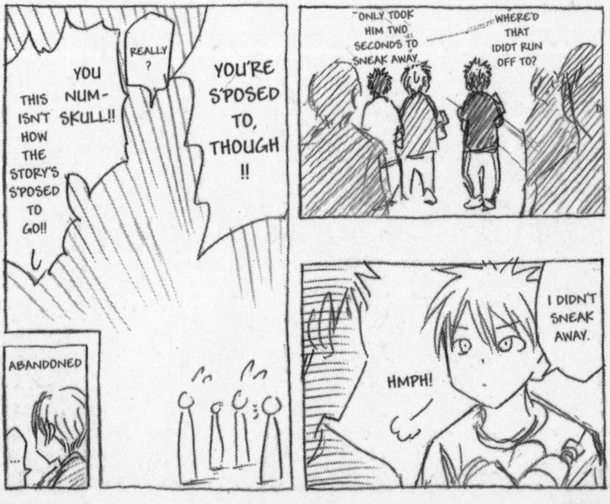
WHERE'D THAT IDIDT RUN OFF TO?
ONLY TOOK HIM TWO SECONDS TO SNEAK AWAY.
I DIDN'T SNEAK AWAY.
HMPH!
YOU'RE S'POSED TO, THOUGH!!
REALLY?
YOU NUMSKULL!!
THIS ISN'T HOW THE STORY'S S'POSED TO GO!!
ABANDONED
...

69TH QUARTER: HOW ABOUT THEN?

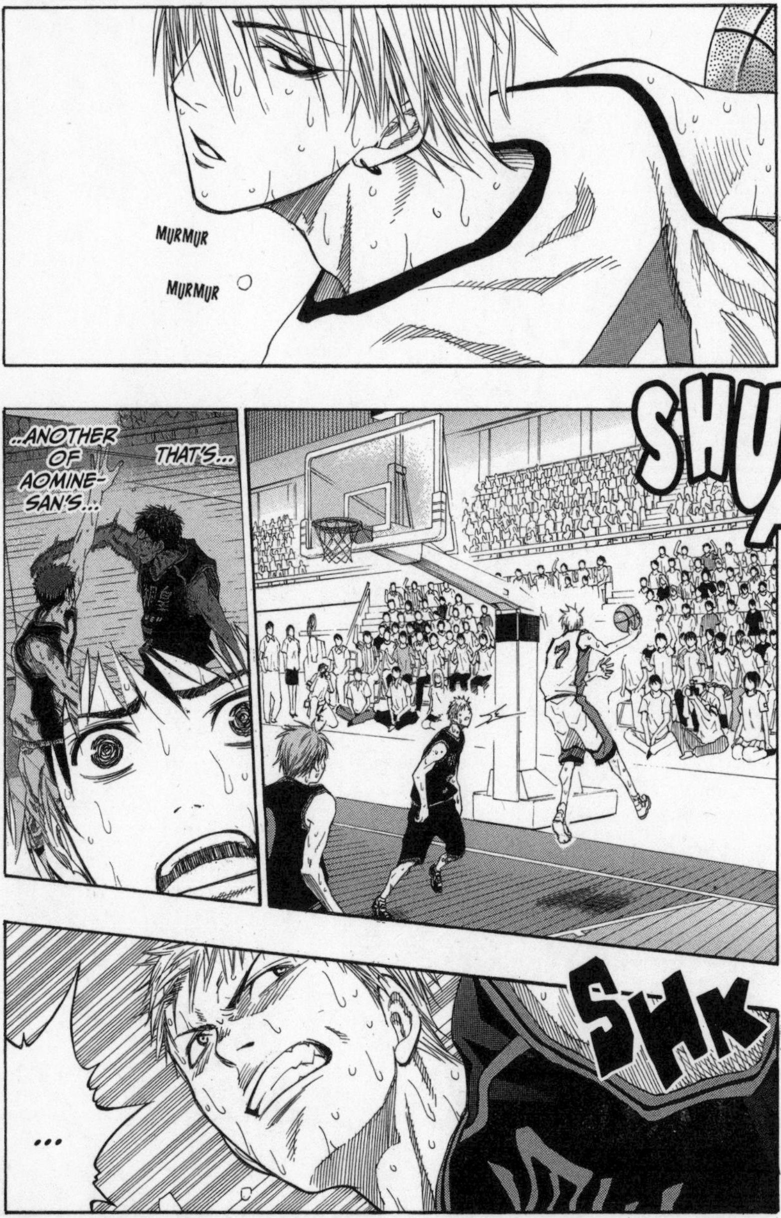
MURMUR
MURMUR
SHUP
THAT'S...
...ANOTHER OF AOMINE-SAN'S...
SHK
...

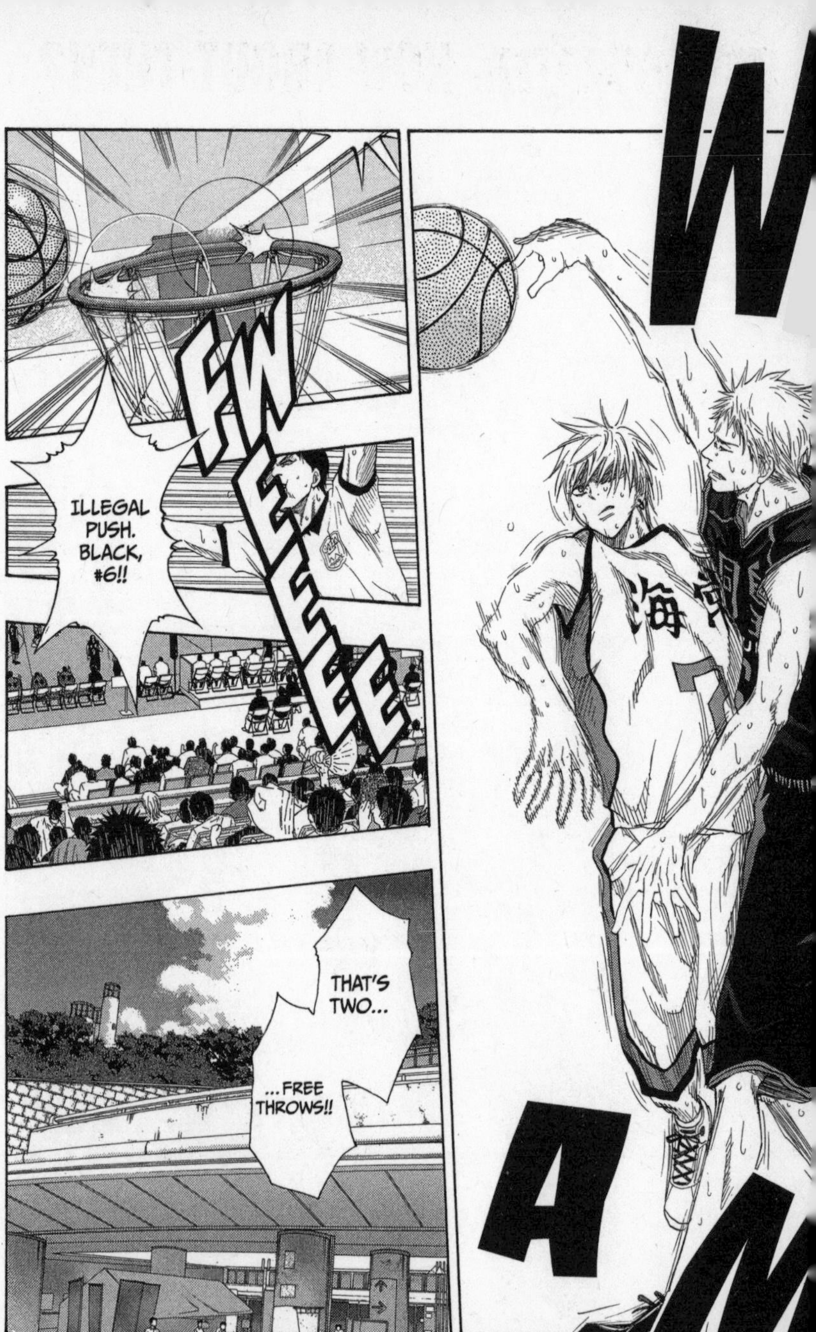
W
AM
FWEEEEE
ILLEGAL PUSH. BLACK, #6!!
THAT'S TWO...
...FREE THROWS!!

69TH QUARTER: HOW ABOUT THEN?

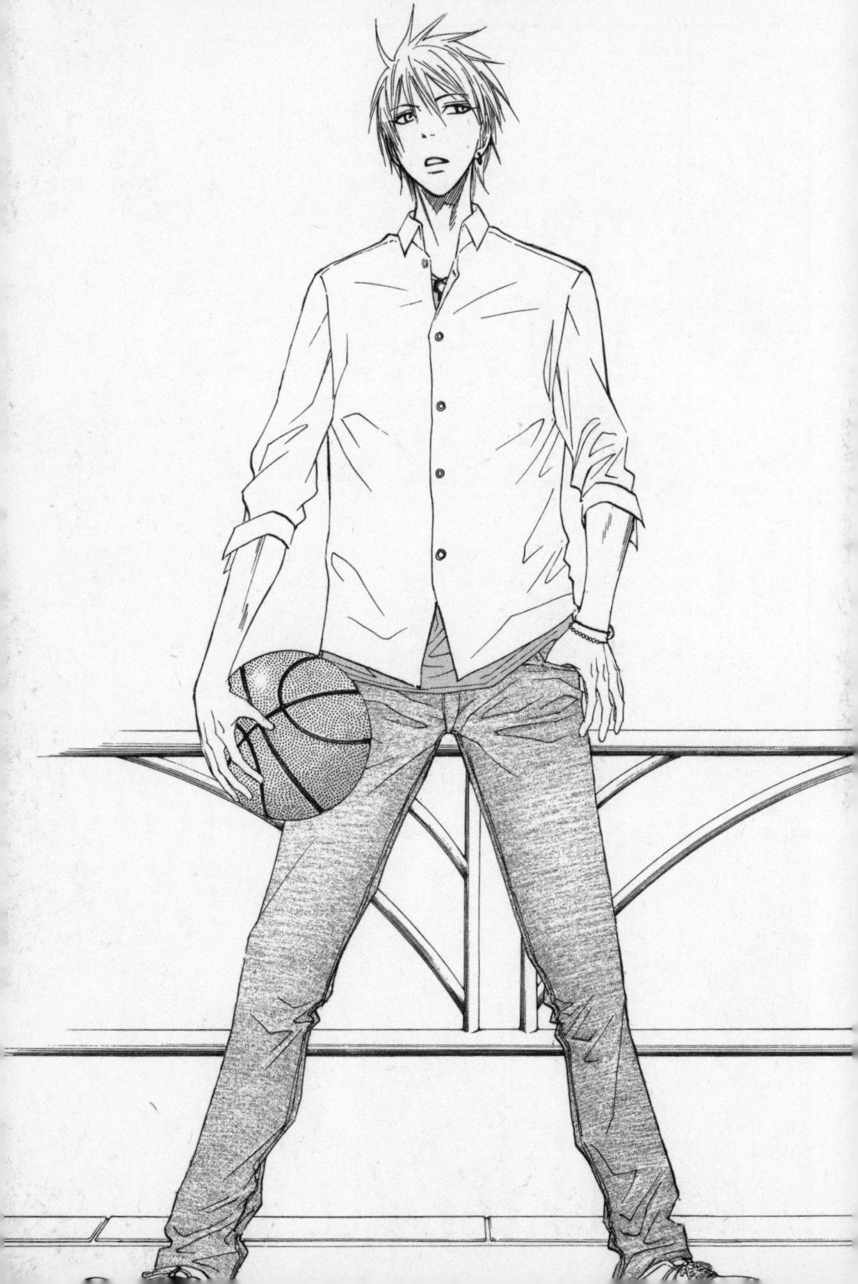

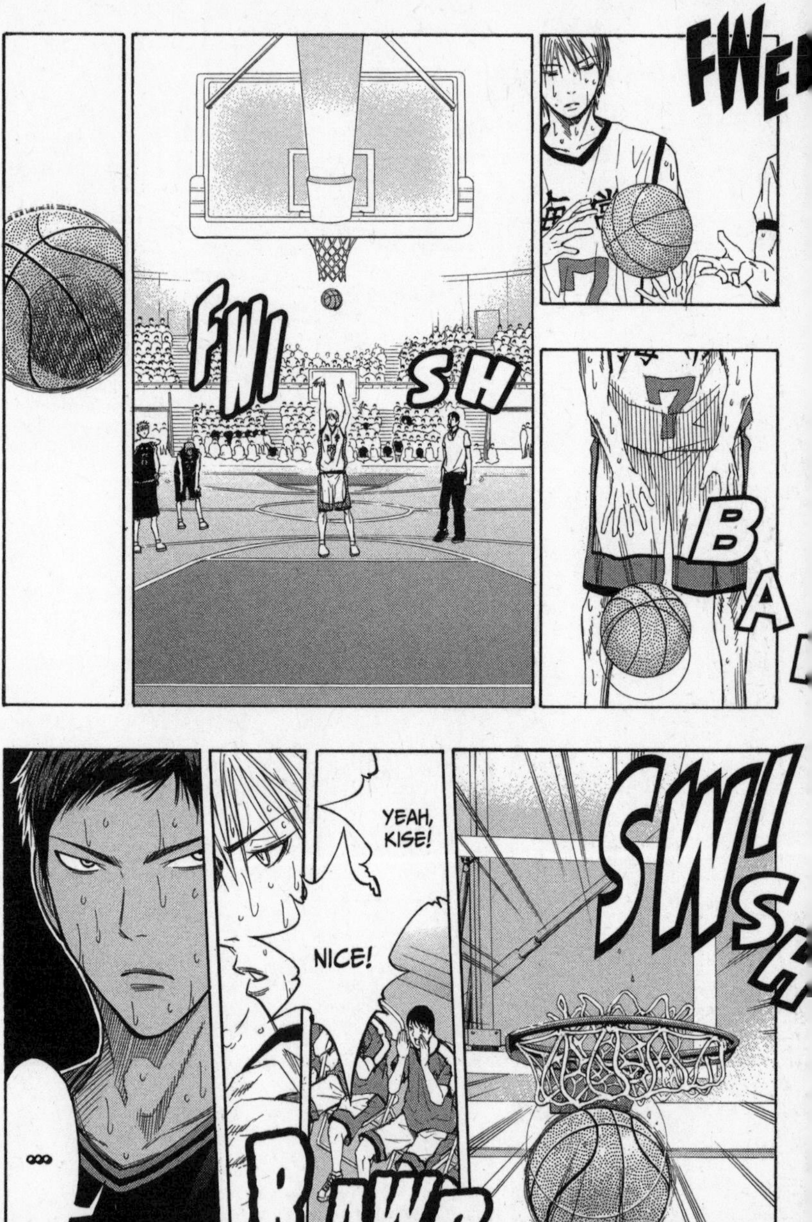
FWE
BA
FWISH
SWISH
YEAH, KISE!
NICE!
RAWR
...

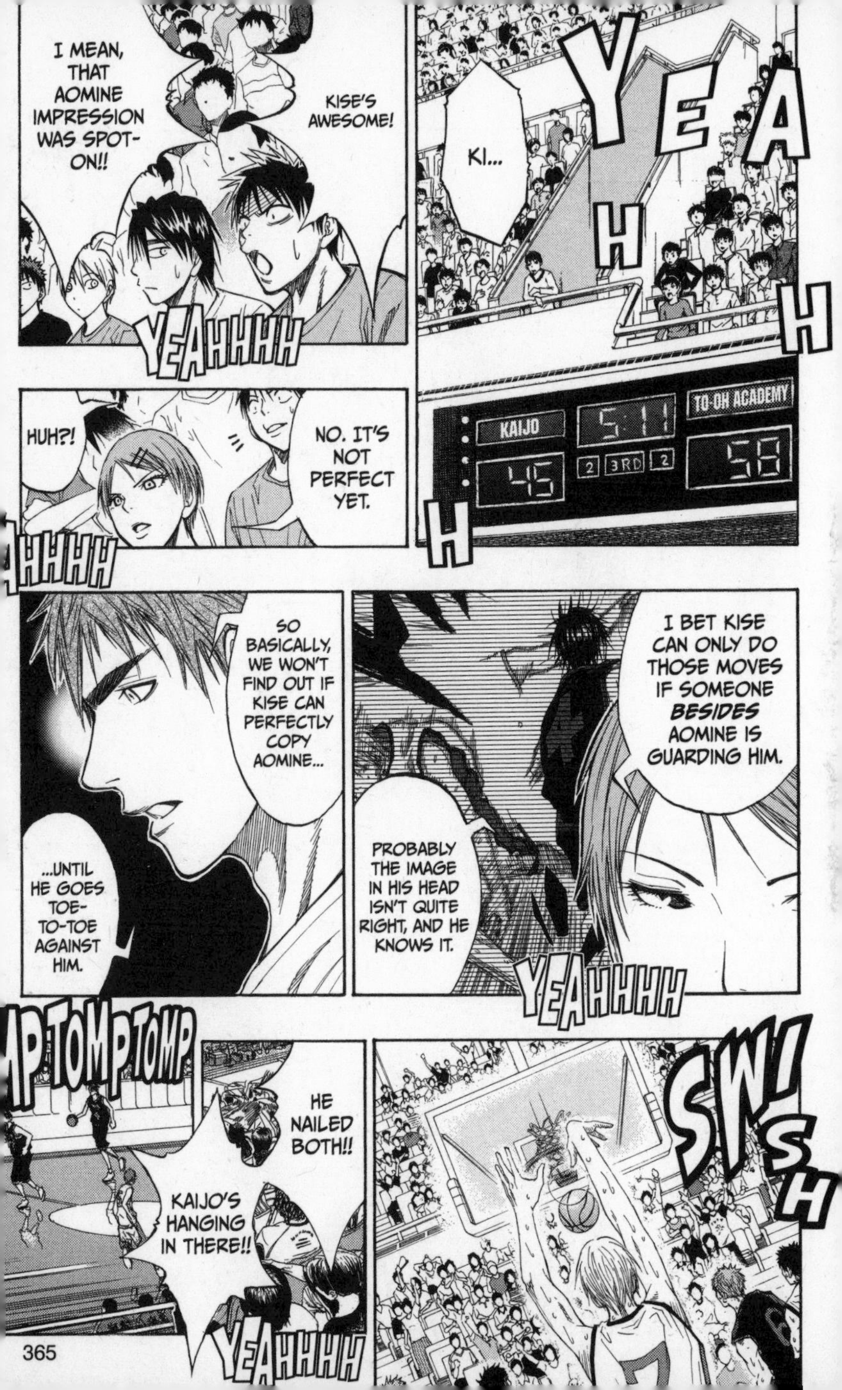
KI...
YEAHHHH
KAIJO
5:11
TO OH ACADEMY
45
2 3RD 2
58
KISE'S AWESOME!
I MEAN, THAT AOMINE IMPRESSION WAS SPOT-ON!!
YEAHHHH
NO. IT'S NOT PERFECT YET.
HUH?!
AHHHHH
I BET KISE CAN ONLY DO THOSE MOVES IF SOMEONE *BESIDES* AOMINE IS GUARDING HIM.
PROBABLY THE IMAGE IN HIS HEAD ISN'T QUITE RIGHT, AND HE KNOWS IT.
YEAHHHH
SO BASICALLY, WE WON'T FIND OUT IF KISE CAN PERFECTLY COPY AOMINE...
...UNTIL HE GOES TOE-TO-TOE AGAINST HIM.
SWISH
HE NAILED BOTH!!
KAIJO'S HANGING IN THERE!!
MP TOMP TOMP
YEAHHHH

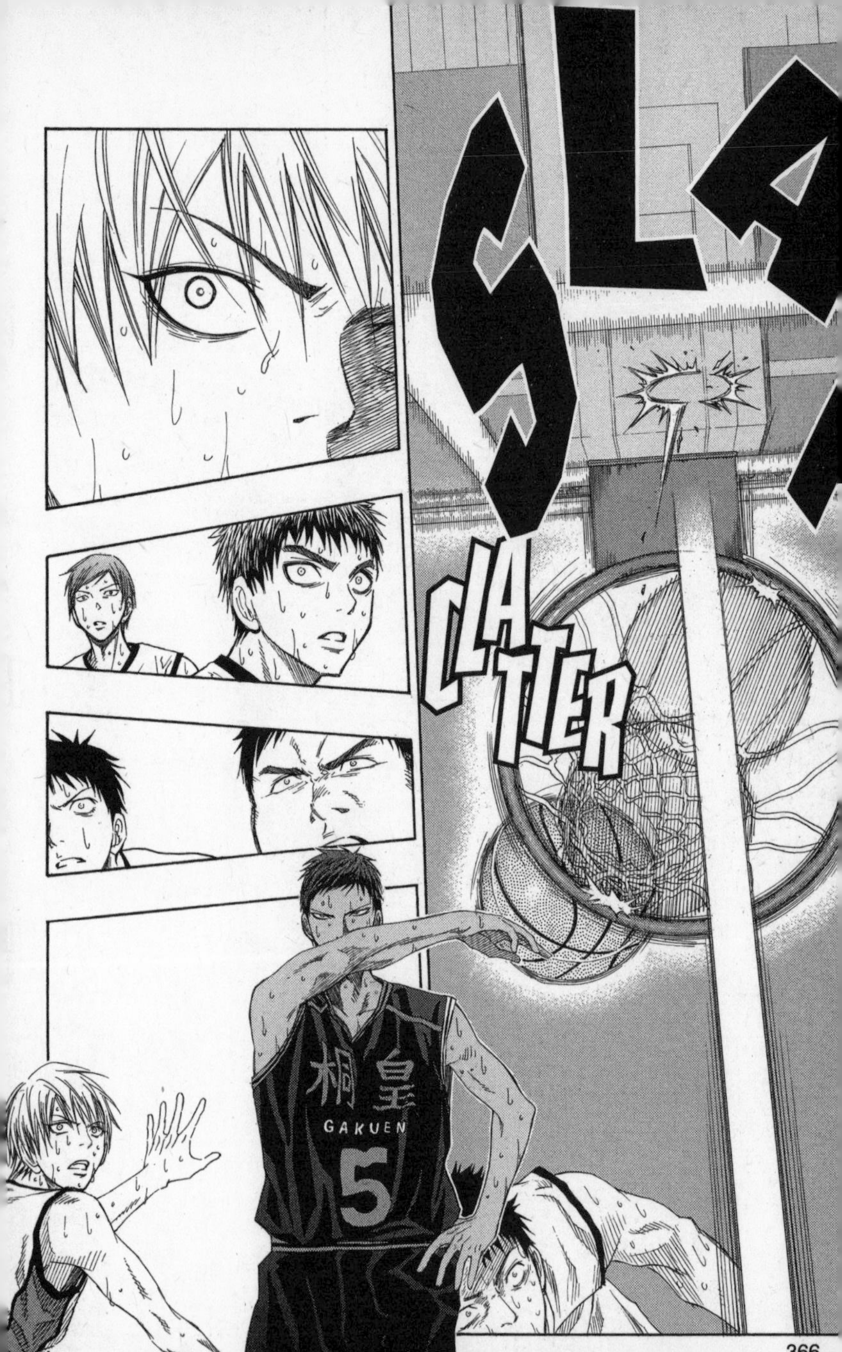
SLAM
CLATTER
桐皇
GAKUEN
5

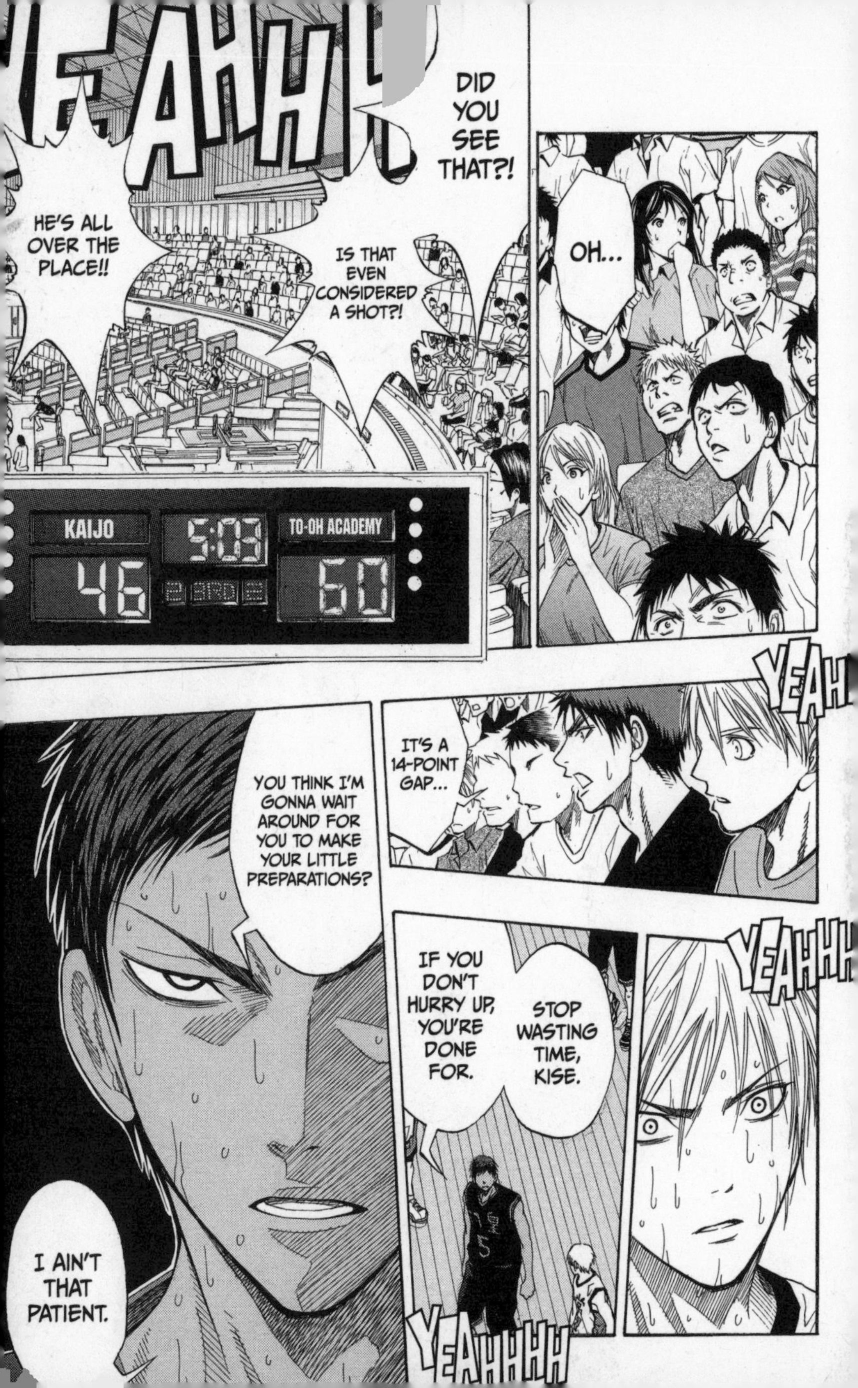

DID YOU SEE THAT?!
OH...
EAHH
IS THAT EVEN CONSIDERED A SHOT?!
HE'S ALL OVER THE PLACE!!
KAIJO
5:03
TO-OH ACADEMY
46
60
YEAHH
IT'S A 14-POINT GAP...
YEAHHH
STOP WASTING TIME, KISE.
IF YOU DON'T HURRY UP, YOU'RE DONE FOR.
YEAHHHH
YOU THINK I'M GONNA WAIT AROUND FOR YOU TO MAKE YOUR LITTLE PREPARATIONS?
I AIN'T THAT PATIENT.

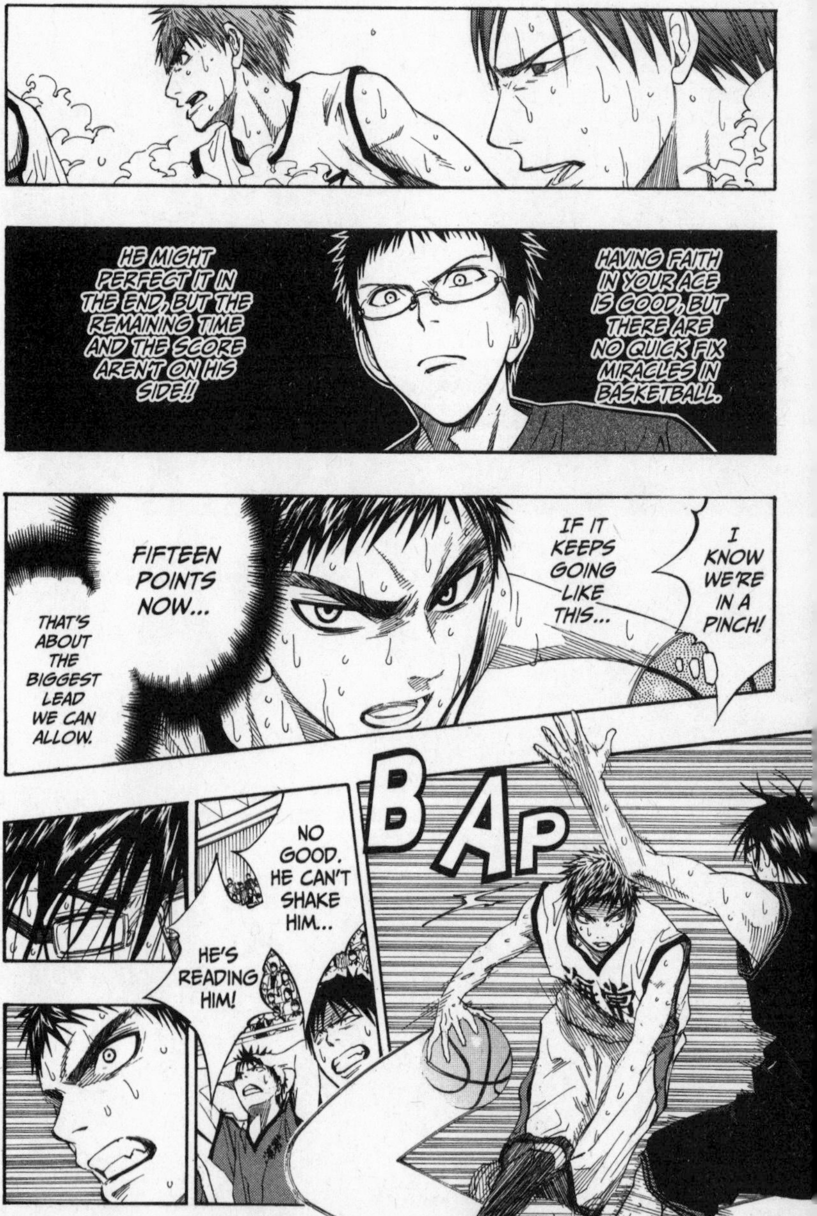
HAVING FAITH IN YOUR ACE IS GOOD, BUT THERE ARE NO QUICK FIX MIRACLES IN BASKETBALL.
HE MIGHT PERFECT IT IN THE END, BUT THE REMAINING TIME AND THE SCORE AREN'T ON HIS SIDE!!
I KNOW WE'RE IN A PINCH!
IF IT KEEPS GOING LIKE THIS...
FIFTEEN POINTS NOW...
THAT'S ABOUT THE BIGGEST LEAD WE CAN ALLOW.
BAP
NO GOOD. HE CAN'T SHAKE HIM...
HE'S READING HIM!

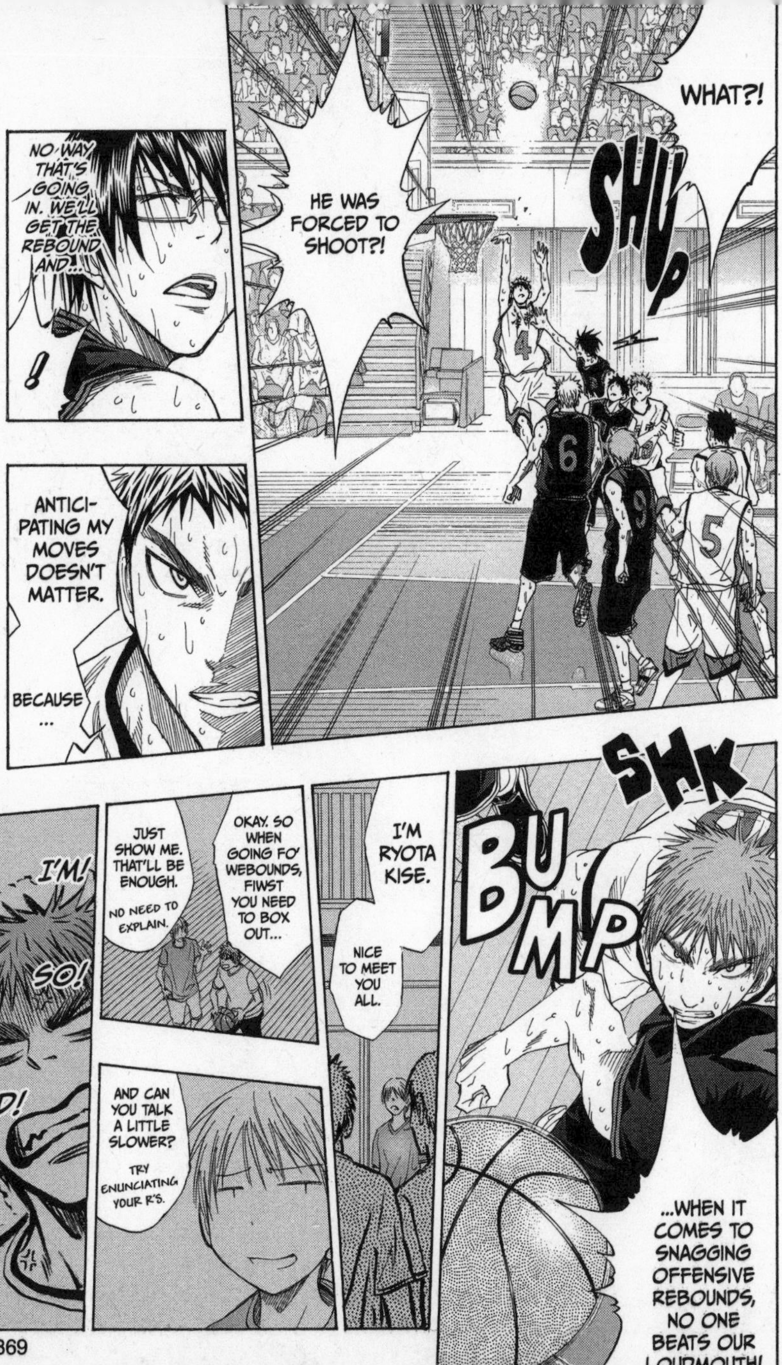
WHAT?!
SHUP
HE WAS FORCED TO SHOOT?!
NO WAY THAT'S GOING IN. WE'LL GET THE REBOUND AND...
!
ANTICI-PATING MY MOVES DOESN'T MATTER.
BECAUSE ...
SHK
BUMP
...WHEN IT COMES TO SNAGGING OFFENSIVE REBOUNDS, NO ONE BEATS OUR LOUDMOUTH!
I'M RYOTA KISE.
NICE TO MEET YOU ALL.
OKAY. SO WHEN GOING FO' WEBOUNDS, FIWST YOU NEED TO BOX OUT...
JUST SHOW ME. THAT'LL BE ENOUGH.
NO NEED TO EXPLAIN.
AND CAN YOU TALK A LITTLE SLOWER?
TRY ENUNCIATING YOUR R'S.
I'M!
SO!
MAD!

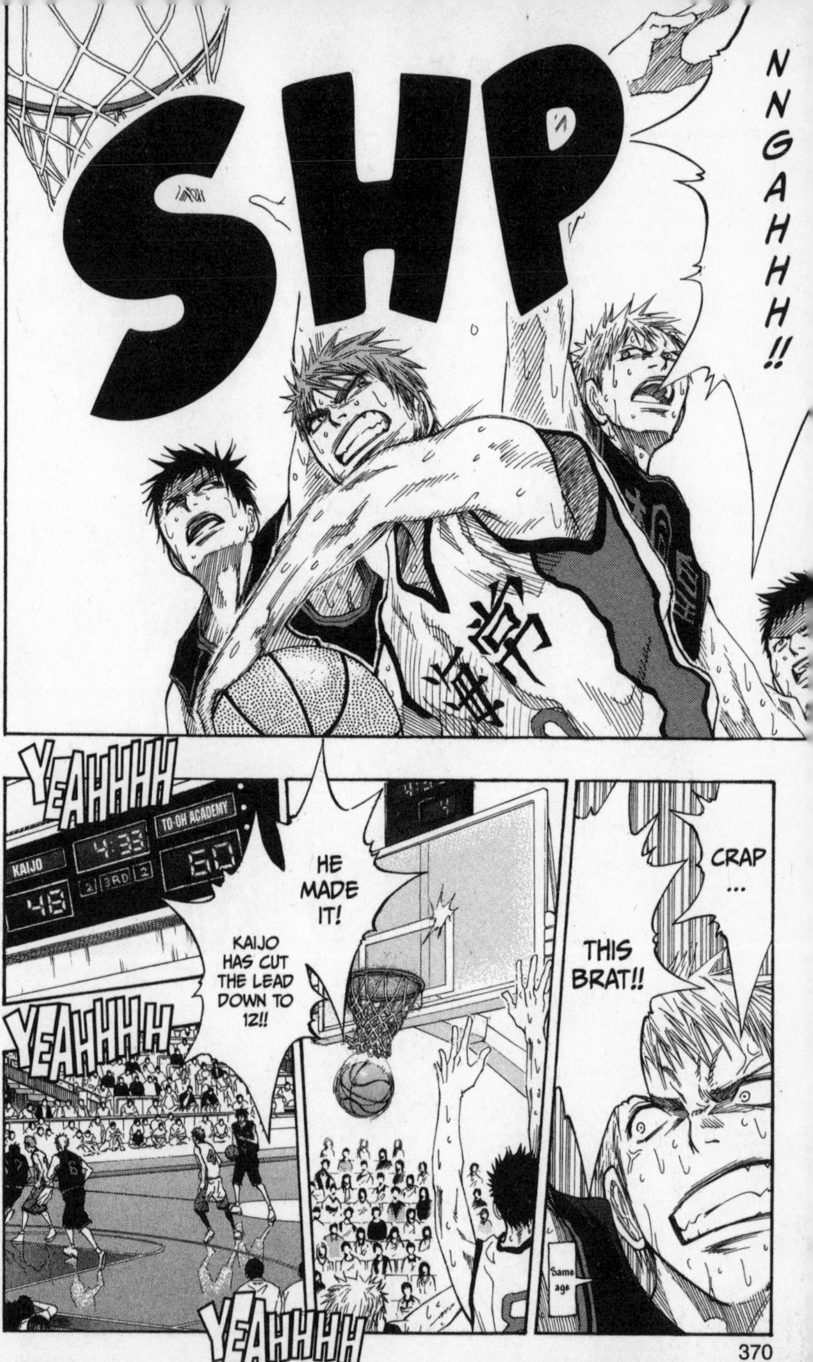
NNGAHHHH!!
SHP
CRAP...
THIS BRAT!!
Same age
HE MADE IT!
KAIJO HAS CUT THE LEAD DOWN TO 12!!
YEAHHHH
TO-OH ACADEMY
KAIJO
4:38
3RD
48
60
YEAHHHH
YEAHHHH

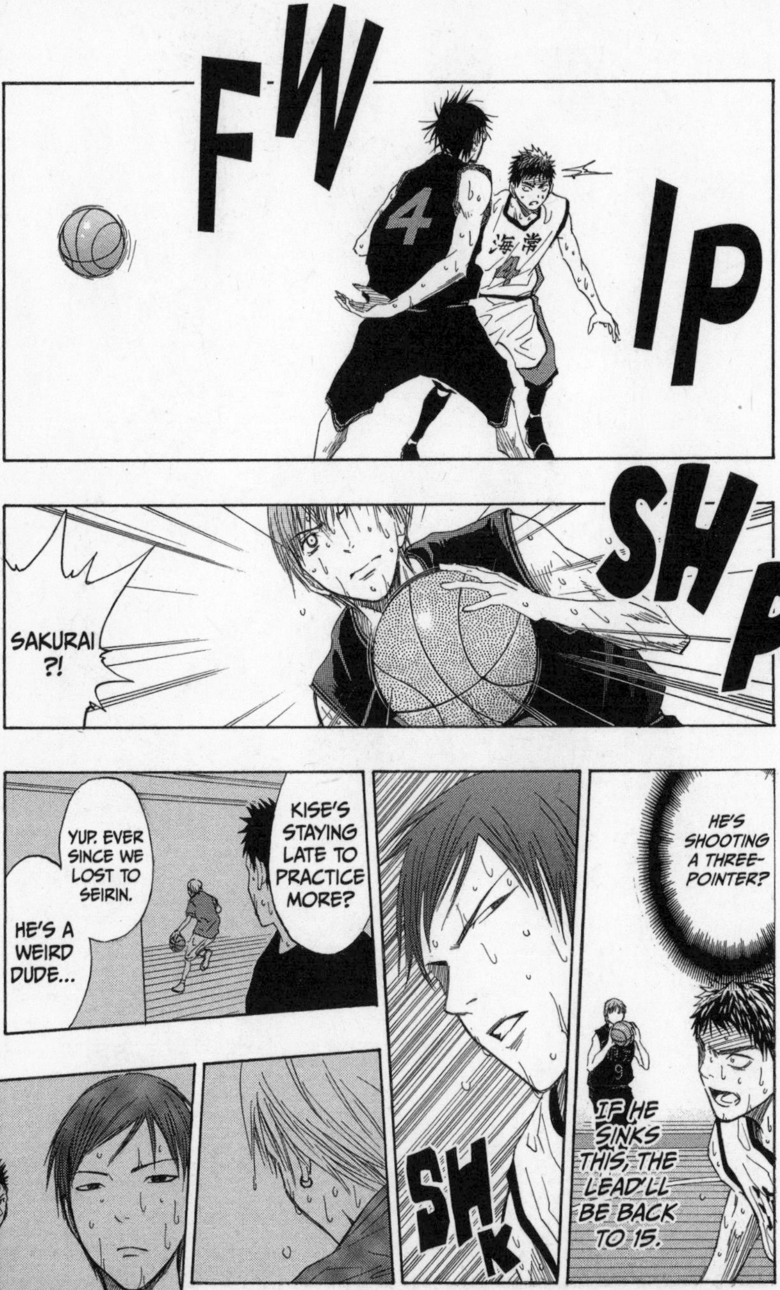
FWIP
SHP
SAKURAI ?!
HE'S SHOOTING A THREE-POINTER?
IF HE SINKS THIS, THE LEAD'LL BE BACK TO 15.
SHK
KISE'S STAYING LATE TO PRACTICE MORE?
YUP. EVER SINCE WE LOST TO SEIRIN.
HE'S A WEIRD DUDE...

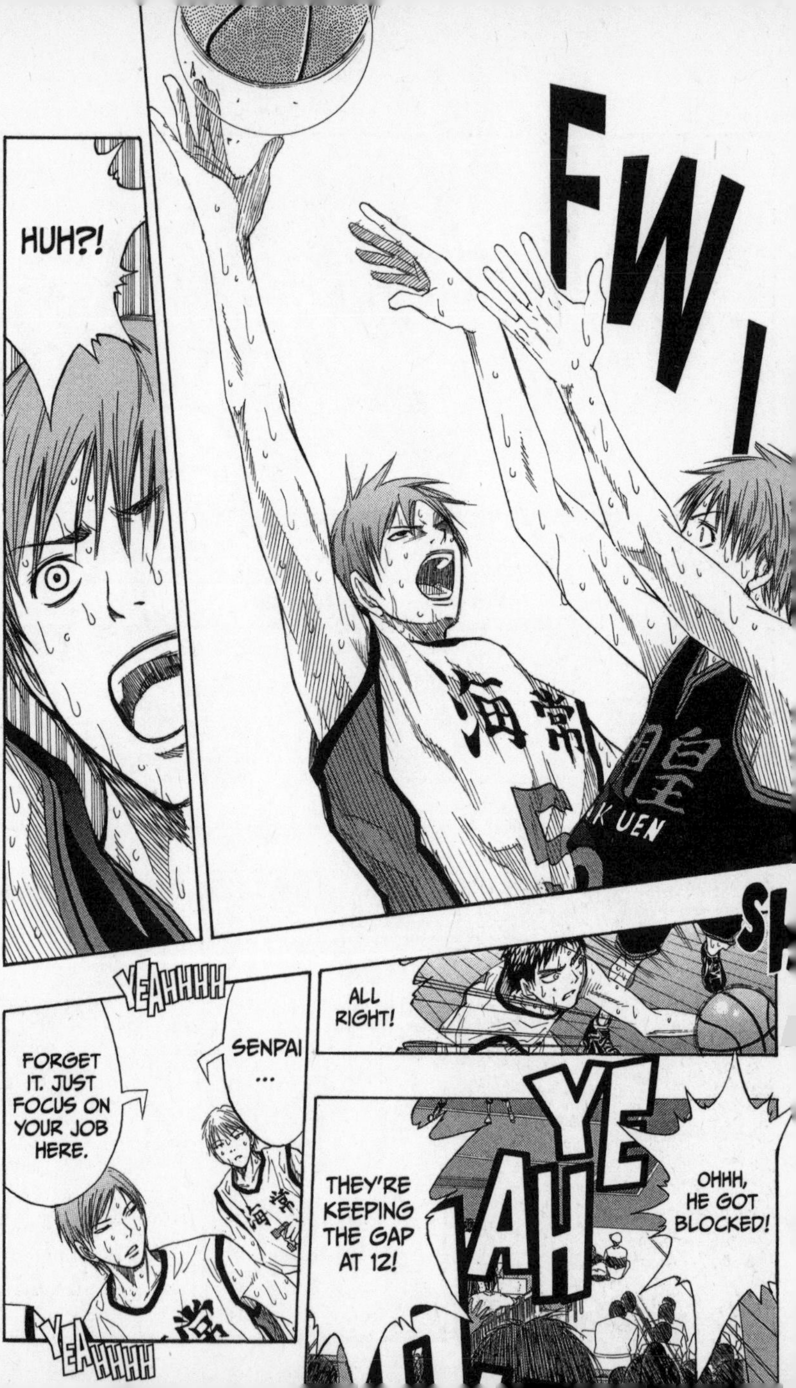

FWI
HUH?!
SH
ALL RIGHT!
YEAH
OHHH, HE GOT BLOCKED!
THEY'RE KEEPING THE GAP AT 12!
YEAHHHH
SENPAI ...
FORGET IT. JUST FOCUS ON YOUR JOB HERE.
YEAHHHH

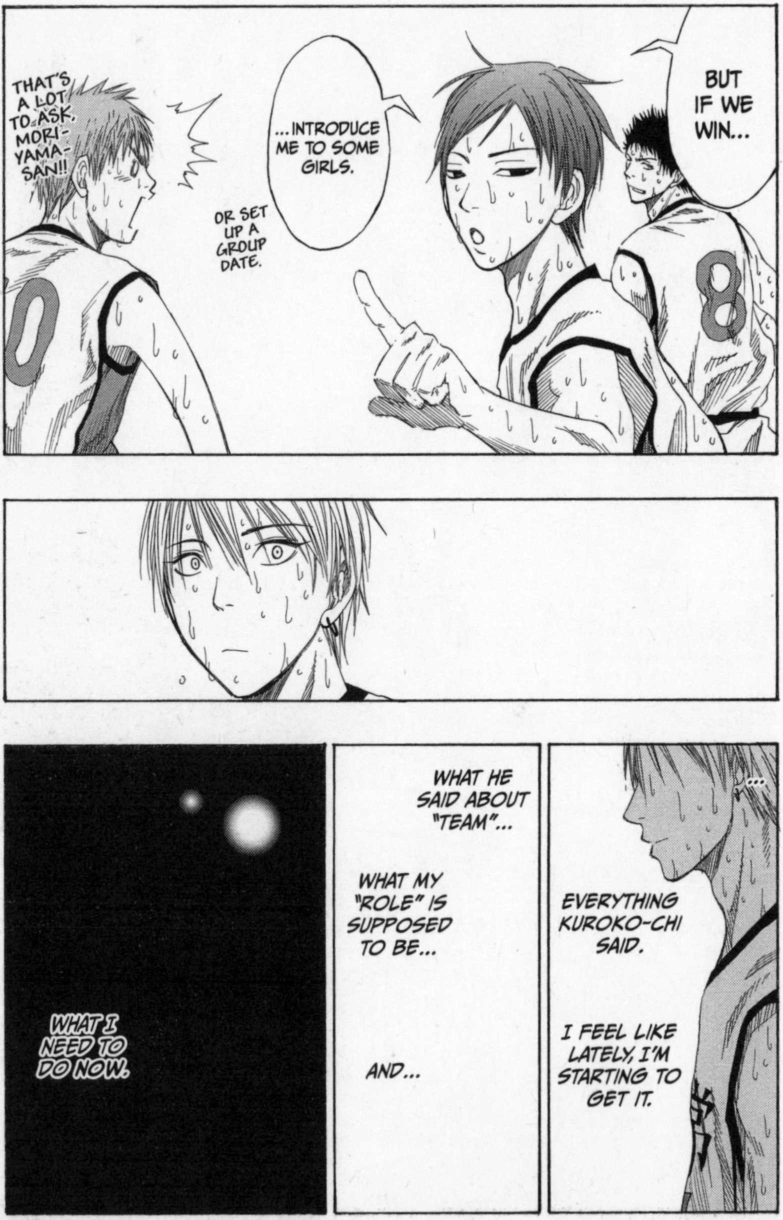
BUT IF WE WIN...
...INTRODUCE ME TO SOME GIRLS.
OR SET UP A GROUP DATE.
THAT'S A LOT TO ASK, MORI-YAMA-SAN!!
...
EVERYTHING KUROKO-CHI SAID.
I FEEL LIKE LATELY, I'M STARTING TO GET IT.
WHAT HE SAID ABOUT "TEAM"...
WHAT MY "ROLE" IS SUPPOSED TO BE...
AND...
WHAT I NEED TO DO NOW.

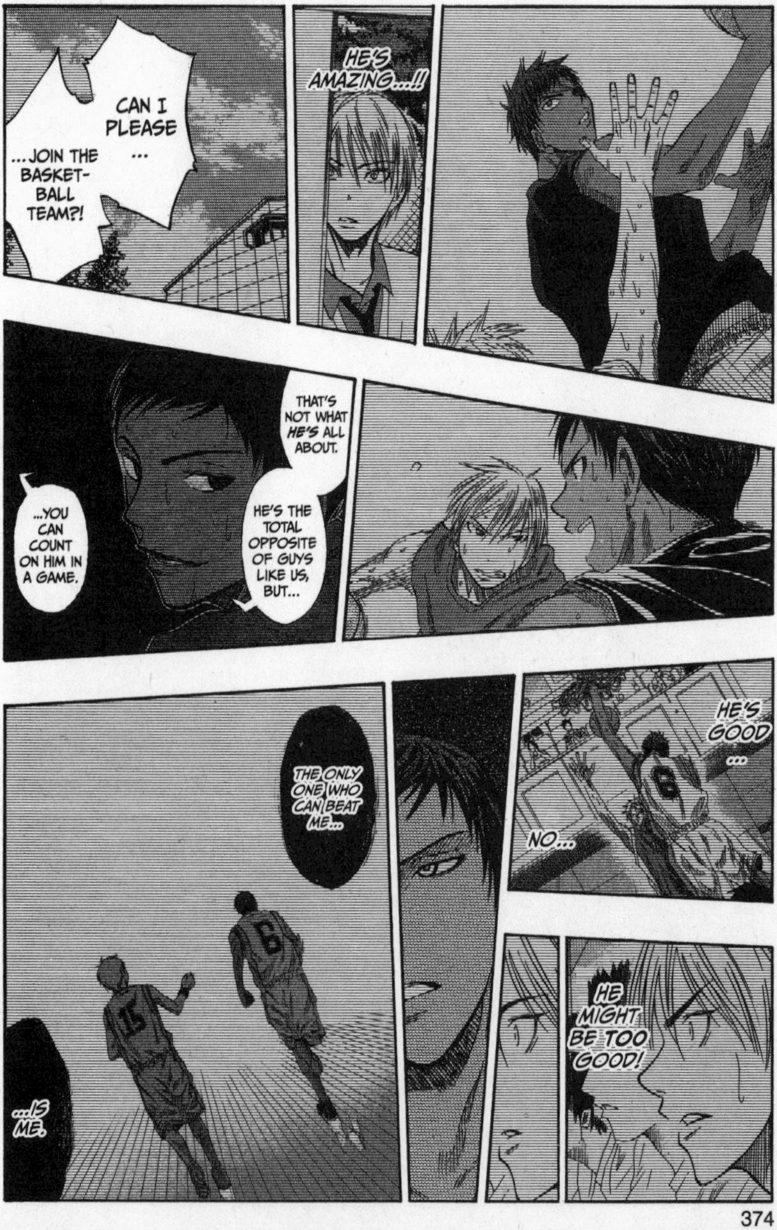
HE'S AMAZING...!!
CAN I PLEASE ...
...JOIN THE BASKET-BALL TEAM?!
THAT'S NOT WHAT HE'S ALL ABOUT.
HE'S THE TOTAL OPPOSITE OF GUYS LIKE US, BUT...
...YOU CAN COUNT ON HIM IN A GAME.
HE'S GOOD...
NO...
HE MIGHT BE TOO GOOD!
THE ONLY ONE WHO CAN BEAT ME...
...IS ME.

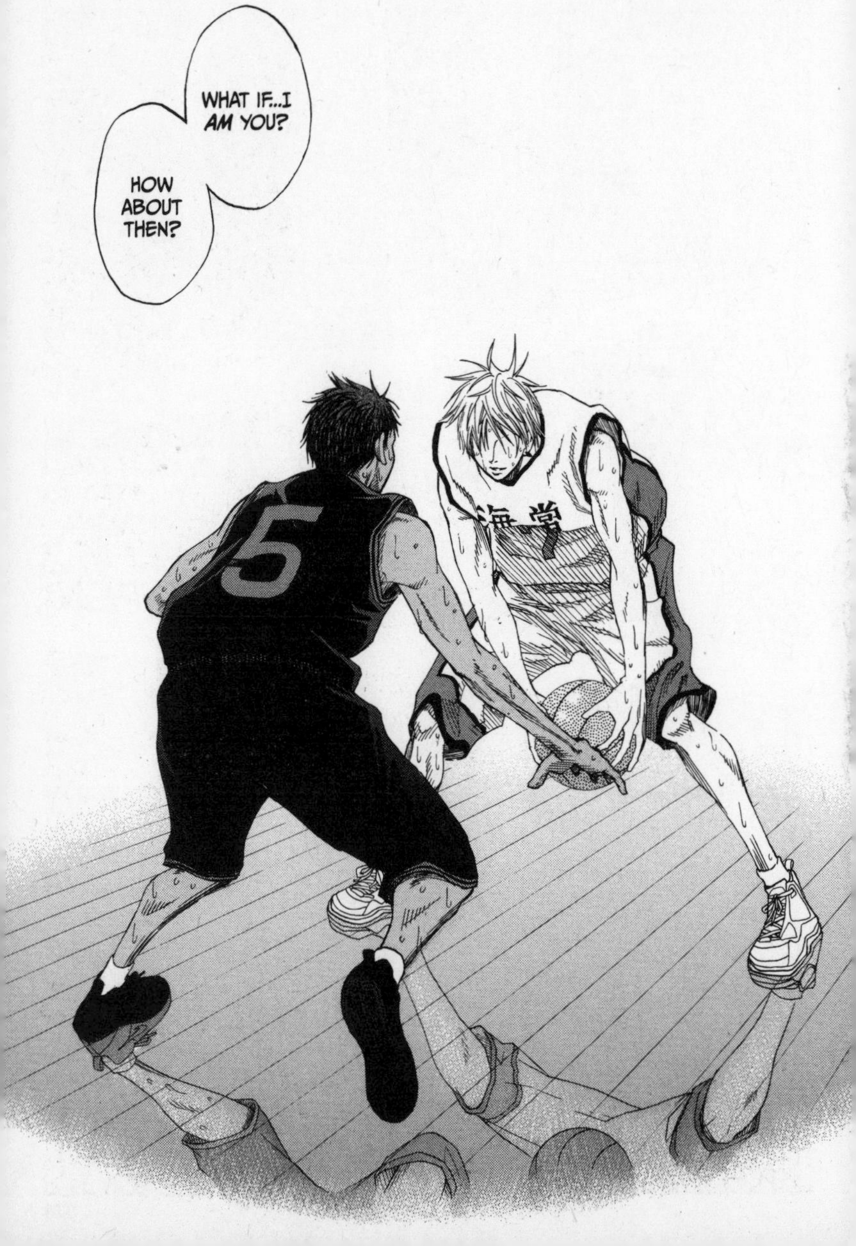
WHAT IF...I AM YOU?
HOW ABOUT THEN?

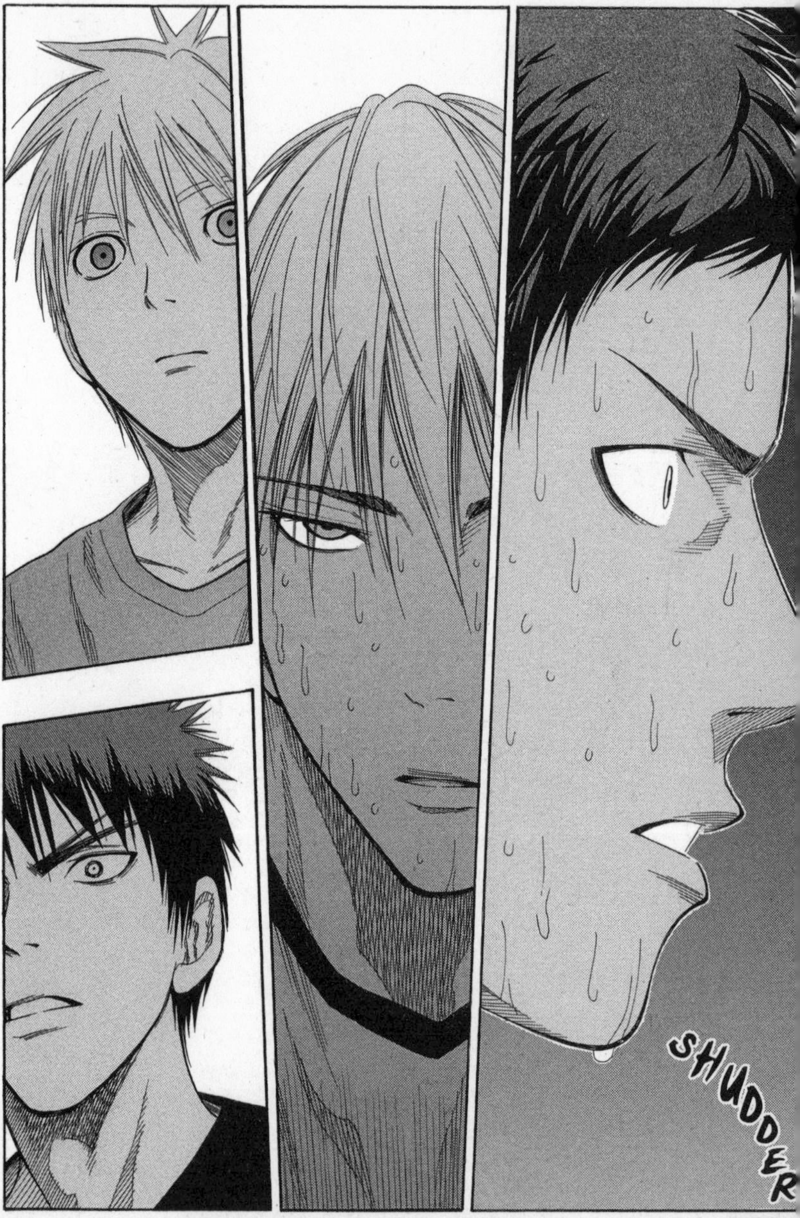
SHUDDER

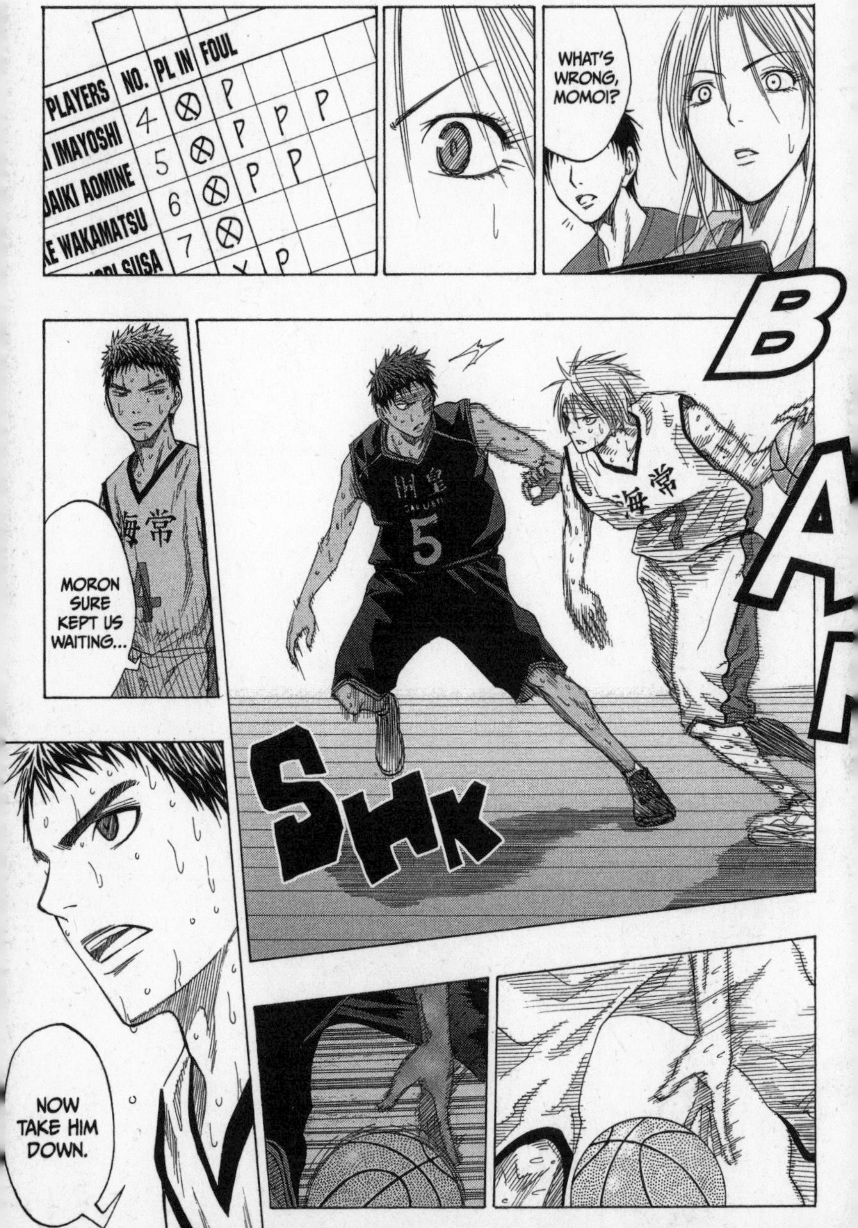
WHAT'S WRONG, MOMOI?
PLAYERS NO. PL IN FOUL
I IMAYOSHI 4
DAIKI AOMINE 5
KE WAKAMATSU 6
7
BA
SHK
MORON SURE KEPT US WAITING...
NOW TAKE HIM DOWN.

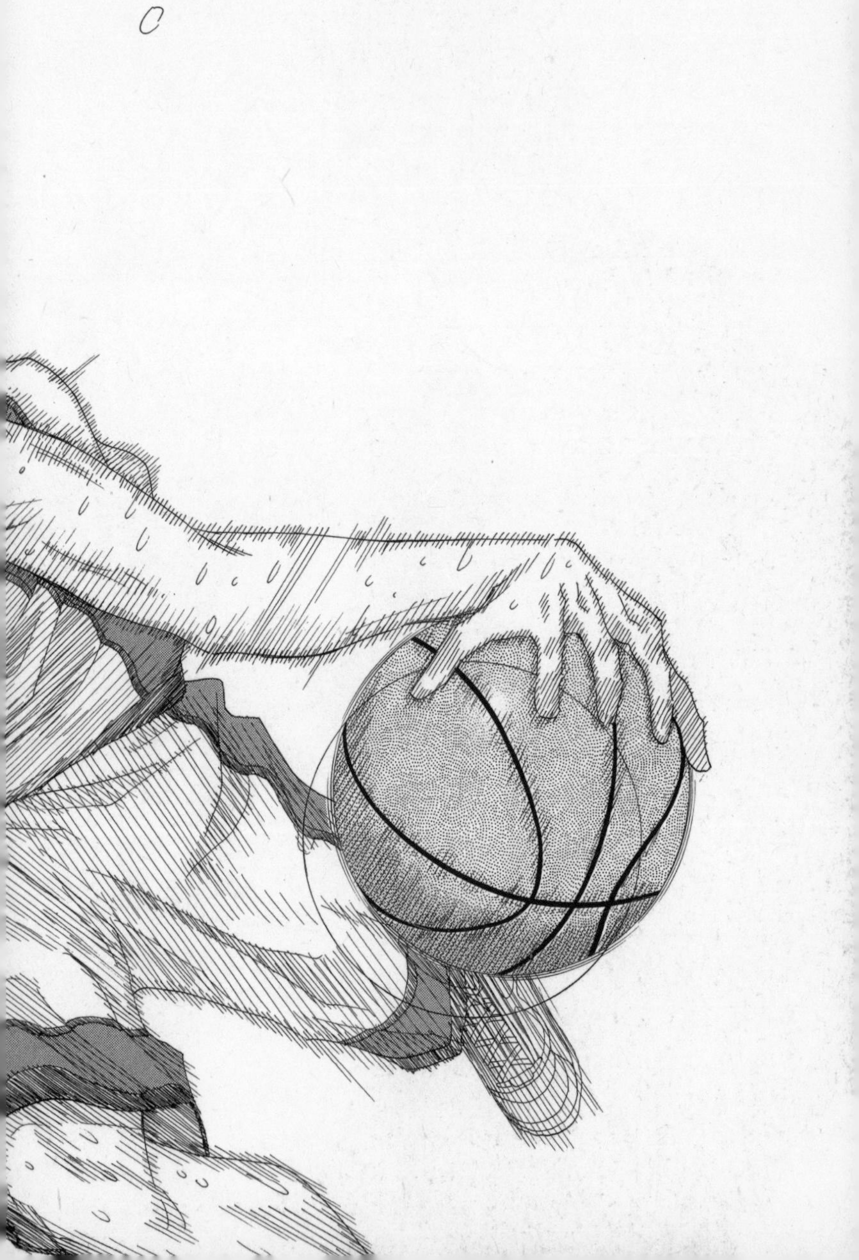

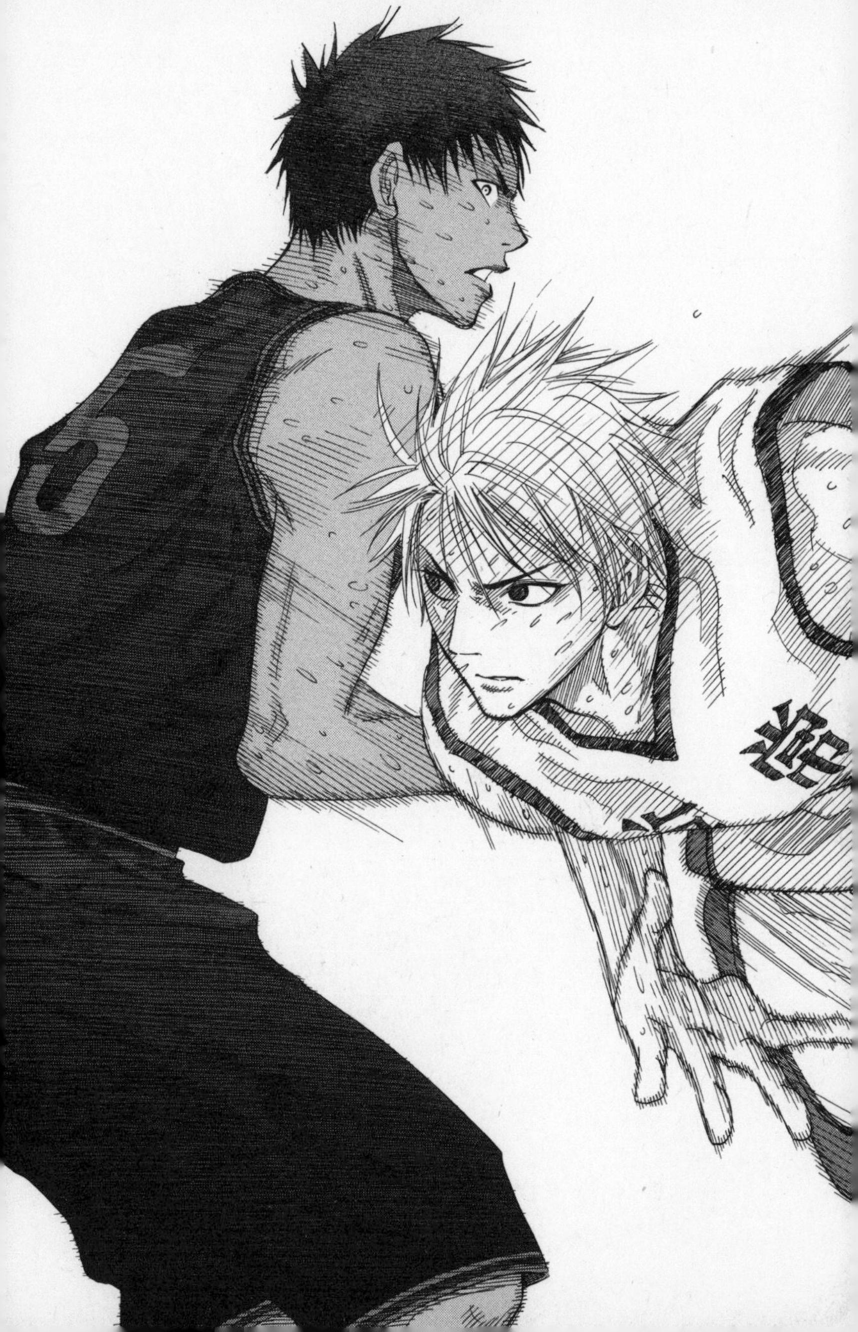

KUROKO'S BASKETBALL BLOOPERS

TAKE 1

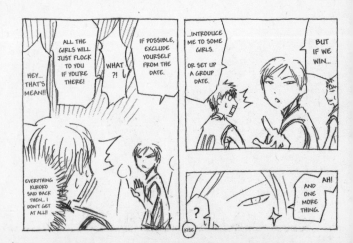

BUT IF WE WIN...
...INTRODUCE ME TO SOME GIRLS.
OR SET UP A GROUP DATE.
AH!
AND ONE MORE THING.
?
KISE
IF POSSIBLE, EXCLUDE YOURSELF FROM THE DATE.
WHAT ?!
ALL THE GIRLS WILL JUST FLOCK TO YOU IF YOU'RE THERE!
HEY... THAT'S MEAN!!
EVERYTHING KUROKO SAID BACK THEN... I DON'T GET AT ALL!!

70TH QUARTER: DON'T FOOL YOURSELVES!

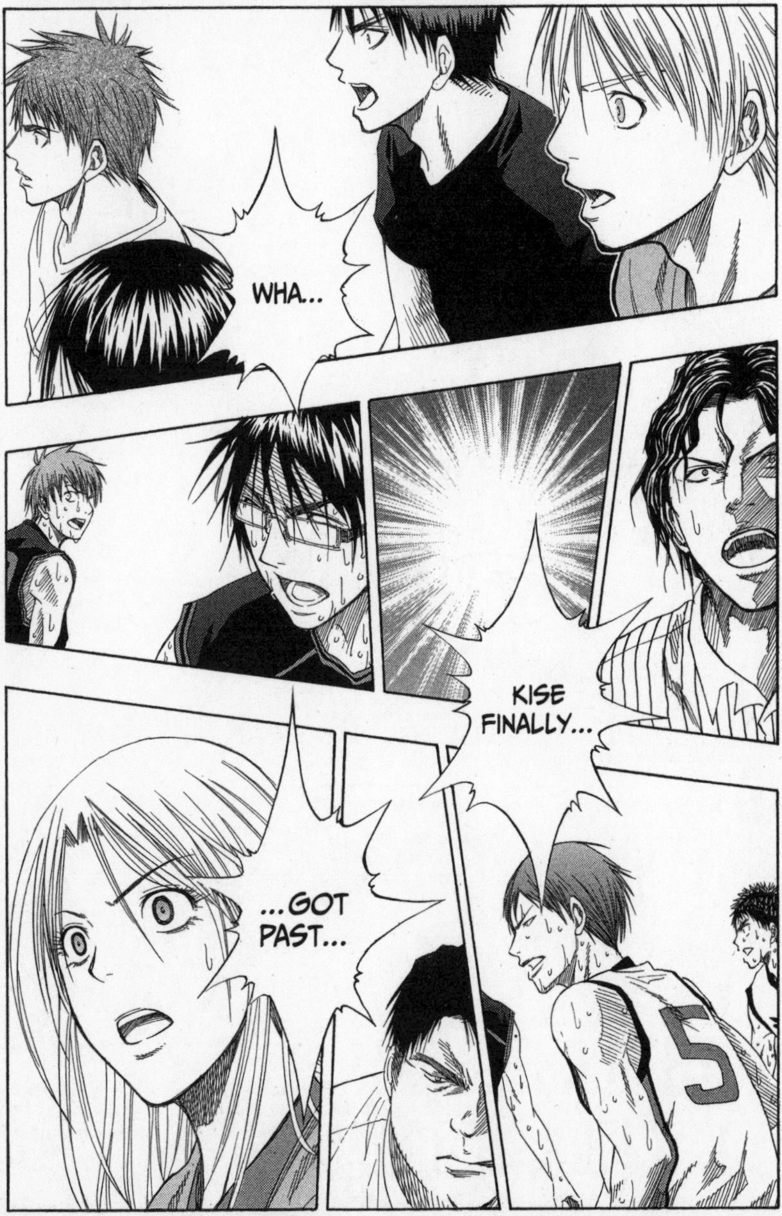
WHA...
KISE FINALLY...
...GOT PAST...

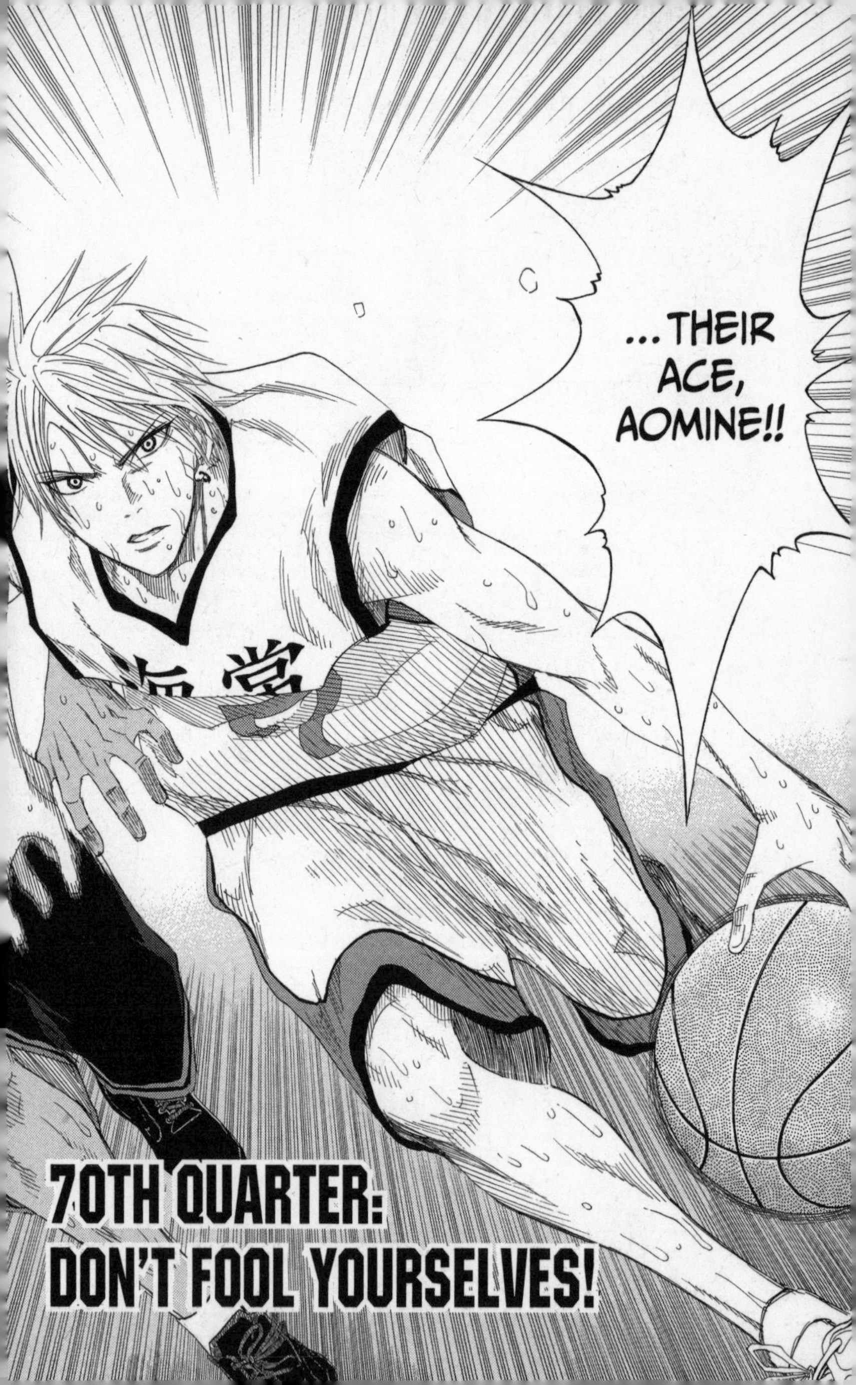
...THEIR ACE, AOMINE!!
70TH QUARTER: DON'T FOOL YOURSELVES!

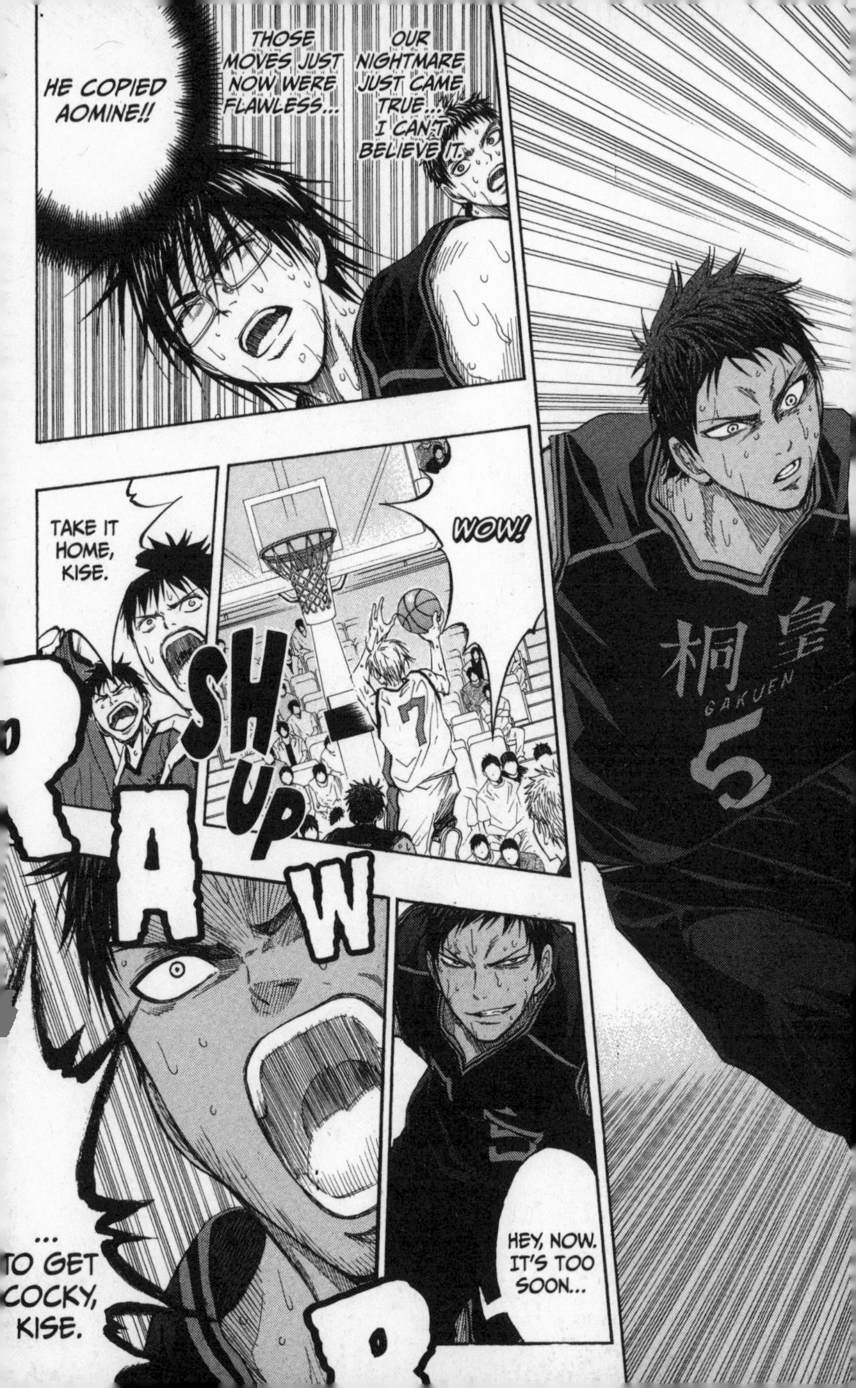
OUR NIGHTMARE JUST CAME TRUE... I CAN'T BELIEVE IT.
THOSE MOVES JUST NOW WERE FLAWLESS...
HE COPIED AOMINE!!
WOW!
SHUP
TAKE IT HOME, KISE.
AW
HEY, NOW. IT'S TOO SOON...
... TO GET COCKY, KISE.

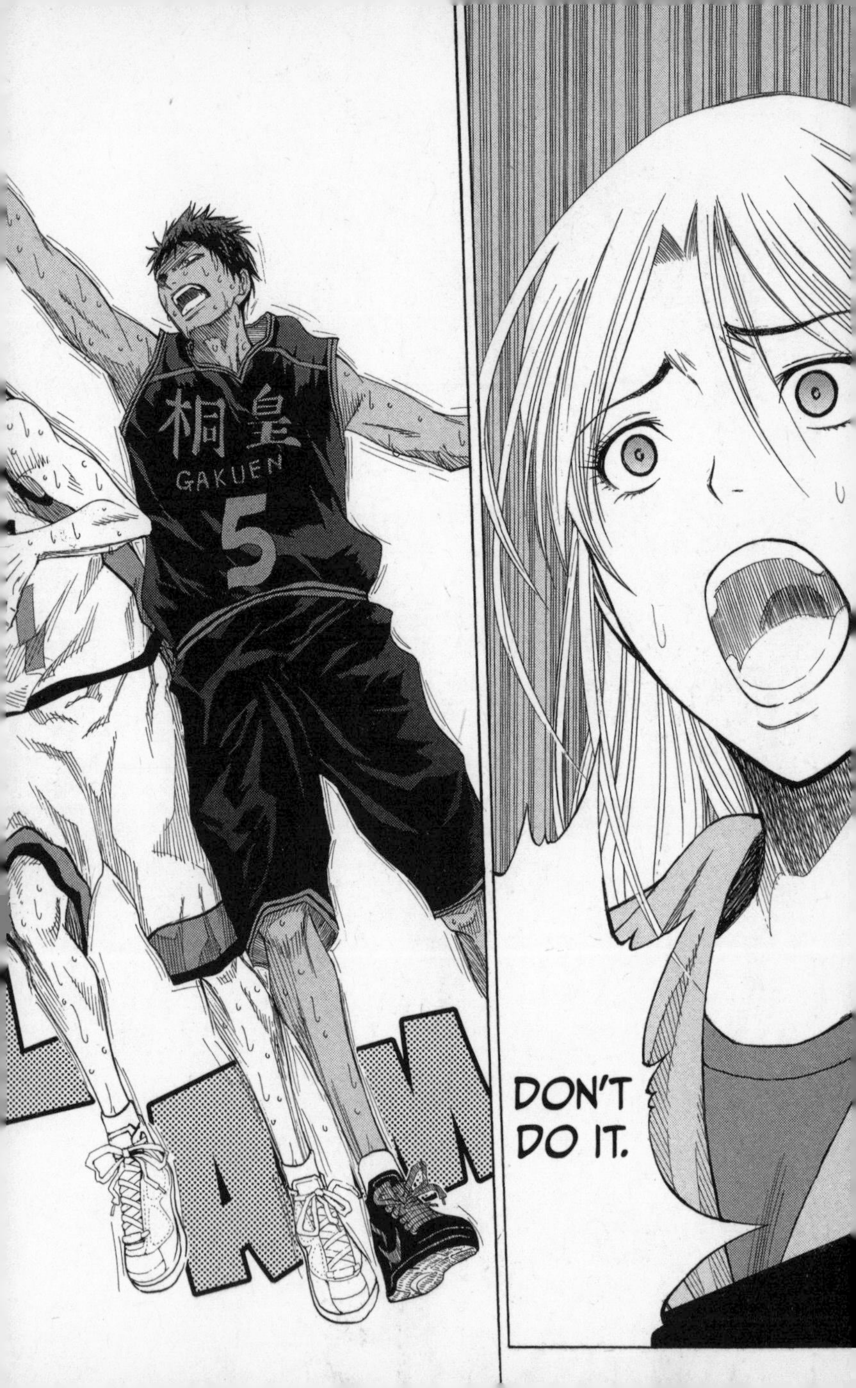
DON'T
DO IT.
桐皇
GAKUEN
5

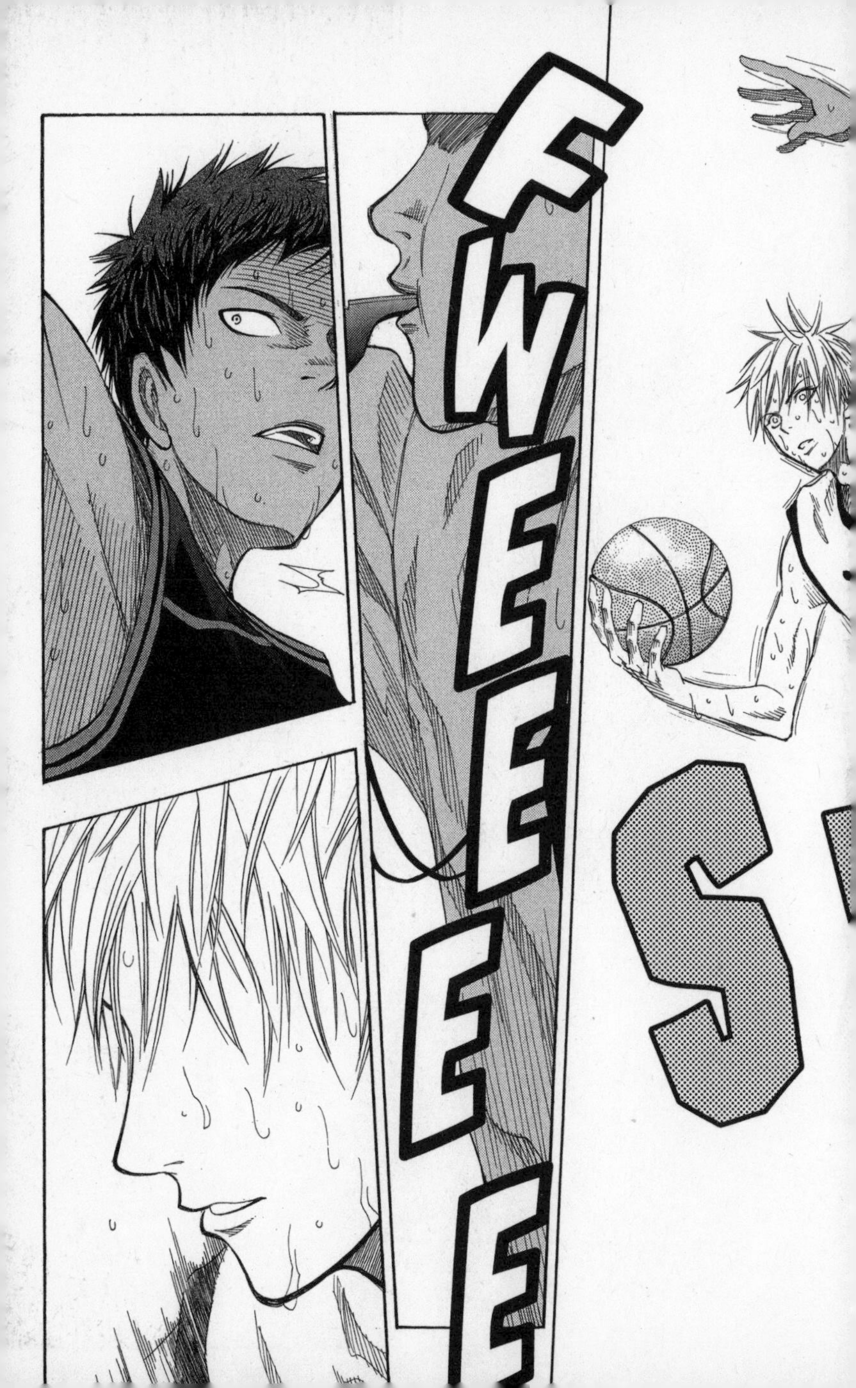
FWEEEE

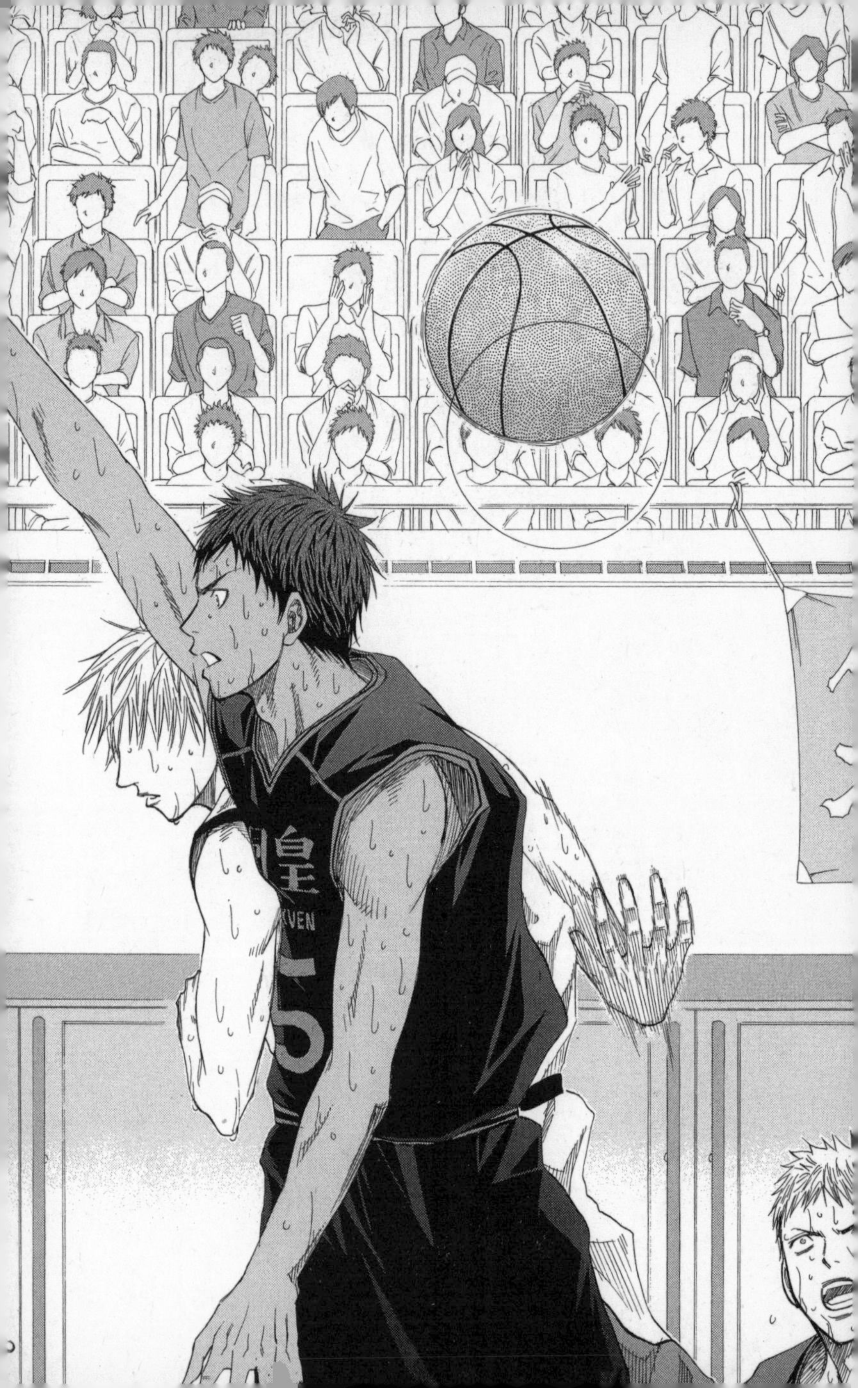

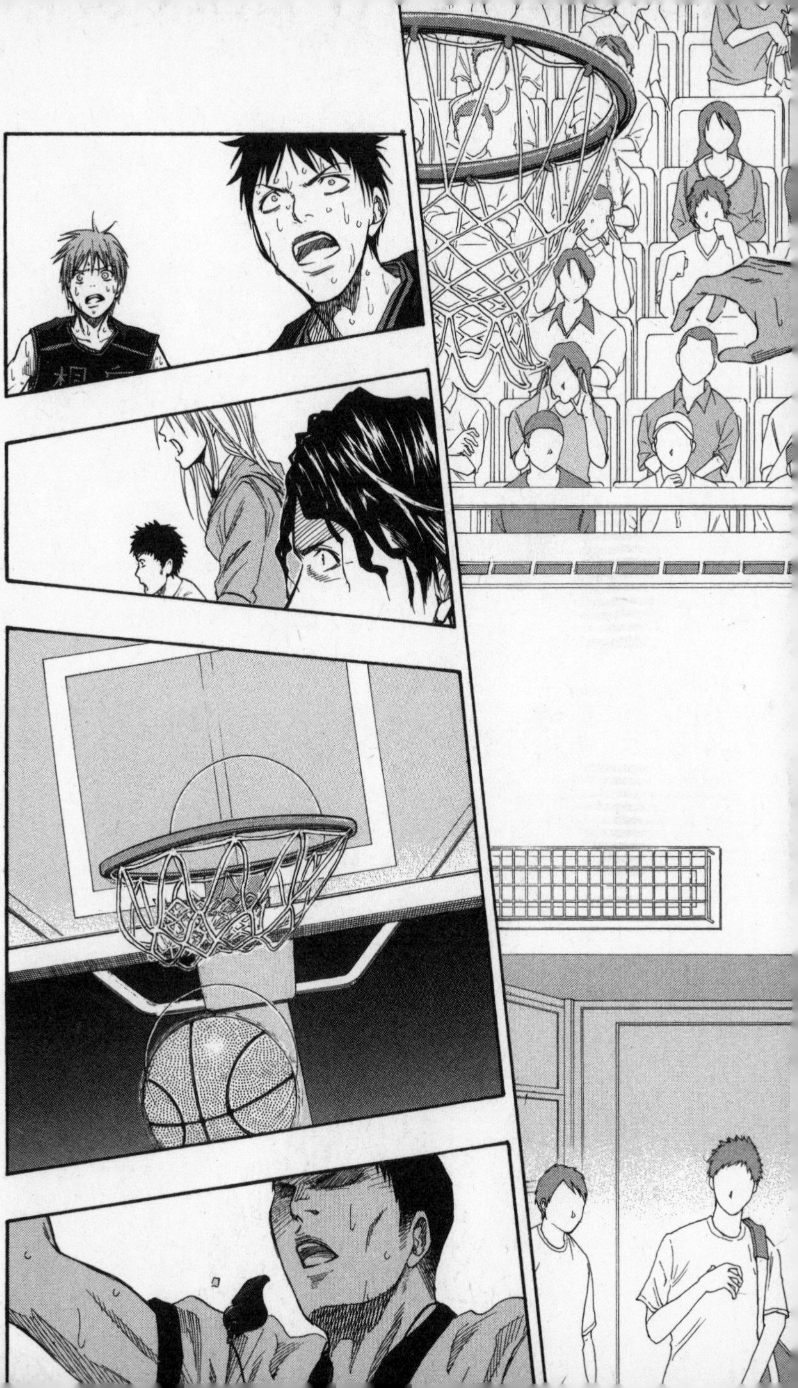

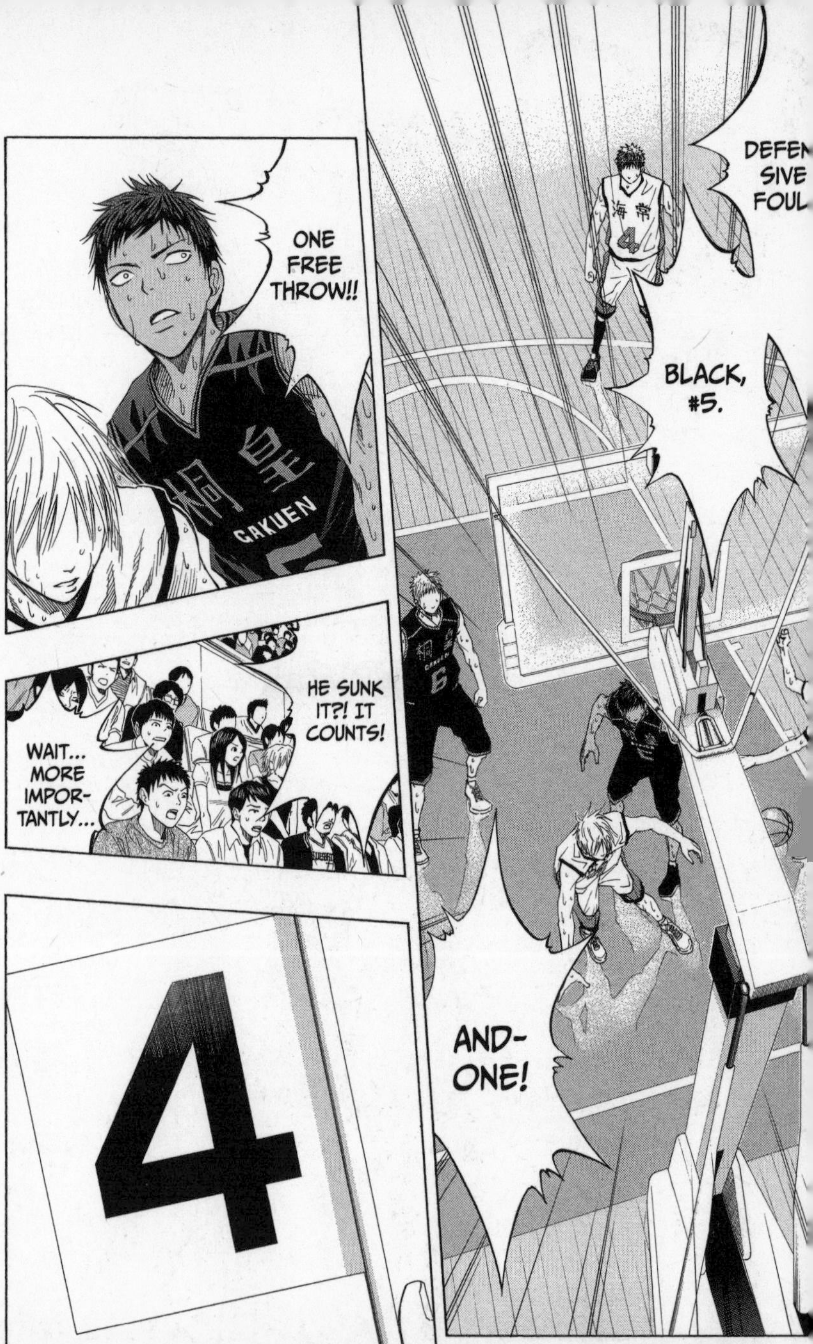
DEFENSIVE FOUL
BLACK, #5.
AND-ONE!
ONE FREE THROW!!
HE SUNK IT?! IT COUNTS!
WAIT... MORE IMPORTANTLY...

*And-one: If a player makes a shot while being fouled, the player is awarded a single

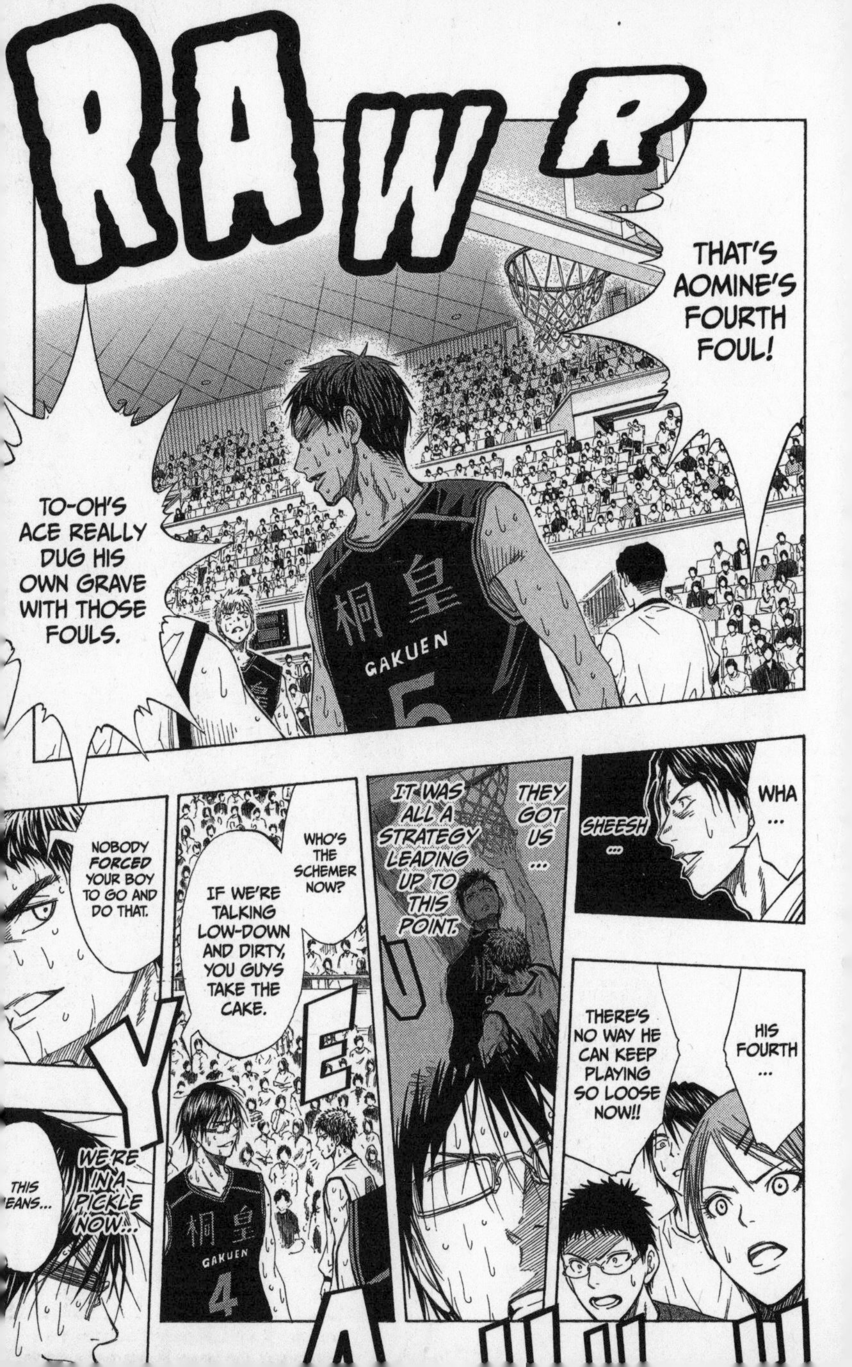
RAWR
THAT'S AOMINE'S FOURTH FOUL!
TO-OH'S ACE REALLY DUG HIS OWN GRAVE WITH THOSE FOULS.
GAKUEN
WHA ...
SHEESH ...
THEY GOT US ...
IT WAS ALL A STRATEGY LEADING UP TO THIS POINT.
WHO'S THE SCHEMER NOW?
IF WE'RE TALKING LOW-DOWN AND DIRTY, YOU GUYS TAKE THE CAKE.
NOBODY FORCED YOUR BOY TO GO AND DO THAT.
HIS FOURTH ...
THERE'S NO WAY HE CAN KEEP PLAYING SO LOOSE NOW!!
WE'RE IN A PICKLE NOW...
GAKUEN
THIS
EANS...

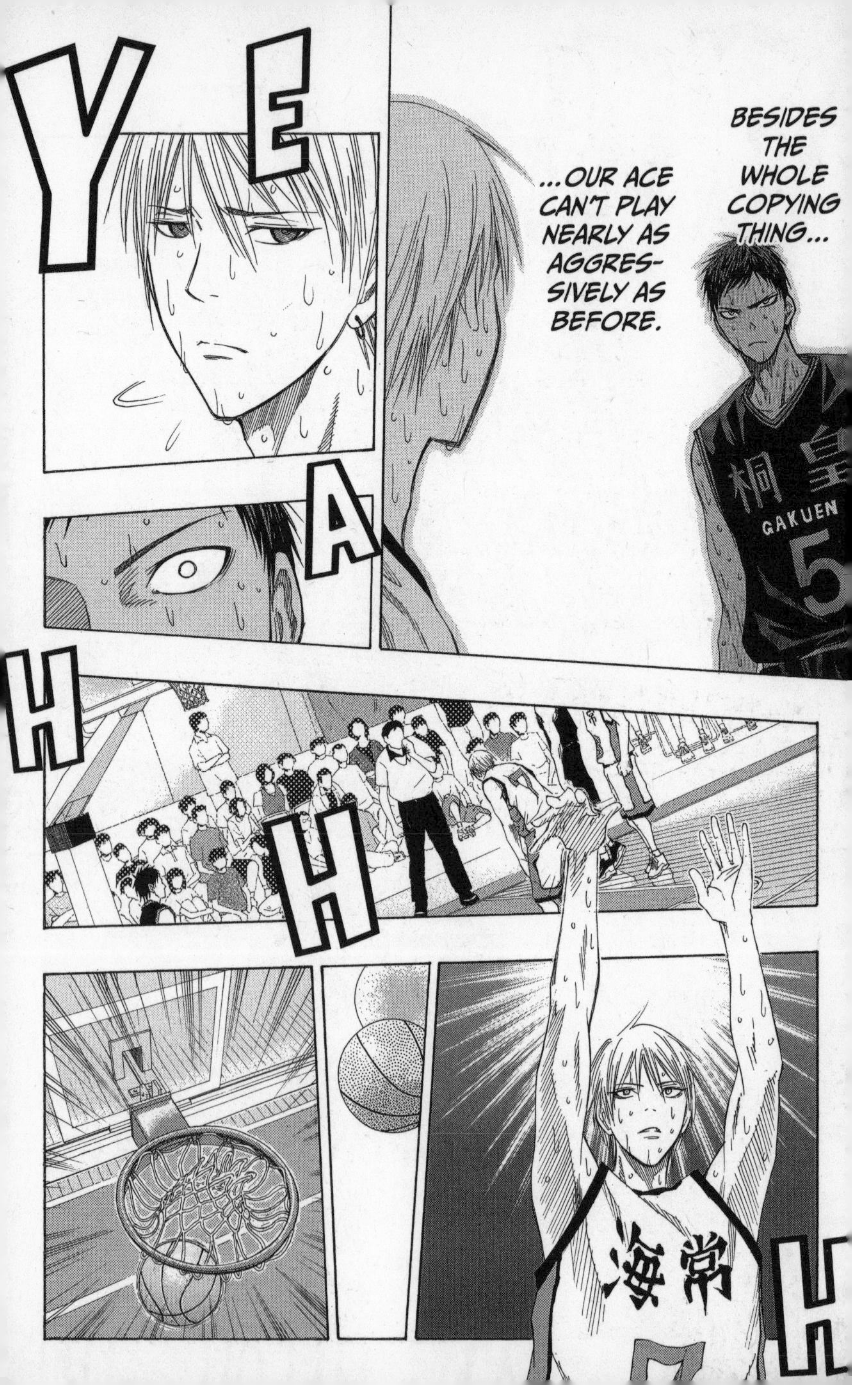
BESIDES THE WHOLE COPYING THING...
...OUR ACE CAN'T PLAY NEARLY AS AGGRES-SIVELY AS BEFORE.
YEAHHH

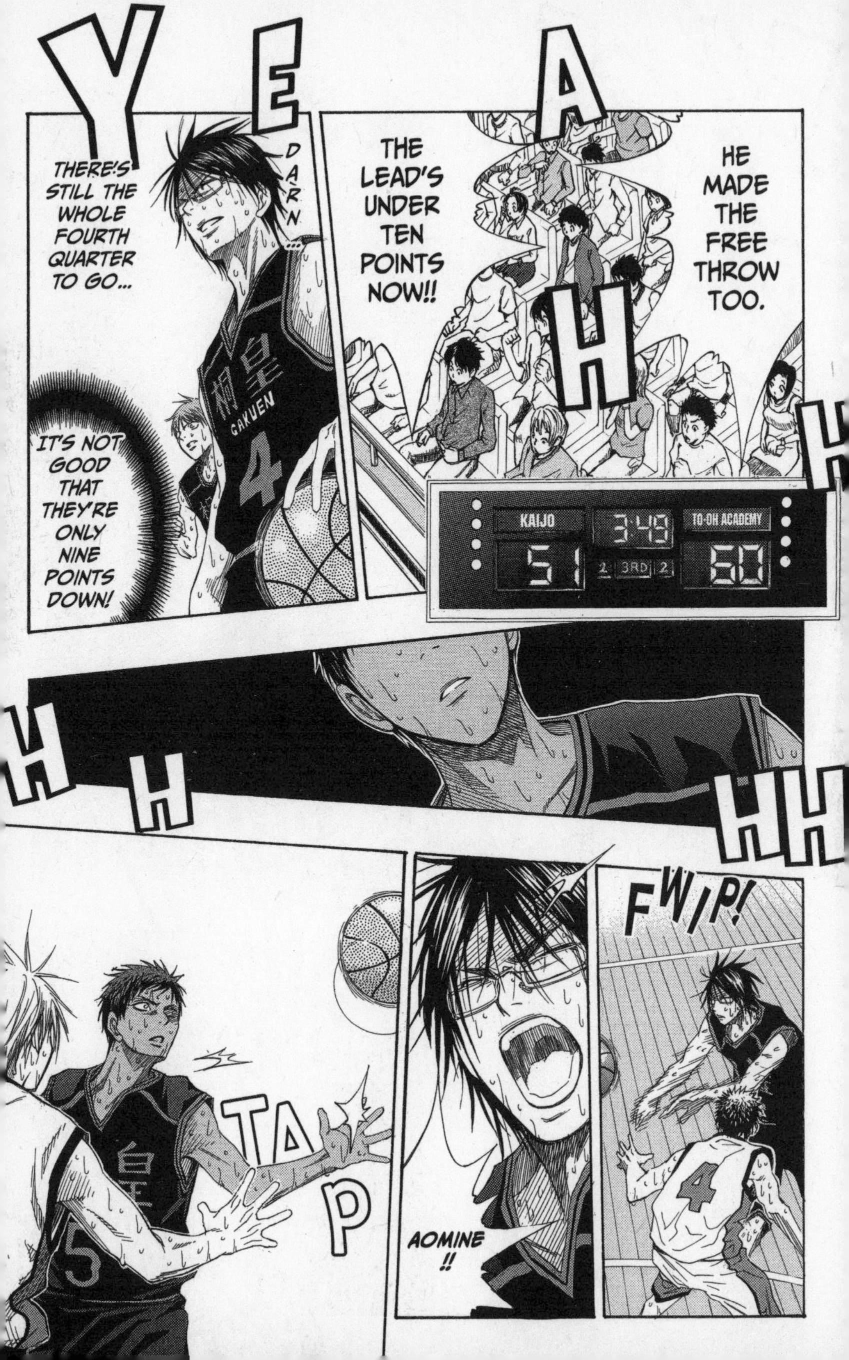
YEAHHHHHHHH
HE MADE THE FREE THROW TOO.
THE LEAD'S UNDER TEN POINTS NOW!!
KAIJO
3:49
TO-OH ACADEMY
51
3RD
60
DARN...
THERE'S STILL THE WHOLE FOURTH QUARTER TO GO...
IT'S NOT GOOD THAT THEY'RE ONLY NINE POINTS DOWN!
GAKUEN
FWIP!
AOMINE!!
TAP

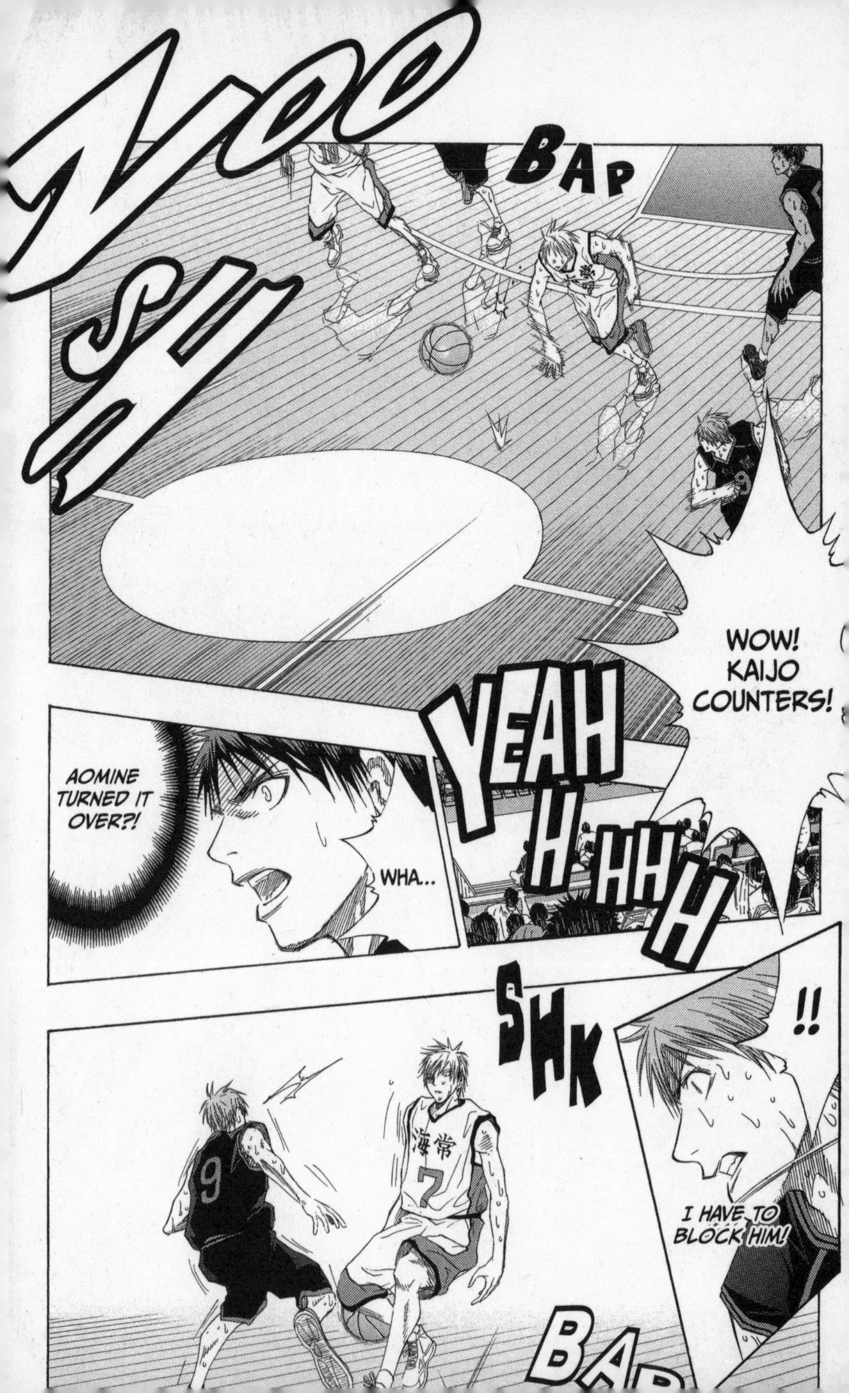
BAP
WOW! KAIJO COUNTERS!
YEAH HHHHH
WHA...
AOMINE TURNED IT OVER?!
!!
I HAVE TO BLOCK HIM!
SHK
BAP

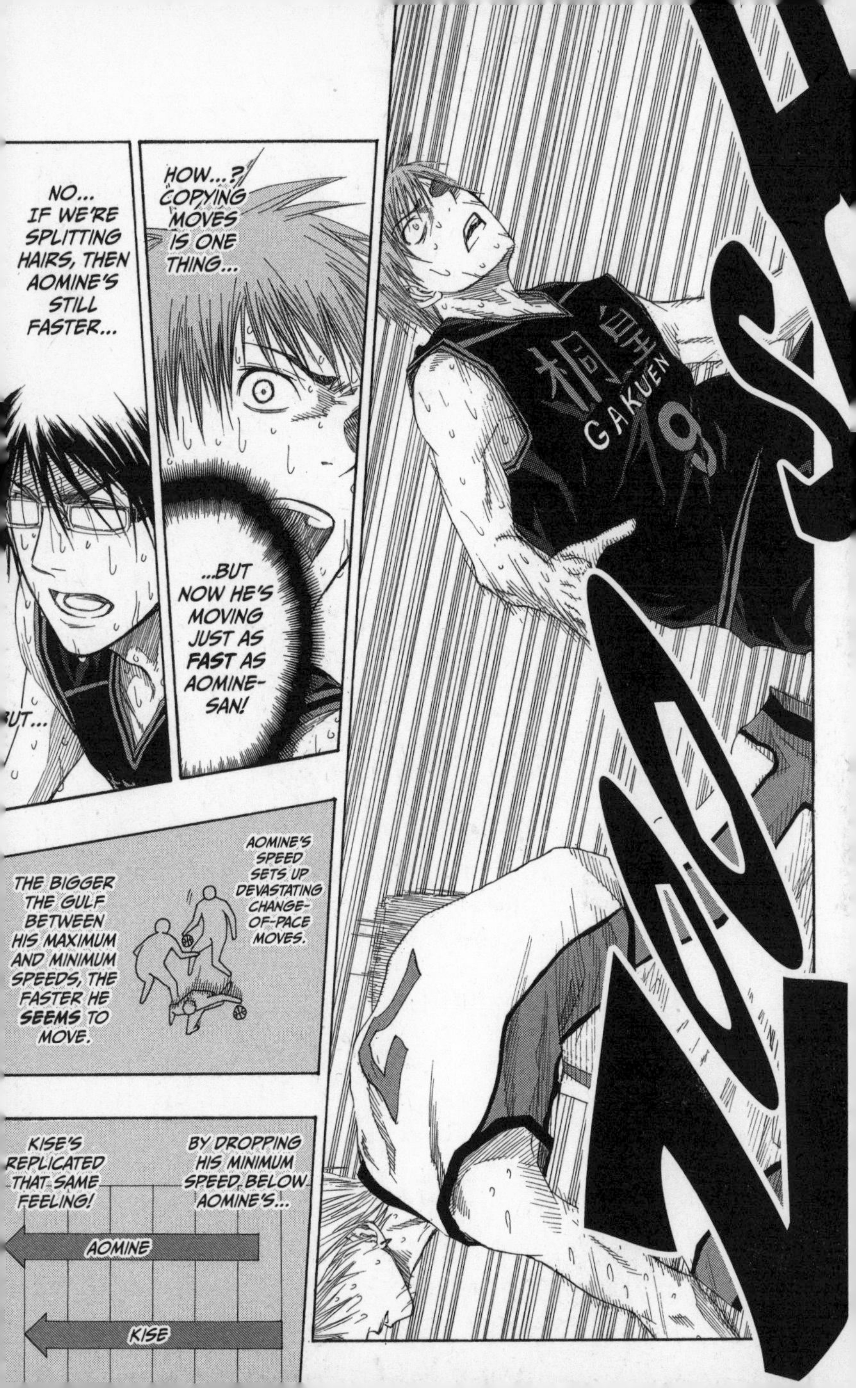
HOW...? COPYING MOVES IS ONE THING...
...BUT NOW HE'S MOVING JUST AS FAST AS AOMINE-SAN!
NO... IF WE'RE SPLITTING HAIRS, THEN AOMINE'S STILL FASTER...
AOMINE'S SPEED SETS UP DEVASTATING CHANGE-OF-PACE MOVES.
THE BIGGER THE GULF BETWEEN HIS MAXIMUM AND MINIMUM SPEEDS, THE FASTER HE SEEMS TO MOVE.
BY DROPPING HIS MINIMUM SPEED BELOW AOMINE'S...
KISE'S REPLICATED THAT SAME FEELING!
AOMINE
KISE

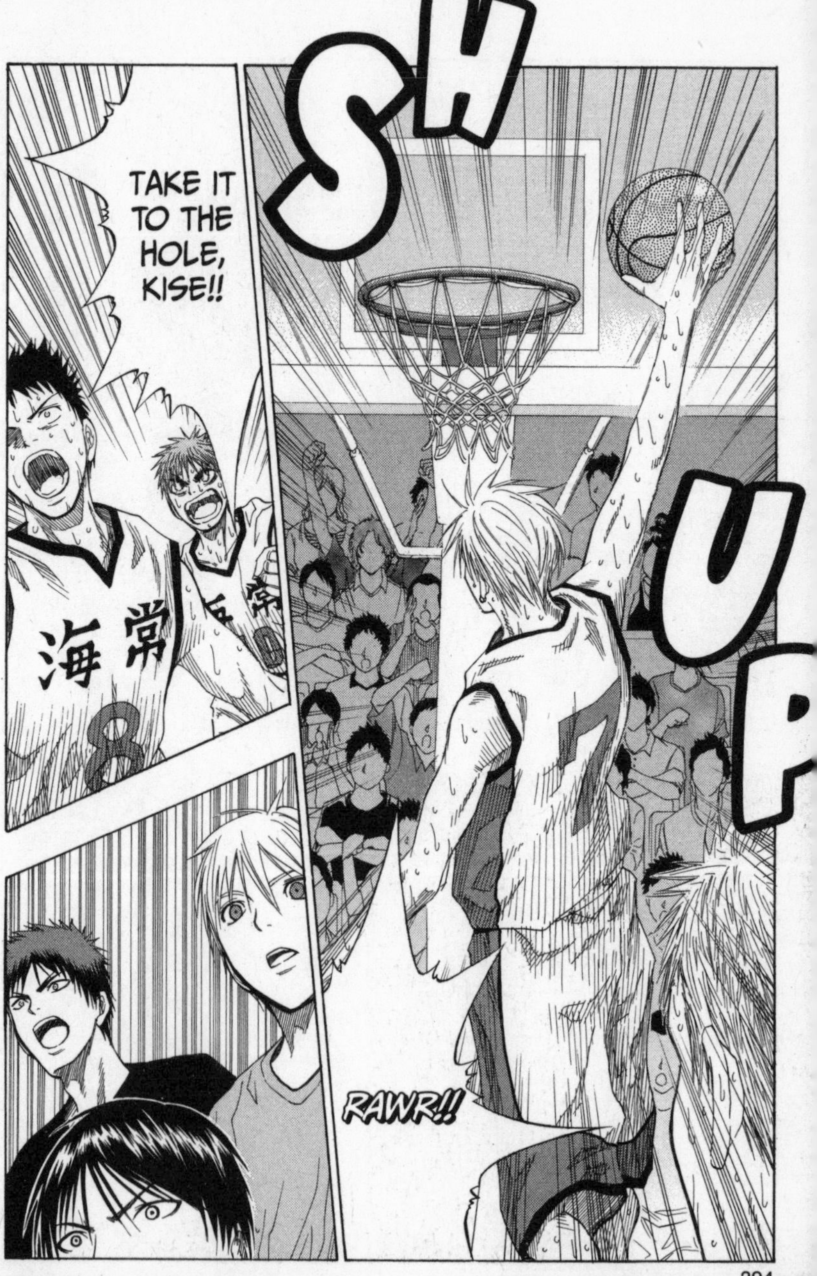
SHUP
RAWR!!
TAKE IT TO THE HOLE, KISE!!

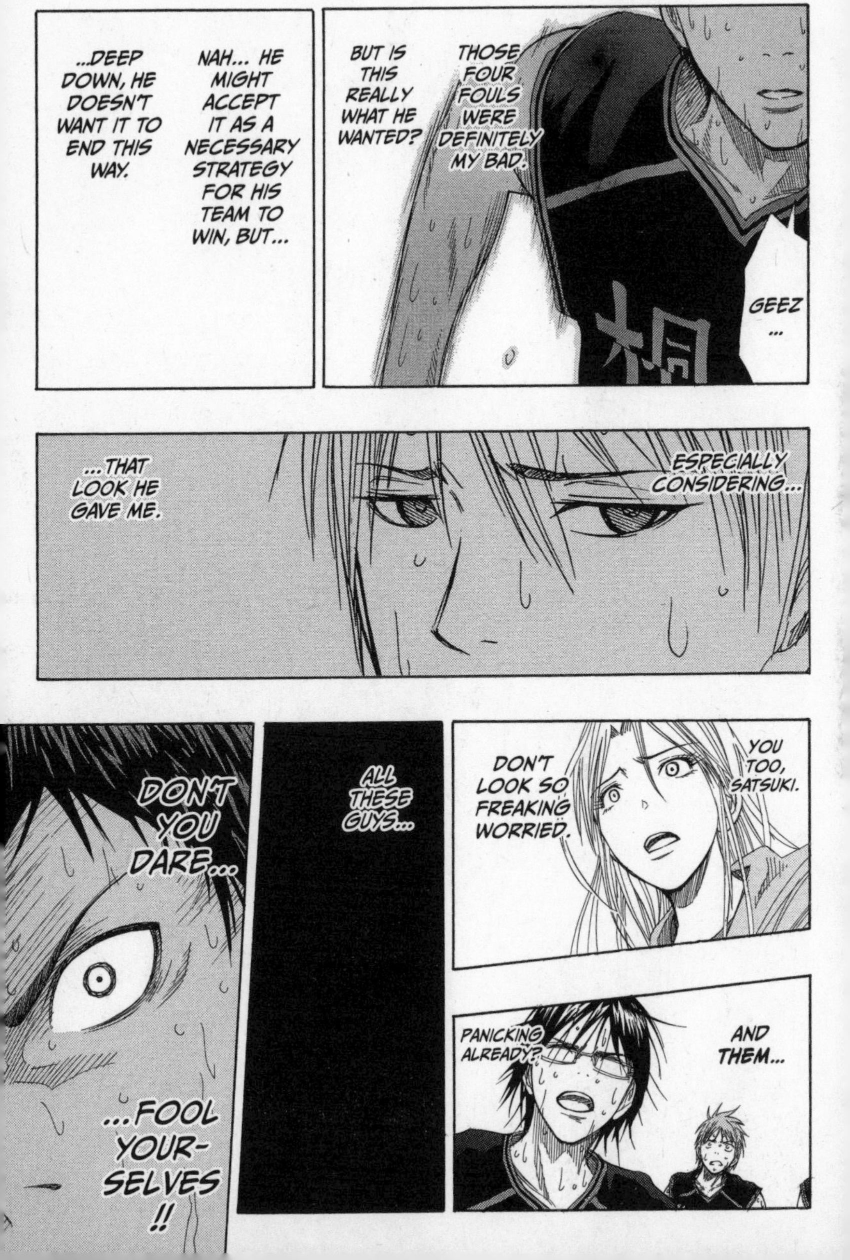
THOSE FOUR FOULS WERE DEFINITELY MY BAD.
BUT IS THIS REALLY WHAT HE WANTED?
GEEZ...
NAH... HE MIGHT ACCEPT IT AS A NECESSARY STRATEGY FOR HIS TEAM TO WIN, BUT...
...DEEP DOWN, HE DOESN'T WANT IT TO END THIS WAY.
ESPECIALLY CONSIDERING...
...THAT LOOK HE GAVE ME.
YOU TOO, SATSUKI.
DON'T LOOK SO FREAKING WORRIED.
AND THEM...
PANICKING ALREADY?
ALL THESE GUYS...
DON'T YOU DARE...
...FOOL YOUR-SELVES!!

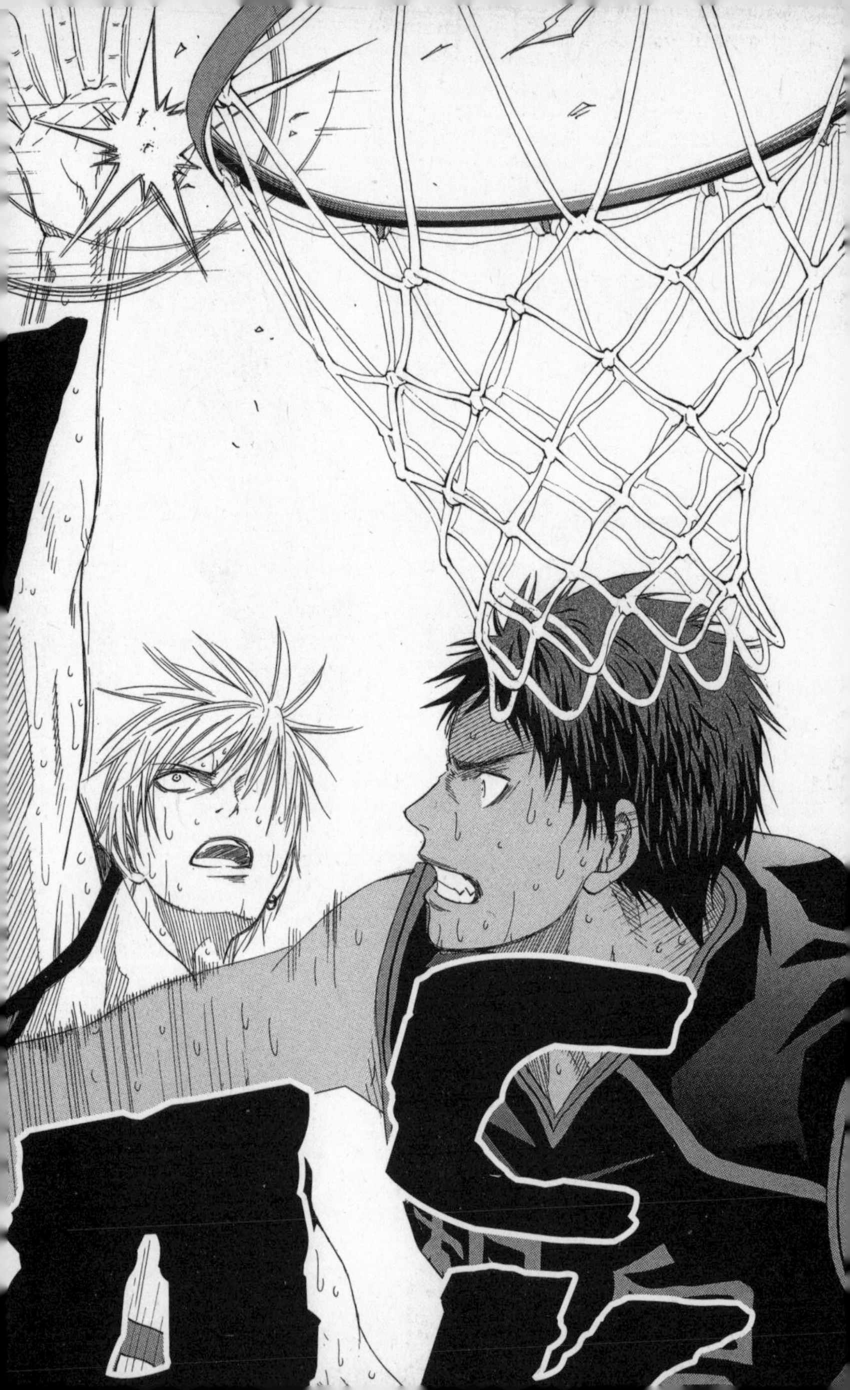

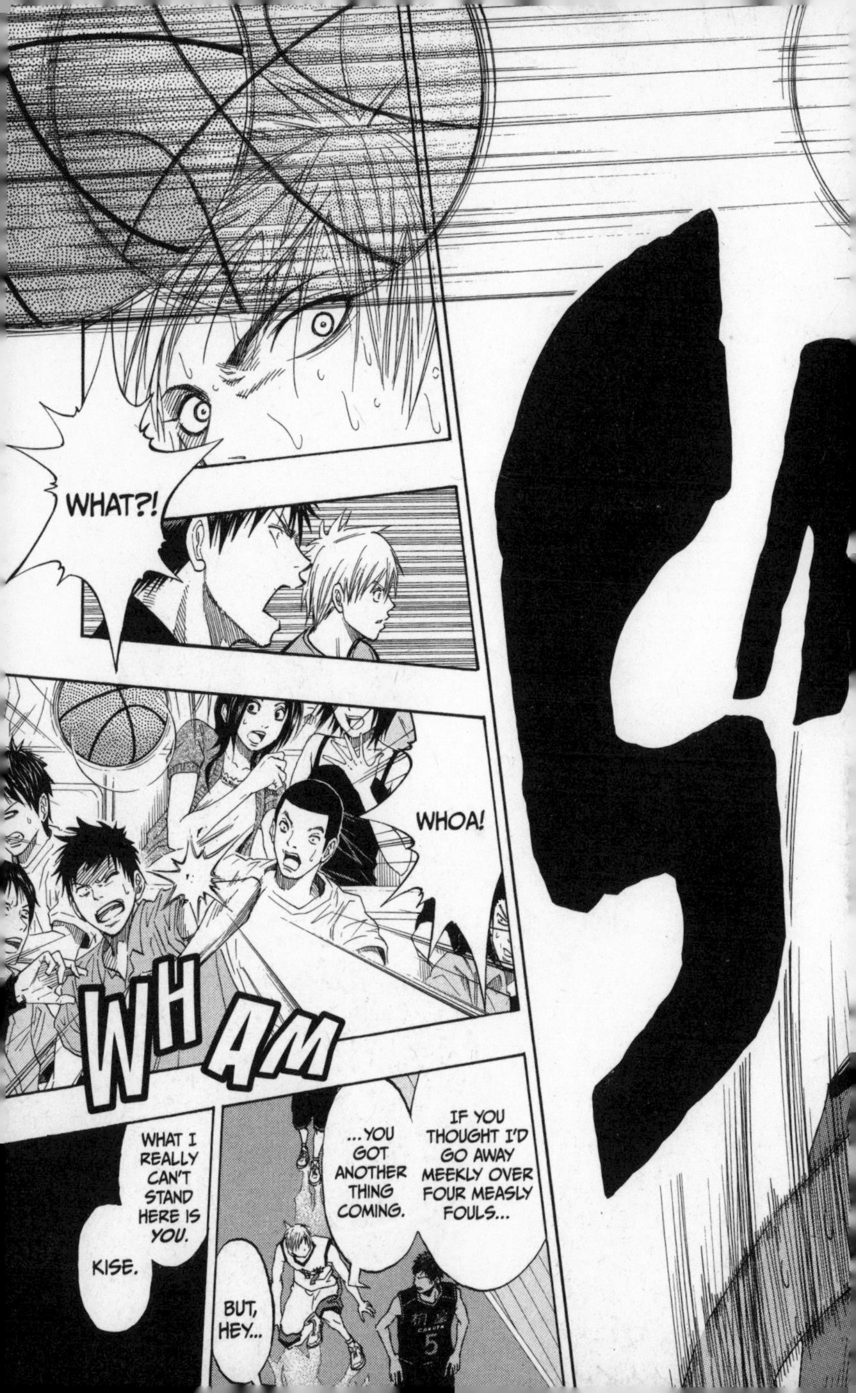
WHAT?!
WHOA!
WHAM
IF YOU THOUGHT I'D GO AWAY MEEKLY OVER FOUR MEASLY FOULS...
...YOU GOT ANOTHER THING COMING.
BUT, HEY...
WHAT I REALLY CAN'T STAND HERE IS YOU.
KISE.

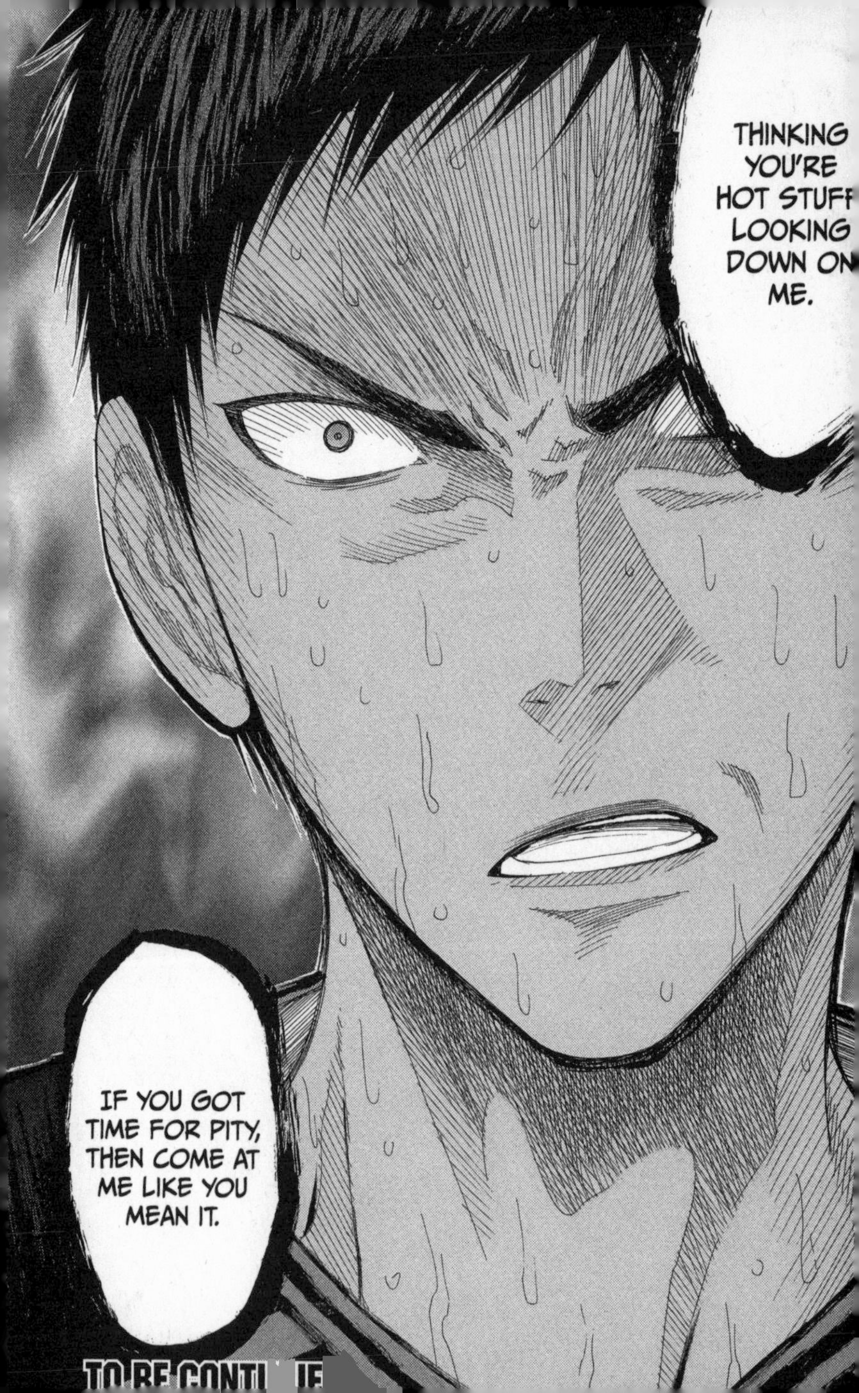
THINKING YOU'RE HOT STUFF LOOKING DOWN ON ME.
IF YOU GOT TIME FOR PITY, THEN COME AT ME LIKE YOU MEAN IT.
TO BE CONTI

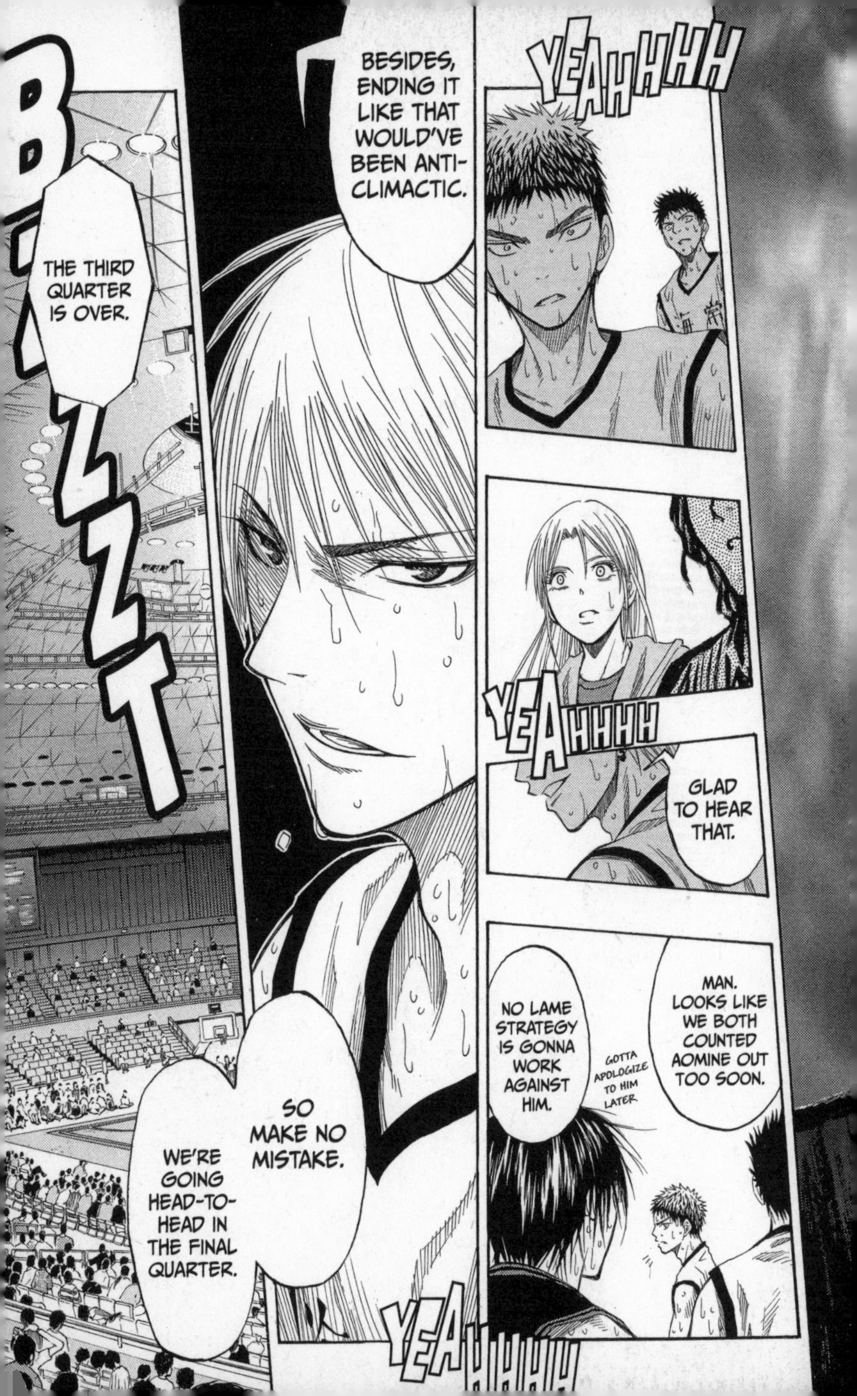
YEAHHHH
YEAHHHH
GLAD TO HEAR THAT.
MAN. LOOKS LIKE WE BOTH COUNTED AOMINE OUT TOO SOON.
NO LAME STRATEGY IS GONNA WORK AGAINST HIM.
GOTTA APOLOGIZE TO HIM LATER
YEAHHHHH
BESIDES, ENDING IT LIKE THAT WOULD'VE BEEN ANTI-CLIMACTIC.
SO MAKE NO MISTAKE.
WE'RE GOING HEAD-TO-HEAD IN THE FINAL QUARTER.
BZZZT
THE THIRD QUARTER IS OVER.

KUROKO'S BASKETBALL BLOOPERS

TAKE 4

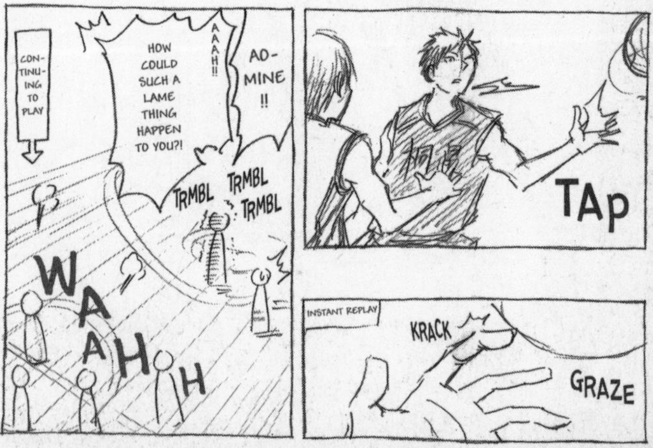
TAp
INSTANT REPLAY
KRACK
GRAZE
AOMINE!!
AAAH!!
HOW COULD SUCH A LAME THING HAPPEN TO YOU?!
CONTINUING TO PLAY
TRMBL TRMBL
TRMBL TRMBL
WAAAHH

COMING NEXT VOLUME

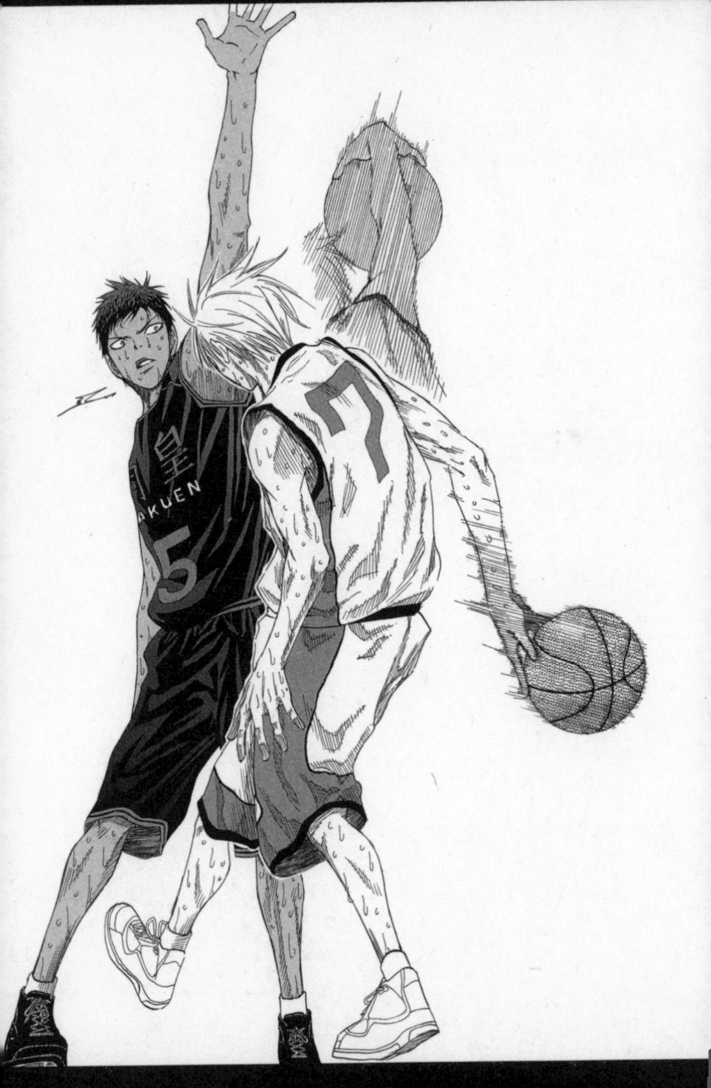

The back-and-forth slugfest between Kise and Aomine continues.
Neither is backing down, but only one winner can emerge at the end

EYESHIELD 21

STORY BY **RIICHIRO INAGAKI**
ART BY **YUSUKE MURATA**

From the artist of *One-Punch Man!*

Wimpy Sena Kobayakawa has been running away from bullies all his life. But when the football gear comes on, things change—Sena's speed and uncanny ability to elude big bullies just might give him what it takes to become a great high school football hero! Catch all the bone-crushing action and slapstick comedy of Japan's hottest football manga!

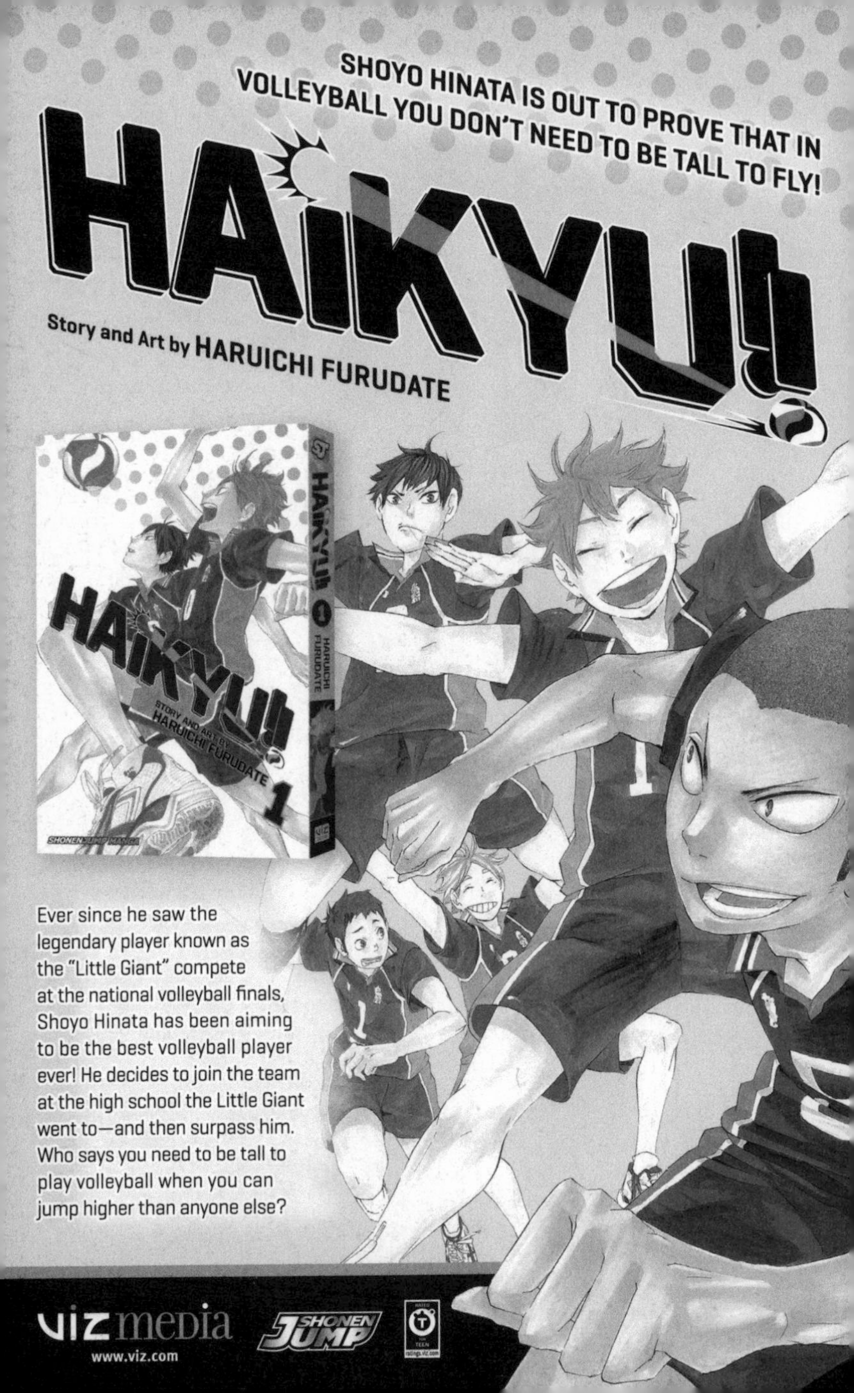
SHOYO HINATA IS OUT TO PROVE THAT IN VOLLEYBALL YOU DON'T NEED TO BE TALL TO FLY!
HAIKYU!!
Story and Art by HARUICHI FURUDATE
HAIKYU!!
STORY AND ART BY HARUICHI FURUDATE
1
SHONEN JUMP MANGA
Ever since he saw the legendary player known as the "Little Giant" compete at the national volleyball finals, Shoyo Hinata has been aiming to be the best volleyball player ever! He decides to join the team at the high school the Little Giant went to—and then surpass him. Who says you need to be tall to play volleyball when you can jump higher than anyone else?
viz media
www.viz.com
SHONEN JUMP
RATED T FOR TEEN
ratings.viz.com

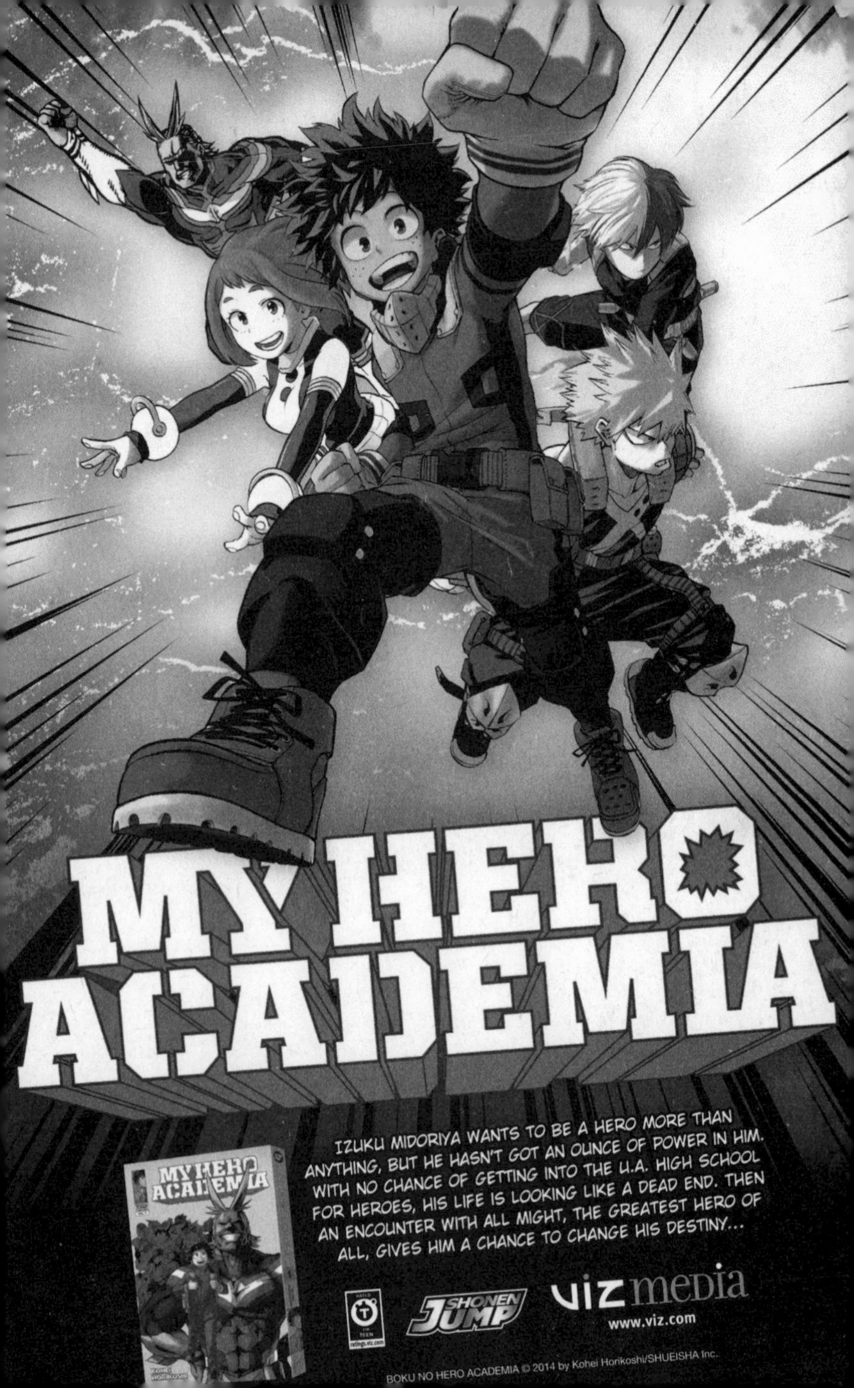
MY HERO ACADEMIA
IZUKU MIDORIYA WANTS TO BE A HERO MORE THAN ANYTHING, BUT HE HASN'T GOT AN OUNCE OF POWER IN HIM. WITH NO CHANCE OF GETTING INTO THE U.A. HIGH SCHOOL FOR HEROES, HIS LIFE IS LOOKING LIKE A DEAD END. THEN AN ENCOUNTER WITH ALL MIGHT, THE GREATEST HERO OF ALL, GIVES HIM A CHANCE TO CHANGE HIS DESTINY...
SHONEN JUMP
viz media
www.viz.com
BOKU NO HERO ACADEMIA © 2014 by Kohei Horikoshi/SHUEISHA Inc.

Black ✤ Clover

STORY & ART BY YŪKI TABATA

Asta is a young boy who dreams of becoming the greatest mage in the kingdom. Only one problem—he can't use any magic! Luckily for Asta, he receives the incredibly rare five-leaf clover grimoire that gives him the power of anti-magic. Can someone who can't use magic really become the Wizard King? One thing's for sure—Asta will never give up!

Food Wars!
SHOKUGEKI NO SOMA

Story by **Yuto Tsukuda**
Art by **Shun Saeki**
Contributor **Yuki Morisaki**

Soma Yukihira's old man runs a small family restaurant in the less savory end of town. Aiming to one day surpass his father's culinary prowess, Soma hones his skills day in and day out until one day, out of the blue, his father decides to enroll Soma in a classy culinary school! Can Soma really cut it in a school that prides itself on a 10 percent graduation rate? And can he convince the beautiful, domineering heiress of the school that he belongs there at all?!

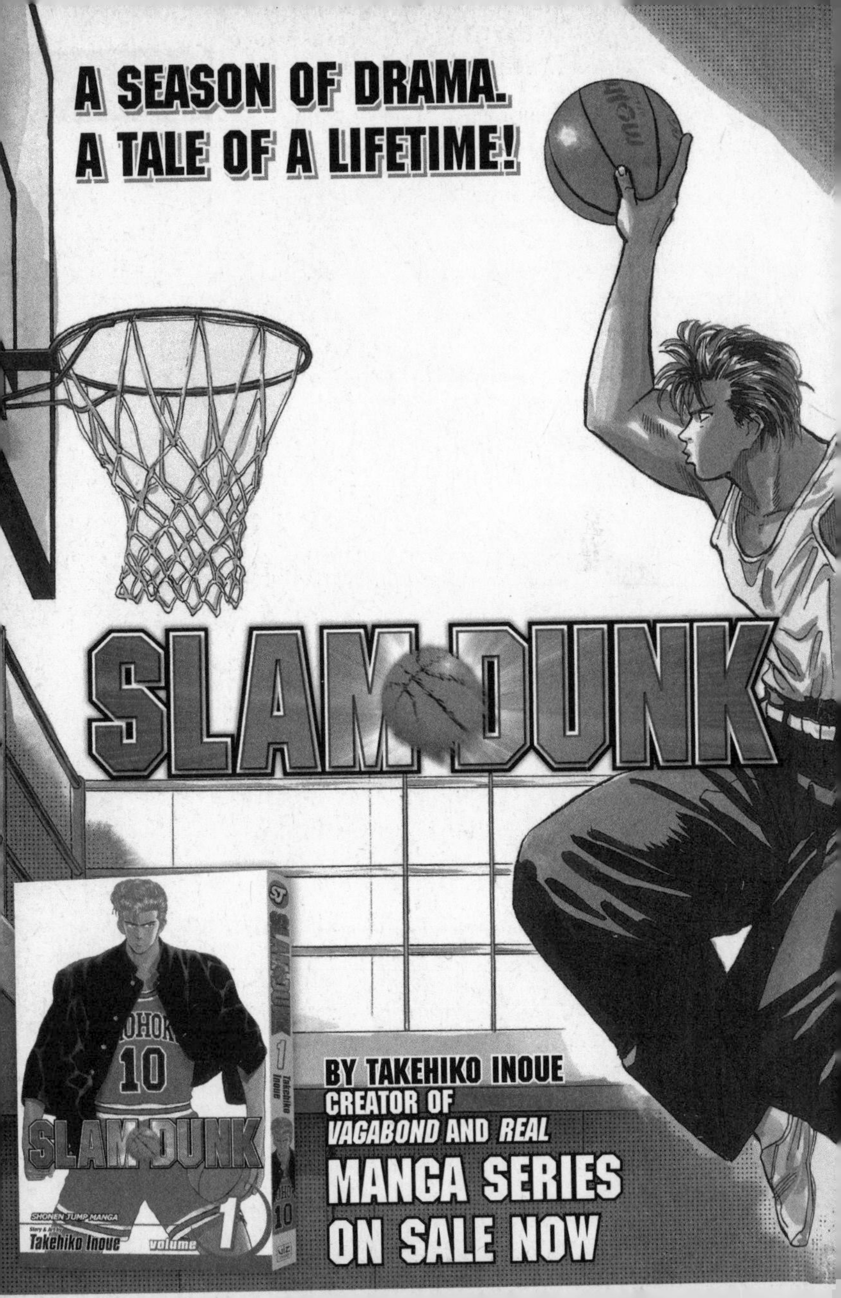
A SEASON OF DRAMA.
A TALE OF A LIFETIME!
SLAM DUNK
SLAM DUNK
SHONEN JUMP MANGA
Story & Art by
Takehiko Inoue
volume 1
BY TAKEHIKO INOUE
CREATOR OF
VAGABOND AND *REAL*
MANGA SERIES
ON SALE NOW

YOU'RE READING THE WRONG WAY!

KUROKO'S BASKETBALL reads from right to left, starting in the upper-right corner. Japanese is read from right to left, meaning that action, sound effects and word-balloon order are completely reversed from English order.

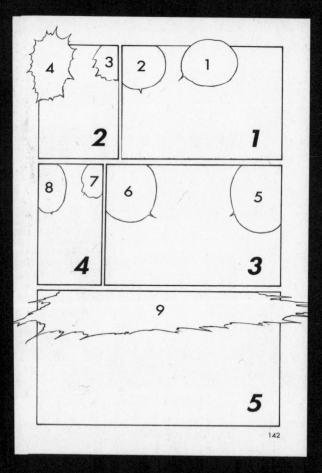

FLIP IT OVER TO GET STARTED!